Then a Miracle Occurs

"I THINK YOU SHOULD BE MORE EXPLICIT HERE IN STEP TWO."

Source: Image courtesy ScienceCartoonPlus.com

Then a Miracle Occurs

Focusing on Behavior in Social Psychological Theory and Research

Purdue Symposium on Psychological Sciences

Edited by
Christopher R. Agnew
Donal E. Carlston
William G. Graziano
Janice R. Kelly

OXFORD
UNIVERSITY PRESS
2010

OXFORD
UNIVERSITY PRESS

Oxford University Press, Inc., publishes works that further
Oxford University's objective of excellence
in research, scholarship, and education.

Oxford   New York
Auckland   Cape Town   Dar es Salaam   Hong Kong   Karachi
Kuala Lumpur   Madrid   Melbourne   Mexico City   Nairobi
New Delhi   Shanghai   Taipei   Toronto

With offices in
Argentina   Austria   Brazil   Chile   Czech Republic   France   Greece
Guatemala   Hungary   Italy   Japan   Poland   Portugal   Singapore
South Korea   Switzerland   Thailand   Turkey   Ukraine   Vietnam

Published by Oxford University Press, Inc.
198 Madison Avenue, New York, New York 10016

www.oup.com

Oxford is a registered trademark of Oxford University Press, Inc.

Library of Congress Cataloging-in-Publication Data
Then a miracle occurs : focusing on behavior in social psychological
   theory and research / edited by Christopher R. Agnew . . . [et al.].
      p.   cm.
   Includes bibliographical references and index.
   ISBN: 978-0-19-537779-8
   1. Interbehavioral psychology.   2. Social psychology.   I. Agnew,
   Christopher Rolfe.
   BF200.T44 2009
   150—dc22
                                                          2009008642

9 8 7 6 5 4 3 2 1

Printed in the United States of America
on acid-free paper

ACKNOWLEDGMENTS

This book emerged as the result of the inaugural Purdue Symposium on Psychological Sciences (PSPS), a two-day gathering held on the West Lafayette, Indiana campus of Purdue University in May of 2008. We are indebted to a number of individuals for helping to make this book a reality. Purdue alumnus James Bradley provided a generous donation to our department, making PSPS financially possible. Our department head, Howard Weiss, spearheaded the creation of PSPS and encouraged our efforts to pursue a broad yet "hot" topic. Erica Wilson handled many of the arrangements for our symposium participants, who traveled from far and wide to attend. Lori Handelman at Oxford has been a supportive and cheerful presence throughout the process. Finally, we wish to thank our Purdue colleagues (faculty and graduate students), particularly those in the social psychology program, who help to make our academic home a happy and productive one.

Christopher R. Agnew
Donal E. Carlston
William G. Graziano
Janice R. Kelly

West Lafayette, Indiana, USA

TABLE OF CONTENTS

III. Behavior and Inter-Individual Processes   273

CONTRIBUTORS

Christopher R. Agnew
Department of Psychological
   Sciences
Purdue University
West Lafayette, Indiana

Jessica L. Alquist
Department of Psychology
Florida State University
Tallahassee, Florida

Arthur Aron
Department of Psychology
Stony Brook University
Stony Brook, New York

John A. Bargh
Department of Psychology
Yale University
New Haven, Connecticut

Reuben M. Baron
Department of Psychology
University of Connecticut
Storrs, Connecticut

Roy F. Baumeister
Department of Psychology
Florida State University
Tallahassee, Florida

Niall Bolger
Department of Psychology
Columbia University
New York, New York

Donal E. Carlston
Department of Psychological Sciences
Purdue University
West Lafayette, Indiana

Justin V. Cavallo,
Department of Psychology
University of Waterloo
Waterloo Ontario
Canada

Anita DeLongis
Department of Psychology
University of British Columbia
Vancouver, British Columbia
Canada

C. Nathan DeWall
Department of Psychology
University of Kentucky
Lexington, Kentucky

Leandre R. Fabrigar
Department of Psychology
Queen's University
Kingston, Ontario, Canada

Joshua D. Fetterman
Department of Psychology
University of Pittsburgh
Pittsburgh, Pennsylvania

Jeffrey J. Flagg
Department of Psychology
University of Pittsburgh
Pittsburgh, Pennsylvania

David C. Funder
Department of Psychology
University of California at Riverside
Riverside, California

R. Michael Furr
Department of Psychology
Wake Forest University
Winston-Salem, North Carolina

Lewis R. Goldberg
Oregon Research Institute
Eugene, Oregon

Peter M. Gollwitzer
Department of Psychology
New York University
New York, USA and
Department of Psychology
University of Konstanz, Germany

William G. Graziano
Department of Psychological
    Sciences
Purdue University
West Lafayette, Indiana

Judith A. Hall
Department of Psychology
Northeastern University
Boston, Massachusetts

Ronald R. Holden
Department of Psychology
Queen's University
Kingston, Ontario, Canada

Andrea B. Hollingshead
School of Communication
University of Southern California
Los Angeles, California

John G. Holmes
Department of Psychology
University of Waterloo
Waterloo, Ontario, Canada

Janice R. Kelly
Department of Psychological Sciences
Purdue University
West Lafayette, Indiana

Tara K. MacDonald
Department of Psychology
Queen's University
Kingston, Ontario, Canada

Sean M. McCrea
Department of Psychology
University of Konstanz
Germany

Mario Mikulincer
New School of Psychology
Interdisciplinary Center (IDC)
Herzliya, Israel

Richard L. Moreland
Department of Psychology
University of Pittsburgh
Pittsburgh, Pennsylvania

Ezequiel Morsella
Department of Psychology
San Francisco State University and
Department of Neurology
UC San Francisco
San Francisco, California

Andrea L. Myers
Department of Psychology
University of Konstanz
Germany

Christine Paprocki
Department of Psychology
Columbia University
New York, New York

Delroy L. Paulhus
Department of Psychology
University of British Columbia
Vancouver, British Columbia
Canada

Harry T. Reis
Department of Clinical and Social
   Sciences in Psychology
University of Rochester
Rochester, New York

Phillip R. Shaver
Department of Psychology
University of California
   at Davis
Davis, California

Gertraud Stadler
Department of Psychology
Columbia University
New York, New York

Kristina L. Swanenburg
Department of Psychology
University of Pittsburgh
Pittsburgh, Pennsylvania

Bas Verplanken
Department of Psychology
University of Bath
Bath, United Kingdom

Kathleen D. Vohs
Department of Marketing
University of Minnesota
Minneapolis, Minnesota

Seth A. Wagerman
Department of Psychology
California Lutheran University
Thousand Oaks, California

Duane T. Wegener
Department of Psychological Sciences
Purdue University
West Lafayette, Indiana

Frank Wieber
Department of Psychology
University of Konstanz
Konstanz, Germany

I

Behavior in Social Psychological Theory and Research

1 Behavior and Miracles

Christopher R. Agnew
Donal E. Carlston
William G. Graziano
Janice R. Kelly

In the Spring of 2007, the social psychology faculty at Purdue University met over lunch to plan the inaugural Purdue Symposium on Psychological Sciences (PSPS), to be held on the West Lafayette campus in Spring of 2008. How the social faculty came to be responsible for such an event is a long story, beginning with a generous donation to the psychological sciences department by Purdue alumnus James Bradley, mediated by an allocation and a directive from department head Howard Weiss, and culminating with the luncheon meeting described here. We had, at that point, everything needed to initiate planning for the symposium—except a topic. And finding one that all of the social faculty could get behind was seemingly going to take a miracle.

The Purdue social psychology faculty encompassed a diverse set of subfields: attitudes, close relationships, group processes, prosocial behavior, social cognition, social influence, and stereotyping and prejudice. Of course, any of these could have served as an attractive domain in which to target our symposium, at least in the eyes of some subset of our faculty. But none offered the kind of broad, overarching "hot topic" that might capture the interest of a majority of our area, to say nothing of our department, or of social psychologists in general.

We chewed on a number of ideas, along with our lunches, until someone (named Don) cried out "How about behavior?" As we were then seven years into the American Psychological Association's "Decade of Behavior," this inspiration fell somewhat short of divine. However, its status grew as those attending the meeting chimed in with their own perspectives on the topic. Someone mentioned the attitude–behavior relationship, someone else, interpersonal behaviors. In quick succession, automaticity, behavioral synchrony, and behavioral coding and measurement were added to the list. As we digested the suggestions, the menu of possible topics grew until it became clear to all that we had identified a general (albeit broad) topic of common interest across subfields.

At some point, someone (named Bill) mentioned the famous Sidney Harris cartoon shown as the frontispiece for this book. The carton shows a scientist drawing an elaborate formula on the blackboard, in which he has embedded the comment, "Then a Miracle Occurs." Some of those present may have felt that the miracle was the manna from heaven that was to finance our little shindig; others that it lay in our ability to find an idea we could all feed on; and still others, thinking more scientifically, that it characterized the theoretical hand waving that so often occurs in science when one or more links in a causal chain haven't been fully specified. Whether this last interpretation is a fair description of the science of behavior is one of many issues debated, at least implicitly, in this volume. In any case, as we finished our discussion and our sandwiches, sentiment converged on using "Then a Miracle Occurs" as the catchphrase for our symposium.

CARTOON AS RORSCHACH: DIVINING THE FOCUS ON BEHAVIOR

Clearly, the Harris cartoon is open to interpretation. Indeed, it appears to act as a kind of projective test: When presented with it, different scholars focus on different aspects of the cartoon itself or the caption underneath. In that caption, a colleague addresses the scientist who apparently generated the miraculous formula: "I think you should be more explicit here in step two." Some social psychologists have emphasized a mediational interpretation, seeing the miracle as reflecting on theories of processing between stimulus and behavior. Others see the miraculous hand waving as more typical of theoretical treatments of situational and contextual precursors of behavior, and still others, as characteristic of the field's treatment of behavior itself. Still other scholars have highlighted the colleagues' advice in the caption, arguing for greater precision in our theoretical constructions, measurements, and empirical tests. Finally, at least a few cynics have found it a "miracle" that social psychologists would focus on behavior at all! You will find these interpretations, and more, in the chapters in this volume.

Whether miraculous or not, we firmly believe that focusing attention on issues surrounding the study of behavior is timely and important. Some scholars believe that, across various subdisciplines of the field, social psychology actually has contributed a great deal to our understanding of behavior and its antecedents. From this perspective, there is considerable utility in drawing together such work in one place. Other scholars suggest that though there has been great progress elucidating the *internal* cognitive, affective, and motivational underpinnings of behavior, much less research focuses on *external* behavior itself. From this perspective, it is important to identify the theoretical gaps, the empirical needs, and the focal issues that still demand attention. This and a number of other controversies enlivened the symposium that eventually materialized on the Purdue campus. In what follows, we try to summarize some of these key issues that emerged and that are examined in greater detail in the pages of this volume.

ISSUES REGARDING BEHAVIOR IN SOCIAL PSYCHOLOGY

Psychologists commonly partition the behavioral chain into three parts that can be roughly characterized as the stimulus environment, mediating processes, and behavioral response. We attempted in our symposium, and in this volume, to ensure that all three of these were well represented by scholars studying each. It is therefore sensible for us to organize the issues facing behavior-related theory and research in much the same way.

What Do We Know About the Stimulus Environment (and Why Don't We Know More)?

At the root of most social psychological examinations of the causal sequence of action is the stimulus environment. People, more often than not, react to what they perceive around them, so knowledge about such stimuli to behavior would seem to be of critical importance to social psychologists. Not only do environmental elements elicit conscious activity, but they can also at times automatically determine behavior (see Bargh & Morsella, Chapter 6). Moreover, from an affordance perspective (see Baron, Chapter 13), objects in the physical and social environment give rise to certain actions; they "afford" it. Given what we know (or at least what our theories tell us), it is more than a little surprising that social psychologists have not focused greater attention on the stimulus environment, often termed "the situation."

Chemistry has its periodic table. Biology has its taxonomic ranks. But what of social psychology? In a field where behavior is held to be a function of the person and the situation, what progress have we made in classifying situations? Personality psychologists have made great strides in delineating basic dimensions of personality (cf. John & Srivastava, 1999), but can the same be said with respect to delineating the basic dimensions of situations? Interdependence theorists (including Harry Reis in Chapter 16 and John Holmes and Justin Cavallo in Chapter 17) have begun the difficult yet necessary work to outline such dimensions. Building on the pioneering theoretical work of Thibaut and Kelley (1959; Kelley & Thibaut, 1978; Kelley, 1983), Reis, Holmes, and Cavallo describe key dimensions of social situations, including the degree of outcome interdependence between actors, the bases of control (exchange versus coordination), and the extent to which actors' outcomes are correspondent (cf. Kelley, Holmes, Kerr, Reis, Rusbult, & Van Lange, 2003). Such painstaking theoretical work is necessary for efforts by the field to truly understand the situational roots of behavior.

Why Don't We Study Real Behaviors (or at Least Important Ones)?

Baumeister, Vohs, and Funder (2007) succinctly captured one major perspective on behavior in a recent article titled, "Psychology as the Science of Self-Reports and Finger Movements: Whatever Happened to Actual Behavior?" We were so taken with this article that we have reprinted it in this volume as Chapter 2. It reflects a view that is common, though not universal, in the field of social psychology today. The chapter and the Moreland, Fetterman, Flagg, & Swanenburg chapter that follows argue that behavior has garnered progressively less interest over the years, both in social psychology at large and in those specific areas of the discipline (e.g., group processes) where one would expect to find more of an emphasis on behavior.

A number of factors have seemingly contributed to this trend. For one, explicit behavioral assessment can be costly and time consuming. In an era when journals typically require packages of multiple studies, more efficient means of assessment (e.g., self-reports) are more practical than more laborious ones. Responses to rating scales are easily collected, easily coded, and easily analyzed, allowing researchers to get on with Studies 2 and 3 (and 4...) while their behaviorally oriented colleagues are still coding videotapes from their initial experiment.

A second factor, according to many, was the emergence of social cognition around 1980, and the prevalence of the social cognition perspective thereafter. One aspect of this new approach was a focus on internal cognitive states that might precede or underlie behavior, without much attention to behavior itself. Eventually, affective and motivational concerns, which social cognitionists were initially accused of ignoring, were brought into the fold, but still with an emphasis on the mediators rather than on the behavioral responses they were thought to mediate.

The social cognition fixation on mental mediation arguably had yet another consequence, as researchers were "encouraged" to add measures to their studies to assess states and processes that served as precursors to the phenomena of interest. This inevitably led to more complex studies involving self-report measures, button presses, and the other "nonbehavioral" assessments about which Baumeister et al. complain. Sometimes something had to give, and too often, what gave was the final, behavioral outcome measure that might complete the causal chain.

And so, according to Baumeister et al., the field degenerated into a science of self-reports and finger movements. Of course, not everyone agrees with this assessment. Some of those self-reports were proxies for behavioral observations, with respondents reporting, summarizing, or predicting their own behavior. Whether such self-reports are a valid source of data about extraexperimental behavior is, of course, an empirical question. As for finger movements, the author of the paragraph you are reading right now would note that such movements represent the only behavior through which he communicated to you the ideas that you are now considering. Add in thumb movements and you may actually have the principal means of communication for an entire generation of young text messagers. Which leads us to the next issue:

What, Exactly, Counts as Behavior Anyway?

When critics of social psychology lament the field's lack of emphasis on real behavior, they often decline to spell out exactly what they mean by "real behavior." One gets the sense sometimes that they mean behaviors that are dramatic, meaningful, and important. One gets the further sense that most behaviors enacted in research laboratory settings probably don't qualify, making laboratory research more or less passé by definition. Perhaps the prototypic real behaviors are acts of aggression, like punching somebody, or acts of altruism, like saving someone's life. Certainly such acts can be dramatic, meaningful, and important. And though creative social psychologists have provoked such responses in the lab, they are probably even more dramatic, meaningful, and important when they occur elsewhere.

But if the goal of social psychology is to understand "everyday behavior," then it should be noted that most everyday behaviors wouldn't qualify as real by this definition. Verplanken notes in Chapter 5 that 45% of all behaviors are enacted in pretty much the same place every day. So much for being dramatic. Verbal behaviors, which probably encompass the vast majority of those studied in the lab, are also probably the most common to occur outside of the lab (see Hollingshead, Chapter 20, in this volume). In fact, our guess would be that more people are regularly affected, in meaningful and important ways, by the words, "I love you," and/or "I'm leaving you," than are punched (though the latter two may sometimes co-occur). Nonverbal behaviors are also meaningful and important, as Hall reminds us in Chapter 21. One conference participant even suggested at the symposium that neural events might qualify as behavior, though that is undoubtedly an extreme view.

It may be more productive to specify what kinds of behaviors are being neglected than to quibble about what constitutes behavior and what does not. Chapters in this volume range from those that detail such neglect to those that emphasize the kinds of behavior that are *not* being neglected in social psychology. As already noted, Baumeister et al. and Moreland et al. provide the strongest exemplars of the former (see also Furr, Wagerman, & Funder, Chapter 10). The latter include Verplanken's chapter on habits, Goldberg's on avocational pursuits (Chapter 11), Bolger, Stadler, Paprocki, and DeLongis's on relationship behaviors (Chapter 19), and Hall's chapter on nonverbal behaviors, among others. Many other chapters deal with difficult issues regarding theories or measures of behavior, especially in terms of possible mediators.

What Kinds of Processes Mediate Behavior?

A main, take-home message of Fishbein and Ajzen's (1975) theory of reasoned action was that intention is the most proximal predictor of action. Several meta-analyses (e.g., Sheppard, Hartwick, & Warshaw, 1988) and decades of research later, we now know that intention accounts for about 50% of the variance in behavior. Accordingly, the march is on to better understand behavioral intentions and how they do what they do. Gollwitzer, Wieber, Myers, and McCrea (Chapter 8) describe a particularly thoughtful approach to understanding parameters of the intention–

behavior relationship. By making important theoretical distinctions among different kinds of intentions, and empirically examining the effectiveness of each, Gollwitzer has helped to contribute to our understanding of this particularly proximal precursor to action.

On the other hand, it would appear that at least 50% of the variance in behavior is *not* accounted for by intention. In fact, in their chapter, Bargh and Morsella (Chapter 6) suggest that the majority of human behaviors probably occur unintentionally, though all such claims depend quite a bit on how one defines behavior. Bargh and Morsella describe four unconscious behavior production systems and detail evidence regarding the existence and effects of each. Their analysis suggests that unconscious behaviors can be studied as systematically as conscious ones can.

A number of other chapters deal with specific mediators of behavior that fall at various points along the unconscious–intentional continuum. Among these are habit (Chapter 5 by Verplanken), emotion (Chapter 7 by Baumeister, DeWall, Vohs, and Alquist), and personality (Chapters 10–13). These chapters hardly exhaust the field's repertoire of possible mediators, but they do raise a number of important, and more general, issues about the nature of mediation. And of course one such issue is how mediators and behaviors are measured.

What Gets Measured, How, and Why?

There are many ways to measure behavior. Perhaps the most obvious is through direct inspection of the overt actions of others by observers. Naturalistic observation is the example that comes to mind easily. Hall (see Chapter 21) also talks about the direct coding of nonverbal behavior, but notes that one of the problems with the research on nonverbal behavior is the atheoretical nature of such investigations. Observer-report data (O-data) has several advantages relative to other forms of behavioral assessment. Often observers have access to information that the actor her/himself may not have. For example, actors may not have as clear a picture of their own standing within a group as do observers, especially in aggregation. Furthermore, an observer can evaluate more than one actor. With multiple observers evaluating multiple actors, research can begin to separate variations and potential biases due to observers from those associated with the observed (Kenny, Kashy, & Cook, 2006). Of course, some observers may be better evaluators of behaviors than others. Just as expert diagnosticians may be more skilled at reading an fMRI (functional magnetic resonance imaging) than garden-variety physicians, knowledgeable informants such as spouses may have special expertise and privileged information, which could give them a predictive edge compared to people who do not know the actor as well.

Another way to measure behavior is through the use of standardized tests (T-data). Examples of T-data include EEG (electroencephalography), EMG (electromyography), and fMRI. A third way to measure behavior is through its residues in the life course. People marry, divorce, receive speeding tickets, and die of heart attacks. These residues can be assessed with L-data. Webb and colleagues (Webb, Campbell, Schwartz, Sechrest, & Grove, 1981) describe the utility of trace measures and archival data—where the residue of actual behavior has been stored for reasons other than research—for assessing behavior in a nonreactive manner. Unfortunately, these measures do not exist for many of the research questions that we are interested in addressing.

By far the most common way of measuring behavior used in social and personality psychology is through self-report (S-data). As Paulhus and Holden (Chapter 12; Paulhus & Vazire, 2007) note, there are good reasons for collecting S-data. For example, Bolger and colleagues (see Chapter 19) describe how S-data can be strengthened by using daily diary methods for assessing everyday behavior, with such advantages as the mitigation of problems associated with biased retrospective reporting.

People have access to a wealth of information that is not available to anyone else. But, as stated in the limitation section of many published articles, S-data is not a perfect assessment method, especially when used without converging data from other sources. S-data is subject to a host of biases, including biases associated with retrospective reports of behavior and with issues of motivated self-presentation (see Chapter 12 by Paulhus and Holden). Retrospective self-reports of behavior may be skewed because of memory loss, whether due to decay or impaired encoding of the behavioral event, or to reconstructive processes, that might emphasize what we think we should or could have done, rather than what actually occurred.

Many of these issues are considered in detail in the chapters that follow. PSPS gathered leading thinkers in social psychology to consider theoretical and empirical issues relevant to behavior, across the field and with respect to various subfields of social psychological inquiry. Each contributor highlights theoretical and/or measurement issues about behavior, including how behavior is treated in current social psychological theory and research.

We divide our coverage of behavior into two overarching sections: (1) Behavior and Intra-Individual Processes, including social cognition and individual differences, and (2) Behavior and Inter-Individual Processes, including close relationships and group dynamics. Despite the imposed sections, you will find significant overlap in issues examined across sections. Considering a wide variety of behavior-related topics within one volume has been its own sort of miracle, one that we are pleased to share with you.

REFERENCES

John, O. P., & Srivastava, S. (1999). The Big Five trait taxonomy: History, measurement, and theoretical perspectives. In L. A. Pervin & O. P. John (Eds.), *Handbook of personality: Theory and research* (2nd ed., pp. 102–138). New York: Guilford Press.

Kelley, H. H. (1983). The situational origins of human tendencies: A further reason for the formal analysis of structures. *Personality and Social Psychology Bulletin, 9*, 8–36.

Kelley, H. H., Holmes, J. G., Kerr, N., Reis, H., Rusbult, C., & Van Lange, P. A. (2003). *An atlas of interpersonal situations.* Cambridge, UK: Cambridge Press.

Kelley, H. H., & Thibaut, J. W. (1978). *Interpersonal relations: A theory of interdependence.* New York: Wiley.

Kenny, D., Kashy, D., & Cook, W. (2006). *Dyadic data analysis.* New York: Guilford.

Paulhus, D. L., & Vazire, S. (2007). The self-report method. In R.W. Robins, R. C. Fraley, & R. F. Krueger (Eds.), *Handbook of research methods in personality psychology* (pp. 224–239). New York: Guilford.

Sheppard, B. H., Hartwick, J., & Warshaw, P. R. (1988). The theory of reasoned action: a meta-analysis of past research with recommendations for modifications and future research. *Journal of Consumer Research, 15*, 325–343.

Thibaut, J. W., & Kelley, H. H. (1959). *The social psychology of groups.* New York: Wiley.

Webb, E. J., Campbell, D. T., Schwartz, R. D., Sechrest, L., & Grove, J. B. (1981). *Nonreactive measures in the social sciences.* Boston: Houghton Mifflin.

2 Psychology as the Science of Self-Reports and Finger Movements: Whatever Happened to Actual Behavior?*

Roy F. Baumeister
Kathleen D. Vohs
David C. Funder

For decades now psychology students have been taught, from the first day of class, that psychology is the science of behavior, and that its ultimate goal is to describe and explain what people do. Is that a fair description? The answer varies with the specific area of psychology. Neuroscience and cognitive psychology have never had much to say about the meaningful activities people perform in their daily lives, nor have they really intended to. These fields are more interested in understanding the internal workings of the mind and brain rather than behavioral outcomes. In contrast, animal learning and developmental psychology (perhaps because participants studied by these fields generally cannot fill out questionnaires or read prompts on a computer screen) have consistently focused on behavior at various levels ranging from increases in bar pressing as a function of rewards to behavioral coordination between small children and their parents.

The fields of social and personality psychology, however, offer a special and discouraging case. Both of these related fields have a mandate to study the important social behaviors that comprise the very texture of

* Baumeister, R. F., Vohs, K. D., & Funder, D. C. (2007). Psychology as the science of self-reports and finger movements: Whatever happened to actual behavior? *Perspectives on Psychological Science, 2,* 396–403. Copyright © 2007 Association for Psychological Science. Reproduced with permission of Blackwell Publishing Ltd.

human life, with personality focusing on individual differences in those behaviors, and social psychology exploring situational influences. But personality psychology has long relied heavily on questionnaires in lieu of behavioral observation, a state of affairs that has begun to change only recently and ever so slowly at that. Even worse, social psychology has actually moved in the opposite direction. At one time focused on direct observations of behaviors that were both fascinating and important—a focus that attracted many researchers to the field in the first place—social psychology has turned in recent years to the study of reaction times and questionnaire responses. These techniques, which promised to help to explain behavior, appear instead to have largely supplanted it. The result is that current research in social and personality psychology pays remarkably little attention to the important things that people do.

The 1990s were named the "Decade of the Brain." This widely advertised rubric, promoted heavily by the American Psychological Association (APA), focused attention on the importance of and advances in research on brain processes. It was wildly successful, to the extent that many funding agencies jettisoned many other research priorities as they poured money into expensive brain research, and articles and conference sessions on brain studies proliferated. Brain researchers have always been more interested in brain and nervous system functioning than in behavioral implications. Ironically, however, their research has benefited hugely from the conviction by funding agencies and the public at large that anything a neuron does must be behaviorally important. Such relevance has been demonstrated once in a great while (e.g., in the work by Damasio, 1994, and his colleagues on the interaction between emotional and cognitive systems in decision making), but more often it has merely been taken on faith. Meanwhile, the increase in study of the brain has helped erode interest in actually observing behavior.

It seemed an extremely wise move, therefore, when, impressed by the success of the brain decade, APA came up with the idea of making the first decade of the new century "The Decade of Behavior." The goal was to focus attention on the contributions of psychology toward understanding and affecting important behaviors and consequent life outcomes, thereby adding relevance, credibility, and (one hoped) big research budgets to the enterprise. This emphasis was—or at least should have been— especially welcome to social and personality psychologists, whose research programs would seem to be in a position to benefit greatly from a renewed recognition of the importance of behavior.

It is now past halfway through the putative Decade of Behavior and therefore a fair time to ask: How's it going? In particular, how are social and personality psychologists doing? To anticipate our answer, we think they are doing fine in many respects—but not in studying behavior.

LOOKING FOR BEHAVIOR

With that question in mind, we picked up a recent (January 2006) issue of the *Journal of Personality and Social Psychology*, by consensus the premier journal in our subdisciplines (we are all social and personality psychologists). It is undeniably a fine issue, offering important advances in the topics the articles address. The methods are rigorous and the discussions thoughtful. The editors, reviewers, and authors did their jobs well.

But behavior is hard to find. Or if it is there, it is rather different than what we had imagined it to be. If this issue offers a representative sample, then human behavior is almost always performed in a seated position—usually seated in front of a computer. Finger movements, as in keystrokes and pencil marks, constitute the vast majority of human action.

In fact, a remarkable amount of "behavior" turns out to be really just marks on a self-report questionnaire. Sometimes these questionnaires ask people to report what they have done, will do, or would do. More often, they ask people to report what they think, how they feel, or *why* they do what they do. In other words, most personality and social psychological studies gather self-reports of inner states.

Nisbett and Wilson (1977) thought they had discredited introspection back in the 1970s, when they reported a series of clever demonstrations that the factors that drive behavior are often invisible to the people who perform it. As their title expressed, most introspective reporting involves "telling more than we can know." Although aspects of this research became controversial, it is abundantly clear from their studies, other research, and everyday observation that people have not always done what they say they have done, will not always do what they say they will do, and often do not even know the real causes of the things they *do* do. These discrepancies mean that self-reports of past behaviors, hypothetical future behaviors, or causes of behavior are not necessarily accurate[1].

Nonetheless, self-report appears to have all but crowded out all other forms of behavior. Behavioral science today, at least as represented in *JPSP*, mostly involves asking people to report on their thoughts, feelings, memories, and attitudes. Occasionally they are asked to report on recent or hypothetical actions. Or, somewhat differently (and more rarely), reaction times, implicit associations, or memory recall might be assessed, in the service of illuminating a cognitive process. But that's as close as most research gets. Direct observation of meaningful behavior is apparently passé.

---

[1] This does not mean they are never accurate, but rather that there is no way without direct observation of behavior to know whether they are accurate or not.

This is certainly quite an ironic turnabout from Nisbett and Wilson's (1977) critical stance. In fact, Wilson's more recent work (2002) has shown that when people introspect to analyze the reasons for their actions, they often mislead themselves. In a choice rhetorical flourish, he advises people who seek self-knowledge to eschew direct inspection and instead consult books on social psychology. Yet the books on social psychology are increasingly based on research that itself is heavily based on introspection.

The move from behavior to an emphasis on introspective self-report and hypothetical responses to imagined events is potentially a hugely important shift in the very nature of psychology. Psychological science started out in the 1800s with introspection (e.g., Wundt, 1894). One major development of the twentieth century was the shift from introspection to direct observation of behavior, widely regarded as an advance in the development of scientific methodology. Did someone, somewhere, decide that that had been a mistake, and that we should all now go back to introspection?

Let's take a closer look at this recent issue of *JPSP*, which was chosen just for convenience and is presumably representative. It contained 11 articles reporting 38 studies. The closest thing to behavior in the dependent measures was making a choice. That is, one study asked participants to choose between two stimulus persons (who were made known to participants via photographs) to give them the postexperimental interview. Apart from that borderline case, not a single one of those 38 studies contained direct observation of behavior. The dependent measures consisted entirely of ratings, either on paper questionnaires or computer-administered stimuli. The ratings were mainly introspective self-reports.

Some of the procedures included hints of behavior along the way. One study had participants read a fictional police report about a violent act and express a (nonbinding) opinion as to the appropriate prison sentence for the perpetrator. (So at least they read about someone else's behavior, albeit fictional behavior.) Four studies had participants take tests, one for the purpose of legitimizing bogus feedback, the other three as a basis for assessing the accuracy of self-ratings of performance. Some of the questionnaires asked people to report on their past behaviors. Several asked people to read things, such as descriptions of hypothetical behavior. One study had participants cross out all instances of the letter *e* in a page of printed text.

So that is behavior today in the leading journal of social and personality psychology. Ratings, and more ratings. Occasionally making a choice. Reading and taking a test. And crossing out the letter *e*.

Behavior fared only slightly better in the previous issue: Out of 38 studies in 13 articles, there was one that measured negotiation moves (Bowles, Babcock, & McGinn, 2005) and one that studied "how an individual actually behaves during an induced conflict" (quoted from Knee, Lonsbary, Canevello, & Patrick, 2005). Note the authors' use of the term "actually," which illustrates their awareness of how unusual it was to observe behavior directly[2]. That study induced and videotaped a disagreement between romantic partners and then coded for understanding versus defensive behaviors (mainly speech acts) (Knee et al., 2005). Those two studies are about real behavior, but again they are only 2 out of 38 studies. One additional study included a behavioral independent variable, sort of, consisting of having people read their e-mail message aloud before sending it (as opposed to just sending it; Kruger, Epley, Parker, & Ng, 2005). And there was one that used a questionnaire for self-report of behavior.

We do not doubt that other surveys would yield similar numbers. Social and personality psychologists do not report much actual behavior in their premier journal, or elsewhere.

WAS IT ALWAYS THUS?

Our impression is that this has been building for a while. In what psychologists from the baby boom generation may remember as a golden age, social psychology for a time was characterized by studies that directly observed important behaviors in vividly evocative contexts (see Aronson, Brewer, & Carlsmith, 1985). We suspect that more than one social psychologist was inspired onto his or her career by an undergraduate class lecture on John Darley's and Bibb Latane's studies of bystander intervention (e.g., Darley & Latané, 1968), or Stanley Milgram's (1975) obedience studies, which put real people into emotionally powerful situations and then *watched what they did.* Even many classic studies of inner variables such as attitudes and guilt contained dramatic behavioral experiences prior to the self-reporting of inner states (e.g., Aronson & Mills, 1959; Festinger & Carlsmith, 1959). Studies like this faded from view, however, when the field embraced the cognitive revolution in the 1980s, and the success (and apparent rigor and prestige, see Rozin, 2001) of cognitively framed studies may have encouraged many researchers to concentrate on the self-report measures that were appropriate for those studies, rather than struggle for difficult and expensive behavioral observation. The impressively successful Decade of the Brain, as we have already noted, also demonstrated to researchers the success, prestige, and funding that could accrue to studies exploring inner psychological

---

[2] Since we wrote this, we have noticed the increasing frequency with which behavior is called "actual behavior," presumably to distinguish from the other, more commonly studied kinds, or perhaps just to dramatize its rarity.

processes while postponing, perhaps indefinitely, examination of the behavioral results of these processes.

In personality, meanwhile, the interest in behavior in some ways was weaker all along, especially given the core emphasis on measurement of traits, for which self-report has long been the prominent method. Although sophisticated psychometric methods have been developed, the primary method for validating a personality questionnaire is still to demonstrate how it correlates with other questionnaires (Funder, 2001). Hundreds of studies of the "structure of personality" seek that structure amongst the correlations between questionnaires. One major recent project that aimed to compare the utility of several major personality inventories in their ability to predict behavior did so by seeing how well each one predicted *self-reports* of behavior; in other words, yet another questionnaire. Even personality psychologists who evince skepticism about personality traits are not immune; their research, too, is based almost exclusively on self-reports or hypothetical predictions, with only rare (and therefore highly notable) exceptions (e.g., Wright & Mischel, 1987). In recent years, a few personality psychologists have begun to look again at behavior in the laboratory (e.g., Borkenau Riemann, Angleitner, & Spinath, 2001), assess "behavioral residue" (e.g., the condition of a student's dorm room or a worker's office cubicle; e.g., Gosling et al., 2002), and develop methods to code directly observed behavior along meaningful dimensions (e.g., the Riverside Behavioral Q-sort, Funder, Furr, & Colvin, 2000). These efforts remain rare, however, and so far have not been particularly influential. The dominant method throughout personality psychology, to this day, is the questionnaire (Funder, 2001).

We were moved by these questions and reflections, as well as some prodding by reviewers, to take a slightly more systematic and quantified look at behavior in JPSP over the decades. Two of the authors went to libraries and selected issues from 1966, 1976, 1986, 1996, and 2006 for coding. We used our birth months (March and May) for each year, and we coded all studies reported in the issue as to whether they included any direct observation of behavior. Coding was deliberately liberal, so that a study qualified as having behavior if any element involved behavior, that is, any manipulation, any dependent measure, or even using behavior as the conduit for manipulating the independent variable (e.g., taking a test and getting feedback on it). Self-reports of general past behaviors or of hypothetical behaviors did not count. Using archival behavioral data (e.g., crime statistics) qualified. Reading about someone else's behavior was not coded as behavior. The two issues for each same year furnished quite similar numbers except for 1966, in which the very young journal had several peculiar features (including mostly one-study papers and some short reports, one of which oddly reported four brief and very similar studies that were ultimately counted as one), and so we coded two

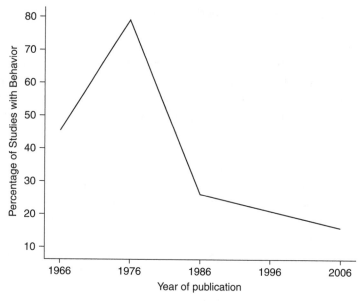

Figure 2.1. Percentage of Studies from the *Journal of Personality and Social Psychology* that Included Behavior, 1966–2006.

additional issues for that year to furnish a broader base); one of the originally coded issues was lost because of catastrophic computer failure. Comment and theory articles were not included. In all, we coded 304 studies across the 11 issues of the journal.

Figure 2.1 shows the results of these codings. Back in 1966, when most articles contained only a single study, about half of these involved actual behavior. The study of behavior increased its share of the journal into the 1970s. But it dropped sharply in 1986, and the subsequent decades have seen a continued downward trend. Apparently, then, behavior has been in a steady decline since the early 1980s.

CAVEAT

We want to be very clear that we see nothing wrong with what social and personality psychologists are doing, as far as it goes. Self-reports of behavior, emotion, intention, and thoughts are often illuminating, may be the method of choice for certain topics (e.g., studies of attitudes or emotional experience), and sometimes are all that is possible. Such measures can and do lead to important and interesting knowledge that will advance theory. But the restriction of methods also serves to constrain the topics that are addressed in the first place (Rozin, 2001). In other words, our complaint is with what social and personality psychologists, and perhaps others in the field, are *not* doing.

Surely some important behavior involves standing up? Or actually talking to another live person, even beyond getting instructions about how to sign a consent form and activate the computer program? Whatever happened to helping, hurting, playing, working, taking, eating, risking, waiting, flirting, goofing off, showing off, giving up, screwing up, compromising, selling, persevering, pleading, tricking, out-hustling, sandbagging, refusing, and the rest? Can't psychology find ways to observe and explain these acts, at least once in a while?

WONDERING WHY

There are probably many reasons for the sorry state of behavioral study during this possibly last-gasp Decade of Behavior. For example, sometimes direct behavioral observations are unethical, unfeasible, or impossible. For the foreseeable future, most studies of everyday behaviors ranging from eating to sexual behavior, exercise habits to drug use, will have to rely primarily on self-report despite the obvious disadvantages. Moreover, if one wants to know what a participant is thinking or feeling, there is little alternative but to ask. And even under the best of circumstances, observing actual social behavior is more difficult, challenging, and inconvenient than just asking for ratings or sitting a participant in front of a computer screen and measuring his or her keystrokes or reaction times. The field is competitive, and the top journals require multiple studies, so struggling with trying to observe behavior, even when it would be possible, may well make it harder to crank out the high volume of data that academic success now requires. Moreover, the sad fact is that many studies fail to show meaningful significant differences. A failed behavioral study is an expensive failure, and could even be a major career setback. Last, and perhaps most important, journals do not seem to give extra points or consideration to studies that observe behavior instead of just getting ratings, so why bother?[3]

Our data on JPSP across the years points to the early 1980s as a turning point, specifically a hugely downward turning for behavior. Several things had changed in the journal between 1976 and 1986. First, the journal had been split into three sections, and they were allocated in ways that might be taken as at best indifferent to behavior.

---

[3]   One author of this paper, in his previous capacities as associate editor of one personality journal and as editor of another, did follow an (unadvertised) policy of trying extra hard to find a way to accept any article that included any direct measurement of behavior, but he received very few such submissions.

Second, editorial policy changed toward explicitly favoring articles with multiple studies, and as we have suggested, it is far easier to do many studies by seating groups in front of computers or questionnaires than to measure behavior over and over. To be sure, other trends in the field at that time may also have contributed. These would include the cognitive revolution (itself a strong push to focus on inner process and downplay so-called "actual" behavior) and the steady increase in restrictive IRBs.

Institutional Review Boards (IRBs) may be more likely to raise objections to behavioral measures than to ratings. From an IRB perspective, it seems far less intrusive to ask someone what she would eat than to observe how much she actually eats[4]. The problem is, of course, that hypothetical behavioral responses may be wildly inaccurate—and, in any case, there is no way to know unless actual behavior is also measured. In a similar vein, it may seem less intrusive to measure "prejudice" as indicated by speed of key presses in response to prompts on a computer screen than by actually seeing how a person interacts with a person against whom he or she might or might not be biased. And it is certainly easier. But, as psychologists bow to pressure from the IRBs to avoid anything that might have the remotest chance of slightly upsetting their research participants, and to competitive pressures to produce lots of studies per paper, they sacrifice the scientific quality of the discipline. Not to mention abandoning its original goal of being the science of behavior.

Ratings, reaction times, and similar measures are surely necessary. The maturation of the field has required a great rise of interest in inner process. In the 1960s, a researcher could manipulate independent variables, measure behavior, and simply speculate about the internal mediating process. Now the researcher is required to demonstrate the inner process, too. Adding ratings surely made for better science. But in principle the ratings and self-reports were supposed to shed light on the behavior—not to replace it.

To put it another way: Once upon a time, perhaps, psychologists observed behavior and reported what they saw, along with their theories about why it happened. The emergence of competing theories and therefore competing explanations led psychologists to push each other to show what happened inside the person to produce the behavior. Gradually the focus shifted on these debates about inner processes, and journals started publishing studies that made significant contributions about

---

[4] One of us spent part of her career studying how much ice cream dieters and nondieters would eat under different conditions. One university's IRB feared that measuring eating behavior—namely, having to admit to participants that their eating was being recorded—might cause dieters to go into a tailspin and develop disordered eating habits.

demonstrating inner processes. Somewhere along the way, it became acceptable to publish data on inner processes without any real behavior included at all. And then it became the norm.

WHAT'S THE PROBLEM?

One might say, is there anything wrong with learning about the inner process? We think not. But behavior matters, too. It cannot be blithely assumed that responding to questionnaires is enough to tell us all we need to know about actual life. It is necessary to study actual behavior some-times. For example, West and Brown (1975) conducted the same experi-ment two different ways—once asking people what they would do in this situation, and once by actually staging the event. The experiment involved an ostensible accident victim standing on the street, asking passersby for money to help pay for medical care at a nearby clinic. Actual and hypothetical behavior differed in two major ways. First, the levels of help were dramatically different. Asked how they would react to such a request, participants said they would give fairly generously, but when the experiment was conducted live, actual donations averaged barely over ten cents in some conditions.

The other difference is even more important for psychology's goal of building sound theories about behavior. The victim's attractiveness did not have a significant effect on hypothetical donations, but it did have a significant effect on real donations. This occurred despite the lower overall generosity in actual behavior (hence overcoming any possible floor effect). A researcher who followed the common contemporary method of relying solely on hypothetical behavior would draw a false conclusion that would omit an important and significant contributor to actual behavior.

In recent years the reasons for doubting self-reports and the resulting need to observe actual behavior have increased. Affective forecasting studies show systematically how inaccurate are people's predictions of how they will react and feel (e.g., Wilson & Gilbert, 2003). Studies on judgment and decision making have likewise shown that people's predic-tions are inaccurate and that hypothetical decisions do not reliably match actual ones. For example, in hypothetical decisions, people are moder-ately risk averse regardless of the amount at stake, but when actual money is used, people become dramatically more risk averse as amounts increase (Holt & Laury, 2002).

This issue has arisen before. During the 1960s and 1970s, both personality traits and attitudes came under vigorous attack on precisely these grounds. Mischel (1968) wrote a famous and influential critique that argued personality trait measures seldom have appreciable correlations with measures of actual behavior. Wicker (1969) went so far as to suggest that attitudes, which had been touted by Gordon Allport as social psychology's most important concept, should be abandoned. The fields responded with impressive programs designed to show that, yes, one could predict some of the people's behavior some of the time from attitudes and trait scales (e.g., Kenrick & Funder, 1988; Ajzen, 2000; Glasman & Albarracín, 2006).

The issues remain today, and indeed the questions of attitude–behavior consistency and behavioral predictability remain important research topics. But in a recent class devoted to examining articles published in JPSP, the students were surprised to find that the latest article on attitude–behavior consistency did not bother measuring behavior. (It asked participants to imagine what they might do in hypothetical situations.) Similarly, we have already mentioned how at least one study has sought to assess the predictive validity of personality trait questionnaires via their correlations with a measure of behavior that was itself a questionnaire. This hardly seems fair. Social psychologists cannot claim that attitudes or personality predict behavior if by behavior they do not really mean behavior.

The problem goes even deeper. While self-reports, reaction times, implicit associations, and the like are good and even ideal methods for examining certain topics, we believe that psychology has tilted toward examining precisely those topics for which these methods are appropriate, and away from everything else (Rozin, 2001). Which leads us to wonder: In our rush to test competing theories of internal processes, as we move away from the description of important behavioral phenomena, what are we missing? What questions are we forgetting to even ask? A partial list is not difficult to generate:

- How do people with different levels of a personality trait behave differently?
- How do situational variables—physical aspects, social relationships, cultural structures—affect what people do?
- How do prejudiced individuals actually treat the objects of their prejudice? How do the discriminated-against respond— behaviorally?
- How and when do women and men act differently in situations ranging from the first date to chairing a meeting?

The reader is invited to make his or her own additions to this list. It is not difficult to do. Again, our point is not that topics like these are never addressed (e.g., see Nisbett & Cohen, 1996, for fascinating studies of the relationship between culture and aggressive behavior), but that they are neglected, relative to the study of cognitive process, and certainly relative to their intrinsic importance. This is why for social and personality psychology, the fields that should benefit the most from this initiative, APA's "Decade of Behavior" risks becoming a laughingstock.

Very possibly, too, the abandonment of behavior could be seriously detrimental to the field's goals and its broad influence. A recent president of the Society for Personality and Social Psychology articulated in the society newsletter that those fields are suffering from failing to get their message across to outsiders. They are seen as not making much interesting progress, even though insiders know that the conferences and journals are filled with exciting new work. But perhaps scholars in other fields, and even undergraduates, find it harder to appreciate the excitement of our work when it rests on correlations among questionnaire items or significant differences in reaction times. The dramatic behaviors of the early years of social psychology experiments are still featured in the textbooks, and probably for good reason.

TODAY'S DILEMMA

Perhaps ironically, psychologists who study behavior today find themselves at a disadvantage. Probably everyone would agree that the ideal paper would report both direct observation of behavior and measurement of inner processes that mediate and produce those behaviors. But if you only have one without the other, preferences are lopsided. Data on behavior without inner process are regarded as unpublishable at the best and even the medium journals. Grant reviewers often behave similarly. One of the present authors submitted a grant proposal for a behavioral study that a reviewer criticized on the grounds that it did not include "psychological variables," apparently meaning internal process measures[5]. By this definition, behavior is not even a psychological variable! Behavior by itself is regarded as only a beginning, an unsolved puzzle. Meanwhile, however, a study of inner process without behavior is acceptable.

Confronted with a study reporting behavior but no inner process, reviewers will immediately ask, why did this happen? You need to show what goes on inside. But confronted with a paper reporting inner process

---

[5] This is not just sour grapes: the study was funded despite a negative review—itself an unusual outcome.

but no overt behavior, reviewers almost never ask, would this actually alter behavior? Inner process is considered interesting and important in its own right, without any proof that it has any implications for what people do.

Given those unequal contingencies, it is not surprising that researchers have turned away from behavior. It is apparently more trouble than it is worth. Ratings are the keys to success, and they are publishable with or without behavior. Behavior, meanwhile, is not publishable by itself without ratings, and moreover, behavior often has a nasty way of complicating the cleaner, more elegant picture that one can get from ratings alone.

AFFIRMATIVE ACTION FOR ACTION?

We wish to suggest, gently and respectfully[6], that social and personality try to put a bit more behavior back into the science of behavior (as psychology still advertises itself). There is no need to stop asking for ratings or analyzing reaction times, but perhaps psychologists could all push themselves to include an occasional study that includes direct observation of what Knee et al. (2005) poignantly called "actual behavior." To be sure, behavioral observation is not always ethical or feasible, as we have mentioned. But when it is, why not include it? Researchers could put a bit more effort into developing methods for observing behavior directly (e.g., Furr & Funder, 2007). We could do more to build on efforts such as those by Jack and Jeanne Block to design behavioral batteries for personality assessment (Block, 1993), the behavior-sampling technologies pioneered by Matthias Mehl and his colleagues (Mehl, Gosling, & Pennebaker, 2006), behavioral observations in real life such as used by James Dabbs, Chris Fraley, and their colleagues (Dabbs, Hargrove, & Heusel, 1996; Fraley & Shaver, 1998), and speech-sampling methods such as those developed by Lisa Feldman-Barrett, James Pennebaker, Lisa Fast, and their colleagues (Feldman-Barrett, Williams, & Fong, 2002; Pennebaker, Mehl, & Niederhoffer, 2003; Fast & Funder, 2008). Not to mention social psychology's long tradition of studying laboratory behavior that involves moving more than fingers.

Perhaps reviewers, editors, and granting agencies could even give a little extra preference to studies that contain behavior, in the spirit of affirmative action for the promotion of methodological diversity. If

---

6 Any attentive reader can tell by now that we are nothing if not gentle and respectful.

others share our view that the current system subtly discourages scientists from observing behavior, then perhaps more vigorous changes might be called for to redress that imbalance. Possibly a new section of JPSP could be earmarked for studies of behavior. Or perhaps one of the new journals that APS is introducing might be devoted to behavioral studies. Having such a devoted outlet would reduce the (apparently crippling) demand that behavioral studies must compete for space with the easier-to-do and therefore correspondingly more rigorous and plentiful studies that use only ratings.

Let us stress that we are not criticizing APA's initiative on the "Decade of Behavior." We support the goal wholeheartedly. But if social and personality psychology has given up on behavior, how can the field expect society as a whole to embrace it? In fact, even if society (or funding agencies at least) were to embrace the Decade of Behavior idea, would that benefit the field? The saddest outcome would be for the powerful and fund-granting authorities to decide that behavior is important after all and then to use that as a reason to disrespect our field. They might say, and not without reason: "We want to support the study of human behavior, but personality and social psychologists don't study behavior."

REFERENCES

Ajzen, I. (2000). Nature and operation of attitudes. *Annual Review of Psychology, 52,* 27–58.

Aronson, E., Brewer, M., & Carlsmith, J. M. (1985). Experimentation in social psychology. In G. Lindzy & E. Aronson (Eds.) *Handbook of Social Psychology,* 3rd ed. (Vol 1., pp. 441–486). New York: Random House, New York.

Aronson, E., & Mills, J. (1959). The effect of severity of initiation on liking for a group. *Journal of Abnormal and Social Psychology, 59,* 177–181.

Block, J. (1993). Studying personality the long way: In D. C. Funder, R. D. Parke, C. Tomlinson-Keasey, & K. Widaman (Eds.), *Studying lives through time: Personality and development* (pp. 9–41). Washington, DC: American Psychological Association.

Borkenau, P., Riemann, R., Angleitner, A., & Spinath, F. M. (2001). Genetic and environmental influences on observed personality: Evidence from the German observational study of adult twins. *Journal of Personality and Social Psychology, 80,* 655–668.

Bowles, H. R., Babcock, L., & McGinn, K. L. (2005). Constraints and triggers: Situational mechanics of gender in negotiation. *Journal of Personality and Social Psychology, 89,* 951–965.

Dabbs, J. M., Jr., Hargrove, M. F., & Heusel, C. (1996). Testosterone differences among college fraternities: Well-behaved vs. rambunctious. *Personality and Individual Differences, 20,* 157–161.

Damasio, A. R. (1994). *Descartes' error: Emotion, reason, and the human brain*. New York: Putnam.

Darley, J. M., & Batson, C. D. (1967). "From Jerusalem to Jericho": A study of situational and dispositional variables in helping behavior. *Journal of Personality and Social Psychology, 27*, 100–108.

Darley, J. M., & Latané, B. (1968). Bystander intervention in emergencies: Diffusion of responsibility. *Journal of Personality and Social Psychology, 28*, 377–383.

Fast, L. G., & Funder, D. C. (2008). Personality as manifest in word use: Correlations with self-report, acquaintance report, and behavior. *Journal of Personality and Social Psychology, 94*, 334–346.

Feldman-Barrett, L., Williams, N. L., & Fong, G. T. (2002). Defensive verbal behavior assessment. *Personality and Social Psychology Bulletin, 28*, 776–788.

Festinger, L., & Carlsmith, J. M. (1959). Cognitive consequences of forced compliance. *Journal of Abnormal and Social Psychology, 58*, 203–210.

Fraley, R. C., & Shaver, P. R. (1998). Airport separations: A naturalistic study of adult attachment dynamics in separating couples. *Journal of Personality and Social Psychology, 75*, 1198–1212.

Funder, D. C. (2001). Personality. *Annual Review of Psychology, 52*, 197–221.

Funder, D. C., Furr, R. M., & Colvin, C. R. (2000). The Riverside Behavioral Q-sort: A tool for the description of social behavior. *Journal of Personality, 68*, 450–489.

Furr, R. M., & Funder, D. C. (2007). Behavioral observation. In R. Robins, C. Fraley, & R. Krueger (Eds.), *Handbook of Research Methods in Personality Psychology* (pp. 273–291). New York: Guilford Press.

Glasman, L. R., & Albarracín, D. (2006). Forming attitudes that predict future behavior: A meta-analysis of the attitude-behavior relation. *Psychological Bulletin, 132*, 778–822.

Gosling, S. D., Kos, S. J., Mannarelli, T., & Morris, M. E. (2002). A room with a cue: Personality judgments based on offices and bedrooms. *Journal of Personality and Social Psychology, 82*, 379–398.

Holt, C. A., & Laury, S. (2002), Risk aversion and incentive effects. Andrew Young School of Policy Studies Research Paper Series No. 06-12. Available at SSRN: http://ssrn.com/abstract=893797

Kenrick, D. T., & Funder, D. C. (1988). Profiting from controversy: Lessons from the person-situation debate. *American Psychologist,43*, 23–34.

Knee, C. R., Lonsbary, C., Canevello, A., & Patrick, H. (2005). Self-determination and conflict in romantic relationships. *Journal of Personality and Social Psychology, 89*, 997–1009.

Kruger, J., Epley, N., Parker, J., & Ng, Z. (2005). Egocentrism over e-mail: Can we communicate as well as we think? *Journal of Personality and Social Psychology, 89*, 925–936.

Mehl, M. R., Gosling, S. D., & Pennebaker, J. W. (2006). Personality in its natural habitat: Manifestations and implicit folk theories of personality in daily life. *Journal of Personality and Social Psychology, 90*, 862–877.

Milgram, S. (1975). *Obedience to authority*. New York: Harper & Row.

Mischel, W. (1968). *Personality and assessment*. New York: Wiley.

Nisbett, R. E., & Cohen, D. (1996). *Culture of honor: The psychology of violence in the south*. Boulder, CO: Westview.

Nisbett, R. E., & Wilson, T. D. (1977). Telling more than we can know: Verbal reports on mental processes. *Psychological Review, 84*, 231–259.

Pennebaker, J., Mehl, M., & Niederhoffer, K. (2003). Psychological aspects of natural language use: Our words, our selves. *Annual Review of Psychology, 54*, 547–77.

Rozin, P. (2001). Social psychology and science: Some lessons from Solomon Asch. *Personality and Social Psychology Review, 5*, 2–14.

West, S. G., & Brown, T. J. (1975). Physical attractiveness, the severity of the emergency and helping: a field experiment and interpersonal simulation. *Journal of Experimental Social Psychology, 11*, 531–538.

Wicker, A. M. (1969). Attitudes vs. actions: The relationship of verbal and overt behavioral responses to attitude objects. *Journal of Social Issues, 22*, 41–78.

Wilson, T. D. (2002). *Strangers to ourselves: Discovering the adaptive unconscious*. Cambridge, MA: Harvard University Press.

Wilson, T. D., & Gilbert, D. T. (2003). Affective forecasting. In M. Zanna (Ed.), *Advances in experimental social psychology*, Vol. 35 (pp. 345–411). New York: Elsevier.

Wright, J. C., & Mischel, W. (1987). A conditional approach to dispositional constructs: The local predictability of social behavior. *Journal of Personality and Social Psychology, 53*, 1159–1177.

Wundt, W. (1894). *Lectures on human and animal psychology* (J. E. Creighton & E. B. Titchener, Trans.). New York: Macmillan.

3 Behavioral Assessment Practices Among Social Psychologists Who Study Small Groups

Richard L. Moreland
Joshua D. Fetterman
Jeffrey J. Flagg
Kristina L. Swanenburg

A recent article on publication trends in social psychology, published by Baumeister, Vohs, and Funder in 2007 and reprinted in this book (see Chapter 2), caught the attention of many people, including us. Baumeister and his colleagues were intrigued by a trend among social psychological researchers, who seem to have moved away from measuring actual behavior (e.g., people talking together, working with one another on a task, displaying or reacting to emotions), toward more trivial (and less social) activities (e.g., ratings of the self and/or others on questionnaires, keyboard strokes in response to artificial stimuli presented on computer monitors).

We are social psychologists whose research focuses on small groups. Although such research is a small portion of all the work done by social psychologists, that portion has been growing. And researchers from different disciplines who study small groups have become more collaborative lately, forming INGROUP, an international association (www.msu.edu/~gwittenb/ingroup.html) that hopes to generate even more research of this sort. So, when we read the paper by Baumeister and his colleagues, our thoughts naturally turned to its possible implications for research on small groups. Traditionally, the assessment of behavior has been a key feature of such research. People who study groups have thus developed a variety of methods for assessing behavior (see, for example, Beck & Lewis,

2002; Dabbs & Ruback, 1987; McGrath & Altermatt, 2001), and resources are available to help those who must analyze data on the behavior of group members (see, for example, Kenny, Mannetti, Pierro, Luvi, & Kashy, 2002). Surely, we thought, the trend that Baumeister and his colleagues observed would not be found in articles describing research on small groups. And if that trend were observed there, then group researchers should be made aware of it and led to consider its implications. Is the trend problematic? If so, then how serious a problem is it and what can be done about it?

OUR DATA SET

One of us (Moreland) has been involved for many years with a special data set that contains information about articles describing research on small groups. The data set involves articles published in the *Journal of Experimental Social Psychology* (*JESP*), the *Journal of Personality and Social Psychology* (*JPSP*), and the *Personality and Social Psychology Bulletin* (*PSPB*). These journals were chosen because of their prominence in social psychology. The original data set (Moreland, Hogg, & Hains, 1994) contained all of the articles that appeared in those journals between 1975 and 1993. The articles were first evaluated to determine whether they described research on small groups. Articles that met that criterion were then evaluated further for a variety of characteristics, including (a) length (number of pages); (b) number of studies reported; (c) primary research methodology; (d) primary substantive focus (group phenomenon); and (e) whether the work was influenced by European and/ or social cognition approaches to groups.

This data set was created with two broad goals in mind. One goal was to provide some descriptive data on small group research. Several interesting, and occasionally worrisome, findings emerged from the data. For example, about 75% of all small group studies involved laboratory experimentation, rather than other methodologies, and this obsession changed little over the years (cf. Haslam & McGarty, 2001). Another interesting finding was that some phenomena, especially those involving intergroup relations, were quite popular among researchers, whereas other phenomena, especially those involving intragroup phenomena, were not. There was, in fact, a general trend over time away from research on intragroup relations and toward research on intergroup relations.[1]

---

[1] Sanna and Parks (1997) later found just the opposite trend, using a data set that contained articles from major organizational psychology journals published over the same period. It would be interesting to investigate levels of behavioral assessment, and changes in those levels over time, among those articles and contrast the findings with the ones reported here.

But there was another goal as well, namely to test some predictions made by Steiner (see Steiner 1974, 1983, 1986) about trends in the overall popularity of research on groups over time. To examine those trends, a simple yearly index was created by first counting all of the pages describing group research that were published by the three journals, then dividing that number by the total number of journal pages published on all topics. The resulting proportion represented how interested social psychologists were in studying small groups that year. Statistical analyses of changes in the index scores over time were then carried out to test Steiner's predictions.

As it turned out, few of Steiner's predictions were confirmed. Yet there *were* clear changes over time in the index scores. That index started, in 1975, at around 15%, and then fell steadily for several years, reaching a low in the early 1980s of around 8%. But then it began to rise steadily, a trend that continued until 1994, when the index reached a high of about 23%. At that point, the future looked bright for small group research.

What caused the surge of interest in studying groups during the early 1980s and the 1990s? Moreland and his colleagues identified two possible factors. One factor was the growing influence during that period of European approaches to studying groups. For example, Tajfel's work on the role of social categorization in intergroup relations (see Tajfel, 1981, 1982; Tajfel & Turner, 1979) influenced such American social psychologists as Brewer (1979) and Wilder (1981, 1986; Wilder & Cooper, 1981). And many other American social psychologists, such as Levine (1980), Nemeth (1986), and others (e.g., Latane & Wolf, 1981; Maass & Clark, 1984; Tanford & Penrod, 1984) became interested around the same time in minority influence because of Moscovici's work on that topic (see Moscovici, 1976; 1980).

Another factor was enthusiasm among social psychologists for theories and research methods associated with social cognition. Consider, for example, Hamilton's (1981) book on cognitive processes in stereotyping, which demonstrated the potential value of cognitive analyses of groups. Other examples of people who took a cognitive approach to groups during this period include Jones (e.g., Jones, Wood, & Quattrone, 1981; Linville & Jones, 1980), who studied perceptions of the variability among group members, and Rothbart (e.g., Howard & Rothbart, 1980; Rothbart, Evans, & Fulero, 1979; Rothbart, Fulero, Jensen, Howard, & Burrell, 1978), who studied the encoding and recall of information about group members. Mullen's (1983) work on group composition and self-awareness also began at about this time.

Moreland, Hogg, and Hains (1994) tested their ideas about the impact of these factors in two ways. First, they showed that articles on groups that were influenced by European and/or social cognition approaches did indeed appear initially in the early 1980s and then became increasingly common as time passed. Second, when those articles were removed from the data set, leaving only articles that described research *not* influenced by either European or social cognition approaches, the surge of interest (from the early 1980s onward) in studying groups more or less disappeared.

Wittenbaum and Moreland (2008) later expanded the original data set by adding articles on group research published between 1996 and 2006. These new articles were evaluated in exactly the same ways as the articles studied by Moreland, Hogg, and Hains (1994), and many of the same analyses were done, often with similar results. One important difference, however, involved changes over time in the index scores. The good news was that research on groups continued to gain popularity, with the scores reaching a high of around 30% in 2003. The bad news was that those scores stabilized for a couple of years afterward, and then actually began to drop. Why? Were social psychologists starting to lose interest in groups? Maybe, but the drop could also have been artifactual. Over the last few years, new journals devoted entirely to group research (e.g., *Group Processes and Intergroup Relations, Group Dynamics: Theory, Research, and Practice*) have appeared, and *Small Group Research*, an older journal devoted to such work, has been revitalized. Maybe articles describing group research that once would have been submitted to more mainstream journals are now appearing in these specialized journals instead. If so, then the recent decline in the popularity of group research may be misleading—if a broader set of journals were examined, then interest among social psychologists in studying small groups might prove to be stronger than ever (cf. Randsley de Moura, Leader, Pelletier, & Abrams, 2008).

For this chapter, we decided to expand the data set yet again and to perform some analyses that explored levels of behavioral assessment among small group researchers. One small change that we made was to incorporate articles on group research published in the three target journals during 2007. These new articles were evaluated exactly as before, and by someone (Moreland) who carried out evaluations of the articles in earlier versions of the data set.

The data set now contains a total of 1,995 articles (398 from *JESP*, 968 from *JPSP*, 560 from *PSPB*) describing 4,067 studies. Index scores were computed in the same way as before. A summary of these scores across the years can be found in Figure 3.1. There are two lines in that figure. The solid line shows the actual index scores, and the dashed line shows the predicted scores derived from a regression analysis. Similar figures will appear later in this chapter, so it's worthwhile to pause now and describe briefly the analyses that generated them.

To explore this issue, three of us (all graduate students in social psychology who do group research themselves) reviewed all 4,067 studies in the data set and evaluated in each case whether behavior was measured or not, and if so, then how that was done. As Baumeister and his colleagues (2007) noted, the first judgment seems simple, but is actually complex. After some discussion, we chose to be conservative in our evaluations, requiring that group-related behavior be included among the *dependent* measures in a study. In other words, it was less important to us whether participants interacted (or exhibited other behavior) during a study than whether some behavior of theirs was measured and later predicted. Like Baumeister and his colleagues, we did not count as "behavioral" any study in which participants merely rated themselves or others on a questionnaire.

When group behavior *was* measured in a study, judging *how* it was measured turned out to be complicated as well. We devised several categories of measurement. These included (a) the direct observation of group interaction; (b) biological measurements, such as heart-rate, GSR, or brainwave recordings of group members; (c) archival data about groups or their members; (d) self-reports by group members about their past or current behavior; (e) reports by others (e.g., friends) about the past or current behavior of group members; (f) fictional behavior, as when group members describe how they might act in some hypothetical situation; and (g) measures of information processing by group members, such as listings of their thoughts, their memory for information (often about hypothetical others) shown to them by researchers, the time they spend looking at such information, how quickly they made whatever judgments researchers require from them, and so on. Finally, there was a large, miscellaneous category (h) that included a variety of methods, each used in just a few studies.

Can specific examples of group research be assigned reliably to these categories? After discussing the categories, three of us (the same persons who coded whether behavioral assessment occured at all or not) independently evaluated 100 articles from the data set. These articles represented all three journals and every publication year. For each study in an article, a coder first decided whether group behavior was measured at all. If not, then the study was assigned a special coding category (i) reserved for that purpose. But if group behavior *was* measured, then a further decision was made about which of the eight measurement techniques [(a) through (h)] described above was used.[2]

---

[2] In some studies, more than one type of behavioral measurement was used. When that happened, just one coding category was chosen, based on which measurement technique the researcher(s) seemed to emphasize.

Because the number of studies varied from one article to the next, only decisions that coders made about the first study in each article were compared for reliability. Following advice from King (2004), we calculated a generalized kappa statistic that compared all three coders' decisions simultaneously (rather than comparing those decisions one pair of coders at a time and then averaging the results across pairs). The generalized kappa was .72, which was significant ($p < .01$), indicating that studies were reliably assigned to the assessment categories.

In our opinion, however, the clearest example of behavioral assessment was (a), the direct observation of group interaction. The other categories varied in plausibility and some seemed arguable. Moreover, across the entire data set, direct observation was used more often than any other single form of behavioral assessment. A conservative decision was thus made to focus on behavioral assessments of this type. For each article, we thus created an index score by counting how many times such observations were made, and then dividing that number by the total number of studies in the article. The resulting score indicated the proportion of studies within an article that involved the direct observation of group behavior.[3]

These index scores were modest in size, with an overall mean of .36 and a standard deviation of .46. Among the 4,067 studies in the data set, 1,175 studies involved direct observations of behavior, 1,260 studies involved behavioral assessment of some other type, and 1,632 studies involved no behavioral assessment at all. Have there been any changes in levels of behavioral assessment over time, as Baumeister and his colleagues (2007) suggested? The answer can be found in Figure 3.2. The solid line there shows the actual behavioral assessment index scores and the dashed line shows predicted index scores. Polynomial regression analyses showed only linear effects of publication year on the index scores. The regression was significant, $F(1,31) = 81.70$, $p < .001$, accounting for about 73% of the variance. The Durbin-Watson statistic was 1.45. The figure shows that behavioral assessment has indeed become less popular over time among group researchers.

We also investigated whether levels of behavioral assessment varied significantly by journal or by group phenomenon. An analysis of variance that compared behavioral assessment index scores across the three journals was indeed significant, $F(2,1923) = 16.68$, $p < .01$. Behavioral assessment was more likely to be found in articles from the *Journal of*

---

[3] A more focused reliability check was done by comparing how many studies containing direct behavioral observation were found in the first study from each of the 100 articles. The resulting intraclass correlation was .71, which was significant ($p < .05$), indicating adequate reliability.

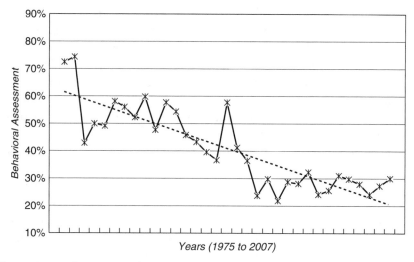

Figure 3.2. Changes over the Years in Behavioral Assessment among Researchers who Study Small Groups.

Experimental Social Psychology (M = .43, SD = .48) or the *Journal of Personality and Social Psychology (M = .38, SD = .47)*, rather than the *Personality and Social Psychology Bulletin. (M = .27, SD = .43)*. A second analysis of variance, one that compared behavioral assessment index scores across the six broad topic areas mentioned earlier (intergroup relations, conflict within groups, group performance, group composition, group structure, and the ecology of groups), was significant as well, $F (5, 1899) = 83.85$, $p < .01$. Behavioral assessment was more likely to be found in articles about group performance ($M = .70, SD = .45$), conflict in groups ($M = .64, SD = .46$), or group composition ($M = .61, SD = .47$), than in articles about group structure ($M = .40, SD = .48$) or the ecology of groups ($M = .32, SD = .45$). Behavioral assessment was least likely to be found in articles about intergroup relations ($M = .20, SD = .38$).

WHY IS THIS HAPPENING?

Baumeister and his colleagues (2007) offered several explanations for the decline of behavioral assessment in social psychology. One explanation involved the "cognitive revolution" in social psychology. That revolution, which began in the 1960s and has grown stronger since, has led many social psychologists to focus on cognitive structure and cognitive processes as the ultimate causes for behavior. As a result, they have naturally tried to measure such things (in addition to, and often even instead of, behavior itself) in their research. There has also been more pressure on researchers, from both reviewers and journal editors, to measure cognitive factors in their work, rather than only speculating about such factors.

Another explanation offered by Baumeister and his colleagues involves an emphasis in the major journals on articles that contain multiple studies. Behavioral assessment can be difficult and time-consuming, so if a researcher's goal were to publish as many articles as possible, then he or she might prefer dependent variables that can be measured quickly and easily. Behavior is seldom such a variable.

Finally, Baumeister and his colleagues noted that Institutional Review Boards (IRBs), which have become stronger in recent years, are often more cautious about research that involves behavioral rather than other measures. To resolve difficult negotiations with IRBs, or even to avoid IRB problems altogether, some researchers may thus have abandoned the assessment of behavior and come to rely instead on measurement techniques that raise fewer ethical concerns.[4]

Our focus in this chapter, however, is small groups. Why have social psychologists who study such groups moved away from assessing behavior? Three explanations, which overlap somewhat with those offered by Baumeister and his colleagues (2007), seem plausible to us. Our explanations involve (a) the growing influence of European approaches to studying groups, especially work involving social identity and self-categorization; (b) the growing influence of social cognition approaches to studying groups; and (c) an increasing pressure on authors to produce journal articles containing multiple studies.

As we noted earlier, all of the articles in our data set were evaluated for the influence of both European and social cognition approaches to studying groups. Why should these influences have anything to do with researchers' decisions about measuring group behavior? Let's begin with European influences, which are strongest in research on intergroup relations. This research often features social identity or social categorization theory. Social identity theory (see Tajfel & Turner, 1979, for an overview), which was developed to explain conflict between groups, argues that people possess both personal and social identities. Personal identities involve the individual qualities (e.g., physical attractiveness, intelligence) that make every person unique, whereas social identities involve group

---

[4] We are skeptical about this explanation, primarily because there is no evidence that the timing of changes in IRB strength matches the timing of changes in behavioral assessment in social psychological research. The latter changes seemed to begin long before the former ones—our own department evaluated much of its own research (the unfunded studies, at least) for ethical concerns until the 1990s, with little input from our university's IRB. Yet the decline in behavioral assessment that Baumeister et al. (2007) identified seemed to begin in the 1960s.

memberships (e.g., gender, religion, ethnicity) that can unite people or separate them from one another. There is considerable evidence from research on self-esteem that people value positive personal identities (see Pyszczynski, Greenberg, Solomon, Arndt, & Schimel, 2004; Yamaguchi et al., 2007). Social identity theory argues that people value positive social identities as well, and that conflicts between groups often reflect efforts to protect or improve the social identities of the people involved.

Self-categorization theory (see Turner Hogg, Oakes, Reicher, & Wetherell, 1987, for an overview) resembles social identity theory in several ways, but focuses more on the social categorization processes through which people come to associate themselves and others with various groups. And uncertainty reduction, rather than self-esteem enhancement, is the primary motive in self-categorization theory (see Hogg, 2001).

Both of these theories have been enormously influential, not just in social psychology, but also in other fields, such as organizational psychology. And in recent years, these theories have been used to explain intragroup relations, as well as intergroup relations (see, for example, Hogg & van Knippenberg, 2003).

For our purposes, a critical feature of both theories is their claim that face-to-face contact is unnecessary for group phenomena to occur. Turner, for example, claims that a psychological group arises, and can influence its members, whenever a set of people simultaneously categorize themselves as members of the same group. Although this may occur more often when people are doing something together, in the same place and at the same time, all of that is unnecessary. People need not interact at all for a "group" to exist. In fact, face-to-face interaction does not guarantee the existence of a group—a shared categorization of the self as a group member is what actually matters. All this has implications for research on small groups. Maybe there is no need to study groups by gathering research participants together and making them interact in some way. Instead, the essential step is to lead participants (who could be studied individually, even at different times and places) to *think* about themselves as members of the same group, and then observe how they react. Behavioral assessment (observing how research participants act toward one another) is unnecessary.

Let us turn now to social cognition influences on group research. As many observers have noted (e.g., Markus & Zajonc, 1985), the impact of cognitive psychology on social psychology has been widespread and powerful. Cognitive theories are discussed and cognitive research methods used in nearly every area of social psychology, even minor areas like groups. What does that have to do with behavioral assessment? For our purposes, a critical feature of the cognitive approach to social psychology is the claim (dating back to Lewin, 1936; Murray, 1938; and others) that behavior depends less on what is actually happening to someone than on what that person *thinks* is happening. In other words, events are less important than *meanings* for predicting behavior. Again, this has implications for research on small groups. To do research on conformity, for example, why is it necessary to observe actual groups, in which people that agree or disagree with one another about an issue express their opinions openly? The same or similar social pressures could be created by simply leading people to believe that their own views are similar or dissimilar to those held by other group members, who need not be present. Once again, behavioral assessment is unnecessary.

To explore these ideas, we went back to the data set and performed analyses guided initially by two questions. First, how often did European and social cognition influences actually occur, and did those influences become stronger over the years? Second, was behavioral assessment indeed less likely to be found in articles displaying either form of influence?

Among the 1,926 articles in the data set that contained at least one study, about 35% were influenced by European approaches to groups, and about 61% were influenced by approaches associated with social cognition. The two forms of influence were not independent, as indicated by a chi-square analysis, $X^2 (1) = 117.04, p < .01$. Articles influenced by European approaches to groups were more likely than not to show a social cognition influence as well ($n = 519$ vs. $n = 147$). Articles without European influence displayed a similar, but weaker trend ($n = 664$ vs. $n = 596$).

We analyzed the impact of European and social cognition influences (separately and together) on changes over time in levels of behavioral assessment. Social cognition influences proved to have a stronger impact; that impact was indeed negative and it has grown.[5] But rather than describe the results from those analyses in detail, we will focus here (because of space constraints) on analyses involving the related impact on behavioral assessment practices of studying intergroup relations. Articles influenced by European or social cognition approaches to groups often seemed to focus on intergroup relations. Could this explain the decline in behavioral assessment among group researchers? Research on intergroup relations has surged in recent years (see Abrams & Hogg, 1998; Wittenbaum & Moreland, 2008), and as we noted earlier, when describing our data set, articles about intergroup relations are less likely than articles about any other group phenomena to involve behavioral assessment.

---

[5] Details about these analyses are available on request.

Are European and social cognition influences indeed stronger in articles describing research on intergroup relations? To find out, we first assigned new topic codes to all the articles in the data set. Articles describing research on social identity, conflict between groups, and stereotyping were classified as work on intergroup relations, whereas articles describing research on group composition, group structure, conflict in groups, and group performance were classified as work on intragroup relations. Articles about research on the ecology of groups or miscellaneous topics did not clearly involve intergroup or intragroup relations, so they were set aside. Next, chi-square analyses were carried out to see whether there were significant relationships between (a) the topic of an article (intergroup or intragroup relations) and (b) any European or social cognition influences on that article. The chi-square values, each with a single degree of freedom, were both significant (European $X^2 = 81.69$; Social Cognition $X^2 = 426.39$), $p < .01$. As expected, articles influenced by European approaches to groups were more likely to focus on intergroup ($n = 488$) than intragroup relations ($n = 163$). Articles without such influence also tended to focus on intergroup relations ($n = 621$ vs. $n = 542$), but to a smaller degree. Articles influenced by social cognition approaches to groups were also more likely to focus on intergroup ($n = 903$) than intragroup relations ($n = 235$), again as we expected. Articles without such influence, in contrast, actually tended to focus on intragroup ($n = 470$), rather than intergroup relations ($n = 206$).

Research on intergroup relations, therefore, seems to embody both European and social cognition approaches to groups. But has such research indeed become more popular over the years? To check, we computed a yearly popularity index for intergroup relations research by adding all of the pages in articles associated with research on that topic, then dividing that number by the number of pages in the group articles.

Polynomial regression analyses of this popularity index, using year of publication as a predictor, revealed significant linear and quadratic trends. The overall analysis was significant, $F (2, 30) = 74.91$, $p < .01$, and accounted for about 86% of the variance. The Durbin-Watson statistic was 2.20. Raw popularity scores (solid line), and the predicted scores (dotted line) generated by the analysis, are shown in Figure 3.3. The popularity of research on intergroup relations has indeed been growing, although that growth seems to have slowed in recent years.[6]

---

[6] We also calculated similar popularity scores for research on intragroup relations, but they were so highly correlated with the intergroup relations popularity scores ($r = -.93, p < .01$) that there was little point in analyzing how they too changed over time.

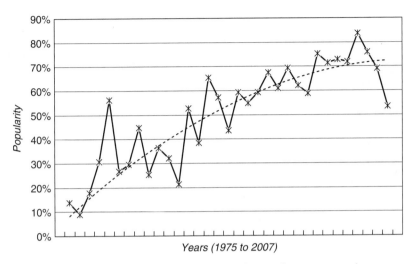

Figure 3.3. Changes over the Years in the Popularity of Intergroup Relations as a Research Topic.

The relationship between behavioral assessment and studying intergroup relations or intragroup relations was investigated through two separate sets of polynomial regression analyses. In both cases, attempts were made to predict behavioral assessment index scores over time. There was a linear effect of publication year on the scores for articles about intragroup relations. The overall regression was significant, $F(1, 31) = 18.06$, $p < .01$, and accounted for about 37% of the variance. The Durbin-Watson statistic was 2.05. The analysis of index scores for articles about intergroup relations produced less clear results. There was evidence of linear, quadratic, and cubic effects of publication year, but the overall analysis was only marginally significant, $F(3, 29) = 2.33$, $p < .10$, and accounted for just 19% of the variance.

Predicted behavioral assessment index scores from the two analyses are shown in Figure 3.4 (actual scores are not shown, in order to simplify the figure). The line for research on intragroup relations research is much higher than the line for intergroup relations research, indicating again that behavioral assessment is less common in the latter type of research. Among articles on intergroup relations, there was a complex pattern of predicted index scores across years—those scores fell at first, then rose gradually for many years, and finally fell again in recent years. But given the weak results of the analysis that generated these scores, they must be interpreted cautiously. Among articles on intragroup relations, the pattern was clearer—the predicted index scores fell steadily over time. This suggests that studying intergroup relations was not the only reason for the decline in behavioral assessment. Even researchers who study intragroup

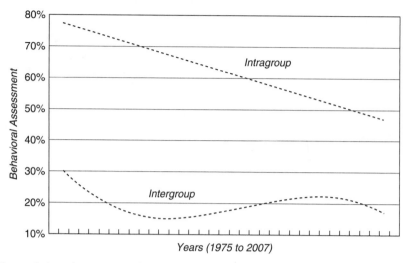

Figure 3.4.   Changes over the Years in Predicted Levels of Behavioral Assessment among Articles on Intergroup versus Intragroup Relations.

relations have gradually abandoned such assessment. Something else, then, must have contributed to the decline as well.

We suggested earlier that another reason for that decline is the growing pressure on all social psychologists to submit articles containing multiple studies. Wegner (1992) and others (e.g., Webster, 2007) have noted this trend, discussed its probable causes, and lamented some of its effects. One likely effect of such pressure on researchers who study groups is to limit the number of articles that are published (by those who measure behavior in their work), and to make it less likely that behavioral assessment will be part of any articles that are published. Assessing group behavior, especially through the direct observation of group members, can be very difficult, requiring considerable time, energy, and money (Weingart, 1997). It may thus be viewed by some researchers as a kind of "luxury" that they cannot afford, if their major goal is to complete multiple studies and thereby publish more articles.

Have group researchers, like other social psychologists, also increased the number of studies contained in their articles? And is the number of studies in an article about groups related to the assessment of behavior in those studies? To answer these questions, we computed the mean number of studies in the articles published each year. Polynomial regression analyses were again used to detect any temporal trends in the data, and a linear effect of publication year was indeed found. The overall analysis was significant, $F(1, 31) = 199.13$, $p < .01$, and accounted for about 87% of the variance. The Durbin-Watson statistic was 1.61. Figure 3.5 shows the mean number of studies actually published in articles over the years (solid

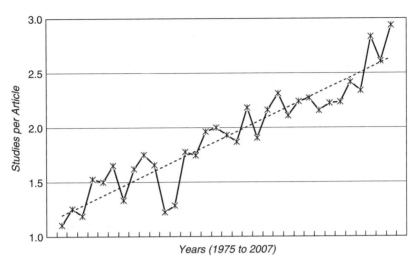

Figure 3.5. Changes over the Years in the Mean Number of Studies Contained in Articles about Small Groups.

line), as well as the predicted number of studies in those articles (dashed line). The trend was remarkably strong—the mean number of studies per article nearly tripled between 1975 and 2007!

To see whether the number of studies in an article was related to the assessment of behavior, we carried out a one-way analysis of variance that compared the behavioral assessment index scores for articles with one study ($n = 810$), two studies ($n = 525$), three studies ($n = 326$), four studies ($n = 156$), and five or more studies ($n = 109$). The analysis was significant, $F(4, 1921) = 35.83, p < .01$, and showed a general decrease in the assessment of behavior as the number of studies contained in an article increased. Behavioral assessment was least likely in articles with five or more studies ($M = .25, SD = .24$) followed by articles with four studies ($M = .34, SD = .34$), and then articles with three studies ($M = .42, SD = .42$). Levels of behavioral assessment were lower (unexpectedly) in articles with two studies ($M = .33, SD = .44$) but then rose again (and reached their highest levels) in articles with just one study ($M = .49, SD = .50$).

Is this enough to explain the results shown in Figure 3.2? To explore that issue, we did some counterfactual thinking. What if the number of studies contained in an article had stayed the same over the years, maybe at a low level that would have discouraged few group researchers? With this in mind, we removed from the data set all articles that contained more than one study, and then re-examined trends in behavioral assessment among the articles that remained. Would the decline in behavioral assessment among social psychologists who study groups have occurred if multistudy articles were not the norm?

A set of polynomial regression analyses was again performed, and significant linear, quadratic, and cubic trends of publication year on behavioral assessment index scores were found. The overall analysis was significant, $F (3,29) = 17.19$, $p < .01$, accounting for about 64% of the variance. The Durbin-Watson statistic was 2.04. A summary of the results can be found in Figure 3.6. The solid line in the figure represents actual behavioral assessment index scores, whereas the dashed line represents predicted scores. The latter scores rose at first, then fell for many years, only to rise again near the end. This pattern indicates that levels of behavioral assessment in research on groups still might have declined over the years, even if authors had felt no pressure to include multiple studies in their articles. And so, behavioral assessment by group researchers must be affected by other factors as well, such as the popularity of intergroup relations as a topic area.

It should not be surprising, given what we've said already, that a focus on intergroup versus intragroup relations, and the pressure to include more studies in each article, are related to one another. Indeed, articles on intergroup relations ($M = 2.34$, $SD = 1.32$) contained significantly more studies, $t (1812) = 9.68$, $p < .01$, than did articles on intragroup relations ($M = 1.76$, $SD = 1.14$). So, did behavioral assessment depend on the topic that a researcher was studying, the number of studies in the article that he or she wrote, or both? To find out, we regressed the behavioral assessment index scores on three variables, namely topic area (intergroup or intragroup relations), article size (number of studies), and their interaction. All of these predictors were significant ($p < .01$), as was the overall

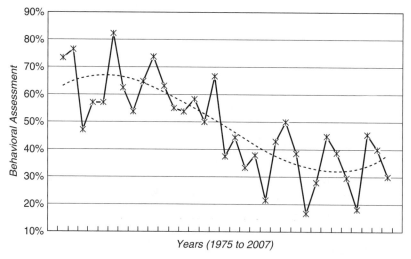

Figure 3.6. Changes in Behavioral Assessment over the Years among Articles in Which Just One Study Appeared.

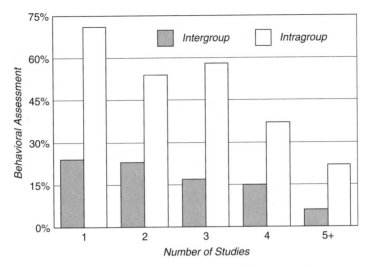

Figure 3.7. The Relationship between the Mean Number of Studies and Levels of Behavioral Assessment in Articles about Intergroup versus Intragroup Relations.

regression, $F(3, 1810) = 177.29, p < .01$, which accounted for about 23% of the variance. The two main effects were just as described earlier (less behavioral assessment in research on intergroup relations and in articles containing more studies). The fact that topic area and article size each had a significant effect, when the effects of the other variable were controlled, implies that both variables are important factors in the choices that researchers make about behavioral assessment. To interpret the interaction effect, we regressed behavioral assessment index scores on article size separately for articles about each topic. Both analyses were significant overall $(p < .01)$, but stronger effects were found in the analysis for articles about intragroup relations, where 6% (versus 2%) of the variance was explained.[7] This difference is illustrated in Figure 3.7.

WHAT'S THE HARM?

We have shown that behavioral assessment is becoming less common among social psychologists who study small groups. But is this a serious problem? What harm is done when behavior is neglected in this way?

We would not argue that behavioral assessment is essential for research on groups. Nevertheless, it seems to us that much can be lost

---

[7] Both of these effects were somewhat weak, probably because of range restrictions in the number of studies per article when only one topic area was considered.

when behavior is not assessed. One drawback, discussed by Baumeister and his colleagues (2007), is that researchers who rely too much on participants' self-reports are sometimes misled. After all, people may have limited access to their thoughts and feelings, so they can either say little about such things, or they describe instead how someone "ought" to think and feel in a given situation (cf. Nisbett & Wilson, 1977). Even when participants *can* tell researchers about their thoughts or feelings, they may decide not to, because of social desirability concerns about themselves and/or their groups. Self-reports can also be influenced by moods and other irrelevant factors (Schwarz, 1999). These may not be salient to participants, so their effects go unnoticed (and are thus unlikely to be controlled) by participants.

Another drawback of neglecting to measure behavior is that certain phenomena may be ignored or misunderstood. Consider, for example, group emotions. There has been much interest in this topic recently (see Kelly & Barsade, 2001). Do group emotions exist (apart from individual emotions), and if so, then how do they affect groups and their members? Such questions are important, but they may be difficult or even impossible to answer if behavior is not measured, because people often have trouble describing their emotions. Other group phenomena that may require behavioral assessment to be understood include implicit coordination (Rico, Sanchez-Manzanares, Gil, & Gibson, 2008; Wittenbaum, Vaughan, & Stasser, 1998), group cultures (Levine & Moreland, 1991), transactive memory (Moreland, 1999), and implicit learning in groups (Wilson, Goodman, & Cronin, 2007). All these phenomena can have a significant impact on groups, yet group members seem to have little awareness of them. Only by observing actual group behavior can phenomena like these be detected and related to other aspects of group life.

Finally, moving away from the "earthy" world of actual group behavior, into the more "ethereal" world of thoughts about groups and their members, can sometimes drain the life out of a phenomenon, making it less interesting. As a result, fewer researchers are motivated to study the phenomenon, which retards understanding of it. A case in point is minority influence, a phenomenon brought to everyone's attention by Moscovici in the 1970s. Moscovici was intrigued by examples of real-world groups containing minorities that were influential, despite their small size and limited power. How is such influence possible? What social psychological processes are involved? A 2001 paper by Levine and Kaarbo described those processes (in the context of political groups), and they are intriguing. But to study such processes, one would probably have to create (or gain access to) actual groups that contain majorities and minorities, and then observe the behavior of group members carefully over time (perhaps collecting other kinds of data too).

Does anyone do such research? Sadly, they do not. Instead, research of quite a different sort is done. Participants in that research (who are often isolated from one another and/or forbidden to interact) are given false information about the opinions of a group to which they belong (usually a large social category, in fact, rather than a small group). Some issue is identified, and participants are told that X% of group members think one way about it, whereas Y% of group members think another way. Persuasive messages (also false) from people on each side of the issue are given to participants, who read the messages, describe their reactions to them, and finally report their own opinions about the issue. Of special interest is how the cognitive processing of the messages interacts with the majority/minority status of their authors to produce attitude change among the participants.

Is this sort of research interesting? Some social psychologists would say so. But the "proof is in the pudding" — minority influence, as a topic area, appears to be dying, in the sense that less research on it is published every year. Other group phenomena, such as group polarization, have already suffered a similar fate. Would interest in phenomena like these be any stronger if researchers had measured actual behavior, rather than just collecting self-reports? We think so.

SOLVING THE PROBLEM

Behavioral assessment is gradually disappearing from research on groups. If the current trends continue, less than one in four articles about groups that are published in the next few years will feature such assessment. We have identified some negative consequences of this trend when it comes to understanding groups. What can be done to solve this problem? Baumeister and his colleagues (2007) offered a few solutions, and we have some ideas of our own as well ...

One solution may be to do little more than warn researchers about the problem and then sit back to see what happens. Perhaps the Baumeister et al. (2007) paper, in combination with our chapter (and the other chapters in this book), will lead researchers to be more thoughtful about their methodological options, and to assess behavior more often as a result. This would certainly be consistent with Moscovici's (1980) theory, and later research (Maass, West, & Cialdini, 1987), on minority influence. Work in that area suggests that a minority (researchers who favor behavioral assessment) ought to state its position forcibly and consistently, then stand back and wait while that message works its way through the minds of the majority (researchers who have abandoned behavioral assessment), eventually changing at least some of the majority's behavior. We would also note a few results from our analyses that suggest things may be improving already. In recent years, for example, fewer articles describing research on intergroup relations have appeared (Figure 3.3). As we have shown, such articles are less likely to feature behavioral assessment, so overall levels of behavioral assessment may soon rise as result. There is no evidence of that as yet (see Figure 3.2), but perhaps the change will take awhile to occur. It is also worth noting that the era of multistudy papers may be ending, according to analyses and arguments offered by Webster (2007). As we have shown, articles containing more studies are less likely to feature behavioral assessment, so once again, overall levels of behavioral assessment may soon rise as a result. We found no evidence in our own data that the preference for more studies per article is weakening (Figure 3.5), but that may be because Webster analyzed articles on many topics from journals throughout psychology, whereas we focused on articles about small groups that appeared in social psychological journals. We saw no evidence that overall levels of behavioral assessment in these articles are rising yet, but that may also take awhile to occur.

Although it is certainly easier to simply publish a few papers about this problem, and then sit back for awhile and hope for the best, a more active approach may be needed. One tactic, suggested by Baumeister and his colleagues (2007), is to make it easier for researchers to include behavioral assessment in their research. This tactic has at least two major components, one educational and the other technological. The educational component involves the lack of training in behavioral assessment among younger social psychologists. Assessing behavior (especially in small groups), and then performing the complex data analyses associated with such assessment, requires skills and knowledge that may no longer be a part of many graduate students' training. And given that journal articles are becoming less likely to feature behavioral assessment as time goes by, the chances that graduate students in years to come will be taught what they need to know seem weak as well. What can be done about this? Several possible solutions come to mind, including (a) including more material about behavioral assessment in the research methods courses taught to graduate students in social psychology; (b) publishing more articles in major social psychological journals that describe how behavioral assessment is done, or describe research projects that feature behavioral assessment, along with material annotating the specific procedures involved; (c) presenting workshops, during conventions or as independent events, where behavioral assessment techniques are taught, preferably in "hands-on" manner.

The technological component of this tactic (making behavioral assessment easier) involves the development of (a) better devices for recording and then editing records of participants' behavior during research projects, and (b) better software for performing some of the more onerous tasks associated with transcribing behavior and then coding transcripts for content. Although some progress has been made along these lines (see Carley, 1997; Ottoni, 2000), more is needed. The technology that is already available must reach more researchers (some of the devices and software are expensive, priced beyond the budgets of many researchers), and often suffers from thorny problems (e.g., certain aspects of oral behavior, such as irony, are too subtle to be detected by anything other than highly trained human coders).

Even if more researchers become capable of assessing behavior, they must still be motivated to do so. Why go to the trouble of assessing behavior if it is not really helpful, and may even be harmful, when it comes to publishing one's work? Where can articles that feature behavioral assessment be submitted, and what are their chances of actually being published there?

Baumeister and his colleagues (2007) suggested that journal editors and reviewers be encouraged to perform a kind of "affirmative action" when it comes to articles that feature behavioral assessment. The people who decide what will be published in the journals should be urged (without sacrificing quality) to look for more articles describing research in which behavior was assessed, even if those articles contain fewer studies or focus on topics that are less popular. We support this tactic, although we are skeptical about the chances of persuading all editors and reviewers to behave in this way, and the tactic might work best if it is implemented quietly, because research on affirmative action programs in other contexts shows that beneficiaries of those programs are often viewed (by others, and even by themselves), as less competent (see Heilman & Haynes, 2006).

Another tactic that might help is to foster a norm favoring research in which behavior is assessed. This could be done by increasing the prominence of journal articles that feature behavioral assessment, say by making them the "lead" articles in journal issues, or by moving them to a special section of the journal. An even stronger version of this same tactic might be to create and/or encourage journals devoted entirely to research in which behavior is assessed. This tactic has our support as well, although two dangers should be kept in mind. First, researchers who do not assess behavior in their own work may not be interested enough in work that features such assessment to read even a special section of their favorite journal, let alone read some separate journal. [Moreover, recall our finding that articles contain fewer studies when they feature behavioral assessment, along with Webster's (2007) finding that journals are less prestigious when their articles contain fewer studies]. If articles that feature behavioral assessment are avoided by readers, then the impact of such articles would obviously be limited. A second danger is that the appearance of too few articles in a special journal section devoted to research involving behavioral assessment, or in a journal devoted entirely to such research, might signal that behavioral research is rare, perhaps because it is very difficult (as, ironically, it is), or unpopular for other reasons. Such signals would probably weaken, not strengthen, the motivation to assess behavior among those who have not yet done so in their own research.

One way to avoid both of these dangers might be to award prizes to especially good research in which behavior was assessed. Division 49 (Group Psychology and Group Psychotherapy) of the American Psychological Association, for example, awards a prize each year for the best dissertation research on groups. Maybe that organization, along with other organizations that award research prizes (prizes that could be won by people who study groups), might be encouraged to focus on research in which attempts were made to assess participants' behavior.

IN CLOSING

More could be said about all this, but it's time now to close the chapter. Our main goal here was to alert social psychologists who study groups about a problem. If that goal has been accomplished, then we are content. We hope that our colleagues will consider the problem carefully, and if it seems serious to them, then develop and try to implement some solutions. We have offered a few suggestions regarding these issues, but a broader and deeper analysis is needed. That analysis is already overdue and should now begin.

REFERENCES

Abrams, D., & Hogg, M. A. (1998). Prospects for research on ingroup processes and intergroup relations. *Group Processes and Intergroup Relations, 1,* 7–20.

Beck, A. P., & Lewis, C. M. (Eds.) (2002). *The process of group psychotherapy: Systems for analyzing change.* Washington, DC: American Psychological Association.

Brewer, M. B. (1979). In-group bias in the minimal inter-group situation: A cognitive-motivational analysis. *Psychological Bulletin, 86,* 307–324.

Carley, K. M. (1997). Extracting team mental models through textual analysis. *Journal of Organizational Behavior, 18,* 533–558.

Dabbs, J. M., & Ruback, R. B. (1987). Dimensions of group process: Amount and structure of vocal interaction. In L. Berkowitz (Ed.), *Advances in experimental social psychology* (Vol. 20, pp. 123–269). New York: Academic Press.

Hamilton, D. C. (Ed.) (1981). *Cognitive processes in stereotyping and intergroup behavior*. Hillsdale, NJ: Erlbaum.

Haslam, S. A., & McGarty, C. (2001). A 100 years of certitude? Social psychology, the experimental method, and the management of scientific uncertainty. *British Journal of Social Psychology, 40*, 1–21.

Heilman, M. E., & Haynes, M. C. (2006). Affirmative action: Unintended adverse effects. In M. F. Karsten (Ed.), *Gender, race, and ethnicity in the workplace* (Vol. 2, pp. 1–24). Westport, CT: Greenwood.

Hogg, M. A. (2001). Self-categorization and subjective uncertainty resolution: Cognitive and motivational facets of social identity and group membership. In J. P. Forgas, K. D. Williams, & L. Wheeler (Eds.), *The social mind: Cognitive and motivational aspects of interpersonal behavior* (pp. 323–349). New York: Cambridge University Press.

Hogg, M. A., & van Knippenberg, D. (2003). Social identity and leadership processes in groups. In M. Zanna (Ed.), *Advances in experimental social psychology* (Vol. 35, pp. 1–52). New York: Elsevier.

Howard, J. W., & Rothbart, M. (1980). Social categorization and memory for in-group and out-group behavior. *Journal of Personality and Social Psychology, 38*, 301–310.

Jones, E. E., Wood, G. C., & Quattrone, G. A. (1981). Perceived variabilitiy of personal characteristics in in-groups and out-groups.: The role of knowledge and evaluation. *Personality and Social Psychology Bulletin, 7*, 523–528.

Kelly, J. R., & Barsade, S. G. (2001). Mood and emotions in small groups and work teams. *Organizational Behavior and Human Decision Processes, 86*, 99–130.

Kenny, D. A., Mannetti, L., Pierro, A., Luvi, S., & Kashy, D. A. (2002). The statistical analysis of data from small groups. *Journal of Personality and Social Psychology, 83*, 125–137.

King, J. E. (2004, February). *Software solutions for obtaining a kappa-type statistic for use with multiple raters*. Paper presented at the annual meeting of the Southwest Educational Research Association, Dallas, TX.

Latane, B., & Wolf, S. (1981). The social impact of majorities and minorities. *Psychological Review, 8*, 438–453.

Levine, J. M. (1980). Reaction to opinion deviance in small groups. In P. Paulus (Ed.), *Psychology of group influence* (pp. 375–429). Hillsdale, NJ: Erlbaum.

Levine, J. M., & Kaarbo, J. (2001). Minority influence in political decision-making groups. In C. K. W. DeDreu & N. K. DeVries (Eds.), *Group consensus and minority influence: Implications for innovation* (pp. 229–257). Malden, MA: Blackwell.

Levine, J. M., & Moreland, R. L. (1991). Culture and socialization in work groups. In L. B. Resnick, J. M. Levine, & S. D. Teasdale (Eds.), *Perspectives on socially shared cognition* (pp. 257–279). Washington, DC: American Psychological Association.

Lewin, K., (1936). *Principles of topological psychology*. New York: McGraw-Hill.

Linville, P. W., & Jones, E. E. (1980). Polarized appraisals of out-group members. *Journal of Personality and Social Psychology, 38*, 689–703.

Maass, A., & Clark, R. D. (1984). Hidden impact of minorities: Fifteen years of minority influence research. *Psychological Bulletin, 95*, 428–450.

Maass, A., West, S. G., & Cialdini, R. B. (1987). Minority influence and conversion. In C. Hendrick (Ed.), *Review of personality and social psychology* (Vol. 9, pp. 55–79). Newbury Park, CA: Sage.

Markus, H., & Zajonc, R. B. (1985). The cognitive perspective in social psychology. In G. Lindzey & E. Aronson (Eds.), *The handbook of social psychology* (Vol. 1, pp. 137–231). New York: Random House.

McGrath, J. E., & Altermatt, T. W. (2001). Observation and analysis of group interaction over time: Some methodological and strategic choices. In M. A. Hogg & R. S. Tindale (Eds.), *Blackwell handbook of social psychology: Group processes* (pp. 525–556). Oxford, UK: Blackwell.

Moreland, R. L. (1999). Transactive memory: Learning who knows what in work groups and organizations. In L. Thompson, D. Messick, & J. Levine (Eds.), *Shared cognition in organizations: The management of knowledge* (pp. 3–31). Mahwah, NJ: Erlbaum

Moreland, R. L., Hogg, M. A., & Hains, S. (1994). Back to the future: Social psychological research on groups. *Journal of Experimental Social Psychology, 30*, 527–555.

Moscovici, S. (1976). *Social influence and social change.* New York: Academic Press.

Moscovici, S. (1980). Toward a theory of conversion behavior. In L. Berkowitz (Ed.), *Advances in experimental social psychology* (Vol. 13, pp. 209–239). New York: Academic Press.

Mullen, B. (1983). Operationalizing the effect of the group on the individual: A self-attention perspective. *Journal of Experimental Social Psychology, 19*, 295–322.

Murray, H. A. (1938). *Explorations in personality: A clinical and experimental study of fifty men of college age.* New York: Oxford University Press.

Nemeth, C. (1986). Differential contributions of majority vs. minority influence. *Psychological Review, 93*, 23–32.

Nisbett, R. E., & Wilson, T. D. (1977). Telling more than we can know: Verbal reports on mental processes. *Psychological Review, 84*, 231–259.

Ottoni, E. B. (2000). EthoLog 2.2: A tool for the transcription and timing of behavior observation sessions. *Behavior Research Methods and Instrumentation, 32*, 446–449.

Pyszczinski, T., Greenberg, J., Solomon, S., Arndt, J., & Schimel, J. (2004). Why do people need self-esteem? A theoretical and empirical review. *Psychological Bulletin, 13*, 435–468.

Randsley de Moura, G., Leader, T., Pelletier, J., & Abrams, D. (2008). Prospects for group processes and intergroup relations research: A review of 70 years' progress. *Group Processes and Intergroup Relations, 11*, 575–596.

Rico, R., Sanchez-Manzanares, M., Gil, F., & Gibson, C. (2008). Team implicit coordination processes: A team-based approach. *Academy of Management Review, 33*, 163–185.

Rothbart, M., Evans, M., & Fulero, S. (1979). Recall for confirming events: Memory processes and the maintenance of social stereotypes. *Journal of Experimental Social Psychology, 15*, 343–355.

Rothbart, M., Fulero, S., Jensen, C., Howard, J., & Burrell, P. (1978). From individual to group impressions: Availability heuristics in stereotype formation. *Journal of Experimental Social Psychology, 14*, 237–255.

Sanna, L. J., & Parks, C. D. (1997). Whatever happened to intragroup research? *Psychological Science, 8*, 261–267.

Schwarz, N. (1999). Self-reports: How the questions shape the answers. *American Psychologist, 54*, 93–105.

Steiner, I. D. (1974). Whatever happened to the group in social psychology? *Journal of Experimental Social Psychology, 10,* 94–108.

Steiner, I. D. (1983). Whatever happened to the touted revival of the group? In H. Blumberg, A. Hare, V. Kent, & M. Davies (Eds.), *Small groups and social interaction* (Vol. 2, pp. 539–548). New York: Wiley.

Steiner, I. D. (1986). Paradigms and groups. In L. Berkowitz (Ed.), *Advances in experimental social psychology* (Vol. 19, pp. 251–289). Orlando, FL: Academic Press.

Tajfel, H. (1981). *Human groups and social categories.* Cambridge: Cambridge University Press.

Tajfel, H. (1982). *Social psychology and intergroup relations.* Cambridge: Cambridge University Press.

Tajfel, H., & Turner, J. C. (1979). An integrative theory of intergroup conflict. In W. G. Austin & S. Worchel (Eds.), *The social psychology of intergroup relations* (pp. 33–47). Monterey, CA: Brooks/Cole.

Tanford, S., & Penrod, S. (1984). Social influence model: A formal integration of research on majority and minority influence processes. *Psychological Bulletin, 95,* 189–225.

Turner, J. C., Hogg, M. A., Oakes, P. J., Reicher, S. D., & Wetherell, M. S. (Eds.) (1987). *Rediscovering the social group: A self-categorization theory.* Oxford: Blackwell.

Webster, G. D. (2007). The demise of the increasingly protracted APA journal article. *American Psychologist, 62,* 255–257.

Wegner, D. M. (1992). The premature demise of the solo experiment. *Personality and Social Psychology Bulletin, 18,* 504–508.

Weingart, L. R. (1997). How did they do that? The ways and means of studying group process. In B. M. Staw & L. L. Cummings (Eds.), *Research in organizational behavior* (Vol. 19, pp. 189–239). Greenwich, CT: JAI Press.

Wilder, D. A. (1981). Perceiving persons as a group: Categorization and intergroup relations. In D. L. Hamilton (Ed.), *Cognitive processes in stereotyping and intergroup behavior* (pp. 213–257). Hillsdale, NJ: Erlbaum.

Wilder, D. A. (1986). Social categorization: Implications for creation and reduction of intergroup bias. In L. Berkowitz (Ed.), *Advances in experimental social psychology* (Vol. 19, pp. 291–355). Orlando: Academic Press.

Wilder, D. A., & Cooper, W. E. (1981). Categorization into groups: Consequences for social perception and attribution. In J. Harvey, W. Ickes, & R. Kidd (Eds.), *New directions in attribution research* (Vol. 3, pp. 247–277). Hillsdale, NJ: Erlbaum.

Wilson, J. M., Goodman, P. S., & Cronin, M. A. (2007). Group learning. *Academy of Management Review, 32,* 1041–1059.

Wittenbaum, G. M., & Moreland, R. L. (2008). Small group research in social psychology: Topics and trends over time. *Social and Personalitiy Psychology Compass, 2,* 187–205.

Wittenbaum, G. M., Vaughan, S. I., & Stasser, G. (1998). Coordination in task-performing groups. In R. S. Tindale & Associates (Eds.), *Theory and research in small groups* (pp. 177–204). New York: Plenum.

Yamaguchi, S., Greenwald, A. G., Banaji, M. R., Murakami, F., Chen, D., Shiomura, K., Kobayashi, C., Cai, H., & Krendl, A. (2007). Apparent universality of positive implicit self-esteem. *Psychological Science, 18,* 498–500.

II

Behavior and
Intra-Individual Processes

4   Individuals, Behavior, and What Lies Between the Two

Donal E. Carlston
William G. Graziano

Miracles arise from our ignorance of nature, not from nature.

—Montaigne (1588).

The Harris cartoon that serves as frontispiece to this volume and the epigraph that serves to introduce this chapter both suggest that sometimes there are gaps in our understanding that are most readily explained by appealing to miracles. In psychology, that gap is often between stimulus environment and behavioral response, in what was once characterized as the "black box" of the mind. In this simple model, stimuli influence the individual's unknown internal workings, which then influence observable behaviors. Doctrinaire behaviorism urged researchers to ignore what was unobservable and unknowable and concentrate on the superordinate link from stimulus to response. Conditioned by decades of behaviorist domination, psychologists came to speak of that black box mostly in hushed tones, until the cognitive revolution came along and freed them to pontificate about it with considerable zeal. So much zeal, in fact, that the stimulus environment and behavioral response, which were once the only socially acceptable topics of scientific discourse, became neglected instead.

After the cognitive revolution, the black box was mostly characterized as a magnificent information processor, which could churn up stimuli, mix and match them with other material from memory, and produce new, more elaborate representations. If the question arose as to how to get from these new representations to actual behavior, there was often a certain amount of hand waving and reference to what would be, in essence, a miracle dressed in scientific clothing. Like William James, more than 100 years ago (1890), psychologists seemed to reason that mental representations of behavior must be linked to motoric representations of behavior, so obviously, if the mind could manufacture the former, the body would enact the latter.

Of course, the information processing characterization of the black box wasn't the only one, and other psychologists came to view it in terms of such concepts as emotions, attitudes, or personality, all of which could mediate between stimulus and response. Like the information processing models, these other concepts served to make the black box seem less inscrutable and mysterious. In many cases, however, clarity regarding one component of the causal chain (the black box) was somewhat negated by vagueness about the next (the link to behavior)—the exact mechanisms through which emotion, attitude, or personality were supposed to affect behavior remained a mystery. So a miracle was still needed.

Many of the contributions in this section of this book serve to clear up these mysteries (and cancel the need for a miracle). Among these are chapters on the mediating role of emotions (Chapter 7: Baumeister, DeWall, Vohs, & Alquist), attitudes (Chapter 9: Fabrigar, Wegener, & MacDonald), and personality (Chapters 10–13: Furr, Wagerman, & Funder; Goldberg; Paulhus & Holden; Baron). In addition, chapters resurrect and clarify two older conceptions of behavior mediation that were largely neglected during the first stages of the cognitive revolution, habit (Chapter 5: Verplanken) and unconscious behavioral guidance (Chapter 6: Bargh & Morsella). Though habit was an acceptable construct to the behaviorists, its considerable impact on behavior has been largely ignored since then (see Triandis, 1980, for an early exception). And the idea of unconscious behavioral guidance was awkward, to say the least, in the era of information processing. With today's interest in implicit social cognition, both concepts have come out of the closet, and the included chapters emphasize how much traction they afford in accounting for large portions of human behavior.

In virtually all of these chapters, the authors challenge either the field's neglect or its misconstrual of the mediator on which they focus. In the process, several authors also raise doubts about the adequacy of the whole causal metaphor with which this chapter began. In Verplanken's construal of habit, behavior is cause as well as effect, as frequently performed behaviors become ingrained and contribute to their own subsequent execution. Baumeister et al. suggest that emotion is not so much the direct cause of behavior as a consequence, which serves to feed back and shape subsequent behaviors. And Baron essentially questions any distinction between the stimulus environment, the individual, and behavior, arguing that all three of these are embodied in the affordances inherent in settings and situations. Such views don't just clarify the causal chain but, rather, melt it down and remold it. Given this perspective, any tendency the field has had to neglect behavior (see Chapter 2 by Baumeister, Vohs, & Funder) becomes a threat to our understanding of all aspects of individual psychology, as these are all bound inextricably together in a coherent system.

Another theme common to many of the chapters in this section is their focus on construct measurement. Verplanken describes a self-report measure of habit, Paulhus and Holden discuss behavioral measures of self-enhancement tendencies, Furr et al. emphasize a method for assessing behavior observationally, and Goldberg reviews an extensive program of research that relies on self-reports of behavioral acts. Measurement issues have also been important, for some of the same reasons, in the attitude-behavior debate covered in the Fabrigar et al. chapter. Perhaps the central reason for this importance is the continued exaltation of behavior as uniquely objective and meaningful (but see Goldberg, this volume) coupled with an appreciation for the difficulty and expense involved in assessing it (see Furr et al., this volume). In any case, given that the adequacy of measures can make or break any attempt to understand the psychology of the individual, this consensual emphasis on behavior measurement makes sense.

SOCIAL CONSTRUCTS AND BEHAVIOR

The first five chapters of this section deal with some possible mediators of behavior. They are ordered in this volume roughly in terms of conceptual level, with Chapters 5 and 6 representing the most basic mechanisms (habit and unconscious behavioral guidance), Chapters 8 and 9 representing the most cognitive (implementation intentions and attitudes), and Chapter 7 (emotions) in between. We here present a brief overview of each.

In Chapter 5, Verplanken notes that 45% of everyday behaviors are repeated in the same location almost every day, and are so "subtly woven" into the fabric of people's lives that they occur outside of awareness. Thus, he makes the case both for the ubiquity of habitual behaviors and for their nonconscious nature. He notes that some models of attitudes, such as the Ajzen and Fishbein (1980) model of behavioral intentions, fail to take into account the habitual effect of past behaviors. In doing so, he essentially distinguishes his emphasis from that of more cognitive approaches, such as those described by in Chapters 8 (implementation intentions) and 9 (attitudes). He then discusses a meta-analysis suggesting that past behavior is the dominant predictor of frequently performed behaviors, though intention is the dominant predictor of infrequent behaviors. This discussion helps to delineate some of the boundary conditions for different mediators of behavior covered in this section of this book.

Verplanken observes that habitual behaviors tend to be externally cued, so that the "center of control over behavior" shifts from the individual to the environment. This view dovetails nicely with Baron's Chapter 13 interpretation of the "affordances" inherent in different environments, as well as with aspects of Bargh and Morsella's Chapter 6 description of an unconscious behavioral guidance system. Verplanken makes the connections with the latter work even more explicit by basing his own Self-Report Habit Index (SRHI) partly on Bargh's (1994) criteria for automaticity. The goal in doing so is to formally recognize that habit cannot be equated solely with past behavioral frequency, as the processes underlying that frequency also matter.

Finally, Verplanken discusses relationships among motivation, goals, and habits, suggesting that higher-level aspects of behaviors (e.g., goals) can become habitual even when lower-level aspects (execution of the behavior) are not. Thus, for example, a person may have a habit of working out, though the days, times, and activities involved may be entirely under intentional control. He concludes this analysis by suggesting that "habits are inherently goal-directed," suggesting further ties between his chapter and the goal-directed properties of unconscious behavioral guidance (Chapter 6) and implementation intentions (Chapter 8).

In Chapter 6, Bargh and Morsella note that in the 1980s (relatively early in the cognitive revolution) psychologists were comfortable with conscious-process accounts of behavior but not with less-conscious process accounts. Consequently, even though consciousness is arguably more mysterious, and more atypical (for animals, especially, but humans as well), arguments regarding nonconscious processes were met with some skepticism. But thanks to several decades of intensive research, models of such processes are now viewed as much more theoretically and empirically tractable than was true earlier.

Bargh and Morsella detail the evidence for four different nonconscious behavioral guidance systems: perceptual, evaluative, motivational, and emotional. In each case evidence is first presented regarding basic priming or activation effects, followed by evidence that these effects actually have behavioral consequences. Consequently, the four systems, as sequenced above, provide partial accounts for phenomena discussed in Chapters 10 (affordances), 9 (attitudes), 8 (implementation intentions), and 7 (emotions), respectively. But the emphasis here on automatic processes that serve to diminish the "role for intentional conscious causation and guidance" provides a rather different perspective towards most of these phenomena than do those that follow.

In Chapter 7, Baumeister et al. challenge the traditional view that emotion directly causes behavior, as represented in the claim that someone did something "because he was angry" or "because she was afraid." Essentially, this is the view that "the impetus for the behavior is contained in the emotion," a premise that still leaves a miraculous gap between feeling the emotion and enacting the behavior. As an alternative, the authors advance the view that "conscious emotion tends to come after behavior and operates as a kind of inner feedback system." This view is consistent with Bargh and Mosella's discussion of emotion, though Baumeister et al. confine themselves to emotions that are "conscious feeling states" distinct from more subtle and less-conscious automatic affect.

The authors bolster their argument against the traditional view with evidence that emotions are not specific enough to serve as impetus for specific behaviors, that emotions seem to have more impact on cognition than on behavior, and that emotional influences on behavior tend to disappear unless people believe that their actions will affect their emotional state. They also note that habit and emotion are negatively correlated, so that rather than developing stronger feelings as behaviors are practiced, emotional reactions actually attenuate. The authors suggest that all of this evidence is more consistent with the premise that emotions serve as feedback that leads people to anticipate the emotional consequences of their behaviors and adjust their actions accordingly than it is with the traditional view of emotions as causes of behavior. They also note that their theory of emotion helps to explain people's tendency to overestimate the strength of future emotional reactions, because such exaggeration serves the adjustment function by increasing the likelihood that people will modify their behavior. Taking into account such adjustments, they conclude that "emotion does have a causal influence on behavior, just not in the direct and immediate manner widely assumed."

In Chapter 8, Gollwitzer et al. focus on one of the more cognitive mediators of behavior, dealing with the extent to which implementation intentions lead to successful execution of an intended behavior. From this viewpoint, automatic processes such as those discussed in the preceding chapters (particularly 5 and 6) are sometimes an unwanted source of interference that must be dealt with for a desired behavior to transpire.

The chapter is framed as a lesson on how to overcome such interferences by creating the most efficacious forms of intentions, though a by-product of such efforts is a better understanding of the "miraculous" translation of intentions into actions.

Among the phenomena discussed is the greater effectiveness of intentions that have more specific antecedent conditions (the "if" in intentions couched in "if-then" form). Thus, an individual is more likely to mail a letter if he or she resolves to do so at the office ("if at office, then mail letter") than if he or she resolves to do so at the office, the nearest mailbox, or the nearest postal substation. The paradox, of course, is that more specific antecedent provides fewer opportunities to fulfill the intention, and the individual may overlook acceptable antecedents not included in the constrained intention statement. But the broader intention dilutes attention by including too many possible antecedents, creating a risk that none will be successfully recognized, and the letter will not get mailed. This example emphasizes the manner in which implementation intentions attempt to take advantage of automatic perceptual processes such as those described by Bargh and Morsella, while overcoming other automatic (and nonautomatic) processes that might interfere with behavioral execution.

In Chapter 9, Fabrigar et al. discuss the best-established mediator of behavior, attitude, for which there is also the most extensive literature on behavioral effects. Historically, attitudes were virtually defined as behavioral influences, as in the tripartite definition (attitudes as cognition, affect, and behavior) or Allport's (1935) characterization of them as "states of readiness" that exert a "directive or dynamic influence" on people's responses. As Fabrigar et al. note, the attitude literature agonized for years over whether people's attitudes really predict their behaviors and discovered a fair number of moderators of the attitude-behavior relationship in the process. However, they note further that the relationship was probably never as tenuous as people imagined, and that under most circumstances, it is reasonably strong.

The authors present a general framework for organizing the moderators that have been suggested in the literature, focusing on several central distinctions. First, they distinguish between predictions of behavior and mechanisms that might actually mediate the underlying attitude-behavior link. The first category of moderators includes the kinds of measurement issues postulated by Fishbein and his colleagues—issues that are potentially germane to efforts to predict behavior from any individual difference variable (such as those described in the personality chapters summarized below). The Fabrigar et al. chapter distinguishes mediational mechanisms further along lines suggested by dual-processing theory, into those involving low-deliberation behaviors and those involving high-deliberation behaviors. The former includes perceptual and behavioral cuing effects that could implicate habitual or nonconscious processes similar to those described in Chapters 5 and 6. The latter arguably encompasses both higher-level propositional reasoning and biased information processing (finally, something to make the hardcore cognitivists happy!).

The Fabrigar et al. chapter provides a comprehensive review of the most elaborate literature on predicting individual behavior, and the implications of the review are potentially relevant to all of the constructs considered in this section of this book. Beyond that, however, the chapter serves as a useful reminder of several central issues. First, measurement matters. The chapters on personality described in the next section of this chapter will certainly drive this home, but even more generally, it is important to remember that how we examine the mediation of behavior may be as central to our findings as the constructs we examine and the theoretical premises of our approach. Second, processing matters. The role of any construct in determining behavior is likely to depend very heavily on what exactly a person is doing. More specifically, given the chapters just reviewed, it is likely to depend on how often the person has engaged in a behavior, how aware he is of engaging in it, how engaging in it makes him feel, how well articulated his intentions of engaging in it are, and whether he is deliberating a lot or a little about engaging in it.

We might add, as well, that the individual matters. And though we can distinguish individuals based on their habits, emotions, intentions, and attitudes, they are also commonly distinguished by their personalities. This is the focus of the next group of chapters.

PERSONALITY CONSTRUCTS AND BEHAVIOR

Four of the chapters address issues linking personality to behavior. Personality psychology brings a distinctive perspective on the issue of behavior. The dominant view in modern research-oriented personality psychology is that personality is more than the study of one individual difference at a time. It is instead the study of the ways individuals organize and structure the entire package of individual differences and processes they possess. Our expectations about the likely social behavior of a person who is intelligent is qualified by additional knowledge that she is also female, and qualified further by knowledge that she is/is not physically attractive, and still further by knowledge that she is/is not dispositionally introverted. Behavior represents one of the adaptive outputs of the structural compromises that constitute the individual's personality. Going a bit further, behavioral demands of certain ecologies, roles, and life stages may affect personality structure.

Furr, Wagerman, and Funder offer a chapter that describes a need for a descriptive foundation (Chapter 10). They—and they alone—explicitly argue for the role of behavior as part of the descriptive foundation of personality and social psychology. Such research addresses the fundamental assumption that "who you are affects what you do." Furr et al. move beyond exhortation to an analysis of why behavior seems to have moved to the back row in psychological research in recent years. It is costly in time, effort, and money to collect behavioral observations relative to reaction times and self-ratings. Moreover, there was a lack of standardized systems for measuring or coding such observations. And finally, the simpler and less expensive methods have indeed yielded good fruit.

Furr et al. assert that the most general benefit of behavioral data is that it permits psychological scientists to address behavior with empirical conviction. Without such data, the ability to claim status as a science of behavior is greatly reduced. Central to direct behavioral observation research is a coding system. Exactly what are the behaviors to be observed and the method of observing and scoring them? They note key considerations in choosing a behavioral observational system, including the context in which the system is to be deployed, and the situational specificity of the behaviors. Within these issues are additional, increasingly concrete considerations. Exactly what behaviors should be observed and at what level of abstraction? For observations that occur in sequences, exactly how should the sequences be ordered? There are, of course, trade-offs. The more concrete and focused the measures, the fewer inferences the observers need to make.

In the words of the philosopher Walter Kaufman, it is easier to detect a rotten egg than to lay a fresh one. Furr et al. eschew the easy task and offer us a fresh egg with the Riverside Behavioral Q-sort. It was originally derived from the California Adult Q-Set. For each personality item on the CAQ, the Riverside researchers wrote items describing behaviors that might be used flexibly in a range of situations relevant to personality and social psychology. Furthermore, the eggs come with sauce béarnaise: They offer also a computer program for coding the behavioral observations.

In Chapter 11 Goldberg presents data that aligns nicely with the Furr, Wagerman, and Funder strategy. Goldberg notes that it is one thing to develop a new measure of some individual difference; it is another to establish its utility as a predictor of important human behaviors. Goldberg shows very explicitly that who you are indeed affects what you do in everyday life. Clearly vocational interest patterns have proven their worth over the years. What about avocational interests, as measured by self-reports of the relative frequency of individuals' engagement in various interest-related activities? Goldberg presents a survey of behavioral act frequencies for a wide-ranging array of daily activities in a community-wide sample. These provide the basic data from which to assess important individual differences in lifestyle. Such patterns of lifestyle differences, then, might ultimately be useful as criteria. A total of 400 behaviors (e.g., "read the Bible or other sacred text;" "played with a pet animal") were reduced to a more manageable set of 22 reliable clusters of avocational behavior. Some of the relations between the avocational interest scales and demographic indices are high. Correlations with gender range up to .60 (housekeeping chores, with women doing more) and .55 (fashion-related activities, again with women doing more). Furthermore, aspects of people's lifestyles (as reflected in the frequency with which they engage in various activities) are differentially related to personality perceptions by *others*, above and beyond the individual's own self-perceptions. That is, the activity clusters seemingly constitute cues that others use to assess targets' personality traits. These cues may be used similarly by oneself and others to assess the same personality trait, but some of them must be used somewhat differently by the two kinds of judges, thus permitting the interest-related scales to predict above and beyond the informants' personality assessments.

The chapters by Paulhus and Holden (Chapter 12) and by Reuben Baron (Chapter 13) take approaches different from the others in the set. Both of these chapters question whether behavior deserves a position at the center of our universe. Paulhus and Holden note that social and personality psychologists address the issue of behavior in rather different ways. Social psychologists tend to exploit behavior as a concrete outcome reflecting the difference in psychological state induced by an experimental manipulation. Within social psychology, behavior appears to hold a more elevated stature in the hierarchy of scientific credibility. It is viewed as more credible and tangible. In contrast, personality psychologists view behavior as only one indicator of psychological constructs. Peer ratings, for example, are in some respects superior to behavioral observation. And self-reports have advantages that explain why they are the most popular of methods (Paulhus & Vazire, 2007).

Paulhus and Holden note that the traditional complaint against self-report measures is their vulnerability to self-presentation effects. The general tendency for people to self-enhance raises concerns that self-reports are just as likely to reflect presentation motives as actual personalities. One solution is to index self-enhancement via behavioral measures. Paulhus and Holden compare the full range of options from self-report to concrete behavioral methods. They also discuss the over-claiming approach, which taps the tendency to claim knowledge of non-existent items. They conclude with the response latency approach, which is purely behavioral in nature. Their summary favors the overclaiming and response latency methods.

Baron offers a far-reaching and integrative chapter in his discussion of affordances. He notes that behavior is a central element of any ecologi-cally-based view of psychology, including J. J. Gibson's (1979/1986) discussions of the visual perception basis of affordances and Barker's (1968) discussion of behavior settings. In both cases, behavior is the "straw that stirs the drink." For Gibson (1979/1986) in particular, seeing is for doing. He views the detection of affordances as embodied in behavior through perceiving–acting cycles. What we see affects what we do and what we do affects what we see.

Baron offers several important insights about the role of behavior in psychology in general, but especially in social and personality psychology. He explores whether his ideas can be turned into a fresh look at a theory of situations. In such a theory, situations are a complementary mirror image of a theory of personality, in the same sense that certain niches imply certain plants and animals, while certain plants and animals imply certain niches. Here are the powerful ideas of coevolution and the self-organization of complex systems. Why are certain opportunities config-ured to support certain dispositions, and/or types of people? He suggests that the social analogue of coevolution is the embedding of personality in the organizational dynamics of behavior to recruit people with the appro-priate personality traits to carry out these roles successfully.

DISCUSSION

The chapters in this section provide a diverse set of views on the relation-ship between various individual differences and behaviors. Some of those individual differences—for example, attitudes, emotions, and person-ality—have been central to social psychology for a long time. And some of the described approaches can be traced back a fair number of years as well. Yet, almost without exception, the clarion cry of these chapters is for more sophisticated theoretical treatment or empirical measurement of those individual differences, of behavior, or of the relationship between the two. With such sophistication, it is hoped, the "nature" of individuals' behavior will become more evident and the need for miracles will diminish.

REFERENCES

Ajzen, I., & Fishbein, M. (1980). *Understanding attitudes and predicting social behavior*. Englewood Cliffs, NJ: Prentice Hall.

Allport, G. W. (1935). Attitudes. In C. Murchinson (Ed.), *A handbook of social psychology* (pp. 798–844). Worcester, MA: Clark University Press.

Bargh, J.A. (1994). The four horsemen of automaticity: Awareness, intention, efficiency, and control in social cognition. In: R.S. Wyer & T.K. Srull (Eds.), *Handbook of social cognition* (vol.1, pp.1–40). Hillsdale, NJ: Erlbaum.

Barker, R. G. (1968).*Ecological psychology*.Palo Alto, CA: Stanford University Press.

James, W. (1890). *The Principles of Psychology*. New York: Henry Holt and Company.

Gibson, J. J.(1986). *The ecological approach to visual perception*. Hillsdale, NJ: Lawrence Erlbaum Associates. (Original work published 1979.)

Montaigne (1588). Of custom. *Essays*.

Paulhus, D. L., & Vazire, S. (2007). The self-report method. In R.W. Robins, R. C.Fraley, & R. F. Krueger (Eds.), *Handbook of research methods in personality psychology* (pp. 224–239). New York: Guilford.

Triandis, H. C. (1980). Values, attitudes, and interpersonal behavior. In: H. E. Howe, Jr., & M. M. Page (Eds.), *Nebraska symposium on motivation, 1979* (pp.195–259). Lincoln, NE: University of Nebraska Press.

5 Habit: From Overt Action to Mental Events

Bas Verplanken

Repetition is the heartbeat of everyday life. We repeat many behaviors over and over again in one way or another. Most people would acknowledge that they have a substantial number of habits. Wood, Quinn, and Kashy (2002) reported on the basis of diary studies that approximately 45% of everyday behaviors are repeated in the same location almost every day. Habits are subtly woven into the fabric of everyday life activities, and we usually are not aware of them. We may experience habits when we can no longer execute them, for instance when we change environment (e.g., relocating), or when a changing environment disrupts behavior (e.g., a power shutdown). In spite of the abundance of habits, the habit construct has not been incorporated in prevalent models of behavior, although there are a few exceptions (e.g., Bamberg & Schmidt, 2003; Eagly & Chaiken, 1993; Triandis, 1980). In this chapter, I will first discuss the role of past behavior, followed by addressing the conceptualization and measurement of habits. I will then extend the habit concept beyond overt behavior, and introduce the concept of "mental habits." Finally, I will discuss a number of outstanding issues concerning habit.

THE ROLE OF PAST BEHAVIOR

Although prevalent models of attitude–behavior relations, in particular the theories of reasoned action (Ajzen & Fishbein, 1980) and planned behavior (Ajzen, 1991), have demonstrated great value in modeling antecedents of behavior, these models do not fully account for the relationship between past and later behavior; past behavior usually appears as the most powerful predictor of later behavior and remains significant even when controlling for the model variables (e.g., Ajzen, 1991, 2002; Ajzen & Fishbein, 2005; Bentler & Speckart, 1979; Conner & Armitage, 1998; Fredricks & Dossett, 1983). This phenomenon is referred to as the residual variance effect (Ajzen, 2002).

An important insight in the role of past behavior was provided by a meta-analysis of studies that incorporated measures of intentions, past behavior, and later behavior (Ouellette & Wood, 1998). Both intentions and past behavior were found significantly related to future behavior. However, the frequency with which behaviors occurred was a moderator; intentions were the dominant predictor of later behavior when behaviors were infrequently performed, whereas past behavior was the dominant predictor when behaviors were frequently performed. This meta-analysis thus suggested a dual process account of the influence of past behavior on future behavior (cf., Triandis, 1980). When behavior is infrequent, the experiences from past behavior are likely to feed into our belief systems and guide future behavior through behavioral intentions. For instance, we may evaluate a previous holiday destination and decide to go there once more. Such an account is fully compatible with the theories of reasoned action and planned behavior. However, when behavior is frequently performed, this loop may not occur anymore. Although behavior may still be in line with previously formed attitudes and intentions, there may not be a need to consciously review past experiences; choices and behavior have become automatic and habitual (Aarts & Dijksterhuis, 2000). For instance, after moving to a new house, it may take some deliberation and experience to find the most efficient way to commute, but once a particular route has proven satisfactory, this becomes highly automatic and does not require any more thought. It is important to note that repetition of behavior does not *necessarily* lead to an automatic and habitual mode per se (Ajzen, 2002). For instance, an investor may be faced with repetitive and similar decisions but is advised to consider each decision carefully.

The dual process view of the influence of past on future behavior thus suggests that repetition and habituation of behavior pose boundary conditions to the influence of intentions and thus to the power of the theories of reasoned action and planned behavior. Triandis (1980) suggested a trade-off between intention and habit in the prediction of behavior and thus was the first to integrate reasoned and habitual action. A number of primary studies have directly demonstrated such Intention × Habit interactions in the prediction of later behavior (de Bruijn et al., 2007;

Ferguson, & Bibby, 2002; Ji & Wood, 2007; Verplanken, Aarts, van Knippenberg, & Moonen, 1998). For instance, in a longitudinal design and using different measures of habit, participants in Verplanken et al.'s (1998) study responded to a questionnaire assessing their intentions to use the car versus public transport during the following week. In addition, their car use habit strength was measured. Under the cover story that the researchers wanted to know where people were traveling, transportation mode choices were recorded in a travel diary, which was kept over the course of the week following the questionnaire. It was found that behavioral intentions to take the car were highly predictive of later behavior, which was in accordance with the theory of planned behavior. However, this was only the case for individuals who did not have strong car use habits. On the other hand, strong habit participants' intentions were unrelated to later behavior. Additional evidence for a shallower decision process under strong habit conditions comes from studies on information acquisition and decision making (Aarts, Verplanken, & van Knippenberg, 1997; Verplanken, Aarts, & van Knippenberg, 1997). These studies demonstrated that habit attenuates information acquisition, such as the amount of information acquired about choice options and about choice situations, and the use of less elaborate decision rules in different stages of the decision-making process.

Practice and repetition thus may make individuals switch from deliberate thinking and decision making to a more automatic mode of behavior. For example, Wood et al. (2002) observed that participants were less likely to think about their behavior when performing habitual acts. An important caveat is that in the "deliberate mode" behavior is largely *internally* cued, that is, by a person's motivation and intention, thus following the principles represented by the theories of reasoned action and planned behavior. This includes the proposition that previous experiences feed into the belief systems, which then form the basis of new deliberations and choices. On the other hand, in the "habitual mode" behavior is largely *externally* cued, that is, by features in the environment where behavior takes place (Wood & Neal, 2007). A diversity of cues may fulfill such a role, for instance time cues, location cues, or people (Wood et al., 2002). Switching from a deliberate to a habitual mode thus moves the center of control over behavior from the individual to the environment. This may have important consequences, for instance, for strategies to influence behavior. Internally cued behaviors may be sensitive to changes in beliefs and attitudes. Changing the balance of perceived advantages and disadvantages may thus lead to intentions to adopt a new behavior. However, such strategies are much less likely to affect habitual behavior. As the latter is externally cued, changing attitudes and intentions will not affect the cue-response mechanism that drives such behavior.

THE CONCEPTUALIZATION AND MEASUREMENT OF HABIT

So far, I equated "habit" with "repeated behavior" or "past behavioral frequency." I thus followed the prevalent view among psychologists, which stems straightforwardly from the behaviorist conception of habits as behavioral responses that are established by learned associations between situational cues and rewards (e.g., Hull, 1943; James, 1890; Skinner, 1938). Most psychologists to date have drawn on this conception (e.g., Ouellette & Wood, 1998; Ronis, Yates, & Kirscht, 1989), although it has been acknowledged that the field lacked adequate measures of habit (e.g., Eagly & Chaiken, 1993). There are two main conceptual problems with equating habit and behavioral frequency. The first is that although repetition is a necessary condition for habits to develop, repetitive behavior is not necessarily habitual (e.g., Ajzen, 2002). A doctor may have sent numerous patients to the operating table, one would hope this has not become a habit. The second problem is that habitual behavior is not only repetitive, but is also characterized by a certain degree of automaticity (Aarts & Dijksterhuis, 2000; Verplanken & Aarts, 1999; Wood & Neal, 2007). Equating habit with behavioral frequency does not capture this aspect. Thus, repetition is a necessary but not a sufficient condition for labeling a behavior as a habit. Although a number of definitions of habit have been proposed (e.g., Ronis et al., 1988; Verplanken & Aarts, 1999; Wood et al., 2002), perhaps the following definition captures the essence of a habit: *"A recurrent, often unconscious pattern of behavior that is acquired through frequent repetition."* (*The American Heritage*® *Dictionary of the English Language*, 2008).

In line with the conception of habit as past behavioral frequency, habit has mostly been assessed by some measure of past behavioral frequency. The prevalent measure has been a one-item self-report, for instance asking respondents to rate how often they performed a particular behavior on a scale ranging from "never" to "always." However, alternative measures of habit have been proposed as well. One measure combines the self-reported frequency measure with self-reported habit into one item, as in the question "How often did you use your seatbelt during the past month by force of habit" (e.g., Mittal, 1988).

Some researchers constructed a habit measure by multiplying self-reported past behavioral frequency with an assessment of context stability (Danner, Aarts, & de Vries, 2008; Wood et al., 2002; Ji & Wood, 2007; Wood, Tam, & Guerrero Wit, 2005). The measure of context stability varies in content, depending on the behavior, and may consist of multiple items, for example, physical location, time, or people (e.g., Ji & Wood, 2007).

Verplanken, Aarts, van Knippenberg, and van Knippenberg (1994) introduced the Response Frequency Measure (RFM). This instrument was developed for measuring habitual choices between multiple alternatives. Participants are presented with a range of hypothetical choice situations (e.g., travel destinations) and are asked to mention as quickly as possible which alternative (e.g., car, bus, walking) they would choose. Assuming that the imposed time pressure elicits schema-based responding, the invariance of a particular choice across the situations (i.e., the number of times an alternative is chosen) is taken as a measure of habit strength.

Finally, Verplanken and Orbell (2003) presented the Self-Report Habit Index (SRHI). The SRHI is a generic 12-item instrument, which assesses the experience of frequency and automaticity of a particular behavior. The experience of automaticity is broken down into a number of facets, that is, the lack of awareness and conscious intent, mental efficiency, and difficulty to control (Bargh, 1994). In addition, the SRHI includes the experience of behavior being self-descriptive. To date the SRHI has been successfully used in a large variety of domains, such as food or snack consumption (Brug, de Vet, de Nooijer, & Verplanken, 2006; Conner, Perugini, O'Gorman, Ayres, & Prestwich, 2007; de Bruijn et al., 2007; Honkanen, Olsen, & Verplanken, 2005; Verplanken, Herabadi, Perry, & Silvera, 2005), consumption of beverages (Kremers, van der Horst, & Brug, 2007), food safety practices (Hinsz, Nickell, & Park, 2007), physical activity (Chatzisarantis & Hagger, 2007; Verplanken & Melkevik, 2008), weight loss (Lally, 2007), internet use (Lintvedt, Sørensen, Østvik, Verplanken, & Wang (2008), and travel mode choices (Verplanken, Myrbakk, & Rudi, 2005). The 12 items show internal reliabilities > 0.90, and satisfactory test-retest reliabilities have been obtained of 0.71 over one week for unhealthy snacking (e.g., Verplanken, 2006), and 0.87 over one month for exercising (Verplanken & Melkevik, 2008). An important piece of evidence that validates the relationship between the SRHI and automaticity came from two studies in which implicit and explicit measures of attitudes and behavior were taken with respect to eating sweets (Conner et al., 2007). These authors showed that the SRHI moderated the relationships between implicit measures of attitude and behavior, while no moderation was found in the relationship between explicit measures and behavior. This suggests that the SRHI indeed taps into the realm of implicit processes.

Which is the best measure? Given that the one-item self-reported past behavioral frequency measure fails to capture any other aspect of habit than behavioral frequency, this seems not an adequate measure of habit. One-item measures are also notoriously unreliable. The combined one-item self-reported frequency and self-reported habit measure suffers from a validity problem due to being double barreled. As for the other measures, each seems to capture some unique aspect of habit. Selecting the best alternative measure depends on the researcher's goal and type of behavior studied. Wood et al.'s (2002) measure captures context stability, in addition to past behavioral frequency. The RFM (if properly taken, i.e., time-pressured responding) is particularly useful for assessing habits in multiple choice contexts. The SRHI captures the experience of both frequency and automaticity. This measure has the advantage of being generic and easy to use and of having excellent psychometric properties.

PROGRESS IN HABIT RESEARCH

In their seminal text on attitudes, Eagly and Chaiken (1993) noted that "... the role of habit *per se* remains indeterminate (...) because of the difficulty of designing adequate measures of habit" (p.181). Indeed, equating habit with past behavioral frequency has stalled the progress of habit research for a long time. The availability of new habit measures is therefore progress in and of itself (Ajzen & Fishbein, 2005), and clears the way for new research. One issue that now can be addressed is the distinction between behavioral frequency and habit. Suppose one wants to investigate habituation in medicine use. A patient is put on medication, and, being a conscientious patient, he takes a pill every evening. The traditional measure of behavioral frequency would not provide information about the degree to which this behavior is or becomes habitual. Only independent measures of habit can distinguish between behavioral frequency and habit. Lally (2007) asked participants to plan a new behavior, and subsequently presented a selection of seven items from the SRHI every day over three months. Monitoring participants' habit strength thus resulted in individual habit-formation curves. Parameters were estimated that described these curves, such as the steepness of the curves (speed of habit formation) and the value at which the curves leveled (degree of perceived automaticity). This pioneering work on habit formation is promising, as it may provide a paradigm to quantify habituation over time.

Another area where progress has been made due to the availability of a habit measure is the residual variance effect. As discussed earlier in this chapter, the residual variance effect refers to the robust finding that measures of past behavioral frequency are strong predictors of later behavior even when the most powerful "psychological" antecedents of behavior, most notably behavioral intentions and perceived behavioral control, are controlled for. Ajzen (2002) proposed a number of explanations of this effect, such as scale compatibility and the stability of behavioral intentions. Habit might be another candidate as a mediator of the residual variance effect. However, this hypothesis cannot be tested when habit is operationalized as frequency of past behavior; only independent measures of habit can provide evidence for a role of habit. Such evidence was provided in a study on snacking (Verplanken, 2006). In a prospective design, participants filled out a questionnaire, which contained the theory of planned behavior variables concerning snacking, a measure of past behavioral frequency, and the SRHI. Subsequently, participants kept a food diary over a week, from which a measure of snacking was derived. A hierarchical multiple regression analysis revealed the power of intentions and perceived behavioral control in predicting later snacking (Step 1), as well as the residual variance effect when past behavioral frequency was entered (Step 2). The SRHI entered at Step 3 served as another independent predictor and, importantly for the present discussion, rendered the effects of all other variables nonsignificant, thus suggesting a statistical mediation effect. It is important to note that although habit mediated the residual variance effect in this particular study, habit needs not necessarily be involved in other residual variance contexts, where one or more of the alternative explanations that Ajzen (2002) proposed may explain the effect.

The availability of independent measures of habit has opened the way to make significant progress in research on habit. This will undoubtedly stimulate research in particular on processes underlying habit formation and change. In the following I will turn to a somewhat unconventional twist in the use of the habit construct: *mental habits*.

MENTAL HABITS

If habits are considered as frequent and automatic responses, it might be argued that habits are not confined to overt behavior, but that we may have mental habits, too. Mental habits can be described as repetitive and recurrent thinking patterns (Verplanken, Friborg, Wang, Trafimow, & Woolf, 2007). Repetitive thoughts may have a large variety of qualities, such as being evaluative, concrete versus abstract, or pertaining to self versus others, and may be constructive or dysfunctional (Watkins, 2008). In order to position the concept of mental habit, it is useful to make a distinction between *content* and *process*. Repetitive thoughts have content, for instance, self-beliefs, self-perceptions, or attributions. However, there are also process aspects to repetitive thinking. For instance, thoughts may be contained in schemas, which are automatically retrieved, or may be part of a response style that is associated with certain conditions such as the occurrence of rumination in depression (e.g., Nolen-Hoeksema, 1991). By referring to the degree to which thoughts occur frequently and automatically, a mental habit can thus be qualified as a process aspect of repetitive thinking. Similar to behavioral habits, mental habits may be automatically triggered by specific cues, for example, specific events, persons, or locations.

In a comprehensive research program, the mental habit concept was explored with respect to negative self-thinking (Verplanken et al., 2007). Instances of negative self-thinking may be constructive and healthy, for instance, when we critically evaluate our actions and learn from past mistakes. However, when negative self-thinking occurs frequently and automatically, it may become dysfunctional, for instance by contributing to low self-esteem. The primary contribution to such negative consequences stems of course from the content of the thinking. For instance, a person may think that he is worthless, messes up relationships, or has an unattractive appearance. However, we assumed that having such thoughts in a habitual fashion poses an additional risk factor. The overall hypothesis of this research was that the habitual component of negative self-thinking independently explains variance in measures of self-worth over and above negative cognitive content.

In one study (Verplanken et al., 2007, Study 2) participants responded to the Automatic Thoughts Questionnaire (ATQ; Hollon & Kendall, 1980). This instrument presents 30 negative self-thoughts, and respondents indicate the degree to which they had those thoughts during the previous week. The ATQ was considered as a measure of content of negative self-thinking. Participants were then presented with an adapted version of the SRHI, which in the present context was labeled the Habit Index of Negative Thinking (HINT). Participants were thus asked to indicate the degree to which the thoughts formulated in the ATQ occur habitually, using the 12 items that specify the perception of frequency, unawareness of the onset of the thoughts, lack of conscious intent, difficulty to control, mental efficiency, and self-descriptiveness. Participants also responded to a measure of self-esteem. Regression of the self-esteem measure on the ATQ (content) and HINT (process) revealed an independent contribution of the HINT. This result was replicated in a study where the ATQ was replaced by a thought-listing task (Verplanken et al., 2007, Study 3). Participants were asked to write down negative self-thoughts they sometimes had, and, similarly to the ATQ, rated the extent to which they had these thoughts during the previous week. The HINT was then presented focused on the set of thoughts. Regressing self-esteem on the number of thoughts written down, the ratings of the perceived prevalence of thoughts, and the HINT revealed that while all predictors were significantly related to self-esteem, the HINT had an independent contribution.[1]

Some further evidence of the validity of the HINT as an independent predictor of unconstructive consequences was provided in a longitudinal study on depression and anxiety among 1,102 participants, based on a representative sample of 5,000 adults in Norway (Verplanken et al., 2007, Study 8). The sample was approached twice with a 9-month interval. In the first wave a host of clinical measures were taken, among which were measures of depressive and anxiety symptoms, home and work stress as well as the Dysfunctional Attitude Scale (Weissman & Beck, 1978), which served as a measure of negative cognitive content, and the HINT. The second measurement included an assessment of the occurrence of a range of negative life events, as well as a reassessment of the presence of depressive and anxiety symptoms. The results showed that the HINT at Time 1 predicted depressive and anxiety symptoms at Time 2 over and above all other measures, thus controlling for symptoms at Time 1. This confirmed the power of the habitual aspect of negative thinking.

Habitual negative self-thinking was also studied with respect to more specific self-evaluations, such as body image. In one study it was found that habitual negative thoughts about one's appearance accounted for variance in body image attitudes over and above the number and negativity of self-generated negative body-related thoughts (Verplanken & Tangelder, 2007). Importantly, whereas body dissatisfaction has always been a highly gendered domain, in that women tend to express more body dissatisfaction than men (e.g., Feingold & Mazzella, 1998), the independent effects of habitual negative body image thinking were present for both sexes. In another study, adolescents aged 12–15 were presented with assessments of body dissatisfaction, a body image HINT, as well as assessments of self-esteem and eating disturbance propensity (Verplanken & Velsvik, 2008). The latter two variables were regressed on body dissatisfaction and negative body image thinking. The body image HINT predicted self-esteem and eating disturbance propensity over and above body dissatisfaction. Again, the effects were gender-unrelated, suggesting that habitual negative thinking posed a risk factor for both sexes.

---

[1]   Of course, there exist other process-oriented constructs in the realm of self-reflection. In one study the HINT was pitted against measures of mental rumination and (lack of) mindfulness in predicting self-esteem (Verplanken et al., 2007, Study 4). While all three predictors were significantly related to self-esteem, the HINT obtained a significant weight, and thus showed discriminant validity.

Habitual Negative Self-Thinking and Implicit Processes

The nature of the mental habit concept, and in particular the automaticity facet, may lead to the hypothesis that habitual thinking has links with implicit cognitions and processes. For instance, in one study habitual negative body image thinking was found to be related to the speed with which negatively valenced food-related words were recognized (Verplanken, Thompson, & Whale, 2008). Participants in this study were presented with a lexical decision task, that is, deciding as quickly as possible whether stimuli were words or nonwords. The words category included stimuli that were related to unhealthy and healthy food items. Participants also responded to a body image HINT and a measure of body image attitude. The latency data revealed a statistically significant interaction between the HINT and body image attitude for the unhealthy food items. Simple slope analyses showed that among participants with negative body images, high HINT scores were associated with shorter response latencies for the unhealthy food items,, whereas no such association was present for participants with positive body images. The were no such effects for healthy food items.

In a number of other studies, habitual negative self-thinking appeared to be associated with implicit measures of self-esteem. Participants in Verplanken et al. (2007, Study 5) were presented with an Implicit Association Test assessing self-esteem (IAT; Greenwald & Farnham, 2000). They also responded to the ATQ and the HINT, in addition to an explicit measure of self-esteem. The results showed that the HINT was statistically significantly related to the IAT ($r = 0.28, p < .01$). Neither the ATQ nor explicit self-esteem correlated significantly with the IAT. These results were replicated in the body image domain (Verplanken & Tangelder, 2007). In this study, participants responded to an IAT assessing body image attitudes. The HINT (focused on thoughts on body dissatisfaction) was significantly correlated with the body image IAT ($r = 0.20, p < .001$).

A conceptual replication of the relationship between habitual negative self-thinking and implicit self-esteem was obtained by using the name letter and birthday number effect as an implicit measure of self-esteem (Verplanken et al., 2007, Study 6). The name letter and birthday number effect refers to the phenomenon that people tend to like their name letters (or initials) and their birthday numbers relatively better compared to people who do not have these name letters or birthday numbers (e.g., Nuttin, 1985). The size of this effect has been interpreted as an implicit measure of self-esteem (Koole, Dijksterhuis, & van Knippenberg, 2001). The HINT correlated weakly but statistically significantly with this effect ($r = 0.17, p < .05$), whereas the number of self-generated negative self-thoughts and the perceived prevalence of these thoughts (taken as assessments of cognitive content) did not. In all, the HINT showed consistent associations with a number of different implicit outcome measures. These findings support the intriguing assumption underlying the HINT that this measure captures the experience of automaticity. I will return to this issue in the next section.

OUTSTANDING ISSUES

In the remainder of this chapter I will discuss four issues concerning habit, which are unresolved and/or require further attention. These are first the question where exactly habits are located, given that most behaviors of interest to social scientists are very complex. Second, I address the issue of breaking and creating habits. The third issue summarizes an ongoing discussion of whether habits are inherently goal-directed. Finally, I will discuss the paradox of conscious reflection on automatic processes.

Where Is the Habit?

The first issue concerns the question whether complex social behaviors such as healthy eating, exercising, media use, or transportation choice are habitual. If we take "exercising" as an example, one may object to qualifying such behavior as habitual, because many people who engage in such activities do this in a deliberate and mindful way (Maddux, 1997). In answering the question of what is habitual in exercising, we may first acknowledge that "exercising" covers a range of different decisions and activities, for example, planning, changing clothes, deciding on which route to take, running, showering, and so on. Each of these activities may or may not be executed in an automatic fashion. The realization that exercising is a complex behavior thus requires the scientist, policy maker, or health worker to designate which of the constituting elements is the interesting or important one to focus on. One may, for example, designate "the decision to exercise" (rather than, e.g., the execution of the activity proper) as the element of interest (Verplanken & Melkevik, 2008). Once this decision has been firmly built into one's everyday routines, it may have acquired all features of a habit, and may thus be qualified as "habitual," while the actual execution of exercising may occur in a mindful fashion. From a health promotion perspective, focusing on the moment of decision, rather than the execution of the activity, would make much sense; making the decision to exercise habitual would be an important contribution to a healthy lifestyle.

Another issue related to the question "where is the habit" concerns the level of construal. Habits may be defined narrowly, such as "using the car to bring the kids to school", or "eating a piece of chocolate at 4pm." However, habits may also be construed at a more general level ("taking the car in any situation", "consuming sweet and fatty food"), thus encompassing a variety of contexts. Such general-level habits may often be more important in terms of their social, health or environmental consequences than specific habits (Dawes, 1998; Verplanken et al., 1994). For instance, persons with a general car use habit produce larger carbon footprints than persons who selectively, but habitually, use the car for some trips and public transport for others. Habitually consuming sweet and fatty food in a large range of food consumption contexts contributes more to an obesity problem than when a person habitually eats a piece of chocolate, but eats healthily otherwise. When considering large-scale problems such as obesity or climate change, habits construed at a general level, encompassing a variety of contexts, thus seem much more important than specific habits.

Breaking and Forming Habits

It often seems to require a miracle to break old habits. However, trivial as this remark may seem, there has been little discussion about exactly why this is the case. The discussion has been hampered by the fact that habits have been defined merely as frequency of past behavior. Taking the element of automaticity on board provides more insight as well as more leverage for interventions to change habitual behavior (Verplanken & Wood, 2006). It is important to note that as many interventions are based on providing information aimed at changing attitudes and behavior, the evidence from habit research does not bode well for the effectiveness of such interventions for two reasons. The first is that habit attenuates attention to, and desire for, information, particularly information about new or alternative options (Verplanken et al., 1997). Whereas attendance to particular mass media campaigns is very low in general (e.g., Weenig & Midden, 1997), target groups with strong habits are even more unlikely to attend to such campaigns. Second, habit attenuates the influence of attitudes and intentions on behavior (de Bruijn et al., 2007; Ferguson, & Bibby, 2002; Ji & Wood, 2007; Ouellette & Wood, 1998; Verplanken et al., 1998). Thus, even if an information campaign changes attitudes and intentions, if these do not connect to behavior, existing habits are unlikely to change.

There are some optimistic caveats to this pessimistic conclusion. One is that behavior may be targeted before it becomes habitual. For instance, it makes much sense to educate young male drivers to abstain from drink and driving in order to prevent them from joining the most dangerous segment of the driving population. A second caveat is that existing habits may temporarily be broken, and thus provide a window of opportunity to influence or promote deliberate thinking. Context change thus provides interesting opportunities for influencing new decisions in more sustainable or healthy directions. For instance, when people relocate, many existing habits (e.g., transportation, shopping, leisure activities) are broken and need to be reviewed. For a short while these individuals may need information and may thus engage in more deliberate decision making (Wood et al., 2005). In a study among commuters, Verplanken, Walker, Davis, and Jurasek (2008) found that participants who were environmentally concerned reported using more sustainable transportation modes after they changed residence, compared to environmentally concerned participants who had not moved house.

The other side of the habit coin is that the very features that make old habits hard to change are advantageous for new behavior to occur. In other words, if an intervention is successful in changing behavior, one would want this new behavior to become habitual. Habit formation may thus be explicitly adopted as an intervention goal (Verplanken & Wood, 2006). This may have consequences for the type and the scope of an intervention. For instance, habit formation requires an environment that cues and maintains the new habit. Behavior change interventions may thus shift from a focus on knowledge and motivation to properties of the environment.

One way to start new habits may be to use implementation intentions. Implementation intentions are explicit formulations of specific cues and responses in the environment where behavior is to take place (e.g., Gollwitzer & Schaal, 1998). Implementation intentions thus represent planned automatic contingencies that may turn into habitual responses when these occur frequently. Aarts and Dijksterhuis (2000) found that implementation intentions resulted in associations between goals and actions that were functionally equivalent to similar habitual associations. However, implementation intentions seem not very effective in breaking established habits (e.g., Aarts & Dijksterhuis, 2000; Verplanken & Faes, 1999; Webb, Sheeran, & Luszczynska, 2008).

Habits and Goals

We develop habits when behavior that fulfills some goal is repeated and becomes automatic. It can therefore be argued that habits are inherently goal directed (Aarts & Dijksterhuis, 2000). For instance, Aarts and

Dijksterhuis (2000, Study 1) presented habitual and nonhabitual cyclists with combinations of travel locations and travel modes, while half of each group was primed with a travel goal. The dependent variable was the speed with which they endorsed the combinations as being realistic. It was found that habitual cyclists responded faster to the stimuli, however, only if they were primed with travel goals. Other scholars have argued against the *necessity* of goal activation in the operation of habits (Wood & Neal, 2007). For instance, the occurrence of action slips (e.g., taking the usual way to work instead of the incidental ride to the airport) suggests that at least the current goal (driving to the airport) is not active, and an old habit unfolds automatically upon encountering a particular cue that is associated with it. The studies that demonstrated Intention × Habit interactions in the prediction of later behavior (de Bruijn et al., 2007; Ferguson & Bibby, 2002; Ji & Wood, 2007; Ouellette & Wood, 1998; Verplanken et al., 1998) provided circumstantial evidence for the notion that habits attenuate the role of goals and motivation. Neal, Pascoe, and Wood (2007) provided more direct evidence for the thesis that goals do not necessarily mediate habitual responses to cues by manipulating the accessibility of performance goals in a probabilistic cue-response task involving weather prediction. In their experiment participants in a habit formation condition learned to perform by means of procedural memory, whereas in a control condition participants learned to use declarative rules. When achievement goals were activated, this facilitated the performance in the control, but not in the habit formation, condition, suggesting that habits are a form of goal-*in*dependent automaticity. Wood and Neal (2007) presented a comprehensive model of how habits and goals may interrelate. The model specifies three principles. The first is that habits are a form of slowly accrued automaticity, which is based on the direct association between context and response. The second is that the context can activate the response without the mediation of a goal. The third principle is that habit formation and performance interface with goals and motivated thinking. The latter may occur in multiple ways. For instance, habits may serve goal accomplishment, goals may activate habits, goals may be inferred from habits, or habits and goals may both operate to guide performance.

The Wood and Neal (2007) model demonstrates that the discussion about how habits and goals are interrelated has gone beyond a perhaps too simplistic dual-process account. The exact nature of the relations between habits and goals will undoubtedly be the focus of future debate and research. A number of issues still remain to be settled. For instance, goals may operate at different levels of consciousness. Since Bargh's (1989) seminal text on conditional automaticity, an impressive literature has accumulated on implicit goal-dependent processes (e.g., Aarts, 2007;

Bargh, 2005; Bargh & Barndollar, 1996). It is as yet not completely clear how habits, explicit goals, and implicit goals interrelate. Another issue is that the distinction between goals and representations of goal-related contexts is not always clear. For instance, my university represents a commuting destination and may thus elicit cycling as my mode of transportation. However, once the association of university and cycling has been established, the question is whether the goal of commuting is still part of the equation when this association is activated. In addition, the university is associated with multiple goals (e.g., academic achievement, social relations) and may therefore not be a sufficient representation of one goal in particular.

Metacognitive Reflection on Habits

Implicit processes are often portrayed like the miracle component of Sidney Harris' cartoon on the frontispiece of this book. The SRHI and HINT presuppose that participants have the ability to reflect on this miracle. This in and of itself may be a controversial and perhaps paradoxical statement. Obviously, I would not want to claim that we have direct access to and awareness of automatic processes (Nisbett & Wilson, 1977). However, the findings that the SRHI moderates relationships between implicit measures of attitude and behavior (Conner et al., 2007) and that HINT correlates with implicit measures such as the IAT, the name letter effect and lexical decision latencies (Verplanken et al., 2007; Verplanken & Tangelder, 2007; Verplanken et al., 2008) all provide strong evidence that these habit measures do relate to implicit processes. Apparently we do have an ability to reflect on such processes. There may be a number of reasons why this is the case. First, the SRHI and HINT break down "automaticity" into more specific facets (e.g., lack of awareness, lack of control), which may be easier to reflect on than the generic term. Second, although we may not be able to directly access the experience of an automatic process, we may be able to reflect on what has *not* happened, such as not having given a decision much thought, or not remembering a conscious intent. Third, implicit processes may do things to us that enter explicit awareness. For instance, implicit low self-esteem may surface in the form of nagging doubts, feelings of uncertainty, or suspicious "intuitions." When such events occur frequently, these may be subject to conscious reflection. Fourth, some people may have more access to their intuitions than others, which makes their self-reports such as the SRHI or HINT reflect more of their implicit processes (Koole & DeHart, 2007). Finally, the distinction between implicit and explicit processes may not be as discrete as the use of these terms suggest. For instance, Sherman et al. (2008) argue that the dichotomy between automatic and controlled processes conceals important differences, and picture a far more nuanced account.

CONCLUSION

It is probably not an uncommon feeling among writers in psychology to read William James, and sigh, "What more is there to contribute?" James (1890) wrote about the essentials of habit; from the imprint that repetitive behavior makes in our brains, habit as a simplifying device that diminishes fatigue, the attenuated attention to habitual acts, the fluency of habitual behavior, to advice on habit formation, and designating habit as "the fly-wheel of society" which keeps our conduct in order. He even referred to mental habits, when he mentioned the sentimental value of emotions, which habitually pass by when indulging in music. And James did not have a problem throwing in some moral messages, such as when he wrote:

> The hell to be endured hereafter, of which theology tells, is no worse than the hell we make for ourselves in this world by habitually fashioning our characters in the wrong way. Could the young but realize how soon they will become mere walking bundles of habits, they would give more heed to their conduct while in the plastic state (p.127).

In spite of James' brilliant insights, the habit concept has long been poorly treated by others after him. The behaviorists provided valuable knowledge but did not step beyond the relatively simple Stimulus-Response scheme (e.g., Hull, 1943). Habit was not part of the cognitive revolution, and social psychologists uncritically adopted the concept of habit as merely repetitive behavior. It took a good century before psychologists again began to appreciate the richness of the habit concept. Although much has still to be done, habit now seems to find its place in models that provide a fuller account of how and why we behave repetitively. We begin to see the broader picture again by recognizing that habits may form part of larger cognitive and behavioral structures, which enable us to self-regulate and interact effectively with the environment. While William James might have been disappointed in the moral side of contemporary society, he would undoubtedly have been excited about the new status of the habit concept in contemporary psychology.

REFERENCES

Aarts, H. (2007). Health and goal-directed behavior: The nonconscious regulation and motivation of goals and their pursuit. *Health Psychology Review, 1*, 53–82.

Aarts, H., & Dijksterhuis, A. (2000). Habits as knowledge structures: Automaticity in goal-directed behavior. *Journal of Personality and Social Psychology, 78*, 53–63.

Aarts, H., Verplanken, B., & van Knippenberg, A. (1997). Habit and information use in travel mode choices. *Acta Psychologica, 96*, 1–14.

Ajzen, I. (1991). The theory of planned behavior. *Organizational Behavior and Human Decision Processes, 50*, 179–211.

Ajzen, I. (2002). Residual effects of past on later behavior: Habituation and reasoned action perspectives. *Personality and Social Psychology Review, 6*, 107–122.

Ajzen, I., & Fishbein, M. (1980). *Understanding attitudes and predicting social behavior.* Englewood Cliffs, NJ: Prentice Hall.

Ajzen, I., & Fishbein, M. (2005). The influence of attitudes on behavior. In D. Albarracín, B. T. Johnson, & M. P. Zanna (Eds.), *The handbook of attitudes* (pp. 173–221). Mahwah, NJ: Erlbaum.

The American Heritage® Dictionary of the English Language, Fourth Edition. Retrieved June 12, 2008, from Dictionary.com website: http://dictionary.reference.com/browse/habit

Bamberg, S., & Schmidt, P. (2003). Incentives, morality, or habit? Predicting students' car use for university routes with the models of Ajzen, Schwartz and Triandis. *Environment and Behavior, 35*, 264–285.

Bargh, J. A. (1989). Conditional automaticity: Varieties of automatic influence in social perception and cognition. In: J. S. Uleman & J. A. Bargh (Eds.), *Unintended thought* (pp. 3–51). New York: The Guilford Press.

Bargh, J. A. (1994). The four horsemen of automaticity: Awareness, intention, efficiency, and control in social cognition. In: R. S. Wyer & T. K. Srull (Eds.), *Handbook of social cognition* (vol.1, pp.1–40). Hillsdale, NJ: Erlbaum.

Bargh, J. A. (2005). Bypassing the will: Toward demystifying the nonconscious control of social behavior. In: R. R. Hassin, J. S. Uleman, & J. A. Bargh (Eds), *The new unconscious* (pp. 37–58). New York: Oxford University Press.

Bargh, J. A., & Barndollar, K. (1996). Automaticity in action: The unconscious as repository of chronic goals and motives. In: P. M. Gollwitzer & J. A. Bargh (Eds.), *The psychology of action: Linking cognition and motivation to behavior* (pp. 457–481). New York: The Guilford Press.

Bentler, P. M., & Speckart, G. (1979). Models of attitude-behavior relations. *Psychological Review, 86*, 452–464.

Brug, J., de Vet, E., de Nooijer, J., & Verplanken, B. (2006). Predicting fruit consumption: Cognitions, intention, and habits. *Journal of Nutrition Education and Behavior, 38*, 73–81.

Chatzisarantis, N. L., & Hagger, M. S. (2007). Mindfulness and the intention-behavior relationship within the theory of planned behavior. *Personality and Social Psychology Bulletin, 33*, 663–676.

Conner, M., & Armitage, C. J. (1998). Extending the theory of planned behavior: A review and avenues for further research. *Journal of Applied Social Psychology, 28,* 1429–1464.

Conner, M. T., Perugini, M., O'Gorman, R., Ayres, K., & Prestwich, A. (2007). Relations between implicit and explicit measures of attitude and behavior: Evidence of moderation by individual difference variables. *Personality and Social Psychology Bulletin, 33,* 1727–1740.

Danner, U., Aarts, H., & de Vries, N.K. (2008). Habit vs. intention in the prediction of future behaviour: The role of frequency, context stability and mental accessibility of past behaviour. *British Journal of Social Psychology, 47,* 245–265.

Dawes, R. M. (1998). Behavioral decision making and judgment. In: D. T. Gilbert, S. T. Fiske, & G. Lindzey (Eds.), *The handbook of social psychology* (4th ed.) (pp. 497–548). Boston: McGraw-Hill.

de Bruijn, G.-J.., Kremers, S., de Vet, E., de Nooijer, J., van Mechelen, W., & Brug, J. (2007). Does habit strength moderate the intention-behaviour relationship in the Theory of Planned Behaviour? The case of fruit consumption. *Psychology and Health, 22,* 899–916.

Eagly, A. H., & Chaiken, S. (1993). *The psychology of attitudes.* Fort Worth, TX: Harcourt Brace Jovanovich.

Feingold, A., & Mazzella, R. (1998). Gender difference in body image is increasing. *Psychological Science, 9,* 190–195.

Ferguson, E., & Bibby, P. A. (2002). Predicting future blood donor returns: Past behavior, intentions, and observer effects. *Health Psychology, 21,* 513–518.

Fredricks, A. J., & Dossett, D. L. (1983). Attitude-behavior relations: A comparison of the Fishbein-Ajzen and the Bentler-Speckart models. *Journal of Personality and Social Psychology, 45,* 501–512.

Gollwitzer, P. M., Schaal, B. (1998). Metacognition in action: the importance of implementation intentions. *Personality and Social Psychology Review, 2,* 124–136.

Greenwald, A. G., & Farnham, S. D. (2000). Using the Implicit Association Test to measure self-esteem and self-concept. *Journal of Personality and Social Psychology, 79,* 1022–1038.

Hinsz, V. B., Nickell, G. S., & Park, E. S. (2007). The role of work habits in the motivation of food safety behaviors. *Journal of Experimental Psychology, 13,* 105–114.

Hollon, S. D., & Kendall, P. (1980). Cognitive self-statements in depression: Development of an Automatic Thoughts Questionnaire. *Cognitive Therapy and Research, 4,* 383–395.

Honkanen, P., Olsen, S. O., & Verplanken, B. (2005). Intention to consume seafood: The importance of habit strength. *Appetite, 45,* 161–168.

Hull, C. L. (1943). *Principles of behaviour: An introduction to behaviour theory.* New York: Appleton-Century Crofts.

James, W. (1890/1950). *The principles of psychology* (vol. 1). New York: Dover Publications.

Ji, M. F., & Wood, W. (2007). Purchase and consumption habits: Not necessarily what you intend. *Journal of Consumer Psychology, 17,* 261–276.

Koole, S., & DeHart, T. (2007). Self-affection without self-reflection: Origins, models, and consequences of implicit self-esteem. In: C. Sedikides & S. J. Spencer (Eds.), *The self* (pp. 21–49). New York: Psychology Press.

Koole, S. L., Dijksterhuis, A., & van Knippenberg, A. (2001). What's in a name: Implicit self-esteem and the automatic self. *Journal of Personality and Social Psychology, 80,* 669–685.

Kremers, S. P., van der Horst, K., & Brug, J. (2007). Adolescent screen-viewing behaviour is associated with consumption of sugar-sweeted beverages: The role of habit strength and perceived parental norms. *Appetite, 48,* 345–350.

Lally, P. J. (2007). *Habitual behavior and weight control.* Unpublished doctoral dissertation, University College London.

Lintvedt, O. K., Sørensen, K., Østvik, A. R., Verplanken, B., & Wang, C. E. (2008). The need for web-based cognitive behaviour therapy among university students. *Journal of Technology and Human Services, 26,* 239–258.

Maddux, J. E. (1997). Habit, health and happiness. *Journal of Sport and Exercise Psychology, 19,* 331–346.

Mittal, B. (1988). Achieving higher seat belt usage: The role of habit in bridging the attitude-behavior gap. *Journal of Applied Social Psychology, 18,* 993–1016.

Neal, D. T., Pascoe, A., & Wood, W. (2007). *Effortless perfection: Paradoxical effects of explicit and implicit goals on habitual responding.* Unpublished manuscript, Duke University, Durham, NC.

Nisbett, R. E., & Wilson, T. D. (1977). Telling more than we can know: Verbal reports on mental processes. *Psychological Review, 84,* 231–259.

Nolen-Hoeksema, S. (1991). Responses to depression and their effects on the duration of depressive episodes. *Journal of Abnormal Psychology, 100,* 569–582.

Nuttin, J. M., Jr. (1985). Narcissism beyond Gestalt and awareness: The name letter effect. *European Journal of Social Psychology, 15,* 353–361.

Ouellette, J. A., & Wood, W. (1998). Habit and intention in everyday life: The multiple processes by which past behavior predicts future behavior. *Psychological Bulletin, 124,* 54–74.

Sherman, J. W., Gawronski, B., Gonsalkorale, K., Hugenberg, K., Allen, T. J., & Groom, C. J. (2008). The self-regulation of automatic associations and behavioral impulses. *Psychological Review, 115,* 314–335.

Skinner, B. F. (1938). *The behavior of organisms: An experimental analysis.* New York: Appleton-Century.

Ronis, D. L., Yates, J. F., & Kirscht, J. P. (1989). Attitudes, decisions, and habits as determinants of repeated behavior. In: A. R. Pratkanis, S. J. Breckler, & A. G. Greenwald (Eds.), *Attitude structure and function* (pp. 213–239). Hillsdale, NJ: Erlbaum.

Triandis, H. C. (1980). Values, attitudes, and interpersonal behavior. In: H. E. Howe, Jr. & M. M. Page (Eds.), *Nebraska symposium on motivation, 1979* (pp. 195–259). Lincoln, NE: University of Nebraska Press.

Verplanken, B. (2006). Beyond frequency: Habit as mental construct. *British Journal of Social Psychology, 45,* 639–656.

Verplanken, B., & Aarts, H. (1999). Habit, attitude, and planned behaviour: Is habit an empty construct or an interesting case of automaticity? *European Review of Social Psychology, 10,* 101–134.

Verplanken, B., Aarts, H., & van Knippenberg, A. (1997). Habit, information acquisition, and the process of making travel mode choices. *European Journal of Social Psychology, 27,* 539–560.

Verplanken, B., Aarts, H., van Knippenberg, A., & Moonen, A. (1998). Habit versus planned behaviour: A field experiment. *British Journal of Social Psychology, 37,* 111–128.

Verplanken, B., Aarts, H., van Knippenberg, A., & van Knippenberg, C. (1994). Attitude versus general habit: Antecedents of travel mode choice. *Journal of Applied Social Psychology, 24,* 285–300.

Verplanken, B., & Faes, S. (1999). Good intentions, bad habits, and effects of forming implementation intentions on healthy eating. *European Journal of Social Psychology, 29,* 591–604.

Verplanken, B., Friborg, O., Wang, C. E., Trafimow, D., & Woolf, K. (2007). Mental habits: Metacognitive reflection on negative self-thinking. *Journal of Personality and Social Psychology, 92,* 526–541.

Verplanken, B., Herabadi, A. G., Perry, J. A., & Silvera, D. H. (2005). Consumer style and health: The role of impulsive buying in unhealthy eating. *Psychology and Health, 20,* 429–441.

Verplanken, B., & Melkevik, O. (2008). Predicting habit: The case of physical exercise. *Psychology of Sport and Exercise, 9,* 15–26.

Verplanken, B., Myrbakk, V., & Rudi, E. (2005). The measurement of habit. In: T. Betsch, & S. Haberstroh (Eds.). *The routines of decision making* (pp. 231–247). Mahwah, NJ: Lawrence Erlbaum.

Verplanken, B., & Orbell, S. (2003). Reflections on past behavior: A self-report index of habit strength. *Journal of Applied Social Psychology, 33,* 1313–1330.

Verplanken, B., & Tangelder, Y. (2007). *No body is perfect: The role of habitual negative thinking in body dissatisfaction and its consequences.* Manuscript submitted for publication.

Verplanken, B., Thompson, M., & Whale, K. (2008). [Habitual negative body image thinking and response latencies in a food-related word recognition task]. Unpublished raw data.

Verplanken, B., & Velsvik, R. (2008). Habitual negative body image thinking as psychological risk factor in adolescents. *Body Image, 5,* 133–140.

Verplanken, B., Walker, I., Davis, A., & Jurasek, M. (2008). Context change and travel mode choice: Combing the habit discontinuity and self-activation hypotheses. *Journal of Environmental Psychology, 9,* 15–26.

Verplanken, B., & Wood, W. (2006). Interventions to break and create consumer habits. *Journal of Public Policy and Marketing, 25,* 90–103.

Watkins, E. R. (2008). Constructive and unconstructive repetitive thought. *Psychological Bulletin, 134,* 163–206.

Webb, T. L., Sheeran, P., & Luszczynska, A. (2008). *Planning to break unwanted habits: Habit strength moderates implementation intention effects on behaviour change.* Manuscript submitted for publication.

Weenig, M. W. H, & Midden, C. J. H. (1997). Mass-media information campaigns and knowledge-gap effects. *Journal of Applied Social Psychology, 27,* 945–958.

Weissman, A., & Beck, A. T. (1978, November). *Development and validation of the dysfunctional attitude scale*. Paper presented at the meeting of the Association for Advancement of Behavior Therapy, Chicago.

Wood, W., & Neal, D. T. (2007). A new look at habits and the habit-goal interface. *Psychological Review, 114*, 843–863.

Wood, W., Quinn, J. M., & Kashy, D. A. (2002). Habits in everyday life: Thought, emotion, and action. *Journal of Personality and Social Psychology, 83*, 1281–1297.

Wood, W., Tam, L., & Guerrero Witt, M. (2005). Changing circumstances, disrupting habits. *Journal of Personality and Social Psychology, 88*, 918–933.

6 Unconscious Behavioral Guidance Systems

John A. Bargh
Ezequiel Morsella

It is the duty of the natural scientist to attempt a natural explanation before he contents himself with drawing upon factors extraneous to nature.
                                        —Konrad Lorenz (1962, p. 23)

INTRODUCTION

In the early days (by which we mean way back in the 1980s), discoveries of nonconscious processes were seen as magical, mysterious—if they were believed at all. The conscious-process account of how one gets from *A* to *B* (say, from attitudes to behavior, or from a witnessed behavior to one's attribution of its cause) involved self-reportable steps or stages, clear and easy for all to see. But when the same effects began to be demonstrated without conscious awareness or involvement, the underlying process was invisible, and quite mysterious (especially mysterious, for some reason, to journal editors and reviewers!). Happily, in the three decades that followed, our understanding of how these nonconscious or automatic processes operate has improved a hundred-fold (see Bargh, 2006). No longer are these effects viewed as miraculous; today they are just as theoretically tractable as conscious or controlled processes, and appeals to divine miracles are no longer necessary to explain them.

Purposive behavior is widespread among living organisms, although only a few possess anything approaching the information-processing capacities of human consciousness (Mayr, 1976; Tomasello et al., 2005). The behavior of most organisms living today—the fly, the Venus flytrap, and perhaps the alligator and its fellow reptiles—is under the guidance of what we humans consider to be *unconscious* control. (For a treatment regarding the presence of consciousness in nonhuman animals, see Gray, 2004.) Moreover, for millions of years prior to the advent of consciousness, the actions of intelligent life forms, both toward the world and toward each other, were under the control of exclusively unconscious systems. Conscious mental processes (e.g., conscious intentions) were relative latecomers in the phylogeny of intelligent behavior (Corballis, 2007; Deacon, 1997; Dennett, 1991; Donald, 1991). Thus, as difficult as it may be for us to imagine—because consciousness encompasses the totality of what "we" are and could ever experience—the history of our planet and its organisms was for the most part one devoid of consciousness: A zombie-like world having colorful plants, streams, and gigantic creatures performing complex acts and communicating with each other, but possessing nothing that could ever be conscious of any of it.

Hence, despite our intuitions and how much consciousness may mean to "us," consciousness is actually an atypical phenomenon and tool with respect to both the natural world and the majority of human nervous functions. Figuratively speaking, it is as atypical regarding the nuts and bolts of intelligent behavior as are the computerized, GPS-based navigational systems in today's automobiles. These devices, and their "reverse engineering," fail to reveal the basic principles of mechanized transport, and, as sophisticated as they may be (interacting with satellites and creating graphical "representations" of one's current driving environment, including traffic conditions), they are not responsible for either powering the car or for conducting it. Just as automobiles could get from one place to another long before the advent of such systems, so did creatures express intelligent behavior before the advent of consciousness. The intelligentsia of this "unconscious fauna" is still within us, and, like the engine and driver of a car, it is working behind the scenes as the prime mover of our behavioral repertoire, in the form of *unconscious behavioral guidance systems*.

Who Is the Real Driver Behind the Wheel of the Cognitive Apparatus?

Because evolution works only gradually, making incremental changes and, if at all possible, "exapting" already-existing structures and processes (Allman, 2000; Bargh & Morsella, 2008), we should be able to find evidence still today of the continued operation of these original unconscious behavioral guidance systems. How would such systems work? The simplest mechanism, present in all living organisms from single-cell paramecia to human beings, is reflexive approach versus withdrawal behaviors, in direct response to external stimuli (Schneirla, 1959). For many animals, incoming stimuli would activate approach or withdrawal behaviors (Roe & Simpson, 1958). These are simple reflex or S–R (stimulus–response) reactions. Humans, of course, are much more complex information processors than this, with sophisticated internal processing systems specializing in producing affective, emotional, cognitive, perceptual, and motivational responses to external stimuli, each of which mediate between the sensation of a stimulus event and its effect on behavior (Bargh, 1997). Despite the claims of the radical behaviorists (e.g., Skinner, 1953; see Bargh & Ferguson, 2000), human behavior is not controlled by such simple S-R, direct stimulus-to-behavior linkages: indeed, the concept of the simple reflex arc on which behaviorist theory was built had long ago been abandoned by physiologists such as Sherrington (1906), who called it "a convenient, if not probable, fiction" (p. 137). Skinner's (1957) attempt to account for the higher mental processes (including language and social interaction) in humans using only such simple S-R associations failed spectacularly and helped in fact to bring about the cognitive revolution (Chomsky, 1959; Koestler, 1967), as he permitted himself no recourse to internal systems to extract the important, situationally- and purpose-relevant meanings from external stimuli, and to prepare the individual for appropriate behavioral responses.

Research on priming and automaticity in social psychology, on the other hand, has examined the direct (unconscious) effect of environmental stimuli on these important internal mediational systems and has shown that the mere, passive perception of environmental events directly triggers higher mental processes in the absence of any involvement by conscious, intentional processes (see reviews in Bargh & Ferguson, 2000; Dijksterhuis, Aarts, & Chartrand, 2007; Higgins, 1996). These automatic effects of environmental stimuli were found to drive evaluation (e.g., Fazio, 1986, 1990), stereotyping and prejudice (Devine, 1989), social behavior (e.g., Bargh, Chen, & Burrows, 1996; Dijksterhuis & van Knippenberg, 1998), and motivated goal pursuit (e.g., Bargh & Gollwitzer, 1994; Chartrand & Bargh, 1996)—in each case, without any awareness by the individual of the role played by these external stimuli in the production of his or her behavior. The ease and ubiquity with which priming effects on these sophisticated higher mental (including executive) processes have been obtained reveal both the openness of the human mind to environmental influences, and a necessarily decreased role for intentional, conscious causation and guidance of the higher mental processes (Bargh & Ferguson, 2000; Huang & Bargh, 2008).

The Present Model

According to the above logic, the human version of unconscious behavioral guidance systems must have (at minimum) two main stages, not just one (i.e., S-R): the initial automatic activation of the mediating system by external stimuli (*Step 1*) *and* that system's effect on behavior (*Step 2*). Both stages must be capable of unconscious operation, that is, with no role played by conscious choice or guidance in the entire sequence, for us to be able to speak of truly *unconscious* behavioral guidance systems (see Figure 6.1).

What are the different mental systems that are directly and unconsciously activated by external stimuli?[1] Research has identified four: perceptual, evaluative, motivational, and emotional. They are considered

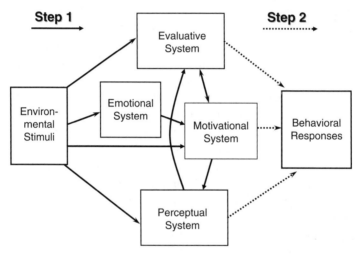

Figure 6.1. Unconscious Behavioral Guidance Systems. "Step 1" (solid lines) refers to automatic activation of distinct internal information processing systems; "Step 2" (dotted lines) refers to automatic influences of these activated systems on behavior.

---

[1] How researchers define the unconscious significantly affects conclusions as to its power over human behavior and other higher mental processes (Bargh & Morsella, 2008). In cognitive science, the powers of the unconscious are often operationally equated with the powers of subliminally presented stimuli (i.e., one must be unaware of the triggering stimulus itself). This practice has led to the conclusion that the unconscious is rather "dumb" (Loftus & Klinger, 1992) because while concept activation and primitive associative learning could occur unconsciously, nothing complex requiring flexible responding, integration of stimuli, or higher mental processes could. But this was not the original meaning of the term "unconscious," which was used by Darwin (1859), Freud (see Brill, 1938), and others to refer to the *unintentional* nature of the behavior or process, with an associated lack of awareness not of the stimuli themselves, but of the influence or consequences of those stimuli. It is this "unintentional" definition that has driven research on unconscious (automatic, nonconscious, implicit) phenomena in social psychology since Nisbett and Wilson (1977) posed their seminal question: "To what extent are people aware of and able to report on the true causes of their behavior?"

distinct systems because they are dissociable—they have different operating characteristics and qualities and are not reducible to each other. For
example, activations in the perceptual system are relatively short lived, and
those in the evaluative system are even shorter, but activated motivational
representations (goal pursuit structures) actually *increase* in strength over
time (until the goal is actively pursued: Atkinson & Birch, 1971; Bargh,
Gollwitzer, Lee-Chai, Barndollar, & Troetschel, 2001, Study 2).

In what follows we will first sketch out the evidentiary support for
these four unconscious behavior guidance systems; within each of the
four types we present the basic evidence for Step 1 priming or activation
effects, followed by the Step 2 evidence that these priming effects extend
to the creation of appropriate behavioral tendencies.

UNCONSCIOUS BEHAVIORAL GUIDANCE SYSTEMS

Perceptual

Theoretical Background. Recent cognitive neuroscience research supports
the dissociation of conscious awareness and intention from the operation of
complex behavioral processes (see Prinz, 2003). First, in a classic study by
Goodale, Milner, Jakobsen, and Carey (1991), patients with lesions in the
parietal lobe region are able to correctly identify an object held up to them
by an experimenter but are not able to reach for it correctly based on its
spatial orientation (horizontal or vertical). Patients with lesions in the
ventral-visual system, on the other hand, could not identify (recognize)
the object, but were still able to reach for it correctly when the experimenter casually asks them to take it. Thus, the one group exhibited
appropriate action tendencies toward the object in the absence of conscious
awareness of what the object was (i.e., action without perception), while
the other group was aware of what the object was but could not act toward
it appropriately (i.e., perception without action). Theorists have concluded
from this and related studies that two different cortical visual pathways are
activated in the course of perception, a dorsal pathway that supports
actional responses ("what to do") and a ventral pathway supporting
semantic knowledge regarding the object ("what it is"; see review in
Westwood, 2009). Importantly, it is the dorsal (actional) system that is
believed to operate largely outside of conscious awareness, while the
operation of the ventral system is normally accessible to awareness
(Decety & Grèzes, 1999; Jeannerod, 2003; Norman, 2002).

Indeed, humans are *generally* unaware of the operations of their
motor system (Fourneret & Jeannerod, 1998; Frith et al., 2000;
Rosenbaum, 2002). This research is revealing a startling lack of awareness

on the part of individual human beings of exactly how one is moving one's body through space. Fourneret and Jeannerod (1998) showed that when one's hand is controlling a computer-drawing device but behind a screen so the individual is prevented from seeing the hand in motion, participants can be easily fooled into thinking their hand moved one direction when it had actually moved in a different direction (through false feedback on the computer display). Participants reported great confidence that their hand had moved in the direction of the line drawn on the screen, when in reality substantial bias had been programmed into the translation of their actual movement into what was displayed. This result is obtainable only if participants had little if any conscious access to their actual hand movements.

One important function of social perception of which people are generally unaware is its direct effect in preparing one's own behavioral responses. The priming effects of people's behavior and other situational features extend to a direct influence on our own behavior, beginning soon after birth. Infants naturally learn much about how to behave by mere passive imitation of fellow children and also their adult caretakers. Meltzoff (2002) concluded from decades of researching this phenomenon that infants can imitate body movements and facial acts at birth, and that this ability represents a "primordial connection between infant and caretaker" (p. 19).

That infants engage in direct imitation of others' behavior indicates that such imitation is likely not a strategic or intentional act on their part, but the outcome of an unconscious tendency to act in harmony with those around us. As Dawkins (1976) pointed out, the best behavioral strategy from the point of view of evolution and adaptation "depends on what the majority of the population is doing" (p. 69; see Maynard Smith, 1982; Maynard Smith & Parker, 1976). Thus, "blindly" or unconsciously adopting what others around you are doing, especially in new situations or with strangers, makes good adaptive sense as a default option or starting point for your own behavior.

Step 1. Automatic or unconscious influences on social perception were among the first experimental demonstrations of automaticity in social information processing. Individuals as social objects are automatically categorized in terms of their social groups (race, gender, roles, etc.), and social behaviors are automatically categorized in trait terms (e.g., Uleman et al., 1996), so that social perceivers naturally "go beyond the information given" (e.g., Brewer, 1988; Bruner, 1957; Fiske, 1982). The *preconscious* analysis of the environment that is continually occurring during normal perceptual activity (e.g., Neisser, 1967) was found, in the case of social information, to extend to a rich activation of knowledge, assumptions, and expectancies concerning the individuals one encounters, much of it at an implicit or unconscious level (as in automatic stereotype activation; e.g., Devine, 1989). The ease and ubiquity of priming effects in social psychology (and now in other fields such as behavioral economics, health psychology, consumer behavior, and political psychology) is testimony to the rich variety of meanings unconsciously activated during normal perceptual activity (see reviews in Bargh, 1989, 2007; Higgins, 1996).

Step 2. These imitative impulses, triggered by the perceived behavior of others, continue to be activated throughout one's life, causing children and adults to have default tendencies to act the same as those around them are acting—producing behavioral and emotional contagion effects. Thus, how other people are acting around us in the present is yet a further unconscious influence or guide as to how we ourselves should act. This tendency, and its unconscious and unintentional nature, has been repeatedly demonstrated in human adults in the research of Chartrand and colleagues (e.g., Chartrand & Bargh, 1999; Chartrand, Maddux, & Lakin, 2005; Lakin & Chartrand, 2003). People don't know and even don't believe once informed that they had engaged in these imitative behaviors. Not only do people tend to adopt the physical behavior (posture, facial gestures, arm and hand movements) of strangers with whom they interact, without intending to or being aware they are doing so, such unconscious imitation also tends to increase liking and bonding between the individuals—serving as a kind of natural "social glue" (see also Giles, Coupland, & Coupland, 1991).

Wiltermuth and Heath (2009) recently extended this finding from the dyadic to the group level. They pointed to the widespread use of synchronous rituals by social groups over thousands of years of human history, and argued that these rituals serve the purpose of promoting cohesiveness within the group: for example, armies marching in lockstep, and worshipers at religious services standing, kneeling, and singing in unison. They provided experimental demonstrations of this natural phenomenon by first manipulating synchronous activity—for example, by having participants walk in step with each other (or not) on a stroll around campus, mouthing song lyrics together (or not) while listening to a well-known song. Compared to those in the control group, those who acted in synchrony with each other then were found to cooperate with each other to a greater extent across a variety of cooperative tasks. Doing the same things at the same time as one's group-mates fosters bonding and cooperative behavior within the group, just as it does within dyads.

Finally, just as the internal meanings that are automatically activated during social perception (Step 1) extend beyond what is directly observable in the current environment (as in stereotype or trait concept activations), so, too, do the automatic behavioral effects (Step 2) of those perceptual activations (see reviews in Dijksterhuis & Bargh, 2001; Dijksterhuis, Aarts, & Chartrand, 2007). Stereotypic content activated during social perception creates behavioral tendencies to act in line with that content, across a wide range of stereotypes and types of behavior studied (e.g., activating the elderly stereotype influences both physical behavior such as walking speed but also cognitive performance such as forgetfulness). The perception of situations also automatically activates behavioral dispositions in line with the particular setting; for example, priming the concept of "library" causes participants (not actually in a library) to speak more quietly (Aarts & Dijksterhuis, 2002). Because the individual is unaware of both the stereotype activation and its influence on action tendencies, these studies show a direct, unconscious influence of the current environment on behavior that is mediated by mundane perceptual activity.

Related Evidence. The discovery of mirror neurons in both macaques (Rizzolatti & Arbib, 1998) and humans (Buccino et al., 2001), in which perception of behavior in a conspecific directly (unconsciously) activates the same premotor cortical regions used to engage in that behavior oneself, is significant further support for the proposed direct, unconscious influence of perception on behavior. This tight, automatic connection between our perceptual and our actional representations suggests that we are prewired to have behavioral and goal pursuit tendencies in line with those around us.

Moreover, related cognitive neuroscience research has indicated as well an automatic connection between behavioral concept representations and their corresponding motor representations. Merely hearing action verbs pronounced out loud activates the same brain region (Brodman 45) as does witnessing a meaningful action (Jeannerod, 1999) and both activate implicit motor representations needed to carry out that type of behavior (Perani et al., 1999). Motor programs thus appear to be part of the very meaning of action-related verbs (Grèzes & Decety, 2001; Pulvermuller, 2005), and this fact is likely responsible for the many successful behavioral priming demonstrations using verbal stimuli (as in the commonly used Scrambled Sentence Test manipulation of priming).

Evaluative

Theoretical Background. Preferences and feelings are unconscious guides to appropriate behavior. A tight connection between immediate, unconscious evaluation and appropriate (approach versus avoidance) actional tendencies is found throughout the animal kingdom; even single-celled paramecia have them (Schneirla, 1959). These "guides" do not arise out of thin air, however. Our present preferences are derived from those that served adaptive ends in the past. Knowledge gained at a lower level of blind selection, the shortcuts and other "good tricks" (Dennett, 1995) that consistently worked over our long-term evolutionary past, is fed upwards as a starting point—appearing as a priori knowledge, the source of which we are unaware. Campbell (1974) called these "shortcut processes" because they save us from having to figure out, each of us individually from scratch, which are the good and helpful things and which are the dangerous.

Step 1. The finding that attitudes can become active automatically upon the perception of the attitude object (Fazio, Sanbonmatsu, Powell, & Kardes, 1986; see also Fiske, 1982) was one of the first demonstrations of automaticity in social psychology. The mere presentation of an attitude object name (prime) was shown to automatically and immediately activate its associated evaluation (good versus bad), in that the activated evaluation facilitated or interfered with evaluation of a second presented attitude object (target) in a Stroop-like fashion. Subsequent research using this and other experimental techniques (e.g., the Implicit Association Test; Nosek et al., 2007) revealed automatic evaluation to be a fairly general and ubiquitous phenomenon, occurring even for novel stimuli (e.g., fragments of abstract art) the participant had not encountered before (Duckworth, Bargh, Garcia, & Chaiken, 2002).

Step 2. Under the present argument that the unconscious evolved as a behavioral guidance system, a source of adaptive and appropriate actional impulses, these unconsciously activated preferences should be found to be directly connected to behavioral mechanisms. Several studies have now established this connection: immediate and unintended evaluation processes are directly linked to approach and avoidance behavioral predispositions in humans, as theorized originally by both Lewin (1935) and Osgood, Suci & Tannenbaum (1957). Chen and Bargh (1999; see also Neumann, Förster, & Strack, 2003) showed that participants are faster to make approach movements of the arm (pulling a lever towards oneself) when responding to positive attitude objects, and faster to make avoidance movements (pushing the lever away) when responding to negative attitude objects. This was true even though their conscious task in the experiment was not to evaluate the objects at all, merely to "knock off the screen" the names of these objects as soon as they appeared. And this unconscious behavioral tendency to approach what is good and avoid what is bad extends even to novel objects never encountered before; Duckworth et al. (2002) obtained the evaluation–action link for the novel as well as the mundane attitude objects in their study.

Related Evidence. This "evaluation-motivation-action" effect appears to be bidirectional: Cacioppo, Priester, and Berntson (1993) found that participants induced into approach-related versus avoidance-related muscular movements while being exposed to novel attitude objects caused evaluations of the objects (i.e., attitude formation) to be consistent with the induced motivational orientation. Recently, van Knippenberg et al. (2007) showed that inducing participants to make avoidance-related (versus approach-related) muscular movements resulted in more effortful cognitive processing on a subsequent task, in line with now-established findings that negative stimuli attract greater attention (Smith, Cacioppo, Larsen, & Chartrand, 2003) than positive stimuli, and negative moods recruit effortful processing to a greater extent than positive moods (e.g., Schwarz & Clore, 1996).

Motivational

Theoretical Background. Goals can be conceptualized as mental representations of desired end-states that include the means through which those states can be attained (Aarts & Dijksterhuis, 2000; Bargh, 1990; Kruglanski et al., 2002; Fishbach & Ferguson, 2007; McCulloch, Ferguson, Kawada, & Bargh, 2008). Theoretically, then, goals can thus be primed, or unconsciously activated by relevant environmental stimuli, just as can other representations (Bargh, 1990).

That a goal can operate independently of conscious awareness of its operation implies the existence of a dissociation between the executive control structures in the brain responsible for "running" that goal's "program" and those that enable conscious awareness of the goal pursuit. Recent cognitive neuroscience research has confirmed that distinct anatomical structures support the operating goal program, on the one hand, and the knowledge of its operation (i.e., consciously held intentions) on the other. As one review concluded, aspects of the processing of conscious intentions appear to be represented in the prefrontal and premotor cortex, but it is the parietal cortex that houses the representation used to guide action (Frith, Blakemore, & Wolpert, 2000).

Moreover, the hypothesis that executive control structures could operate without the person's awareness of their operation requires the existence of dissociable component processes within executive control or working memory structures (Baddeley, 2003; Baddeley & Hitch, 1974;

Buchsbaum & D'Esposito, 2008). Evidence of such dissociations had been reported in stroke patients with "environmental dependency syndrome" (Lhermitte, 1986; also Bogen, 1995), whose behavior was almost entirely driven by situational cues. This hypothesis is supported as well by research in which incentives associated with various goal pursuits were manipulated outside of participants' awareness and nonetheless influenced effort expenditure at the task (Aarts, Custers, & Marien, 2008; Pessiglione et al., 2007).

Step 1. Research on unconscious goal pursuit has typically primed a goal representation and then measured its predicted effect on behavior. However, this is the same method used to demonstrate perception–behavior effects, and so from the behavioral effects alone it can be difficult to tell if the responsible mechanism is an activated motivational state or a straight, nonmotivational activation of a behavioral predisposition (see discussion in Dijksterhuis & Bargh, 2001). Therefore, other means must be found in order to be able to tell one system's operation from the other.

Fortunately, the pioneering theoretical and empirical work of Kurt Lewin (1926, 1935) provided us with signature qualities of motivational states that permit us to classify an effect as motivational instead of cognitive, evaluative, or perceptual. Classic research on conscious goal pursuit confirmed the existence of the signature phenomenal qualities of motivational as posited by Lewin (Bandura, 1977, 1986; Gollwitzer & Moskowitz, 1996; Heckhausen, 1991; Lewin, 1926), and more recent research has confirmed that these qualities hold as well for unconscious goal pursuit. These qualities include persistence in the face of obstacles, resumption of interrupted goal pursuits despite the availability of intrinsically more attractive activities (Bargh et al., 2001; Chartrand & Bargh, 2002; Custers, Maas, Wildenbeest, & Aarts, 2008; Ferguson, Hassin, & Bargh, 2007), increase in goal strength over time (Atkinson & Birch, 1971; Bargh et al., 2001, Study 2), and changes in mood and goal strength depending on the success versus failure of the goal attempt (Bongers, Dijksterhuis, & Spears 2009; Chartrand & Bargh, 2002).

Cognitive neuroscience studies of the brain regions involved in motivated behavior support the hypothesis that the same underlying mechanisms are implicated in unconscious as in conscious goal pursuit. Pessiglione et al. (2007) showed an automatic effort increase effect in response to increases in incentive or reward on a hand grip exertion task, both when the reward cue (amount of money to be won on that trial) was presented to conscious awareness as when it was presented subliminally. They also found that the same region of the basal forebrain moderates task effort level in response to both the consciously perceived and the subliminally presented reward signal. The authors concluded that "the motivational processes involved in boosting behavior are qualitatively similar, whether subjects are conscious or not of the reward at stake" (p. 906). Neurophysiological recordings also show that the same brain regions are invoked whether the goal pursuit is conscious or unconscious (Pessiglione et al., 2007).

Moreover, just as perceptual-priming effects on social behavior are relatively short lived and decrease over time (e.g., Higgins, Bargh, & Lombardi, 1985), perceptually driven unconscious effects on behavior decrease over time as well, but goal or motivation priming effects actually increase over time (Atkinson & Birch, 1971) until the goal is pursued. Bargh et al. (2001; Study 2) demonstrated this dissociation of these two effects over a time delay: effects of an achievement prime on social perception (impression formation) decreased and disappeared after a 5 min delay, but its effects on task performance behavior increased over the same time interval. Taken together, research has revealed unconscious goal pursuit to produce the same outcomes, through the same underlying processes and involvement of the same brain regions, and to possess the same phenomenal qualities as in conscious goal pursuit (see Huang & Bargh, 2008), supporting the present conclusion that goal representations were indeed automatically activated (*Step 1*) and responsible for the behavioral effects described next under "Step 2".

Step 2. The goal-priming literature has shown that these representations can be activated without the individual knowing about or intending it and then impact the individual's evaluations, emotions, and behaviors. A variety of environmental stimuli have been employed as activation triggers in these studies: not only verbal stimuli semantically related to the goal (as in many studies), but also material objects such as backpacks and briefcases to prime cooperation and competitiveness, respectively (Kay, Wheeler, Bargh, & Ross, 2004); candy bars to prime tempting hedonic goals (Fisbach, Friedman, & Kruglanski, 2003); dollar bills to prime greed (Vohs, Mead, & Goode, 2006); scents such as cleaning fluids to prime cleanliness goals (Holland, Hendriks, & Aarts, 2005); power-related features of the social context (Chen, Lee-Chai, & Bargh, 2002; Custers, Maas, Wildenbeest, & Aarts, 2008); and the names of close relationship partners (e.g., mother, friend) to prime the goals they have for the individual as well as those the individual characteristically pursues when with the significant other (Fitzsimons & Bargh, 2003; Shah, 2003).

Related Evidence. In recent experimental work by Custers and Aarts (2005, 2007), a positive affective response was classically conditioned to the name of a particular goal. This manipulation increased the probability that the participant would pursue that goal over other possible alternatives, with the participant unaware of this influence on their goal pursuits. Extending this finding, Aarts, Custers, and Marien (2008) unconsciously manipulated both the goal of high performance (exertion) and the incentive attached to that goal; participants who had been subliminally primed with the goal of exertion did outperform a control group on the hand-grip squeezing task, but those primed simultaneously with both the exertion goal and positive stimuli outperformed everyone else. Moreover, Aarts, Custers, and Holland (2007) obtained the complementary effect: pairing negative stimuli with a goal increased the probability that the participant would disengage from the goal. Thus, both the goal itself and the incentives associated with the goal can be manipulated unconsciously and will then influence task performance just as if the participant had been aware of the incentives and had consciously chosen the goal to pursue. These findings provide additional support for the hypothesis that the same underlying brain regions and processes are mobilized in unconscious as in conscious goal pursuit, and that conscious goal pursuit makes use of preexisting unconscious motivational structures.

Emotional

Theoretical Background. Emotions have long been taken to be the least controllable automatic activation event; Mowrer (1960) originally argued that emotions served to simulate the expected or anticipated outcomes of environmental events in a "safe," internal manner so that behavior could be guided without having to actually experience those outcomes. For example, fear is an unpleasant, noxious emotional state that we seek to dissipate—but it is better to experience fear than the greater unpleasantness of actual physical attack and damage that we might have stumbled into without the warning emotion. Accordingly, it would make a poor functional arrangement if our emotional states were instead under our own control; this would mitigate their important signaling function (see also Damasio, 1994). And if emotions were not automatically activated (Step 1) and difficult to prevent (Öhman & Mineka, 2001), we would not need to engage so often in the regulation of emotions after the fact (Gross, 1998).

Step 1. Emotional states can automatically trigger goals and motivational states of which the individual is not aware and does not consciously intend; *anger*, for example, induces approach motivation with associated feelings of greater efficacy and confidence; *disgust* induces a strong avoidance motivation towards all present stimuli; *sadness* triggers a motivation to change state (e.g., Haidt, 2001; Lerner & Keltner, 2000).

Step 2. Clues that this activation is unconscious and automatic include the participant's lack of awareness of any carryover influence of the prior emotional state on the subsequent task or decision, plus the finding that these emotion-induced goals produce outcomes that go against the rational, best interests of the individual. For example, in the "endowment effect" in behavioral economics research, people place a higher value on objects they possess than those they do not yet possess, resulting in the setting of higher prices to sell something they already have, compared to the price they'd be willing to pay to acquire the same object if they didn't already own it. Selling an object for a higher price than one would pay for it makes perfect, rational economic sense.

However, Lerner, Small, and Loewenstein (2004) showed that the endowment effect can be moved around—even reversed—by manipulating the emotional states of participants. In an ostensibly unrelated first experiment, the researchers had participants think about something sad, or something disgusting, or neither, in the control condition. Sad moods are known to trigger a goal to change one's state. This goal was found to operate in the subsequent economic game, so that compared to the control condition, sad participants in the "buy" condition were willing to spend more money (apparently to change state by acquiring the new object), and in the "sell" condition were willing to take less money (to change state by getting rid of the object)—thus reversing the usual endowment effect.

The disgust condition produced relevant findings as well. Disgust is an emotion known to trigger the goal of protection or rejecting objects from coming into contact with the body (e.g., Haidt, 2001). As would be expected if this protection motive had been unconsciously activated by the disgust prime, participants in the Lerner et al. (2004) study induced to recently feel disgust showed both lower buy (reducing chances of acquiring the object) and lower sell (increasing chances of expelling the object) prices, compared to the control condition.

THE UNCONSCIOUS AS THE SOURCE OF BEHAVIORAL IMPULSES

The present approach to the sources of human behavior is in harmony with contemporary theory and research in evolutionary biology, in which unconscious forces are understood to drive the behavior of all living organisms. In the case of humans, these structures must have existed long before the advent of conscious information-processing capabilities. From these starting points the hypothesis of unconscious behavioral guidance systems can be derived. Social cognition research over the past quarter century has confirmed the existence of these unconscious guidance systems, in that each variety of automatic process of relevance to social psychology—in the domains of evaluation and attitude activation, social perception, and goal pursuit—has been found to be directly connected to behavioral tendencies, without any need for conscious intention or awareness in the production of these adaptive behaviors. Together, these findings support the present argument that unconscious processes for adaptively guiding human behavior existed prior to the advent of consciousness and continue to generate behavioral tendencies today.

Such an idea is not new. Several theorists have suggested that the conscious mind is not the source or origin of our behavior; rather, impulses to act are unconsciously activated, and the role of consciousness is as gate-keeper and sense-maker after the fact (Eagleman, 2004; Gazzaniga, 1985; James, 1890; Libet, 1986; Wegner, 2002). In this model, conscious processes kick in *after* a behavioral impulse has occurred in the brain—that is, the impulse is first generated unconsciously, and then consciousness claims (and experiences) it as its own. Take, for example, Libet's (1986) *time of intention* studies. In the Libet paradigm, participants are free to make a button-pressing or other response whenever they choose (simulating the state of free will) and are asked only to note when (by referring to a sweep-hand clock in front of them) they had made the intention to respond. At the same time, the experimenter was measuring brain activation potentials associated with the instigation of action. The finding, surprising at the time, was that the action potential consistently came hundreds of milliseconds *before* the participant's conscious awareness of intending to make the response. Consistent with the present argument that our action impulses are generated for us through unconscious mechanisms, the impulses, even in this paradigm emphasizing free will or action, came prior to the person's conscious awareness of having made them.

Eagleman (2004) hypothesized from the Libet experiments that people do not generate intentions consciously but *infer* them based on perceptions of their own behavior. Recently, Banks and Isham (2009) tested this hypothesis in a new paradigm in which deceptive feedback was given to participants regarding the timing of their behavioral responses. When this feedback was slightly delayed (using an auditory beep representing when the participant began his or her behavioral response), participants' estimates of when they initiated their action were also delayed. The estimate was thus an *inference* based on the perceived time of response initiation, and therefore participants could be "fooled" by manipulations of that perception. These authors concluded from their experiments that "... the intuitive model of volition is overly simplistic—it assumes a causal model by which an intention is consciously generated and is the immediate cause of an action. *Our results imply that the intuitive model has it backwards; generation of responses is largely unconscious, and we infer the moment of decision from the perceived moment of action"* (our italics).

Wegner and colleagues (2002; Wegner & Wheatley, 1999) had already made this point in a different way, by showing how people's feeling of having willed a given event to occur is an *attribution* or inference (not a direct readout of actual causation) based on key variables such as the timing of their thoughts of performing the action relative to the action occurring, through a novel paradigm in which these variables could be manipulated without the person's knowledge. The right combination of these variables produced feelings in the participants of having willed the event when in fact it had not been under their control.

Thus, many have proposed that consciousness is not the source of impulses to act. Yet to date there has been little said about where, exactly, those impulses *do* come from. Given the evidence reviewed above, however, there now seems to be an answer to this question. There are a multitude of behavioral impulses generated at any given time from our unconsciously operating motives, preferences and their associated approach and avoidance behavioral tendencies, emotional reactions and their associated motivations, and mimicry and other behavior priming effects triggered by the mere perception of others' behavior. There certainly seems to be no shortage of suggestions from our unconscious as to what to do in any given situation.

All of these separate types of input have their own direct connections to behavioral mechanisms, and they operate in parallel (see Bargh, 1997). And so there also must have been some mechanism to integrate the multiple parallel unconscious inputs into serial responses because this is a problem we must have faced as a species in the distant past before the development of consciousness.

How Do Multiple, Parallel Unconscious Behavioral Guidance Systems Interact?

How do these parallel influences get channeled back through the bottleneck of having to act in real time? To presage the argument which follows, language is behavior (Clark, 1996): it is for doing things, for accomplishing goals with others (as opposed to by oneself), and so we might want to look to language production models—how ideas and thoughts are expressed—for insights as to how (other forms of) behavior are expressed. These linguistic production models have already tackled the problem of how parallel processes (thoughts, ideas, intentions) are transformed into serial speech acts (Dell, Burger, & Svec, 1997). It may be that serial, real-time behavior *in general* follows the same principles, and even uses the same or a similar mechanism.

In other words, if language *is* action, then how language is produced may well be how behavior in general is produced. The relevant point about language production is that we do not usually formulate sentences in our mind prior to saying them. Rather, we may have some vague ideas about what we want to say, the ideas or points we want to make, and these guide what we say, but the ways in which we express these intentions, out loud, with words, are opaque to us. That is, language is complex yet spontaneous, in most cases: it has a goal, but no preset concrete plan, yet it is nevertheless produced automatically and unconsciously (Bock & Levelt, 1994; Levelt, 1989).

Language Probably Made Use of Pre-existing *Behavioral* Structures

An important clue in this regard is how quickly and suddenly, in terms of evolutionary time scales, we acquired language (Pinker, 1994). It was not gradual and did not depend on our brains growing to a certain critical size, for Neanderthal brains, which did not have language capabilities, were if anything larger than our contemporary brains (Calvin, 1989). Language is a complex skill that could not possibly be acquired so quickly in young children through normal, slow, trial-and-error learning processes (Chomsky, 1959); it develops spontaneously in nearly all children world-wide regardless of their levels of intelligence. The language production mechanism "takes a web of thoughts and outputs them in form of words spoken one at a time, without a conscious effort or formal instruction, and is deployed without awareness of its underlying logic" (Pinker, 1994, pp. 101–102). In other words, it faced the same problem now posed to us in the case of behavior more generally: how to take multiple parallel behavioral suggestions and map them onto a world in which we can only do one thing at a time (see Bargh, 1997).

The speed with which we acquired language as a species, and the exponential advances in culture and knowledge we've made since then (see Diamond, 1992), suggests that as an ability it piggybacked or was "scaffolded" (Williams, Huang, & Bargh, in press) onto an existing structure, or what Dennett (1995) called a "good trick"—a solution that nature has come up with for a problem that tends to be used over and over again in nature (for example, eyes evolved independently in over 30 different species). The evolutionary theorist Calvin (1989) argued similarly that innate language abilities themselves are quite recent, even rushed, additions to our genetic makeup and as such are very likely exaptations of previously existing sequencing circuitry in the brain. What this means for present purposes is that not only did sophisticated, unconscious modules evolve that give us today the building blocks of adaptive motives, preferences, and behavioral impulses, all operating unconsciously, but there also evolved (indeed, *had* to evolve) a mechanism to integrate or interface these separate, parallel inputs into serial behavioral and judgmental responses. (Indeed, it has been proposed that the primary function of consciousness is to integrate the outputs of different action-oriented systems that are vying for skeletal muscle control [Morsella, 2005]). Our ability to take a vague thought and have it come out of our mouths in a complete coherent sentence, the production of which happens unconsciously, is a paramount example of this.

MIRACLES OR MECHANISMS? SOME CONCLUDING THOUGHTS

We began this chapter by pointing out how unconscious processes are no longer considered as miraculous as they once were. But how *conscious* human cognition produces behavior might well seem miraculous as well given the standard cognitive science approach to mental concepts—what Clark (1996, p. 55) termed the "product tradition," or the *intellectual* aspect of concepts. In the product tradition, concepts are studied for what they contain, how they define the external objects, events, and qualities they stand for. Concepts, in this research tradition, are not for doing, they are for knowing. By contrast, the action tradition (typified by the work of Vygotsky and Goffman) has been concerned with how people use concepts (and language) to get things done in their daily lives; that is, the *experiential* aspect of concepts. The traditional cognitive science approach to concepts is all about their intellectual function and does not attempt to connect concepts to action—for example, in one recent magnus opus on concepts (Murphy, 2002), there is no mention of the development or nature of behavioral or action concepts—the term *action* does not even appear in the index. As Lakoff and Johnson (1980/2003, p. 269) noted, "cognitive psychology is dominated by the old idea that concepts are all literal and disembodied."

    In contrast, for those who have been focusing on action itself for many years, and especially those of us who have focused on automatic or unconscious uses of activated concepts, they are all about the mediation of higher mental processes, including complex action and behavior in social settings. As showcased in the *Oxford Handbook of Human Action* (Morsella, Bargh, & Gollwitzer, 2009), these are exciting times as science is beginning to unravel the basic nuts and bolts of human action, the majority of which are unconscious. People are generally unaware of the sources of their behavioral impulses and of how their actions are successfully guided to completion; it is difficult indeed then to understand how conscious awareness can effectively guide action *without* massive support by unconscious guidance systems.

In the rest of the natural sciences, especially evolutionary biology and neuroscience, complex and highly intelligent design in living things is not assumed to be driven by conscious, intentional processes on the part of the plant or animal (e.g., Dawkins, 1976). As Dennett (1991, p. 251) put it, "in biology, we have learned to resist the temptation to explain *design in organisms* by positing a single great Intelligence that does all the work... We must build up the same resistance to the temptation to explain *action* as arising from the imperatives of an internal action-orderer who does too much of the work." Especially, we would add, when there now exist such promising leads to how human behavior is generated and guided within the domain of unconscious processes.

REFERENCES

Aarts, H., Custers, R., & Holland, R. W. (2007). The nonconscious cessation of goal pursuit: When goals and negative affect are coactivated. *Journal of Personality and Social Psychology, 92*, 165–178.

Aarts, H., & Dijksterhuis, A. (2000). Habits as knowledge structures: Automaticity in goal-directed behavior. *Journal of Personality and Social Psychology, 78*, 53–63.

Aarts, H., Custers, R., & Marien, H. (2008). Preparing and motivating behavior outside of awareness. *Science, 319*, 1639.

Aguiar, A., & Baillargeon, R. (1999). 2.5-month-old infants' reasoning about when objects should and should not be occluded. *Cognitive Psychology, 39*, 116–157.

Allman, J. M. (2000). *Evolving brains.* New York: Scientific American Library.

Asch, S. E. (1946). Forming impressions of personality. *Journal of Abnormal and Social Psychology, 41*, 258–290.

Asch, S. E. (1955). The metaphor: A psychological inquiry. In R. Taguiri & L. Petrullo (Eds.), *Person perception and interpersonal behavior* (pp. 86–94). Stanford, CA: Stanford University Press.

Atkinson, J. W., & Birch, D. (1978). *Introduction to motivation, seventh edition.* New York: D Van Nostrand Company.

Baddeley, A. D. & Hitch, G. J. (1974). Working memory. In G. Bower (Ed.), *The psychology of learning and motivation, vol. VIII.* (pp. 521–539). Hillsdale, NJ: Lawrence Erlbaum Associates Inc.

Baddeley, A. D. (2000). The episodic buffer: A new component of working memory? *Trends in Cognitive Sciences, 4*, 417–423.

Baddeley, A.D. (2003) Working memory: Looking back and looking forward. *Nature Reviews Neuroscience, 4,* 829–839.

Baillargeon, R. (2004). Infants' physical world. *Current Directions in Psychological Science, 13,* 89–94.

Bandura A. (1977). Self-efficacy: Toward a unifying theory of behavioral change. *Psychological Review, 84,* 191–215.

Banks, W.P., & Isham, E.A. (2009). We infer rather than perceive the moment we decided to act. *Psychological Science, 20,*17–21

Bargh, J.A. (1989). Conditional automaticity: Varieties of automatic influence on social perception and cognition. In J. Uleman & J. Bargh (Eds.), *Unintended thought.* New York: Guilford.

Bargh, J. A. (1990). Auto-motives: Preconscious determinants of social interaction. In E. T. Higgins & R. M. Sorrentino (Eds.), *Handbook of motivation and cognition* (Vol. 2, pp. 93–130). New York: Guilford.

Bargh, J. A. (1997). The automaticity of everyday life. In R. S. Wyer, Jr. (Ed.), *The automaticity of everyday life: Advances in social cognition, 10,* (pp. 1–61). Mahwah, NJ: Erlbaum.

Bargh, J. A. (2006). What have we been priming all these years? On the development, mechanisms, and ecology of nonconscious social behavior. *European Journal of Social Psychology, 36,* 147–168.

Bargh, J.A. (2007). Social psychological approaches to consciousness. In P. Zelazo, M. Moscovitch, & E. Thompson (Eds.), *The Cambridge handbook of consciousness.* New York: Cambridge University Press.

Bargh, J. A., Chen, M. & Burrows, L. (1996). Automaticity of social behavior: Direct effects of trait construct and stereotype activation on action. *Journal of Personality and Social Psychology, 71,* 230–244.

Bargh, J.A. & Ferguson, M.J. (2000). Beyond behaviorism: The automaticity of higher mental processes. Psychological Bulletin, *126,* 925–945.

Bargh, J. A., & Gollwitzer, P. M. (1994). Environmental control of goal-directed action: Automatic and strategic contingencies between situations and behavior. In W. D. Spaulding (Ed.), Integrative views of motivation, cognition, and emotion. Nebraska symposium on motivation (Vol. 41) (pp. 71–124). Lincoln, NE: University of Nebraska Press.

Bargh, J.A., Gollwitzer, P.M., Lee-Chai, A., Barndollar, K., & Trotschel, R. (2001). The automated will: Unconscious activation and pursuit of behavioral goals. Journal of Personality and Social Psychology, 81, 1004–1027.

Bargh, J. A., & Morsella, E. (2008). The unconscious mind. Perspectives on Psychological Science, 3, 73–79.

Barrett, H. C., & Kurzban, R. (2006). Modularity in cognition: Framing the debate. Psychological Review, 113, 628–647.

Barsalou, L. W. (1999). Perceptual symbol systems. *Behavioral and Brain Sciences, 22,* 577–660.

Barsalou, L. W., Simmons, W. K., Barbey, A. K., & Wilson, C. D. (2003). Grounding conceptual knowledge in modality-specific systems. *Trends in Cognitive Sciences, 7,* 84–91.

Baumeister, R. (2005). *The cultural animal: Human nature, meaning, and social life.* New York: Oxford University Press.

Bock, K., & Levelt, W. (1994). Language production: Grammatical encoding. In M.A. Gernsbacher (Ed.), *Handbook of psycholinguistics* (pp. 945–983). San Diego: Academic Press.

Bongers, K.C.A., Dijksterhuis, A. & Spears, R. (2009). Self-esteem regulation after success or failure to attain unconsciously activated goals. *Journal of Experimental Social Psychology, 45,* 468–477.

Bogen, J. E. (1995). On the neurophysiology of consciousness: II. Constraining the semantic problem. *Consciousness and Cognition, 4,* 137–158.

Boroditsky, L. (2000). Metaphoric structuring: Understanding time through spatial metaphors. *Cognition, 75,* 1–28.

Boroditsky, L., & Ramscar, M. (2002). The roles of body and mind in abstract thought. *Psychological Science, 13,* 185–189.

Bowlby, J. (1969). *Attachment and loss.* London: Hogarth Press.

Brewer, M. B. (1988). A dual process model of impression formation. In T. Srull & R.Wyer (Eds.). *Advances in Social Cognition. Vol. 1,* Earlbaum.

Brill, A. A. (1938). Introduction. In A. A. Brill (Ed. & transl.), *The basic writings of Sigmund Freud* (pp. 1–32). New York: Modern Library.

Brown, D.E. (1991). *Human universals.* Philadelphia: Temple University Press.

Bruner, J.S. (1957). Going beyond the information given. In J.S. Bruner, E, Brunswik, L. Festinger, F. Heider, K.F. Muenzinger, C.E. Osgood, & D. Rapaport, (Eds.), *Contemporary approaches to cognition* (pp. 41–69). Cambridge, MA: Harvard University Press.

Buccino, G., Binkofski, G., Fink, G. R., Fadiga, L., Fogassi, L., Gallese, V., Seitz, R. J., Zilles, K., Rizzolatti, G., & Greund, H.-J. (2001). Action observation activates premotor and parietal areas in somatotopic manner: An fMRI study. *European Journal of Neuroscience, 13,* 400–404.

Buchsbaum, B. R., & D'Esposito, M. (2008). The search for the phonological store: From loop to convolution. *Journal of Cognitive Neuroscience, 20,* 762–778.

Bugental, D. (2000). Acquisition of the algorithms of social life: A domain based approach. *Psychological Bulletin, 126,* 187–219.

Buss, D. M., Haselton, M.G., Shackelford, T.K., Bleske, A.L., & Wakefield, J.C. (1998). Adaptations, exaptations, and spandrels. *American Psychologist, 53,* 533–548.

Cacioppo, J. T., Priester, J. R., & Berntson, G. G. (1993). Rudimentary determinants of attitudes: II. Arm flexion and extension have differential effects on attitudes. *Journal of Personality and Social Psychology, 65,* 5–17.

Calvin, W. H. (1989). *The cerebral symphony: Seashore reflections on the structure of consciousness.* New York: Bantam.

Campbell, D. T. (1956). Perception as substitute trial and error. *Psychological Review, 63,* 330–342.

Campbell, D. T. (1974). Evolutionary epistemology. In P. A. Schilpp (ed.), *The philosophy of Karl Popper* (pp. 413–463). La Salle, IL: Open Court Publishing.

Chartrand, T.L. & Bargh, J.A. (1996). Automaticity of impression formation and memorization goals. *Journal of Personality and Social Psychology, 71,* 464–478.

Chartrand, T. L., & Bargh, J.A. (1999). The chameleon effect: The perception-behavior Link and social interaction. *Journal of Personality and Social Psychology, 76,* 893–910.

Chartrand, T. L., & Bargh, J. A. (2002). Nonconscious motivations: Their activation, operation, and consequences. In A. Tesser, D. Stapel, & J. Wood (Eds.), *Self and motivation: Emerging psychological perspectives* (pp. 13–41). Washington, DC: American Psychological Association Press.

Chartrand, T. L., Maddux, W., & Lakin, J. (2005). Beyond the perception-behavior link: The ubiquitous utility and motivational moderators of unconscious mimicry. In R. Hassin, J. Uleman, & J. A. Bargh (Eds.), *The new unconscious* (pp. 334–361). New York: Oxford University Press.

Chen, M., & Bargh, J. A. (1999). Consequences of automatic evaluation: Immediate behavioral predispositions to approach or avoid the stimulus. *Personality and Social Psychology Bulletin, 25,* 215–224.

Chen, S., Lee-Chai A. Y., & Bargh J. A. (2001). Relationship orientation as a moderator of the effects of social power. *Journal of Personality and Social Psychology, 80,* 173–187.

Chomsky, N. (1959). Review of "Verbal Behavior" by Skinner, B. F. *Language, 35,* 26–58.

Clark, A. (1998). Where brain, body, and world collide. *Daedalus, 127,* 257–280.

Clark, H. H. (1973) Space, time, semantics, and the child. In T. E. Moore (Ed.), *Cognitive development and the acquisition of language* (pp. 27–63). New York: Academic Press.

Clark, H. H. (1996). *Using language.* Cambridge: Cambridge University Press.

Corballis, M. C. (2007). The evolution of consciousness. In P. D. Zelazo, M. Moscovitch, & E. Thompson (Eds.), *The Cambridge handbook of consciousness* (pp. 571–595). New York: Cambridge University Press.

Cosmides, L., & Tooby, J. (1992). Cognitive adaptations for social exchange. In J. H. Barkow, L. Cosmides, & J. Tooby (Eds.), *The adapted mind: Evolutionary psychology and the generation of culture* (pp. 163–228). New York: Oxford University Press.

Custers, R., & Aarts, H. (2005). Positive affect as implicit motivator: On the nonconscious operation of behavioral goals. *Journal of Personality and Social Psychology, 89,* 129–142.

Custers, R., & Aarts, H. (2007). In search of the nonconscious sources of goal pursuit: Accessibility and positive affective valence of the goal state. *Journal of Experimental Social Psychology, 43,* 312–318.

Custers, R., Maas, M., Wildenbeest, M., & Aarts, H. (2008). Nonconscious goal pursuit and the surmounting of physical and social obstacles. *European Journal of Social Psychology,* 1013–1022.

Damasio, A. R. (1994). *Descartes' error: Emotion, reason, and the human brain.* New York: Avon.

Darwin, C. (1859). *On the origin of species.* London: John Murray.

Dawkins, R. (1976). *The selfish gene.* New York: Oxford University Press.

de Waal, F.B.M. (2002). *Evolutionary psychology: The wheat and the chaff.* Current Directions

Deacon, T. (1997). *The symbolic species: The co-evolution of language and the human brain.* London, UK: The Penguin Group.

Decety, J., & Grezes, J. (1999). Neural mechanisms subserving the perception of human actions. *Trends in Cognitive Sciences, 3*, 172–178.

Dell, G. S., Burger, L. K., & Svec, W. R. (1997). Language production and serial order: A functional analysis and a model. *Psychological Review, 104*, 123–147.

Dennett, D. C. (1991). *Consciousness explained.* Boston: Little, Brown.

Dennett, D. C. (1995). *Darwin's dangerous idea: Evolution and the meanings of life.* New York: Simon & Schuster.

Devine, P. G., (1989). Stereotypes and prejudice: Their automatic and controlled components. *Journal of Personality and Social Psychology, 56*, 5–18.

DeWall, C. N., & Baumeister, R. F. (2006). Alone but feeling no pain: Effects of social exclusion on physical pain tolerance and pain threshold, affective forecasting, and interpersonal empathy. *Journal of Personality and Social Psychology, 91*, 1–15.

Diamond, J. (1992). *The third chimpanzee: The evolution and future of the human animal.* New York: Harper Perennial.

Dijksterhuis, A. & Bargh, J.A. (2001). The perception-behavior expressway: Automatic effects of social perception on social behavior. In M. Zanna (Ed.), *Advances in experimental social psychology* (vol. 33, pp. 1–40). New York: Academic Press.

Dijksterhuis, A., & Aarts, H. (2003). On wildebeests and humans: The preferential detection of negative stimuli. *Psychological Science, 14*, 14–18.

Dijksterhuis, A., Aarts, H., Chartrand, T.L. (2007). Automatic behavior. In J. A. Bargh (Ed.), *Social psychology and the unconscious: The automaticity of higher mental processes.* Philadelphia: Psychology Press.

Donald, M. (1991). *Origins of the modern mind.* Cambridge, MA: Harvard University Press.

Duckworth, K.L., Bargh, J.A., Garcia, M., & Chaiken, S. (2002). The automatic evaluation of novel stimuli. *Psychological Science, 6*, 515–519.

Eagleman, D. M., (2004). The where and when of intention. *Science, 303*, 1144–1146.

Eisenberger, N.I., Jarcho, J.M., Lieberman, M.D., & Naliboff, B.D. (2006). An experimental study of shared sensitivity to physical pain and social rejection. *Pain, 126*, 132–138.

Eisenberger, N.I., Lieberman, M.D., & Williams, K.D. (2003). Does rejection hurt? An fMRI study of social exclusion. *Science, 203*, 290–292.

Fauconnier, G. (1997). *Mappings in thought and language.* New York: Cambridge University Press.

Fazio, R. (1986). How do attitudes guide behavior? In R. H. Sorrentino & E.T. Higgins. (Eds.), *The handbook of motivation and cognition: Foundation of social behavior.* (pp. 204–243). New York: Guilford.

Fazio, R. H. (1990). Multiple processes by which attitudes guide behavior: The MODE model as an integrative framework. In M. P. Zanna (Ed.), *Advances in experimental social psychology* (Vol. 23, pp. 75–109). New York: Academic Press.

Fazio, R. H., Sanbonmatsu, D. M., Powell, M. C., & Kardes, F. R. (1986). On the automatic activation of attitudes. *Journal of Personality and Social Psychology, 50*, 229–238.

Ferguson, M. J., Hassin, R., & Bargh, J. A. (2007). Implicit motivation: Past, present, and future. In J. Shah & W. Gardner (Eds.), *Handbook of motivational science* (pp. 150–166). New York: Guilford.

Fishbach, A., & Ferguson, M. J. (in press). The goal construct in social psychology. In A. W. Kruglanski & E. T. Higgins (Eds.), *Social psychology: Handbook of basic principles (Vol. 2)*. New York: Guilford Press.

Fishbach, A., Friedman, R. S., & Kruglanski, A. W. (2003). Leading us not unto temptation: Momentary allurements elicit overriding goal activation. *Journal of Personality and Social Psychology, 84*, 296–309.

Fiske, A.P. (2002). The four elementary forms of sociality: Framework for a united theory of social relations. *Psychological Review, 99*, 689–723.

Fiske, S. T. (1982). Schema-triggered affect: Applications to social perception. In M. S. Clark & S. T. Fiske (Eds.), *Affect and cognition: The 17th annual Carnegie Symposium on cognition* (pp. 55–78). Hillsdale, NJ: Erlbaum.

Fiske, S. T., Cuddy, A. J. C., & Glick, P. (2007). Universal dimensions of social cognition: Warmth and competence. *Trends in Cognitive Sciences, 11*, 77–83.

Fiske, S. T., Cuddy, A. J. C., Glick, P., & Xu, J. (2002). A model of (often mixed) stereotype content: Competence and warmth respectively follow from perceived status and competition. *Journal of Personality and Social Psychology, 82*, 878–902.

Fitzsimons, G. M. & Bargh, J. A. (2003). Thinking of you: Nonconscious pursuit of interpersonal goals associated with relationship partners. *Journal of Personality and Social Psychology, 84*, 148–163.

Forster, J., Liberman, N., & Friedman, R.S. (2007). Seven principles of goal activation: A systematic approach to distinguishing goal priming from priming of non-goal constructs. *Personality and Social Psychology Review, 11*, 211–233.

Forster, J., Liberman, N., & Higgins, E.T. (2005). Accessibility from active and fulfilled goals. *Journal of Experimental Social Psychology, 41*, 220–239.

Fourneret, P., & Jeannerod, M. (1998). Limited conscious monitoring of motor performance in normal subjects. *Neuropsychologia, 36*, 1133–1140.

Frith, C. D., Blakemore, S.-J., & Wolpert, D. M. (2000). Abnormalities in the awareness and control of action. *Philosophical Transactions of the Royal Society of London, 355*, 1771–1788.

Gazzaniga, M. (1985). *The social brain*. New York: Basic Books.

Giles, H., Coupland, J., & Coupland, N. (1991). *Contexts of accommodation: Developments in applied sociolinguistics*. New York: Cambridge University Press.

Gollwitzer, P. M., & Moskowitz, G. B.(1996). Goal effects on action and cognition. In E.T. Higgins & A. W. Kruglanski (Eds.), *Social psychology: Handbook of basic principles*. (pp. 361–399) New York: Guilford Press.

Goodale, M. A., Milner, A. D., Jakobsen, L. S., & Carey, D. P. (1991). Perceiving the world and grasping it: A neurological dissociation. *Nature, 349*, 154–156.

Gray, J. (2004). *Consciousness: Creeping up on the hard problem*. New York: Oxford University Press.

Grèzes, J., & Decety, J. (2001). Functional anatomy of execution, mental simulation, observation, and verb generation of actions: A meta-analysis. *Human Brain Mapping, 12*, 1–19.

Gross, J. J. (1998). The emerging field of emotion regulation: An integrative review. *Review of General Psychology, 2,* 271–299.

Haidt, J. (2001). The emotional dog and its rational tail: A social intuitionist approach to moral judgment. *Psychological Review, 108,* 814–834.

Haidt, J. (2007). The new synthesis in moral psychology. *Science, 316,* 998–1001.

Haidt, J., McCauley, C.M., & Rozin, P. (1994). Individual differences in sensitivity to disgust: A scale sampling seven domains of disgust elicitors. *Personality and Individual Differences, 16,* 701–713.

Hall, E. T. (1966). *The hidden dimension.* Garden City, NY: Doubleday.

Hamilton, W. D. (1971). Geometry for the selfish herd. *Journal of Theoretical Biology, 31,* 295–311.

Harlow, H. (1958). The nature of love. *American Psychologist, 13,* 673–685.

Heckhausen, H. (1991). *Motivation and action.* New York: Springer.

Higgins, E. T. (1996). Knowledge activation: Accessibility, applicability, and salience. In E. T. Higgins & A. W. Kruglanski (Eds.), *Social psychology: Handbook of basic principles* (pp. 133–168). New York: Guilford Press.

Higgins, E. T., Bargh, J. A., & Lombardi, W. (1985). Nature of priming effects on categorization. *Journal of Experimental Social Psychology, 11,* 59–69.

Holland, R. W., Hendriks, M., & Aarts, H. A. G. (2005). Smells like clean spirit: Nonconscious effects of scent on cognition and behavior. *Psychological Science, 16,* 689–693.

Huang, J. Y., & Bargh, J. A. (2008). Peak of desire: Activating the mating goal changes life stage preferences across living kinds. *Psychological Science, 19,* 573–578.

James, W. (1890). *Principles of Psychology.* New York: Holt.

Jeannerod, M. (1999). To act or not to act: Perspectives on the representation of actions. *Quarterly Journal of Experimental Psychology, 52A,* 1–29.

Jeannerod, M. (2003). Simulation of action as a unifying concept for motor cognition. In S. H. Johnson-Frey (Ed.), *Taking action: Cognitive neuroscience perspectives on intentional acts.* Cambridge, MA: MIT Press.

Kay, A. C., Wheeler, S. C., Bargh, J. A., & Ross, L. (2004). Material priming: The influence of mundane physical objects on situational construal and competitive behavioral choice. *Organizational Behavior and Human Decision Processes, 95,* 83–96.

Koestler, A. (1967). *The ghost in the machine.* London: Hutchinson.

Kruglanski, A.W., Shah, J.Y., Fishbach, A., Friedman, R., Chun, W.Y., & Sleeth-Keppler, D. (2002). A theory of goal systems. In M.P. Zanna (Ed.) *Advances in experimental social psychology* (vol. 34, pp. 331–378). San Diego: Academic Press.

Lakin, J., & Chartrand, T. L. (2003). Using unconscious behavioral mimicry to create affiliation and rapport. *Psychological Science, 14,* 334–339.

Lakoff, G., & Johnson, M. (1980). *Metaphors we live by.* Chicago: University of Chicago Press.

Landis, S., & Insel, T. R. (2008, 7 Nov.). The "neuro" in neurogenetics. *Science, 322,* 821.

Leary, M.R., Tambor, E.S., Terdal, S.K., & Downs, D.L. (1995). Self-esteem as interpersonal monitor: The sociometer hypothesis. *Journal of Personality and Social Psychology, 68,* 518–530.

Lerner, J. S., & Keltner, D. (2000). Beyond valence: Toward a model of emotion-specific Influences on judgment and choice. *Cognition and Emotion, 14,* 473–493.

Lerner, J. S., Small, D. A., & Loewenstein, G. (2004). Heart strings and purse strings: Carryover effects of emotions on economic decisions. *Psychological Science, 15,* 337–341.

Levelt, W. J. M. (1989). *Speaking: From intention to articulation.* Cambridge, MA: The MIT Press.

Lewin, K. (1926). Vorsatz, wille, und bedürfnis [Intention, will, and need]. *Psychologische Forschung, 7,* 330–385.

Lewin, K. (1935). *A dynamic theory of personality.* New York: McGraw-Hill.

Lhermitte, F. (1986). Human anatomy and the frontal lobes: Part II: Patient behavior in complex and social situations: The 'environmental dependency syndrome.' *Annals of Neurology, 19,* 335–343.

Libet, B. (1986). Unconscious cerebral initiative and the role of conscious will in voluntary action. *Behavioral and Brain Sciences, 8,* 529–566.

Loftus, E. F., & Klinger, M. R. (1992). Is the unconscious smart or dumb? *American Psychologist, 47,* 761–765.

Lorenz, K. (1962). Kant's doctrine of the a priori in the light of contemporary biology. *General Systems, 7,* 23–35.

MacDonald, G. & Leary M. R. (2005). Why does social exclusion hurt? The relationship between social and physical pain. *Psychological Bulletin, 131,* 202–223.

MacDonald, G., & Leary, M.R. (2005). Roles of social pain and defense mechanisms in response to social exclusion: Reply to Panksepp (2005) and Corr (2005). *Psychological Bulletin, 131,* 237–240.

Mandler, J. M. (1992). How to build a baby: II. Conceptual primitives. *Psychological Review, 99,* 587–604.

Maner, J. K., Kenrick, D.T., Becker, D.V., Delton, A.W., Hofer, B., Wilbur, C.J., & Neuberg, S.L. (2003). Sexually selective cognition: Beauty captures the mind of the beholder. *Journal of Personality and Social Psychology, 85,* 1107–1120.

Maner, J. K., Kenrick, D.T., Becker, D.V., Robertson, T.E., Hofer, B., Neuberg, S.L., Delton, A.W., & Butner, J. (2005). Functional projection: How fundamental social motives can bias interpersonal perception. *Journal of Personality and Social Psychology, 88,* 63–78.

Maynard Smith, J. (1982). *Evolution and the theory of games.* New York: Cambridge University Press.

Maynard Smith, J., & Parker, G. A. (1976). The logic of asymmetric contests. *Animal Behaviour, 24,* 159–175.

Mayr, E. (1976). *Evolution and the diversity of life.* Cambridge, MA: Harvard University Press.

McCulloch, K. C., Ferguson, M. J., Kawada, C. C. K., & Bargh, J. A. (2008). Taking a closer look: On the operation of nonconscious impression formation. *Journal of Experimental Social Psychology, 44,* 614–623.

Meier, B. P., & Robinson, M. D. (2004). Why the sunny side is up: Associations between affect and vertical position. *Psychological Science, 15,* 243–247.

Meier, B. P., Robinson, M. D., & Clore, G. L. (2004). Why good guys wear white: Automatic inferences about stimulus valence based on brightness. *Psychological Science, 15*, 82–87.

Meier, B.P., Hauser, D.J., Robinson, M.D., Friesen, C.K., & Schjeldahl, K. (2007). What's "up" with God? Vertical space as a representation of the divine. *Journal of Personality and Social Psychology, 93*, 699–710.

Meltzoff, A. N. (2002). Elements of a developmental theory of imitation. In A. N. Meltzoff, & W. Prinz (Eds.), 2002). *The imitative mind: Development, evolution, and brain bases* (pp. 19–41). New York: Cambridge University Press.

Moll, J., de Oliveira-Souza, R., Moll, F.T., Ignacio, F.A., Bramati, I.E., Caparelli-Daquer, E.M., & Eslinger, P.J. (2005). The moral affiliations of disgust: A functional MRI study. *Cognitive Behavioral Neurology, 18*, 68–78.

Mooring, M. S., & Hart, B. L. (1992). Animal grouping for protection from parasites: Selfish herd and encounter-dilution effects. *Behaviour, 123*, 173–193.

Morsella, E. (2005). The function of phenomenal states: Supramodular interaction theory. *Psychological Review, 112*, 1000–1021.

Morsella, E., Bargh, J. A., & Gollwitzer, P. M. (Eds., 2009). *The Oxford handbook of human action.* New York: Oxford University Press.

Morsella, E., & Krauss, R. M. (2004). The role of gestures in spatial working memory and speech. *American Journal of Psychology, 117*, 411–424.

Mowrer, O. H. (1960). *Learning theory and behavior.* New York: Wiley.

Neisser, U. (1967). *Cognitive psychology.* New York: Appleton-Century-Crofts.

Neuberg, S.L., Kenrick, D.T., Maner, J.K., & Schaller, M. (2004). From evolved motives to everyday mentation: Evolution, goals, and cognition. In J.P. Forgas and K.D. Williams (Eds.), *Social motivation: Conscious and unconscious processes* (pp.133–152). New York: Cambridge University Press.

Neumann, R., Forster, J., Strack, F. (2003). Motor compatibility: The bidirectional link between behavior and evaluation. In J. Musch, K. C. Klauer (Eds.). *The psychology of evaluation: Affective processes in cognition and emotion* (pp. 371–391). Mahwah, New Jersey: Lawrence Erlbaum Associates Publishers.

Niedenthal, P. M., Barsalou, L. W., Winkielman, P., Krauth-Gruber, S., & Ric, F. (2005). Embodiment in attitudes, social perception, and emotion. *Personality and Social Psychology Review, 9*, 184–211.

Nisbett, R. E., & Wilson, T. D. (1977). Telling more than we can know: Verbal reports on mental processes. *Psychological Review, 84*, 231–259.

Norman, J. (2002). Two visual systems and two theories of perception: An attempt to reconcile the constructivist and ecological approaches. *Behavioral and Brain Science, 24*, 73–96.

Öhman, A., & Mineka, S. (2001). Fears, phobias, and preparedness: Toward an evolved module of fear and fear learning. *Psychological Review, 108*, 483–522.

Osgood, C. E., Suci, G., & Tannenbaum, P. (1957). *The measurement of meaning.* Champaign: University of Illinois Press.

Panksepp, J. (2003). Feeling the pain of social loss. *Science, 302*, 237–239.

Panksepp, J. (2005). Why does separation distress hurt? Comment on MacDonald and Leary (2005). *Psychological Bulletin, 131*, 224–230.

Perani, D., Cappa, S. F., Schnur, T., Tettamanti, M., Collina, S., Rosa, M. M., & Fazio, F. (1999). The neural correlates of verb and noun processing: A PET study. *Brain, 122,* 2337–2344.

Pessiglione, M., Schmidt, L., Draganski, B., Kalisch, R., Lau, H., Dolan, R. J., & Frith, C. D. (2007). How the brain translates money into force: a neuroimaging study of subliminal motivation. *Science, 11,* 904–906.

Piaget, J., & Inhelder, B. (1969). *The psychology of the child* (H. Weaver, Trans.). New York: Basic Books. (Original work published 1966)

Pinker, S. (1994). *The language instinct.* New York: William Morrow.

Pinker, S., & Bloom, P. (1990). Natural language and natural selection. *Behavioral and Brain Sciences, 13,* 707–784.

Popper, K. R. (1972). *Objective knowledge: An evolutionary approach* (pp 281–284). Oxford, UK: Oxford University Press.

Prinz, W. (2003). How do we know about our own actions? In S. Maasen, W. Prinz, & G. Rogh (Eds.), *Voluntary action: Brains, minds, and sociality* (pp. 21–33). New York: Oxford University Press.

Pulvermuller, F. (2005). Brain mechanisms linking language and action. *Nature Reviews Neuroscience, 6,* 576–582.

Rizzolatti, G., & Arbib, M. A. (1998). Language within our grasp. Trends in *Neuroscience, 21,* 188–194.

Roe, A., & Simpson, G. G. (1958). *Behavior and evolution.* New Haven, CT: Yale University Press.

Rosenbaum, D. A. (2002). Motor control. In H. Pashler (Series Ed.) & S. Yantis (Vol. Ed.), *Stevens' handbook of experimental psychology: Vol. 1. Sensation and perception* (3rd ed., pp. 315–339). New York: Wiley.

Rozin, P., & Fallon, A.E. (1987). A perspective on disgust. *Psychological Review, 94,* 23–41.

Rozin, P., Lowery, L., Imada, S., & Haidt, J. (1999). The CAD triad hypothesis: A mapping between three moral emotions (contempt, anger, disgust) and three moral codes (community, autonomy, divinity). *Journal of Personality and Social Psychology, 76,* 574–586.

Rozin, P., Millman, L. & Nemeroff, C. (1986). Operation of the laws of sympathetic magic in disgust and other domains. *Journal of Personality and Social Psychology, 50,* 703–712.

Schaller, M., Park, J. H., & Faulkner, J. (2003). Prehistoric dangers and contemporary prejudices. *European Review of Social Psychology, 14,* 105–137.

Schnall, S., Haidt, J., Clore, G.L., & Jordan, A.H. (2008). Disgust as embodied moral judgment. *Personality and Social Psychology, 34,* 1096–1109.

Schneirla T. C. (1959). An evolutionary and developmental theory of biphasic processes underlying approach and withdrawal. In Jones M. R. (Ed.), *Nebraska Symposium on Motivation* (Vol. 7, pp. 1–42). Lincoln: University of Nebraska Press.

Schwarz, N., & Clore, G. L. (1996). Feelings and phenomenal experiences. In E. T. Higgins & A. W. Kruglanski (Eds.), *Social psychology: Handbook of basic principles* (pp. 433–465). New York: Guilford.

Shah, J. Y (2003). The motivational looking glass: How significant others implicitly affect goal appraisals. *Journal of Personality and Social Psychology, 85,* 424–439.

Shepard, R.N. (1984). Ecological constraints on internal representation: Resonant kinematics of perceiving, imagining, thinking and dreaming. *Psychological Review, 91,* 417–447.

Sherrington, C. (1906). *Integrative action of the nervous system.* New York: Holt.

Skinner, B. F. (1953). *Science and human behavior.* New York: Macmillan.

Skinner, B. F. (1957). *Verbal behavior.* New York: Appleton-Century-Crofts.

Smith, N. K., Cacioppo, J., Larsen, J., & Chartrand, T. L. (2003). May I have your attention, please: Electrocortical responses to positive and negative stimuli. *Neuropsychologia, 41,* 171–183.

Symons, D. (1992). On the use and misuse of Darwinism in the study of human behavior. In J. H. Barkow, L. Cosmides, & J. Tooby (Eds.), *The adapted mind: Evolutionary psychology and the generation of culture* (pp. 137–159). New York: Oxford University Press.

Tetlock, P. E. (2002). Social functionalist frameworks for judgments and choice: Intuitive politicians, theologians, and prosecutors. *Psychological Review, 109,* 451–471.

Tetlock, P.E., Kristel, O.V., Elson, S.B., Green, M.C., & Lerner, J.S. (2000). The psychology of the unthinkable: Taboo trade-offs, forbidden base rates, and heretical counterfactuals. *Journal of Personality and Social Psychology, 78,* 853–870.

Tomasello, M., Carpenter, M., Call, J., Behne, T., & Moll, H. (2005). Understanding and sharing intentions: The origins of cultural cognition. *Behavioral and Brain Sciences, 28,* 675–691.

Tomasello, M., Carpenter, M., Call, J., Behne, T., & Moll, H. (2005). Understanding and sharing intentions: The origins of cultural cognition. *Behavioral and Brain Sciences, 28,* 675–691.

Tooby, J. & Cosmides, L. (1992). The psychological foundations of culture. In J. Barkow, L. Cosmides, & J. Tooby (Eds.), *The adapted mind: Evolutionary psychology and the generation of culture* (pp. 19–136). New York: Oxford University Press.

Trope, Y., & Liberman, N. (2003). Temporal construal. *Psychological Review, 110,* 403–421.

Uleman, J. S., Newman, L. S., & Moskowitz, G. B. (1996). People as flexible interpreters: Evidence and issues from spontaneous trait inference. In M. P. Zanna (Ed.), *Advances in experimental social psychology* (Vol. 28, pp. 211–279). San Diego, CA: Academic Press.

Vohs, K. D., Mead, N. L., & Goode, M. R. (2006). The psychological consequences of money. *Science, 314,* 1154–1156.

Vygotsky, F. (1962). *Thought and language* (E. Hanfmann & G. Vakar, Trans.). Cambridge, MA: MIT Press. (Original work published 1934)

Wegner, D. M. (2002). *The illusion of conscious will.* Cambridge, MA: MIT Press.

Wegner, D. M., & Wheatley, T. P. (1999). Apparent mental causation: Sources of the experience of will. *American Psychologist, 54,* 480–492.

Westwood, D. A. (2009). The visual control of object manipulation. In E. Morsella, J. A. Bargh, & P. M. Gollwitzer (Eds.), *The Oxford handbook of human action* (pp. 88–103). New York: Oxford University Press.

Wheatley, T., & Haidt, J. (2005). Hypnotic disgust makes moral judgments more severe. *Psychological Science, 16*, 780–784.

Williams, L. E., & Bargh, J. A. (2008). Keeping one's distance: The influence of spatial distance cues on affect and evaluation. *Psychological Science, 19*, 302–308.

Williams, L. E., & Bargh, J. A. (2008, 24 October). Experiencing physical warmth influences interpersonal warmth. *Science. 322*, 606–607.

Wilson, M. (2001). The case for sensorimotor coding in working memory. *Psychonomic Bulletin and Review, 8*, 44–57.

Wilson, M. (2002). Six views of embodied cognition. *Psychonomic Bulletin and Review, 9*, 625–636.

Wiltermuth, S. S., & Heath, C. (2009). Synchrony and cooperation. *Psychological Science, 20*, 1–15.

Zhong, C.-B., & Leonardelli, G. J. (2008). Cold and lonely: Does social exclusion literally feel cold? *Psychological Science, 19*, 838–842.

Zhong, C.-B., & Liljenquist, K. (2006). Washing away your sins: Threatened morality and physical cleansing. *Science, 313*, 1451–1452.

7   Does Emotion Cause Behavior (Apart from Making People Do Stupid, Destructive Things)?

Roy F. Baumeister
C. Nathan DeWall
Kathleen D. Vohs
Jessica L. Alquist

Psychology is often described as the scientific study of behavior. In practice it studies many other things, including thoughts and feelings, and indeed by some measures the direct observation of behavior has been disappearing from many laboratories and journals (Baumeister, Vohs, & Funder, 2007; see Chapter 2). Yet in principle, the study of thoughts, feelings, and other phenomena is justified partly on the basis that understanding these things will help illuminate behavior.

This chapter focuses on the relationship between emotion and behavior. It will present two main theories about that relationship. They are not equals. One is widely accepted, is simple, and enjoys the benefits of tradition and parsimony. The other has none of those advantages. By rights, therefore, the one deserves to be given the benefit of the doubt, and the second theory should only be considered seriously if the first one is found to be seriously inadequate to account for the evidence. But I shall propose that it has finally been revealed by the gradual accumulation of evidence to be seriously inadequate if not downright wrong. Hence a new theory is needed—preferably one that can fit the observed facts, especially including the ones that have gradually discredited the standard theory.

In a nutshell, the two theories are as follows. The first holds that emotion directly causes behavior. Actions can be explained by citing the emotional state that gave rise to them: Someone did something "because he was angry" or "because she was happy" or "because he was afraid" or "because she was sad." The evolved purpose and function of emotions was to cause people to act in particular ways.

The second theory, in contrast, holds that conscious emotion tends to come after behavior and operates as a kind of inner feedback system that prompts the person to reflect on the act and its consequences, and possibly learn lessons that could be useful on future occasions. People may choose their actions based on the emotional outcomes they anticipate. The influence of emotion on behavior is thus indirect.

The title of this book, "Then a Miracle Occurs," suggests a mystery if not a miracle intervening between antecedent situational causes and behavioral response. The two theories construe this miracle quite differently. In the first theory, the emotional state is itself sufficient, or almost, to account for the miracle. Once the emotion arises, the behavior cannot be far behind, because the impetus for the behavior is contained in the emotion. The blackboard in the cartoon could be simplified. The second theory, on the other hand, may require considerably more writing and perhaps a larger blackboard. Emotion is stimulated by actions and outcomes, and emotion in turn stimulates cognitive processing, reappraisal, and simulations, all of which then may interact with the banks of programs that the person's executive function consults in order to know how to act on nonspecific future occasions. Consideration of current behavioral options may be influenced by mental simulations of action and their anticipated emotional consequences.

The chapter will be organized as follows. Before we lay out the two theories, it is necessary to grapple with what is meant by emotion. This is more than a definitional conundrum or chore, because there are at least two major classes of phenomena that are understood as emotion, and they are quite different in feeling, function, process—and relation to behavior. After this we shall outline the first theory, along with the arguments against it. Then the second theory and some of the relevant evidence.

This chapter presents an overview of the main ideas. Readers interested in a more detailed explication, as well as a fuller presentation of relevant evidence, should consult the article by some of us published in 2007 (Baumeister, Vohs, DeWall, & Zhang, 2007).

TWO TYPES OF EMOTION PROCESSES

Many phenomena are grouped under the rubric of emotion: vague moods, intense feeling states, twinges of liking and disliking, and more. They do not necessarily all have the same processes, nor the same effects on behavior.

For present purposes, it is useful to distinguish two broad categories. Our main focus will be on what ordinary people (i.e., not specialists in the psychology of emotion) call emotions. These are conscious feeling states. A person normally has one at a time. Often it is characterized by a bodily response, such as physiological arousal. These states are highly differentiated, and people have a wealth of terms they use to denote many different emotions: fear, anger, jealousy, joy, surprise, anger, disgust, and many more. These states tend to be slow to arise and slow to dissipate.

Such states must be distinguished from automatic affects, which are possibly far more common than full-blown emotions but are perhaps less frequently recognized. These can be subtle, possibly not even conscious. They are activated quickly and may come (and go) within a fraction of a second. Because these are linked by simple associations, and a person may have multiple associations, a person may have several affective reactions at the same time. They may not be as differentiated as conscious emotions, and in some views affects are simply on a single dimension of positive to negative, although some recent work has begun to suggest that even nonconscious affective reactions fall into various distinct categories that are demonstrably different (Ruys & Stapel, 2008).

Because conscious emotion typically involves a bodily response, including arousal that can take some time to develop, it may not be effective for providing input into behavioral decisions in a fast-changing or newly emerging situation. In contrast, the automatic affects arise within milliseconds and thus are plenty fast enough to contribute even to quick reactions.

One more difference has to do with the amount of cognition involved. In the 1980s, psychologists debated whether emotion depended on cognition (cf. Lazarus, 1982; Zajonc, 1980). The two sides in the debate seemed to refer to different kinds of phenomena. Zajonc's (1980) title "Preferences need no inferences" argued that emotion was independent of cognition, but he was referring chiefly to the automatic, affective reactions. One often has a reaction of liking or disliking almost as soon as one recognizes what the object is. Therefore, very little cognitive processing was required beyond knowing what something is and perhaps having one simple association. In contrast, full-blown emotional reactions tend to be saturated with cognitions, insofar as they depend on interpreting and appraising the eliciting events.

THE STANDARD THEORY: EMOTION DIRECTLY CAUSES BEHAVIOR

The idea that emotion directly causes behavior, and moreover that that is the proper function of emotion, is well established in psychology. It has been asserted in various forms by many theorists (see Baumeister, Vohs,

DeWall, & Zhang, 2007, for partial review). It makes intuitive sense—which may be part of the problem because the intuitive appeal has likely prevented the idea from being scrutinized critically.

The frequently used example is that fear causes one to run away. This view resonates with personal experience. It also lends itself to convincing evolutionary arguments. Thus, an ancestor who lacked a fear response might approach a dangerous snake or tiger and be killed, thereby failing to pass along his or her genes. In contrast, fearful ancestors would flee those predators and as a result would survive long enough to reproduce. Hence today's human population would be descended from ancestors who had emotions such as fear.

Other examples can be suggested (though many theorists seem not to bother). Anger might cause animals and ancestors to fight, thereby protecting or gaining resources and status. Frustration might stimulate aggressive goal pursuit. Love might cause people to engage in sex, thereby increasing reproduction.

Direct causation implies that the behavior, or at least the beginnings of it, is somehow contained in the emotional state. For example, anger might inherently contain incipient motor movements associated with struggling and fighting. Alternatively, the emotional reaction in the brain might directly activate other brain regions to initiate activity.

Given the widespread popularity of the direct causation theory, as well as its plausibility and parsimony, there would not seem to be much justification for developing a rival theory unless the direct causation theory were shown to fail in some way. Therefore, we turn next to delineate some of the problems with that theory.

CRITIQUE OF DIRECT CAUSATION THEORY

The direct causation theory suffers from multiple problems, both in terms of its internal plausibility and in terms of its fit to the available evidence. We ourselves embraced that theory for some time uncritically, and so we share the understanding of that theory's appeal.

The example that fear causes fleeing and thereby promotes survival has both theoretical and intuitive appeal, and so we think many researchers have considered the matter settled. However, that example has gradually come to seem a poor one, for multiple reasons. First, fear makes a poor prototype of emotion, and there is some evidence that it is not a typical emotion (Robinson, 1998). Second, many anecdotal reports of intensely frightening experiences contain the curious theme that the person remained calm and clear headed during the crisis but then was overcome with intense emotion when it was over (e.g., Gollwitzer, personal communication, 2003). Meanwhile, many animals do not flee when afraid but instead freeze. Humans, remarkably, sometimes do the opposite, such as when soldiers walk toward people who are shooting at them (e.g., Holmes, 1985).

Third, the delayed response reported anecdotally is, on reflection, possibly inevitable, and the delay reduces the plausibility of the standard evolutionary argument. When an animal encounters a predator, immediate flight is often vital for survival. Immediate flight does not allow time for the body to develop an arousal reaction that then serves as input into the behavioral decision process. Anyone who jogs in the woods has likely noticed that wildlife take flight as soon as the jogger's approach is perceived, rather than after the perception of the jogger has stimulated a slowly building bodily reaction of arousal that is then perceived by the brain and taken as impetus to skedaddle.

Another theoretical objection to the direct causation view is that, in human life at least, there are many, many behaviors but not nearly as many emotions. Emotions are thus not specific enough to give rise to specific behaviors, as the direct causation theory requires. This point has been articulated eloquently by Schwarz and Clore (2007): Based on knowing that people are afraid, it is impossible to predict their precise behaviors, which might well include starting to run but might instead involve things as different as listening to weather reports or selling their stocks.

Schwarz and Clore did not elaborate on this point, but it is a devastating objection to the direct causation theory. Specific behaviors depend on the situation and its structure of opportunities, constraints, and affordances (see chapters by Reis, by Holmes & Cavallo, and by Baron in this volume). Behavior cannot be driven by the emotion alone because behavioral choices can only be negotiated between the person and the situation. At most, emotions might activate broad tendencies toward approach and avoidance, but what specific form the behaviors take would depend on the situation.

Perhaps some readers may find these theoretical objections unconvincing. Let us turn, then, to consider actual evidence. Surely, one thinks (as we did), there must be plenty of evidence that emotional states cause behavior? An excellent and highly influential review by Loewenstein, Weber, Hsee, and Welch (2001) claimed that "the idea that emotions exert a direct and powerful influence on behavior receives ample support in the psychological literature" (2001, p. 272). Yet it is revealing that when Loewenstein et al. (2001) made that statement, they did not provide a long list of references, or indeed any. They simply assumed it was true. Such an assumption seems reasonable (and indeed the editors and reviewers of that paper, which was published in a highly rigorous journal, seemed to find the statement so uncontroversial that they did not challenge the authors to provide specific findings).

What happens when one looks for findings? Let us return to Schwarz and Clore, who were tasked with providing a review of the effects of emotion. Their 1996 review was 27 pages long, but it devoted barely half a page to the effects of emotion on behavior. The rest was spent on how emotion affects cognition. They were aware of how scant this seemed and said, with a slightly apologetic tone, that the imbalance in their coverage reflected the state of the empirical literature. A decade later, they revisited the same literature, and this time they were more confident than apologetic: "The effects of emotion . . . are more mental than behavioral" (2007, p. 402). Our search led to similar conclusions. Emotion seems to have its impact on cognition, not often directly on behavior.

To be sure, we did find some studies in which emotion as independent variable (or mediating variable) produced significant effects on behavior as dependent variable. But a close look at these raised further problems for the direct causation view.

One problem is that even when emotion does affect behavior, the results are often less than optimal and sometimes downright counterproductive. Among the general population, emotion has the stereotype of causing people to do irrational, sometimes destructive and even self-destructive things. This stereotype is not undeserved. A review of psychology's research on self-defeating behavior found that emotional distress was often implicated (Baumeister & Scher, 1988). That is, when people are in intense emotional states, they sometimes do things that bring suffering, harm, or failure to themselves. There are various processes by which this occurs. For example, when people are upset, they take foolish risks, often selecting a course of action that offers a small chance of a very good payoff but carries a substantial probability of producing a bad outcome, as opposed to playing it safe as people in neutral emotional states tend to do (Leith & Baumeister, 1996).

The links between emotion and self-defeating behavior explain the second part of the title of this chapter. Emotion apparently does make people do stupid, destructive things, at least sometimes.

Why are the irrational, destructive effects of emotion a problem for the direct causation theory? At first blush, one might look upon such findings as supporting the direct causation theory: It seems that emotion does cause behavior, after all. But evolution would not likely build the psyche with mechanisms that cause it to harm itself. Self-harm is maladaptive. If emotion directly caused such behavior, then natural selection would have favored ancestors who had fewer and weaker emotions, and so emotion might gradually have been phased out of the human psyche.

To put this argument more precisely: The observations about self-defeating behavior could support the idea that emotion does sometimes cause behavior, but they contradict the idea that that is its main function.

Self-defeating behaviors are almost by definition an unwanted side effect of processes that serve other, adaptive functions. If emotions do cause behavior in the form of self-defeating behavior, that indicates that their main function lies elsewhere.

A recent meta-analytic investigation by DeWall, Baumeister, and Bushman (2008) involved a systematic and detailed search for direct causation of behavior by emotion. The search was narrowly focused on articles in the *Journal of Personality and Social Psychology*, which is generally acknowledged to be the most prestigious and influential journal devoted to those two fields (i.e., personality and social psychology). It compiled tests for mediation by emotion. That is, it surveyed studies examining the effects of various situational factors (as independent variables) on behaviors and/or judgments (the dependent variables), and that included measures of emotion as possible mediators. To illustrate, Twenge, Baumeister, Tice, & Stucke (2001) showed that randomly assigned experiences of social rejection and exclusion caused increases in subsequent aggressive behavior, and they reported mediation analyses to test the theory that rejection would cause emotional distress, which in turn would cause increases in aggression. Thus, the direct cause of aggression would be the emotional distress.

Over 4,000 articles in the journal were consulted. These included nearly 400 tests for mediation by emotion. Over half of these looked for effects on behaviors. Of them, only 17% were significant at the .05 level (which means that random variation would produce such results about 5% of the time). The remaining studies examined effects on judgments, and the results were no better: Only 18% reached significance.

This result is shocking. Space in that journal is highly competitive, and by consensus only the best, most important results have a chance of being published there. Despite these high standards, the journal appears to report a great many null results—specifically, results testing hypotheses that the direct cause of behavior would be emotion. Apparently, authors, reviewers, and/or editors have believed that it is vital to test for mediation by emotion, as if that were the most likely explanation that needed to be ruled out before any other explanation could be asserted.

Thus, there were indeed some findings indicating that emotion did lead directly to behavior. But not very many, and certainly not nearly as many as somebody (again, one cannot know whether authors, editors, or reviewers thought those tests needed to be done) expected.

Let us turn now to consider those few cases in which emotion does apparently cause behavior. Do these indicate that emotion at least sometimes directly causes behavior? On close inspection, some of these turn out to be misleading as well.

The inherent ambiguity in studying the effects of emotion, or at least negative emotions, was articulated in the 1980s by Isen (1984, 1987). She pointed out that when emotional distress leads to a behavioral response, there are almost always at least two possible explanations. One is direct causation: The emotion makes the person act in a certain way. The other is mood regulation. A person who is upset may act in a particular way in the hope or expectation that the behavior will produce a change, presumably an improvement, in the emotional state. For example, if severe disappointment leads to an increase in the consumption of alcoholic beverages, it may signify that distress makes people thirsty for intoxicants—or it could mean that disappointed people choose to drink because they think that intoxication will make them feel better.

It is quite difficult to tease those two explanations apart, which led Isen to recommend that researchers study positive emotions instead. However, one ingenious procedure for separating those two explanations was devised by Manucia, Baumann, and Cialdini (1984). They dubbed it the "mood-freezing pill," which is to say a pill that supposedly will cause a person's emotional state to remain the same for an hour or two regardless of what else might happen. Of course there is no such pill, but it is possible to make naïve research participants believe that one exists and to give them a placebo with that cover story.

Manucia et al. (1984) sought to explain one well-documented effect of emotion on behavior, namely that sadness leads to an increase in helping. They induced sadness in many participants and by random assignment administered the mood-freezing pill manipulation to half of them. If sadness directly causes helping, then the mood-freezing pill should make no difference: Sadness would still cause helping regardless of whether one's mood is frozen or changeable. But they found that the mood-freezing pill eliminated the effect of sadness on helping. The implication is that sad people help others because they believe that helping will cheer them up. The mood-freezing pill means that one cannot be cheered up whether one helps or not, and under those circumstances, helping disappeared.

The finding is important because it undermines some of the remaining evidence that emotion directly causes behavior. Sadness had been shown to lead to helping. But the findings of Manucia et al. (1984) indicated that sadness does not directly cause helping. Rather, sadness makes people look for some opportunity to escape from sadness, and they strategically decide to do good deeds in order to achieve this goal. The operative relevant effect of emotion is that emotion is the goal and the outcome of the behavior, not its direct cause.

Researchers have begun to apply the mood-freezing manipulations in other settings. One of the best replicated effects of emotion on behavior in all the social sciences is that anger leads to aggression. Although the fact is not widely remarked, in practice aggression researchers have found it nearly impossible to get laboratory participants to behave aggressively unless they are provoked and angered in some way. Hence all the thousands of studies of the causes of aggression are in fact demonstrations of what variables increase or decrease the basic effect of angry provocation on aggression. To be sure, purists have pointed out that anger is neither necessary nor sufficient for aggression and that much anger does not lead to aggression (Averill, 1982). (The last observation is actually relevant here, for it suggests that anger does not directly or inevitably cause aggression; but one might retort that perhaps anger naturally causes aggression, but sometimes people manage to self-regulate and override the aggressive impulse, thereby thwarting the natural tendency for anger to cause aggression. See Baumeister, 1997.)

Yet when Bushman, Baumeister, and Phillips (2001) administered the mood-freezing pill manipulation to several samples of research participants, the time-honored effect of anger on aggression disappeared. Thus, anger does not directly cause aggression. Rather, angry people only aggress when they believe they can change their emotional state. The implication is that angry aggression is a strategic effort to improve one's mood.

Other standard findings have likewise withered under mood-freeze manipulations. Sadness and emotional upset lead to increased eating of sweets and junk food—but only because people think the tasty and unhealthy treats will make them feel better (Tice, Bratslavsky, & Baumeister, 2001). Likewise, emotional distress undermines prudent delaying of gratification, causing people to choose immediate rewards instead of larger, delayed ones—but not if their moods are frozen. The impact of distress on delay of gratification is in fact a strategic effort to improve one's mood (Tice et al., 2001). Sadness leads to procrastination, but only if people can procrastinate with pleasant, entertaining tasks that promise to cheer them up, and (again) only if their moods are believed to be changeable (Tice et al., 2001).

Thus, of the cases in which emotion does seem to cause behavior, further study with appropriate control groups again disconfirms the direct causation theory. What looks at first glance like emotion causing behavior is in fact behavior pursuing emotional outcomes. This brings us to the second, feedback theory, which proposes precisely that: Emotion functions as the outcome of behavior.

EMOTION AS FEEDBACK

Thus far we have surveyed multiple reasons to reject the standard theory that the proper or primary function of emotion is for the direct causation of behavior. The theory had serious inadequacies on conceptual grounds and also has failed to find much empirical support. What ostensible support there was turned out on closer inspection to suggest, instead, that emotion is the goal rather than the driver of behavior. In this section we will build on that insight to flesh out the theory of emotion as a feedback system.

The core idea is that full-fledged, conscious emotion serves mainly to provide feedback after behavior, by stimulating the person to reflect on recent actions and their consequences and possibly to learn lessons for the future. This approach deals effectively with several of the observations that plagued the direct causation theory. The lack of specificity is not a problem because emotion serves to stimulate cognitive processing about what has already happened, and so the behavior is already existent. The slow-arising nature of emotion is not a problem because there is no urgent rush to make decisions, only an open-ended opportunity to think about what happened and what might have happened. The fact that emotion sometimes directly leads to self-defeating behaviors is not a problem because that involved the direct effects of emotion on current choices, and emotion is not supposed to facilitate current choices, only retroactive reflection.

We reported Schwarz and Clore's (2007) observation that the research literature has shown the effects of emotion to be much more centered on cognition than on behavior. This fits the feedback theory, which holds that emotion is for stimulating learning (thus cognition).

In all this, our emphasis has been on the full-blown, conscious emotional states rather than on automatic affect. Automatic affect may be part of the story, however. The full-blown emotional states may create affective memories and associations that can be useful in the future. Return for a moment to the suggestion that the full-blown conscious emotion of fear may often arise only after the crisis or emergency has passed because it is too slow to drive behavior during a fast-occurring occasion of danger. One might well wonder, what use would there be in being afraid after the danger has passed? But the strong wash of fear may leave strong associations to the circumstances that contained the danger. The next time one approaches or notices signs of similar circumstances, those associations may produce automatic affective twinges of fear that can help steer the person to take preventive action. Full-blown fear is not needed on that later occasion, just the automatic affective reminder.

Feedback may come as a surprise at first, but over time people develop rather elaborate and thorough knowledge of what kinds of actions in various situations bring what emotional outcomes. They can thus learn to anticipate how they will feel if they do this or that. Crucially, we think these anticipated emotions can help guide behavioral choices. In that sense, we have suggested behavior comes to pursue emotion, rather than emotion directly causing behavior.

The idea that behavior pursues emotion can account for the mood-freezing findings. People come to know, for example, that helping will make them feel good, and so when they are sad and an opportunity arises to help someone, they help, and as a result they feel better. Researchers can thus show that sad moods lead to increased helping, and some may be misled into thinking that sadness somehow directly causes helping. The truth, however, as revealed by the mood-freezing studies by Manucia et al. (1984), is that the crucial factor is people's knowledge of their emotional lives and their anticipation of what actions will make them feel certain ways. They choose their actions strategically to produce the emotional outcomes they desire.

We have noted that the favorite example of theorists advocating the direct causation theory involved fear causing someone to flee. Guilt is a good example to illustrate the feedback theory. Guilt does not directly cause any behavior, although it has been shown to lead people to do various things that may reduce their guilt, such as apologizing, making amends, promising to refrain from repeating the transgression, and doing various good deeds (for review, see Baumeister, Stillwell, & Heatherton, 1994).

The ordinary sequence involving guilt goes something like this. The person performs some misdeed, possibly for selfish reasons or in many cases simply because the person fails to realize the adverse effects of the action on others. Afterward, the person feels guilty, especially insofar as the unhappy effects of the action become apparent. Guilt stimulates the person to reflect on the misdeed, including replaying the episode mentally multiple times, and in particular imagining counterfactual scenarios by which other possible actions would have produced better, less harmful outcomes (and hence no guilt). By virtue of these ruminations and reflections, the person learns some lesson about how to avoid a repeat of this unhappy scenario. At some point in the future, a similar situation arises, and a recognition of the similarity produces associations that bring automatic affect, including twinges of guilt that help the person realize that to act in the same way as before will bring guilt again. Anticipating that possible and unwelcome feeling, the person selects a course of action that will bring a better result (including no guilt).

Evidence supports this scenario. A pair of studies by Baumeister, Stillwell, and Heatherton (1995) compared accounts of transgressions that produced guilt with transgressions that did not. Although the two sets were similar in many respects including type and apparent severity of outcome, the ones involving guilt were more likely than the others to include reference to learning lessons and changing behavior subsequently. These findings suggest that guilt does indeed function to make people reflect on what they did wrong, extract a relevant lesson or moral for the future, and change their behavior on subsequent occasions.

EVIDENCE: EMOTION AND LEARNING

This section will cover some of the evidence that makes the feedback theory plausible. In view of the fact that this chapter is intended as an introductory overview, it cannot provide a full treatment of such evidence, and interested readers are referred to the more thorough presentation by Baumeister, Vohs, DeWall, & Zhang (2007).

We have already mentioned the fact that research has been much more successful and prolific at demonstrating effects of emotion on cognition than on behavior, and this fact is quite congenial to the idea that emotion is for stimulating learning. Some of the particular facts about the effects of emotion on cognition lend further credence to the idea that emotion promotes learning. Emotion appears to strengthen the memory traces that are formed, such that information with emotional impact is remembered better than other information. There is abundant evidence for this so-called emotional modulation of memory (for reviews, see McGaugh, 2000, 2002). Also, emotional states seem to focus people's attention better, so that they zero in on the most relevant aspects of an event and thus learn the crucial lesson better (as compared to learning that occurs in the absence of emotion).

One of the most important mental processes for social learning is counterfactual thinking. This appears to be rather distinctively human, although it is difficult to know for certain what can occur in the minds of various animals. Still, humans seem especially likely to replay events mentally while altering various aspects or steps in the unfolding sequence. Counterfactual thinking has the potential power to multiply the learning benefits of an event many times over. Even just replaying an event repeatedly exactly as it happened could improve learning, insofar as each replay creates a new memory trace and thus possibly strengthens the total impact on memory. But counterfactual replays allow the person, in effect, to experience a full range of the behavioral contingencies, imagining at least every possible action and what outcome it might have produced. For the highly complex events that occur in human social life, counterfactual replaying can help the person work through all the possible aspects of a situation and the various possible courses of action, and thus can ideally produce useful learning well suited to the unique demands of human society.

Emotion contributes to counterfactual thinking in multiple, important ways. First and foremost, emotion, especially aversive emotion, appears to be a powerful stimulus to engage in counterfactual thinking. Roese's (1997) authoritative review of counterfactual thinking concluded that negative emotional states were a, if not the, "chief determinant" of such thought. Thus, one vital function and consequence of unpleasant emotional states is to make people reflect back on what they did, on what went wrong, and on how things might have gone differently.

The link between emotion and habit is also instructive here. The link is strikingly negative. Wood, Quinn, and Kashy (2002) have shown that when people perform habitual actions, they tend to experience little or no emotion, as compared to when people perform activities that are not habitual. By definition, habits are behaviors that are very well learned (see chapter by Verplanken, this volume). The implication is that people feel emotions when they are learning patterns of behavior, but when the learning is done, the emotion is gone.

The link between emotion and learning could also have implications for how people judge and infer learning. If emotion is generally useful for stimulating learning, then people might infer from emotion that they learned something. One of us first began to suspect this when watching game shows and hearing the characters say how much they had learned. In this particular case, the possible lessons (which were never spelled out by the contestant) seemed unpromising. He said the experience had taught him a lot about himself. Perhaps he had learned that he (the eponymous bachelor in a show about choosing a romantic partner) enjoyed riding around in limousines, drinking champagne, and having a dozen beautiful women competing for his affections. Big insight! But no doubt he had had quite a set of unusual emotions during this experience, and perhaps these emotions create the illusion of learning.

To study the illusions of learning, Baumeister, Alquist, and Tice (2008, unpublished) have conducted an initial study. Participants first read a biographical article about George Bernard Shaw, ostensibly for a study of reading comprehension. Then they performed an emotion induction exercise (presented as a writing exercise) in which they vividly imagined an episode that would produce a strong emotion. After this, they were asked to rate how much they had learned from the article. Then they completed a mood measure. Participants who had been induced into highly aroused emotional states reported feeling that they learned more than participants in other conditions. In further studies we are obtaining objective measures of learning to compare with the self-reports of learning.

Thus, a dose of emotion, in this case generated by a completely irrelevant task, increased the extent to which people believed they had learned much from reading an article. Such a pattern suggests that emotion operates as a subtle cue to the self about learning. Emotion may generate an illusion of learning, which could be highly relevant to many phenomena, including teacher ratings in undergraduate courses. Many instructors have suspected that students will give higher marks to a lecture that uses vivid stories and exciting audiovisual materials to dramatize a pedestrian point than they will to a relatively dry lecture that is packed with information. Administrative pressure on college faculty to obtain high course ratings may gradually shift the educational process away from providing information and toward stimulating emotional responses in students.

ANTICIPATED EMOTION

An important aspect of the feedback theory of emotion is that people learn to anticipate emotional outcomes and adjust their behavior accordingly. In a sense, this could render most human behavior a form of emotion regulation, insofar as people decide what to do as a strategic effort to pursue and achieve emotional outcomes. We proposed guilt as a useful prototype of how the feedback theory could operate, and guilt can guide behavior effectively even if people quite rarely actually feel guilty, insofar as they anticipate what actions would bring guilt and change their behaviors so as to avoid that unpleasant outcome. Indeed, one of the surprising findings to emerge from the research literature on guilt is that guilt and guilt proneness tend to produce more positive and beneficial outcomes than negative ones, despite the prevailing cultural stereotype of guilt as a useless, self-destructive emotion (for reviews, see Baumeister et al., 1994; Tangney & Dearing, 2002).

Several important sets of findings about anticipated emotion lend credence to the feedback theory. One is the evidence that anticipated regret, in particular, can influence decisions, mostly in beneficial, advantageous ways. That is, people make choices based on anticipating what will bring them regret, and the impact of this anticipation on the choices is generally to steer people to choose in ways that will benefit them (see Mellers, Schwartz, & Ritov, 1999).

More generally, anticipated emotion tends to shift decisions toward two types of choices, which sometimes will be less than the optimal one but which, by and large, seem likely to be beneficial. The first is that anticipated emotion (including anticipated regret) makes people facing uncertain circumstances choose relatively safe options (e.g., Richard, De Vries, & van der Pligt, 1998; Simonson, 1992; Tetlock & Boettger, 1994). These can be shown to depart sometimes from what would be economically optimal and might produce the best outcome, such as pursuing a risky but promising opportunity. Still, playing it safe cannot really be characterized as a foolish, irrational, or self-defeating strategy in general, and so to the extent that anticipated emotion makes people play it safe, they are probably doing reasonably well.

Second, anticipated regret or other anticipated emotion can shift people toward favoring the status quo, as long as it is acceptable (Anderson, 2003;

Kruger, Wirtz, & Miller, 2005). That is, they do not choose options that produce change but rather stick with known options as long as those are acceptable. Again, this can sometimes mean forgoing a promising opportunity, but again staying with an acceptable status quo is a form of playing it safe and thus seems likely to avoid the worst possible outcomes.

Research on affective forecasting is also relevant. Affective forecasting refers to people's predictions of how they will feel under future or hypothetical circumstances. The standard finding from that literature, which has been replicated many times, is that people tend to predict that their emotional reactions to future events will be relatively long lasting, whereas when such events occur the emotions tend to dissipate. In a sense, people overpredict their emotions (Wilson & Gilbert, 2003).

The overprediction of emotion indicates the importance of anticipation. If people underpredicted their emotional reactions, it would be very difficult to suggest that anticipation of emotion is important because anticipation would tend to be small and trivial whereas the experienced reality would be relatively large and impactful. In a sense, then, the biggest emotion is the expected one, rather than the actually experienced one. Emotion looms larger and thus presumably has more impact in anticipation than in actual experience.

And sure enough, anticipated emotion does seem to have more impact on behavior than actually experienced emotion. Earlier we cited the compilation of *JPSP* mediation analyses indicating that experienced emotion only significantly mediated behavior about 17% of the time (DeWall, Baumeister, & Bushman, 2008). In that same investigation, in contrast, anticipated emotion significantly mediated emotion 90% of the time! The success rate of anticipated emotion was thus even greater than the shocking failure rate of experienced emotion.

To be sure, there were far fewer studies testing for mediation by anticipated emotion than by experienced emotion, and the 90% figure is thus a less reliable estimate than the other numbers. Still, the contrast between the two is so striking that it strongly recommends that future researchers pay more attention to the relevance of anticipated emotion in mediating behavior. For present purposes, at any rate, it certainly underscores the importance of anticipated emotion specifically, and the feedback theory generally, as deserving further, prospective tests.

SUMMARY AND CONCLUSION

This chapter presented two theories of emotion. We made no attempt to present them as equal rivals in a fair fight. One is well established, and indeed for a long time we subscribed to it ourselves. Yet the accumulating evidence of its inadequacy compelled us to search for an alternative, which led to the development of the second theory. We reviewed the research literature with an open-minded search for evidence that would enable us to develop a new and correct theory, but our presentation here has been organized so as to present the best research evidence and most compelling reasons that we think the second theory is better. As we said, a more nuanced and thorough presentation is available in Baumeister, Vohs, DeWall, and Zhang (2007).

The first theory was that emotion directly causes behavior and that, moreover, direct causation of behavior is a principal function of emotion. We have believed this in the past and we think many researchers continue to believe it. There are many signs of the widespread belief in this theory, including the fact that so many *JPSP* authors almost routinely report analyses for mediation of behavior by currently felt emotion.

We presented conceptual and empirical reasons to reject that theory. Considered carefully, it has serious gaps, including the inability of the relatively few emotions to directly cause the many different behaviors that people show. The majority of findings reported in the field's premier journal fail to show that emotion is the (mediating) direct cause of behavior. And even when emotion does seem to cause behavior, replication with appropriate control conditions often shows that the behavioral effects depend on strategic attempts to regulate emotion.

Instead, we think the available evidence suggests that emotion operates as a feedback system. After behavior has occurred, emotion drives appraisal and reflection, often including counterfactual replays, which can promote learning. Moreover, people learn to anticipate what actions will lead to what emotions, and they adjust their behaviors accordingly. Behavior pursues emotion.

The feedback theory does in a way provide a positive answer to our titular question of whether emotion causes behavior. Emotion does have a causal influence on behavior, just not in the direct and immediate manner widely assumed. Rather, emotion stimulates learning from behavior, and this learning can have beneficial effects on behavior in the undefined future. The effect of emotion on behavior is thus indirect. Nonetheless, it can be powerfully beneficial.

REFERENCES

Anderson, C. J. (2003). The psychology of doing nothing: Forms of decision avoidance result from reason and emotion. *Psychological Bulletin, 129,* 139–167.

Averill, J. (1982). *Anger and aggression: An essay on emotion.* New York: Springer-Verlag.

Baumeister, R. F. (1997). *Evil: Inside human violence and cruelty*. New York: W.H. Freeman.

Baumeister, R. F., & Scher, S. J. (1988). Self-defeating behavior patterns among normal individuals: Review and analysis of common self-destructive tendencies. *Psychological Bulletin, 104*, 3–22.

Baumeister, R. F., Stillwell, A. M., & Heatherton, T. F. (1994). Guilt: An interpersonal approach. *Psychological Bulletin, 115*, 243–267.

Baumeister, R. F., Stillwell, A. M., & Heatherton, T. F. (1995). Personal narratives about guilt: Role in action control and interpersonal relationships. *Basic and Applied Social Psychology, 17*, 173–198.

Baumeister, R. F., Vohs, K. D., DeWall, C. N., & Zhang, L. (2007). How emotion shapes behavior: Feedback, anticipation, and reflection, rather than direct causation. *Personality and Social Psychology Review, 11*, 167–203.

Baumeister, R. F., Vohs, K. D., & Funder, D. C. (2007). Psychology as the science of self-reports and finger movements: Whatever happened to actual behavior? *Perspectives on Psychological Science, 2*, 396–403.

Baumeister, R. F., Alquist, J., & Tice, D. M. (2008). *Unpublished research findings*, Tallahassee, FL: Florida State University.

Bushman, B. J., Baumeister, R. F., & Phillips, C. M. (2001). Do people aggress to improve their mood? Catharsis beliefs, affect regulation opportunity, and aggressive responding. *Journal of Personality and Social Psychology, 81*, 17–32.

DeWall, C. N., Baumeister, R. F., and Bushman, B. J. (2008). Meta-analyses of mediation by current and anticipated emotion: Is today's behavior based on today's or tomorrow's emotion? Manuscript submitted for publication.

Holmes, R. (1985). *Acts of war: The behavior of men in battle*. New York: Free Press.

Isen, A. M. (1984). Toward understanding the role of affect in cognition. In R. S. Wyer & T. K. Srull (Eds.) *Handbook of Social Cognition* (Vol. 3, pp. 179–236). Hillsdale, N.J.: Erlbaum.

Isen, A.M. (1987). Positive affect, cognitive processes, and social behavior. In L. Berkowitz (Ed.), *Advances in experimental social psychology* (Vol. 20, pp. 203–253). New York: Academic Press.

Kruger, J., Wirtz, D., & Miller, D. T. (2005). Counterfactual thinking and the first instinct fallacy. *Journal of Personality and Social Psychology, 88*, 725–735.

Lazarus, R. S. (1982). Thoughts on the relations between emotion and cognition. *American Psychologist, 37*, 1019–1024.

Leith, K. P., & Baumeister, R. F. (1996). Why do bad moods increase self-defeating behavior? Emotion, risk taking, and self-regulation. *Journal of Personality and Social Psychology, 71*, 1250–1267.

Loewenstein, G. F., Weber, E. U., Hsee, C. K., & Welch, N. (2001). Risk as feelings. *Psychological Bulletin, 127*, 267–286.

Manucia, G. K., Baumann, D. J., & Cialdini, R. B. (1984). Mood influences on helping: Direct effects or side effects? *Journal of Personality and Social Psychology, 46*, 357–364.

McGaugh, J. L. (2000). Memory—a century of consolidation. *Science, 287*, 248–251.

McGaugh, J. L. (2002). Memory consolidation and the amygdala: A systems perspective. *Trends in Neuroscience, 25*, 456–461.

Mellers, B., Schwartz, A., & Ritov, I. (1999). Emotion-based choice. *Journal of Experimental Psychology: General, 128,* 332–345.

Richard, R., de Vries, N. K., & van der Pligt, J. (1998). Anticipated regret and precautionary sexual behavior. *Journal of Applied Social Psychology, 28,* 1411–1428.

Robinson, M. D. (1998). Running from William James' bear: A review of preattentive mechanisms and their contributions to emotional experience. *Cognition & Emotion, 12,* 667–696.

Roese, N. J. (1997). Counterfactual thinking. *Psychological Bulletin, 121,* 133–148.

Ruys, K. I., & Stapel, D. A. (2008). The secret life of emotions. *Psychological Science, 19,* 385–391.

Schwarz, N., & Clore, G. L. (1996). Feelings and phenomenal experiences. In E. T. Higgins & A. Kruglanski (Eds.), *Social psychology: Handbook of basic principles* (pp. 433–465). New York: Guilford.

Schwarz, N., & Clore, G. L. (2007). Feelings and phenomenal experiences. In E. T. Higgins & A. Kruglanski (Eds.), *Social psychology: Handbook of basic principles* (2nd Edition), pp. 385–407. New York: Guilford.

Simonson, I. (1992). The influence of anticipating regret and responsibility on purchase decisions. *Journal of Consumer Research, 19,* 105–118.

Tangney, J. P., & Dearing, R. L. (2002). *Shame and guilt.* New York: Guilford.

Tetlock, P. E., & Boettger, R. (1994). Accountability amplifies the status quo effect when change creates victims. *Journal of Behavioral Decision Making, 7,* 1–23.

Tice, D. M., Bratslavsky, E., & Baumeister, R. F. (2001). Emotional distress regulation takes precedence over impulse control: If you feel bad, do it! *Journal of Personality and Social Psychology, 80,* 53–67.

Twenge, J. M., Baumeister, R. F., Tice, D. M., & Stucke, T. S. (2001). If you can't join them, beat them: Effects of social exclusion on aggressive behavior. *Journal of Personality and Social Psychology, 81,* 1058–1069.

Wilson, T. D., & Gilbert, D. T. (2003). Affective forecasting. In M. Zanna (Ed.), *Advances in experimental social psychology,* Vol. 35 (pp. 345–411). New York: Elsevier.

Wood, W., Quinn, J., & Kashy, D. (2002). Habits in everyday life: Thought, emotion, and action. *Journal of Personality and Social Psychology, 83,* 1281–1297.

Zajonc, R. B. (1980). Feeling and thinking: Preferences need no inferences. *American Psychologist, 35,* 151–175.

8   How to Maximize Implementation Intention Effects

Peter M. Gollwitzer
Frank Wieber
Andrea L. Myers
Sean M. McCrea

How do people turn their intentions into behavior? This miracle is clarified in the present chapter by analyzing how if-then planning (i.e., implementation intentions; Gollwitzer, 1993, 1999) supports the translation of intentions into actions. In addition, we will examine how if-then plans should be worded best to maximize their effectiveness. Subsequently, we will address the importance of the if-then format when wording implementation intentions by inspecting the extension of such plans into an if-then-why format, and by inspecting upward counterfactuals as an if-then format directed at past goal pursuits.

IMPLEMENTATION INTENTIONS AND DIFFICULT GOAL STRIVING

Whereas goal intentions merely specify desired end states ("I want to achieve goal X!"), implementation intentions in the format "If situation Y arises, then I will initiate behavior Z!" additionally specify when, where, and how a person intends to pursue a goal. Implementation intentions delegate control over the initiation of the intended goal-directed behavior to a specified opportunity by creating a strong link between a situational cue and a goal-directed response. For example, a person who has the goal to become physically fit can form the implementation intention "If

I come home after work on Friday, then I will immediately go for a 30 min run!" Implementation intentions have been found to be beneficial with respect to four major obstacles that have to be overcome to bridge the gap from initial goal setting and meeting that goal (i.e., not getting started to act on one's goals, getting derailed during goal striving, not disengaging when courses of action are failing, and overextending oneself during goal striving). Recent meta-analyses revealed a medium-to-large effect size (Cohen, 1992) of implementation intentions on goal achievement on top of the effects of mere goal intentions (Gollwitzer & Sheeran, 2006; Webb & Sheeran, 2008).

Knowing this, can implementation intentions clarify the miraculous translation of intentions (goals) into behavior, even in situations that do not seem responsive to self-regulation? Indeed, implementation intentions have been found to help overcome several problems people might encounter during goal realization. Implementation intentions are capable of prompting particular motivational states or efforts. For example, in a study on solving analytic reasoning tasks, they improved participants' performance by strengthening self-efficacy (Bayer & Gollwitzer, 2007). Secondly, implementation intentions helped people protect themselves from inner states that interrupt goal striving. In a study by Achtziger, Gollwitzer, and Sheeran (2008), implementation intentions were shown to help tennis players regulate disruptive cognitive, motivational, physiological, and emotional states in order to better compete against an opponent. Implementation intentions also support peoples' attainment of prosocial goals in cognitively demanding situations. For example, when people find themselves in loss-framed negotiations, implementation intentions can support the use of more integrative negotiation strategies (Trötschel & Gollwitzer, 2007). Moreover, implementation intentions can be used to replace bad behavioral habits that threaten the realization of attractive goals (e.g., wasteful recycling behaviors for people with the goal to protect the environment) with more appropriate behaviors (e.g., recycling; Holland, Aarts, & Langendam, 2006).

Lastly, there are three ways in which unwanted automatic processes that cause problems for goal realization can be controlled by using implementation intentions. First, these plans help suppress unwanted cognitive responses. For example, they can reduce automatic stereotyping by automating counterstereotypic thoughts (Stewart & Payne, 2008). Second, they can improve emotion regulation in aversive and fear-triggering situations. For example, implementation intentions were shown to reduce arousal when fear or disgust-triggering stimuli were presented (Schweiger Gallo, Keil, McCulloch, Rockstroh, & Gollwitzer, 2009). That this strategic emotion regulation by if-then plans operates in an automatic fashion was supported by evidence from early electrocortical correlates. Finally, implementation intentions can enhance behavioral inhibition. For example, inhibition performance in a neuropsychological task (i.e., stop task) was improved among children with ADHD by using implementation intentions (Gawrilow & Gollwitzer, 2008).

HOW ARE IMPLEMENTATION INTENTIONS WORDED MOST EFFECTIVELY?

The implementation intentions used in the reported experimental research were always found to be highly effective; other research has demonstrated that this effectiveness does not produce costs in terms of rigidity (Gollwitzer, Parks-Stamm, Jaudas, & Sheeran, 2008) or ego depletion (Bayer & Gollwitzer, 2009; Webb & Sheeran, 2003). Does this connote that implementation intentions are always effective in terms of meeting one's goals? Several limits of the effectiveness of implementation intentions have been found in terms of goal attributes, self-beliefs, and personality factors. First, a weak commitment to the respective goal intention limits the effectiveness of implementation intentions (Sheeran, Webb, & Gollwitzer, 2005). This goal-dependence of implementation intentions may generally protect people from rigidly enacting plans directed at goals that are obsolete or not vitally important. However, it may also occasionally counter people's intentions. For example, when a person has the goal of becoming physically fit but has rather weak goal commitment, even implementation intentions will not work wonders. Second, low self-efficacy beliefs concerning the respective goal intention have been demonstrated to limit the effectiveness of implementation intentions (Wieber, Odenthal, & Gollwitzer, in press). Although low self-efficacy beliefs may often represent a correct indication that a goal cannot be successfully realized, they may also limit people's goal striving. For instance, when a person unwarrantedly doubts his or her ability to run for 30 minutes, a relevant implementation intention may not support goal attainment. Moreover, individuals who preferably evaluate their behavior according to others' standards (i.e., people who score high on socially prescribed perfectionism; Powers, Koestner, & Topciu, 2005) do not seem to benefit from forming implementation intentions. Possibly, the personality attribute of socially prescribed perfectionism hinders full commitment to if-then plans, thus reducing the effectiveness of these plans. Finally, the personality trait of conscientiousness has been found to limit implementation intentions' effectiveness (Webb, Christian, & Armitage, 2007). Whereas persons with a low level of conscientiousness immensely benefited from forming implementation intentions, those with a high level of conscientiousness did not; the superior performance of high conscientious individuals left little room for improvement (ceiling effect; Webb et al., 2007).

In addition to the limitations caused by these moderators of implementation intention effects, attributes of implementation intentions themselves (namely the wording and format of these plans) might limit their effects on goal-striving behavior. In everyday life, people may not succeed in forming effective implementation intentions either because the if-component or the then-component is specified suboptimally or because the format of the implementation intention as a whole is inappropriate. The remainder of this chapter will inspect these potential limits and how implementation intentions should be formed to maximize goal attainment.

How to Word the If-Component of Implementation Intentions?

According to the theory of intentional action control (Gollwitzer, 1993; 1999), planning a situation in which one intends to act on a goal via the formation of an implementation intention leads to heightened cognitive accessibility of the mental representation of the situation. This accessibility persists over time until the plan is enacted or the goal is achieved or dismissed. The heightened activation of the critical situation helps people to easily recall the specified situation (Achtziger, Bayer, & Gollwitzer, 2009, Study 1) and leads to swift attention when the situation arises (Aarts, Dijksterhuis, & Midden, 1999; Achtziger et al., 2009, Study 2). For example, Webb and Sheeran (2004, Study 2 and 3) observed that implementation intentions improve cue detection (fewer misses and more hits) without stimulating erroneous responses to similar cues (false alarms and correct rejections). However, because attentional and cognitive resources are limited (Wegner & Bargh, 1998), the increased readiness to attend to an implementation intention's critical cues should reduce attention to other cues (Broadbent, 1958; Kahneman, 1973). Given this consequence, can specifying situational cues in the implementation intention's if-component both support and hamper goal attainment? Three studies tested this hypothesis.

Cue Detection During Goal Pursuit. In a Story Listening Study (Parks-Stamm, Gollwitzer, & Oettingen, 2007), participants had to identify five-letter words in a recorded story that was quickly read aloud. Before listening to the story, all participants familiarized themselves with the two most common five-letter words "Laura" and "mouse." In the implementation intention condition, they additionally included these words in if-then plans ("If I hear the word 'Laura,' then I will immediately press the L; if I hear the word 'mouse,' then I will immediately press the M!"). The facilitated detection of the critical five-letter words would indicate a shift in attention to the implementation intention cues. As attentional resources are limited, it was predicted that implementation intentions would increase performance in response to the two critical five-letter words but impair performance in response to the remaining five-letter words. In line with these assumptions, implementation intentions increased performance in response to the critical words but at the cost of reduced performance in response to the remaining five-letter words. Thus, preferring one situational means by including it in an implementation intention may compromise the use of alternative means to the goal.

Attention Attraction During the Pursuit of Unrelated Goals. Will critical cues even attract attention when they occur during the pursuit of an unrelated goal? To test this, Wieber and Sassenberg (2006) conducted two attention disruption studies. In both studies, the disruption of attention through implementation intentions was investigated by presenting critical situations (stimuli that were part of an implementation intention for an unrelated task) as task-irrelevant distractors along with task-relevant stimuli in a so-called flanker paradigm (Eriksen & Eriksen, 1974). In the first study, half of the participants formed implementation intentions ("If I see [the word] 'flower', then I will press the left control key!" and "If I see 'insect', then I will press the right control key!"). The other half of the participants formed control intentions ("I will respond to 'flower' as quickly and accurately as possible!", "I will respond to 'insect' as quickly and accurately as possible!", "I will press the left control key as quickly and accurately as possible!", and "I will press the right control key as quickly and accurately as possible!"). These intentions were directed at the goal of performing well on a subsequent categorization task (a flower vs. insect implicit association task). Next, participants worked on the ostensibly unrelated flanker task, in which they had to make word versus nonword decisions while both neutral and critical stimuli were presented as task-irrelevant distractors. The results indicated that the presence of a critical stimulus slowed down participants' responses; however, this effect only occurred when they had formed implementation intentions, not when they had formed control intentions. In the second study, these findings were replicated using a flanker task with vowel versus consonant classifications.

Taken together, these findings imply that critical situations will not escape a person's attention when they have been included in an implementation intention, regardless of whether the implementation intention is goal relevant or not. This may, however, compromise attention to other goal-relevant cues, as attention is a limited resource. Thus, one has to be careful which critical situational cues one includes in the if-component of an implementation intention.

One way to prevent missing alternative opportunities would be to formulate rather inclusive situational descriptions in the if-component of one's implementation intentions. For example, to ensure one uses an unexpected good opportunity on Tuesday to go for a run, one may simply specify "Once a week after work" in the if-component instead of "If I arrive at home after work on Fridays at 5pm". However, a potential problem of using more inclusive formulation is that the critical situation may not acquire a sufficiently high state of activation and thus not allow effortless identification of the situation once it occurs. Consequently, more inclusively formulated if-components might not ensure that a good opportunity to act is captured, especially when an immediate recognition of the opportunity is required.

Inclusive If-Components. The effectiveness of inclusive, as compared to specific, formulations of the if-component was tested in a Car Race Study (Wieber, Odenthal, & Gollwitzer, 2009, Study 1). The participants' task was to drive as fast as possible on a computer-based car race simulation without damaging the car in potentially dangerous situations, such as on slippery racetracks, around competing cars, and in sharp curves. After completing two laps around the racetrack, participants worked on a so-called intention training, which served to manipulate their intentions. All participants formed the goal intention "I will complete the race track as fast and damage-free as possible!" Participants in the specific implementation intention condition additionally added the implementation intention "If I see a black and white curve road sign, then I will immediately adapt my speed!" Participants in the inclusive implementation intention condition added the implementation intention "If I enter a dangerous situation, then I will immediately adapt my speed!" After this intention manipulation, they drove two more laps around the racetrack. Although the inclusive implementation intention included various dangerous situations, it was predicted that specific if-component formulations would lead to an increased performance compared to an unspecific if-component, as the classification of a dangerous situation requires the effortful assessment of the actual situation and might not be completed swiftly enough to prevent car damage.

The results indeed supported the assumptions. Whereas the driving performance of those participants who used abstract formulations of the if-component did not differentiate from the mere goal intention condition, participants with specific implementation intentions caused less damage to their cars without slowing down than those in the other two conditions. Thus, forming more inclusive if-components does not seem to represent a viable alternative to forming specific ones, at least when the swift recognition of the situation is crucial for successful action initiation.

Summary. When identifying an alternative opportunity to act is crucial, forming specific and exclusive if-components might not be ideal, as they cannot ensure the detection of all crucial opportunities. However, when representative situations can be identified that account for a large proportion of the situations appropriate to pursue an intended goal (e.g., sharp curves in the reported study), the benefits of forming specific implementation intentions should generally outweigh the costs of overlooking alternative opportunities. This should especially be true when one is prone to miss the critical opportunity, either because it is difficult to detect (e.g., it presents itself only shortly and thus requires immediate recognition) or because one is exhausted and therefore lacks focused attention.

How to Word the Then-Component of an Implementation Intention?

In addition to the heightened accessibility of the if-component, a second process underlies the implementation intention effect on goal attainment. Implementation intentions create a strong link between the if-component and the then-component (Gollwitzer, 1993; 1999). As a result, the initiation of the action specified in the then-component in response to the critical situation acquires features of automaticity. Responses are initiated immediately (Gollwitzer & Brandstätter, 1997), efficiently (Brandstätter, Lengfelder, & Gollwitzer, 2001), and without the need of a further conscious intent (Bayer, Achtziger, Gollwitzer, & Moskowitz, 2009).

How can this process best be utilized when wording the then-component of an implementation intention? Specifying concrete behaviors seems appropriate whenever a whole array of specific operationalizations is possible. Planning in advance which type of goal-directed behavior is to be executed prevents disruptive deliberation once the critical situation is encountered (with respect to choosing one behavior over another). For example, when one holds the goal of exercising regularly and decides in advance to go to the gym, then one inevitably prevents the deliberation of whether to go to the gym, run, or possibly question the plan of exercising once the situation arises. In this way, implementation intentions help one to act in line with one's valued long-term goals, even when the necessary means require overcoming short-term costs like initial reluctance to engage in unpleasant behavior (i.e., when one runs only for the result of being physically fit but does not like running per se).

To reduce disruptive deliberation during goal striving above and beyond the mere initiation of a behavior, simple behaviors should be included into the then-component that are easily carried out (without requiring reflective thought). Such simple behaviors can refer to single operations (e.g., pressing a keyboard button) or several operations that have been learned well (scripts like going to the gym, flossing teeth; see Gollwitzer & Sheeran, 2006). But in addition to simple behaviors, people's goal striving at times requires the initiation and enactment of complex actions, like applying abstract rules or enacting a sequence of actions that are taxing to automate (Hull, 1951). Does specifying complex behaviors in the then-component of an implementation intention still support goal attainment? Two recent studies examined this question.

Switching Task Strategies. In a Water Jar Study (Wieber, Odenthal, et al., 2009, Study 2), participants had to allocate a predetermined amount of water from an initial jar (A) to a target jar (E) by using three jars (B, C, and D) with specified volumes (Luchins, 1942). Five trials required the application of one specific strategy $(A - C + 2 \times D$ or $A - B + 2 \times C)$ and five trials required the other. All participants learned about these strategies in the task instructions. Before the task began, participants were put in one of four intention conditions. In one condition, participants formed mere goal intentions "I want to find the right solution as fast as possible!" whereas participants in the remaining conditions added an implementation intention comprising the strategies explicated in the instructions in an if-then format. In the remaining three conditions, implementation intentions specified either one of the two pouring strategies in the then-component ("If I start working on a new task, then I will first try to pour water from jar A to jar C!"; "If I start working on a new task, then I will first try to pour water from jar A to jar B!") or both strategies combined ("If I start working on a new task, then I will first try to pour water from jar A to jar C or from jar A to jar B!"). The results revealed that implementation intentions specifying both pouring strategies improved participants' performance more than those specifying one pouring strategy or those who merely formed goal intentions.

Action Sequences. A further aspect of complex behaviors relates to the enactment of action sequences. Do implementation intentions only automate the initiation of the first action of a sequence or do they additionally automate the initiation of subsequent actions in the sequence (like scripts)? To test if the enactment of an action sequence addressed in the then-component of an implementation intention acquires features of automaticity, an Action Sequence Study was conducted (Wieber, Odenthal, et al., 2009, Study 3). Participants worked on a computer-based lexical decision task that required pressing the left control key in response to nonwords and the right control key in response to words. As an exception, the word "jug" required pressing the "l" key (with the right hand), followed by the mouse button (with the left hand) and the right floor-based button (with their right foot). In addition, all participants were assigned goal intentions ("I want to perform as well as possible on the task!") and either added implementation intentions or not. Half of the implementation intentions only spelled out the initial action response to the word "jug" ("If the word 'jug' shows up, then I will first press the 'l' key!"), while the other half spelled out all three sequential action responses in the then-component ("If the word 'jug' shows up, then I will first press the 'l' key, followed by the right mouse key, and the right floor key!"). As participants had to respond as quickly and correctly as possible, the immediacy of their reactions indicated the automaticity of the behavior. As expected, implementation intentions specifying the initial action response accelerated the initial action response time compared to mere goal intentions, but not those of the second and third response (i.e., mouse and floor key press). Most importantly, participants who formed implementation intentions specifying all three behavioral responses in the then-component reacted faster to the complete action sequence than those who formed mere goal intentions.

Summary. In addition to simple behaviors, complex behaviors can also be fruitfully included in the then-component of implementation intentions. People should benefit from this possibility as it allows them to effectively tackle more complex problems like flexible switching between task strategies and the enactment of action sequences.

THE IMPORTANCE OF THE FORMAT OF IMPLEMENTATION INTENTIONS

So far, we have examined how to best specify the if-component and the then-component of implementation intentions. But in addition to the content, the format per se might also contribute to implementation intentions' effectiveness. Generally, the if-then format seems to represent an elementary component of human cognition. If-then conditionals are integral parts of information processing frameworks that are designed to model higher-order cognition (e.g., mathematics, language, reasoning, memory, and problem solving) in psychology, computer science, language science, and philosophy. Examples include production system theories such as cognitive stimulus-response theories (ACT; Anderson, 1983; Anderson et al., 2004), symbolic programming languages (e.g., Java, Perl, PHP), scientific speech theories (e.g., König & van der Auwera, 1988), and philosophical approaches (e.g., Stalnaker, 1968). To clarify the importance of the if-then format for the effectiveness of implementation intentions, we now address three emergent questions: (a) Is the if-then format of implementation intentions necessary?, (b) Is an if-then-why format even more effective?, and (c) Do if-then conditionals have to be directed at the future?

Is the If-Then Format Necessary for Strong Implementation Intention Effects?

If-Then versus When, Where, and How. The contribution of the if-then format was recently tested in a Fruit and Vegetable Promotion Intervention Study (Chapman, Armitage, & Norman, 2008). Participants were randomly assigned to a control condition, a "global" implementation intention condition (in which participants freely chose how to make their plan) or an if-then implementation intention (in which participants were additionally required to plan using the if-then format). One week later, participants filled out a second questionnaire indicating their fruit and vegetable intake during the previous week. As a key result, participants in the control condition did not manage to increase their fruit and vegetable intake, whereas those with global implementation intentions did, although only when their initial intake was low. However, with if-then implementation intentions, even participants with high initial fruit and vegetable intake were able to improve their goal attainment. Similarly, in a study by Oettingen, Hönig, and Gollwitzer, 2000 (Study 3), if-then implementation intentions were more effective than specified goal intentions explicating the when and where of an intended goal-directed behavior (i.e., doing regular math homework). In summary, then, implementation planning that uses an if-then format seems particularly effective.

Is an If-Then-Why Format Even More Effective?

One important prerequisite of implementation intention effects is a strong commitment to the respective goal intention (see also goal-dependent automaticity, Gollwitzer & Schaal, 1998; Sheeran et al., 2005). Implementation intentions per se do not affect the strength of people's goal intentions (Webb & Sheeran, 2008, Study 1). Therefore, one might ask if the if-then format can be expanded to ensure sufficient motivation. One possible way to achieve this is to remind oneself of the desired long-term consequences of goal pursuit. This strategy may be especially helpful when the major problem encountered during goal striving is to overcome an initial reluctance to act on a goal. For example, one may seriously aspire to speak Italian as a foreign language to enjoy vacations in Italy but does not like learning vocabulary or grammar. How could one remind oneself of the positive consequences of a goal? One strategy suggested by Freitas, Gollwitzer, and Trope (2004) is to simply ask oneself why one intends to perform a certain goal-directed action. Thus, an if-then-why format might be a suitable way to increase people's motivation and thereby make implementation intentions particularly effective. Four studies tested this hypothesis.

If-Then-Why and Assigned Goals. In an Analytical Reasoning Study (Wieber, Gollwitzer, Gawrilow, Odenthal, & Oettingen, 2009, Study 1), participants worked on 20 Raven matrices (Raven, 1977, 2000), in which they had to select one of eight possible result patterns that logically completed a 3×3 matrix pattern. All participants first learned that double-checking was a useful strategy to improve one's performance on the upcoming task. Participants then either formed a mere goal intention ("I will correctly solve as many trials as possible!") or added an implementation intention to it ("If I have a first idea for the solution to a trial, then I will double-check it!"). To vary motivation, participants either added a reason to their goal or implementation intention ("because I want to achieve a good performance!") or not. The results revealed that implementation intentions without the motivation intervention as well as goal intentions with the motivation intervention were effective in improving participants' performance. However, the combination of implementation intentions and the motivation intervention did not result in the expected improvement in participants' performance; they did not solve more matrices correctly than did participants in the goal intention group.

If-Then-Why and Self-Set Goals. To replicate these effects with self-set goals, a Dieting Behavior Study was conducted, in which participants formed self-set goal intentions for the highly valued goal of losing weight (Wieber, Gollwitzer, et al., 2009, Study 2). As a baseline, participants' weight and body fat were measured in a first session, and they were required to document their eating habits for 2 weeks. In a subsequent second session, participants were randomly assigned to one of four intention conditions. In the goal intention conditions, they either formed the mere goal intention "I want to lose weight" or additionally added their three foremost motivations for wanting to lose weight (e.g., "I want to lose weight because I want to stay healthy!"). In both implementation intention conditions, participants had to write down three critical situations (e.g., at a party, watching TV) that might jeopardize their goal, define suitable means of counteracting these critical situations, and merge them into three implementation intentions (i.e., in the if-then format). In the implementation intention plus why-component condition, they furthermore added their three foremost motivations for wanting to lose weight (e.g., "If I am sitting in front of the TV, then I will eat fruit because I want to become more attractive!"). After four weeks, participants' body weight, body fat percentage, and body mass index (BMI) were again collected. Moreover, the average calorie and fat content of their weekly meals was computed based on their food diary. Results replicated the findings from the Analytical Reasoning Study. Whereas participants who formed goal intentions without motivational reasons did not manage to change their eating habits (no weight difference), participants who formed implementation intentions without motivational reasons lost on average more than two pounds. Whereas supporting goal intentions with motivational reasons produced an average weight loss of more than two pounds, the implementation intentions plus motivational reasons again did not achieve a significant weight loss.

Adding a why-component to the if-then plans did not result in improved performance in either study, but rather offset the previously observed positive effects for implementation intentions without the why-component. Conversely, adding a why-component to the goal intention improved participants' goal striving in both studies. These findings do not support the notion of additive effects of thinking of motivational reasons when forming implementation intentions. A plausible explanation is that adding the why-reasoning not only focuses people's attention on the beneficial long-term goals but also impacts their cognitive orientation (i.e., mindset) during goal striving. Mindsets are defined as cognitive orientations that accompany the different action phases proposed by the mindset theory of action phases (Gollwitzer, 1990). During goal setting, a deliberative mindset prevails that is characterized by an increased openness to new information and an impartial and realistic assessment of this information. This benefits the main task during this action phase, namely weighing the desirability (i.e., incentives) and feasibility (i.e., expectancies) of one's wishes in order to commit only to the realization of the most desirable and feasible ones (e.g., Gollwitzer &

Bayer, 1999; Gollwitzer & Kinney, 1989; Puca & Schmalt, 2001). Goal striving, in contrast, is accompanied by an implemental mindset that is characterized by closed-mindedness to new information. This again is functional because it helps to shield goal striving from interfering or distracting information (e.g., attention to competing goals, deliberating pros and cons; Puca & Schmalt, 2001; Taylor & Gollwitzer, 1995). Thus, within the pursuit of a single goal, goal intentions are best formed against the backdrop of deliberative mindsets, and implementation intentions are best formed against the backdrop of implemental mindsets. Asking "Why?" during implementation intention formation might impact one's motivation by reminding oneself of the positive consequences of a goal; however, it might also induce a switch from an implemental to a deliberative mindset (Freitas et al., 2004). Wieber, Gollwitzer, et al. (2009) therefore postulated a matching principle of intention formation and mindsets: goal intention formation should work best when people are in a deliberative mindset, whereas implementation intention formation should work best when people are in an implemental mindset. In other words, inducing an implemental mindset during goal intention formation and inducing a deliberative mindset during implementation intention formation should weaken goal setting and if-then planning, respectively, and thus impair subsequent goal attainment.

Do We Have to Assume a Matching Principle Between Mindsets and Intentions?

If-Then-Why and Self-Control. Two studies tested the matching principle by separately manipulating intention formation and mindset induction. In the Handgrip Self-Control Study (Wieber, Gollwitzer, et al., 2009, Study 3), a well-established test of self-control was applied, namely the handgrip trainer task (Muraven, Tice, & Baumeister, 1998). The task requires clutching the handles of a handgrip closed as long possible, despite the increasing discomfort and taxing physical endurance (i.e., required exertion of self-control). All participants learned that the pain experienced is harmless and can be ignored. As a manipulation of participants' intentions, they either received no training (i.e., no intention) or a paper-based hand trainer task training including a goal intention ("I will press the handgrip as long as possible!") or a goal intention plus implementation intention ("If my muscles hurt, then I will ignore the pain!"). As a manipulation of participants' mindsets, they either received no mindset manipulation or one of two versions of an ostensibly unrelated paper-based study on "personal relationships." Participants either thought about reasons "why" it is important to establish and keep personal friendships (deliberative mindset) or about ways "how" to establish and keep personal friendships (implemental mindset; for a similar manipulation, see Freitas et al., 2004). By asking why versus how questions four successive times in a sequence (e.g., asking why/ how the answer to the first why/how question is helpful), increasingly deliberate or implemental thoughts are produced step by step. Subsequently, they performed the handgrip task.

Results indicated that overall, mindsets alone did not impact performance, but intentions did. Implementation intentions lead to better self-control in comparison to goal intentions. Most importantly, this effect was qualified by mindsets. In line with the matching hypotheses, being in a deliberative mindset improved the performance of participants who formed a goal intention compared to those in an implemental mindset or no mindset. Being in an implemental mindset, on the other hand, improved the performance of participants who formed an implementation intention compared to those who were in a deliberative mindset or the control condition. In summary, this study provides initial evidence for the postulated matching principle of intention formation and mindset. As this study does not allow for the disentangling of motivational (i.e., ego depletion) and cognitive processes (i.e., suboptimal cognitive processing), another study was conducted.

If-Then-Why and Automaticity. The Dual Task Study (Wieber, Gollwitzer, et al., 2009, Study 4) sought to replicate the results of the Handgrip Self-Control Study in a more cognitively demanding speed-accuracy performance task. It was additionally intended to shed light on the processes underlying the effects of matching mindset–intention combinations with goal attainment. Derived from the theory of intentional action control (Gollwitzer, 1999) and the mindset theory of action phases (Gollwitzer, 1990), goal intention–deliberative mindset combinations were expected to improve goal attainment via resource-demanding deliberation processes; conversely, implementation intention-implemental mindset combinations were expected to improve goal attainment via automated processes. To test the automaticity of the performance, a dual-task paradigm was employed in accordance with Brandstätter et al. (2001, Studies 3 and 4). Participants had to simultaneously work on a primary tracking task (enclosing a target circle that moved across the computer screen with a mouse-controlled second circle) and a secondary go/no-go task (pressing the left mouse button as quickly as possible in response to numbers [in particular number 3], but not to letters) that both relied on the same resources (i.e., visual attention and motor responses). As attentional capacities are limited, an improved performance on one task is expected to carry features of automaticity only when the performance on the other task is not compromised.

To manipulate participants' intention, they formed the goal intention "I want to react to numbers as quickly as possible" and either added an implementation intention ("And if the number 3 appears, then I will press the left mouse button particularly fast") or a control intention ("I will particularly memorize the number 3"). Subsequently, participants' deliberative or implemental mindsets were induced using the task from the previous study (Wieber, Gollwitzer, et al., 2009, Study 3). Next, participants worked on the dual-task trials with high task complexity (cognitive load), followed by trials with moderate task complexity (no cognitive load).

The results confirmed the hypotheses. When the primary task was easy and thus no automaticity was required for responding, participants in both matching mindset-intention combinations were able to improve performance on the secondary task (i.e., faster responses to critical cues on the go/no-go task) without suffering impaired performance on the primary task (tracking task). Those in the mismatching mindset–intention combinations were less able to improve their performance on the tasks. However, when the primary task was difficult and thus automaticity was required for responding, only those in the implementation intention–implemental mindset combination condition, and not those in the goal intention–deliberative mindset condition, were able to improve their performance on the secondary task without suffering impaired performance on the primary task. Those in the mismatching mindset–intention combinations were again less able to improve their performance on the tasks. These results suggest that the proposed matching principle cannot be completely explained by the depletion of self-regulatory resources, but that the cognitive orientation (mindset) explanation is also required.

Summary. Taken together, these studies provide evidence for the importance of the proposed matching principle for successful goal attainment (Wieber, Gollwitzer, et al., 2009, Studies 1–4) rather than the effectiveness of an if-then-why format. Compared to mismatching intention–mindset combinations, matching intention–mindset combinations improve goal attainment. Thereby, matching mindset–intention combinations impact performance either through effortful processes (goal intentions with deliberative mindsets) or automatic processes (implementation intentions with implemental mindsets). Moreover, mismatching mindset–intention combinations limit goal striving, no matter how the mismatching mindsets are induced (i.e., during the pursuit of the focal goal or of a nonfocal goal). As people commonly pursue multiple goals, is it important to ensure that intentions and mindsets match during goal pursuit. Thus, the present findings suggest that instead of using an if-then-why format during planning, people should either combine tasks requiring concrete implemental actions or abstract deliberating. For example, sorting one's e-mail and organizing a conference trip in one work session should prevent cognitive processing mismatches, thereby resulting in enhanced performance.

Thinking About the Future Versus Thinking About the Past: Implementation Intentions and Upward Counterfactual Thoughts

Deliberating over whether and why to pursue a goal during the formation of an implementation intention undermines its effectiveness. But what if such considerations are completed prior to the formation of the plan, thus avoiding the problem of mismatching mindsets? In this case, motivation could be increased and the strength of subsequently formed implementation intentions enhanced. Such deliberation could be accomplished through upward counterfactual thinking. Upward counterfactuals are if-then statements indicating how a previous outcome could have been better. For example, a student might consider the thought "If only I had attended every lecture, then I would not have failed the exam!" Numerous studies have found that considering upward counterfactuals improves subsequent performance (Markman, McMullen, & Elizaga, 2008; Roese, 1994).

Several explanations for this effect have been postulated. Roese and colleagues (Epstude & Roese, 2008; Roese, 1994; Smallman & Roese, 2007) have suggested that counterfactual thoughts could affect performance by identifying useful strategies and supporting the formation of plans. For example, one could convert the counterfactual "If only I had attended every lecture, then I would not have failed the exam" into the implementation intention "Whenever there is a lecture, then I will attend." There is evidence from several studies that considering upward counterfactuals increases the accessibility of corresponding behavioral intentions (Smallman & Roese, 2007). However, the intentions (i.e., "I will do X") examined in these studies did not take the if-then format of an implementation intention. Thus, it is unclear whether counterfactual thinking is sufficient to support the spontaneous formation of specific if-then plans. Past work (Roese, 1994) examining whether individuals enact the behavioral strategy contained in the counterfactual has produced mixed results. Moreover, these studies were correlational in nature, raising the possibility that the counterfactuals generated by participants merely reflected previously held behavioral intentions.

A second manner in which counterfactual thoughts might improve performance is by mobilizing effort (Epstude & Roese, 2008; Markman & McMullen, 2003). Upward counterfactual thinking involves evaluating the outcome relative to a higher standard. These comparisons are likely to cause disappointment with one's goal progress. Theories of effort mobilization (Brehm & Self, 1989; Carver & Scheier, 1999) suggest that such perceived goal discrepancies will increase effort and persistence. Consistent with this account, performance benefits of upward counterfactual thinking appear to be limited to situations in which the individual is dissatisfied with the outcome (Markman et al., 2008). Conversely, upward counterfactual thoughts reduce persistence and effort when they serve to excuse failure (McCrea, 2008).

Myers and McCrea (2009) conducted several studies directly comparing the effects of upward counterfactuals and implementation intentions that shared a behavioral strategy. If upward counterfactuals improve performance by supporting the spontaneous generation of specific if-then plans, then forming an implementation intention should have no additional benefits. However, based on the notion that counterfactuals mobilize effort, Myers and McCrea (2009) predicted that these thoughts would increase persistence and performance, particularly when accompanied by more negative affect. Furthermore, these effects should be independent of the behavior specified in the thought. In contrast, implementation intentions should lead to enactment of the specified behavior, independent of affect. Thus, both types of thoughts were expected to additively improve goal attainment.

Assigned Counterfactuals and Implementation Intentions. In an initial study, participants were told they would be taking part in a study on decision making under time pressure. Participants were required to quickly select from a pair of pictures the one with the higher point value (adapted from Jaudas & Gollwitzer, 2004). Correct identifications were rewarded with the point value of the picture, minus a time penalty. Importantly, a picture of a water lily was of the highest point value, such that responding quickly on trials in which this picture appeared was a particularly effective strategy. Participants were provided with feedback after the first task and then assigned to one of two counterfactual conditions; those in the counterfactual group were asked to consider the thought "If I had pressed the corresponding key every time I saw the water lily, then I would have done better," whereas those in the control condition were asked to consider the statement "I would like to know how my friends would do on the test." Participants were then randomly assigned to one of two implementation intention conditions; those in the implementation intention group were asked to consider the plan "Every time I see the water lily, then I will immediately press the corresponding key," whereas those in the control condition proceeded to the next phase of the experiment. All participants completed a measure of mood and a second block of the task. Performance on this block relative to the initial block was examined. Participants in the counterfactual condition who also reported less positive affect responded faster on the critical (water lily) trials, compared to those in the control condition or who reported more positive affect. Furthermore, they made fewer errors on noncritical trials and improved their overall score more than did the latter groups. As expected, the beneficial effects of upward counterfactual thinking generalized to aspects of performance not mentioned by the thought and appeared dependent upon experiencing dissatisfaction with one's performance. Both of these findings are more consistent with increased effort mobilization rather than with the spontaneous formation of a plan. Indeed, implementation intentions were found to improve reaction times on the critical trials, suggesting that these plans had an additional (albeit specific) effect on performance. In other words, those who listed both the counterfactual thought and the implementation intention improved the most.

Self-Set Counterfactuals and Implementation Intentions. In a second study, effort mobilization in the form of task persistence was directly examined. Participants were given two word completion tasks. Two insolvable items were included in each task, such that the amount of time spent working on the task constituted a true measure of persistence. As in the previous study, participants were assigned to counterfactual and no counterfactual conditions and implementation intention and no implementation intention conditions prior to completing a second block of items. However, participants freely generated these statements, rather than being provided the statements by the experimenter. Consistent with the initial study, individuals persisted more in the counterfactual condition than in the control condition, but only when they reported experiencing more negative affect. Moreover, analyses classifying the statements generated by participants revealed that this effect was not limited to those counterfactuals concerning time spent on the task. Those assigned to form an implementation intention also persisted longer compared to those in a control condition, but this effect was not moderated by mood. Furthermore, classifying the implementation intentions generated by participants revealed that only those statements related to time spent on the task increased persistence.

In summary, implementation intentions and counterfactual thoughts had additive effects on goal striving, with counterfactuals increasing effort mobilization and implementation intentions increasing the enactment of specified behaviors. In addition to explaining how counterfactual thoughts improve performance, these findings imply that implementation intentions can be made more powerful by first considering how a past performance could have been better. Because counterfactuals increase effort mobilization, subsequently formed implementation intentions become more effective, making it more likely that individuals will overcome the intention–behavior gap. It appears to be critical that counterfactuals are made prior to the formation of implementation intentions, thereby avoiding the problem of mismatching mindsets presented by the if-then-why phasing. Finally, these results once again demonstrate the unique qualities of the if-then format of implementation intentions. Although both counterfactuals and implementation intentions share a conditional phrasing, only implementation intentions commit one to act in a specified manner in a future situation. As a result, counterfactuals do not appear to be as effective in promoting the enactment of specific goal-directed behaviors.

Conclusion and Outlook

In the past, implementation intentions (if-then plans) have been observed to effectively reduce the gap between intentions and behavior. But how should one formulate one's implementation plans to maximize their effectiveness for goal attainment? In the present chapter, we first raised the question of how the components of implementation intentions should be worded. Regarding the if-component, including a specific situational cue in the if-component ensures that the critical cue does not escape one's attention. However, as this attention attraction effect compromises the attention given to alternative cues, people have to carefully choose what kind of situational cue they want to specify in an implementation intention. Specifying more inclusive (abstract) situational cues in the if-component does not qualify as a solution, as such integrative specifications no longer ensure that swift attraction of attention occurs. Thus, the if-component of implementation intentions should be worded by using specific but "representative" good opportunities to act towards the goal. Regarding the then-component, specifying simple behaviors (such as pressing a response key) as well as complex behaviors (such as switching between different action strategies or enacting a sequence of behaviors) seems to be effective in promoting goal attainment. Thus, people can also utilize implementation intentions to facilitate the initiation of complex behaviors.

The format of implementation intentions was subsequently examined. As the if-then format was more effective than merely specifying when, where, and how one intends to pursue a goal, people should apply the if-then format when forming implementation intentions. Conversely, an if-then-why format does not promote goal striving via implementation intentions. Instead, a matching principle between mindsets and intentions was extracted. This finding implies that people should not engage in too much deliberating during the formation or the enactment of an implementation intention, as an implemental, but not a deliberative, mindset supports goal striving with implementation intentions. Finally, applying the if-then format when thinking about past goal pursuits via upward counterfactual thoughts (i.e., conditional if-then statements indicating how a previous outcome could have been better) represents a powerful method to strengthen the motivational basis for subsequently formed implementation intentions

Which venues should future research address in order to expand knowledge on maximizing the effectiveness of implementation intention? A closer look should be given to the situational context in which goal striving with implementation intentions takes place. People pursue their goals in a vast array of different situations, in which intrapersonal differences may be relevant to the maximizing of implementation intention effects. People may only experience problems during goal striving in some domains but not others. For example, a person may encounter problems exercising self-control in the domain of professional goals (e.g., writing an essay) but may have no problem exerting self-control within the domain of a health goals (e.g., resisting tempting chocolates). Thus, making people sensitive to the domains in which they experience difficulty with self-control should allow them to tailor their implementation intentions to the action control problems they most likely encounter.

Finally, future research should systematically develop procedures to ensure that the moderators of implementation intentions do not limit their effects on goal attainment. For instance, only when people are strongly committed to a goal intention can implementation intention effects be expected (e.g., Sheeran et al., 2005). To guarantee such strong goal commitment, people can either form upward counterfactuals or complement the use of implementation intentions with the mental contrasting technique (i.e., contrasting desired future states with the present negative reality to identify potential obstacles and ensure strong motivation; Stadler, Oettingen, & Gollwitzer, 2009). Interventions may also target a second prerequisite for strong implementation intention effects, namely a strong commitment to the plan. A promising route to ensure strong commitment to the plan is to form implementation intentions collaboratively (Prestwich et al., 2005). The collaborative discussion should increase the quality of the plans as more options are considered and inappropriate specifications of situations and behaviors can be prevented. Moreover, the public commitment of an implementation intention should increase people's commitment to the plan. Finally, low efficacy should also be considered as a limit of implementation intention effects. One way to strengthen people's self-efficacy beliefs is to form implementation intentions that include motivational self-speech (e.g., to improve performance on an analytical reasoning test, "When I start a new problem, then I will tell myself: I can solve it!"; Bayer & Gollwitzer, 2007). In other words, people may use implementation intentions to favorably modulate the moderators of implementation intention effects.

REFERENCES

Aarts, H., Dijksterhuis, A., & Midden, C. (1999). To plan or not to plan? Goal achievement or interrupting the performance of mundane behaviors. *European Journal of Social Psychology, 29,* 971–979.

Achtziger, A., Bayer, U. C., & Gollwitzer, P. M. (2009). *Committing oneself to implementation intentions: Attention and memory effects for selected situational cues.* Manuscript submitted for publication.

Achtziger, A., Gollwitzer, P. M., & Sheeran, P. (2008). Implementation intentions and shielding goal striving from unwanted thoughts and feelings. *Personality and Social Psychology Bulletin, 34,* 381–393.

Anderson, J. R. (1983). *The architecture of cognition.* Cambridge, MA: Harvard University Press.

Anderson, J. R., Bothell, D., Byrne, M. D., Douglass, S., Lebiere, C., & Qin, Y. (2004). An integrated theory of the mind. *Psychological Review, 111,* 1036–1060.

Bayer, U. C., Achtziger, A., Gollwitzer, P. M., & Moskowitz, G. B. (2009). Responding to subliminal cues: Do if-then plans facilitate action preparation and initiation without conscious intent? *Social Cognition, 27,* 183–201.

Bayer, U. C., & Gollwitzer, P. M. (2007). Boosting scholastic test scores by willpower: The role of implementation intentions. *Self and Identity, 6,* 1–19.

Bayer, U. C., & Gollwitzer, P. M. (2009). *Staying on track: Planned goal striving is protected from disruptive internal states.* Manuscript under review.

Brandstätter, V., Lengfelder, A., & Gollwitzer, P. M. (2001). Implementation intentions and efficient action initiation. *Journal of Personality and Social Psychology, 81,* 946–960.

Brehm, J. W., & Self, E. A. (1989). The intensity of motivation. *Annual Review of Psychology, 40,* 109–131.

Broadbent, D. E. (1958). *Perception and communication*. Elmsford, NY: Pergamon Press.

Carver, C. S., & Scheier, M. F. (1999). Themes and issues in the self-regulation of behavior. In R. S. Wyer (Ed.), *Perspectives on behavioral self-regulation* (pp. 1–105). Mahweh, NJ: Lawrence Erlbaum.

Chapman, J., Armitage, C. J., & Norman, P. (2009). Comparing implementation intention interventions in relation to young adults' intake of fruit and vegetables, *Psychology and Health, 24*, 317–332.

Cohen, J. (1992). A power primer. *Psychological Bulletin, 112*, 155–159.

Epstude, K., & Roese, N. J. (2008). The functional theory of counterfactual thinking. *Personality and Social Psychology Review, 12*, 168–192.

Eriksen, B. A., & Eriksen, C. W. (1974). Effects of noise letters upon the identification of a target letter in a nonsearch task. *Perception and Psychophysics, 16*, 143–149.

Freitas, A. L., Gollwitzer, P. M., & Trope, Y. (2004). The influence of abstract and concrete mindsets on anticipating and guiding others' self-regulatory efforts. *Journal of Experimental Social Psychology, 40*, 739–752.

Gawrilow, C., & Gollwitzer, P. M. (2008). Implementation intentions facilitate response inhibition in children with ADHD. *Cognitive Therapy and Research, 32*, 261–280.

Gollwitzer, P. M. (1990). Action phases and mindsets. In E. T. Higgins & J. R. M. Sorrentino (Eds.), *The handbook of motivation and cognition* (Vol. 2, pp. 53–92). New York: Guilford.

Gollwitzer, P. M. (1993). Goal achievement: The role of intentions. In W. H. Stroebe & M. Hewstone (Eds.), *European review of social psychology.* (Vol. 4, pp. 141–185). UK: Wiley: Chichester.

Gollwitzer, P. M. (1999). Implementation intentions: Strong effects of simple plans. *American Psychologist, 54*, 493–503.

Gollwitzer, P. M., & Bayer, U. (1999). Deliberative versus implemental mindsets in the control of action. In S. Chaiken & Y. Trope (Eds.), *Dual-process theories in social psychology* (pp. 403–422). New York: Guilford.

Gollwitzer, P. M., Bayer, U., & McCulloch, K. (2005). The control of the unwanted. In R. Hassin, J. Uleman, & J. A. Bargh (Eds.), *The new unconscious* (pp. 485–515). Oxford: Oxford University Press.

Gollwitzer, P. M., & Brandstätter, V. (1997). Implementation intentions and effective goal pursuit. *Journal of Personality and Social Psychology, 73*, 186–199.

Gollwitzer, P. M., & Kinney, R. F. (1989). Effects of deliberative and implemental mind-sets on illusion of control. *Journal of Personality and Social Psychology, 56*, 531–542.

Gollwitzer, P. M., Parks-Stamm, E. J., Jaudas, A., & Sheeran, P. (2008). Flexible tenacity in goal pursuit. In J. Shah & W. Gardner (Eds.), *Handbook of motivation science* (pp. 325–341). New York: Guilford Press.

Gollwitzer, P. M., & Schaal, B. (1998). Metacognition in action: The importance of implementation intentions. *Personality and Social Psychology Review, 2*, 124–136.

Gollwitzer, P. M., & Sheeran, P. (2006). Implementation intentions and goal achievement: A meta-analysis of effects and processes. *Advances in Experimental Social Psychology, 38*, 69–119.

Holland, R., Aarts, H., & Langendam, D. (2006). Breaking and creating habits on the workfloor: A field experiment on the power of implementation intentions. *Journal of Experimental Social Psychology, 42,* 776–783.

Hull, C. L. (1951). *Essentials of behavior.* New Haven, CT: Yale University Press.

Jaudas, A., & Gollwitzer, P. M. (2004, March). *Fuehren Vorsaetze zu Rigiditaet im Zielstreben?* Paper presented at the Meeting of Experimental Psychologists, Giessen, Germany.

Kahneman, D. (1973). *Attention and effort.* Englewood Cliffs, NJ: Prentice-Hall.

König, E., & van der Auwera, J. (1988). Clause integration in German and Dutch: Conditionals, concessive conditionals, and concessives. In J. Haiman & S. Thompson (Eds.), *Clause Combining in Grammar and Discourse* (pp. 101–133). Amsterdam: John Benjamins.

Luchins, A. S. (1942). Mechanization in problem solving—the effect of Einstellung. *Psychological Monographs, 54,* 1–95.

Markman, K. D., & McMullen, M. N. (2003). A reflection and evaluation model of comparative thinking. *Personality and Social Psychology Review, 7,* 244–267.

Markman, K. D., McMullen, M. N., & Elizaga, R. A. (2008). Counterfactual thinking, persistence, and performance: A test of the Reflection and Evaluation Model. *Journal of Experimental Social Psychology, 44,* 421–428.

McCrea, S. M. (2008). Self-handicapping, excuse-making, and counterfactual thinking: Consequences for self-esteem and future motivation. *Journal of Personality and Social Psychology, 95,* 274–292.

Muraven, M., Tice, D. M, & Baumeister, R. F. (1998). Self-control as limited resource: Regulatory depletion patterns. *Journal of Personality and Social Psychology, 74,* 774–789.

Myers, A. L., & McCrea, S. M. (2009). *The preparative function of counterfactual thinking: Providing useful strategies or enhancing motivation.* Unpublished manuscript. Konstanz, Germany.

Oettingen, G., Hönig, G., & Gollwitzer, P. M. (2000). Effective self-regulation of goal attainment. *International Journal of Educational Research, 33,* 705–732.

Parks-Stamm, E. J., Gollwitzer, P. M., & Oettingen, G. (2007). Action control by implementation intentions: Effective cue detection and efficient response initiation. *Social Cognition, 25,* 248–266.

Powers, T. A., Koestner, R., & Topciu, R. A. (2005). Implementation intentions, perfectionism, and goal progress: Perhaps the road to hell is paved with good intentions. *Personality and Social Psychology Bulletin, 31,* 902–912.

Prestwich, A., Conner, M., Lawton, R., Bailey, W., Litman, J., & Molyneaux, V. (2005). Individual and collaborative implementation intentions and the promotion of breast self-examination. *Psychology and Health Education Research, 20,* 743–760.

Puca, R. M., & Schmalt, H.-D. (2001). The influence of the achievement motive on spontaneous thoughts in pre- and postdecisional action phases. *Personality and Social Psychology Bulletin, 27,* 302–308.

Raven, J. (1977). *Raven's Coloured Progressive Matrices.* London: H. K. Lewis.

Raven, J. (2000). The Raven's Progressive Matrices: Change and stability over culture and time. *Cognitive Psychology, 41,* 1–48.

Roese, N. J. (1994). The functional basis of counterfactual thinking. *Journal of Personality and Social Psychology, 66,* 805–818.

Schweiger Gallo, I., Keil, A., McCulloch, K. C., Rockstroh, B., & Gollwitzer, P. M. (2009). Strategic automation of emotion control. *Journal of Personality and Social Psychology, 96,* 11–31.

Sheeran, P. (2002). Intention-behavior relations: A conceptual and empirical review. In W. H. Stroebe (Ed.), *European review of social psychology.* (Vol. 12, pp. 1–36). Chichester, UK:Wiley.

Sheeran, P., Webb, T. L., & Gollwitzer, P. M. (2005). The interplay between goal intentions and implementation intentions. *Personality and Social Psychology Bulletin, 31,* 87–98.

Smallman, R., & Roese, N. J. (2007, January). *Counterfactual thinking facilitates the formation of intentions: Evidence for a content-specific pathway in behavioral regulation.* Paper presented at the Annual Meeting of the Society for Personality and Social Psychology, Memphis, TN.

Stadler, G., Oettingen, G., & Gollwitzer, P. M. (2009). Physical activity in women. Effects of a self-regulation intervention. *American Journal of Preventive Medicine, 36,* 29–34.

Stalnaker, R. C. (1968). A theory of conditionals. In N. Rescher (Ed.), *Studies in logical theory (American Philosophical Quarterly Monograph No. 2).* Oxford, England: Blackwell.

Stewart, B. D., & Payne, K. B. (2008). Bringing automatic stereotyping under control: Implementation intentions as efficient means of thought control. *Personality and Social Psychology Bulletin, 34,* 1332–1345.

Taylor, S. E., & Gollwitzer, P. M. (1995). Effects of mindset on positive illusions. *Journal of Personality and Social Psychology, 69,* 213–226.

Trötschel, R., & Gollwitzer, P. M. (2007). Implementation intentions and the willful pursuit of prosocial goals in negotiations. *Journal of Experimental Social Psychology, 43,* 579–598.

Webb, T. L., Christian, J., & Armitage, C. J. (2007). Helping students turn up for class: Does personality moderate the effectiveness of an implementation intention intervention? *Learning and Individual Differences, 17,* 316–327.

Webb, T. L., & Sheeran, P. (2003). Can implementation intentions help to overcome ego-depletion? *Journal of Experimental Social Psychology, 39,* 279–286.

Webb, T. L., & Sheeran, P. (2004). Identifying good opportunities to act: Implementation intentions and cue discrimination. *European Journal of Social Psychology, 34,* 407–419.

Webb, T. L., & Sheeran, P. (2008). Mechanisms of implementation intention effects: The role of goal intentions, self-efficacy, and accessibility of plan components. *British Journal of Social Psychology, 47,* 373–395.

Wegner, D. M., & Bargh, J. A. (1998). Control and automaticity in social life. In D. T. Gilbert, S. T. Fiske, & G. Lindzey (Eds.), *The handbook of social psychology, Vols. 1 and 2 (4th ed.)* (pp. 446–496). New York: McGraw-Hill.

Wieber, F., Gollwitzer, P. M., Gawrilow, C., Odenthal, G., & Oettingen, G. (2009). *Matching principles in action control.* Unpublished manuscript, Universität Konstanz.

Wieber, F., Odenthal, G., & Gollwitzer (2009). *How to word implementation intentions*. Unpublished manuscript, Universität Konstanz.

Wieber, F., Odenthal, G., & Gollwitzer, P. M. (in press). Self-efficacy feelings moderate implementation intention effects. *Self and Identity*.

Wieber, F., & Sassenberg, K. (2006). I can't take my eyes off of it - Attention attraction effects of implementation intentions. *Social Cognition, 24*, 723–752.

9 Distinguishing Between Prediction and Influence: Multiple Processes Underlying Attitude-Behavior Consistency

Leandre R. Fabrigar
Duane T. Wegener
Tara K. MacDonald

THE HISTORICAL CONTEXT OF ATTITUDE-BEHAVIOR CONSISTENCY RESEARCH

Attitude researchers have long recognized the importance of understanding the relation between attitudes and behavior. Indeed, since the earliest days of attitude research, theorists have speculated about how attitudes might relate to behavior. Early conceptual perspectives generally assumed a close association between the constructs. For example, in his highly influential chapter on attitude theory, Gordon Allport (1935) defined attitudes as "mental and neural states of readiness" that exert "directive or dynamic influence upon the individual's responses to all objects and situations with which it is related." Other early definitions also conceptualized attitudes in terms of their presumed directive impact on behavior (e.g., F. H. Allport, 1924; Bogardus, 1931; Chave, 1928; Doob, 1947; Droba, 1933).

Moreover, early theories of attitude structure also explicitly postulated that behavior was closely intertwined with attitudes. Most notably, the well-known tripartite theory of attitudes went so far as to postulate that behavior was actually a component of attitudes (Insko & Schopler, 1967; Katz & Stotland, 1959; Rosenberg & Hovland, 1960). Likewise, early indirect measures of attitudes such as the information error technique and the lost-letter technique relied on directly observable behaviors that were presumed to be manifestations of attitudes (Hammond, 1948; Millgram, Mann, & Harter, 1965). Thus, these measurement approaches implicitly assumed that attitudes were strongly related to behavior.

The Attitude-Behavior Problem

Unfortunately, by the late 1960s, data had begun to accumulate challenging the assumption of a strong association between attitudes and behavior (e.g., see Deutscher, 1966; 1973). Perhaps the most influential expression of what came to be known as the "attitude-behavior problem" was published by Wicker (1969). Wicker reviewed the results of 46 studies in which attitude-behavior associations were reported. He concluded that correlations between attitudes and behavior were rarely larger than .30 and on average only about .15. Wicker thus argued that there was little evidence that attitudes were strong predictors of behavior.

Rather than discouraging the study of attitudes, the ultimate result of Wicker's (1969) challenge and other criticisms of the utility of the attitude construct (e.g., Wicker, 1971) was to encourage researchers to think in more sophisticated ways regarding why correlations between attitudes and behavior often seemed to fall short of what might be expected. The answer to this question took a number of forms. Some researchers disputed the accuracy of the conclusion itself (e.g., see Kelman, 1974; Schuman & Johnson, 1976), noting that inclusion of a broader set of studies than those examined in Wicker (1969) suggested that attitude-behavior correlations were often substantially larger than he concluded. Another response to this challenge was to note methodological limitations in past studies (e.g., mismatches in specificity of attitudes and behavior, error of measurement) that might account for weak correlations (e.g., Ajzen & Fishbein, 1977; Fishbein & Ajzen, 1974; Kelman, 1974; Schuman & Johnson, 1976; Weigel & Newman, 1976). Still other research, most notably under the auspices of the theory of reasoned action (Ajzen & Fishbein, 1980; Fishbein & Azjen, 1975) and later the theory of planned behavior (Ajzen, 1991), suggested that attitudes might sometimes fail to translate into behavior when attitudes were in conflict with other important determinants of behavior.

Although each of these responses generated significant interest, perhaps the response that produced the largest and most varied body of research and that continues to receive significant attention is the work on moderators of attitude-behavior associations. Researchers in this literature have postulated that the strength of association between an attitude and behavior might be regulated by a host of dispositional characteristics of the person, situational factors present at the time the attitude is assessed and/or the behavior is performed, and properties of the attitude or behavior themselves. For example, attitude-behavior associations have been found to be stronger when situational factors that are likely to make people internally focused are present at the time of behavior (Gibbons, 1978; Snyder & Swann, 1976) or when people are dispositionally inclined to be more internally focused when determining how they should behave (Ajzen, Timko, & White, 1982; Snyder & Swann, 1976; Zanna, Olson, & Fazio, 1980). Likewise, attitude-behavior associations have been found to be stronger in situations where the relevance of the attitude to behavior is very clear (Snyder, 1982; Snyder & Kendzierski, 1982). Still other research has suggested that attitudes are better predictors of behavior if people are simply asked to report their attitudes rather than to carefully introspect about their reasons for their attitudes prior to reporting them (Wilson & Dunn, 1986; Wilson, Dunn, Bybee, Hyman, Rotondo, 1984; Wilson, Dunn, Kraft, & Lisle, 1989; Wilson, Kraft, & Dunn, 1989). A sizable body of research, sometimes referred to under the broad label of "attitude strength" research (for reviews, see Petty & Krosnick, 1995), has indicated that structural features of attitudes (e.g., accessibility, ambivalence, amount of attitude-relevant knowledge), properties of the evaluation itself (i.e., attitude extremity), subjective beliefs regarding the attitude (e.g., certainty, importance), and the process by which an attitude is formed or changed (e.g., amount of cognitive elaboration, direct behavioral experience) moderate the strength of attitude-behavior associations. Finally, a smaller body of research has suggested that attitude-behavior relations are strongest when the basis of the attitude matches the type of behavior (e.g., affectively-based attitudes with consummatory behaviors and cognitively-based attitudes with instrumental behaviors, Millar & Tesser, 1986).

Current Status of Attitude-Behavior Consistency Research

Social psychologists' understanding of attitude-behavior consistency has come a long way since Wicker's influential challenge. Attitude theorists now no longer seriously entertain the extremely pessimistic conclusions advanced in the late 1960s, and general consensus exists among attitude researchers that attitudes can often be useful predictors of behavior (e.g., see Eagly & Chaiken, 1993; Fabrigar, MacDonald, & Wegener, 2005; Fazio & Roskos-Ewoldsen, 2005; Kraus, 1995). Indeed, attitude researchers (e.g., Eagly & Chaiken, 1993) have sometimes expressed surprise that, in light of the large body of empirical evidence that has been amassed to the contrary over the past 40 years, some social psychologists continue to believe that attitudes are only weakly related to behavior.

Moreover, research has moved well beyond the simple question of whether attitudes are related to behavior. Formal theories such as the theory of reasoned action (Ajzen & Fishbein, 1980; Fishbein & Ajzen,

1975), the theory of planned behavior (Ajzen, 1991), and the MODE model (Fazio, 1990; Fazio & Towles-Schwen, 1999) have been proposed to explain the processes by which attitudes guide behavior. Likewise, it is now recognized that characterizing the association of attitudes and behavior as generally weak or strong is misleading because conditions exist in which associations between attitudes and behavior can be extremely large or nonexistent (Fazio & Zanna, 1981; Kraus, 1995). Researchers have compiled an impressive list of moderators that can readily account for this variability in attitude-behavior associations. Indeed, the list of moderators of attitude-behavior consistency has grown so lengthy that it borders on overwhelming. For example, consider simply one area of attitude-behavior consistency research: the attitude strength literature. In this literature, no less than a dozen properties of attitudes have been documented as moderators of attitude-behavior associations.

Thus, it is fair to say that it is now acknowledged that attitudes can be useful predictors of behavior and that significant progress has been made in understanding the processes that account for why attitudes are predictive of behavior. A great deal is also known about what factors regulate how well attitudes will predict behavior. However, although the list of moderators of attitude-behavior consistency is quite lengthy, many of the mechanisms responsible for the moderation effects have never been tested, and the psychological mechanisms underlying many of these moderator effects are not well understood (see also Fabrigar et al., 2005; Fazio & Roskos-Ewoldsen, 2005). Moreover, theories of attitude-behavior consistency (e.g., the MODE model) were not specifically formulated to provide a general organizing framework for understanding when and why many variables moderate attitude-behavior associations (even when these theories have provided insights into the effects of some moderators).

Following the metaphor of the Sidney Harris cartoon presented on the cover of this book, herein lies the remaining "miraculous" component of the attitude-behavior consistency equation. We know quite well what factors determine the strength of the attitude-behavior associations but much can be learned about why these moderating factors have their effects. As such, it is unclear to what extent various moderators reflect similar versus distinct underlying processes and thus no general conceptual framework exists to organize these seemingly diverse moderators.

A CONCEPTUAL FRAMEWORK FOR MODERATORS OF ATTITUDE-BEHAVIOR CONSISTENCY

The goal of the present chapter is to provide the general outlines of a theoretical framework that might organize moderators of attitude-behavior consistency. Our perspective focuses on mechanisms responsible for prediction and influence (MRPI) and postulates that, although the list of documented moderators is lengthy and diverse, six primary mechanisms are responsible for the effects of these moderators. The MRPI does not restrict the effects of a given moderator to operate through only a single mechanism, nor does it assume that a given moderator must necessarily involve all six mechanisms. However, we propose that any given moderator will exert its effects on attitude-behavior associations via these six processes or some subset of them.

Distinguishing Between Prediction and Influence

In considering why moderators of attitude-behavior consistency exert their effects, we begin with the premise that it is important for researchers to be clear about what is meant by the term "attitude-behavior consistency." Typically, this term has been construed in one of two ways (see Fabrigar et al., 2005). First, it is sometimes used to refer to the extent to which a measure of an attitude *predicts* some subsequent behavior (i.e., the degree of association between an attitude measure and a measure of subsequent behavior). Second, it is often used to refer to the degree to which an attitude *influences* or *guides* some subsequent behavior (i.e., the extent to which an attitude exerts a causal influence on the performance of a behavior). These two construals, though related, are not the same.

Variations in the extent to which an attitude influences behavior do generally imply corresponding variations in the extent to which an attitude measure predicts that behavior. However, variations in prediction do not necessarily imply corresponding variations in influence. Interestingly, although most discussions of moderators of attitude-behavior consistency have used the term to refer to the magnitude of influence of an attitude on behavior, few studies have included design features that permitted this construal to be differentiated from mere variations in prediction. Specifically, most attitude-behavior studies measure a target attitude, and then at some later point in time a target behavior is assessed. Attitude-behavior consistency is evaluated by computing a measure of association (usually a correlation or regression coefficient) between the attitude measure and the behavioral measure. Hypotheses about various moderators are then tested by comparing the strength of this association at different levels of the proposed moderator. Thus, at the operational level, attitude-behavior consistency is defined in most studies in terms of prediction.

Processes Involving Variations in Prediction of Behaviors by Attitudes

The first important distinction that can be made among our six underlying processes is between those mechanisms that solely reflect variations in prediction and those that reflect actual variations in the influence of attitudes on behavior. We postulate that there are two processes by which an attitude measure might fail to predict some subsequent behavior without implying that an attitude failed to influence a behavior (see Table 9.1). First, an attitude measure might not predict a subsequent behavior because that measure fails to adequately assess the intended attitude. In such a case, the failure to observe a strong attitude-behavior association does not necessarily imply that people have failed to rely on their attitudes as guides to behavior. For example, imagine a case in which the attitude in question involves a socially sensitive topic such as attitudes toward a particular ethnic group. People holding negative attitudes might be reluctant to report their true attitudes and hence their responses might suggest positive attitudes toward the group. However, when some target behavior toward members of that group is assessed, they might engage in negative behaviors toward the group member. In such a case then, there might be little association between the attitude measure and subsequent behavior, but this lack of association would not imply that people were not relying on their attitudes. Indeed, the opposite might well be true. People's negative attitudes could be exerting a substantial impact on their behavior and, had these attitudes been properly captured by the measure,

Table 9.1. Mechanisms to Organize Moderators of Attitude-Behavior Consistency

Mechanisms Responsible for Prediction and Influence:

Prediction Mechanisms:

1. Measurement Error: Influences the accuracy or relevance of the attitude measure to the behavior of interest.
2. Attitude Stability: Influences the stability of the attitude over the time between the initial attitude measure and the behavior.

Influence Mechanisms (for Low-Deliberation Behaviors):

3. Indirect Judgmental Cue: Influences the extent to which the attitude biases people's perceptions of the target of the behavior.
4. Direct Judgmental Cue: Influences the extent to which the attitude directly informs the person whether they should enact the behavior.

Influence Mechanisms (for High-Deliberation Behaviors):

5. Central Merit of the Behavior: Influences the extent to which the attitude serves as an argument supporting or opposing the behavior.
6. Biasing Processing of Behavior-Relevant Information: Influences the extent to which the attitude biases assessments of the merits of the behavior.

a strong association would have been found. Thus, this possible mechanism represents a parallel but more general version of the point previously made by Fishbein and Ajzen (1972) when they noted that adequate (correspondent, or compatible) measures of attitudes were more likely to predict behavior. When measures of attitudes do not adequately tap the relevant attitude (because the wrong attitude is targeted, because people are unmotivated or unable to provide their true attitude, etc.), then attitude-behavior relations are likely to be relatively weak.

Thus, when investigating any moderator of the strength of attitude-behavior associations, it is important to consider whether that moderator could in some way alter the accuracy of attitude measurement. Indeed, a number of previously documented moderators might plausibly be interpreted in light of this measurement process. For instance, consider the attitude-behavior consistency research on the personality trait of self-monitoring (Ajzen et al., 1982; Snyder & Swann, 1976; Zanna et al., 1980). The finding that low self-monitoring leads to stronger attitude-behavior associations has often been interpreted to be a result of these people being more likely to access their attitudes at the time of behavior and thus to rely on these attitudes as a guide to how they should act. Such an interpretation is entirely plausible and of course implies that increases in the actual impact of attitudes on behavior have occurred. However, a second and not mutually exclusive explanation could be that these people are more likely to access their attitudes at the time of measurement (e.g., see Kardes, Sanbonmatsu, Voss, & Fazio, 1987) and thus to base their responses to the attitude measure on their stored evaluation rather than transient contextual factors at the time of measurement. Importantly, in many studies of attitude-behavior consistency, this explanation has not been considered.

In some cases, the attitude might be appropriately assessed, but the underlying attitude might change in the intervening time between when the attitude is measured and performance of the behavior. Thus, attitude instability could be a second mechanism that weakens the attitude-behavior relation without necessarily implying that attitudes fail to guide behaviors. In such a case, because the response provided at the earlier point in time no longer accurately reflects that person's attitude, the measure might be a poor predictor of behavior. However, it is possible that the new attitude the person holds at the time of behavior could be exerting a strong impact on behavior. Thus, if the attitude had been measured shortly before the behavior, a strong association might have been obtained.

Obviously, attitude instability is only likely to be a plausible process in situations where delays between the measurement of attitudes and the performance of behavior are sufficiently long. Hence, attitude instability is unlikely to account for the results of many laboratory studies of attitude-behavior consistency in which measures of attitudes and behavior were separated by only a few minutes. However, many field studies and some laboratory studies have involved delays of a few days or even several weeks. In some circumstances, during the time between attitude measure and behavior, additional social influence or available attitude-relevant information might have changed attitudes. Thus, instability might well be a viable explanation for observed lack of attitude-behavior consistency in such studies.

Many moderators of attitude-behavior relations could be related to attitude stability. Perhaps most notably, in the attitude strength literature, nearly all of the properties known to moderate attitude-behavior associations also predict the persistence of attitudes over time and the resistance of the attitude to persuasion (see Petty & Krosnick, 1995). Indeed, stability explanations have been proposed to account for the moderating effects of some strength-related properties of attitudes (e.g., see Ajzen & Fishbein, 1980; Davidson, Yantis, Norwood, & Montano, 1985; Doll & Ajzen, 1992; Eagly & Chaiken, 1993). However, empirical demonstrations of attitude stability accounting for moderation of attitude-behavior relations have been very rare.

Processes Involving Variations in Influence of Attitudes on Relatively Nondeliberative Behaviors

Four of our six proposed mechanisms involve variation in the impact of attitudes on behavior. In considering these four mechanisms, we further distinguish between processes in which the influence of attitudes on behaviors occurs when people are highly deliberative about the behavior and processes in which attitudes guide behavior with little deliberation about the behavior. Thus, our theoretical perspective draws upon an important premise first featured in the MODE model within the domain of attitude-behavior consistency (Fazio, 1990; Fazio & Towles-Schwen, 1999) and also long prominently featured in theories of attitude change such as the elaboration likelihood model (ELM: Petty & Cacioppo, 1986; Petty & Wegener, 1999) and the heuristic-systematic model (HSM; Chaiken, 1987; Chaiken, Liberman, & Eagly, 1989). We postulate that the precise process by which an attitude is likely to influence subsequent behavior depends on the extent to which that behavior is performed in a deliberative versus nondeliberative manner. By extension, we also assume that the mechanisms by which moderators regulate the strength of an attitude's influence on behavior will also vary as a result of the degree to which the behavior is based on relatively thoughtful versus nonthoughtful (i.e., deliberative vs. nondeliberative) processes.

When people are relatively nondeliberative in the performance of behaviors (either as a result of low motivation and/or ability to engage in careful thought while performing the behavior), attitudes may influence behavior in two ways (Table 9.1). First, attitudes might guide behavior by biasing people's perceptions of the target of the behavior (Fazio, 1990; Fazio & Towles-Schwen, 1999; Fazio & Roskos-Ewoldsen, 2005). Specifically, attitudes are likely to bias people to perceive the target in attitude-congruent ways (Fazio & Dunton, 1997; Fazio, Ledbetter, & Towles-Schwen, 2000; Smith, Fazio, & Cejka, 1996). These perceptions of the target may then serve as a basis for how the person defines the current behavioral context and thus responds to that situation. Importantly, this process is assumed to be relatively automatic and thus involve little cognitive effort. As such, the attitude can be conceptualized as serving as an "indirect judgmental cue" regarding how to respond to the behavioral situation.[1] That is, the behavioral response is not directly based on the attitude, but the attitude may direct attention to simple features of the object that do directly serve as a basis for the behavioral response.

Although attitudes might sometimes serve as an indirect cue, attitudes could also serve as a "direct judgmental cue" for inferring an appropriate behavior independent of any biasing effects on perception (Fabrigar et al., 2005; Fabrigar, Petty, Smith, & Crites, 2006). For instance, information in the behavioral context may be unambiguous and thus unlikely to be distorted (see Chaiken & Maheswaran, 1994). Alternatively, some behavioral or decision contexts may contain relatively little information to be distorted (see Lord & Lepper, 1999). In such cases, attitudes might still influence behaviors in a nondeliberative way by serving as a direct cue telling the person whether a particular behavior toward the attitude object is appropriate (see Petty & Cacioppo,

---

[1]   In the MODE model of attitude–behavior consistency, nondeliberative attitude–behavior consistency is primarily conceptualized as a result of the attitude biasing perception of the attitude object, which in turn influences how a person perceives a particular behavioral context. In our discussion of nondeliberative attitude–behavior processes, we deviate slightly from the MODE perspective in two ways. First, we allow for the possibility that an attitude could also sometimes serve as a direct cue for inferring an appropriate behavior independent of any biasing effects on perception. Second, we use the term "indirect cue" to refer to the sorts of low-effort biasing processes discussed in the MODE. We use this term to differentiate this process from "biased elaboration" or "biased processing," which has typically been used in the ELM to refer to the process by which a given factor biases thoughts about the central merits of an attitude object. Such biasing of effortful thinking is discussed in the MODE model under the rubric of mixed models of attitude–behavior processes (i.e., automatic components within deliberative processes).

1986; Petty & Wegener, 1999). For example, imagine a case where a person is planning to purchase a particular type of product from one of two companies, but the person is not sufficiently motivated or able to think carefully about the purchase. The person's general attitudes toward those two companies could serve as simple cues to select between two competing products from those companies in the absence of any scrutiny of the merits of the two specific products under consideration (cf., Sanbonmatsu & Fazio, 1990).

Thus, when investigating a moderator of the strength of attitude-behavior associations, it is also important to consider whether that moderator could alter the likelihood of using the attitude as a direct or indirect cue. Of course, for the attitude to serve as a direct or indirect cue, the attitude must be activated at the time of the behavior (Fazio, 1990; 1995; Fazio & Towles-Schwen, 1999). Thus, moderators of attitude-behavior consistency under low-deliberation conditions may exert their effects in part via their relation to attitude accessibility. Indeed, a number of moderators of attitude-behavior associations might be related to attitude accessibility, and in many cases these relations have been empirically established (Fabrigar et al., 2005).

Processes Involving Variations in Influence of Attitudes on Deliberative Behaviors

Nondeliberative behaviors are certainly common, but in many cases people are highly motivated and able to think about their behavior. For example, a person may be motivated because the behavior has significant consequences for the person or because the behavior is related to something about which the person cares a great deal (see Petty & Cacioppo, 1990). The person may be able to think when he or she has substantial time and few distractions when considering his or her actions (e.g., Petty & Wegener, 1999; Petty, Wells, & Brock, 1976).

When people deliberate about their behaviors, we believe that attitudes can influence behaviors via two additional mechanisms. Attitudes may influence behavior by serving as a direct argument for a particular action or by biasing the interpretation and evaluation of information about the merits of a given behavior (see Table 9.1; see Fabrigar et al., 2005; cf., Petty & Cacioppo, 1986; Petty & Wegener, 1999). If the attitude is perceived as directly relevant to the behavior in question, it may serve as a direct argument in favor of or against a course of action (i.e., the attitude may be a piece of information directly pertinent to assessing the merits of a particular behavior; Fabrigar et al., 2005; Fabrigar et al., 2006). For example, one's relative liking for two people could be seen as an argument in favor of one person versus the other when deciding which of two competing social invitations to accept.

It is important to note, however, that even if the attitude is not perceived as directly relevant to evaluating the merits of a behavior, it could still influence behavior by biasing the interpretation and assessment of information that is directly relevant to the behavior (assuming that information is sufficiently ambiguous to allow for more than one interpretation; Chaiken & Maheswaran, 1994). For example, imagine a situation where a person is encouraged by a friend to donate money to a particular charitable cause. The person's positive attitude toward the friend might positively bias assessment of information about the merits of that charitable cause thereby leading to the behavior.

A number of factors could regulate the extent to which attitudes influence behaviors via these two high-deliberation processes. For example, as with nondeliberative behaviors, attitudes must be activated at the time of the behavior if they are to bias processing of information relevant to the behavior or serve as a direct argument for or against the behavior. However, under high levels of deliberation, merely activating the attitude may not be sufficient to ensure that attitude influences behavior. The attitude must also be judged as applicable or relevant to the behavior (e.g., see Fabrigar et al., 2006; Lord, Lepper, & Mackie, 1984; Snyder & Kendzierski, 1982). If an attitude is viewed as irrelevant or inappropriate, it will be disregarded as an argument in favor of or against a particular course of action. People may also try to eliminate any inappropriate or "biasing" impact that this attitude might have on their decision to engage in the behavior (cf., Wegener & Petty, 1997). Thus, even if an attitude is activated, if the attitude is judged to be irrelevant or inappropriate, people may work to avoid use of the attitude when interpreting information relevant to the behavior (e.g., Dunton & Fazio, 1997; Schuette & Fazio, 1995; Towles-Schwen & Fazio, 2003).

These applicability mechanisms should most likely come into play when behaviors are highly deliberative. The metacognitive process of judging the applicability of an attitude to a given behavior and disregarding it or correcting for its influence is likely to require considerable cognitive resources (see Petty, Briñol, Tormala, & Wegener, 2007). Supporting this perspective, corrections for perceived biases in social judgments often require relatively high motivation and ability to think (e.g., Martin, Seta, & Crelia, 1990; Sczesny & Kühnen, 2004). Research has also revealed that when people are unable or unmotivated to think extensively about decisions, they often rely on attitudes even if, on logical grounds, it is inappropriate to do so (Fabrigar et al., 2006; Sanbonmatsu & Fazio, 1990; Schuette & Fazio, 1995). Reliance on inapplicable attitudes is less common when people are highly deliberative in their decisions.

There are reasons to suspect that many moderators of attitude-behavior associations might be related to the extent to which attitudes are perceived as appropriate guides to behavior. For example, a person who is highly certain of his or her attitude might be much more likely to perceive that attitude as an appropriate guide to behavior than someone who is not certain. Likewise, an attitude arrived at via extensive thought might be seen as more generally informative than an attitude arrived at with little thought. Unfortunately, there have only been a few cases in which this mechanism has been examined. In recent research on attitude complexity, complexity of the attitude has been found to strengthen the attitude's effect on behavior at least in part because the attitude is viewed as more applicable when based on information that is more complex (i.e., covering a greater number of behavior-relevant dimensions, Fabrigar et al., 2006).

Even when attitudes are activated and deemed to be appropriate as a reason to support the behavior, not all attitudes will be equivalent in the strength of bias they exert. For example, a person with an attitude based on extensive knowledge or careful thought might be capable of engaging in more extensive attitude-congruent distortion of behavioral information than someone who has little knowledge or who has given little thought to the attitude. To date, this possible mechanism has not been tested. However, there is a substantial theoretical and empirical basis to argue that many known moderators of attitude-behavior associations may also regulate the extent to which attitudes can distort the interpretation of information. For example, some properties of attitudes, such as the extent to which the attitude is based on cognitive elaboration (e.g., Haugtvedt & Petty, 1992; Haugtvedt & Wegener, 1994) or the extent of knowledge associated with the attitude (Biek, Wood, & Chaiken, 1996) have been related to the degree to which people can counterargue persuasive messages.

ILLUSTRATING MODERATOR PROCESSES IN THE CONTEXT OF INTROSPECTION

In summary, the MRPI approach postulates that the many diverse moderators of attitude-behavior associations exert their effects through a comparatively parsimonious set of underlying mechanisms (see Table 9.1). Assuming that these six processes account for many moderators of attitude-behavior associations, a natural question that might arise is to what extent the MRPI generates novel insights into past effects and new predictions regarding effects yet to be demonstrated. This question is perhaps best answered by illustrating in detail how the framework might be applied to a single moderator of attitude-behavior associations. Thus, in the sections that follow, we discuss the MRPI in the context of one well-documented variable known to alter attitude-behavior associations: introspection.

Summary of the Introspection and Attitude-Behavior Consistency Literature

Over the past 25 years, much research suggests that consistency between attitudes (or beliefs) and behaviors is lower when people are asked to introspect about their reasons for holding their attitudes before or during the attitude measure (Wilson & Dunn, 1986; Wilson et al., 1984; Wilson, Dunn, Kraft, & Lisle, 1989; Wilson, Kraft, & Dunn, 1989; Wilson & LaFleur, 1995). This effect of introspection has been demonstrated using novel attitude objects (e.g., puzzles) and familiar attitude objects (e.g., dating partners) and with delays between attitude measures and behavior ranging from a few minutes to several months.

Before discussing how this finding might be explained by the MRPI mechanisms, it is useful to consider how the typical introspection experiment is conducted. With novel attitude objects, under introspection conditions, participants are usually first instructed to think about their reasons for their reactions to the object and then are exposed to the object. Following exposure, participants are again instructed to think about their reasons for their attitudes and then to report their attitudes. Later, participants are provided with an opportunity to engage in some object-relevant behavior or to provide a self-report of the behavior. Under control conditions, the procedures are similar with the exception that participants are not prompted to consider their reasons for their reactions prior to exposure to the object or prior to reporting their attitudes. Introspection studies involving familiar attitude objects are similar but without an exposure stage. In both types of studies, the amount of attitude-behavior consistency is typically assessed by computing attitude-behavior correlations.

Introspection and Prediction Processes

Although the effects of introspection have long been established, the psychological processes responsible for these effects have been less definitively documented. Wilson and his colleagues have speculated that introspection about the reasons for one's attitudes or beliefs focuses people on attributes that are readily accessible in memory and reasons that are easily verbalized and intuitively plausible (see Wilson, Dunn, Kraft, & Lisle, 1989; Wilson, Hodges, & LaFleur, 1995). These generated attributes and reasons may not imply the same attitude held by people prior to introspection. Therefore, within the MRPI approach, one way to view this phenomenon is to say that attitude measures in introspection conditions are not accurate (i.e., not tapping the stored attitude most likely to guide later behaviors). Instead, attitude measures in introspection conditions may reflect mere transitory beliefs rather than people's more stable general evaluations of the object, resulting in poorer prediction of subsequent behavior.

One interesting implication of this explanation is that it suggests that the timing of introspection is critical. Past studies have instructed people to introspect immediately prior to reporting their attitudes. If the attitude-measurement-error process is responsible for introspection effects, then having participants introspect after they have reported their attitudes should have little effect on the strength of attitude-behavior associations. To date, introspection studies have not investigated this possibility or measurement error processes more generally.

To take another MRPI process, one could instead say that introspection temporarily changed the attitude, making it relatively unstable. Indeed, attitude stability processes have been the primary explanation offered for introspection's effects on attitude-behavior associations (see Wilson, Dunn, Kraft, & Lisle, 1989). As noted, Wilson and colleagues have argued that introspection leads people to focus on attributes that are readily accessible in memory and on reasons for the attitude that are easily verbalized and intuitively plausible. They further argue that this process results in people temporarily changing their attitudes. The temporary attitude serves as the basis for responses to the initial (postintrospection) measure. However, the attitude is assumed to rapidly decay, and the original attitude reasserts itself by the time the behavior is assessed. Hence, attitude reports following introspection are poor predictors because responses to the attitude measure reflect an attitude that no longer exists at the time of behavior.

To date, there have been no direct tests of this hypothesis (i.e., meditational analyses involving stability). However, there is indirect evidence for this mechanism. Experiments have confirmed that inducing people to introspect about their attitudes can produce different attitude reports than would be obtained had people not introspected (Hodges & Wilson, 1993; Wilson & Kraft, 1993; Wilson, Kraft, & Dunn, 1989). Moreover, situations in which introspection fails to alter attitude reports (e.g., when attitudes are based on extensive knowledge) also fail to produce the typical lower level of attitude-behavior association for introspection conditions (Wilson, Kraft, & Dunn, 1989).

Of course, it is worth noting that these same findings are also consistent with the predictions one might generate using an error-of-measurement explanation. Indeed, the distinctions between these two explanations are somewhat subtle. In the error-of-measurement explanation, the assumption is that the original attitude has not been altered but that its influence on the response to the measure has been weakened as a result of other constructs (extraneous to the attitude) influencing responses to the measure. For the attitude stability explanation, one would assume that the actual attitude has been altered and this new attitude is reflected in the initial attitude measure, but the attitude is unstable and changes back to the prestudy attitude by the time the behavior takes place.

If one assumes that the attitude stability explanation is viable, it suggests some interesting implications. First, it implies that attitudes can be relatively resilient psychological entities. Although it can be temporarily altered by introspection, the original attitude will reassert itself (often in a matter of minutes), and that original attitude will ultimately be a relatively strong determinant of behavior. A second interesting implication is that the stability explanation makes somewhat different predictions than a measurement explanation regarding the timing of introspection. The stability explanation implies that assessing attitudes in the normal way and later asking people to introspect immediately prior to the behavior would decrease the attitude-behavior association. Presumably this would happen because, at the time of behavior, a new attitude is created, and this new attitude influences the behavior (rather than the original attitude reflected in the initial measure). An attitude measurement explanation would not make the same prediction, unless one assumed that the newly created beliefs extraneous to the attitude were sufficiently strong to directly influence the subsequent behavior (without affecting the attitude).

Introspection and Attitudinal Impact Under Low Deliberation

When deliberation about the behavior is low, introspection might lower the likelihood of attitude activation at the time of behavior. Specifically, Wilson and colleagues have noted that some of the attributes and reasons generated during introspection are not consistent with the original attitudes. Activating an evaluative construct tends to facilitate the activation of other evaluatively consistent constructs and inhibit the activation of evaluatively inconsistent constructs (Bargh, Chaiken, Govender, & Pratto, 1992; Fazio, Powell, & Herr, 1983; Fazio, Sanbonmatsu, Powell, & Kardes, 1986). Thus, if introspection produces cognitions inconsistent with the attitude, this might diminish the likelihood of the attitude being activated and thus the likelihood that the attitude can serve as a direct or an indirect judgmental cue.

Though untested, the attitude activation explanation has several interesting implications. First, the effects of introspection should only diminish attitude-behavior associations when the cognitions generated are inconsistent with the attitude. Were consistent cognitions generated, one would predict no decrease and perhaps an increase in the likelihood of attitude activation. This might be one reason that introspection does not decrease attitude-behavior consistency for high-accessibility attitudes (Hodges & Wilson, 1993). A second implication is that the effects of introspection on attitude-behavior associations should be comparatively short lived. Because activation of constructs is generally thought to be comparatively brief in duration, especially in a changing environment, any inhibition or facilitation effects of introspection should not last very long (Forbach, Stanners, & Hochhaus, 1974; Warren, 1972; cf., Srull & Wyer, 1980). Thus, activation mechanisms could potentially explain some lab studies in which behaviors were assessed only a few minutes following the attitude report but would have a harder time accounting for studies in which delays were days or months in length.

Introspection and Attitudinal Impact Under High Deliberation

Under high deliberation, introspection might once again be expected to influence attitude-behavior associations via its impact on attitude activation. Introspection might also exert its effects by altering the extent to which attitudes are seen as appropriate guides to behavior. Specifically, introspection might induce people to think about the attitude object more broadly than they typically would. Because people want to appear rational to themselves and to others, introspection might encourage people to generate as extensive a set of reasons as possible for their attitudes. This process could result in people strengthening or elaborating upon some beliefs that were originally only weakly associated with the attitude object and in some cases constructing new beliefs regarding the attitude object. The result of this process might be to produce attitudes that are more complex (i.e., more multidimensional in their underlying bases) than was true prior to introspection.

Research suggests that increasing the complexity of beliefs underlying attitudes can alter the extent to which attitudes influence behaviors (Fabrigar et al., 2005; Fabrigar et al., 2006; Fabrigar et al., in preparation). When the newly generated or strengthened dimensions are evaluatively consistent with the overall attitude, increased complexity could lead the person to view the attitude as a particularly valid guide for behavior. On the other hand, if the newly generated or strengthened dimensions are evaluatively inconsistent with the attitude, this can decrease attitude-behavior associations by leading people to see their attitudes as an inappropriate guide to action (Fabrigar et al., in preparation).

For instance, when the behavior in question is closely related to a dimension that is evaluatively inconsistent with the global attitude, people may judge their global attitude to be an inappropriate guide and instead follow their evaluation of the more specific dimension. Also, when behaviors or decisions are not directly relevant to any dimension upon which their attitude is currently based, the existence of evaluative inconsistency among dimensions may make people reluctant to assume that their global evaluation is generally informative. Thus, they may be unwilling to rely upon it, unless the behavior is highly relevant to the specific dimensions upon which the attitude is based. Increased complexity could also alter the extent to which people's attitudes bias interpretation of information relevant to the behavior. When introspection produces additional evaluative reactions that contradict the attitude, these conflicting reactions may weaken or undermine the extent to which people are motivated or able to distort behavioral information in an attitude-congruent fashion.[2]

To date, although research has demonstrated that complexity regulates attitude-behavior associations in the manner described, there has been little attempt to examine whether introspection alters attitude complexity and complexity might account for the effects of introspection on attitude-behavior associations. Some unpublished data have failed to produce evidence that introspection changes complexity (see Wilson, Dunn, Kraft, & Lisle, 1989), but the measure of complexity was not especially sensitive.

If complexity is one of the mechanisms responsible for the effects of introspection, it suggests two interesting implications. First, presuming that the newly strengthened or created dimensions underlying the attitude produced by introspection persist over time, one might expect the effects of introspection on attitude-behavior associations to be relatively long lasting under highly deliberative conditions. Second, this explanation suggests that there should be contexts in which introspection actually increases attitude-behavior associations when behaviors are highly deliberative.

Specifically, research has established that increased complexity involving dimensions that are evaluatively consistent tends to strengthen

---

[2] In some circumstances, however, increasing ambivalence may increase motives to process new information in a way that favors attitude-consistent information and avoids or opposes attitude-inconsistent information (see Clark, Wegener, & Fabrigar, 2008; Nordgren, van Harreveld, & van der Pligt, 2006).

attitude-behavior associations by causing people to see their attitudes as generally informative guides to behaviors relevant to the target. This enhanced impact of attitudes on behaviors is a result of one of two processes (see Fabrigar et al., 2006). First, when attitudes are based on many distinct dimensions of beliefs, the likelihood that the attitude will be based on at least one dimension directly relevant to a given behavior is greater than when the attitude is based on only a single dimension. Second, even in situations in which a behavior is not directly relevant to any dimension upon which the attitude is based, increasing the number of evaluatively consistent dimensions leads people to assume the object is evaluatively similar on other dimensions for which they have no knowledge and thus to conclude their attitude is a generally informative guide to behavior.

Based on these two processes, it follows that attitude-behavior associations should be stronger when introspection results in people generating or elaborating upon dimensions that are consistent with each other and the original dimensions. Similarly, when introspection produces attitude-consistent cognitions, it also suggests that the ability of attitudes to bias information regarding the behavior could be enhanced. This should occur because people presumably should have a more extensive knowledge base underlying their attitude and thus should have greater ability to distort behavioral information.

CONCLUSIONS

Attitude-behavior consistency has been of interest to attitude researchers nearly as long as attitudes have been a topic of scientific inquiry. There is no doubt that major advances have been made in understanding attitude-behavior consistency processes. The question of whether attitudes can predict behavior has largely been put to rest, and influential theories designed to explain the processes by which attitudes exert their influence on behavior have been proposed. Moreover, researchers have documented an impressive array of moderators of the extent to which attitudes are associated with behavior.

It is this later contribution that in some ways poses one of the great remaining challenges. Although the field has produced an extensive catalog of moderators, there has been little attempt to develop a theoretical framework in which to organize them. The six-process framework offered in this chapter is intended to be a first step toward addressing this gap.

If ultimately supported by empirical research, the MRPI approach could advance understanding of attitude-behavior consistency in notable ways. First, by providing a relatively finite set of processes to account for the effects of a wide range of variables, it could provide a basis for a parsimonious categorization of the many moderators of attitude-behavior associations. Specifically, although our illustration involved a variable (i.e., introspection) whose effects could involve all six processes (across different circumstances), this would not be true of all moderators. Rather, our perspective merely postulates that a given moderator will exert its effects via a least one of these processes and that the possible processes at work will vary depending on the level of deliberation involved. Each moderator and each behavior setting must be considered in light of its specific conceptual properties and how they relate to the processes outlined in the framework. In some cases, these properties will suggest that a given moderator could exert effects via multiple processes. For example, a moderator could influence not only measurement properties but also the likelihood of the attitude serving as a direct or indirect cue (when deliberation is low) or the likelihood of the attitude biasing processing of behavior-relevant information (when deliberation is high). In other cases, a given moderator may have its effects via only one or a small subset of the six processes. As such, the MRPI is intended as a framework to guide the questions researchers ask about moderators of attitude-behavior associations and the methods they use to investigate these questions rather than to provide the answers themselves. By undertaking research guided by these questions and methods, it might ultimately be possible to produce a categorization of moderators based on the extent to which they reflect common versus distinct underlying processes.

A second potential contribution of the MRPI approach is its utility for generating novel hypotheses. To date, most moderators of attitude-behavior associations have been presumed to have fairly unitary effects (e.g., introspection about reasons leads to weaker attitude-behavior associations, increased amounts of knowledge lead to stronger attitude-behavior associations, etc.). With few exceptions, there has been little attempt to specify conditions under which the effects of these moderators might disappear or perhaps even reverse. As we have illustrated in this chapter, when moderators are considered in light of the MRPI, a number of novel predictions along these lines can be generated.

In closing, it is important to acknowledge that testing of the MRPI mechanisms is still in the very early stages. Evidence exists for each of the six processes in the context of some moderators of attitude-behavior associations. However, currently no single moderator has been examined in light of all six processes, and some moderators have yet to be examined in light of any of these processes. Thus, much research remains to be conducted. However, regardless of the ultimate outcome of these tests, the process of testing the MRPI is likely to further the goal of turning "miraculous effects" of moderators of attitude-behavior consistency into enhanced scientific understanding of those moderators.

REFERENCES

Ajzen, I. (1991). The theory of planned behavior. *Organizational Behavior and Human Decision Processes, 50,* 179–211.

Ajzen, I., & Fishbein, M. (1977). Attitude-behavior relations: A theoretical analysis and review of empirical research. *Psychological Bulletin, 84,* 888–918.

Ajzen, I., & Fishbein, M. (1980). *Understanding attitudes and predicting social behavior.* Englewood Cliffs, NJ: Prentice Hall.

Ajzen, I., Timko, C., & White, J. B. (1982). Self-monitoring and the attitude-behavior relation. *Journal of Personality and Social Psychology, 42,* 426–435.

Allport, F. H. (1924). *Social psychology.* Boston, MA: Houghton Mifflin.

Allport, G. W. (1935). Attitudes. In C. Murchinson (Ed.), *A handbook of social psychology* (pp. 798–844). Worcester, MA: Clark University Press.

Bargh, J. A., Chaiken, S., Govender, R., & Pratto, F. (1992). The generality of the automatic attitude activation effect. *Journal of Personality and Social Psychology, 62,* 893–912.

Biek, M., Wood, W., & Chaiken, S. (1996). Working knowledge, cognitive processing, and attitudes: On the determinants of bias. *Personality and Social Psychology Bulletin, 22,* 547–556.

Bogardus, E. S. (1931). *Fundamentals of social psychology* (2nd Edition). New York, NY: Appleton-Century-Crofts.

Chaiken, S. (1987). The heuristic model of persuasion. In M. P. Zanna, J. M. Olson, & C. P. Herman (Eds.), *Social influence: The Ontario symposium* (Vol. 3, pp. 143–177). Hillsdale, NJ: Erlbaum.

Chaiken, S., Liberman, A., & Eagly, A. H. (1989). Heuristic and systematic processing within and beyond the persuasion context. In J. S. Uleman & J. A. Bargh (Eds.), *Unintended thought* (pp. 212–252). New York, NY: Guilford Press.

Chaiken, S., & Maheswaran, D. (1994). Heuristic processing can bias systematic processing: Effects of source credibility, argument ambiguity, and task importance on attitude judgment. *Journal of Personality and Social Psychology, 66,* 460–473.

Chave. E. G. (1928). A new type of scale for measuring attitudes. *Religious Education, 23,* 364–369.

Clark, J. K., Wegener, D. T., & Fabrigar, L. R. (2008). Attitude ambivalence and message-based persuasion: Motivated processing of proattitudinal information and avoidance of counterattitudinal information. *Personality and Social Psychology Bulletin, 34,* 565–577.

Davidson, A. R., Yantis, S., Norwood, M., & Montano, D. E. (1985). Amount of information about the attitude object and attitude-behavior consistency. *Journal of Personality and Social Psychology, 49,* 1184–1198.

Deutscher, I. (1966). Words and deeds: Social science and social policy. *Social Problems, 13,* 235–254.

Deutscher, I. (1973). *What we say/what we do.* Glenview, IL: Scott, Foresman.

Doll, J., & Ajzen, I. (1992). Accessibility and stability of predictors in the theory of planned behavior. *Journal of Personality and Social Psychology, 63,* 754–765.

Doob (1947). The behavior of attitudes. *Psychological Review, 54,* 135–156.

Droba (1933). The nature of attitude. *Journal of Social Psychology, 4,* 444–463.

Dunton, B. C., & Fazio, R. H. (1997). An individual difference measure of motivation to control prejudiced reactions. *Personality and Social Psychology Bulletin, 23,* 316–326.

Eagly, A. H., & Chaiken, S. (1993). *The psychology of attitudes.* Fort Worth, TX: Harcourt Brace Jovanovich.

Fabrigar, L. R., MacDonald, T. K., & Wegener, D. T. (2005). The structure of attitudes. In D. Albarracin, B. T. Johnson, & M. P. Zanna (Eds.), *Handbook of attitudes and attitude change* (pp. 79–124). Mahwah, NJ: Erlbaum.

Fabrigar, L. R., Petty, R. E., Smith, S. M., & Crites, S. L., Jr. (2006). Understanding knowledge effects on attitude-behavior consistency: The role of relevance, complexity, and amount of knowledge. *Journal of Personality and Social Psychology, 90,* 556–577.

Fabrigar, L. R., Petty, R. E., Smith, S. M., Crites, S. L., Jr., & Wood, J. K. (2009). *Exploring the role of complexity and between-dimension evaluative consistency of knowledge on attitude-behavior consistency.* Unpublished manuscript, Queen's University, Kingston, Ontario, Canada.

Fazio, R. H. (1990). Multiple processes by which attitudes guide behavior: The MODE model as an integrative framework. In L. Berkowitz (Ed.), *Advances in experimental social psychology* (Vol. 23, pp. 75–109). San Diego, CA: Academic Press.

Fazio, R. H. (1995). Attitudes as object-evaluation associations: Determinants, consequences, and correlates of attitude accessibility. In R. E. Petty & J. A. Krosnick (Eds.), *Attitude strength: Antecedents and consequences* (pp. 247–282). Mahwah, NJ: Lawrence Erlbaum Associates.

Fazio, R. H., & Dunton, B. C. (1997). Categorization by race: The impact of automatic and controlled components of racial prejudice. *Journal of Experimental Social Psychology, 33,* 451–470.

Fazio, R. H., Ledbetter, J. E., & Towles-Schwen, T. (2000). On the costs of accessible attitudes: Detecting that the attitude object has changed. *Journal of Personality and Social Psychology, 78,* 197–210.

Fazio, R. H., Powell, M. C., & Herr, P. M. (1983). Toward a process model of the atittude-behavior relation: Accessing one's attitude upon mere observation of the attitude object. *Journal of Personality and Social Psychology, 44,* 723–735.

Fazio, R. H., & Roskos-Ewoldsen, D. R. (2005). Acting as we feel: When and how attitudes guide behavior. In T. C. Brock & M. C. Green (Eds.), *Persuasion: Psychological insights and perspectives* (pp. 41–62). Thousand Oaks, CA: Sage Publications.

Fazio, R. H., Sanbonmatsu, D. M., Powell, M. C., & Kardes, F. R. (1986). On the automatic activation of attitudes. *Journal of Personality and Social Psychology, 50,* 229–238.

Fazio, R. H., & Towles-Schwen, T. (1999). The MODE model of attitude-behavior processes. In S. Chaiken & Y. Trope (Eds.), *Dual-process theories in social psychology* (pp. 97–116). New York, NY: Guilford Press.

Fazio, R. H., & Zanna, M. P. (1981). Direct experience and attitude-behavior consistency. In L. Berkowitz (Ed.), *Advances in experimental social psychology* (Vol. 14, pp. 162–202). New York, NY: Academic Press.

Fishbein, M., & Ajzen, I. (1972). Attitudes and opinions. *Annual Review of Psychology, 23*, 487–544.

Fishbein, M., & Ajzen, I. (1974). Attitudes toward objects as predictors of single and multiple criteria behavior. *Psychological Review, 81*, 59–74.

Fishbein, M., & Ajzen, I. (1975). *Belief, attitude, intention, and behavior: An introduction to theory and research.* Reading, MA: Addison-Wesley.

Forbach, G. B., Stanners, R. F., & Hochhaus, L. (1974). Repetition and practice effects in a lexical decision task. *Memory and Cognition, 2*, 337–339.

Gibbons, F. X. (1978). Sexual standards and reactions to pornography: Enhancing behavioral consistency through self-focused attention. *Journal of Personality and Social Psychology, 36*, 976–987.

Hammond, K. R. (1948). Measuring attitudes by error-choice: An indirect method. *Journal of Abnormal and Social Psychology, 43*, 38–48.

Haugtvedt, C. P., & Petty, R. E. (1992). Personality and persuasion: Need for cognition moderates the persistence and resistance of attitude changes. *Journal of Personality and Social Psychology, 63*, 308–319.

Haugtvedt, C. P., & Wegener, D. T. (1994). Message order effects in persuasion: An attitude strength perspective. *Journal of Consumer Research, 21*, 205–218.

Hodges, S. D., & Wilson, T. D. (1993). Effects of analyzing reasons on attitude change: The moderating role of attitude accessibility. *Social Cognition, 11*, 353–366.

Insko, C. A., & Schopler, J. (1967). Triadic consistency: A statement of affective-cognitive-conative consistency. *Psychological Review, 74*, 361–376.

Kardes, F. R., Sanbonmatsu, D. M., Voss, R. T., & Fazio, R. H. (1986). Self-monitoring and attitude accessibility. *Personality and Social Psychology, 12*, 468–474.

Katz, D., & Stotland, E. (1959). A preliminary statement to a theory of attitude structure and change. In S. Koch (Ed.), *Psychology: A study of a science: Vol. 3 Formulations of the person and the social context* (pp. 423–475). New York, NY: McGraw-Hill.

Kelman, H. C. (1974). Attitudes are alive and well and gainfully employed in the sphere of action. *American Psychologist, 29*, 310–324.

Kraus, S. J. (1995). Attitudes and the prediction of behavior: A meta-analysis of the empirical literature. *Personality and Social Psychology Bulletin, 21*, 58–75.

Lord, C. G., & Lepper, M. R. (1999). Attitude representation theory. In M. P. Zanna (Ed.), *Advances in experimental social psychology* (Vol. 31, pp. 265–343). San Diego, CA: Academic Press.

Lord, C. G., Lepper, M. R., & Mackie, D. (1984). Attitude prototypes as determinants of attitude-behavior consistency. *Journal of Personality and Social Psychology, 46*, 1254–1266.

Martin, L. L., Seta, J. J., & Crelia, R. A. (1990). Assimilation and contrast as a function of people's willingness and ability to expend effort in forming an impression. *Journal of Personality and Social Psychology, 59*, 27–37.

Millar, M. G., & Tesser, A. (1986). Effects of affective and cognitive focus on the attitude-behavior relationship. *Journal of Personality and Social Psychology, 51*, 270–276.

Millgram, S., Mann, L., & Harter, S. (1965). The lost-letter technique: A tool for social research. *Public Opinion Quarterly, 29*, 437–438.

Nordgren, L. F., van Harreveld, F., & van der Pligt, J. (2006). Ambivalence, discomfort, and motivated information processing. *Journal of Experimental Social Psychology, 42*, 252–258.

Petty, R. E., Briñol, P., Tormala, Z. L., & Wegener, D. T. (2007). The role of meta-cognition in social judgment. In E. T. Higgins & A. W. Kruglanski (Eds.) *Social psychology: handbook of basic principles* (2nd ed., pp. 254–294). New York: Guilford Press, 254–284.

Petty, R. E., & Cacioppo, J. T. (1986). *Communication and persuasion: Central and peripheral routes to attitude change.* New York, NY: Springer-Verlag.

Petty, R. E., & Cacioppo, J. T. (1990). Involvement and persuasion: Tradition versus integration. *Psychological Bulletin, 107*, 367–74.

Petty, R. E., & Krosnick, J. A. (Eds.). (1995). *Attitude strength: Antecedents and consequences.* Mahwah, NJ: Lawrence Erlbaum Associates.

Petty, R. E., & Wegener, D. T. (1999). The Elaboration Likelihood Model: Current status and controversies. In S. Chaiken & Y. Trope (Eds.), *Dual-process theories in social psychology* (pp. 41–72). New York, NY: Guilford Press.

Petty, R. E., Wells, G. L., & Brock, T. C. (1976). Distraction can enhance or reduce yielding to propaganda: Thought disruption versus effort justification. *Journal of Personality and Social Psychology, 34*, 874–884.

Rosenberg, M. J., & Hovland, C. I. (1960). Cognitive, affective, and behavioral components of attitudes. In M. Rosenberg, C. Hovland, W. McGuire, R. Abelson, & J. Brehm (Eds.), *Attitude organization and change* (pp. 1–14). New Haven, CT: Yale University Press.

Sanbonmatsu, D. M., & Fazio, R. H. (1990). The role of attitudes in memory-based decision making. *Journal of Personality and Social Psychology, 59*, 614–622.

Schuette, R. A., & Fazio, R. H. (1995). Attitude accessibility and motivation as determinants of biased processing: A test of the MODE model. *Personality and Social Psychology Bulletin, 21*, 704–710.

Schuman, H., & Johnson, M. P. (1976). Attitudes and behavior. *Annual Review of Sociology, 2*, 161–207.

Sczesny, S., & Kühnen, U. (2004). Meta-cognition about biological sex and gender-stereotypic physical appearance: Consequences for the assessment of leadership competence. *Personality and Social Psychology Bulletin, 30*, 13–21.

Smith, E. R., Fazio, R. H., & Cejka, M. A. (1996). Accessible attitudes influence categorization of multiply categorizable objects. *Journal of Personality and Social Psychology, 71*, 888–898.

Snyder, M. (1982). When believing means doing: Creating links between attitudes and behavior. In M. P. Zanna, E. T. Higgins, & C. P. Herman (Eds.), *Consistency in social behavior: The Ontario symposium* (Vol. 2, pp. 105–130). Hillsdale, NJ: Lawrence Erlbaum Associates.

Snyder, M., & Kendzierski, D. (1982). Acting on one's attitudes: Procedures for linking attitude to behavior. *Journal of Experimental Social Psychology, 18*, 165–183.

Snyder, M., & Swann, W. B. (1976). When actions reflect attitudes: The politics of impression management. *Journal of Personality and Social Psychology, 34*, 1034–1042.

Srull, T. K., & Wyer, R. S. (1980). Category accessibility and social perception: Some implications for the study of person memory and interpersonal judgments. *Journal of Personality and Social Psychology, 38,* 841–856.

Towles-Schwen, T., & Fazio, R. H. (2003). Choosing social situations: The relation between automatically activated racial attitudes and anticipated comfort interacting with African Americans. *Personality and Social Psychology Bulletin, 29,* 170–182.

Warren, R. E. (1972). Stimulus encoding and memory. *Journal of Experimental Psychology, 94,* 90–100.

Wegener, D. T., & Petty, R. E. (1997). The flexible correction model: The role of naive theories of bias in bias correction. In M. P. Zanna (Ed.), *Advances in experimental social psychology* (Vol. 29, pp. 141–208). San Diego, CA: Academic Press.

Weigel, R. H., & Newman, L. S. (1976). Increasing attitude-behavior correspondence by broadening the scope of the behavioral measure. *Journal of Personality and Social Psychology, 33,* 793–802.

Wicker, A. W. (1969). Attitude versus actions: The relationship of verbal and overt behavioral responses to attitude objects. *Journal of Social Issues, 25,* 41–78.

Wicker, A. W. (1971). An examination of the "other variable" explanation of attitude-behavior inconsistency. *Journal of Personality and Social Psychology, 19,* 18–30.

Wilson, T. D., & Dunn, D. S. (1986). Effects of introspection on attitude-behavior consistency: Analyzing reasons versus focusing on feelings. *Journal of Experimental Social Psychology, 22,* 249–263.

Wilson, T. D., Dunn, D. S., Bybee, J. A., Hyman, D. B., & Rotondo, J. A. (1984). Effects of analyzing reasons on attitude-behavior consistency. *Journal of Personality and Social Psychology, 47,* 5–16.

Wilson, T. D., Dunn, D. S., Kraft, D., & Lisle, D. J. (1989). Introspection, attitude change, and attitude-behavior consistency: The disruptive effects of explaining why we feel the way we do. In L. Berkowitz (Ed.), *Advances in experimental social psychology* (Vol. 22, pp. 287–343). Orlando, FL: Academic Press.

Wilson, T. D., Hodges, S. D., & LaFleur, S. J. (1995). Effects of introspecting about reasons: Inferring attitudes from accessible thoughts. *Journal of Personality and Social Psychology, 69,* 16–28.

Wilson, T. D., & Kraft, D. (1993). Why do I love thee?: Effects of repeated introspections about a dating relationship on attitudes toward the relationship. *Personality and Social Psychology Bulletin, 19,* 409–418.

Wilson, T. D., Kraft, D., & Dunn, D. S. (1989). The disruptive effects of explaining attitudes: The moderating effect of knowledge about the attitude object. *Journal of Experimental Social Psychology, 25,* 379–400.

Wilson, T. D., & LaFleur, S. J. (1995). Knowing what you'll do: Effects of analyzing reasons on self-prediction. *Journal of Personality and Social Psychology, 68,* 21–35.

Zanna, M. P., Olson, J. M., & Fazio, R. H. (1980). Attitude-behavior consistency: An individual difference perspective. *Journal of Personality and Social Psychology, 38,* 432–440.

10 Personality as Manifest in Behavior: Direct Behavioral Observation Using the Revised Riverside Behavioral Q-Sort (RBQ-3.0)

R. Michael Furr
Seth A. Wagerman
David C. Funder

If one accepts the standard definition given by most introductory texts, psychology is the study of "behavior and mental processes" (Myers, 2007, p. 2). Relatedly, personality can be described as "an individual's characteristic pattern of thought, emotion, and behavior, together with the psychological mechanisms... behind those patterns" (Funder, 2007, p. 5). Clearly, behavior is central to psychology in general and to personality psychology in particular.

In recent years, however, the study of directly observed behaviors with robust psychological meaning has become relatively rare (Baumeister, Vohs, & Funder, 2007; Furr, in press a; see Chapter 2 in this volume). Recent research appears to be increasingly dominated by studies of dependent variables such as reaction time, memory recall, and self-report, which are chosen for their relevance to hypothesized underlying cognitive processes rather than because of their intrinsic importance. Historically, one could argue that the field has never dedicated itself to a comprehensive and coherent examination of basic social behaviors. Even the classic studies of social psychology in the 1960s and 1970s, which did focus on consequential actions, generally examined but one behavior or aspect of behavior, such as how much time was taken to help someone ostensibly in need, how intensely a participant ostensibly shocked someone, or whether people on the street stopped to join a group that was ostensibly looking intently at something. While these studies were important, single behaviors provide a very narrow window into what people are doing, which at any given moment is multifaceted.

In the current paper, we discuss direct behavioral observation of meaningful social behavior in personality psychology. By *direct behavioral observation* we refer to data provided by independent observers who supply systematic descriptions of something they have actually seen a person do. Our goals are to convince readers that direct behavioral observation is an important facet of psychological research in general and of personality psychology in particular, to outline important considerations in planning or choosing a system for organizing and coding behaviors in such research, and to describe a particular method that researchers may find useful in examining personality as manifest in behavior.

THE COST AND BENEFIT OF BEHAVIORAL OBSERVATION IN PERSONALITY PSYCHOLOGY

The Cost of Behavioral Observation

Any serious attempt to study a range of meaningful social behaviors in an objective way is likely to be costly, and direct behavioral observation may be the most demanding of all assessment strategies. Indeed, the potential benefits of direct behavioral observation must be weighed against their sometimes-significant costs (for additional discussion, see Furr, in press a, in press b).

One challenge is that the process of directly observing a range of meaningful social behaviors can be expensive in terms of time, money, and effort. Depending on one's goals and the scope of one's project, the process of obtaining, preparing, and analyzing direct behavioral observations can require a huge investment. In some research, such observations are made as behavior unfolds, by having observers watch and immediately rate participants' actions. In other research, participants' behavior is recorded, and observers later watch and rate the recorded behavior. In either form of direct behavioral observation, the work requires significant time—both in terms of organizing the observers (e.g., creating a schedule, conducting training, preparing materials) and in terms of the actual collection of the observers' ratings. In fact, the process can take years—literally—though this depends heavily on the scope of one's project. Along with an investment of time comes a potential investment of money for obtaining and preparing adequate infrastructure (e.g., recording devices or room configuration), salaries of people who oversee the process, and payments to people who serve as observers. By contrast, pencils and paper for self-report questionnaires cost little.

Moreover, the less-expensive methods *have* produced important findings. For example, questionnaires and tests are tried-and-true methods for gathering extensive information about self-perceptions, self-reported attitudes, perceptions of other people, abilities, and so on. Such data have provided important insights such as the dimensional structure of personality (or at least the structure of perceived individual differences in personality characteristics), the accuracy of personality judgments (or at least the degree to which people agree in their personality judgments), and the nature of cognitive ability (or at least a reasonable proxy thereof). To be sure, psychology has learned much while relying largely on a variety of relatively simple and inexpensive methods.

The downside is that much of psychology seems to have turned away from studying behavior at all. Cognitive science and neuroscience give the impression of having little interest in what people actually do, often focusing instead on which portion of the participants' brain "lights up" an fMRI (functional magnetic resonance imaging) when performing certain cognitive tasks. Even social psychology, in its move towards "social cognition," risks becoming more interested in cognitive mediators of behavior than behavior itself. As a result, current research sometimes seems to seek behaviors that can test proposed mediators rather than mediators that can explain important behaviors.

Another reason for the rarity of direct behavioral observations may be a lack of tools available to researchers interested in such work. Given the demands of direct behavioral observations, researchers may feel that the hill is too steep to climb—where does one even begin? What should one measure? How does one plan a system for collecting behavioral observations? What are the key considerations in conducting such work? There are few places that researchers may turn to for answers to these kinds of questions (Furr & Funder, 2007). Furthermore, few behavioral coding systems are available to researchers, as very few have been carefully developed with an eye toward a broad range of social behaviors, and as few have been psychometrically evaluated through rigorous use and examination.

An important goal of the current paper is to address these final impediments to broader use of direct behavioral observation. Specifically, we outline important considerations in planning or choosing a system for direct behavioral observations, and we present a system reflecting years of development, application, evaluation, and refinement—the revised Riverside Behavioral Q-Sort (RBQ-3.0). Our hope is that our outline, system, and experience help pave the way for others to pursue the important benefits of behavioral observations.

The Benefit of Behavioral Observation

As students sometimes remind us, psychology is interesting precisely because it is supposed to reveal "why people do what they do." If we truly want to understand "what people do" in a broad and meaningful way, then we must study a wide range of social behaviors. The most general benefit of direct behavioral observation, then, is that it offers particularly strong insight into the social behaviors that people actually enact.

Behavioral observation is essential for the theoretical and empirical well-being of psychology. As a science dedicated, at least in part, to explaining consequential behaviors and outcomes, psychology's value rests heavily on the production of research directly bearing on meaningful behavior. Personality psychology provides a particularly poignant example of this point. In 1968, a book was published that challenged the very core of the field (Mischel, 1968). It reviewed some empirical evidence regarding the consistency or specificity of presumably trait-relevant behavior (e.g., the correlation between two behaviors ostensibly related to dependency, p. 27). The book concluded that such evidence was sorely lacking, which was interpreted to mean that personality traits, as they had been traditionally conceptualized, do not exist. By extension, some people—perhaps many people—interpreted this to mean that per-sonality *itself* does not exist in a substantive way—that one's behavior is almost entirely attributable to situational forces.

It should go without saying that such conclusions were destructive to those who believed that personality actually figured prominently in the equation (e.g., some graduate programs in personality psychology closed their doors, and have not yet reopened). Although personality psychology long ago reasserted and solidified its foundation (Kenrick & Funder, 1988), psychologists are still, nearly 40 years after Mischel's book, dis-cussing the dramatic decline and "comeback" of personality psychology (Swann & Seyle, 2005). In retrospect, it is clear that a major contributing factor to the temporary diminishment of personality psychology was the lack of behavioral research that could be used to rebut Mischel's asser-tions. That is, there was a dearth of well-implemented studies that included a sufficient range of social behaviors; thus, personality psy-chology was left exposed (fairly or unfairly, Block, 1977) to this assault with very little behavioral data to provide cover. Perhaps if more high-quality data had been available, personality psychology would never have suffered this setback and faced a struggle to re-emerge. Fortunately, after Mischel's book, personality researchers did begin collecting more behavioral data (e.g., Asendorpf, Banse & Mücke, 2002; Borkenau, Riemann, Angleitner, & Spinath, 2001; Funder & Colvin, 1991; Furr & Funder, 2004), but such work remains relatively rare.

In sum, the most general and powerful benefit of behavioral data is that it allows psychological scientists to speak of behavior with empirical conviction. Without such data, our ability to claim status as a science of behavior (in a broad, coherent, and generalizable sense) is weakened. For reasons outlined above, the field has been reluctant to collect good, wide-ranging behavioral data; however, we believe that greater familiarity with basic issues in direct behavioral observation can improve the situation. At the heart of any direct behavioral observation research is the coding system—the behaviors to be observed and the method of observing and scoring them.

Researchers willing to pursue this task face several important considerations. The next section describes key issues in planning, creating, or choosing a behavioral coding system. Our description reflects issues we have found compelling in the context of personality and social psychology, but we suspect that they apply to many potential applications of direct behavioral coding. Other sources provide additional perspectives on behavioral observation across psychology (e.g., Bakeman, 2000; Bakeman & Gottman, 1997; Margolin et al., 1998; Thompson, Symons, & Felce, 2000). In addition, Furr and Funder (2007) outline additional considerations in the implementation and evaluation of direct behavioral observations.

PLANNING, CREATING, OR CHOOSING A BEHAVIORAL CODING SYSTEM

Researchers must consider several important issues in planning a coding system for direct behavioral observation. Again, whether a new coding system will be created or an existing system will be chosen and adapted, there are at least three key sets of planning-related considerations (see Table 10.1).

Observational Context

One key consideration in planning a behavioral coding system is the context within which it will be used (Rosenblum, 1978). This consideration has at least two facets. First, observations might be made in a lab

Table 10.1. Considerations in Design of the Revised Riverside Behavioral Q-Sort

Considerations in Planning the Design or Selection of a Behavioral Coding System	RBQ-3.0
Contextual considerations	
In-lab or out-of-lab	Either
Specific or general situations	General
Behavioral considerations	
Behavioral domain – narrow or broad	Broad
Level of analysis – micro or macro	In-between
Amount of psychological interpretation	Moderate
Temporal considerations	
Sequential or global	Global[*]

[*] The RBQ-R has been used in a global or nonsequential manner to date; however, it could be used in sequential analysis as well.

setting or in a more "real-world" context. Lab settings afford greater control for the researcher in terms of when the behavior in question (or the observation of it) is meant to begin and end, the number of observers involved, the physical location of observers or recording devices, the physical layout of the observational area, the number of participants observed at a given time, and so on. In contrast, field settings afford much less control than in-lab settings, but they may offer greater ecological representativeness.

For example, the Electronically Activated Recorder (EAR) is a relatively new technological development used to capture real-world verbal behavior (Mehl & Pennebaker, 2003). The EAR is an unobtrusive digital recording device worn by participants, and it records the sounds in the participant's environment, including whatever they might be saying or hearing. In one study, Mehl and Pennebaker (2003) coded each segment of sound recorded by a participant's EAR, categorizing the information in terms of the interaction, activity, and location. Results indicated, among other things, that "people's everyday lives are not only coherent from the agent's perspective but also show a high degree of consistency from an outsider's perspective" (p. 867). That is, the EAR method provided important real-world confirmation of previous findings of personality stability—findings that had previously been obtained via methods more reliant on participants' self-report.

A second contextual consideration is situational specificity versus generality of the coding system. For some purposes, a coding system needs to be applicable only to a narrow range of situations, perhaps even only a single, specific context, and so only a few, specific behaviors might be assessed. For other purposes, a coding system might need to be applicable across a wide range of situations; in such cases, researchers might examine a variety of behaviors potentially applicable across a range of situations.

Behaviors in the Coding System

When designing, choosing, or adapting a new coding system, researchers face important choices about the nature of the behaviors contained therein. A key decision is the behavioral domains to include. Naturally, this decision should arise from theory and from the researchers' purposes. Some coding systems might focus on a single behavioral domain with specific relevance to a particular research question. For example, Asendorpf, Banse, and Mücke (2002) studied behavioral manifestations of shyness, videotaping participants engaged in activities intended to induce shyness. After watching the videotapes, observers coded six behaviors hypothesized as manifestations of shyness (e.g., speech duration, gaze aversion). Such domain-focused coding systems include a few specific behaviors with direct theoretical relevance. Others could be more wide ranging, reflecting many domains of behavior. Of course, coding systems that include many behaviors require more time and effort from observers than do more focused ones; however, such wide-ranging systems provide a wealth of information with potential relevance for many domains of psychology (e.g., Furr & Funder, 1998; 2004).

Along with the behavioral domains covered by a coding system, a second important issue is the level of abstraction of the behaviors coded. At a microanalytic level, behaviors are defined in very narrow—sometimes simple physical—terms. For example, the Facial Action Coding System (FACS; Ekman, Friesen, & Hager, 2002) is the standard coding system for facial displays of emotion (Rosenberg, 1997). The FACS and similar microanalytic systems include highly specific physical behaviors such as eyeblinks, eyewinks, and the amount of "backward lean" (Ekman et al., 2002; Ellgring, 1989; Kalbaugh & Haviland, 1994). At the other end of the spectrum, some behavioral coding strategies are more macroanalytic. For example, some behavioral research has examined broad behavioral styles such as "managerial-autocratic," "blunt-aggressive," or "cold and socially avoidant" (e.g., Alden & Phillips, 1990; Hokanson, Lowenstein, Hedeen, & Howes, 1986).

Bakeman and Gottman (1997) recommend a coding system at a level of analysis that is slightly more molecular or microanalytic than the level at which the research questions are articulated. They suggest that relatively molecular behaviors can be aggregated into more molar or macroanalytic behavioral categories, but not vice versa (pp. 24–26). This logic is appealing, but researchers should consider such behavioral aggregations carefully—items in a coding system may appear to share meaning with each other, but an item's meaning may shift from one social context to another. Consider a potential behavioral item such as "Competes with others"; the psychological implication of competitiveness observed in a game-playing interaction could be quite different from competitiveness in a typical "getting acquainted" interaction. Given the potentially shifting meaning of competitiveness, with which items should it be aggregated? The answer to this question may vary consequentially, both conceptually and empirically. Thus, aggregation could produce behavioral composites without coherence or psychological meaning across situations, compromising researchers' ability to generalize across situations and/or studies. Although item aggregation might have some psychometric and statistical benefits (e.g., potentially increasing reliability), it may discard information of potential psychological importance and create new psychometric problems (e.g., lack of factorial invariance across situations). Researchers interested in the possibility of aggregating behavioral items might be well advised to analyze data at the item level before aggregating. This allows evaluation of potential lost psychological meaning arising from aggregation.

A coding system's level of abstraction is linked closely to the amount of psychological inference required by coders. In some coding systems, observers make minimal inferences regarding the meaning of participants' behavior. For example, microanalytic systems require no inference about the psychological meaning of an eyeblink, eyewink, or backward lean. Although such codings may be subjective in terms of whether the blink, wink, or lean actually occurred, they do not require coders to interpret the psychological implications of the events—coders need not decide whether the events convey friendliness, nervousness, coquettishness, competitiveness, or simply a sneeze. In contrast, other coding strategies require a great deal of psychological inference. For example, a more macroanalytic rating of behavioral styles such as "managerial-autocratic," "blunt-aggressive," or "cold and socially avoidant" requires coders to make highly inferential judgments of the general psychological quality of a participant's behavior. The "level of inference" issue has been recognized in previous discussions of behavioral observation—Cairns and Green (1979) distinguish between behavioral observations (recording of actual activities) and behavioral ratings (social judgments that observers make, regarding the target's standing on a psychological dimension), and Bakeman and Gottman (1997) distinguish physical and social behaviors (pp. 17–22).

Thus, researchers face a trade-off in choosing appropriate levels of abstraction and inference within a coding system. On one hand, a

physically oriented coding system might require less psychological inference on the part of the coders; on the other hand, the data derived from
such a system might produce results with ambiguous psychological
meaning, or none at all. In contrast, a coding system that is based partly
on reliable, consensual social inferences might lead more directly to
interesting and important psychological implications.

Temporal Units in the Coding System

The temporal units to be coded are a third issue to be addressed in
planning or choosing a behavioral coding system. Specifically, researchers
must consider how the flow of a participant's observed behavior will be
segmented during the coding process, if at all.

Some coding systems are used sequentially, parsing the moment-by-
moment flow of behavior into segments. Within each segment of the
behavioral sequence, observers use the behavioral coding system to
describe the target participant's behavior during that segment.
Segments can be defined in several ways, including event sequential,
state sequential, timed event sequences, and interval sequences
(Bakeman, 2000). Perhaps most well-known in this form of behavioral
coding is Gottman's work with married couples. For example, Gottman,
Markman, and Notarius (1977) were interested in "the marital dyad as an
interacting system" (p. 463), observing husbands and wives while discussing marital problems. To capture the interactive and reciprocal
nature of the behavioral flow of a marital conversation, Gottman and
his colleagues parsed each marital conversation into a sequence of behavioral units, each of which was coded in terms of several verbal/content
and nonverbal/affect codes. These codes were then examined sequentially, revealing patterns of behavior as they unfolded during marital
conversation. Results revealed, for example, that "unsatisfied" couples
showed a more maladaptive sequence of behavior than did satisfied
couples.

Whereas some coding systems are used sequentially, others are used
in a nonsequential or temporally global manner. That is, behavioral codes
are derived to characterize the entirety of a person's behavior during the
period of observation. For example, Furr and Funder (1998) asked coders
to observe videotapes of participants in several 5-minute dyadic interactions with an opposite-sex stranger. For each participant, coders watched
an entire 5-minute interaction and rated the degree to which the participant generally exhibited 64 specific behaviors during the interaction.
That is, rather than recording a participant's talkativeness (or timidity
or degree of smiling, etc.) during specific segments of the interaction,

coders described the participant's overall level of talkativeness (and timidity, etc) across the entire interaction. Such data produced interesting results, revealing, for example, that women self-reporting a negative view of themselves tended to express insecurity, irritation, and feelings of victimization during their interactions with a male stranger.

In planning the temporal units for a coding system, researchers face yet another trade-off. A highly segmented, sequential approach is extremely demanding in terms of time and energy, whereas a more global approach is somewhat less demanding. However, some have argued that a sequential approach reveals "process" more effectively than a global approach, in terms of "behavior unfolding in time" (Bakeman, 2000, p. 140). Although it is true that a sequential approach reveals the unfolding of an interpersonal process within the context of a single interaction or period of observation, a global approach can also provide insight into interpersonal processes, albeit at a more macro level. For example, Furr and Funder's (1998) research included not only participants' self-reported personality judgments, but also behavioral observations of those participants, behavioral observations of the participants' interaction partners, and "informant-report" personality ratings of the participants provided by their close acquaintances. The overall pattern of results, including the global behavioral observations, implied that a negative self-perception (i.e., "personal negativity") manifests itself quickly in maladaptive behavioral style, eliciting negative behavioral responses from interaction partners, and ultimately producing a negative social reputation. Thus, this research provides potential insight into an interpersonal process transcending a single interaction.

In sum, as with all decisions regarding the design or selection of a behavioral coding system, the decision regarding the appropriate temporal unit of analysis should rest on a blend of conceptual and practical considerations. Certainly, researchers should consider the temporal orientation reflecting their theoretical interests; if they are interested in understanding the moment-by-moment process through which behavior emerges, then a sequential approach may be appropriate. However, researchers should also consider carefully the significant investment of time and energy required by such approaches. And indeed, perhaps the first issue a researcher should consider is whether to go through the effort of developing an entirely new coding system or to simply use/adapt an existing system.

UNDERWEAR: NEW OR USED?

Some might plunge headlong into the process of developing a new system for coding behavioral observations. Fortunately, such effort might not be necessary; although few coding systems are available, researchers might discover one that fits their needs. Perhaps more likely, researchers might find a system that, with a bit of revision, works quite well. Indeed, time spent searching for existing coding systems might more than pay for itself by eliminating the extensive effort required to develop an entirely new coding system.

In their extensive discussion of behavioral observation, Bakeman and Gottman assert that using someone else's coding system might initially feel like "wearing someone else's underwear" (1997, p. 15). Frankly, we do not know if this is true (none of us have tried to use someone else's coding system). That said, we suspect that a little alteration might produce a fairly comfortable fit.

In that spirit, we invite researchers to consider the Revised Riverside Behavioral Q-Sort (RBQ-3.0) as a tool, process, and even software for conducting direct behavioral observations. The RBQ-3.0 is a revision of a behavioral coding system described by Funder, Furr, and Colvin (2000; see also Funder & Colvin, 1991), meant to include a wide range of behaviors applicable to many personality characteristics and many social situations.[1]

Researchers are invited to adapt the RBQ-3.0 to suit their needs, but any adaptation represents a trade-off. On one hand, adaptation allows researchers to tailor the RBQ-3.0 items and methods to fit closely their particular interests and theories; on the other hand, close continuity with the RBQ-3.0 allows coherence across studies. The field may benefit from a coherent accumulation of empirical findings related to a common core of social behaviors, and we believe that the RBQ-3.0 is a strong candidate for that core. Thus, we recommend that researchers use and expand the RBQ-3.0 to fit their needs, but that they maintain the core set of RBQ-3.0 items as completely as possible.

THE REVISED RIVERSIDE BEHAVIORAL Q-SORT

The Riverside Behavioral Q-Sort was originally derived—somewhat indirectly— from the items of the California Adult Q-Set (CAQ; Bem & Funder, 1978; Block, 1961), a well-validated and widely used measure of personality. For each personality item, we sought to write items

---

[1] Funder, Furr, and Colvin (2000) formally presented the 64-item second version of the Riverside Behavioral Q-sort, but a 62-item initial version had been used in earlier research (e.g., Funder & Colvin, 1991). Thus, the current chapter presents the third and most widely applicable version of the RBQ.

describing one or more behaviors that might be relevant. For example, the first item in the CAQ read "is critical, skeptical, not easily impressed." The associated RBQ-3.0 items reads "expresses criticism (of anybody or anything)." Because behavior is multiply determined (Funder, 1991), some behavioral items pertain to more than one CAQ item, and thus the RBQ-3.0 is shorter in length than the (100-item) original. Advantages to measuring constructs through use of a Q-sort tool are that (a) it reduces the difficulty of response biases (participants, being forced to categorize cards in a manner that results in a quasinormal distribution, are not free to overuse any particular point on the scale) and (b) it encourages the sorter to consider whether one item is more descriptive of a person than another item (a within-person comparison across all behaviors, in this case), which may be importantly different than considering whether an item is more descriptive of one individual than another individual (a between-person comparison for each behavior).

Other, more microlevel measurements of social behavior (e.g., counting the number of smiles or noting foot-tapping behavior) seem less informative in that they do little to illuminate the underlying psychological processes that cause them, and because they—by themselves—may be inconsistent across situations (Funder et al., 2000). An advantage of the RBQ-3.0 is that it assesses behaviors that can be displayed by a number of microlevel manifestations, being itself a tool aimed at a mid-level of analysis (see Table 10.1). RBQ-3.0 item 37 for example, "Is expressive in face, voice, and gesture," might be used by an observer to indicate any number of smiles or foot taps but, being superordinate to these types of behaviors, is less likely to miss the connection between any particular tic or twitch and its psychological origin.

One problem with the earlier item set (Funder & Colvin, 1991; Funder et al., 2000), however, is that it was constructed for the purposes of examining social behavior in the context of videotaped, experimental sessions, often dyadic or triadic in nature. It has been successful in this capacity, but when aiming to conduct a direct observation of behavior outside of such a setting, the original RBQ becomes less than ideal. Partly, this is due to the presence of items that are much less salient in the field (e.g., an item in the original set was "Expresses awareness of being on camera and/or in an experiment"), and partly due to the absence of items that might be used to describe behavior outside of this environment. It is for this purpose that the recent revision was undertaken.

In order to move the behaviors from the original RBQ outside of the narrow setting for which they were constructed, each item was examined carefully in relation to its potential utility in describing the social behaviors of people *in their everyday lives*. There were three possible outcomes:

1. The item was fine as it was, capturing a behavior that might occur as well outside a laboratory as within one,
2. The item captured the essence of such a behavior, but needed modification of its wording in order to be more broadly applicable, or
3. The item was too narrow in nature and needed to be deleted entirely.

More than half of the original 64 items were deemed usable as written; 27 items were altered to be more flexible in their usability, and only 1 item (the one relating to being on camera) was deleted entirely. Four completely new items were added, bringing the number of items in the newly modified RBQ-3.0 up to 67. The complete item set of the RBQ-3.0 is presented in the Appendix.

As mentioned earlier, one of the largest impediments to direct behavioral observation has been that it required a great deal of time and effort. In response and as a further inducement to consider using the RBQ-3.0, we offer an avenue by which it (or another Q-sort-style coding scheme of the researcher's own devising) might be used in a quicker and more efficient manner. Benefits of the Q-sort method aside, it can by its very nature be a cognitively taxing process. A rater needs to be able to think about and remember which items have been used and where they have been placed, not to mention the general messiness of having small pieces of paper arrayed in front of the user on a (necessarily large) tabletop and the potential for error in recording the final result.

In an attempt to alleviate these difficulties, a computer program was developed to allow the RBQ-3.0—and other Q-sorts—to be completed and recorded on a computer.[2] The Riverside Accuracy Project's Q-Sorter Program runs on Windows XP, and it is currently available online at *http://rap.ucr.edu/qsorter* as freeware. The program retains the same basic procedure as the classic Q-sort (items are first sorted into three piles—characteristic, uncharacteristic, and neutral—and from there into the chosen distribution) but now operates with the convenience of a drag-and-drop interface that allows the sorter to move items from their initial piles into the appropriate category or from one category to another (see Figure 10.1). The program supports certain useful safety features, such as warning flags that indicate when the number of items in a category

---

[2] Our thanks to Matthew Fast for his effort and the outstanding results.

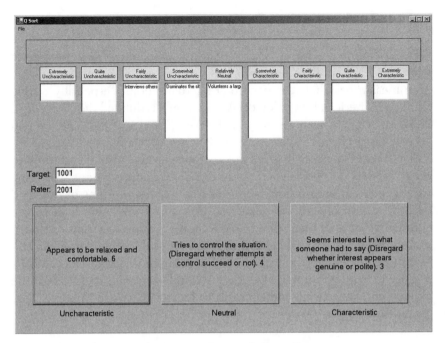

Figure 10.1. The Riverside Accuracy Project Q-Sorter Program.

exceeds its prescribed maximum and the automatic blocking of saving a sort that is improperly formatted or incomplete. Data from the Q-sorter program are saved directly into an easy-to-use text file that appends each additional sort into the same .txt file.

Perhaps the best feature of the program, however, is simply its adaptability. While the deck files for the three currently active Q-sorts (the original CAQ, the RBQ-3.0, and the newly developed Situational Q-Sort or RSQ) are available for download on the RAP website, the program is flexible with respect to the number of items in the Q-deck, the content of the items, the number of categories in the distribution, and the shape of distribution. Thus, anyone with a rudimentary understanding of how the program works could easily alter any existing deck to suit their needs or create and load a Q-deck of their own. Indeed, while the items of the RBQ-3.0 were based upon one particular foundation (the CAQ) for a particular purpose (to see what behaviors are associated with the CAQ personality characteristics), other items with other bases and intended for other purposes could and should be written. The Q-sorter program was designed partially with the goal in mind of encouraging the use of Q-methodology in general, and to make the use of such instruments more user friendly.

CONCLUSION

For a discipline ostensibly dedicated to understanding "why people do what they do," modern psychological science seems to have spent little time measuring what it is people are actually doing, especially during what the American Psychological Association has dubbed the "Decade of Behavior." It has been asserted in the past (Funder, 2000) and we will entreat researchers here again: there is a need for a body of descriptive research within personality that links personality traits and dispositions to their real-world consequences and behavioral manifestations. Not only would such research solidify the fundamental assumptions of our field (that who you are affects what you do), but it also will lead to the cumulative development of a foundation for a more coherent organization of meaningful social behaviors. Without such a foundation, we risk finding ourselves in the place of the scientists in the Harris cartoon. While it's nice to believe that miracles occur, it is indeed our business to be more explicit in "step two," metaphorically located between "people" and "what they do."

APPENDIX

Items of the RBQ-3.0

1. Interviews others (if present). (E.g., asks a series of questions).
2. Volunteers a large amount of information about self.
3. Seems interested in what someone had to say. (Disregard whether interest appears "genuine" or "polite.")
4. Tries to control the situation. (Disregard whether attempts at control succeed or not.)
5. Dominates the situation. (Disregard intention, e.g., if P dominates the situation "by default" because other(s) present do very little, this item should receive high placement.)
6. Appears to be relaxed and comfortable.
7. Exhibits social skills. (E.g., does things to make other(s) comfortable, keeps conversation moving, entertains or charms other(s).)
8. Is reserved and unexpressive. (E.g., expresses little affect; acts in a stiff, formal manner.)
9. Laughs frequently. (Disregard whether laughter appears to be "nervous" or "genuine.")
10. Smiles frequently.
11. Is physically animated; moves around a great deal.
12. Seems to like other(s) present. (E.g., would probably like to be friends with them.)

13. Exhibits an awkward interpersonal style. (E.g., seems to have difficulty knowing what to say, mumbles, fails to respond to other(s)' conversational advances.)
14. Compares self to other(s) (whether others are present or not).
15. Shows high enthusiasm and a high energy level.
16. Shows a wide range of interests. (E.g., talks about many topics.)
17. Talks at rather than with other(s). (E.g., conducts a monologue, ignores what others say.)
18. Expresses agreement frequently. (High placement implies agreement is expressed unusually often, e.g., in response to each and every statement made. Low placement implies unusual lack of expression of agreement.)
19. Expresses criticism (of anybody or anything). (Low placement implies expresses praise.)
20. Is talkative (as observed in this situation).
21. Expresses insecurity. (E.g., seems touchy or overly sensitive.)
22. Show physical signs of tension or anxiety. (E.g., fidgets nervously, voice wavers.) (Lack of signs of anxiety = middle placement; low placement = lack of signs under circumstances where you would expect to see them.)
23. Exhibits a high degree of intelligence. (NB: At issue is what is displayed in the interaction not what may or may not be latent. Thus, give this item high placement only if P actually says or does something of high intelligence. Low placement implies exhibition of low intelligence; medium placement = no information one way or the other.)
24. Expresses sympathy (to anyone, i.e., including conversational references). (Low placement implies unusual lack of sympathy.)
25. Initiates humor.
26. Seeks reassurance. (E.g., asks for agreement, fishes for praise.)
27. Exhibits condescending behavior. (E.g., acts as if self is superior to others [present, or otherwise].) (Low placement implies acting inferior.)
28. Seems likable (to other(s) present).
29. Seeks advice.
30. Appears to regard self as physically attractive.
31. Acts irritated.
32. Expresses warmth (to anyone, e.g., include any references to "my close friend," etc).
33. Tries to undermine, sabotage or obstruct.
34. Expresses hostility (no matter toward whom or what).
35. Is unusual or unconventional in appearance.
36. Behaves in a fearful or timid manner.
37. Is expressive in face, voice, or gestures.
38. Expresses interest in fantasy or daydreams. (Low placement only if such interest is explicitly disavowed.)
39. Expresses guilt (about anything).

40. Keeps other(s) at a distance; avoids development of any sort of interpersonal relationship. (Low placement implies behavior to get close to other(s).)
41. Shows interest in intellectual or cognitive matters. (E.g., by discussing an intellectual idea in detail or with enthusiasm.)
42. Seems to enjoy the situation.
43. Says or does something interesting.
44. Says negative things about self. (E.g., is self-critical; expresses feelings of inadequacy.)
45. Displays ambition. (E.g., passionate discussion of career plans, course grades, opportunities to make money.)
46. Blames others (for anything).
47. Expresses self-pity or feelings of victimization.
48. Expresses sexual interest. (E.g., acts attracted to someone present; expresses interest in dating or sexual matters in general.)
49. Behaves in a cheerful manner.
50. Gives up when faced with obstacles. (Low placement implies unusual persistence.)
51. Behaves in a stereotypically masculine/feminine style or manner. (Apply the usual stereotypes appropriate to the P's sex. Low placement implies behavior stereotypical of the opposite sex.)
52. Offers advice.
53. Speaks fluently and expresses ideas well.
54. Emphasizes accomplishments of self, family, or acquaintances. (Low placement = emphasizes failures of these individuals.)
55. Behaves in a competitive manner. (Low placement implies cooperative behavior.)
56. Speaks in a loud voice.
57. Speaks sarcastically. (E.g., says things (s)he does not mean; makes facetious comments that are not necessarily funny.)
58. Makes or approaches physical contact with other(s). (Of any sort, including sitting unusually close without touching.) (Low placement implies unusual avoidance of physical contact, such as large interpersonal distance).
59. Engages in constant eye contact with someone. (Low placement implies unusual lack of eye contact.)
60. Seems detached from the situation.
61. Speaks quickly. (Low placement = speaks slowly.)
62. Acts playful.
63. Other(s) seek advice from P.
64. Concentrates on/works hard at a task. (Low placement implies loafing.)
65. Engages in physical activity. (E.g., works up a sweat.) (Low placement = almost completely sedentary.)
66. Acts in a self-indulgent manner. (E.g., spending, eating, or drinking.) (Low placement implies self-denial.)
67. Exhibits physical discomfort or pain. (High placement = in excess of what seems proportionate; low placement implies lack of these signs where expected.)

REFERENCES

Alden, L. E., & Phillips, N. (1990). An interpersonal analysis of social anxiety and depression. *Cognitive Therapy and Research, 14*, 499–513.

Asendorpf, J. B., Banse, R., & Mücke, D. (2002). Double dissociation between implicit and explicit personality self-concept: The case of shy behavior. *Journal of Personality and Social Psychology, 83*, 380–393.

Bakeman, R. (2000). Behavioral observations and coding. In H. T. Reis & C. K. Judd (Eds.), *Handbook of research methods in social psychology* (pp. 138–159). New York: Cambridge University Press.

Bakeman, R., & Gottman, J. M. (1997). *Observing interaction: An introduction to sequential analysis* (2nd ed). New York: Cambridge University Press

Baumeister, R. F., Vohs, K. D., & Funder, D. C. (2007). Psychology as the science of self-reports and finger movements. Whatever happened to actual behavior? *Perspectives on Psychological Science, 2*, 396–403.

Bem, D. J., & Funder, D. C. (1978). Predicting more of the people more of the time: Assessing the personality of situations. *Psychological Review, 85*, 485–500

Block, J. (1977). Advancing the psychology of personality: Paradigmatic shift or improving the quality of research? In D. Magnusson & N. S. Endler (Eds.), *Psychology at the crossroads: Current issues in interactional psychology* (pp. 37–63). Hillsdale, NJ: Erlbaum.

Borkenau, P., Riemann, R., Angleitner, A., & Spinath, F.M. (2001). Genetic and environmental influences on observed personality: Evidence from the German observational study of adult twins. *Journal of Personality and Social Psychology, 80*, 655–668.

Cairns, R. B., & Green, J. A. (1979). How to assess personality and social patterns: Observations or ratings? In R. B. Cairns (Ed.), *The analysis of social interactions: Methods, issues and illustrations* (pp. 209–226). Hillsdale, NJ: Erlbaum.

Ekman, P., Friesen, W.V., & Hager, J. C. (2002). *The facial action coding system* (2nd ed.). Salt Lake City, UT: Research Nexus eBook. Retrieved from http://face-and-emotion.com/dataface/facs/description.jsp

Ellgring, H. (1989). *Nonverbal communication in depression.* Cambridge: Cambridge University Press.

Funder, D. C. (2000). Personality. *Annual Review of Psychology, 52*, 197–221.

Funder, D.C. (2007). *The personality puzzle* (4th ed.). New York: Norton.

Funder, D. C., & Colvin, C. R. (1991). Explorations in behavioral consistency: Properties of persons, situations, and behaviors. *Journal of Personality and Social Psychology, 60*, 773–794.

Funder, D. C., Furr, R. M., & Colvin, C. R. (2000). The Riverside behavioral q-sort: A tool for the description of social behavior. *Journal of Personality, 68*, 451–489.

Furr, R. M. (In press a). Personality psychology as a truly behavioral science. *European Journal of Personality.*

Furr, R. M. (In press b). The study of behavior in personality psychology: Meaning, importance, and measurement. *European Journal of Personality.*

Furr, R. M., & Funder, D. C. (1998). A multi-modal analysis of personal negativity. *Journal of Personality and Social Psychology, 74*, 1580–1591.

Furr, R. M., & Funder, D. C. (2004). Situational similarity and behavioral consistency: Subjective, objective, variable-centered, and person-centered approaches. *Journal of Research in Personality, 38*, 421–447.

Furr, R. M., & Funder, D. C. (2007). Behavioral observation. In R. Robins, C. Fraley, & R. Krueger (Eds). *Handbook of research methods in personality psychology* (pp. 273–291). New York: Guilford Press.

Gottman, J. M., Markman, H., & Notarius, C. (1977). The topography of marital conflict: A sequential analysis of verbal and nonverbal behavior. *Journal of Marriage and the Family, 39*, 461–477.

Hokanson, J. E., Lowenstein, D. A., Hedeen, C., & Howes, M. J. (1986). Dysphoric college students and roommates: A study of social behaviors over a three-month period. *Personality and Social Psychology Bulletin, 12*, 311–324.

Kalbaugh, P. E., & Haviland, J. M. (1994). Nonverbal communication between parents and adolescents: A study of approach and avoidance behaviors. *Journal of Nonverbal Behavior, 18*, 91–113.

Kenrick, D. T., & Funder, D. C. (1988). Profiting from controversy: Lessons from the person-situation debate. *American Psychologist, 43*, 23–34.

Margolin, G., Oliver, P. H., Gordis, E. B., O'Hearn, H. G., Medina, A. M., Ghosh, C. M., & Morland, L. (1998). The nuts and bolts of behavioral observation of marital and family interaction. *Clinical Child and Family Psychology Review, 4*, 195–213.

Mehl, M. R., & Pennebaker, J. W. (2003). The sounds of social life: A psychometric analysis of students' daily social environments and natural conversations. *Journal of Personality and Social Psychology, 84*, 857–870.

Mischel, W. (1968) *Personality and assessment*. New York: Wiley.

Myers, D. G. (2007). *Psychology* (8th ed.). New York: Worth.

Rosenberg, E. L (1997). Introduction: The study of spontaneous facial expressions in psychology. In P. Ekman & E. L. Rosenberg (Eds.), *What the face reveals: Basic and applied studies of spontaneous expression using the Facial Action Coding System (FACS)* (pp. 3–17). London: Oxford University Press.

Rosenblum, L. (1978). The creation of a behavioral taxonomy. In G. P. Sackett (Ed.), *Observing behavior (Vol. 2): Data collection and analysis methods* (pp. 15–24). Baltimore: University Park Press.

Swann, W. B., & Seyle, C. (2005). Personality psychology's comeback and its emerging symbiosis with social psychology. *Personality and Social Psychology Bulletin, 31*, 155–165.

Thompson, T., Symons, F. J., & Felce, D. (2000). Principles of behavioral observation: Assumptions and strategies. In T. Thompson, D. Felce, & F. J. Symons (Eds.) *Behavioral observation: Technology and applications in developmental disabilities* (pp. 3–16). Baltimore, MD: Brookes.

11 Personality, Demographics, and Self-Reported Behavioral Acts: The Development of Avocational Interest Scales from Estimates of the Amount of Time Spent in Interest-Related Activities

Lewis R. Goldberg

HOW DOES ONE STUDY "BEHAVIOR"?

Periodically, social psychologists suffer troublesome and often baffling spasms of guilt and self-flagellation. One of their most common laments is not studying real "behavior," at least recently as compared with the good old days (e.g., Baumeister, Vohs, & Funder, 2007).

But, all of us "behave" all day, every day—so what? Behavior must be transduced through some medium before measurement occurs and the resulting measures can then be used for scientific purposes. Even the classic bar presses of rats and pigeons had to be mechanically transformed into graphical recordings, which then had to be interpreted by human observers.

Although some of the media through which behavior can be transduced include various kinds of mechanical apparatus (e.g., activity counts, dial settings), by far the most common medium for converting behaviors to measures is the human brain. Behavioral observers are used for this purpose in various contexts, including (a) short-term versus long-term periods of behavioral observation, (b) in experimental or laboratory settings versus in more normal life settings, and (c) observing the behaviors of others directly or from audio or video transcriptions. Each of these modes of transduction has advantages and disadvantages, many of which are discussed in methodological textbooks. In all cases, however, humans are used at some stage of the measurement process to filter, schematize, organize, classify, conceptualize, and/or categorize their observations into a format suitable for that context.

USING SELF-REPORTS AS TRANSDUCERS OF BEHAVIORAL ACTS

There are some kinds of research contexts when the most accurate observer of a person's thoughts, feelings, or behaviors is the person himself or herself (e.g., Buss & Craik, 1983). At the most basic level, one can characterize those contexts as ones when (a) there is nothing for the self-observer to gain by *not* being accurate; and (b) the task is relatively easy for most people. In addition, people are likely to be more accurate (1) when recalling the past, rather than predicting the future; (2) when asked about real past events, not hypothetical scenarios; (3) when the questions are short and clearly stated; and (4) when the response options fit the questions.

Some caveats are in order: First of all, it is important to realize that we may not know all the reasons *why* we behave as we do (e.g., Nisbett & Wilson, 1977). Moreover, we certainly differ in our ability to recall events, and in the kind of events that we recall most accurately. Indeed, we may sometimes forget important lifetime events, perhaps even highly traumatic events (Freyd, 1996; Gleaves, Smith, Butler, & Spiegel, 2004). But, all in all, we are probably pretty accurate recorders of our past activities, at least to differentiate between those things that we did a lot and those that we did rarely if at all.

A BOTTOM-UP APPROACH TO DEVELOPING AGGREGATES OF SELF-REPORTED BEHAVIORAL ACTS: FROM 400 ACTS TO 60 ACT CLUSTERS

To the extent that individuals are reasonably accurate reporters of the relative frequency with which they have engaged in various behavioral acts, a survey of their act frequencies in a wide-ranging array of such activities should provide the basic data from which to assess important individual differences in lifestyle. Such patterns of lifestyle differences, then, might ultimately be useful as criteria for assessing the comparative validity of measures of personality traits.

As a first step in that direction, we examined the large set of activities included in the research surveys developed by the National Merit Scholarship Corporation and administered to college student samples during 1962–1963 (Loehlin & Nichols, 1976). All of those acts that involved school-related behaviors (e.g., went to sleep in class) were either omitted or rewritten so that the resulting activity pool would be potentially relevant to an adult community sample, most of whom would no longer be associated with any educational institution. In addition, we employed focus groups of adults to examine preliminary act lists and provide additional examples of common behavioral acts that had not yet been included. Through an iterative series of such forums, we settled on a set of 400 activities, some examples of which are included in Table 11.1.

In the Fall of 1997, the 400 act descriptions were included in a longer questionnaire that was administered by mail to approximately 800 members of the Eugene-Springfield Community Sample (ESCS). The ESCS had been recruited in 1993 from lists of homeowners in this Oregon community, all of whom had agreed to complete one or two questionnaires per year for at least 5 to 10 years. ESCS participants are paid for each completed survey they return to Oregon Research Institute; they are identified only by a precoded number, and they are always requested to not include their names on their questionnaires. As of 2008, the ESCS

Table 11.1. Some Examples of the 400 Activities

Played chess.	Had a hangover.	Read the newspaper.
Shot a gun.	Cried.	Had my back rubbed.
Lied about my age.	Consulted a lawyer.	Played with a child.
Polished my toenails.	Walked on a beach.	Went to a night club.
Sang in a bath or shower.	Planned a party.	Chewed gum.
	Skipped a meal.	Bought new clothes.
Gave money to a panhandler.	Read the Bible (or other holy book).	Slept more than 10 hours at a time.
Was late for work.		

Instructions and Response Options:

Here are things that people sometimes do. Please indicate HOW FREQUENTLY you have done each of them.

(1) NEVER in my life.
(2) Not in the past year.
(3) ONCE or TWICE in the past year.
(4) THREE or MORE times in the past year, but not more than 15 times.
(5) MORE THAN 15 TIMES in the past year.

Note: Adapted from Loehlin and Nichols (1976).

Table 11.2. Some Example Clusters (with an Example Item)

Alcohol and drug usage (Had a hangover).
Religious practices (Said grace before a meal).
Computer usage (Surfed the Internet).
Sports (Played golf).
Housekeeping chores (Washed dishes).
Physical exercise (Lifted weights).
Cultural event attendance (Visited a museum).
Travel and leisure activities (Rode in a taxi).
Gardening chores (Did yard work).
Summer activities (Went on a picnic).
Anger manifestations (Hit or slapped someone).
Friendliness manifestations (Made a new friend).
Literary pursuits (Read poetry).
Child-care activities (Played with a child).

participants have completed over 30 assessment measures, and the questionnaire containing the 400 act descriptions was the 14th in this sequence.

Based on a series of hierarchical cluster analyses of the intercorrelations across subjects of the frequency ratings to each of the 400 activity items, we settled on a preliminary set of 60 act clusters. These clusters ranged in size from 3 to 14 acts. Their mean item intercorrelations ranged from .15 to .60, and the coefficient alpha reliability estimates for each act cluster ranged from .40 to .90. The 14 clusters with the highest reliabilities are included in Table 11.2, along with an example activity in each cluster.

PREDICTING EACH OF THE 22 MOST RELIABLE ACT CLUSTERS FROM DEMOGRAPHIC AND PERSONALITY VARIABLES

The mean frequency across all of the acts within each cluster was calculated for each of the ESCS participants, and these activity cluster scores were correlated with their gender, age, and educational level. The gender correlations ranged up to .70 (Housekeeping chores: women reporting more). The age correlations ranged up to .50 (Anger manifestations: younger participants reporting more). The correlations with educational level ranged up to .45 (Cultural activities: the more highly educated participants reporting more).

Multiple correlations based on the three demographic indices ranged from .10 (Religious practices) to .75 (Housekeeping chores) and averaged about .40. When the most highly correlating single scale from virtually any of the broad bandwidth personality inventories (e.g., the NEO-PI-R) was added to each regression equation, the average multiple correlation increased to about .50. Adding the five most highly correlating personality scales from that inventory increased the mean multiple correlation to around .55.

In summary, then, unlike many criterion variables used in personality research, these self-reported act clusters tend to be highly associated with demographic indices. However, for most of the act clusters one or two personality measures can serve to increase their predictability beyond that provided by the demographic indices alone. Indeed, for some of these clusters the predictability from both demographic and personality measures appears to be almost as high as seems possible, given the reliabilities of the clusters and the personality scales.

USING ACT CLUSTERS AS ONE TYPE OF CRITERION FOR THE EVALUATION OF PERSONALITY MEASURES

In what is probably the most comprehensive comparative-validity study ever attempted, Grucza and Goldberg (2007) compared 11 multiscale personality inventories (e.g., the NEO-PI-R, CPI, 16PF, HPI, MPQ, TCI, JPI) as predictors of three types of criteria: (a) six of the most highly reliable act clusters of those described above; (b) five Big-Five assessments by two to three knowledgeable informants; and (c) six self-reported indicators of potential psychopathology. The six activity clusters were selected to include two that were rather undesirable (Drug use and Undependability), two that included quite desirable acts (Friendliness and Creativity), and two that were more middling in their desirability implications (Communication and Erudition). Findings from a series of analyses indicated that there was little difference in the predictability of the six act clusters, with mean cross-validities ranging only from .48 to .54.

And, remarkably, when averaged across the 17 criteria of all three types combined, there was little difference in the mean cross-validities among the 11 inventories, with the cross-validated multiple correlations ranging between .40 and .45. Seemingly, then, there is much in common at the core of most modern personality inventories, despite substantial differences in the ways that they are commercially marketed.

DEVELOPING MEASURES OF AVOCATIONAL INTERESTS AS INDEXED BY THE REPORTED AMOUNT OF TIME SPENT ENGAGING IN DIFFERENT TYPES OF INTEREST-RELATED ACTIVITIES

There are few, if any, public domain inventories measuring either avocational or vocational interests, yet both of these types of individual differences are likely to be quite useful as predictors of important human outcomes. To begin to correct this lacuna, we have now developed public domain measures of eight vocational orientations, which we propose as potential improvements over Holland's (1973) classic 6-domain RIASEC model. Using only 89 items, these 8 new scales have alpha reliabilities ranging from .80 to .90, averaging about .85. They are provided here in Appendix A. They were included in a questionnaire administered to the ESCS in the Fall of 2006.

We measure vocational interests by asking people to indicate how much they would *like* to engage in various activities and occupations if they had their lives to live over again, and if there were no constraints on their skills or training. That is a form of hypothetical scenario that is probably not conducive to optimal self-reporting accuracy, but vocational choices are determined by so many factors beyond one's interests that it makes sense to try to get at those interest patterns in such an "as-if" fashion.

Not so for avocational interests, which should be more directly linked to the frequency with which one engages in different types of interest-related activities. To test that conjecture, we have developed 33 avocational interest scales, each of which includes from 4 to 8 behavioral acts as items. There are 200 items in this new public-domain inventory, roughly 6 acts per scale.

In contrast to the 60 activity clusters developed from the 400 behavior acts—which were based on a bottom-up strategy—the avocational scales were developed using a top-down approach: We began with an analysis of potential categories of avocational interests, and then sought the specific activities that would be representative of each such interest domain.

The items included in each of these new scales are provided in Appendix B. The instructions and response options include: "Here are some things that people sometimes do. Please indicate how frequently you have done each of them, using the following scale: (1) Never in my life; (2) Not in the past year; (3) One or two times in the past year; (4) Three to ten times in the past year; (5) More than ten times in the past year." These activity items were administered to the ESCS in the fall of 2007.

As would be expected from the findings from our analyses of the first set of activity clusters, some of the relations between the avocational interest scales and demographic indices are quite high: Correlations with gender range up to .60 (Housekeeping chores, with women reporting more) and .55 (Fashion-related activities, again with women reporting more). Correlations with age range up to .55 (Food and eating, with younger persons reporting more) and .40 (Computing, with younger persons again reporting more). And, correlations with educational level range up to .40 (Cultural activities) and .35 (Political/Organizational acts), with more educated persons more likely to engage in such pursuits.

Because of the strong correlations between activity patterns and demographic indices, we had assumed that a substantial source of the internal consistency within the act clusters stems from demographic variance, and therefore that estimates of internal-consistency reliability would be substantially attenuated in demographically distinct subsamples (e.g., men versus women). One remarkable finding from this project is that such an assumption is incorrect: The internal-consistency reliabilities of the scales do not differ much between same-sex and pooled samples. For example, the coefficient alpha reliability of the 5-act Fashion scale is .78 in the pooled sample as compared to .75 and .79 in the female and male subsamples, respectively. For the 7-act Housekeeping scale, the coefficient is .63 in the pooled sample as compared to .60 and .67 in each of the two gender-separated subsamples. What this suggests is that although demographically different subsamples may differ in their activity patterns, this is not the source of the cohesion among activities of the same sort.

Obviously not all activity patterns are equally prevalent within the ESCS; indeed, mean differences among the act clusters are quite substantial. At one extreme are activities such as Reading, Housekeeping, Gardening, Computing, Understanding, Food-related, and Shopping, which many of the ESCS participants engage in frequently; at the other extreme are activities such as Automotive, Social Networking, Gambling, Creating, Collecting, Financial, and Romantic, which are engaged in relatively rarely in this adult community sample.

For the purposes of predicting important lifestyle differences, clusters that elicit a large range of individual differences may be far more useful than those that elicit relatively little variation among the ESCS participants. The highest-variance categories include Computing, Exercise, Religion, and Drinking, whereas the lowest-variance categories include Romance, Automotive, Green-related, and Political/organizational activities.

RELATIONS BETWEEN AVOCATIONAL INTEREST PATTERNS AND OTHER INDIVIDUAL DIFFERENCES

Because of the enormous amount of information available on each of the ESCS participants, it is possible to examine the correlations of both avocational and vocational interest patterns with a wide array of other types of individual differences. Although most of those findings are beyond the limited scope of this chapter, a few of them may be of interest to readers of this volume.

One such topic concerns the relations between avocational interest patterns and personality traits. Using Goldberg's (1992) 100-item Big-Five factor markers as measures of personality, we can examine the avocational interest correlates of self-reported personality factors. Overall, the correlations between measures of interest and personality are quite modest, certainly less substantial than the relations between interest patterns and demographic indices. Unsurprisingly, the highest interest correlates of Extraversion are Partying ($r = .25$) and Romance ($r = .20$). For Agreeableness, the highest correlates are Housekeeping (positively related) and Financial (negatively related), both with correlations about .20. For Conscientiousness, the highest correlate is Financial ($r = .15$), and for Emotional Stability it is Fashion ($r = -.20$). Finally, for Intellect/Imagination the correlations are more substantial: .40 for Creating, .30 for Culture, and around .25 for Self-Improvement, Understanding, and Being Alone.

NOW TO THE BOTTOM LINE: CAN AVOCATIONAL INTEREST PATTERNS ADD TO THE VALIDITY OF PREDICTIONS OF REPORTS BY KNOWLEDGEABLE INFORMANTS?

It is one thing to develop a new measure of some individual difference; it is another to establish its utility as a predictor of important human outcomes. Clearly vocational interest patterns have proven their worth over the years as predictors of job satisfaction and other work-related attitudes. But what about avocational interests? And specifically what about avocational interests as measured by self-reports of the relative frequency of individuals' engagement in various interest-related activities? Because there has been little previous research on the utility of such measures, it is important to demonstrate their incremental validity.

But what should we use as criteria? Probably the most difficult type of criterion is one that shares no method variance with the avocational interest measures and is not related in content in any sort of one-to-one manner. Of the three types of criteria used in the comparative-validity studies of Grucza and Goldberg (2007), one type (act frequency self-reports) shares both method and content overlap, whereas another type (self-reports of aspects of psychopathology) shares a reliance on self-reports. The third type of criteria, on the other hand, personality assessments by knowledgeable informants, would seem to be as distal a type of criterion as one could imagine.

Moreover, we know from past research that (a) assessments by knowledgeable informants are highly related to self-reports on the same or similar personality traits, and (b) self-reported activity frequencies are highly related to various demographic indices, such as gender, age, and educational level. As a consequence, it is far from obvious that any avocational interest scale scores could be incrementally associated with personality assessments by knowledgeable others, after controlling *both* for demographic variables and for self-reports on the same personality traits. Indeed, one might argue a priori that this would constitute an unusually challenging validity test.

Each of the participants in the ESCS had been asked to recruit the "three persons who know you best" to provide personality descriptions of that participant, to be mailed directly to Oregon Research Institute in return for an honorarium check. In a letter that the participants gave the informants, they were requested to be as candid as possible, and to refrain from sharing any of their assessments with the participants, who in turn received a bonus check if all three informants returned their completed forms within a specified period of time. Most participants were described by three informants, a few by two, and a very few by only one; the average of the ratings by the informants were used in our analyses.

The informants described the personalities of the ESCS participants using two separate sets of Big-Five factor markers: (a) The 44-item Big-Five Inventory (BFI) developed by Oliver John (e.g., John & Srivastava, 1999), and (b) the 40-item Big Five Mini-Markers (SMM) developed by Gerard Saucier (1994). Both inventories were augmented by two additional items tapping physical attractiveness, so the informant questionnaire included 88 items. A varimax rotation of six components derived from these 88 items, which is included as Table 5 in Grucza and Goldberg (2007), is as clean and clear a representation of the Big Five factor structure as can be found in the literature. Orthogonal factor scores on the five personality factors were used as criteria in the present analysis.

To examine the incremental validity of the avocational interest scales as predictors of informants' reports, each of the five orthogonal factor scores was used as the criterion in a hierarchical analysis in which at Step 1 the three demographic indices (gender, age, and educational level) were first entered in a multiple regression analysis, followed at Step 2 by the orthogonal factor scores derived from self-reports to Goldberg's (1992) 100 Big-Five factor markers, and then finally followed at Step 3 by the 33 avocational interest scales, entered in a stepwise fashion, but stopping when no further variable was significantly associated with the criterion at the p < .001 level of statistical significance. Findings from each of the five hierarchical regression analyses are presented in Table 11.3. Those avocational interest scales that provided incremental validity, above and beyond the demographic indices and the self-reported personality traits, are listed in Table 11.4.

At Step 1, the demographic indices predicted the five informant factors with multiple correlations that ranged from .05 (Conscientiousness) to about .35 (Emotional Stability and Intellect). By Step 2, the introduction of the five self-reported personality factors increased the multiple correlations substantially, and the resulting coefficients now ranged from about .50 (Agreeableness and Emotional Stability) to .70 (Extraversion). Remarkably, however, at Step 3 the provision of one or more avocational interest scales served to increase the multiple correlation statistically significantly in every case—a quite small amount in the

Table 11.3. Predicting Assessments by Knowledgeable Informants from Demographic, Personality, and Avocational Interest Measures: Multiple Correlations at Each Stage from Five Hierarchical Regression Analyses

	EXT	AGR	CON	STA	INT
Step 1: 3 Demographics	.20	.28	.05	.37	.35
Step 2: Big-Five self-reports	.70	.49	.54	.52	.61
Step 3: 33 Avoc. int. scales	.71	.53	.57	.55	.66

Note: EXT = Extraversion. AGR = Agreeableness. CON = Conscientiousness. STA = Emotional Stability. INT = Intellect/Imagination/Openness to Experience.

Table 11.4. Significant (p < .01) Avocational Interest Predictors AFTER Controlling for Demographic Indices AND for Self-Reported Personality Traits

EXTRAVERSION:	+ Sports; - Exercising
AGREEABLENESS:	- Drinking; + Food/Eating;
	- Games; + Children
CONSCIENTIOUSNESS:	- Pets; + Housekeeping;
	- Self-Improvement; + Reading
EMOT. STABILITY:	+ Sports; - Automotive;
	- Culture; - Gambling
INTELLECT:	+ Creating; + Housekeeping;
	- Sports; - Fashion;
	+ Reading; - Exercising

case of Extraversion but by quite a substantial amount (.03 to .05) in the case of the other four factors.

The avocational interest scales that provided these significant increments in validity, which are listed in Table 11.4, suggest aspects of people's lifestyles (as reflected in the frequency with which they engage in various activities) that are differentially related to personality perceptions by others, above and beyond the individual's own self-perceptions. That is, one can think of the activity clusters as some of the cues used by others to assess our personality traits. Many of these cues may be used similarly by oneself and others to assess the same personality trait, but some of them must be used at least somewhat differently by the two kinds of judges, thus permitting the interest-related scales to predict incrementally the informants' personality assessments.

Can one achieve the same results using alternative kinds of activity clusters and/or alternative measures of self-reported personality traits? One potential problem with the analyses reported in Tables 11.3 and 11.4 is that each of the three major sets of variables (informants' reports, self-reports, and avocational interest scales) were administered to the ESCS at different times. To make sure that our findings were not an artifact of time differences in variable administration, we repeated the hierarchical regression analyses using data collected at roughly the same time (1997–1998). Because the ESCS participants had completed the exact same set of Big-Five assessments (BFI and SMM) as their knowledgeable informants, and during the same period of time, we used the five factor scores from those self-reports in Step 2 of our analyses. And, then, in place of the 33 avocational interest scales in Step 3, we used the 33 activity clusters with the highest item intercorrelations, based on the analyses described earlier in this chapter.

At Step 1, the findings were identical to those presented in Table 11.3; the demographic indices predicted the five informant factors with multiple correlations that ranged from .05 (Conscientiousness) to about .35 (Emotional Stability and Intellect). At Step 2, however, the introduction of the five new self-reported personality factors increased the multiple correlations even more substantially than before, with the resulting coefficients now ranging from about .60 (Agreeableness, Conscientiousness, and Emotional Stability) to .72 (Extraversion). Remarkably, however, once again at Step 3 the provision of one or more of the activity clusters served to significantly increase the multiple correlation in every case—again by only a quite small amount in the case of Extraversion but by quite a substantial amount (.05) in the case of Intellect/Openness.

SOME CONCLUSIONS AND IMPLICATIONS

Why are some aspects of people's lifestyles (as reflected in the frequency with which they engage in various activities) significantly related to personality trait inferences by others, above and beyond the individual's own self-ascriptions? Avocational pursuits are among the most easily observable aspects of our lifestyles, and thus they are likely to be highly salient cues used by others to infer our personality traits. On the other hand, the things that we do a lot are likely to be highly automatic routines, to which we may pay little attention. Moreover, we may assume that what we do is pretty much the same as what is done by others, and therefore that our avocational interest patterns have little to say about our basic personality traits. As a consequence of these two cognitive processes, the assessment of avocational interest patterns may provide particularly useful variables in understanding the differences between the personality trait inferences made by ourselves versus others.

More generally, one implication of these findings is that we may need to be far more inclusive in the types of individual differences included in our assessment batteries if we are to substantially increase the predictability of important human outcomes. Measures of cognitive abilities have a long history of utility in predicting educational and vocational outcomes, and more recently measures of personality traits have been linked to a wide range of health-related criteria, including mortality versus longevity (e.g., Roberts, Kuncel, Shiner, Caspi, & Goldberg, 2007). Although measures of vocational interests are popular in counseling settings, they are rarely included in research-oriented assessment batteries. And, measures of avocational interests are virtually never included in research in either social or personality psychology. Part of the reason for this neglect may have been stemmed from the lack of availability of public-domain inventories for assessing vocational and avocational interest patterns. Hopefully, the measures described in this chapter will help to solve that problem.

ACKNOWLEDGMENTS

Funds for this project have been provided by Grant AG20048 from the National Institute on Aging, National Institutes of Health, U.S. Public Health Service.

APPENDIX A: THE ITEMS IN EIGHT NEW VOCATIONAL INTEREST SCALES (89 ITEMS)

Instructions: For each of the following activities and occupations, decide how much you would like doing it if you had your life to live over again. Disregard whether you have the necessary skills or training. Please use the following scale for your responses: (1) Strongly dislike; (2) Dislike; (3) Neutral; (4) Like; (5) Strongly like.

Adventure (CISS: Adventuring; Holland: Realistic)

> Be a professional athlete
> Engage in exciting adventures
> Survive in the wilderness
> Be a racing car driver
> Face physical danger
> Be a military officer
> Compete in athletic events
> Be a bounty hunter
> Be a long-distance bicycle rider
> Be a police officer

Production (CISS: Producing; Holland: Realistic)

> Care for cattle or horses
> Be a farmer
> Construct new buildings
> Be a forest ranger
> Cultivate plants
> Go on nature walks
> Do woodworking
> Raise flowers
> Repair cars or trucks
> Work with tools and machinery

Creativity (CISS: Creating; Holland: Artistic)

> Create works of art
> Create new fashion designs
> Be a professional dancer
> Write short stories or novels
> Play an instrument in a symphony
> Redecorate one's house
> Select art works for a museum
> Sing professionally
> Be an actor or actress

Be an artist or architect
Act in a play
Write songs
Paint or draw

Erudition

Be a translator or interpreter
Be a librarian
Be a professor of English
Make up word puzzles
Edit a newspaper
Know many languages
Be a foreign correspondent
Speak fluently on any subject
Read many books
Keep a diary or journal

Altruism (CISS: Helping; Holland: Social)

Help others learn new ideas
Care for sick people
Be an elementary school teacher
Be a social worker
Be a minister, priest, rabbi, or other religious teacher
Counsel persons who need help
Instruct parents on child care
Be a doctor or nurse
Be a physical therapist
Provide comfort and support to others
Participate in charity events
Help people make career decisions
Be a counselor or therapist

Leadership (CISS: Influencing; Holland: Enterprising)

Make important things happen
Lead other people
Be a sales or marketing director
Be the chief executive of a large company
Organize a political campaign
Be the master of ceremonies at a meeting
Plan an advertising campaign
Debate topics in a public meeting
Persuade others to change their views
Be a state governor or senator
Run for political office
Make decisions that affect a lot of people

Organization (CISS: Organizing; Holland: Conventional)

Be the financial officer for a company
Be an office manager
Plan budgets
Prepare financial contracts
Develop an office filing system
Supervise the work of others
Plan investment strategies
Establish time schedules
Monitor business expenses
Be a purchasing agent
Keep track of a company's inventory
Manage a computer database
Keep detailed records

Analysis (CISS: Analyzing; Holland: Investigative)

Be a chemist
Design a laboratory experiment
Be a mathematician
Explain scientific concepts to others
Be a physicist
Carry out medical research
Be a scientific reporter
Solve complex puzzles
Develop a computer program
Be a statistician

CISS = Campbell Interest and Skill Survey (Campbell, Hyne, & Nilsen, 1992).

APPENDIX B: THIRTY-THREE PRELIMINARY AVOCATIONAL INTEREST SCALES

Instructions: Here are some things that people sometimes do. Please indicate how frequently you have done each of them, using the following scale: (1) Never in my life; (2) Not in the past year; (3) One or two times in the past year; (4) Three to ten times in the past year; (5) More than ten times in the past year.

Being Alone (6 Items [Alpha = .73])

Ate dinner alone.
Went to the movies alone.
Went to a concert or theater alone.
Chose to spend a day by myself.

Went on a trip by myself.
Spent an entire vacation by myself.

Child-Related (6 Items [.86])

Played with a child.
Let a child win a game.
Took a child on an outing.
Served as a baby sitter.
Read a story to a child.
Read the comics to a child.

Collecting (5 Items [.84])

Worked on my collection.
Bought something for my collection.
Traded something in my collection.
Read a book about the things that I collect.
Bought a book about the things that I collect.

Computing (6 Items [.89])

Used a computer.
Sent a message by electronic mail (e-mail).
Surfed the Internet.
Read news on the Internet.
Played a computer game.
Looked up information on the Internet.

Creativity (7 Items [.69])

Tried something completely new.
Produced a work of art.
Wrote poetry.
Acted in a play.
Painted a picture.
Played a musical instrument.
Sang or played an instrument in public.

Culture (6 Items [.82])

Attended a public lecture.
Visited an art exhibition.
Visited a museum.
Attended a ballet performance.
Attended an opera or a concert.
Attended a stage play or musical.

Drinking (5 Items [.84])

Drank beer or wine.
Drank whiskey, vodka, gin, or other hard liquor.
Drank in a bar or nightclub.
Became intoxicated.
Had a hangover.

Exercise (7 Items [.85])

Went running or jogging.
Lifted weights.
Used an exercise machine.
Exercised for 40 minutes or longer.
Did aerobic exercise.
Did yoga or other movement exercises.
Participated in an exercise program.

Fashion (5 Items [.76])

Spent more than 10 minutes thinking about what to wear.
Spent more than an hour thinking about what to wear.
Read a fashion-related magazine.
Read a fashion-related book.
Bought a fashionable item of clothing.

Financial (6 Items [.75])

Obtained stock market prices.
Read a book on a financial topic.
Bought or sold stocks or bonds.
Bought or sold real estate.
Purchased a commodity as an investment.
Worked on a retirement plan.

Food-Related (7 Items [.64])

Chewed gum.
Ate candy.
Ate in a restaurant.
Ordered food to be delivered.
Ate food while walking or working.
Ate too much.
Ate or drank while driving.

Gambling (6 Items [.79])

Played bingo for money.
Gambled with cards or dice.

Purchased a scratch ticket.
Gambled on a slot machine or video poker game.
Went to a casino.
Bet money on a sports event.

Game Playing (5 Items [.65])

Worked on a jigsaw puzzle.
Played cards.
Played a board game.
Played chess or checkers.
Learned a new board or card game.

Gardening (6 items [.85])

Cared for a potted plant.
Gardened.
Did yard work.
Planted or transplanted a plant.
Bought or picked flowers.
Bought plants for a garden or yard.

Green Activities (7 Items [.52])

Used public transportation.
Composted food scraps or yard waste.
Walked or rode a bicycle to work.
Changed a habit to have less impact on the environment.
Used both sides of a piece of paper before discarding it.
Picked up litter.
Recycled one or more items.

Housekeeping (7 Items [.75])

Washed dishes.
Made a bed.
Cleaned the house.
Ironed linens or clothes.
Cooked a meal.
Baked a cake, pie, cookies, or bread.
Knitted, quilted, sewed, or crocheted.

Music (8 Items [.77])

Listened to music on the radio.
Listened to music while working.
Downloaded music from the Internet.
Traded music with a friend.

Purchased a musical album.
Shopped in a music store.
Read music-related news.
Used an MP3 player or iPod.

Partying (5 Items [.82])

Had someone over for dinner.
Went to a small party.
Went to a large party.
Planned a party.
Entertained six or more people.

Pets (5 Items [.84])

Played with a pet animal.
Fed a pet animal.
Cared for a pet animal.
Bathed or groomed a pet animal.
Purchased a pet animal.

Political/Organizational (7 Items [.70])

Signed a petition.
Attended a rally or demonstration.
Donated money to charity.
Donated money to a political campaign or cause.
Volunteered for a club or organization.
Attended a town meeting.
Wrote a letter to a newspaper or politician.

Reading (5 Items [.75])

Read a book.
Bought a book.
Read in bed before going to sleep.
Read an entire book in one sitting.
Visited a public library.

Religious/Spiritual Practices (7 Items [.89])

Discussed religion or spirituality.
Prayed (not including blessings at meals).
Read the Bible or other sacred text.
Gave a blessing at a meal.
Attended a church or religious service.
Listened to a religious program on the radio or TV.
Read a book about religion or spirituality.

Romance (6 Items [.57])

Wrote a love letter.
Went on a date.
Went dancing.
Dined by candlelight.
Attended a formal dance.
Wore formal clothing.

Self-Improvement (5 Items [.66])

Read a self-help book.
Bought a self-help book.
Studied some subject.
Learned a new skill.
Enrolled in a course of study.

Shopping (7 Items [.66])

Spent 10 minutes or more in a nongrocery store.
Spent an hour or more in a nongrocery store.
Bought something other than groceries.
Checked the sales ads in a newspaper.
Read newspaper ads for nongrocery items.
Shopped on the Web.
Used eBay to buy or sell something.

Social Networking (5 Items [.69])

Used a computer for social networking.
Read someone's personal web page.
Made an entry on a personal web page.
Participated in an online discussion group.
Used instant messaging to chat online.

Sports (6 Items [.79])

Discussed sports.
Watched a televised sports event.
Attended an athletic event.
Played a team sport.
Played basketball.
Played tennis or golf.

Summer Activities (7 Items [.74])

Went on a picnic.
Went on a hike.
Walked on a beach.

Went swimming.
Went backpacking or camping.
Went boating or rafting.
Went fishing or hunting.

Travel (6 Items [.79])

Took a trip.
Went sightseeing.
Took travel photographs.
Stayed in a hotel, motel, or resort.
Traveled by train or plane.
Went on a cruise or tour.

TV (7 Items [.61])

Watched television.
Watched television news.
Watched a television soap opera.
Watched a television talk show.
Watched a television reality show.
Recorded a television program.
Watched too much television.

Understanding (6 Items [.61])

Read a news magazine.
Watched an educational channel on TV.
Looked up a word in a dictionary.
Read the editorial page of a newspaper.
Looked something up in an encyclopedia.
Read poetry.

Vehicles (4 Items [.50])

Rode a motorcycle.
Read a car magazine or book.
Bought a car, truck, or motorcycle.
Raced a car, truck, or motorcycle.

Writing/Remembering (7 Items [.69])

Made an entry in a diary or journal.
Wrote a postcard.
Wrote a handwritten letter.
Wrote poetry.
Wrote a thank-you note.
Put pictures in a photo album.
Worked on a scrapbook.

REFERENCES

Baumeister, R. F., Vohs, K. D., & Funder, D. C. (2007). Psychology as the science of self-reports and finger movements: Whatever happened to actual behavior? *Perspectives on Psychological Science, 2,* 396–403.

Buss, D. M., & Craik, K. H. (1983). The act frequency approach to personality. *Psychological Review, 90,* 105–126.

Campbell, D. P., Hyne, S. A., & Nilsen, D. L. (1992). *Manual for the Campbell Interest and Skill Survey: CISS.* Minneapolis, MN: National Computer Systems.

Freyd, J. J. (1996). *Betrayal trauma: The logic of forgetting childhood abuse.* Cambridge, MA: Harvard University.

Gleaves, D. H., Smith, S. M., Butler, L. D., & Spiegel, D. (2004). False and recovered memories in the laboratory and clinic: A review of experimental and clinical evidence. *Clinical Psychology: Science and Practice, 11,* 3–28.

Goldberg, L. R. (1992). The development of markers for the Big-Five factor structure. *Psychological Assessment, 4,* 26–42.

Grucza, R. A., & Goldberg, L. R. (2007). The comparative validity of 11 modern personality inventories: Predictions of behavioral acts, informant reports, and clinical indicators. *Journal of Personality Assessment, 89,* 167–187.

Holland, J. L. (1973). *Making vocational choices: A theory of careers.* Englewood Cliffs, NJ: Prentice-Hall.

John, O. P., & Srivastava, S. (1999). The Big Five trait taxonomy: History, measurement, and theoretical perspectives. In L. A. Pervin & O. P. John (Eds.), *Handbook of personality: theory and research* (2nd ed.: pp. 102–138). New York: Guilford.

Loehlin, J. C., & Nichols, R. C. (1976). *Heredity, environment, and personality: A study of 850 sets of twins.* Austin, TX: University of Texas.

Nisbett, R. E., & Wilson, T. D. (1977). Telling more than we can know: Verbal reports on mental processes. *Psychological Review, 84,* 231–259.

Roberts, B. W., Kuncel, N. R., Shiner, R., Caspi, A., & Goldberg, L. R. (2007). The power of personality: The comparative validity of personality traits, socioeconomic status, and cognitive ability for predicting important life outcomes. *Perspectives on Psychological Science, 2,* 313–345.

Saucier, G. (1994). Mini-markers: A brief version of Goldberg's unipolar Big-Five markers. *Journal of Personality Assessment, 63,* 506–516.

12 Measuring Self-Enhancement: From Self-Report to Concrete Behavior

Delroy L. Paulhus
Ronald R. Holden

OVERVIEW

Self-enhancement is the tendency to exaggerate one's positive qualities. In the context of questionnaire styles, self-enhancement is typically referred to as socially desirable responding and is tapped by measures such as the Marlowe-Crowne scale (Crowne & Marlowe, 1964). A second category of measures incorporates a criterion by contrasting self-evaluations with intrapsychic or external criteria. By contrast, we highlight two behavioral methods: (1) a reaction-time technique, and (2) a knowledge overclaiming technique. Paulhus's overclaiming method relies on the fact that self-enhancers tend to claim knowledge of nonexistent foils (e.g., people, places, events). Holden's response-latency method exploits the fact that the response times of fakers exhibit a pattern distinct from those of individuals who respond honestly. Our taxonomy of assessment methods is discussed in terms of the continuum running from self-report to concrete behavioral measures.

INTRODUCTION

The chapters in this collection illustrate that social and personality psychologists tend to address the issue of behavior in rather different ways.

This difference is not surprising given the variety of ways in which the two fields differ in method and theory (Tracy, Robins, & Sherman, in press). Social psychologists tend to view behavior as a concrete outcome reflecting the difference in psychological state induced by an experimental manipulation. In that field, behavior appears to have an exalted status in the hierarchy of scientific credibility. Because it is more tangible, and can be scored more objectively, concrete behavior is commonly viewed as more valid.

By contrast, personality psychologists tend to view behavior as only one of a family of indicators. Two other modes of measuring psychological constructs are considered at least as credible. Ratings by knowledgeable informants, for example, are viewed as superior in some respects (see McCrae & Weiss, 2007; Vazire, 2007). Self-reports too have a variety of advantages that help explain why they remain the single most popular method for measuring personality traits (Paulhus & Vazire, 2007).

The traditional complaint against self-report measures is their vulnerability to self-presentation effects. The general tendency for people to self-enhance continues to raise concerns that self-reports are contaminated with an extraneous source of variance. Thus interest in the concept of self-enhancement arose in the context of controlling for bias in self-reports. That reason alone justifies the prolonged attention given to the development of valid self-enhancement measures. However, the tendency to self-enhance in self-reports has also turned out to be of interest in its own right. For both these reasons, the search continues for improved measures of self-enhancing tendencies.

In this chapter, we consider the potential for indexing self-enhancement via behavioral measures. To properly situate this possibility, our chapter will compare the full range of options from self-report to concrete behavioral methods. We begin with traditional social desirability scales, which rest on the notion that individuals who tend to give extremely desirable responses are not to be trusted. Next we consider measures that incorporate a criterion by contrasting self-evaluations with intrapsychic or external criteria. Closer to the behavioral end of the continuum, the overclaiming approach taps the tendency to claim knowledge of nonexistent items. Finally, we turn to the response latency approach, which is purely behavioral in nature. Our conclusion favors the overclaiming and response latency methods.

Note that our choice of the term self-enhancement is purposely restrictive. We consider those indexes measuring the promotion of positive qualities. We do not include measures of minimizing one's faults. The latter would include concepts such as malingering, self-effacement, and defensiveness and denial (see Paulhus, Fridhandler, & Hayes, 1997).

STANDARD METHODS

Socially Desirable Responding

Socially desirable responding (SDR) is the term applied to positive self-presentation on self-report questionnaires (for a review, see Paulhus, 1991). When asked to rate their own personalities, people tend to bias their ratings in the favorable direction (Edwards, 1970). When measured as a stable individual difference, this tendency is often called a *social desirability (SD) response style* [1] (Jackson & Messick, 1962). The broader concept of SD *response set* includes context-driven motivations to respond desirably. Whether construed as a set or style, the purpose for measuring SDR is concern over dissimulation. A respondent who scores high on an SDR measure is likely to have responded desirably on other questionnaires administered at the same time.

This concern extends to response tendencies beyond a simple favorability bias. People may purposely fabricate an unfavorable image, for example, misrepresenting themselves as mentally ill (Baer et al., 1992) or incompetent (Furnham & Henderson, 1982). Again, we do not address such tendencies in this chapter.

Factors of SDR. Early factor analyses had suggested that socially desirable responding was not a uniform unidimensional construct (Edwards, 1970; Wiggins, 1959). Some coherence was brought to the field by Paulhus's (1984) comprehensive factor analyses. He found that extant SDR measures could be arrayed in a two-factor space framed by axes labeled *Self-Deception* and *Impression Management*. The label, Impression Management, was based on the rationale argued by Sackeim and Gur (1978): Exaggerated claims for desirable behaviors that are public must be consciously tailored: After all, such responses such as "I always pick up my litter" must be made with full awareness of distorting the truth. Items on the Self-Deception scale, by contrast, concern more ambiguous internal events ("My first impressions about people always turn out to be right."). Such claims are more easily rationalized without blatant awarenesss.

These two sets of items were incororporated into early versions of the Balanced Inventory of Desirable Responding (Paulhus, 1986). The correlation between the two subscales was positive but only modest in size.

---

[1] Abbreviating the term further to "social desirability" leads to misleading characterizations such as "high in social desirability." That terminology should be reserved for labeling individuals who possess desirable attributes.

The Self Deception scale was later subdivided into Self-Deceptive Enhancement and Self-Deceptive Denial (Paulhus & Reid, 1991).

That development eventuated in the development of Version 6 of the BIDR (Paulhus, 1991). The standard version comprised the Impression Management and Self-Deceptive Enhancement scales. The BIDR-6 has enjoyed wide usage and now approaches the popularity of the Marlowe-Crowne scale. The commercial version, BIDR-7 (also known as the Paulhus Deception Scales), is distributed for financially profitable applications (Paulhus, 1998b). A comprehensive measure that incorporates content domains (agency & communion) is now under development (Paulhus, 2002; 2005).

The acknowledgement of content in SDR measures reinforces long-standing concerns that they contain more substance than style (e.g., McCrae & Costa, 1983). The difficulty of distinguishing SDR from forth-right self-descriptions provided by people with socially desirable attributes was exemplified in a series of studies by Graziano and Tobin (2002).

Indeed, it is difficult to conceive of measuring SDR without asking respondents about their personality or abilities. One exception is worth noting. The final item on Costa and McCrae's (1992) NEO-PI-R is "Were you being honest in completing this questionnaire?". The psychometric properties of the self-report measures were weaker among those answering "no" (Carter, Herbst, Stoller, Kidorf, King, Costa, & Brooner, 2001).

Krueger's Method. More sophisticated is the idiosyncratic-weighting method (Krueger, 1998; Sinha & Krueger, 1998). Here, self-enhancement is indexed by the correlation between a respondent's self-ratings and his or her desirability ratings of the same items. Effectively, this method weights each item rating by its desirability as judged by the respondent. By contrast, other methods assume implicitly that the social consensus regarding the social desirability of items is shared by all respondents.

The method also has the advantage of adaptability because the weights can be adjusted to address group and context differences. For example, judgments of social desirability differ between psychopaths and non-psychopaths (Kitching & Paulhus, 2008). The disadvantage in such research is that respondents have to judge the same items twice: Once for the desirability ratings; then again for their self-ratings. Moreover, the order of these two tasks influences the self-ratings (Kitching & Paulhus, 2009).

One might argue that this method has a behavioral aspect. Implicitly, respondents are demonstrating the degree to which they value their own responses. In a sense, they are providing a key template for their own responses.

Contrast Methods: Intrapsychic and External Criteria

The methods in this section differ from SDR measures in several respects. Whereas SDR measures infer self-enhancement from the positivity of self-descriptions, the contrast measures compare self-descriptions with a credible criterion. Because a direct comparison is involved, the latter measures promise to be more effective than are SDR scales in distinguishing distortion from truth.

The primary application of SDR measures has been to determine whether to trust answers on concurrently administered self-report scales. Contrast methods were targeted at something deeper, namely, a characteriological tendency toward self-favorability. Issues garnering the most attention are whether self-enhancement is commonplace, adaptive, and unitary.

The Taylor and Brown (1988) review provoked interest in measuring the concept of self-enhancement via contrast methods. Measured in this fashion, self-enhancement can be demonstrated even on anonymous self-descriptions (Baumeister, 1982; Brown, 1998). As such, the phenomenon corresponds to the private audience component of SDR (Paulhus & Trapnell, 2008).

Three issues have dominated the literature. One is the ideal operationalization. A second addresses the adaptiveness of self-enhancement. The third concerns the breadth and structure of self-enhancement.

Competing Operationalizations. Although the concept might seem straightforward, much controversy has arisen over the choice of operationalization. Here, we will entertain two that warrant special attention.

Intrapsychic Comparisons. The most popular choice has been to index self-enhancement as the tendency to view oneself more positively than one views others. [Kwan, John, Kenny, Bond, and Robins (2004) refer to this operationalization as *social comparison.*] A well-replicated body of research indicates that a majority of people tend to rate themselves above average on lists of evaluative traits (e.g., Brown, 1998). If pervasive, this tendency certainly implies an illusion: After all, it is not possible for a large majority of people to actually be better than average.[2]

To index a general tendency, self-enhancement scores are typically aggregated across a wide set of evaluative traits. Respondents may be asked for separate ratings of self and others or, alternatively, a direct comparison of themselves relative to the average other. A number of

---

[2] Although impossible if everyone were referring to the same dimension, individuals tend to define evaluative traits (e.g., intelligence) in an idiosyncratic fashion to ensure that they score high (Dunning, 2005). In that sense, everyone can legitimately report being above average.

studies have confirmed that individuals scoring high on such indexes of self-enhancement tend to be well adjusted (Brown, 1986; Kurt & Paulhus, 2008; Taylor Lerner, Sherman, Sage, & McDowell, 2003).

Note, however, that this operationalization makes it difficult to distinguish self-enhancement from true differences in positive traits. After all, many people are actually above average—even across a large set of traits (Colvin & Block, 1994). In short, the intrapsychic operationalization lacks a reality criterion against which the validity of the self-descriptions can be evaluated.

External Criterion Discrepancies. This limitation led a number of other researchers to operationalize self-enhancement as a *criterion discrepancy*, that is, the overestimation of one's positivity relative to a credible criterion. This category of measures includes both difference scores and residual scores. Rather than absolute values, higher numbers indicate the degree to which respondents' self-ratings exceed their criterion scores. Almost invariably, discrepancy measures of self-enhancement have shown negative associations with long-term adjustment outcomes (e.g., Colvin, Block, & Funder, 1995; John & Robins, 1994; Kwan et al., 2004; Paulhus, 1998a; Robins & Beer, 2001; Shedler, Mayman, & Manis, 1993; but see Bonanno, Field, Kovacevic, & Kaltman, 2002).

The most sophisticated version is the SRM approach developed by Virginia Kwan and her colleagues (Kwan, John, Kenny, Bond, & Robins, 2004). It fully exploits the statistical sophistication of Kenny's (1994) social relations model (SRM). The technique decomposes personality ratings into perceiver effects, target effects, and unique self-perception components.

SRM analyses typically draw on round-robin data: That is, all participants rate each other. In one typical application, all members of a task group rate each other and themselves (Paulhus & Reynolds, 1995). All three rating components showed a significant contribution to rating scores.

To measure self-enhancement, Kwan and colleagues took the SRM approach one step further. They included controls for several factors that plague its competitors. The criterion discrepancy method omits a control for the tendency to rate targets high versus low. The intrapsychic method omits a control for the tendency to receive high versus low ratings. The SRM method controls for both in asking, "Is the target's self-rating higher than would be expected from his/her tendency to give and receive high ratings?"

Adaptiveness of Self-Enhancement. As noted above, Taylor and Brown (1988) claimed that tendencies toward self-enhancement ("positive illusions") were adaptive in most respects. Two decades of further research have revealed that the validity of that claim turns on the choice of operationalizations of self-enhancement.

For example, the Taylor-Brown claim appeared to be supported by such research as the Brown (1986) study: He showed that individuals who claimed to be above average across a wide variety of traits also scored high on a standard self-esteem scale. A number of subsequent studies have supported the Taylor-Brown claim for adaptive outcomes (e.g., Bonanno et al., 2002; Sedikides et al., 2004).

Critics pointed specifically to Taylor and Brown's use of the intrapsychic operationalization, which lacks a reality criterion against which the validity of the self-descriptions can be evaluated (Colvin et al., 1995; Robins & John, 1997). Critics also pointed to the problem of using self-report outcomes when studying self-report predictors. If individual differences in self-favorability bias contaminate both the predictor and outcome, this common method variance will induce an artifactual positive correlation (Colvin & Block, 1994). For that reason, many critics have insisted that the criterion measures for adaptiveness be independent external measures such as peer-rated adjustment (Paulhus, 1998a), expert ratings of adjustment (Colvin et al., 1995), or school grades (Gramzow, Elliot, Asher, & McGregor, 2003; Robins & Beer, 2001).

Such criticism led many researchers to turn to the criterion discrepancy operationalization of self-enhancement. When external criteria were used to evaluate outcomes, discrepancy measures of self-enhancement showed long-term maladaptive outcomes (e.g., Colvin et al., 1995; John & Robins, 1994; Paulhus, 1998a; Robins & Beer, 2001).

Even with the discrepancy operationalization, however, the outcomes of self-enhancement are not uniformly negative. For example, Paulhus (1998a) investigated reactions to self-enhancers in two longitudinal studies where small groups met weekly for a total of 7 weeks. Results showed that, although high self-enhancers were initially perceived favorably, those perceptions became more and more negative over time. Paulhus concluded that self-enhancing tendencies were a "mixed blessing" (p. 1207).

This mixed blessing was also evident in subsequent research reported by Robins and Beer (2001). They showed, in two studies, that self-enhancing tendencies had short-term affective benefits but did long-term damage to self-esteem and task engagement as disconfirmation of overly positive self-assessments became evident. Even with concrete behavioral criteria, then, the research seems to dispute claims that self-enhancement has any long-term adaptive outcomes.

Recently, Kurt and Paulhus (2008) have provided a head-to-head comparison of the intrapsychic and criterion discrepancy methods. They also expanded the outcomes to include four different measures of psychological adjustment. Results showed that, in the same sample, intrapsychic measures had positive associations and discrepancy measures had negative associations with externally evaluated adjustment—except self-rated self-esteem.

In sum, the literature indicates that the criterion discrepancy measure is more valid than the intrapsychic method for tapping chronic self-enhancement. Based on research with the more valid measure, we conclude that chronic self-enhancement is linked to maladaptive attributes. The jury is still out on the direction of causation.

Three exceptions are noteworthy. One is that chronic self-enhancement may promote intrapsychic forms of adjustment such as self-esteem and happiness. Second is that self-enhancement may promote short-term interpersonal adjustment in the sense of engagement with strangers. Third, self-enhancement may pay off in severe settings (e.g., refugee victims), where a formidable self-confidence is required for psychological survival.

In sum, no absolute conclusion can be drawn regarding the Taylor-Brown claim for the adaptiveness of self-enhancement. In retrospect, this outcome is not surprising: It simply confirms the inherent complexity of defining psychological adjustment (Asendorpf & Ostendorf, 1998; Paulhus, Fridhandler, & Hayes, 1997; Scott, 1968).

Structure of Self-Enhancement. Does the domain of self-enhancement make a difference? Recent work is converging on the importance of distinguishing between agentic and communal content. Paulhus and John (1998) initiated this work with a factor analysis of self-criterion discrepancies. The two primary factors mapped clearly onto the agency versus communion distinction.

Other researchers have elaborated on this distinction (e.g., Lonnqvist, Verkasalo, & Bezmenova, 2007). It has proved especially useful in the study of cross-cultural issues (Church et al., 2006; Kurman, 2001).

A recent chapter by Paulhus and Trapnell (2008) illustrated the parallel between the structure of socially desirable responding measures and that of self-enhancement measures. In both cases, the distinction between agentic and communal content helped organize the available measures. The organizational robustness of these two dimensions may derive from the underlying impact of agentic and comunal values (Trapnell & Paulhus, in press).

THE OVERCLAIMING TECHNIQUE (OCT)

The methods reviewed so far have both advantages and disadvantages. SDR scales offer easy administration but lack a criterion. Criterion discrepancy measures appear more credible but are impractical in standard administration settings because they require collection of the criterion. The overclaiming technique (OCT) was designed as a compromise between these approaches (Paulhus, Harms, Bruce, & Lysy, 2003).

The OCT also incorporates departure from reality, but in a different fashion from the criterion discrepancy method. Respondents are asked to rate their familiarity with a set of persons, places, items, or events. Twenty percent of the items are foils: that is, they do not actually exist. Such responses can be scored via signal detection method to yield both accuracy and bias scores for each respondent.

Respondents receive high accuracy scores to the extent that they claim real items and disclaim foils. A high bias score ensues from an overall tendency to claim items—especially foils. In short, the credibility of this measure derives from the argument that claiming nonexistent items is an a priori index of self-enhancement.

A variety of formulas are provided by Paulhus et al. (2003). Of these, the most intuitively evident are the so called "common-sense measures." Accuracy is the difference between the hit rate (PH) and the false-alarm rate (PFA). Bias is indexed by PFA (or the mean of PH and PFA). The inclusion of PH in the latter formula is based on the assumption that those who self-enhance on the foils also self-enhance on the reals: that is, such respondents inflate their familiarity ratings on both sets of items.

Item Content

The original overclaiming questionnaire comprised 15 items in each of 10 academic categories (e.g., science, law, philosophy, history, literature, language). A series of studies demonstrated that the accuracy index predicted verbal IQ scores in the .40–.60 range (Paulhus & Harms, 2004). The bias index correlated moderately (.25–.38) with trait self-enhancement measures such as narcissism and the Self-Deceptive Enhancement scale (Paulhus et al., 2003). When the items concerned such lay topics such as sports, music, and films, the bias link was more nuanced. Correlations with narcissism were significant only for topics that the respondent valued. Interestingly, the accuracy scores predicted IQ for virtually any of the lay topics.

Several advantages of the OCT have already been demonstrated. For example, the validity of accuracy scores is sustained under faking conditions, where bias scores increase (Paulhus & Harms, 2004). On the other hand, bias validities are sustained under warning conditions, where the presence of foils is made salient (Paulhus et al., 2003).

A recent practical application is to the field of marketing surveys (Nathanson, Westlake, & Paulhus, 2007). In the traditional approach to indexing product familiarity, a survey with a list of product names is administered. But foils are rarely included. We developed a marketing survey comprising 12 product categories (e.g., wine, cars, fashion designers, cosmetics brands). Following the OCT, 20% of the items in each category were foils. We administered the consumer version under a variety of instructional sets. Our results indicated that the validity of the accuracy index held up even when the bias index was inflated, for example, under instructions to fake good.

Some work has begun on clarifying the processes underlying over-claiming. What would make individuals claim knowledge of nonexistent foils under anonymous circumstances? Preliminary evidence suggests both motivational and cognitive elements at work. Independent of narcissism scores, bias scores tend to correlate with a global memory bias.

In short, the overclaiming technique offers an efficient and robust method for indexing self-enhancement. It is robust across a variety of administration conditions. Finally, the method is largely nonthreatening and unobtrusive because the apparent purpose is a survey of personal familiarities.

RESPONSE LATENCIES

As an assessment tool for detecting response biases, response times have a long history. Consider that in 1908, Munsterberg (p. 86) stated that deceptive responses have an "involuntary retardation by emotional influence." Although intuitively appealing as a indicator of dissimulation, empirical evidence for the use of *raw* response latencies as indicators of lying suggests that the effects tend to be small and subject to moderating influences (DePaulo et al., 2003). A more refined approach to the use of response times arose in the 1980s: It sought to reduce the low signal-to-noise ratio inherent in latency data (Fazio, 1990). In particular, as information processing models came to be applied to personality, schema theory and notions of self-schema led to the use of adjusted rather than raw response times for assessing standing on personality traits (Erdle & Lalonde, 1986).

Consider that a schema is a cognitive structure that directs the acquisition, organization, and application of knowledge; that a self-schema is one based on past experiences and representative of the self; and that a personality trait represents a structural component of a schema (Fekken & Holden, 1992). A prominent self-schema (e.g., a salient personality trait), will induce differential processing of schema-relevant and schema-irrelevant information. Schema-consistent information will be accepted faster (and rejected more slowly) and schema-inconsistent information will be rejected faster (and accepted more slowly). As a result, individuals at the high end of a personality trait will endorse a relevant positively-keyed personality item more quickly than they reject it and will reject a relevant negatively-keyed personality item more quickly than they endorse it.

Of course, the response time for a specific individual answering a specific item is determined by myriad factors, many of which are not directly relevant to the personality trait being measured (Holden, Fekken, & Cotton, 1991). Most specific about these factors is Rogers's (1974a, b) independent stage model of responding to personality items. In identifying distinct stages for stimulus encoding, stimulus comprehension, self-referent decision making, and response selection, he served to highlight various item properties that influence the speed of processing for specific stages. Examples of item factors included item length, item ambiguity, item controversiality, number of response options, and so forth. Holden et al. extended Rogers's model by identifying corresponding person factors that affect processing speed for these same stages. Examples of person factors included reading speed, verbal ability, schema organization, motor speed, and so forth. Subsequent work by Holden and colleagues demonstrated that the key factors in measuring personality traits are not the main effects attributable to items or to persons but, rather, the interaction of the schema-relevant item and the respondent's relevant schema.

In addition to controlling for main effects for items and for persons, the use of response times must also take into account whether a respondent endorses or rejects a trait-relevant personality item (Erdle & Lalonde, 1986). Endorsement and rejection represent opposite sides of the "inverted-U RT" effect found for decision times for self-ratings of adjective descriptors (Kuiper, 1981) and personality items (Akrami, Hedlund, & Ekehammar, 2007). Further, because single latencies tend to be unreliable, more reliable response latencies are obtained by averaging over related trait-specific items. When these adjustments are undertaken (see Appendix for a detailed example), response latencies will demonstrate appropriate patterns of validity for scales of personality and psychopathology in adults, children, and psychiatric patients (Holden et al., 1991) and will generally demonstrate the presence of construct validity (Fekken & Holden, 1994; Holden & Fekken, 1993).

Although relevant for assessing personality self-schemas, this response latency approach for response times has been extended to adopted schemas associated with faking (Holden & Hibbs, 1995; Holden & Kroner, 1992; Holden, Kroner, Fekken, & Popham, 1992). Individuals faking good will take relatively longer in providing responses that make them look bad rather than good. (Individuals faking good will provide some negative information about themselves. If they offer only favorable responses, standard validity scales will detect this.) Respondents who fake bad will take relatively longer to give answers that make them look good rather than bad. (Again, individuals faking bad will offer some positive responses to avoid being caught by standard validity scales.) In short, these within-respondent response latency differences represent relatively longer response times for answers that are incompatible with a faking schema than for compatible answers, and these response time differences can generate summary scores that successfully differentiate between honest and dissimulating respondents.

Holden (1995), for example, demonstrated this response incompatibility effect for faking in samples drawn from two distinct populations. Using a job application scenario, 64 university students were randomly assigned to complete a validated personnel selection test under either honest instructions or instructions to maximize their chances of being hired (i.e., fake) for a government job. Item content for the test included 81 items related to delinquency (e.g., employment trouble, illegal drug use). Not surprisingly, individuals instructed to maximize their chances of being hired scored an average of more than one standard deviation lower on an overall measure of delinquency. Importantly, however, although giving keyed responses to many fewer delinquency items, fakers were relatively much slower in providing these relatively fewer "delinquent" responses (i.e., answers incompatible with their schema to fake). Similar findings emerged for a second sample comprising 100 unemployed adults actively seeking employment who were also randomly assigned either to answer honestly or to fake.

More recent research has attempted to explore and expand on the associations between response latencies and faking, but not always successfully. Although some have argued that socially desirable responding is a response-editing process that requires more time than that for honest responding (Holtgraves, 2004; McDaniel & Timm, 1990), there is no evidence to indicate that controlling response times can prevent or reduce faking. Holden, Wood, and Tomashewski (2001) limited response time to 1.5 s per personality test item and found that the deleterious effects of faking on validity were not diminished. Further, Holden (2005) set a limit of 0.5 s per item and similarly reported that the disruption of validity by faking remained unabated. It appears, therefore, that faking is a primitive process requiring little cognitive load.

In an innovative undertaking using a variation of the Implicit Association Test, Gregg (2007) sought to refine the schema incompatibility effect on response times by enhancing antagonistic responding associated with not answering truthfully. To date, this approach has focused on distinguishing liars and truth-tellers for obviously true and false factual (e.g., "The sky is blue"; "The sky is purple") and self-descriptive (e.g., "My name is Ron"; "My name is George") statements. Reported effect sizes were very impressive. Whether this technique can be applied to faking on personality items is unknown but certainly worthy of future investigation.

In sum, we place the response latency approach at the behavioral end of the continuum. Unlike rational scale construction strategies, which emphasize a one-to-one correspondence between verbal reports and reality, response latencies are more indirect because they tap into personality-relevant cognitive processes. In this regard, response latencies, particularly statistically adjusted, aggregated ones, seem less susceptible to deliberate response distortion than standard verbal reports of behavior.

SUMMARY

This chapter has focused on the potential for measuring self-enhancement via behavioral as opposed to self-report methods. To this end, we organized extant methods into three categories, in increasing order of emphasis on concrete external criteria. These were social desirability scales, criterion comparison methods (intrapsychic and external criterion measures), and behavioral approaches (overclaiming and response latency techniques).

We conclude that the behavioral element of the latter two methods advances their credibility as indexes of self-enhancement. The response latency method is clearly superior to the others with respect to behavioral concreteness. The validity of the overclaiming technique rests on the proposition that any claim to recognize foils is inherently indicative of exaggeration. In both cases, self-reports are still required but it is the behavioral coding of these reports that leads us to recommend them over alternative measures of self-enhancement.

APPENDIX: AN EXAMPLE OF THE COMPUTATION OF ADJUSTED RESPONSE LATENCIES

Note: Data would normally comprise many more items and respondents.

Personality Items:

1. I like to be the first to apologize after an argument.
2. I get a kick out of seeing someone I dislike appear foolish in front of others.
3. If public opinion is against me, I usually decide that I am wrong.
4. I get annoyed with people who never want to go anywhere different.
5. I live from day to day without trying to fit my activities into a pattern.

Raw response time latencies (in seconds) for five respondents:

			Item				
Respondent	1	2	3	4	5	Mean	SD
1	4.12	19.82	4.50	6.42	5.06	7.98	6.67
2	9.61	10.43	6.81	6.59	5.83	7.85	2.03
3	3.95	10.66	4.51	14.23	3.40	7.35	4.84
4	4.45	9.45	0.30	3.79	4.28	4.45	3.27
5	10.77	76.31	12.14	6.29	4.50	22.00	30.52
Mean	6.58	25.33	5.65	7.46	4.61		
SD	3.33	28.80	4.32	3.95	0.90		

Step 1. Reset maximum latencies to 40 seconds and minimum latencies to 0.5 seconds (values outside this range are regarded as outliers that will unduly influence analyses).

			Item				
Respondent	1	2	3	4	5	Mean	SD
1	4.12	19.82	4.50	6.42	5.06	7.98	6.67
2	9.61	10.43	6.81	6.59	5.83	7.85	2.03
3	3.95	10.66	4.51	14.23	3.40	7.35	4.84
4	4.45	9.45	0.50	3.79	4.28	4.49	3.20
5	10.77	40.00	12.14	6.29	4.50	14.74	14.47
Mean	6.58	18.07	5.69	7.46	4.61		
SD	3.33	12.96	4.26	3.95	0.90		

Step 2. Standardize within a respondent to adjust for irrelevant person factors such as reading speed, verbal ability, motor speed, etc.

			Item				
Respondent	1	2	3	4	5	Mean	SD
1	-0.58	1.77	-0.52	-0.23	-0.44	0.00	1.00
2	0.86	1.27	-0.51	-0.62	-1.00	0.00	1.00
3	-0.70	0.68	-0.59	1.42	-0.82	0.00	1.00
4	-0.01	1.55	-1.25	-0.22	-0.07	0.00	1.00
5	-0.27	1.75	-0.18	-0.58	-0.71	0.00	1.00
Mean	-0.14	1.40	-0.61	-0.05	-0.61		
SD	0.62	0.45	0.39	0.84	0.36		

Step 3. Standardize within an item to correct for irrelevant item factors such as item length, complexity, order, etc. [Note: For experimental groups, standardizing within an item should use item means and standard deviations associated with a control or normative group]. Results are standardized times that represent latencies relative to the respondent and relative to the item.

			Item				
Respondent	1	2	3	4	5	Mean	SD
1	-0.71	0.82	0.23	-0.22	0.46	0.12	0.60
2	1.61	-0.30	0.25	-0.68	-1.08	-0.04	1.05
3	-0.90	-1.60	0.06	1.74	-0.58	-0.26	1.27
4	0.20	0.32	-1.63	-0.20	1.48	0.03	1.12
5	-0.21	0.76	1.10	-0.64	-0.28	0.15	0.75
Mean	0.00	0.00	0.00	0.00	0.00		
SD	1.00	1.00	1.00	1.00	1.00		

Step 4. These are standardized times. Reset maximum latencies to 3.00 and minimum latencies to -3.00 (values outside this range are regarded as outliers that will unduly influence analyses). [Not necessary for this example].

Step 5. Aggregate data by computing mean latencies within a respondent. Usually done separately for endorsements and rejections of a specific trait (or response style) and done separately for answering true and for answering false to true/false items.

REFERENCES

Akrami, N., Hedlund, L., & Ekehammar, B. (2007). Personality scale response latencies as self-schema indicators: The inverted-U effect revisited. *Personality and Individual Differences, 43,* 611–618.

Asendorpf, J. B., & Ostendorf, F. (1998). Is self-enhancement healthy? Conceptual, psychometric, and empirical analysis. *Journal of Personality and Social Psychology 74*, 955–966.

Baer, R. A., Wetter, M. W., & Berry, D. T. (1992). Detection of underreporting of psychopathology on the MMPI: A meta-analysis. *Clinical Psychology Review, 12*, 509–525.

Baumeister, R. F. (1982). A self-presentational view of social phenomena. *Psychological Bulletin, 91*, 3–26.

Bonanno, G. A., Field, N. P., Kovacevic, A., & Kaltman, S. (2002). Self-enhancement as a buffer against extreme adversity: Civil war in Bosnia and traumatic loss in the United States. *Personality and Social Psychology Bulletin, 28*, 184–196.

Brown, J. D. (1986). Evaluations of self and others: Self-enhancement biases in social judgments. *Social Cognition, 4*, 353–376.

Brown, J. D. (1998). *The self.* Boston: McGraw-Hill.

Carter, J. A., Herbst, J. H., Stoller, K. B., King, V. L., Kidorf, M. S., Costa, P. T., Jr., & Brooner, R. K. (2001). Short-term stability of NEO-PI-R personality trait scores in opioid-dependent outpatients. *Psychology of Addictive Behaviors, 15*, 255–260.

Church, A. T., Katigbak, M. S., del Prado, A. M., Valdez-Medina, J. L., Miramontes, L. G., & Ortiz, F. A. (2006). A cross-cultural study of trait self-enhancement, explanatory variables, and adjustment. *Journal of Research in Personality, 40*, 1169–1201.

Colvin, C. R., & Block, J. (1994). Do positive illusions foster mental health? An examination of the Taylor and Brown formulation. *Psychological Bulletin, 116*, 3–20.

Colvin, C. R., Block, J., & Funder, D. C. (1995). Overly positive self-evaluations and personality: Negative implications for mental health. *Journal of Personality and Social Psychology, 68*, 1152–1162.

Costa, P. T., Jr., & McCrae, R. R. (1992). *Revised NEO Personality Inventory(NEO-PI-R) and NEO Five-Factor Inventory (NEO-FFI): Professional manual.* Odessa, FL: Psychological Assessment Resources.

Crowne, D. P., & Marlowe, D. (1964). *The approval motive.* New York: Wiley.

DePaulo, B. M., Lindsay, J. J., Malone, B. E., Muhlenbruck, L., Charlton, K., & Harris, C. (2003). Cues to deception. *Psychological Bulletin, 129*, 74–118.

Dunning, D. (2005). *Self-insight: Roadblocks and detours on the road to knowing thyself.* New York: Psychology Press.

Edwards, A. L. (1970). *The measurement of personality traits by scales and inventories.* Oxford, England: Holt, Rinehart & Winston.

Erdle, S., & Lalonde, R. N. (1986, June). *Processing information about the self: Evidence for personality traits as cognitive prototypes.* Presented at the Canadian Psychological Association Annual Convention, Toronto.

Fazio, R. H. (1990). A practical guide to the use of response latency in social psychological research. In C. Hendrick & M. S. Clark (Eds.), *Research methods in personality and social psychology* (pp. 74–97). Newbury Park, CA: Sage.

Fekken, G. C., & Holden, R. R. (1992). Response latency evidence for viewing personality traits as schema indicators. *Journal of Research in Personality, 26*, 103–120.

Fekken, G. C., & Holden, R. R. (1994). The construct validity of differential response latencies in structured personality tests. *Canadian Journal of Behavioural Science*, *26*, 104–120.

Furnham, A., & Henderson, M. (1982). The good, the bad, and the mad: Response bias in self-report measures. *Personality and Individual Differences*, *3*, 311–320.

Gramzow, R. H., Elliot, A. J., Asher, E., & McGregor, H. A. (2003). Self-evaluation bias and academic performance: Some ways and some reasons why. *Journal of Research in Personality*, *37*, 41–61.

Graziano, W. G., & Tobin, R. (2002). Agreeableness: Dimension of personality or social desirability artifact? *Journal of Personality*, *70*, 695–727.

Gregg, A. P. (2007). When vying reveals lying: The timed antagonistic response alethiometer. *Applied Cognitive Psychology*, *21*, 621–647.

Holden, R. R. (1995). Response latency detection of fakers on personnel tests. *Canadian Journal of Behavioural Science*, *27*, 343–355.

Holden, R. R. (2005, August). *Response time restrictions, faking, and personality inventory validity.* Paper presented at the American Psychological Association Annual Convention. Washington, DC.

Holden, R. R., & Fekken, G. C. (1993). Can personality test item response latencies have construct validity? Issues of reliability and convergent and discriminant validity. *Personality and Individual Differences*, *15*, 243–248.

Holden, R. R., Fekken, G. C., & Cotton, D. H. G. (1991). Assessing psychopathology using structured test-item response latencies. *Psychological Assessment*, *3*, 111–118.

Holden, R. R., & Hibbs, N. (1995). Incremental validity of response latencies for detecting fakers on a personality test. *Journal of Research in Personality*, *29*, 362–372.

Holden, R. R., & Kroner, D. G. (1992). Relative efficacy of differential response latencies for detecting faking on a self-report measure of psychopathology. *Psychological Assessment*, *4*, 170–173.

Holden, R. R., Kroner, D. G., Fekken, G. C., & Popham, S. M. (1992). A model of personality test item response dissimulation. *Journal of Personality and Social Psychology*, *63*, 272–279.

Holden, R. R., Wood, L. L., & Tomashewski, L. (2001). Do response time limitations counteract the effect of faking on personality inventory validity? *Journal of Personality and Social Psychology*, *81*, 160–169.

Holtgraves, T. (2004). Social desirability and self-reports: Testing models of socially desirable responding. *Personality and Social Psychology Bulletin*, *30*, 161–172.

Jackson, D. N., & Messick, S. (1962). Response styles and the measurement of psychopathology *Psychological Bulletin*, *55*, 243–252.

John, O. P., & Robins, R. W. (1994). Accuracy and bias in self-perception: Individual differences in self-enhancement and the role of narcissism. *Journal of Personality and Social Psychology*, *66*, 206–219.

Kenny, D. T. (1994). *Interpersonal perception: A social relations analysis.* New York: Guilford.

Kitching, S., & Paulhus, D. L. (2008, June). *Do psychopaths really impression manage?* Presented at the meeting of the Canadian Psychological Association, Halifax, Nova Scotia.

Kitching, S., & Paulhus, D. L. (2009, August). *Order effects in the measurement of socially desirable responding.* Presented at the meeting of the American Psychological Association, Toronto.

Krueger, J. (1998). Enhancement bias in descriptions of self and others. *Personality and Social Psychology Bulletin, 24,* 505–516.

Kuiper, N. (1981). Convergent evidence for the self as prototype: The "Inverted U RT Effect" for self and other judgments. *Personality and Social Psychology Bulletin, 7,* 438–443.

Kurt, A., & Paulhus, D. L. (2008). Moderators of the adaptiveness of self-enhancement: Operationalization, motivational domain, adjustment facet, and evaluator. *Journal of Research in Personality, 42,* 839–853.

Kurman, J. (2001). Self-enhancement: Is it restricted to individualistic cultures? *Personality and Social Psychology Bulletin, 27,* 1705–1716.

Kwan, V. S. Y., John, O. P., Kenny, D. A., Bond, M. H., & Robins, R.W. (2004). Reconceptualizing individual differences in self-enhancement bias: An interpersonal approach. *Psychological Review, 111,* 94–110.

Lonnqvist, J. E., Verkasalo, M., & Bezmenova, I. (2007). Agentic and communal bias in socially desirable responding. *European Journal of Personality, 21,* 853–868.

McCrae, R. R., & Costa, P. T. (1983). Social desirability scales: More substance than style. *Journal of Consulting & Clinical Psychology, 51,* 882–888.

McCrae, R. R., & Weiss, A. (2007). Observer ratings of personality. In R. W. Robins, R. C. Fraley, & R. F. Krueger (Eds.), *Handbook of research methods in personality psychology* (pp. 259–272). New York: Guilford.

McDaniel, M. A., & Timm, H. (1990, August). *Lying takes time: Predicting deception in biodata using response latency.* Paper presented at the American Psychological Association Annual Convention, Boston.

Nathanson, C., Westlake, B., & Paulhus, D. L. (2007, May). *Controlling response bias in the measurement of consumer knowledge.* Presented at the meeting of the Association for Psychological Science, Washington, DC.

Paulhus, D. L. (1984). Two-component models of socially desirable responding. *Journal of Personality and Social Psychology, 46,* 598–609

Paulhus, D. L. (1986). Self-deception and impression management in test responses. In A. Angleitner & J. S. Wiggins (Eds.), *Personality assessment via questionnaire* (p. 143–165). New York: Springer-Verlag.

Paulhus, D. L. (1991). Measurement and control of response bias. In J. P. Robinson, P. R. Shaver, & L. S. Wrightsman (Eds.), *Measures of personality and social psychological attitudes* (pp. 17–60). San Diego: Academic Press.

Paulhus, D. L. (1998a). Interpersonal and intrapsychic adaptiveness of trait self-enhancement: A mixed blessing? *Journal of Personality and Social Psychology, 74,* 1197–1208.

Paulhus, D. L. (1998b). *Manual for Balanced Inventory of Desirable Responding* (BIDR-7). Toronto: Multi-Health Systems.

Paulhus, D. L. (2002). Socially desirable responding: The evolution of a construct. In H. Braun, D. N. Jackson, & D. E. Wiley (Eds.), *The role of constructs in psychological and educational measurement* (pp. 67–88). Hillsdale, NJ: Erlbaum.

Paulhus, D. L. (2005). *The Comprehensive Inventory of Desirable Responding.* Presented at the meeting of the Society for Personality and Social Psychology, Memphis, TN.

Paulhus, D. L., Fridhandler, B., & Hayes, S. (1997). Psychological defense: Contemporary theory and research. In R. Hogan, J. A. Johnson, & S. R. Briggs (Eds.), *Handbook of personality psychology* (pp. 543–579). San Diego: Academic Press.

Paulhus, D. L., & Harms, P. D. (2004). Measuring cognitive ability with the over-claiming technique. *Intelligence, 32,* 297–314.

Paulhus, D. L., Harms, P. D., Bruce, M. N., & Lysy, D. C. (2003). The over-claiming technique: Measuring self-enhancement independent of ability. *Journal of Personality and Social Psychology, 84,* 681–693.

Paulhus, D. L., & John, O. P. (1998). Egoistic and moralistic biases in self-perception: The interplay of self-deceptive styles with basic traits and motives. *Journal of Personality, 66,* 1025–1060.

Paulhus, D. L., & Reid, D. B. (1991). Enhancement and denial in socially desirable responding. *Journal of Personality and Social Psychology, 60,* 307–317.

Paulhus, D. L., & Reynolds, S. R. (1995). Enhancing target variance in personality impressions: Highlighting the person in person perception. *Journal of Personality and Social Psychology, 69,* 1233–1242.

Paulhus, D. L., & Trapnell, P. D. (2008). Self-presentation of personality: An agency-communion perspective. In O. P. John, R. W. Robins, & L. A. Pervin (Eds.), *Handbook of personality psychology* (pp. 777–790). New York: Guilford.

Paulhus, D. L., & Vazire, S. (2007). The self-report method. In R. W. Robins, R. C. Fraley, & R. F. Krueger (Eds.), *Handbook of research methods in personality psychology* (pp. 224–239). New York: Guilford.

Robins, R. W., & Beer, J. S. (2001). Positive illusions about the self: Short-term benefits and long-term costs. *Journal of Personality and Social Psychology, 80,* 340–352.

Robins, R. W., & John, O. P. (1997). The quest for self-insight: Theory and research on the accuracy of self-perceptions. In R. Hogan, J. A. Johnson, & S. R. Briggs (Eds.), *Handbook of personality psychology* (pp. 649–679). San Diego, CA: Academic Press.

Rogers, T. B. (1974a). An analysis of two central stages underlying responding to personality items: The self-referent decision and response selection. *Journal of Research in Personality, 8,* 128–138.

Rogers, T. B. (1974b). An analysis of the stages underlying the process of responding to personality items. *Acta Psychologica, 38,* 205–213.

Sackeim, H. A., & Gur, R. C. (1978). Self-deception, self-confrontation, and consciousness. In G. E. Schwartz & D. Shapiro (Eds.), *Consciousness and self-regulation: Advances in research* (Vol. 2, pp. 139–197). New York: Plenum Press.

Scott, W. A. (1968). Concepts of normality. In E. F. Borgatta & W. W. Lambert (Eds.), *Handbook of personality: Theory and research* (pp. 974–1006). Chicago: Rand-McNally.

Shedler, J., Mayman, M., & Manis, M. (1993). The illusion of mental health. *American Psychologist, 48,* 1117–1131.

Sinha, R. R., & Krueger, J. (1998). Idiographic self-evaluation and bias. *Journal of Research in Personality, 32,* 131–155.

Taylor, S. E., & Brown, J. D. (1988). Illusion and well-being: A social psychological perspective on mental health. *Psychological Bulletin, 103,* 193–210.

Taylor, S. E., Lerner, J. S., Sherman, D. K., Sage, R. M., & McDowell, N. K. (2003). Portrait of the self-enhancer: Well adjusted and well liked or maladjusted and friendless? *Journal of Personality and Social Psychology, 84,* 165–176.

Tracy, J. L., Robins, R. W., & Sherman, J. W. (in press). The practice of psychological science: Searching for Cronbach's two streams in social-personality psychology. *Journal of Personality and Social Psychology.*

Trapnell, P. D., & Paulhus, D. L. (in press). Agentic and communal values: Their scope and measurement. *Journal of Personality Assessment.*

Vazire, S. (2007). Informant reports: A cheap, fast, easy method for personality assessment. *Journal of Research in Personality, 40,* 472–481.

Wiggins, J. S. (1959). Interrelationships among MMPI measures of dissimulation under standard and social desirability instructions. *Journal of Consulting Psychology, 23,* 419–427.

13 Developing an Ecological Framework for Establishing Connections Among Dispositions, Behaviors, and Environments: From Affordances to Behavior Settings

Reuben M. Baron

First, the problem. Behavior, be it at the individual or group level, is not a central concern of mainstream social psychology. We have become so concerned with *why* the chicken crosses the road that we don't bother to ascertain whether the chicken has actually crossed the road. Sticking with the chicken metaphor, we can ask which comes first, the chicken or the egg? I think it is the Lewinian egg in the modern form of ever more sophisticated cognitive modeling of social phenomena and processes. I offer a brief historical explanation and a longer investigation of a multi-level strategy for making behavior more central to our enterprise. To be a bit melodramatic, if we are looking at Humpty Dumpty after the fall, I am suggesting a rationale for putting him back together again.

But first, let us look at a possible narrative for how behavior became not the victim of some conspiracy, but rather an incidental victim of success. Specifically, from the mid-fifties to the mid-sixties psychology was the scene of "Mortal Kombat", as the computer game puts it, between the forces of the dark side—the Skinnerian Behaviorists and the forces of light and good, the cognitivists (cf. Miller, Galanter, & Pribram, 1960). As with most revolutions, the triumph of the cognitivists brought with it excesses. In this case, along with diminishing the relevance of Skinnerian Behaviorism, the relevance of behavior itself was also lessened. In effect, the baby (i.e., behavior) was thrown out with the bath water, both in the mainstream and in social psychology.

In contradistinction to Zajonc's (1980) warning that "preferences need no inferences," inferences and cognitive rule-based models, in general, became dominant. Rather than focus on behavior, there were a predominance of computer-based or computer-inspired models of cognition (cf. Wyer & Srull, 1986). Such models told us how people should think if they were rational, thereby implying that people are biased and a bit stupid if they violate these conceptual axioms. At this point, I want to make it clear that I do not want to make the reverse error. When I shortly offer an ecologically-based strategy for returning behavior to prominence, I am not saying that the cognitive revolution has not been extremely useful as one model for social psychology. Rather, I am proposing that there are complementary approaches that are perhaps better suited to restoring the importance of behavior.

Specifically, I will be advocating a broadened ecological perspective that has been run through a social filter. Why is an ecological approach particularly relevant to this problem? Because behavior is a central tenet of any ecologically-based view of psychology whether it is James J. Gibson's (1979/1986) view of the visual perception basis of affordances or Roger Barker's (1968) discussion of behavior settings. In both cases, behavior is the "straw that stirs the drink." For Gibson (1979/1986), seeing is for doing. He views the detection of affordances (opportunities for action specified in the structure of the environment) as fundamental to our navigating the world. Specifically, Gibson postulates perceiving–acting cycles—that is, what we see affects what we do and what we do affects what we see. Further, for Barker (1968) behavior–environment congruence, what he refers to as synomorphy, is foundational to his whole approach. For example, if a school is the behavior setting of interest, the shape or structure of students' ". . . desks and seats fits the sitting and studying behavior patterns" (Schoggen, 1989, p. 385). Similarly, the desks face the teachers to facilitate successful lecturing. In general, Barker focuses on extra-individual or group-level behaviors, including the importance of what Heft (2001) refers to as collective affordances, that is, affordances specified at the level of a behavior setting. In the examples given above, these would include Barker's synomorphs.

However. I recognize that the ecological approach in an unreconstructed form is itself too narrow for making a case for the centrality of social behavior. Indeed, I have become increasingly concerned not only with making social psychology more ecological (Baron & Boudreau, 1987, McArthur & Baron, 1983) but rather with making ecological psychology more social (Baron, 2007). It is in this spirit that I offer a broader way to frame the present problem. Social psychology needs to move from the

Cartesian—"I think therefore I am" to Heidegger's "I act therefore I am". Or better yet—as social psychologists, we should say—I act with others therefore I am. As Buber (1970, p.69) so aptly wrote, "In the beginning is the relation". I believe that the gap between dispositions (be they cognitions, traits, feelings, attitudes, etc.) and behavior has occurred because not only are certain computer-based models nonbehavioral (if not antibehavioral), but they are also asocial. Cognitions do not enter into relationships or join groups.

Indeed, in an earlier work I suggested that the "group is mind's environment" (Caporeal & Baron, 1997). That is, cognitions are constrained by the need to solve basic social problems. For example, there is data that supports an evolutionary supposition that it was the organization of people into ever-larger groups that accelerated the development of language as well as the development of categorical thinking including stereotyping (Dunbar, 1993). Viewed this way, it is the constraints of social functioning that drive both cognitive functioning and the organization of behavior. When action is socially situated, behavior is both input and output; groups not only demand proper thoughts, they demand proper actions. This is particularly true of group contexts that have an extended duration such as a behavior setting. Settings such as schools or churches exert "environmental force units" (Schoggen, 1989, p. 163), which direct action toward the collective goals of the setting. Neither rats nor people are left buried in thought at choice points when people act collectively as part of a social unit. Only when we treat people in isolation do we ask questions such as: How do we explain how internal states such as cognitions, emotions, and motivations evoke behavior? When we are part of a social unit, the pressures to maintain that unit constrain both dispositions and behavior.

In this sense, all social action is to a certain extent "groupthink" (Janis, 1972). In effect, to answer a number of questions raised in the Purdue Symposium agenda, we need to recall that *the person is in the group and the group is in the person*. In this sense, even when we are engaging in a supposedly nonsocial behavior such as eating, we are always eating with others in mind. For example, even when eating alone we follow social scripts. We do not ordinarily eat with our hands or throw food around. People, in effect, produce their own environmental force units; this is the sense in which the group is in the individual.

From this analysis of the general problems facing the Purdue Symposium, I would like to offer a more specific framing of my particular approach to these issues. My goal is to develop a common affordance-based framework for indicating connections among dispositional concepts, behavior, and the impact of the environment. In this context, by affordance I mean "the perceived functional significance of an object, event, or place for an individual" (Heft, 2001, p. 123), taken in relation to the functional capabilities of that person. (I will add to this mix personality traits, a topic I will address later in this chapter). Thus, even in regard to nonsocial objects, for example, the sitability of a chair, the graspability of a cup, and so forth, the affordances are relational. Such meanings do not require categories or representations. "They emerge from my relationships to environmental entities and exist in this relationship" (Schmidt, 2007, p. 136). For example, when a chair affords sitability, what this means is that "the ability to sit on the chair is between the person and the chair and is not part of either separately" (Chemero, 2003). That is, affordances are neither subjective nor objective. They have a kind of *betweenness* that makes such dualisms irrelevant. The physical sciences long ago accepted such states. For example, an electron has both particle and wave properties. Like an affordance, it is not "this or that"; rather, it is "this and that". Thus, Buber (1970, p.69), even though he had people in mind was, in effect, framing the meaning of all affordances when he said that "in the beginning there is the relation". Affordances are both relational and embodied. They are scaled with reference to what the organism brings—size, strength, and inclinations based on past encounters with the environment. That is, opportunities for action found in specific objects, places, and so forth, can only be exploited in regard to the action modes that the person is capable of making in that environment. For example, the climability of an incline may require people with a certain level of leg strength. Further, the information specifying such affordances is outside the head—to be detected in the optic array in the course of perceiving–acting cycles of engagements with the environment. Perceiving the relation is just as real as perceiving that John is taller than Mary (paraphrase of Chemero, 2003). Indeed, Mark (2007) has demonstrated that one can perceive when a chair will be sitable for another person.

DISTINGUISHING SOCIAL FROM NONSOCIAL AFFORDANCES

Given this interpretation of affordances, what distinguishes social from nonsocial affordances, given that they are both relational? First, when the environment consists of other people, there are different types of affordances available. For example, we may want to know what another person's dispositional properties would afford, particularly in regard to specific possibilities for relating to that person (Reis, 2008b). The Gibsonian affordance framework in this context has demonstrated that extensional information exists for perceiving whether another person is vulnerable to attack (Gunns, Johnson, & Hudson, 2002), whether they would be able to help you move an object (Richardson, Marsh, & Baron, 2007), whether they are acting deceptively (Runeson & Frykholm, 1983), or whether they are capable of carrying a baby carefully (Hodges & Lindhiem, 2006). It is important to understand that from an ecological perspective dispositions are not conceptualized at a mentalistic level. They are viewed as embodied intentions or inclinations that are the product of a person's unique encounters with the environment. For example, we may hold a baby more closely to our bodies or more tightly as compared to a bag of groceries of the same weight (Hodges & Lindheim, 2006).

Another type of social affordance study (Schmidt, Christianson, Carello, & Baron, 1994) frames social affordances in a somewhat different way that offers a direct bridge to one of the major concerns of this conference—Personality × Situation Interactions and how they can be treated at a behavioral level. Specifically, these investigators measured social dominance and created three conditions: High-Low, High-High, and Low-Low. All participants were asked to coordinate the movements of their limbs with the person they were interacting with. The highest level of coordination was achieved with the asymmetrical as opposed to the symmetrical pairing—that is, the best combination was a High Dominant and Low Dominant person. Coordination may be best in this condition because in it people find a kind of *mutual comfort zone*. That is, taken together, this condition provides a complementarity structure for each person's dispositions. It allows people who want to dominate an opportunity to lead and people who want to follow an opportunity to follow.

These studies can be interpreted in ways that are useful for distinguishing social from physical affordances. Chairs do not seek out sitters in order to have their affordances fulfilled. By contrast, people both individually and collectively may select people to interact with because they are perceived as offering the right kind of interaction possibilities as in the above dominance example. Thus, social affordances have a different, more active and reciprocal organizational structure than physical affordances, a point that becomes critical when we offer an affordance interpretation of personality.

Now, I would like to clarify further the relationship between intrapersonal and interpersonal affordances (Richardson, Marsh, & Baron, 2007). My formulation of affordances allows me to use the same relational concept to deal with both the problem of individuals lifting an object by themselves and lifting it with the help of another person. At issue again are scaling relationships between the demands of what is being lifted (e.g., length or weight) and the response capabilities of the lifter (e.g., arm span). That is, certain situations afford individual-based lifting, while others afford joint lifting, just as different sized groups allow different types of affordances to be fulfilled (Caporeal & Baron, 1997). Another way to frame these results is that the presence of another person alters the physical affordance for lifting by changing response capabilities. In effect, *many physical affordances take a loan on sociality* (Baron, 2007).

More formally, the boundaries between liftable and nonliftable change when another person is available to help with the lifting. The affordance formulation shifts from what "I" am capable of lifting to what "we" are capable of lifting. This shift from "I" to "we" in orientation is the hinge for the emergence of social affordances. For example, mother–child breastfeeding interactions involve more than physical coodinations. Breastfeeding is likely facilitated where there is a joint perception of caring viewed as a social (or proto- "we") affordance. I propose that caring functions as a reciprocal relationship between mother and child as embodied in the *jointness* of breastfeeding. From this perspective, caring becomes a property of a self-organized dynamical social system which, in turn, will modify subsequent physical coordinations top-down—what Campbell (1990) referred to as downward causation. Thus, the invariant of all social affordances may be the emergence of a "we" level of coordination, what Marsh, Richardson, Baron, & Schmidt (2006) refer to as a *social synergy*. Such cyclical mutuality may, in turn, become the prototype of more complex social affordances such as trusting and cooperation. Further, in line with Buber's "In the beginning there is the relation", we may view the mother–child relation as the basic matrix for how personality interacts with situation.

TRAITS AND SITUATIONS: AN AFFORDANCE INTERPRETATION

In order to better understand the reciprocity of Personality and Situation, I propose that traits can be reconceptualized in affordance terms. This move also allows one to deal directly with how to go from traits to behavior in that traits can be viewed in an affordance perspective as affecting response capability, a critical factor in the actualization of affordances. For example, extroverts may have a greater range of social skills than introverts. Given such skills they will likely be better than introverts at exploiting environments that offer limited opportunities for social interaction such as small-sized schools. Further, affordances, because they have one foot in the individual and one foot in the environment (including other people), help us understand how the environment evokes behavior. More generally, different situations afford different behaviors in many ways including what types of traits they require. For example, while many school settings may select for open-mindedness, church settings may recruit for dispositions that support faith. Further, it may be argued that situations can be derived from the objective environmental organizations that Barker (1968) referred to as behavior settings, that is, "behavior settings are the immediate environments of human behavior—their time and place boundaries can be pointed out precisely" (Wicker, 1979, p. 9).

Behavior Settings, Situations and Collective Affordances. Settings, in turn, are organized in ways that allow people to achieve certain collective goals. Such goals need to be achieved if behavior settings are to persist and be effective. For example, a classroom is only likely to be a successful setting for learning if the right combination of teacher, student, and arrangement of physical properties exists. Further, such settings have collective goals and plans—what Barker (1968) refers to as the settings' programs. Behavior settings are organized around specific functions or positions (e.g., roles or standing patterns of behavior) that need to be carried out if the setting is to survive (paraphrase of Wicker, 1979, p.11). Viewed thusly, behavior settings are *constellations of affordances* with a crucial difference. Settings reflect affordances at a *collective* level. Here we truly have a situation where the group is in the individual and the individual is in the group. Further, whereas the affordances at the level of the individual *invite* proper actions, the affordances of a behavior setting have a certain *coercive* character to them (Barker's 1968 environmental force units). These affordances are embedded in the standing patterns of behavior that define proper action as normative in a setting such as a classroom. In its daily operating mode we may speak of a behavior setting as a situation. That is, situations are nested in behavior settings and reflect what properties—from actions to traits—are likely to be salient and in some cases, required in the current space–time slice, what Warren and Shaw (1985) refer to as an event. Situations then are transient environments as compared to behavior settings that have an extended duration and a specific geography in space–time.

Roles, Situations and Behavior. In this section, I will use affordances to explore the relationships among roles, situations, and behavior. From my perspective, a situation refers to what specific affordances are needed at this particular time in the daily functioning of a behavior setting. The concept of behavior setting also allows us to relate *roles* to behaviors. That is, at issue is not only what is afforded to us as individuals but is what is afforded to us as role occupants. Role, what Barker (1968) refers to as a standing pattern of behavior, is not merely a social construction. It requires a specific spatio-temporal grounding such as a teacher in a small school in a small town in the

Midwest. Here, I go beyond Gibson and assume that role affects our response capabilities, much as the arrival of another person may be perceived as affording the liftability of a log at a dyadic level (Asch, 1952). It is this type of naturalistic example that inspired Richardson et al.'s (2007) demonstration that social factors alter physical affordances; that is, the presence of another person changes the boundaries for what is liftable. Similarly, if, as a teacher, I can assume the help of a teaching assistant, this can radically change the types of assignments I can provide to my students. Given my augmented response capabilities, more hands-on types of exercises will be possible. Thus, role-based affordances may moderate between situation and behavior.

Role then is one of the ways that situations evoke behavior, where *by evoke we mean to change the perceived availability of certain affordances*, given that roles potentially alter our response capabilities. Further, roles are one of the loci of organization that guides specific behaviors in a group context. For example, whatever the personality of a point guard on a basketball team, his/her major role (standing pattern of behavior) is not to shoot the basketball but to assist the other players in getting good shots. In this context, role organizes the distribution of passing affordances including shaping response capabilities. It is postulated that good point guards readily provide information that they possess social affordances for passing both by the positioning of their bodies and the nature of their eye contact. Personality, in this case, affects style but not substance. For example, an extroverted point guard might favor making a behind-the-back pass while a more introverted point guard might favor a simple bounce pass. But making the right pass at the right time is what is crucial for this behavior setting, not how it is done.

The individualism of a given player is evidenced in how he or she carries out his or her role as well as in that player's judgments as to whether this is a good time to fast-break. For example, extroverted and/or more aggressive players may be more likely to fast-break at the slightest opportunity because the fast break facilitates spectacular plays like the "dunk." Other players being more introverted and/or conscientious may wait for the more ideal circumstances before looking to fast-break. However, role is still the meta-constraint because if players, because of personality, fast-break at inappropriate times, the coach will pull them out of the game. Specifically, I am suggesting that *personality can make for non-interchangeable* role performance at the behavioral level but within the limits of that role. The classic Barker treatment of role or position is that occupants are interchangeable. In contradistinction, Larry Bird, a great Indiana State and Boston Celtics basketball player, had sufficient passing and leadership skills as a forward that he created a new position—the point forward. Thus, role influences behavior and can, in turn, be modified by occupants' personality-relevant dispositional behaviors. This reflects a particular way in which a Personality × Situation interaction might occur.

Viewed thusly, a basketball game is a behavior setting that provides situations that in Reis' (2008a) terms "affords the expression of personality" as moderated by role expectations. That is, specific cognitions, etc., are nested within traits, which are nested within roles. Given that extroverts may have different intentions, goals, skills, and so forth, than introverts in the same situation, one may speak of Role × Personality interactions. Further, people with different personalities may seek out different behavior settings. Athletic extroverts may, for example, seek out mass audience sports such as football or basketball, whereas athletic introverts may prefer small audience sports such as swimming or college wrestling. What affordance contributes to this kind of analysis is that it provides a way of talking about the selectivity of behavior that is both *embodied* and *embedded socially*. Here, personality functions as a filter or organizer of what affordances are focused on, given a person's inclinations. From this perspective, *personality carries with it situational preferences.*

Suitable Circumstances and the Lock and Key Model

My strategy up until now has been to present my case in broad strokes to give people a feel for my kind of approach. I would now like to be more analytical. Let's begin with Harry Reis' (2008a) suggestion that situations are the settings that afford the expression of personality. That is, "they provide opportunities for certain traits to be expressed" (Reis, 2008a). What might a "stricter" affordance perspective make of this proposition? First, I propose that situations, in effect, are samplings of the broader universe of group-based social affordances that constitutes the core of a behavior setting. Specifically, what does it mean for a situation to afford opportunities? In Barker & Gump's (1964) *Big School, Small School,* school size dictates the opportunity structure. For example, in a large school, the universe of affordances is likely to be greater, more specialized, and allow more opportunities for meeting people in more situations. However, opportunities for one-on-one, more intimate exchanges both academically and personally might be fewer. That is, people may be more spread out and busier.

Reframing Personality × Situation Interactions. At this point, I want to apply the affordance approach to Personality × Situation relationships at a more formal level. First, generally speaking we can use Baron & Boudreau's (1987) notion of a *lock and key* relationship between people and situations to reframe Reis' (2008a) proposition. Specially, if behavior settings include constellations of affordances or opportunities for taking specific actions that allow one to take advantage of the functional utilities of a setting, we can treat personalities in trait terms as offering keys that will unlock the opportunity doors. For example, if a large campus provides a large range of affordances for meeting people in a range of settings, then people with certain traits are more likely to be able to take full advantage of such opportunities—for example, extroverts rather than introverts. Further, in large campuses the social organizations may be more selective, given the large pool of people. By contrast, given that an organization needs a certain minimal number of people to function effectively and carry out its goals, etc., on a small campus, clubs may have to compromise their standards lest they be undermanned. That is, size affects staffing rules or what Barker & Schoggen (1973) referred to as the theory of manning, involving undermanning, optimal manning, and overmanning.

I want to use affordances to reframe traits both structurally and functionally in ways that will allow us to do away with the dualism between trait and situation where situation includes other people. For example, while information specifying the affordance for edibility is available in the fruit to be detected by the animal, the affordance for cooperativeness does not reside exclusively in any single object or entity, it is a "we"-level affordance. It only exists in the reciprocal, mutually facilitated actions of two or more people. Similarly, helpfulness requires a helper and a recipient person in need, competition requires a rival, and dominance requires a subordinate. Such relations are social synomorphs (defined as a perceived congruence between what one person offers and the other person needs) analogous to desks affording writing. These examples are not to be viewed as metaphorical; rather, it is proposed that *such relational structures exist in the world to be detected*. For example, Kean (2000) was able to demonstrate that people are able to accurately discriminate between whether people are cooperating or competing given only point light data regarding patterns of movement for tasks that range from joint folding to a pulling of different ends of a blanket as in a tug of war. Such perceptions are highly accurate even when the images are reduced to pixels so that only abstract dynamic information is available to specify the joint social intentions underlying cooperation.

More generally, in arguing for sociality as a necessary condition to specify certain social motives or traits, we are arguing that, for dispositions to be identified behaviorally, we need *"suitable circumstances,"* what Baron and Misovich (1993) referred to as event activity tests (EATs). For example, seeing a person high in shyness interact with a close friend is less informative then seeing him interact with a stranger.

Suitable circumstances, in effect, move us from a nonobservable disposition to one that is clearly behaviorally specified. Similar arguments can be made for other Big Five traits. For example, even aggressive people do not always act aggressively (Wright & Mischel, 1987).

While this approach is relatively straightforward for traits high in socialness, the more intrapersonal traits such as conscientiousness and information seeking involve a more difficult challenge. However, I propose the problem again is to find "suitable circumstances" or, in my earlier metaphor, "the right key for the right lock." This may involve different time slices. For example, to bring out conscientiousness we may require tasks that need to be performed over time in situations that are important. For example, one tennis player may practice hard for only a few days before an important tournament. In this context, another player who begins to practice several weeks before such a tournament will be perceived as more conscientious than the first one. Finally, I do not wish to imply that conscientiousness does not have social implications. Who better to trust than a conscientious person (see Hogan & Ones, 1997)? Rather, my point is that variations in conscientiousness are ordinarily not readily observable in single social encounters.

Viewing dispositions in these terms suggests that an affordance analysis for the concept of trait allows us to get away from the static, stand-alone character of traits that creates what we theoretically see as a gap to be explained between disposition and behavior. Following McArthur & Baron (1983) and Baron & Boudreau (1987) it may be claimed that an affordance view does a better of job of capturing the situational specificity of traits than do traditional trait approaches (Mischel, 1968). The concept of "suitable circumstances" as manifested in EATS has an advantage over the general Mischelian (Mischel, 1973) approach that personality-related behavior is situationally contingent because the suitable circumstances approach provides a more principled rationale for Personality X Situation interactions. Only certain situations are relevant for certain dispositions. Just as salt is soluble in some liquids and not in others (e.g., in water, but not oil), I claim that "specifically, many personality dispositions have suitable circumstances that are likely to reveal the individual's standing on that disposition" (Baron & Misovich, 1999, p.600).

In sum, "suitable circumstances" encompasses the relational structure of affordances, whereby personality "... is a key in the search of the right lock." Reciprocally, the environment (e.g., a behavior setting) is the lock waiting to be opened so that its affordances can be realized (paraphrased from Baron & Boudreau, 1987, p.1227). The basic idea here is that personality and setting interactions are not arbitrary. Personality and settings, including other people, exhibit reciprocity or mutuality because *each is incomplete without the other*. A further derivation from this approach is that we parse the Big Five traits into dispositions that facilitate or inhibit the transformation of "I"- to "we"-based affordances by virtue of the settings they favor.

The connectivity and selectivity of personality. Personality from such a perspective is jointly defined by the range of affordances people can activate as keys and the range of opportunities that occur for unlocking settings including groupings of people (Baron & Boudreau, 1987). More specifically, different personality traits provide different response capabilities for connecting to subsets of affordances in a given behavior setting. *The specificity of these connections is the defining ecological behavioral property of this new view of personality.* That is, any given behavior setting has a plethora of affordances, which are differentially available to people with differing response capabilities. Complex settings offer a range of affordance, including "I"- versus "We"-favoring affordances, only some of which (a) will be detected by specific people, or (b) will be actualized by still a smaller subject of people. Settings in this view are not passive, just as people select situations to use as a way of satisfying personality-driven needs, goals, motives, and so forth, so settings recruit certain types of people. For example, competitive people may select settings that reward competitiveness ranging from sports to chess—both introverts and extroverts can be competitive but differ in how they seek to express that competitiveness—chess versus team sports, for example. In regard to settings, basketball coaches may selectively search for highly competitive, outgoing players. On the other hand, the Peace Corps may prefer people with a cooperative bent as ambassadors of the United States. Settings, in effect, recruit occupants who will fit in. Indeed, settings may signal their affordance availabilities both verbally in their program description and nonverbally in terms of the subtle cues they give in interviews to make people feel comfortable or uncomfortable. Moreover, the work of Price & Bouffard (1974) demonstrates that a strong consensus exists regarding peoples' perceptions of what activities are afforded by different settings. For example, churches afford both worshiping and socializing, which may differ in the sociality of the affordances they reflect—for example, individual prayer versus communal activities.

In sum, in this view personality is a set of dispositions (e.g., traits, motives, attitudes, emotions) collectively viewed as inclinations (Heft, 2008) that attune the person to select, detect, and realize certain affordances rather than others. This interpretation also assumes that personality includes effectivities (Turvey & Shaw, 1979) or response capabilities for actualizing the affordances of the physical and social environment. For example, people who detect affordances for nurturance need to be both willing and able to dispense caring. It should be noted that this model is highly ecological in that we are modeling a successful ecosystem in the sense that "each niche requires a particular kind of plant or animal and each animal requires a particular niche" (Baron & Boudreau, 1987, p. 1227). Most importantly, *an ecosystem is the meta-model of an affordance-based analysis*—it is the ultimate example of the lock and key metaphor. We can use it to describe the general properties of all affordances—a fit or connection between response capabilities and environmental opportunities. More specifically, the model can be used to describe a specific application such as a Disposition × Situation interaction. It is also the model behind the idea of suitable circumstances—that is, *dispositions are linked to behavior because they are both parts of a broader system*. We now turn to how such a system model might work.

Personality and the Development of Behavior Settings

Given this analysis I want to explore whether these ideas can be turned into the basis for a fresh look at the idea of a theory of situations. In such a theory, situations are a complementary mirror image of a theory of personality in the same sense that certain niches imply certain plants and animals, while certain plants and animals imply certain niches. At issue is the powerful idea of co-evolution, which, in turn, is likely to be an example of what we now refer to as the self-organization of complex systems. With regard to social settings, we need to understand why certain opportunities are configured in certain ways to support certain dispositions, and/or, types of people. What I suggest is that the social analogue of co-evolution is the embedding of personality in the organizational dynamics of behavior settings in regard to (a) what roles need to be performed for the maintenance of a behavior setting, and (b) the ability of the setting to recruit people with the appropriate personality traits to carry out these roles successfully.[1]

It should also be noted that in line with Kelley et al's (2003) meta-concept of an atlas of interpersonal situations, the requirement of interdependence is a basic system property of my approach. That is, *dynamic interdependence* is what systems are all about. Further, in regard to my affordance analysis that complex settings have multiple nestings of affordances, which are likely to be differentially sampled by people with different dispositions (keys), a very similar view is taken in the atlas in

---

[1] This is my formulation, not Barker's; he eschews personality, given his focus on collective behavior.

the chapter on encounters with strangers. Here, Ickes' (1982) view that such situations (locks) are unstructured is reinterpreted as a situation that is multiply structured—or "hyperstructured"—"affording persons with very different social tendencies, unique opportunities to express themselves" (Kelley, 2003, p. 348).

This idea is very close to both Baron & Boudreau's 1987 use of a lock and key metaphor and more specifically to their proposition that "settings therefore offer many possible worlds through their affordance structures" (p. 1227). The fact that Kelley arrived at this analysis independently is encouraging. It is encouraging because it shows that the utility of affordance can be arrived at in multiple ways. The next step, I believe, is to "use affordances to group phenotypically different settings that share important affordances" (Baron & Boudreau 1987, p. 1227). For example, both art museum openings and church suppers may afford opportunities for meeting people. It is time to attempt this move because it is perhaps a path through which one builds both a typology of settings and a typology of behavior, where behavior is not written individually but is embedded in the roles and affordances of behavior settings. Further, I propose that the kind of ordering of affordances within the setting that I present holds at the level of both phylogeny and ontogeny, thereby giving the kind of developmental or narrative organization that has been lacking until now.

TOWARD A TYPOLOGY OF SITUATIONS AND BEHAVIOR

Current approaches to building such typologies have followed two major strategies. One is a bottom-up approach, which codes natural language (Saucier & Goldberg, 2008); the other is a theoretically driven approach that Kelley has pioneered. Kelley's approach involves analyzing interpersonal situations through their basic property—interdependence—and then parsing interdependence into various situations that reflect major problems that are raised by interdependence such as conflicting and corresponding mutual joint control, "me" versus "we," threat, and asymmetric dependence. One of the unusual characteristics of Kelley's (2003) analysis is that it took into consideration group size as a moderator of certain effects, for example, single person versus two- and three-person games.

Group Size and Affordances

I would like to build on this idea that group size is a moderator of certain situational effects to *make group size an engine that organizes the distribution of affordances*, taking as my points of departure Caporeal and Baron's (1997) use of the group as mind's environment and Barker's use of the size of behavior settings as a key constraint on the structures and processes that regulate behavior settings. For example, deviants in a large behavior setting are expelled whereas in a small setting they are corrected and resocialized. Further, size matters sufficiently that Dunbar's (1993) analysis suggests that it was increasing group size that produced a phase transition from nonverbal communication to the point where language developed. The meta-assumption that such a model makes is that because we are dealing with relationships that can be modeled as complex dynamical systems, even a small change in the triggering independent variable (control parameter), such as size, "is able to produce a qualitative change or phase transition all at once (i.e., without moving through intermediate stages)" (Baron & Misovich, 1999, pp. 595). Viewed thusly, our typology of situations is also a process model such that group size differences change affordances in ways that radically alter their meaning and availability. Thus, in a sense, size gives a kind of developmental or evolutionary description of what happens to dynamical systems as they become more complex. Moreover, this progression occurs in both top-down and bottom-up processes. The top-down effects of size constrain affordances by affecting resource availability and allocation, while the bottom-up effects involve the output from one phase serving as the input to the next phase. For example, size stresses certain affordance boundaries because beyond a certain size face-to-face interaction is difficult. Specifically, when memory load is strained and/or sufficient nonverbal information is lacking, processing then becomes categorical and the group develops role differentiation. Each of these changes, in turn, affects the type and amount of affordances available. Note that cognitive processes are, in these examples, constrained by social challenges.

Group Size and the Evolution of Affordances

In the next sections, I draw upon a systems-based evolutionary model suggested by Caporeal & Baron (1997). This model is reinterpreted as an affordance-based typology of situations and behavior. For example, when group size is two, that is, a dyad, different social action is afforded from when the group size escalates to five. Major dyadic affordances flow from forming a basic social unit. For example, assuming that the interactants are post-pubescent, mating is afforded, which in turn can lead to parent–child affordances typically involving caring, which shape basic personality dispositions. This type of relationship is also a prototype for expert–novice relations involving affective and behavioral synchronizing, which likely begins to shape traits such as agreeableness, shyness, and openness to new information. Interpersonal affordances for trust are also likely to begin at this basic level of social interdependence. Vygotsky, Cole, John-Steiner, & Scriber's (1978) proposition that social scaffolding accelerates cognitive development (the zone of proximal development) can also be interpreted in these terms.

When we shift to five or more members (but less than ten), group- or team-level type affordances become possible beginning with distributed cognition. Here, shareability functions as a constraint on cognition and role differentiation. The opportunity to cooperate in the form of role coordination becomes possible. For the first time, the issue of whether each person is "pulling his or her own weight" becomes important so that conscientiousness becomes socially relevant and perhaps becomes transformed into dependability. Further, the major behavioral setting shifts from the family to secondary settings like school or work. In classic evolutionary analyses, examples include foraging, hunting, and gathering. In the contemporary setting, examples include study groups and work teams, as well as sports teams. The next level of size, the band 10–30 (which is the first group size to move from place to place[2]) is key to our broader social functioning. Two basic collective affordance problems emerge: (a) maintaining group stability and (b) building coalitions between social units, ranging from dyads, to families, to work teams, and so forth. Problems such as building group cohesion become prominent and with it affordances relevant to in-group, out-group stereotyping and majority and minority issues become salient.

Most broadly, as group size increases, two simultaneous processes occur. First, aspects of the lower-order affordance problems persist and become nested in a broader set of issues. For example, trust remains a problem as does role coordination, but these problems now have to be viewed within the context of a higher level of problems dealing with intergroup issues. Thus, the progression is from the intrapersonal to interpersonal, then from intragroup to intergroup affordance problems. One of the key constraints to note at this point flows from our meta-assumption that we are dealing not simply with more complex aggregates of people but with more complex dynamical systems. One of the most important implications of this recognition is that the highest level of organization feeds back and modifies the functioning of the lower levels. Consider a simple example—an eco-niche comprised of grass, plants, and then trees will have a different pattern of growth from a

---

[2] Caporeal & Baron (1997) also deal with a macroband the size of 300 or larger, a unit beyond the scope of the present analysis.

situation where trees do not exist. Similarly, the intragroup affordances will change importantly when intergroup processes emerge. For example, intra-group affordances that favor divergent thinking and the acceptance of minority views may be suppressed as a kind of groupthink mentality emerges. Further, with a larger behavior setting, deviants are no longer likely to be tolerated. They will be rejected and expelled from the group (Barker & Schoggen, 1973; Wicker, 1979). Thus, staffing theory (Wicker, 1979) and groupthink theory (Janis, 1972) make similar predictions regarding the toleration of opinion deviants.

Further at the intergoup level, distinctiveness motives (Brewer, 1991) are likely to be suppressed in favor of people wanting to fit in. People want to belong as the group orients itself to dealing with out-group level conflict and threat. Most generally, the individual is acting less and less as an individual and more as a group member. In such large-group situations, knowing personality traits may be less predictive of behavior than knowing the individual's roles and how strongly people have internalized group norms and values (Baron, 2002). It should be noted in this context that I am not talking about the relative salience of agentic versus communion types of motives. Rather, I am hypothesizing that, in multiple regression terms, role or group-based variables will be more predictive of behavior variance than individual-based variables. Further, given that my general approach is to favor "this and that" over "either/or" formulations, conceptually, my stance would be that as group size increases, individual motives become embedded in or entrained by group-level demands. For example, individual traits such as introversion-extroversion become expressed in terms of role selection and/or in how roles are performed (see my basketball example in this chapter).

Note that this is analogous to our tree, plant, and grass problem. For example, to predict the growth of grass, we now need to know how the grass is affected by the creation of shade and the growth of trees' roots. Knowing about the properties of different grasses independent of these system-level contexts will be of limited utility. Similarly, in the interpersonal settings, affordances for trust are nested in the dynamic between intra- and intergroup processes. Framing the problem in this way is, in turn, useful in understanding group organization and processes such as Granovetter's (1973) "strength of weak ties." This phenomenon occurs when intragroup cohesion is limited (the opposite of groupthink). These issues become more salient as group size increases and group-intergroup relations are between macrobands, for example, tribes, or business organization, or nations.

Specifically, weak within-group ties allow a greater role of individual personality traits as predictors, with trust becoming a matter of interpersonal experiences as opposed to group-constructed social reality. In such groups, personal identity is more related to intragroup than intergroup processes. Further, weak within-group ties encourage subgroup formation. In general, affordances become more a matter of satisfying individual needs and subgroup roles. But, we should always remember that from a complex systems framework even when an organization allows subgroup formation, size will affect lower-order processes. The role of personality and the nature of trust function differently in large and small groups. Thus, size, as Barker has emphasized, has its own constraints both in terms of advantages and disadvantages.

Affordances and Dynamical Systems. I would like to conclude my exploration of the interphase of behavior, settings, and dispositions with an overview of what the concept of affordances, when linked to a dynamical systems view of a relationship between parts and wholes, buys us. Perhaps the most important insight is that there is really *no useful individual level of analysis* for the behaviors we are interested in; that is, behaviors that go beyond reflexes, habits, or largely hormonally-driven actions. The Big Five type traits, if viewed in an affordance context, are relational at the level of behavior either directly or indirectly. For example, even if we begin with something like a neurological basis for sensation-seeking (Zuckerman, 1978) or a brain-based analysis of introversion (Eysenck and Levey, 1972), I would argue that at a behavioral level, what is critical is a seeking after an environment that allows such people to avoid highly stimulating events such as the presence of other people. That is, such people seek affordances for quiet, given their limited response capabilities for handling stimulation, and in a complementary manner such people may give off affordance information that they want to be left alone. Similarly, while conscientiousness appears to be a largely intrapersonal trait, people with this trait are likely to be recruited into certain social situations such as the formation of a study group in settings such as law school. Specifically, such people may afford reliable performance of an important group-based affordance involving distributed cognition (Hogan & Ones, 1997). And as we suggested earlier, traits such as dominance directly imply the presence of a person to be dominated (Schmidt, Christianson, Carillo, & Baron, 1994).

Further, it is likely that as group size increases, more individualistic traits like conscientiousness become transformed at the level of social affordances into social actions such as dependability, which, in turn, become the building blocks for social-unit level processes such as trust. Thus, dependability is embodied in the reliability of reciprocally relevant actions over time, which in turn leads to perceptions of trustworthiness. Moreover, as we scale up in terms of group size, dependability is likely to move into role-based phenomena. That is, at issue then is the reliability of role-constrained actions. For example, on a basketball team, can the point guard be trusted to look to pass to an open teammate as opposed to looking first for his or her own shot? Dependability is reorganized at a group-role level in terms of cooperative team play. That is, dependability contributes to conceptions of trustworthiness, which in turn affords cooperation. And as I have noted earlier, cooperativeness can, in itself, be directly perceived as a joint social action (Kean, 2000).

New Behavioral Paradigms for Studying Social Affordances

My own recent research is direct evidence for the inherent behavior-orientedness of the ecological approach. Richardson, Marsh, & Baron (2007) carried out a series of studies designed to demonstrate what the boundaries were for the transition from intrapersonal to interpersonal affordances for lifting planks of wood, and in some conditions carrying the wood across the room. Most relevant to our present analysis, the effects we found were relational; the key parameters for grasping were captured by the ratio of physical properties like the length of wood and a person's arm span. That is, the point at which participants switched modes of grasping, be it one versus two hands or one-person versus two-person lifting and carrying, occurred at similar action-scaled ratios (i.e., plank length to hand span, plank length to arm span). Basically, this research demonstrated that when peoples' own effectivities are insufficient to utilize a given affordance for lifting, they resort to joint lifting, thereby defining the boundaries for a shift from intra- to interpersonal affordances for lifting. More generally, such data suggest that the perception and actualization of affordances should be understood from the perspective of dynamical systems theory (Richardson et al., 2007), with the presence of others functioning as a higher-order control parameter that changes the affordance boundaries for liftability.

In social psychological terms, the two-person action system is a situation in which a social unit emerges over time to form a "fragile we" within a "mutually shared social field" (Asch, 1952). In effect, the 2P condition moves the individual from simple embodiment (acting alone) toward joint activity—what we might call socially-embodied coopera-tion. More broadly at issue is determining the point at which mere behavioral coordination of movement with another person can be viewed as teamwork, a situation not so different from when a team of basketball players moves from physical synchronies to playing as a team, where a team is a kind of *social synergy* (Marsh et al., 2006).

What this research design does is to give us is a behavioral paradigm within which one could input, for example, variations on the Big Five traits. For example, do shy people take longer—that is, need greater discrepancies between hand or arm size and plank length before they turn to joint lifting than outgoing people? Or do people who are high on conscientiousness, persist longer in trying to lift the plank by themselves because they try harder? Even more to the point, I predict that people high in agreeableness may move from an intrapersonal to an interpersonal lifting *before* they are physically unable to do the lifting. A study by Isenhower (2009) provides a physical analogue to such personality pairings. He created pairs of individuals matched for either short or long arms or mismatched in arm span. It was found that the lifting process was dictated by the participant with the smaller arm span for each pair in all three groups. Specifically, liftability for a pair was more constrained by what the person with the shorter arm span person could do.

Researching the Shift to "We"-Based Affordances

In this context, perhaps the most interesting direction for affordance-oriented research that comes out of such hybrid studies, which mix social and physical affordances and are described above, is how physical coordinations might become an occasion for forming a relationship. Given the foundational nature of trust for extended social interaction (Baron, 2007), do people who are led to trust the other person switch to a two-person mode earlier? That is, when and how are our physical limitations embedded in social prompts and constraints? We also need to look at the consequences of effective passing in sports like basketball or soccer. Specifically, what kinds of social affordances emerge with teamwork? For example, are affordances more coercive in a situation that increases joint outcomes? Here, behaving in synch with other people may create a situation that induces Barker-like environmental force units, a precondition for collective affordances. The team is, in effect, a social niche where the person is in the group and the group is in the person. "I" affordances become "we" affordances.

Further, my analysis of the relationship between group size and the emergence of social affordances suggests that at the level of the relation or group, these affordances are no less real than physical affordances like a desk affording writing (Barker's, 1968 synomorph). At issue in all such social situations are constrained opportunities for social interaction. This suggests research that turns coordinations between individuals into group processes, thereby providing a new level of constraint ranging from group norms to group roles.

This group-level interpretation of social affordances moves us beyond focusing research on physical coordinations that secondarily take on social meaning to exploring situations where the physical coordinations are socially or group embedded from the start. For example, groupness can be created in two ways:

(1) Subjects could be told that they and their lifting partners will be compared with other lifting combinations in regard to the speed with which they carry the planks across the room with a valuable prize for the winning team.

(2) Following Horwitz (1954), lifters can be told in one condition that they will be interacting with these same people in future experiments versus being told that they will not interact with them in the future. Horwitz (1954) found that those expecting to interact again formed a stronger group identity in the form of remembering incomplete group tasks better than interrupted individual tasks while the reverse was true for people not expecting to interact in the future.

Each of these paradigms has something to recommend it. The Horwitz (1954) procedure simulates a key characteristic of being part of a behavior setting—the continuity over time. On the other hand, the competition paradigm captures a central characteristic of ongoing teams—the occurrence of joint outcomes, which turn coordinations into cooperation (Baron, 2007). Taken together, such procedures can perhaps simulate the collective affordances that characterize behavior settings.

Finally, it is perhaps not an accident that Aronson (Aronson, Stephan, Sikes, Barney, & Snapp, 1978) called his cooperation paradigm a jigsaw strategy. Here each member of a group has only part of the necessary information needed for the problem to be completed. What occurs is the creation of social synomorphs where people are both locks and keys. In the jigsaw example, success is rooted in reciprocity. Just as the desk and chair are shaped to support writing and studying, so each of the cooperative constituents in such systems are fragile "we's" in the making (Baron, 2007).

SUMMARY AND CONCLUSIONS

One route for reinstating behavior into social psychology is the recognition that dispositions and behaviors are embedded or situated in settings that provide affordances for socially-embodied activities. From this perspective, embodied cognition is, in most cases, a necessary but not sufficient condition for achieving socially-embodied behavior. The most important things we do are as parts of social units. Sociality is the meta-constraint on dispositions, behavior, and settings. A new social cognition will be behavioral if we abandon the Cartesian mantra "I think therefore I am" and replace it with "I act with others, therefore I am." It is from this perspective that I propose we parse the Big Five personality traits into dispositions that facilitate or inhibit the transformation from "I" to "we" affordances.

Finally, I do not wish to throw out the baby with the bath water. Cognitivism has a role in all of this—it allows us some distance between what we notice in the world and what we do (or don't) do about it. Perceptions of affordances invite, but do not force, appropriate or proper behaviors. In certain situations such perceptions need to be moderated cognitively (note, not mediated). For example, when I notice injustice in the world I might have an inclination to exact immediate revenge, but this may not be a wise or practical behavior. The adaptive value of thinking in such situations is considerable (Hodges, personal communication, 2008). Just as perceptions may constrain, so may thinking alter the perception–action cycle. Thus, the final take-away message is that the mystery is no mystery. One misplaces behavior only when one conceptualizes the phenomena of interest in social psychology in ways that ignore the role of bodies, relations, and groups. The value of the present affordance-based framework is that it makes the relevance of these factors inescapable.

ACKNOWLEDGMENTS

I wish to acknowledge the helpful comments and suggestions of William G. Graziano, Bert H. Hodges, and Joan Boykoff Baron on earlier drafts of this chapter and the thoughtful responses of the participants at the Purdue Symposium.

REFERENCES

Aronson, E., Stephan, C. Sikes, J., Barney, N., & Snapp, M. (1978). *The jigsaw classroom*. Beverly Hills, CA: Sage.

Asch, S. (1952). *Social psychology*. New York: Prentice Hall.

Barker, R. G. (1968). *Ecological psychology*. Palo Alto, CA: Stanford University Press.

Barker, R. G., & Gump, P. (1964). *Big school, small school: High school size and student behavior*. Palo Alto: CA: Stanford University Press.

Barker, R. G., & Schoggen, P. (1973). *Qualities of community life: Methods of measuring environment and behavior applied to an American and an English town*. San Francisco, CA: Jossey-Bass.

Baron, R. M. (2002). *A dynamical systems perspective on individual-group relations: Theoretical and applied considerations.* Paper presented at the meeting of the Society for Experimental Social Psychology, Columbus, Ohio.

Baron, R. M. (2007). Situating coordination and cooperation between ecological and social psychology. *Ecological Psychology, 19,* 179–199.

Baron, R. M., & Boudreau, L. (1987). An ecological perspective on integrating personality and social psychology. *Journal of Personality and Social Psychology, 53,* 122–128.

Baron, R. M., & Misovich, S. J. (1993). Dispositional knowing from an ecological perspective. *Personality and Social Psychology Bulletin, 19,* 541–542.

Baron, R. M., & Misovich, S. J. (1999). On the relationship between social and cognitive modes of organization. In S. Chaiken & Y. Trope (Eds.), *Dual-processes in social psychology* (pp. 586–605). New York: The Guilford Press.

Brewer, M. B. (1991). The social self: On being the same and different at the same time. *Personality and Social Psychology Bulletin, 17,* 475–482.

Buber, M. (1970). *I and thou.* New York: Scribner.

Campbell, D. T. (1990). Levels of organization, downward causation and selection-theory approach to ecological psychology. In G. Greenberg & E. Tobach (Eds.), *Theories of the evolution of knowing. The T. C. Scheirla Conference Series, Vol. 4* (pp. 1–17). Hillsdale, NJ: Lawrence Erlbaum Associates, Inc.

Caporeal, L. R., & Baron, R. M. (1997). Group as mind's environment. In J. A. Simpson & D. T. Kenrick (Eds.), *Evolutionary social psychology* (pp. 317–344). Hillsdale, NJ: Lawrence Erlbaum Associates, Inc.

Chemero, T. (2003). Radical empiricism through the ages. *Contemporary Psychology, 48,* 18–20.

Dunbar, R. I. M. (1993). Coevolution of neocortical size, group size and language in humans. *Behavioral and Brain Science, 16,* 681–735.

Eysenck, H. J. & Levey, A. (1972). Conditioning, introversion-extroversion and the strength of the nervous system. In V. D. Nebylitsyn & J. A. Gray (Eds.), *Biological basis of individual behaviour* (pp. 206–220). London: Academic Press.

Gibson, J. J. (1986). *The ecological approach to visual perception.* Hillsdale, NJ: Lawrence Erlbaum Associate. (Original work published 1979.)

Granovetter, M. S. (1973). The strength of weak ties. *American Journal of Sociology, 78,* 1360–1380.

Gunns, R. E., Johnston, L., & Hudson, S. M. (2002). Victim selection and kinematics: A point-light investigation of vulnerability to attack. *Journal of Nonverbal Behavior, 26,* 129–158.

Heft, H. H. (2001). *Ecological psychology in context: James Gibson, Roger Barker and the legacy of William James' radical empiricism.* Mahwah, NJ: Erlbaum.

Heft, H. H. (2008). *The participatory character of landscape.* Unpublished manuscript.

Hodges, B. H., & Lindheim, O. (2006). Carrying babies and groceries: The effect of moral and social weight on caring. *Ecological Psychology, 16.* 93–111.

Hogan, J., & Ones, D. S. (1997). Conscientiousness and integrity at work. In R. Hogan, R. Johnson, & S. Briggs (Eds.), *Handbook of personality psychology* (pp. 849–870). CA: Academic Press Inc.

Horwitz, M. (1954). The recall of interrupted tasks: An experimental study of individual motivation in relation to group goals. *Human Relations, 7,* 3–28.

Ickes, W. (1982). A basic paradigm for the study of personality, roles, and social behavior. W. Ickes & E. S. Knowles (Eds.). *Intergroup cognition and intergroup behavior* (pp. 75–107). Mahwah, NJ: Erlbaum.

Isenhower, R. W., Richardson, M. J., Carello, C., Baron, R. M, & Marsh, K. L. (2009). *Affording cooperation: Embodied constraints, dynamics, and action-scaled invariance in joint lifting.* Unpublished manuscript.

Janis, I. L. (1972). *Victims of Groupthink.* Boston: Houghton Mifflin.

Kean, K. J. (2000). An investigation into the interpersonal kinematics of cooperation and competition. *Dissertation Abstracts International Section B: The Sciences and Engineering, 60,* 4965.

Kelley, H. H. (2003). Encounters with strangers. In H. H. Kelley, J. G. Holmes, N. L. Kerr, H. T. Reis, C. E. Rusbult, P. A. M. Van Lange (Eds.), *An atlas of interpersonal relations.* Cambridge, UK: Cambridge University Press (pp. 338–352).

Mark, L. S. (2007). Perceiving the actions of other people. *Ecological Psychology, 19,* 107–136.

Marsh, K. L., Richardson, M. J., Baron, R. M., & Schmidt, R. C. (2006). Contrasting approaches to perceiving and acting with others. *Ecological Psychology, 18,* 1–37.

McArthur, L. Z., & Baron, R. M. (1983). Toward an ecological theory of social perception. *Psychological Review, 90,* 215–228.

Miller, G. A., Galanter, E., & Pribram, K. H. (1960). *Plans and the structure of behavior.* New York: Holt, Rinehart, & Winston.

Mischel, W. (1968). *Personality and assessment.* New York: Wiley.

Mischel, W. (1973). Toward a cognitive social learning reconceptualization of personality. *Psychological Review, 80,* 252–283.

Price, R. H., & Bouffard, D. L. (1974). Behavioral appropriateness and situational constraint as dimensions of social behavior. *Journal of Personality and Social Psychology, 30,* 579–586.

Reis, H. T. (2008a, February 2). *Towards a psychology of situations.* Discussant comments in response to symposium. Annual meeting of the Society of Personality and Social Psychology, Albuquerque, New Mexico.

Reis, H. T. (2008b). Reinvigorating the concept of situation in social psychology. *Personality and Social Psychology Review, 12,* 311–329.

Richardson, M. J., Marsh, K. L., & Baron, R. M. (2007). Judging and actualizing intrapersonal and interpersonal affordances. *Journal of Experimental Psychology, 33,* 845–859.

Runeson, S., & Frykholm, G. (1983). Kinematic specification of dynamics as an informational basis for person-and-action perception: Expectation, gender recognition and deceptive intention. *Journal of Experimental Psychology, 112,* 585–615.

Saucier, G., & Goldberg, L. R. (2008). Lexical studies of indigenous personality factors: Premises, products, and prospects. *Journal of Personality, 69,* 847–879.

Schmidt, R. C. (2007). Scaffolds for social meaning. *Ecological Psychology, 19,* 137–151.

Schmidt, R. C., Christianson, N., Carrillo, C., & Baron, R. M. (1994). Effects of social and physical variables on between-person visual coordination. *Ecological Psychology, 6,* 154–184.

Schoggen, P. C. (1989). *Behavior settings: A revision and extension of Roger Barker's ecological psychology.* Stanford, CA: Stanford University Press.

Turvey, M. T., & Shaw, R. (1979). The primacy of perceiving: An ecological reformulation of perception for understanding memory. In L. G. Nilsson (Ed.), *Perspectives on memory research: Essays in honor of Uppsala University's 500th anniversary* (pp. 167–221). Hillsdale, NJ: Lawrence Erlbaum Associates, Inc.

Vygotsky, L. S., Cole, M., John-Steiner, V., & Scriber, S. (1978). *Mind in society: Development of higher psychological processes.* Cambridge, MA: Harvard University Press.

Warren, W. H., & Shaw, R. (1985). Events and encounters as units of analysis for ecological psychology. In W. H. Warren, Jr. & R. Shaw (Eds.), *Persistence and change; Proceedings of the First International Conference on Event Perception* (pp. 1–27). Hillsdale, NJ: Lawrence Erlbaum Associates, Inc.

Wicker, A. W. (1979). *An introduction to ecological psychology* (pp. 9–10). Monterey, CA: Brooks/Cole.

Wright, J. C., & Mischel, W. (1987). A conditional approach to dispositional constructs: The local predictability of social behavior. *Journal of Personality and Social Psychology, 55,* 454–469.

Wyer, R. S., & Srull, T. K. (1986). Human cognition in its social context. *Psychological Review, 93,* 322–339.

Zajonc, R. B. (1980). Feelings and thinking: preferences need no inferences. *American Psychologist, 35,* 157–175.

Zuckerman, M. (1978). Dimensions of sensation seeking. In H. London & J. Exner (Eds.), *Dimensions of personality* (pp. 487–549). New York: Wiley.

III

Behavior and
Inter-Individual Processes

14 Behavior Between People: Emphasizing the "Act" in Interaction

Christopher R. Agnew
Janice R. Kelly

Understanding behavior has always been a defining goal of social psychology. Behaviors involving others, whether in their initiation, their enactment, or their consequences, are of particular interest to social psychologists. Not surprisingly, behaviors featuring the intertwining of outcomes of actors can be a theoretical and measurement challenge, though not one that has resulted in reduced enthusiasm for the attempt (e.g., Kelley et al., 2003). This section contains a number of chapters that focus on behavior, both broadly and specifically defined, and inter-individual processes.

Of course, not all behaviors are the same; they differ in fundamental and dramatic ways. For example, one way in which behaviors differ is in their relative independence versus interdependence (Agnew, 1999). Some actions require other people for enactment (e.g., intercourse) while other actions can be performed without outside assistance or co-action (e.g., tooth brushing). Behavior also differs depending on the context in which it is generated. Reading a book on particle physics while sitting alone in a library is quite different from reading it while surrounded by a group of friends at a party. Wincing at a colleague's less than sensitive remark at a faculty meeting is markedly different from fluttering one's eyes in response to a sand storm. In these examples, the outward behaviors may be the same (reading, wincing), but enactment in one setting versus another conveys vastly different sentiments, has different social implications, and generates markedly different attributions on the part of behavioral observers.

Interpersonal interaction adds yet another layer of complexity to the study of behavior. In interpersonal interaction, behaviors are enacted with varying degrees of fidelity with respect to the communicator's intentions. That behavior is then decoded or interpreted by the receiver, again with varying degrees of precision, and a response is generated. An interaction sequence repeats these patterns of enactment, interpretation, and response. Even the important social behavior of verbal communication requires interpretation and response, with accordant difficulties for both actors and those who wish to study those behaviors.

Moreover, the very definition of what constitutes "behavior" becomes challenging in interpersonal contexts. For example, consider ending a romantic relationship, or "breaking up." "Breakup" is often considered a key dependent variable in close relationship research and is used to validate a number of relationship process variables. It is particularly prized among social psychological researchers given that it is considered behavioral in nature, in contrast to the multiplicity of psychological variables often investigated. But what is "breakup," behaviorally? Is it an individual's action(s) or a dyadic outcome? A number of researchers have treated it as the latter, ignoring the discrete behaviors that may be said to constitute the action of breakup. Recent work has begun to address this theoretical and measurement limitation (VanderDrift, Agnew, & Wilson, in press), but there are a constellation of interpersonal behaviors that defy easy, clean, and clear definition and present a corresponding measurement challenge.

Behavior is an exceptionally broad concept that, not surprisingly, fills different niches within the field. Art Aron's chapter (Chapter 15) serves as a useful reminder of the multiple roles served by behavior in social psychological research. All too often, behavior is considered important only as a key dependent variable. Certainly understanding the determinants or precursors of important and consequential behavior is a critical aim of the field. But behavior is also often used as a criterion variable for validating self-report measures. Behavior measures are seen as desirable given that they are seen as being relatively "objective," and less susceptible to purposeful bias. Moreover, at times behavior is used as a means of operationalizing a specific affective, cognitive, or motivational state, at the individual level (e.g., smiling face as operationalization of happiness), dyad level (e.g., mutual eye gazing as an operationalization of shared romantic interest), or group level (e.g., audience applause as an operationalization of popular approval).

Behavior also may be seen as playing a mediating role, providing the necessary middle step(s) in a process involving multiple steps (and, often, multiple actors). Behavioral confirmation (Snyder, Tanke, & Berscheid, 1977) is a perfect example of this role. Aron also reminds us of the classic role of behavior as an experimental manipulation, such as the actions taken by a confederate in a lab study. In fact, the use of behavior as independent variable may be more common in social psychological research than its use as a dependent one. Finally, Aron describes how neuroscience methods often serve the same function for social psychologist studying neural activity as traditional behavior measures do.

Regardless of the niche filled by behavior, Harry Reis (Chapter 16) argues that the relationship context of behavior should be of central concern to social psychologist. He reviews findings from a number of studies demonstrating how behavior varies as context varies. For example, the Reis and Shaver (1988) model of intimacy clearly delineates that when self-disclosure is not met with sensitivity on the part of a listener, feelings of intimacy will not develop. Thus, behavioral consequences differ as a function of perceived responsiveness (for more on the general importance of perceived responsiveness in understanding interpersonal behavior, see Reis, Clark, & Holmes, 2004).

In addition, Reis outlines the unique and integrative orientation of social psychology with respect to other disciplines in its approach to behavior. In its emphasis on situational factors underlying behavior, social psychology blends elements from various "macro" orientations, including sociology, political science, and economics. In its emphasis on person factors, social psychology blends elements from the realms of neuroscience, biology, and biochemistry. Reis also provides a clear overview of aspects of interdependence theory that are particularly relevant to behavior: (a) the degree of one's outcome interdependence with an interaction partner, and (b) whether a situation is characterized as being one of exchange or of coordination. These aspects suggest the values of an interdependence analysis in helping understand how relationship context shapes individual and dyadic behavior.

John Holmes and Justin Cavallo describe other key elements of interdependence theory in their chapter (Chapter 17). Building on the cognitive-affective personality system (CAPS) framework offered by Mischel and Shoda (1995), Holmes and Cavallo emphasize the importance of considering abstract properties of situations to improve behavioral prediction. As illustrated in Chapter 17, the CAPS model incorporates a person-by-situation interactionist perspective, holding that specific features of situations activate specific cognitive and affective elements in individuals that then produce responses to situations. Holmes and Cavallo argue that the notion of "situation" in the CAPS model is not at an appropriately abstract level to allow for a priori prediction of what specific cognitive-affective elements would be activated. To help overcome this limitation, they review recent developments by interdependence theorists to produce a comprehensive "theory of situations."

True to its origins as a theory crafted by students of Kurt Lewin, interdependence theory is ultimately concerned with the social psychological determinants of interpersonal behavior. It expands on Lewin's oft-cited behavior formula [b = ƒ (p, e)] by explicitly taking into account person and relational elements that influence the interaction occurring between two people. They describe six key dimensions of situations identified to date (as elaborated in Kelley et al., 2003). Holmes and Cavallo also review recent work on the risk regulation model (Murray, Holmes, & Collins, 2006), a model that describes the delicate balancing act of being dependent on a relational partner (and vulnerable to their negative actions) and the need to simultaneously maintain positive feelings about the self.

The interdependence existing between relational actors is particularly evident in parent–infant interactions. Given the massive dependency of infants combined with their enormous cerebral cortex, it is reasonable to surmise that the perceived responsiveness of caregivers might act to shape a child's orientation toward relationships with others throughout life. Building on the pioneering theoretical work of Bowlby on attachment theory, caregiver–infant relationships, and the attendant development of guiding mental relational models (Bowlby, 1982), social psychological researchers have broadened the original focus of attachment theory to include more of an emphasis on adult relationships (cf., Mikulincer & Shaver, 2007). In Chapter 18, Phil Shaver and Mario Mikulincer describe the reciprocal association between mental processes and behavior within attachment theory. Just as mental states of an individual guide behavioral enactment toward others, behaviors often give rise to changes in mental processes. Shaver and Mikuliner review Bowlby's notion of a behavioral system, including its evolutionary roots and biological function. They also describe both normative features of the attachment system and individual differences in the functioning of the system that arise in response to exposure to differing experiences with others.

Shaver and Mikuliner argue that relational experience can be characterized as a long chain of mental states and observable behaviors, linked with reciprocal causal arrows. Viewed in this way, behavior can be seen as a vehicle between motivational states. Rather than emphasize the particular importance or primacy of behavior, Shaver and Mikulincer stress the importance of considering both, in combination. This position strikes a reasonable middle ground between the pointedly one-sided behaviorist and cognitivist camps of yore, and places social psychology at the nexus envisioned by its earliest proponents (Lewin, 1936).

The Bolger, Stadler, and Paprocki chapter (Chapter 19) challenges the field to overcome its focus on internal states and behavioral precursors as a substitute for behavior and offers instead a method for studying behavior in everyday contexts. Using marital conflict as a specific instantiation of an important social behavior, the authors describe the utility of daily diaries as an important tool for the assessment of these behaviors. Diary studies offer the important advantages of overcoming various biases produced by retrospective reports of behavior and increasing the possibility of sampling infrequent behaviors through sampling a universe of behaviors. They argue that studying variability in behavior is as essential to understanding behavior as studying mean levels, and offer possibilities for statistical analysis of diary data that focus on such variability.

The authors report a reanalysis of couples' diary data originally published in Bolger et al. (1989) that focuses on questions of variability in marital conflict and reactions to those conflicts. They use husband and wife diary reports and estimate a multilevel logistic regression model to specify a population distribution of probabilities of reporting marital conflict across the days of the diary study. Thus, this approach clearly assumes that interpersonal behavior is interdependent, and that differences can occur in how the same behavior is interpreted by two interdependent individuals. They find that husbands' and wives' reports of conflict generally agree, suggesting that the behavior is being reported accurately, and that, although marital conflict is fairly rare, there is large variability between couples in conflict level. In terms of distress level, there was little evidence for high distress levels to occur in both couple members, as distress levels were only weakly correlated. Similarly, there was both between and within-couple heterogeneity in distress on days with no conflict. The authors describe how this analysis of variability led to insight about couple conflict that was not apparent from the original analyses reported in Bolger et al. (1989). More generally, the authors argue for moving beyond a focus on the typical person, to a closer examination of variability across time and across contexts.

One of the most important forms of social behavior is communication, as it is through our communication with others that we reveal our thoughts and emotions and dispositions toward the world around us. In Chapter 20, Andrea Hollingshead discusses the importance of communication, which she defines broadly as involving both verbal and nonverbal features, in coordinating people's actions within groups. The interdependent nature of social communication is illustrated as she discusses the relationship between coordinated action, cognitive synchrony, and communication, and discusses how communication can enhance or impair coordinated action depending on various features of the situation. For example, successful coordination can be achieved in the absence of communication in situations where there are salient focal points—prominent or conspicuous characteristics of people or situations—that can serve to unite action. On the other hand, communication is essential for coordination action in situations where salient focal points do not exist. Hollingshead illustrates the relationships between coordinated action, communication, and focal points in research where social stereotypes functioned as salient focal points in diverse dyads. For example, dyads were asked to memorize information, some of which was stereotype consistent with the dimension that defined the dyad's diversity (e.g., gender, culture). Members of diverse dyads compared to members of similar dyads were more likely to use the social stereotype as a salient focal point and were therefore better able to remember stereotype-consistent information in the absence of communication. Additional research demonstrated that when communication between partners was allowed, performance was impaired. Hollinghead closes the chapter with a description of her current research involving the coordination of teams of first responders, where the lack of interpersonal communication among responder groups was directly related to poor coordination. She also speculated on how developing technologies may possibly serve as an aid to coordinated action.

Our book closes with a chapter by Judy Hall on nonverbal communication in social psychology (Chapter 21). Nonverbal behavior is generally defined as almost any potentially communicative behavior that is not purely linguistic in form, including visible and auditory nonverbal cues, speech patterns and dysfluencies, as well as various physical attributes. As she states at the beginning of her chapter, the study of nonverbal communication is noncontroversially the study of social behavior, as nonverbal communication usually involves the expression and interpretation of nonverbal behaviors and subsequent responses to those behaviors. The study of nonverbal communication generally follows one of two main research traditions. The first tradition involves the description of nonverbal behavior, with the research goal of attempting to understand the antecedents, consequences, and sometimes the correlates of that behavior. The second primary research tradition involves the study of nonverbal communication skills in expression (encoding) and judgment (decoding), with the research goals of being able to differentiate skill levels, and to understand other person and situation correlates of skill level. Hall also explores the good, the bad, and the ugly of nonverbal communication research. The good includes an explicit focus on behavior, the intrinsic interest that people show toward this research area, the relevance of this research across disciplines, and the recent publication surge that indicates a renewal or newfound interest in the area. The bad includes an atheoretical approach, a lack of professional identity created by its multidisciplinary nature, and its labor-intensive nature. Finally, the ugly of nonverbal communication research lies in its complexity. Nonverbal cues take meaning only in a specific context. Furthermore, meaning also depends on the perspective of the interactants—is meaning derived from the intent of the expressor or the interpretation of the receiver? Despite these difficulties, this field clearly demonstrates the possibilities and utilities of a focus on actual social behavior.

This section provides readers with a thorough sense of the many ways in which behavior is considered in social psychological theory and research. Each of the chapters highlights the complexities and the challenges inherent in the study of inter-individual behavior. At the same time, each reflects the genuine enthusiasm of those whose own scholarly motivation and actions push us closer to a more complete understanding of the underpinnings and nuances of behavior in its various forms.

REFERENCES

Agnew, C. R. (1999). Power over interdependent behavior within the dyad: Who decides what a couple does? In L. J. Severy & W. B. Miller (Eds.), *Advances in population: Psychosocial perspectives* (Vol. 3, pp. 163–188). London: Jessica Kingsley.

Bolger, N., DeLongis, A., Kessler, R. C., & Schilling, E. A. (1989). Effects of daily stress on negative mood. *Journal of Personality and Social Psychology, 57,* 808–818.

Bowlby, J. (1982). *Attachment and loss: Vol. 1. Attachment (2nd ed.).* New York: Basic Books.

Kelley, H. H., Holmes, J. G., Kerr, N. L., Reis, H. T., Rusbult, C. E., & Van Lange, P. A. M. (2003). *An atlas of interpersonal situations.* New York: Cambridge University Press.

Lewin, K. (1936). *Principles of topological psychology.* New York: McGraw-Hill.

Mikulincer, M., & Shaver, P. R. (2007). *Attachment patterns in adulthood: Structure, dynamics, and change.* New York: Guilford Press.

Mischel, W., & Shoda, Y. (1995). A cognitive-affective system theory of personality: Reconceptualizing situations, dispositions, dynamics, and invariance in personality structure. *Psychological Review, 102,* 246–268.

Murray, S. L., Holmes, J. G., & Collins, N. L. (2006). Optimizing assurance: The risk regulation system in relationships. *Psychological Bulletin, 132,* 641–666.

Reis, H. T., Clark, M. S., & Holmes, J. G. (2004). Perceived partner responsiveness as an organizing construct in the study of intimacy and closeness. In D. Mashek & A. Aron (Eds), *The handbook of closeness and intimacy* (pp. 201–225). Mahwah, NJ: Lawrence Erlbaum Associates.

Reis, H.T., & Shaver, P. (1988). Intimacy as an interpersonal process. In S. W. Duck (Ed.), *Handbook of personal relationships* (pp. 367–389). Chichester, England: John Wiley and Sons, Ltd.

Snyder, M., Tanke, E. D., & Berscheid, E. (1977). Social perception and interpersonal behavior: On the self-fulfilling nature of social stereotypes. *Journal of Personality and Social Psychology, 35*, 656–666.

VanderDrift, L. E., Agnew, C. R., & Wilson, J. E. (2009). Non-marital romantic relationship commitment and leave behavior: The mediating role of dissolution consideration. *Personality and Social Psychology Bulletin, 35*, 1220–1232.

15 Behavior, the Brain, and the Social Psychology of Close Relationships

Arthur Aron

This chapter considers the roles of behavior and neuroscience in social psychology, focusing on the study of close relationships, the area of the field with which I am most familiar, as a representative example. I first consider the major roles of behavior in this field and then focus on central ways in which neuroscience methods fill parallel roles.

THE ROLES OF BEHAVIOR IN SOCIAL PSYCHOLOGY RELATIONSHIP RESEARCH

I take the term "behavior" to refer to objectively observable actions and patterns of actions. In practice, social psychologists tend to include as "behavioral" most anything other than self-reports of internal states, although internal physiology (including neural activity) is usually not meant to be included. In this section I focus on three major roles of behavior broadly construed in this way in the social psychology of close relationships: behavior as operationalization of dependent variables (including behavior as criterion variables for validating self-report measures and cases in which particular behaviors are uniquely important variables in their own right), behavior as operationalization of intervening variables, and manipulation of behavior as a powerful way of operationalizing independent variables.

Behavior as Operationalization of Dependent Variables

The main role of behavior, broadly construed, in the social psychology of close relationships has been a way of operationalizing dependent variables, as an alternative to self-report that is more objectively measured and avoids problems of various kinds of response bias. In many cases involving behavioral measures, participants are not aware they are being assessed at all (as in nonobtrusive measures or the use of archival information), or they are not aware of or misled about the purpose of their tasks (as in implicit measures).

Here are some examples of behavior used in this way, mainly from my own close relationships research. In the Dutton and Aron (1974) suspension bridge arousal/attraction study, a key dependent variable was whether or not the person who met the confederate on the different bridges (shaky vs. solid) telephoned that night to the phone number they had been led to believe was the confederate's phone number. This is a direct, real-world behavior (phoning or not) that the participant was not aware of being a measure of anything. A related type of behavioral measure is based on asking the participant to report retrospectively on an objective (behavioral) event. For example, in testing our method for creating closeness between strangers experimentally (Aron, Melinat, Aron, Vallone, & Bator, 1997), participants first completed the closeness (or control) activity in a classroom setting early in the semester. Then, at the end of the semester, they were asked if they had any further interaction with their partner over the semester. This kind of approach (often with phone or e-mail contact; and often with the purpose of assessing whether a person has remained in a relationship with a marital or dating partner) has become fairly common in relationship research.

Perhaps what many think of as the quintessential "behavioral" approach in the relationship area is videotaping couples discussing some issue in a laboratory context and later, independent coders rate the interactions for diverse variables ranging from the micro (e.g., number of interruptions) to the macro (e.g., overall warmth). The task developed early on by Weiss and colleagues (e.g., Weiss & Heyman, 1990) and made most prominent by Gottman and colleagues (e.g., Gottman, 1979) involves couples discussing an issue on which they disagree. In our own research we used this kind of approach as a dependent variable in one of our studies (Aron, Norman, Aron, McKenna, & Heyman, 2000, Study 5). In that research, couples engaged together in either a mundane or in a novel and challenging activity. In this particular study, before and after the task, couples were videotaped discussing a topic we assigned them. These discussions were then coded with a focus on overall positivity and negativity of the discussion. In previous experiments in this series, we had already shown the effect using self-report measures. We added the behavioral observation measure to reassure ourselves (and readers) that the effects were not somehow simply a matter of people in one condition *saying* they were happier with their partner. That is, the role of the behavioral measure here, as often, was simply to add to the confidence in the effect by the measure being more objectively assessed and with presumably less opportunity for response bias.

This kind of observation of interpersonal interactions is especially persuasive when participants are not even aware they are being observed. We have not used this method in any of our own research, but the approach has been quite successfully applied in the relationship area. For example, Fraley and Shaver (1998) observed attachment behaviors of couples parting at the airport, comparing those in which both members were leaving to those in which only one was leaving. Another example is the fruitful procedure developed by Ickes (1983). In this method, pairs of participants are videotaped interacting when they arrive at the laboratory and are supposedly awaiting the experiment. (Ickes avoids violating participants' privacy by having the video recording done mechanically and later giving each participant, separately, the opportunity to have the recording destroyed before any human being sees it.)

Another much more common approach is simply to ask participants about whether some objective behavior occurred or its frequency. Thus, participants might be asked how much time they spend per week with a close friend or how often they kiss their spouse. For example, in each of two surveys (Aron et al., 2000, Studies 1 and 2), we asked participants how often they do "exciting" activities with their partner (as predicted, this correlated positively with satisfaction and was mediated by relationship boredom). Indeed, perhaps the most persuasive use of asking participants about objective events is diary methods, particularly event-related or experience-sampling methods in which people indicate what they are doing right then. For example, Graham (2008) in a 1-week experience sampling study found that when couples were signaled at random intervals, the degree of excitement when doing an activity with their partner predicted later experience-level relationship quality.

Perhaps the most common behavioral-type approach to operationalization of a dependent variable throughout social psychology, including the close relationship area, is the use of laboratory tasks involving response time or memory or eye movement or some other response about which the participant either has no conscious control or is unaware of the relation of the response to the focal variable of interest. For example, as part of our original research program on including other in the self (Aron, Aron, Tudor, & Nelson, 1991, Study 3), we used a method in which participants responded to a series of trait words presented on a computer screen. For each word, participants were instructed to indicate as quickly as possible whether the trait was or was not true of themselves (a "me"-"not-me" decision). The prediction (and finding) was that people are slower in deciding a trait is true of themselves if it is not also true of a close other (and the closer they subjectively report being to the close other, the stronger the effect). The idea is that if the other is part of me, then when something is true of me but not of the other, there is a part of myself that it is not true of, so there is interference. The point here is simply that participants were not aware of what was being measured and had minimal control over differences in milliseconds between words. Again, the main role of measuring "behavior" (in this case, how quickly one presses a key) is to provide greater confidence in the objectivity of measurement.

Having emphasized this usage, I also want to note that there are contexts in which the behavior is not just a way of operationalizing some internal state or abstract relational property. Sometimes the behavior is itself the key variable of interest. The most obvious examples in the relationship area are whether and with whom a relationship is formed, whether a relationship breaks up, and how long it lasts. Some other, more dramatic examples are violent acts towards the partner, protected versus unprotected sex, and pregnancy. Somewhat less dramatic, but highly important (and widely studied) are effects on such variables as health outcomes and health behaviors (exercise, diet, etc.), economic behaviors (purchases, investments), and leisure activities and time spent with various close others. That is, the purpose of much social psychology research is to understand the causes or processes associated with these behavioral events because these behavioral events are of great practical significance in their own right or because they are part of a causal network that ultimately affects experience (or other behaviors).

Behavior may also function as a criterion variable for validating a self-report measure. For example, Rubin (1970) used the amount of gazing into the partner's eyes as a measure to validate his love scale; Rusbult, Martz, and Agnew (1998) used whether or not a relationship persisted to validate their measure of commitment; and Agnew, Van Lange, Rusbult, and Langston (1998) provided validation for Aron, Aron, and Smollan's (1992) self-report measure of "including other in the self" by showing it had a strong correlation with the number of times participants used first person plural pronouns (we, us, etc.) when writing about their relationship.

Behavior as Intervening Variable

Intervening variables, variables that are somewhere in the middle of a multistage process, are sometimes conceptualized as behaviors. For example, in a dating or conflict or social support script, the partner's overt observable response (or typical response pattern) may play a central mediating role between external circumstances or one's own actions and one's subsequent actions or feelings. Another kind of example is behavioral confirmation, as in Snyder, Tanke, and Berscheid's (1977) classic study in which (a) the extent to which one is led to believe an interaction partner is good looking leads to (b) a pattern of behaviors towards the partner that (c) lead to the partner behaving like a more attractive person (as rated by blind observers). A more direct relationship example is Drigotas, Rusbult, Wieselquist, and Whittin's (1999) research on the "Michelangelo Effect." In this work, one's partner's behavioral reactions to one's own behavior serve to reinforce one's own behavior patterns and characteristics.

This kind of approach is also central to major theoretical models. For example, Reis and Shaver's (1998) intimacy model posits a system in which whether one's self-disclosure leads to high or low levels of partner's responsiveness (understanding, validation, and caring) determines the extent to which one's experienced intimacy escalates or declines. A more general model of this kind is a systems type account of how attachment styles develop, as classically proposed by Bowlby (1969). In this model, following an experienced threat, the infant turns to the caregiver, and the extent to which the caregiver is available and responsive leads to subsequent steps in which one develops either a sense of security or insecurity. Indeed, in even the most general relationship-relevant models, behavior often plays a central intervening role. For example, in evolutionary models, mate choice, a clearly behavioral variable, is a very key factor in the development of a species.

Behavioral Manipulations as Operationalizations of Independent Variables

It is almost a quintessential social psychological method to operationalize an independent variable by manipulating the behavior of a confederate. Perhaps the most classic example is the Asch (1956) conformity study. In the relationship domain, sometimes a relationship partner is recruited as a confederate. In other studies, the researcher simply manipulates behavior that the subject believes is coming from the partner, as in whether or not the partner sends a supportive or nonsupportive note when the subject is facing a stressful situation (Collins & Feeney, 2004). It is also possible to manipulate the participant's own behavior. For example, in White and Kight's (1984) arousal-attraction-effect study, individuals ran in place for a few minutes (or did not) prior to meeting the confederate. Finally, in some studies, the behavior of an interacting pair is manipulated. For example, in our studies of creating closeness between strangers (Aron et al., 1997), pairs of individuals are instructed to ask each other a set of questions that are structured to be either rapidly escalating in degree of personalness (high closeness induction condition) or involve mundane superficial disclosures (low closeness induction condition). More concretely, in our shared self-expanding activities experiments (Aron et al., 2000, Studies 3–5), participants carry out together a physical activity that is either novel and challenging (high self-expansion condition) or enjoyable but mundane (low self-expansion condition). For example, in the novel/challenging condition, the couple is first tied together with Velcro straps at the wrist and ankles, then they push a foam cylinder together, without using hands or teeth, across a 10 meter gym mat, over a barrier (a rolled up gym mat) and back, trying to beat a time limit.

Summary

In this first main section we argued (and provided illustrative examples) that the major roles of behavior in the social psychology of close relationships are (a) operationalizations of dependent variables that are used mainly because of their virtues of being objective, (b) intervening processes in multistep theoretical models, and (c) powerful ways of manipulating independent variables.

HOW NEUROSCIENCE METHODS PLAY PARALLEL ROLES TO BEHAVIOR

Neuroscientists typically call something a "behavioral study" if it uses any systematic method other than a neural or physiological one. Thus, they tend to include among behavioral studies what social psychologists would call cognitive or self-report. On the other hand, there is a sense in which social psychologists, as we have seen, tend to define anything that is not an explicit self-report as behavioral—so that one could call neuroscience studies behavioral in that sense. Indeed, there is a sense in which neuroscience methods are literally studying behaviors, in the sense of objectively observable actions, of neural systems in the brain.

In any case, what I want instead to emphasize here is that in many ways neuroscience methods can and sometimes do serve for social psychologists, including social psychologists studying relationships, the same functions as traditional behavioral measures of the types we have been considering. Neuroscience methods are objectively assessed and usually minimally subject to response biases, and the variables observed are closely linked with emotions, motivations, cognitions, and bodily actions.

Thus, I will focus on illustrating how brain activity has been used to provide objective operationalizations of dependent variables, conceptualized as intervening variables in multistep models, and as powerful manipulations of independent variables. (However, before turning to these themes, I also want to note that it is my experience that most researchers using neuroscience methods are doing so to understand the brain, and not as a tool to understand human experience and behavior. In that light, collaborations with social psychologists can be very important for neuroscientists by providing sophistication about the kinds of social and psychological phenomena associated with neural processes. However, again, my focus here is on the role of neuroscience in facilitating advances in understanding the social psychology of close relationships, in which brain responses are used as a means to this end, not as the main purpose of the research.)

Neural Activity as Objective Operationalization of Dependent Variables

Neuroscience methods can provide data to triangulate with behavioral methods and, most importantly, to apply to variables difficult to operationalize behaviorally, permitting objective, nonobvious measurement of variables such as degree of passionate love, closeness, or stress. The main procedures used are brain imaging, such as functional magnetic resonance imaging (fMRI), to identify localized regions of the brain that respond specifically to an experimentally manipulated task or stimulus (versus an otherwise comparable control task or stimulus). For example, Coan, Schaefer, and Davidson (2006) used fMRI methods to create, in effect, an implicit, objective operationalization of response to stress— activation of a particular brain region (the HAP-axis) known from both animal and human research to be active when under stressful stimuli. (It is the starting point of a hormonal stress cascade to regulate bodily threat response.) In their study, participants were put in a stressful situation, and then the researchers assessed whether these areas of the brain were less active when holding the hand of one's spouse versus when holding the hand of a stranger (the experimenter). They also tested how the degree of reduction of this brain response when holding the spouse's hand differs as a function of the quality of the relationship. (That is, Coan et al. correlated the brain response reduction for spouse versus control hand with a standard self-report measure of relationships satisfaction.) Note that in

this example, the independent variable—who was holding the participant's hand—was also behavioral.

Another widely used neuroscience method (although one with relatively few applications so far to relationships) is evoked response potential (ERP). ERP measures the brain's electrical activity from the scalp,
focusing on the pattern of response over fractions of a second to repeated
stimuli of a given type. For example, in a study exploring responses to face
images of a new beloved, Langeslag, Jansma, Franken, and Van Strien
(2007) found significantly larger responses (late positive potentials) for a
beloved partner versus a familiar control or another unknown beautiful
face, suggesting increased motivated attention for the beloved. That is, in
this study, the particular pattern of response, known from other research
to be an indicator of attention, served as an implicit, objective operationalization of attention.

Other widely used neuroscience methods, such as single cell
recording, have been used primarily with nonhuman animals and have
been minimally applied to relationship contexts. (However, I will briefly
mention some relevant work using some of these methods in the section
on manipulation of independent variables.)

Detailed Example

To illustrate the possibilities, I will describe in a bit more detail some of
the research my collaborators and I have been doing on romantic love. In
the initial study (Aron et al., 2005), we sought to address the question of
whether passionate love should be understood as a particular emotion like
anger or happiness versus as a strong desire like intense hunger or an
ardent quest for fame. This emotion-versus-motivation issue is one of
longstanding interest to emotion and relationship researchers. On the one
hand, love is certainly highly emotional, in lay understanding it is a
prototypical example of an emotion, and it is included in many standard
lists of basic emotions. On the other hand, unlike particular emotions,
passionate love has no specific facial expression; and like most motivations (goal-oriented states), passionate love is especially hard to control,
yields diverse emotions according to whether or not it is satisfied, and is
very highly focused on a specific outcome. There are also considerable
theoretical implications to this distinction, including whether one should
apply to love the various things we know about emotions (e.g., emotion
regulation processes) or the various things we know about motivations
(e.g., abstract vs. concrete mindsets). However, this issue has been quite
hard to sort out using existing methods, both because the differences in
behavior between emotions and motivations are relatively subtle (and

overlapping) and because in a case such as love, self-reports are likely to be especially biased by one's lay beliefs about how it operates. In contrast, neuroscience methods offered us a strong opportunity to address this issue because emotions and motivations are associated with the activity of quite distinct brain regions.

A second longstanding issue this research sought to address was whether passionate love is just a fancy name for sexual desire. Passionate love has been defined as an intense desire for a highly intimate, close relationship with specific other; sexual desire, as an intense drive to have sex with someone. On the one hand, the two are typically correlated, although people sometimes report experiencing one without the other (especially sexual desire without passionate love). Other relevant evidence is that young children report intense passionate love (without sex), and some animal research (see Fisher, 1998) suggests the sex drive evolved to motivate sexual union with any appropriate other, but the equivalent to passionate love (focused attraction to a particular other) evolved to promote pursuit of a specific mating partner. However, like the emotion/motivation issue, this is-love-just-sex issue has been particularly difficult to sort out using existing social psychological methods given the difficulty of people distinguishing these experiences subjectively (as well as their questionable ability or willingness to report on them without bias). But once again, neuroscience methods seemed like a hopeful way to address this issue, as there have been clearly identified brain regions associated with sexual arousal.

More generally, neuroscience methods may be particularly useful for addressing issues of these kinds (emotion vs. motivation, love vs. sex). Neuroscience methods have been particularly successful in other domains for evaluating whether two related processes are qualitatively the same or different (Posner & DiGirolamo, 2000). For example, it was neuroscience methods that finally permitted a clear, persuasive answer to the question of whether implicit and explicit memory are really different. (It turns out they are different in that they engage quite different brain regions.) And it was neuroscience methods that clearly and persuasively sorted out the extent to which subjectively visualizing something is basically the same as actual visual perception of an external object. (It turns out they have a lot in common in that they largely engage the same central brain regions, though peripheral regions that first process stimuli are clearly different.)

In the present example, neuroimaging seemed likely to be very helpful for addressing the emotion versus motivation question because, as noted, there is good evidence from multiple sources that quite different brain regions are engaged. Emotion is known to engage areas such as the amygdale, orbital frontal cortex, and the insular cortex. For example, these regions have been found to be active in human neuroimaging studies when viewing emotional faces or pictures of scenes known to create positive or negative feelings. Motivation (reward and seeking reward), on the other hand, is known to engage quite different areas, notably the ventral tegmental area (VTA), caudate, and related areas especially associated with dopamine. For example, in human studies, these areas are active following cocaine ingestion or when anticipating or receiving a monetary reward.

Similarly, while little was known about what areas are engaged by passionate love, there was good evidence from some previous human fMRI studies, as well as from extensive work with animals, as to what brain regions are involved in sexual arousal (e.g., the hypothalamus). For example, these areas have been found to be active when people view erotic versus neutral pictures, and to correlate with bodily indicators of sexual arousal.

Finally, we had one additional question: How valid are subjective reports of passionate love? The Passionate Love Scale (PLS; Hatfield & Sprecher, 1986), the most widely used measure, is clearly reliable and yields theoretically appropriate results in correlational and experimental studies. However, social desirability and other response biases seem highly likely to affect reports of such a quintessentially subjective experience. Neuroimaging provides a unique opportunity to assess convergent validity of self-report scales. That is, in the present case, if we did find regions that were clearly associated with passionate love from the overall mean comparisons across conditions, it would be possible to see if activation in these regions were most strongly activated for those whose scores were highest on the PLS.

Thus, to address these three questions (motivation/emotion, sex/love, PLS validity), we conducted an fMRI study (Aron et al., 2005). We recruited 10 women and 7 men who reported they were "madly in love" and thought about their partner at least 80% of their waking hours, and who also seemed to be intensely in love based on interviews and questionnaire responses. Relationship length in our sample ranged from a month to a little over a year, with a mean of 7 months.

We asked these intensely in-love individuals to provide us with a photo of their beloved and of an equally familiar person of the same age and sex as their beloved, but about whom they had no special feelings. These pictures were the basis of the key experimental manipulation. In the fMRI scanner, participants alternatively viewed pictures of their partner and of the familiar neutral person for 30 seconds each, interspersed with a countback task. (The countback task was a standard serial subtraction task in which participants were given a high number and asked to count back by sevens. The countback task was interspersed between the two types of photos to prevent carry over from one picture to the next. It also provided an additional condition that permitted us to control for attentional demand.)

The whole 2-minute series—partner, countback, neutral-familiar, countback—was repeated six times for a total of 12 minutes. (Whether each series started with the partner photo or neutral-familiar photo was counterbalanced across participants.) Using standard social psychological terminology, this was a within-subject design in which the independent variable consisted of the three experimental conditions (viewing partner, viewing familiar-neutral, and countback), and the dependent variables were activation in the various focal brain regions known to be associated with emotion, motivation, and sexual arousal.

The results were quite straightforward. Planned contrasts of partner versus familiar-neutral and also of partner versus countback both showed significant, strong activations in motivation areas (VTA and caudate) but virtually no mean difference across subjects between conditions in brain areas known to be associated with emotion or sexual arousal. Interestingly, in light of the arguments about love being a motivation that leads to diverse emotions, there were indeed significant effects within individual subjects in emotion areas. However, the particular emotion areas differed from subject to subject, while the motivation areas were quite consistent across subjects.

Because the participants were selected for high levels of passionate love, there was minimal variation in PLS scores. All subjects had means of at least 7 on a 9-point scale. Nevertheless, even within this restricted range variance, there was a strong, significant correlation between PLS scores and activation (that is, the difference in activation between viewing the partner minus either of the control conditions) in focal areas of the caudate.

Thus, this study is an example of how neuroscience methods were used to operationalize dependent variables (and to provide validation of a self-report measure) in the context of addressing important social psychological issues in a way that, like traditional behavioral measures, is implicit and objective.

Further, as is typical in social psychology, once a paradigm has been developed, it is often applied to extend the original findings into new contexts. This has also proven true in relationship neuroscience (and in social, cognitive, and affective neuroscience more generally). Two extensions of the Aron et al. early-stage love paradigm provide examples. First, Xu et al. (2008) recently replicated the exact Aron et al. (2005) study in Beijing, China. The purpose of the study was to provide for the first time a direct assessment of the cross-cultural similarities or differences in passionate love using a method that does not rely primarily on language or subjective report. That is, again, neuroscience methods served the function that behavioral measures do of being nonobvious and objective (and in this case, not even relying on language—a particularly important feature in cross-cultural work). The findings were a very close replication overall, but also some interesting correlations with questionnaire measures in which the degree of effect in particular brain regions was correlated with Chinese traditionalism.

As yet another example, Acevedo, Aron, Fisher, and Brown (2008) replicated the basic Aron et al. (2005) design, but with long-term (mean = 21 years) married individuals recruited because they claimed to have very high levels of passionate love. This was yet another case in which the ability of neuroscience methods to function as nonobvious and objective indicators was especially important. That is, relationship theorists, like the general public, have generally assumed that intense passionate love inevitably dies out over time and that claims of a few individuals in long-term involvements to have achieved it are probably due to either trying to make a good impression or to self-deception. Thus, Acevedo et al. sought to see if the pattern of neural responses to the partner in these cases would be the same as had been found in the Aron et al. study of newly in love participants. Preliminary findings suggest that, surprisingly, results are remarkably similar. There were also some interesting differences. The findings from the long-term in-love participants compared to the original short-term findings showed (a) somewhat less activation in some secondary regions associated with obsession and (b) somewhat greater activation in regions associated in animal studies with long-term connection and bonding. However, the overall basic pattern seems the same—and consistent with the claim of these people to be intensely engaged with their partner, including strong attraction, a lively sex life, and a general sense of passion associated with their relationship. Presuming final results confirm the initial analyses, it is hard to imagine that any self-report methods would be nearly as convincing. Of course, more traditional nonobvious, objective behavioral measures might also be convincing, but in the present case the brain-based measures seem the most straightforward.

Variables of Ultimate Interest

In the case of behavior, we noted that in some cases behavior was not just an especially apt operationalization of a conceptually interesting variable, but that behavior may be a variable of ultimate interest—such as forming or ending a relationship. This may be a case in which neuroscience methods less often serve a parallel role to behavioral measures. However, there are a few possible exceptions, such as brain function disability, enhancement, or other permanent change due to relationship factors (e.g., possible effects of social support, support for self-expansion, stress from conflict, violence, or abandonment). For example, it is possible that high quality relationships may slow Alzheimer's or other dementia or facilitate "rewiring" neural systems after brain injuries; or, at the other extreme, that traumatic relationships may undermine brain system development in children or adolescents.

Neural Activity as an Intervening Variable

We saw that a key role of behavior in social psychology, and perhaps particularly in relationship research, involves its function as a central step in some multistep process. In this context, there are some clear parallels with the role of neural activity. That is, the operation of the nervous system mediates between external stimuli and action, and presumably between external stimuli and experience and between experience and action. Understanding brain response to stimuli (such as a partner's actions) can in principle tell us about expected response and experience. There has been relatively little work of this kind directly in the relationship domain. But an interesting example of the possibilities from a related domain is a study by Knutson, Wimmer, Kuhnen, and Winkielman, (2008), in which exposure to sexual stimuli (erotic pictures) yielded activation of a key reward area (nucleus accumbens), which in turn led to more risky decisions in a monetary choice task. That is, a mediational analysis showed that, for example, controlling for the accumbens activation, there was no increase in risky decisions.

Brain Manipulations as Operationalizations of Independent Variables

In principle, manipulation of brain states (like manipulation of own or relevant other's behavior) provides an exciting opportunity to test important theoretical questions. This is in part because, like behavioral manipulations, such manipulations are likely to be powerful and minimally likely for the participant to be aware of the purpose of the study or what is being manipulated. In practice, there has been almost no such research to date with humans. There are several methods that are starting to be used in human work in cognitive and perceptual domains (e.g., see Pascual-Leone, Davey, Rothwell, Wassermann, & Puri, 2002) that could well be adapted to the social and relationship context. These include transcranial magnetic stimulation (TMS), in which a cerebral region is safely deactivated for a fraction of a second during which focal stimuli can be introduced), drugs that increase (agonists) or decrease (antagonists) the functioning of key neural chemicals, and possibly even neural stimulation during surgery. In animal research, including importantly for relationship researchers the influential work done on prairie voles (a rare monogamous mammalian species), more drastic methods are proving quite productive (e.g., Curtis, Liu, Aragona, & Wang, 2006). Such methods include focused brain lesions, genetic manipulations, and brain stimulation.

CONCLUSION

In this chapter I suggest (and provide illustrative examples) that the key roles of behavior in social psychology, particularly in its study of close relationships, are a means to create objective, nonobvious operationalizations of dependent variables (including for validation of measures and occasionally as important outcomes in their own right); intervening steps in theoretical articulations of multistep processes; and a particularly powerful way to manipulate independent variables. I also argue, and provide some relatively detailed illustrative examples, that neuroscience methods often fill these same roles. That is, methods that focus on brain functioning have been applied to the social psychology of close relationships largely as objective, nonobvious operationalizations of key dependent variables and are conceptualized as intervening steps in multistep processes, and there is some potential even of using them as a means to create powerful manipulations of independent variables.

As neuroscience methods become increasing common in social psychology, they promise to offer triangulation with existing methods, including behavioral methods. More importantly, they promise to be an important supplement to behavioral methods, permitting us in some cases to do what we often use behavioral methods to do, but opening up opportunities in contexts in which behavioral methods are not optimal or available for the specific variables at hand.

It seems a miracle that social psychologists would pay attention again to behavior after ignoring it ever since the reign of behaviorism ended decades ago. Yet this miracle is happening all the time in our field, perhaps quietly, yet surely, even in the midst of the reign of (social) cognition that replaced it. In particular, we have used behavior very effectively and creatively to operationalize dependent and intervening variables in ways that are uniquely objective and nonobvious, and also to construct uniquely powerful manipulations of independent variables. It may seem even more miraculous if social psychologists today can use neuroscience methods effectively as another way to accomplish these things for which behavioral methods have served us so especially well. My goal in this chapter has been to use examples from relationship research to be explicit about some ways this Step 2 miracle might happen.

REFERENCES

Acevedo, B., Aron, A., Fisher, H., & Brown, L. (2008, February). *The neural basis of long-term romantic love.* Presented at the Society for Personality and Social Psychology, Albuquerque, NM.

Agnew, C. R., Van Lange, P. A. M., Rusbult, C. E., & Langston, C. A. (1998). Cognitive interdependence: Commitment and the mental representation of close relationships. *Journal of Personality and Social Psychology, 74,* 939–954.

Aron, A., Aron, E. N., Tudor, M., & Nelson, G. (1991). Close relationships as including other in the self. *Journal of Personality and Social Psychology, 60,* 241–253.

Aron, A., Fisher, H., Mashek, D., Strong, G., Li, H., & Brown, L. (2005). Reward, motivation and emotion systems associated with early-stage intense romantic love. *Journal of Neurophysiology, 93,* 327–337.

Aron, A., Melinat, E., Aron, E. N., Vallone, R., & Bator, R. (1997). The experimental generation of interpersonal closeness: A procedure and some preliminary findings. *Personality and Social Psychology Bulletin, 23,* 363–377.

Aron, A., Norman, C. C., Aron, E. N., McKenna, C., & Heyman, R. (2000). Couples shared participation in novel and arousing activities and experienced relationship quality. *Journal of Personality and Social Psychology, 78,* 273–283.

Asch, S. E. (1956). Studies of independence and conformity: A minority of one against a unanimous majority. *Psychological Monographs, 70* (Whole no. 416).

Bowlby J. (1969). *Attachment.* Attachment and loss. Vol. I. London: Hogarth.

Coan, J. A., Schaefer, H. S., & Davidson, R. J. (2006). Lending a hand: Social regulation of the neural response to threat. *Psychological Science, 17,* 1032–1039.

Collins, N. L., & Feeney, B. C. (2004). Working models of attachment shape perceptions of social support: Evidence from experimental and observational studies. *Journal of Personality and Social Psychology, 87,* 363–383.

Curtis, J. T., Liu, Y., Aragona, B. J., & Wang, Z. (2006). Dopamine and monogamy. *Brain Research, 1126,* 76–90.

Drigotas, S. M., Rusbult, C. E., Wieselquist, J., & Whitton, S. W. (1999). Close partner as sculptor of the ideal self: behavioral affirmation and the Michelangelo phenomenon. *Journal of Personality and Social Psychology, 77,* 293–323.

Dutton, D. G., & Aron, A. (1974). Some evidence for heightened sexual attraction under conditions of high anxiety. *Journal of Personality and Social Psychology, 30,* 510–517.

Fisher, H. E. (1998). Lust, attraction, and attachment in mammalian reproduction. *Human Nature, 9,* 23–52.

Fraley, R. C., & Shaver, P. R. (1998). Airport separations: A naturalistic study of adult attachment: Dynamics in separating couples. *Journal of Personality and Social Psychology, 75,* 1198–1212.

Gottman, J. M. (1979). *Marital interaction: Experimental investigations*. San Diego, CA: Academic Press.

Graham, J. M. (2008). Self-expansion and flow in couples' momentary experiences: An experience sampling study. *Journal of Personality and Social Psychology, 95,* 679–694.

Hatfield, E., & Sprecher, S. (1986). Measuring passionate love in intimate relations. *Journal of Adolescelnce, 9,* 383–410.

Ickes, W. (1983). A basic paradigm for the study of unstructured dyadic interaction. In H. Reis (Issue Ed.), *New directions for methodology of behavioral science: Naturalistic approaches to studying social interaction* (pp. 5–21). San Francisco: Jossey-Bass.

Knutson, B., Wimmer, G. E., Kuhnen, C. M., & Winkielman, P. (2008). Nucleus accumbens activation mediates the influence of reward cues on financial risk taking. *NeuroReport, 19,* 509–513.

Langeslag, S. J. E., Jansma, B. M., Franken, I. H. A., & Strien, J. W. V. (2007). Event-related potential responses to love-related facial stimuli. *Biological Psychology, 76,* 109–115.

Pascual-Leone, A., Davey, N., Rothwell, J., Wassermann, E. M., & Puri, B. K. (2002). *Handbook of Transcranial Magnetic Stimulation*. London: Arnold.

Posner, M. I., & DiGirolamo, G. J. (2000). Cognitive neuroscience: Origins and promise. *Psychological Bulletin, 126,* 873–889.

Reis, H. T., & Shaver, P. R. (1988). Intimacy as an interpersonal process. In S. Duck (Ed.), *Handbook of research in personal relationships* (pp. 367–389). London: Wiley.

Rubin, Z. (1970). Measurement of romantic love. *Journal of Personality and Social Psychology, 10,* 265–273.

Rusbult, C. E., Martz, J. M., & Agnew, C. R. (1998). The investment model scale: Measuring commitment level, satisfaction level, quality of alternatives, and investment size. *Personal Relationships, 5,* 357–391.

Snyder, M., Tanke, E. D., & Berscheid, E. (1977). Social perception and interpersonal behavior: On the self-fulfilling nature of social stereotypes. *Journal of Personality and Social Psychology, 35,* 656–666.

Weiss, R.L., & Heyman, R. E. (1990). Observation of marital interaction. In F. D. Fincham and T. N. Bradbury (Eds.) *The psychology of marriage: basic issues and applications.* (pp. 87–117). New York: Guilford.

White, G. L., & Kight, T. D. (1984). Misattribution of arousal and attraction: Effects of salience of explanations for arousal. *Journal of Experimental Social Psychology, 20,* 55–64.

Xu, X., Aron, A., Cao, G., Feng, T., Fisher, F., Brown, L., & Weng, W. (2008, February). *Is love universal? An fMRI study of early-stage intense romantic love in China*. Presented at the Society for Personality and Social Psychology, Albuquerque, NM.

16 The Relationship Context of Social Behavior

Harry T. Reis

The individualistic orientation of Western psychology is well known. Within this tradition, psychologists investigate processes governing the behavior of individuals, on the assumption that the most important mechanisms for understanding human behavior reside within the individual. Even social psychology, the subdiscipline within the psychological sciences that is most concerned with the external environment, relies on perceptual, cognitive, affective, and motivational systems that reside exclusively within the individual.

There is little reason to question the integrity of the individual person as a biologically based organism composed of integrated operating systems that act in concert to produce adaptive responses to environmental events. No comparable larger units possessing similar levels of organismic integrity or motivational coherence have yet been identified, at least with direct tangible evidence of their impact. Even culture, the most systemic concept in the behavioral sciences, is understood by Western psychologists largely in terms of its impact on the individual, an understanding that represents the mind of the individual as a mediating variable between culture and behavior.

This individualistic orientation presents something of a challenge to social psychology. If the causal mechanisms for behavior reside within the individual, how do we conceptualize the fact that situations—factors external to the person—have strong influence on behavior? Even more challenging, how do we account for the fact of interdependence—that many, if not most, important human behaviors involve interacting individuals who influence each other, and that the outcome of a given interaction often depends on the behavior of both, as well as how well those behaviors fit together?

This chapter reviews concepts central to one way in which social psychology might address this challenge. To provide historical context, I first review definitions of the scope of social psychology. I then discuss several lines of evidence and theory suggesting why the relationship context of behavior ought to be a focal construct in social psychology. This section includes a selective review of diverse phenomena showing how behavior varies systematically as a function of relationship contexts. The next and final section provides a brief overview of one conceptually based approach for understanding relationship contexts, based on the interdependence analysis of situations. Throughout, the larger goal of this chapter is to suggest that social psychology's traditional mission of articulating the impact of situations on behavior would be best served by emphasizing their fundamentally interpersonal nature.

DEFINING SOCIAL PSYCHOLOGY

Although the details vary, most textbooks define social psychology in terms of people's impact on one another. For example, Gilovich, Keltner and Nisbett define social psychology as "The scientific study of the feelings, thoughts, and behaviors of individuals in social situations" (2006, p. 5)[1]. Taylor, Peplau, and Sears describe the field by stating that "Social psychologists use scientific methods to study how we perceive people and social events, how we influence others, and the nature of human relationships" (2000, p. 3). Myers refers to social psychology as "the scientific study of how people think about, influence, and relate to one another" (1999, p. 3). Smith and Mackie offer a similar characterization: Social psychology is "the scientific study of the effects of social and cognitive processes on the way individuals perceive, influence, and relate to others" (2000, p. 3). Common to these (and most other) definitions is the idea that what people think, feel, and do is affected by other people. Or, as Roger Brown wryly put it, "roughly speaking, social psychology is concerned with the mental processes (or behavior) of persons insofar as these are determined by past or present interaction with other persons . . . this is not a definition that excludes very much" (1965, p. xx).

---

[1] The New American Heritage Dictionary defines "social" as "living in an organized group or similar close aggregate."

These definitions can be seen as emerging from the field's historical roots. In one of the first two textbooks traditionally cited as inaugurating the birth of social psychology, Edward Alsworth Ross defined social psychology as dealing with "uniformities due to *social* causes, i.e., to *mental contacts* or *mental interactions* ... It is *social* only insofar as it arises out of the interplay of minds" (1908, p. 3). What Ross called "uniformities" attributable to the "conditions of life"—features of the environment not subject to mental interplay between persons, such as the physical setting, visual cues, culture, or race—were explicitly excluded. The other inaugural volume, by William McDougall, was somewhat less explicit, charging social psychology with the task of showing "how, given the native propensities and capacities of the individual human mind, all the complex mental life of societies is shaped by them and in turn reacts upon the course of their development and operation in the individual" (1908, p. 18).

About a half-century later, Solomon Asch borrowed elements from both McDougall and Ross, albeit without offering a formal definition of the field: "To discover the full potentialities of men we must observe them in the social medium . . . the basic problems of psychology require the extension of observation into the region of social processes" (1952, p. 34). At roughly the same time, in the first edition of the *Handbook of Social Psychology*, Gordon Allport proposed a definition that has been more influential among contemporary researchers: "Social psychologists regard their discipline as an attempt to understand and explain how the thought, feeling, and behavior of individuals are influenced by the actual, imagined, or implied presence of other human beings" (1954, p. 5).

Although all of these definitions mention how people are affected by other people, over the years a subtle shift occurred, codifying the social psychological mission in terms of situationism, or in a phrase that Ross and Nisbett (1991) made famous, as showing "the power of the situation." This shift reflected the pervasive influence of Kurt Lewin's "life space" theorizing on the field. Lewin coined what is probably the second-most cited equation of the 20th century, $B = f(P, E)$[2]. To Lewin, behavior was the result of two sets of causal factors, some rooted in the Person and others in the Environment, more precisely the psychological environment, or in other words, the psychological significance of the "total concrete situation" for the individual. Somewhat ironically, Lewin appears not to have intended for P and E to be independent causal agents

---

[2] Unlike the first-most cited equation, Einstein's $E = mc^2$, this one has yet to demonstrate mathematical rigor.

whose effects could be isolated from each other in the statistical analysis of variance sense. Rather, he theorized that $E = f(P)$ and $P = f(E)$, or in other words: "The person and his environment have to be considered as *one* constellation of interdependent factors" (Lewin, 1951, pp. 239–240). Nevertheless, the dualism of person and situation as distinct, separable factors became entrenched as the field grew rapidly in the 1950s and 1960s, following the influence of Lewin and his students.

This dualism has had certain epistemological advantages. As shown in Figure 16.1, the Lewinian equation positioned social and personality psychology squarely between traditional "macrolevel" disciplines that examine complex, systemic processes whose explanations depended on units greater than the individual (such as political science, economics, and sociology) and "microlevel" sciences that investigate more elementary mechanisms residing within the person (such as biology and the disciplines that have come to be known as cognitive science and neuroscience). That is, by focusing on external, environmental factors, the social psychological level of explanation pointed to the ways in which the outside world operates on individuals. Personality explanations were, in a complementary manner, concerned with the ways in which the individual acted on the outside world, partly as a function of accumulated experiences. Both were closer to the idea of the individual as an integrated nexus of explanatory mechanisms for understanding behavior than any other discipline. In the conceptual hierarchy of disciplines, this niche allowed social-personality psychology to provide a novel and useful level of explanation for behavior. (See Hinde, 1997, and Myers, 1999, for related examples of explanatory hierarchies.)

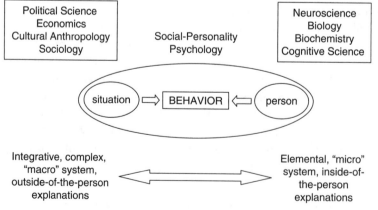

Figure 16.1. The Social-Personality Psychology Level of Explanation.

WHICH ASPECTS OF THE SITUATION SHOULD SOCIAL PSYCHOLOGY STUDY?

If situations and their influence on behavior are the identified province for social psychological inquiry, it might be asked, which aspects of situations should social psychologists study? If the Lewinian metaphor were a guide, any and all conditions and circumstances external to the individual would have to be considered (cf., Pervin, 1978; Magnusson, 1981), although this seems overly inclusive. Mischel and Shoda (1995) proposed a useful distinction between nominal and psychological situations. Nominal situations describe basic features of the context in which behavior occurs, such as place and activity (similar to Roger Barker's, 1965, pioneering work on behavior settings, the foundation of what he named ecological psychology, but became better known as environmental psychology). Psychological situations, in contrast, concern those features of situations that give rise to the expression of basic psychological processes. It is not surprising that the vast majority of social psychological research has focused on these.

My premise in this chapter is that social psychological research has been too much focused on nonsocial aspects of situations (the above-mentioned definitions notwithstanding) and not enough focused on a particular fundamentally social aspect of situations, the relationship context. As Reis, Collins, and Berscheid (2000) explain, who one is with, one's history with this and similar partners in related situations, and what one is trying to accomplish with this partner, exert a potent causal impact on behavior. Many lines of theory and evidence converge to support this principle, a few of which will be briefly mentioned here.

- Many of people's most common goals and motives involve other people, especially those with whom they have an ongoing relationship, either as the target of those goals or motives (e.g., to initiate, develop, modify, or terminate a relationship with that person), or as an agent who facilitates or constrains the attainment of personal goals (e.g., support or interference from parents, romantic partners, teachers, or work supervisors).
- Because most human activity involves coordinating one's actions with the actions of others, success or failure in those processes of coordination are a principal determinant of achievement, productivity, and well-being.
- Relationships figure prominently in attention and thought, both in consciously controlled cognition and also in cognition that takes place outside of awareness. Cognition is an action control system designed to facilitate goal-directed behavior (Fiske, 1992;

Gollwitzer & Moskowitz, 1996), and coordination with relationship partners is often required (Bugental, 2000).

- In an influential review, Ekman and Davidson concluded that "emotions are brought into play most often by the actions of others, and, once aroused, emotions influence the course of interpersonal transactions" (1994, p. 139). Many theories stress the social regulating functions of emotion (for example, to communicate internal states to others) and, in turn, the influence of relationship partners on emotional experience and regulation.
- Abundant evidence indicates that the ability to relate successfully to others is a principal determinant of success in nearly all domains of human activity and during all stages of the life cycle (Hartup & Stevens, 1997). Most, if not all, theories of life span development assign central roles to relationships.
- Early relationships (primarily with caregivers during the first two years of life) exert profound and pervasive effects on development, evidence of which can be seen throughout the life span. These effects, which follow from the effects of interactions with caregivers on the maturing infant's brain structures and psyche, span cognitive, affective, and personality development.
- Evolutionary theorists increasingly recognize that social life provided the principal mechanisms for human adaptation, and that many of the human mind's most important processes evolved for the purpose of regulating social interactions and relationships (e.g., Buss & Kenrick, 1998; Cosmides & Tooby, 1992).

Smith and Semin's recent (2004, 2007) model of socially situated cognition suggests a somewhat more abstract rationale for the importance of relationships as a context for behavior. Their analysis brings together two highly influential lines of research, that of situated cognition—that cognition emerges from the interaction of agents and their environment, rather than existing purely in the mind of the agent—and of social cognition, arguably the dominant theme in social psychology during the past two or three decades. In their theoretical synthesis, social-cognitive processes "constitute an adaptive regulatory process that ultimately serves survival needs" (2004, p. 56)—that is, social cognition is the natural vehicle for self-regulation, or in other words, the individual's attempts to interact effectively with the social environment. Behavior is the action expression of these adaptive efforts. Most relevant for present purposes is the idea that socially situated cognition is based on transactions between actors and their social environment, which, most typically, means interactions with relationship partners.

Smith and Semin offer four themes as guiding principles for the study of socially situated cognition. These principles illuminate the need for social psychology to understand relationship contexts:

1. Social Cognition Exists to Further Adaptive Action.

Although adaptive action takes many forms, most important life activities involve coordinating one's actions with the actions of others. Thus, human adaptive action is rarely conducted solus ipse (alone, by oneself). For example, school and work tasks are commonly distributed across multiple persons, and success or failure depends on how well these persons synchronize and carry out their activities. Similarly, family life usually requires that family members coordinate their instrumental, social, and affective activities. In most circumstances, the others with whom adaptive action is coordinated are relationship partners—friends, lovers, coworkers, schoolmates, neighbors, teammates, family members, and so on. The nature of those affiliations, including one's history and imagined future with them, is likely to influence how activities are coordinated.

2. Social Cognition is Embodied in Our Neural-Physical Architecture.

Because relationships provided the context for most reproductive and survival-oriented activities in human evolutionary history, our species has evolved numerous biologically based mechanisms geared toward the tasks of living, working, and reproducing with others. Increasing evidence identifies many genetic, neural, and hormonal systems that underlie diverse social behaviors, including empathy and synchrony, attachment, emotion regulation and contagion, face recognition, love, sexual attraction, warmth and affection, trust, loneliness, coping with stress, stereotyping, helping, and dominance and submission. These mechanisms are central to everyday interactions within relationships, emphasizing the role of relationships in shaping the human mind during evolution and suggesting that functional analyses of these social behaviors should consider how their expression varies across relationship contexts.

3. Social Cognition Involves a Dynamic Process of Continuous Reciprocal Influence Between the Self and the Social/Physical Environment.

The transmission of information among interacting persons represents some of the more common and potent of these dynamic influences, including relatively direct mechanisms such as communication, persuasion, leadership, and self-presentation, and also more subtle examples such as situated identity, social referencing, shared construction of reality, social comparison, and behavioral confirmation. In each case, actors construct meaning or understanding out of their interactions with the social environment. Relationship partners are in most instances more salient and influential in these processes than strangers; and, more importantly, the nature of the relationship often dictates the manner in which these processes unfold. For example, persuasion and social comparison processes differ among close friends than among acquaintances (Beach, Tesser, Fincham, Jones, Johnson, & Whitaker, 1998; Cialdini & Trost, 1998).

4. Social Cognition is More Than Individual Cognition; It Is Distributed Across Tools, People, and Groups.

Not all useful knowledge is stored in our heads; some of it resides in tools (e.g., books, the internet), some in other people (e.g., a spouse or friend), and some in groups of people (e.g., statistical consultants). What people know is thereby distributed throughout the social and physical environment, and our ability to use this knowledge effectively depends on tools and skills for accessing it (e.g., computers, language, telephones). Distributed information processing is most often studied in work settings, such as studies of how members of a task-oriented group with different expertise interact. These systems may be profoundly influenced by the nature of the relationship between team members (e.g., Moreland, Argote, & Krishnan, 1996; Thompson & Fine, 1999). Socially shared knowledge is also common in more personal relationships. For example, spouses and family members often rely on each other for specialized information, as has been shown experimentally in several studies of transactive memory (e.g., Hollingshead, 1998; Wegner, Erber, & Raymond, 1991). Key to accessing socially shared information is knowing who knows what and believing that they will openly share their knowledge. Both of these factors reflect the nature of relationships.

DO RELATIONSHIP CONTEXTS REALLY AFFECT SOCIAL PSYCHOLOGICAL PROCESSES?

My premise to this point has been that social psychological research on the impact of situations would benefit from greater attention to the relational aspects of situations. That is, I argue that the explanatory power of social psychological theories would gain by considering the impact of who else is present or who else is affected by, or has an effect on, the individual. Social psychologists are by nature skeptical; exhortations (even those as well-grounded as this one!) are less compelling than demonstrations. The question then becomes, to what extent do the findings of existing social psychological research depend on relationship contexts?

Note that this question asks something more complex than whether relationships affect behavior. That relationships affect behavior seems unquestionable; people behave differently when interacting with their lovers, best friends, subordinates, in-laws, teenage daughters, rivals, insurance agents, and neighbors (Reis et al., 2000). The more consequential question being asked here is whether the processes that define well-known social psychological theories might vary as a function of the relationship context in which they are studied. For example, consider attributional egotism, the tendency to take credit for success and deny responsibility for failure. Does this tendency vary as a function of *whose* success and failure one's own is being compared to? If it does, then the relevant finding, considered a staple of the field in most textbooks, would need to be qualified in theoretical accounts of when and why it occurs. In other words, if relationship contexts moderate so-called "basic" social psychological findings, then our theories will need to view these phenomena less as general (i.e., acontextual) human tendencies and more as reflections of processes that are grounded in relationship circumstances.

A few examples selected from differing areas of social psychological research may help illustrate this general point.

1. As mentioned above, people typically take credit for success and deny responsibility for failure. Sedikides, Campbell, Reeder, and Elliot (1998) found this pattern in self-rated personal responsibility for test results, but only in distant dyads. In close dyads, no such bias was evident, suggesting that self-serving attributional biases may not dominate when they imply comparisons with close others. Beach et al. (1998) similarly found that self-evaluation maintenance processes such as jealousy when being outperformed and pride at outperforming others were attenuated when the other was a romantic partner (see also Scinta & Gable, 2005).
2. Memory is enhanced when information is encoded with regard to the self compared to others. However, meta-analysis of 65 studies indicates that the magnitude of this effect is twice as large for distant others than it is for intimate others (Symons & Johnson, 1997).

3. All other things being equal, there is said to be an asymmetry in explanations for the behavior of self and others: People tend to explain their own behavior with situational explanations and other people's behavior with dispositional (person) explanations. Malle's (2006) meta-analysis showed that this asymmetry occurs only for close others (romantic partners, friends, parents); when the other is a stranger or acquaintance, there is no evidence of such an asymmetry.

4. Gender differences in language-related behavior are commonly cited in textbooks. Leaper and Ayres's (2007) recent meta-analysis indicated that some of the most popular of these gender differences are moderated by the relationship among conversational partners. For example, women are more talkative in studies of classmates and families (i.e., parents with their children), whereas men are more talkative in studies of romantic partners, mixed-familiarity groups, and strangers. Also, women are more likely than men to use affiliative speech with strangers but not with close others, whereas men are more likely than women to use assertive speech with strangers but not with close others.

5. An oft-stated reason for helping another person is to remedy their sad mood. Consistent with this idea, Clark, Ouellette, Powell and Milberg (1987) found that the sadder the needy recipient's mood, the more help participants offered—but only when there was a communal relationship between them. When they had an exchange relationship, the recipient's mood had no effect on the amount of help offered.

6. Attachment security is reflected in the capacity for and comfort with closeness. Tidwell, Reis, and Shaver (1996) supported this hypothesis in a diary study of college students' everyday social interactions. Secure people reported higher levels of intimacy than anxious people, who in turn reported higher levels of intimacy than avoidant people, but only in interactions with romantic partners. In interactions with nonromantic opposite sex others, the pattern was reversed: avoidant individuals reported higher levels of intimacy than anxious individuals, who in turn reported higher levels of intimacy than secure individuals. Tidwell et al. explain this reversal by noting that security may involve differentiating between appropriate and inappropriate partners for intimacy (consistent with research showing that institutionalized children may indiscriminately seek soothing from anyone available; Rutter et al., 2007).

7. Narcissism predisposes individuals to be sensitive to ego threat. In one study, high-narcissism individuals were more aggressive (levels of noise delivered) than low-narcissism individuals toward a partner who had negatively evaluated their work but only when that partner was described as having a different birthday from themselves (Konrath, Bushman, & Campbell, 2006). When the critical partner shared one's birthday, the level of aggression delivered by high narcissism individuals did not differ from that of low-narcissism individuals in either condition, suggesting that a sense of shared identity may alter the perception of ego threat by narcissistic individuals.

Many other examples exist, cutting across nearly all of the phenomena that social psychologists traditionally study. (Table 1 in Reis, 2008, provides further examples.) Of course, this listing is highly selective and more systematic scrutiny is needed. I suspect that the impact of relationship contexts may be more widely appreciated, albeit implicitly so, than is acknowledged. That is, researchers design studies to be run in settings that are likely to activate certain processes—for example, studies designed to test hypotheses about self-centered egotism, competition, dominance, or intergroup threat may create contexts in which participants are distant from one another, whereas studies designed to test hypotheses about empathy and perspective taking, cooperation, belongingness, security, and trust may be more likely to create contexts in which participants are able to identify and/or feel a sense of connection with one another. If so, this is a legitimate and important part of theory building, but it should become an explicit part of the field's theories, by specifying boundary conditions for phenomena. The failure to identify contextual conditions that contribute to a given effect or process means that a theory is underspecified and lessens the likelihood that its findings can be successfully generalized in other research or in applied settings.

A THEORY OF INTERDEPENDENT SITUATIONS

Another approach to thinking about the role of situations in social psychology is more conceptually grounded. Interdependence theory (Kelley & Thibaut, 1978; Thibaut & Kelley, 1959) proposes that situations be described and understood in terms of abstract properties that define how partners must interact in order to achieve desired outcomes. That is, in a given interaction, interacting partners influence each other's actions as they pursue whatever outcomes are most salient at the moment.

Situations structure this influence in certain ways; for example, inter-acting partners' outcomes might correspond (both succeed if either one succeeds) or conflict (one's success dictates the other's failure). The interdependent nature of situations creates an adaptive problem: A person must determine not merely what to do oneself but also how to coordinate with interaction partners in order to arrive at the most favor-able outcomes. How this coordination is accomplished, and to what effect, will vary according to the properties defining the situation. Importantly, in interdependence theory, the key features of situations are defined interpersonally—the nature and kind of interdependence that partners have, what they know about each other and the situation, and the behavioral options that are open to them.

An important element in interdependence theory analyses is that situa-tional causes are not isolated from personal causes but rather are inextric-ably linked (which, as noted above, is what Lewin intended). Situations present individuals with behavioral options, thereby making certain beha-viors more likely, others less likely, and still others irrelevant. This occurs because situations activate within the individual relevant cognitive and affective processing systems for selecting among them (Mischel & Shoda, 1999). Situations, in other words, offer a kind of "affordance" (to use terminology introduced by Gibson, 1979, in a different context). This analysis begins with the actual properties that define interdependence in a given situation (these will be discussed below; see Holmes & Cavallo, Chapter 17, Figure 17.1). Particular situations afford certain responses and preclude others. For example, when one is likely to benefit personally from a partner's goal attainment, one can show encouragement but not benevolence (In as much as benevolence requires benefitting the other at some cost to the self). Which of the available options is enacted reflects the actor's choice (made with or without deliberate awareness), depending on several types of "person variables": stable personal attributes (e.g., traits, values), transitory moods and beliefs, relational qualities (e.g., trust of the partner), or social norms. The situation thereby does not "cause" behavior, as many other models suggest, but rather alters the likelihood of a given behavior by making certain alternatives more relevant and others irrelevant.

To illustrate this principle, consider the well-known experiments on obedience to authority, conducted by Stanley Milgram in the 1960s (Milgram, 1974). This research is often used as the prototype for demon-strating "the power of the situation"—that is, for showing how situations "cause" obedience. The interdependence analysis is more nuanced. Two key features of this situation are the aura of scientific legitimacy that Milgram's paradigm painstakingly created, and the experimenter's per-sistent demands that the participant continue delivering increasingly intense shocks to the confederate. These afford the participant at least two behavioral options: to obey or to resist (which about 40% of participants did). To interdependence theorists, the participant's interaction with a domineering authority figure is seen as activating certain motives and goals (to please the experimenter, to do no harm, and so on), affording him or her an opportunity to select between the options of obedience or resistance. The situation, in other words, contributes to the causal analysis but is not itself causative independent of person factors.

Earlier in this chapter I argued that relationship contexts were central to understanding human behavior. Supplementing this contention with the insights of interdependence theory suggests that relationship contexts be analyzed in terms of their abstract properties of interdependence, describing the particular ways in which interacting partners influence each other's outcomes and goal-directed behavior. In *An Atlas of Interpersonal Situations*, Kelley, Holmes, Kerr, Reis, Rusbult, and Van Lange (2003) describe 20 common interpersonal situations that can be differentiated according to various combinations of six key properties, four of which concern interdependence directly (the other two concern timing and information). These six properties are as follows:

- The extent to which an individual's outcomes depend on the actions of others. High independence indicates that a person's outcomes are strongly affected by the other's behavior, whereas low interdependence means that the partner's behavior has little or no effect on one's outcomes.
- Whether individuals have mutual or asymmetric power over each other's outcomes. Mutual (equal and nontrivial) dependence implicates processes such as reciprocity and sharing, whereas asymmetric dependence, in which one partner is more dependent on the other for outcomes, implicates displays of dominance or benevolence by the more powerful person, and submission or reactance by the less powerful person.
- Whether one individual's outcomes correspond or conflict with the other's. Corresponding interests encourage cooperation and harmony, whereas competing interests foster competition, although it also provides an opportunity for partners to demonstrate caring by placing the partner's interests above one's own.
- Whether partners must coordinate their activities to produce satisfactory outcomes, or whether each one's actions are sufficient to determine the other's outcomes. In coordination situations, interacting parties must synchronize their activities, prioritizing processes relevant to communication and social coordination (e.g., perspective taking, negotiation, responsiveness). In contrast, exchange situations allow each person to effectively control the

other's outcomes, giving rise to norms about responsibility and not hurting others, as well as equity.

- The situation's temporal structure: Whether the situation is a one-time occurrence whose outcomes are immediately available, or involves interaction over the long-term. Time-extended situations allow individuals to forego immediate rewards in anticipation of later gains, implicating self-regulatory skills such as delay of gratification and allowing investment in the relationship.
- Information certainty: Whether partners have the information needed to make good decisions, or whether uncertainty exists about the future. When information is adequate and public, decisions can usually be made on that basis. On the other hand, uncertainty often requires risk—a choice between loss avoidance and gain seeking—and provides an opportunity for examining how partners adjudicate discrepant preferences (e.g., by invoking procedural norms, by negotiating, or by exerting power and control).

To illustrate the value of this analysis for social psychological research, I will explain two of these dimensions in somewhat more detail. The first illustration shows how the first of these dimensions, degree of interdependence, has already yielded many findings in the social-psychological literature, although not in an integrated way. In the second example, I discuss a dimension that has received relatively little explicit attention, although it underlies several important social psychological constructs, basis of control (also see Holmes and Cavallo, Chapter 17, for discussion of another dimension: correspondence of outcomes). In passing, I note briefly that most real-world situations are best characterized not along a single dimension but rather in terms of permutations of several factors (e.g., high, asymmetric interdependence). Although the application of this analysis to actual research situations requires considering these more complex permutations, for clarity the present analysis examines only single dimensions. Readers interested in the more complex analysis are referred to the *Atlas* (Kelley et al., 2003).

Example 1: Degree of Outcome Interdependence

When outcome interdependence is low, parties exert little or no influence on each other's outcomes; each person does what makes the most sense to him or her, on a personal basis, with little regard to the other. On the other hand, when outcome interdependence is high, one person's outcomes are strongly influenced by the other's actions. This would be the case, for example, when people work together on a task to which both must contribute; when family members share instrumental and socio-emotional life tasks; and when friends depend on each other for support, advice, recreation, and satisfaction of relatedness needs.

The social-psychological literature includes many studies documenting changes in social behavior that reflect varying degrees of outcome interdependence. For example, all other things being equal, when outcome interdependence is high, people pay more attention to interaction partners and are more attracted to them (Berscheid, Graziano, Monson, & Dermer, 1976); make more individuated, less stereotypic judgments about others (Fiske, 1993); are more generous in attributions for the other's performance (Sedikides et al., 1998); identify more closely with the other person (Rabbie, Schot, & Visser, 1989); enact a greater number of prosocial acts to benefit the other (Batson, 1998) and display lesser aggression (Geen, 1998); are less prejudiced and engage in fewer discriminatory acts (Pettigrew, 1998); make more attempts to persuade the other or induce conformity, and are in turn more persuasible (Cialdini & Trost, 1998; Mackie et al., 1990); and are more committed to close relationships (Rusbult, 1983).

These studies show that high interdependence predicts greater involvement with, interest in, and positivity toward others. Importantly, the foundation shared by these various findings is rarely seen or mentioned in theoretical analyses or textbooks. By highlighting the role of abstract properties of interdependence, their conceptual linkage, as well as the possibility that this is a foundational principle for understanding social behavior, becomes apparent.

Example 2: Basis of Control: Exchange Versus Coordination

In exchange situations, outcomes are determined by the other's actions, the value of which is fixed irrespective of one's own actions; typically, outcomes in exchange situations have similar value regardless of who provides them. For example, it usually doesn't matter who provides a ride to pick up one's car at the repair shop. Exchange situations encourage trading and reciprocity and are often impersonal. In coordination situations, on the other hand, outcomes depend on what both partners do and how they coordinate their actions. Collaborating on research with a colleague, for example, depends on each partner contributing specific and interlocking expertise so that the resulting project is optimally conceptualized and designed. In this case, value tends to be partner specific because the project would likely look different if one were to collaborate with a different partner. Effective coordination depends on the fit between each partner's expertise, whether they have common goals, how well they communicate, and so forth.

Coordination situations are not often studied in social psychology, although there are examples, notably in organizational settings. Steiner (1972) distinguished two forms of process loss that occur in work groups, one regarding motivational deficits, the other concerned with poor organization and deployment of resources. These two forms correspond to exchange and coordination situations, respectively. Coordination situations are far more common in everyday social life than the research literature implies. For example, friends and romantic partners often interact (either with each other or with third parties) in ways that reflect shared knowledge about each other (e.g., Hardin & Higgins, 1996; Hollingshead, 2001), and juggling household and family responsibilities is a major task that couples face. The ability to manage coordination situations effectively is key to social life.

Coordination situations may also be more subtle. Consider self-disclosure. Effective self-disclosure requires ascertaining suitable targets (e.g., others likely to be receptive to one's openings) and appropriate timing and contexts. For example, highly self-disclosing statements are normative with close friends but not with strangers (Wortman, Adesman, Herman, & Greenberg, 1976). Whether or not self-disclosure meets its goals (e.g., promoting intimacy, obtaining information or advice; Miller & Read, 1987) depends on the listener's response, which is in turn a function of various dispositional (e.g., perspective-taking skill, warmth) and situational (e.g., willingness to be supportive to the discloser at this time) (Reis & Patrick, 1996; Reis & Shaver, 1988). For example, an offer of tangible assistance may be experienced as comforting in one context, and as a sign of perceived inadequacy in another (Burleson, 1994). Thus, as shown in Figure 16.2, the intimacy process involves synchronizing one

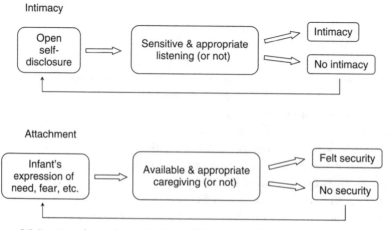

Figure 16.2. Interdependence Analysis of Two Coordination Situations.

partner's openness with the other partner's responsiveness, coordinating the discloser's goals and abilities with those of the responder. Importantly, success in this process is determined less by individual properties of the persons involved and more by their willingness to be open or responsive, respectively, with that partner at that moment—in other words, by relational and situational factors. Miller and Kenny (1986) showed that the large majority of variance in self-disclosure is attributable to relationship variance rather than to actor or partner effects—that is, most people have some partners to whom they disclose little and others to whom they disclose a lot.[3] Self-disclosure, like friendship in general, is a highly particularistic resource (Foa, Converse, Tornblom, & Foa, 1993).

A similar analysis applies to other well-known phenomena. For example, in attachment theory, a secure attachment relationship develops when an infant's expressions of need or fear are met by a caregiver's sensitive and appropriate responses. Caregivers who ignore the infant's needs, or alternatively who are overprotective or intrusive, are both considered nonresponsive and tend to foster insecure attachments. The key, in other words, is for caregivers to be perceptive in assessing the infant's needs, and willing and able to respond appropriately to them. Caregiving motivated primarily by the caregiver's own needs (for example, to be seen by others as a good caregiver) is likely to be mistimed, ill matched to the particular distress, or insensitive to the infant's emerging autonomy (Stern, 1985). Similar arguments have been made for caregiving in adult attachment relationships (e.g., Mikulincer & Shaver, 2004). At the most general level, numerous processes relevant to interaction in close relationships depend on this kind of coordinated behavior, in which effective interaction depends on partners' attention to each other's signals, and their mutual ability and willingness to respond sensitively and appropriately—processes such as empathy, communication (including nonverbal synchrony and certain types of conversational interaction), supportiveness, and sexuality, to name only a few, come readily to mind.

Let me conclude this section by reiterating the purpose of this analysis. In each case, the nature of the interpersonal situation, characterized in terms of the abstract properties of interdependence between interacting partners, shapes the social and personality processes that regulate behavior. Thus, this model provides a systematic and useful framework for organizing and understanding the ways in which interpersonal situations affect behavior. Rather than a more or less listlike accumulation of

---

[3] I am aware of no studies that conduct the same sort of analysis on responsiveness, though I would expect a similar result.

findings, as situational effects are commonly reported, this framework offers a systematic and theoretically grounded scheme for organizing research on relationship contexts as situations.

CONCLUSION

Social psychology has a long and venerable history of investigating the impact of situations on behavior. One hundred and one years after the publication of McDougall's and Ross's seminal volumes, the field has accumulated a wealth of important and influential studies, well-known not only among behavioral researchers but by most educated persons. Nearly every college-educated American is at least superficially aware of the classic Asch and Milgram studies and the Stanford Prison Study; and many know about Darley and Latané's helping studies (e.g., Darley & Latane, 1968), learned helplessness, and the Implicit Association Test (IAT). Social psychological studies are reported often by most major media, and there is even a situationist website, thesituationist.word-press.com, managed by a group called the Project on Law and Mind Sciences at Harvard Law School.

Yet little systematic theory, or even a comprehensive descriptive tax-onomy, about situations exists (see Reis, 2008, for elaboration; Kenny, Mohr, and Levesque, 2001, and Rozin, 2001, reach a similar conclusion), giving most accounts a somewhat happenstance or idiosyncratic tone. Part of the reason for this lacuna is the need to identify just which types of situations are most important, and what their conceptual properties are. Although there are a great many situational factors that influence behavior and that therefore ought to be the subject of social psychological research, the premise of this chapter is that social-psychological situations are at their core interpersonal. (Apparently, based on the definitions cited at the beginning of this chapter, most textbooks agree.) Thus, to fail to consider the role of interpersonal factors in behavior, arguably the focal feature of the situational context from the individual's perspective, is to underesti-mate situational influences on behavior.

The "miracle" in the Sidney Harris cartoon that provides the theme for this book, then, is the miracle by which individuals band together in dyads, groups, and social networks to form interdependent entities that, in one way or another, together go about performing the important behaviors of living, learning, working, playing, and reproducing. Further attention to the inherently interpersonal nature of human behavior is likely to advance the validity and usefulness of social-psychological theory and research.

REFERENCES

Allport, G. W. (1954). The historical background of modern social psychology. In G. Lindzey (Ed.), *Handbook of social psychology* (vol. 1, pp. 3–56). Reading, MA: Addison-Wesley Publishing Co.

Asch, S. E. (1952). *Social Psychology*. New York: Prentice Hall.

Barker, R. G. (1965). Explorations in ecological psychology. *American Psychologist, 20*, 1–14.

Batson, C. D. (1998). Altruism and prosocial behavior. In D. Gilbert, S. T. Fiske, & G. Lindzey, (Eds.), *The handbook of social psychology* (4th ed., Vol. 2, pp. 282–316). New York: McGraw-Hill.

Beach, S. R. H., Tesser, A., Fincham, F. D., Jones, D. J., Johnson, D., & Whitaker, D. J. (1998). Pleasure and pain in doing well, together: An investigation of performance-related affect in close relationships. *Journal of Personality and Social Psychology, 74*, 923–938.

Berscheid, E., Graziano, W., Monson, T., & Dermer, M. (1976). Outcome dependency: Attention, attribution, and attraction. *Journal of Personality and Social Psychology, 34*, 978–989.

Brown, R. (1965). *Social psychology*. New York: The Free Press.

Bugental, D. B. (2000). Acquisition of the algorithms of social life: A domain-based approach. *Psychological Bulletin, 126*, 187–219.

Burleson, B. R. (1994). Comforting messages: Significance, approaches, and effects. In B. R. Burleson, T. L. Albrecht, & I. G. Sarason (Eds.), *Communication of social support: Messages, interactions, relationships, and community* (pp. 3–28). Thousand Oaks, CA: Sage.

Buss, D. M. & Kenrick, D. T. (1998). Evolutionary social psychology. In D. Gilbert & S. Fiske (Eds.), *The handbook of social psychology*, (4th ed., Vol. 2, pp. 982–1026). Boston: McGraw-Hill.

Cialdini, R. B., & Trost, M. R. (1998). "Social influence: Social norms, conformity, and compliance." In D. Gilbert, S. Fiske, & G. Lindzey (Eds.) *The handbook of social psychology* (4th ed., Vol. 2, pp. 151–192). New York: McGraw-Hill.

Clark, M. S., Oullette, R., Powell, M. C., & Milberg, S. (1987). Recipient's mood, relationship type, & helping. *Journal of Personality and Social Psychology, 53*, 94–103.

Cosmides, L., & Tooby, J. (1992). Cognitive adaptations for social exchange. In J. H. Barkow, L. Cosmides, & J. Tooby (Eds.), *The adapted mind: Evolutionary psychology and the generation of culture* (pp. 163–228). New York: Oxford University Press.

Darley, J. M., and Latane, B. (1968). Bystander intervention in emergencies: Diffusion of responsibility. *Journal of Personality and Social Psychology, 8*, 377–383.

Ekman, P., & Davidson, R. J. (1994). Afterword: How is evidence of universals in antecedents of emotion explained? In P. Ekman & R. J. Davidson (Eds.), *The nature of emotion: Fundamental questions* (pp. 176–177). New York: Oxford University Press.

Fiske, S. T. (1992). Thinking is for doing: Portraits of social cognition from Daguerreotype to laserphoto. *Journal of Personality and Social Psychology, 63,* 877–889.

Fiske, S. T. (1993). Controlling other people: The impact of power on stereotyping. *American Psychologist, 48,* 621–628.

Foa, U. G., Converse, Jr., J., Tornblom, K. Y., & Foa, E. B. (1993). *Resource theory: Explorations and applications.* San Diego, CA: Academic Press.

Geen, R. G. (1998). Aggression and antisocial behavior. In D. Gilbert, S. T. Fiske, & G. Lindzey, (Eds.), *The handbook of social psychology* (4th ed., Vol. 2, pp. 317–356). New York: McGraw-Hill.

Gibson, J. J. (1979). *The ecological approach to visual perception.* Boston, MA: Houghton-Mifflin.

Gilovich, T., Keltner, D., & Nisbett, R. E. (2006). *Social psychology.* New York: W. W. Norton.

Gollwitzer, P. M., & Moskowitz, G. B. (1996). Goal effects on action and cognition. In E. T. Higgins & A. W. Kruglanski (Eds.), *Social psychology: Handbook of basic principles* (pp. 361–399). New York, NY: The Guilford Press.

Hardin, C. D., & Higgins, E. T. (1996). Shared reality: How social verification makes the subjective objective. In R. M. Sorrentino & E. T. Higgins (Eds.), *Handbook of motivation and cognition* (pp. 28–84). New York: The Guilford Press.

Hartup, W. W., & Stevens, N. (1997). Friendships and adaptation in the life course. *Psychological Bulletin, 121,* 355–370.

Hinde, R. A. (1997). *Relationships: A dialectical perspective.* East Sussex, England: Psychology Press.

Hollingshead, A. B. (1998). Retrieval in transactive memory systems. *Journal of Personality and Social Psychology, 74,* 659–671.

Hollingshead, A. B. (2001). Cognitive interdependence and convergent expectations in transactive memory. *Journal of Personality and Social Psychology, 81,* 1080–1089.

Kelley, H. H., Holmes, J. G., Kerr, N. L., Reis, H. T., Rusbult, C. E., & Van Lange, P. A. M. (2003). *An atlas of interpersonal situations.* New York: Cambridge University Press.

Kelley, H. H., & Thibaut, J. W. (1978). *Interpersonal relations: A theory of interdependence.* New York: Wiley.

Kenny, D. A., Mohr, C. D., and Levesque, M. J. (2001). A social relations variance partitioning of dyadic behavior. *Psychological Bulletin, 127,* 128–141.

Konrath, S., Bushman, B. J., & Campbell, W. K. (2006). Attenuating the link between threatened egotism and aggression. *Psychological Science, 17,* 995–1001.

Leaper, C., & Ayres, M. M. (2007). A meta-analytic review of gender variations in adults' language use: Talkativeness, affiliative speech, and assertive speech. *Personality and Social Psychology Review, 11,* 328–363.

Lewin K. (1951). Behavior and development as a function of the total situation. In D. Cartwright (Ed.), *Field theory in social science* (pp. 238–297). New York: Harper & Row.

Mackie, D. M., Worth, L. T. & Asuncion, A. G. (1990). Processing of persuasive in-group messages. *Journal of Personality and Social Psychology, 58,* 812–822.

Magnusson, D. (1981). *Toward a psychology of situations: an interactional perspective.* Hillsdale, N.J.: Erlbaum Associates.

Malle, B. F. (2006). The actor-observer asymmetry in attribution: A (surprising) meta-analysis. *Psychological Bulletin, 132,* 895–919.

McDougall, W. (1908). *Introduction to social psychology.* Boston: Luce.

Mikulincer, M., & Shaver, P. R. (2004). Security-based self-representations in adulthood: Contents and processes. In S. W. Rholes & J. A. Simpson (Eds.), *Adult attachment: Theory, research, and clinical implications* (pp. 159–195). New York, NY: Guilford Publications.

Milgram, S. (1974). *Obedience to authority.* New York: Harper & Row.

Miller, L. C., & Kenny, D. A. (1986). Reciprocity of self disclosure at the individual and dyadic levels: A social relations analysis. *Journal of Personality and Social Psychology, 50,* 713–719.

Miller, L. C., & Read, S. J. (1987). Why am I telling you this?: Self-disclosure in a goal-based model of personality. In V. J. Derlega & J. H. Berg (Eds.), *Self-disclosure: Theory, research, and therapy (Perspectives in social psychology)* (pp. 35–58). New York: Plenum.

Mischel, W., & Shoda, Y. (1995). A cognitive-affective system theory of personality: Reconceptualizing situations, dispositions, dynamics, and invariance in personality structure. *Psychological Review, 102,* 246–268.

Mischel, W., & Shoda, Y. (1999). Integrating dispositions and processing dynamics within a unified theory of personality: The cognitive-affective personality system. In L. A. Pervin & O. P. John (Eds.), *Handbook of Personality* (2nd ed., pp. 197–218). New York: Guilford.

Moreland, R. L., Argote, L., & Krishnan, R. (1996). Socially shared cognition at work: Transactive memory and group performance. In J. L. Nye & A. M. Brower (Eds.), *What's social about social cognition? Research on socially shared cognition in small groups* (pp. 57–84). Thousand Oaks, CA: Sage Publications, Inc.

Myers, D. G. (1999). *Social psychology* (6th ed.). Boston: McGraw-Hill College.

Pervin, L. A. (1978). Definitions, measurements, and classifications of stimuli, situations, and environments. *Human Ecology, 6,* 71–105.

Pettigrew, T. F. (1998). Intergroup contact theory. *Annual Review of Psychology, 49,* 65–85.

Rabbie, J. M., Schot, J. C., & Visser, L. (1989). Social identity theory: A conceptual and empirical critique from the perspective of a behavioural interaction model. *European Journal of Social Psychology, 19,* 171–202.

Reis, H. T. (2008). Reinvigorating the concept of situation in social psychology. *Personality and Social Psychology Review, 12,* 311–329.

Reis, H. T., Collins, W. A., & Berscheid, E. (2000). The relationship context of human behavior and development. *Psychological Bulletin, 126,* 844–872.

Reis, H. T., & Patrick, B. C. (1996). Attachment and intimacy: Component processes. In A. Kruglanski & E. T. Higgins (Eds.), *Social psychology: Handbook of basic principles* (pp. 523–563). New York: Guilford.

Reis, H. T., & Shaver, P. (1988). Intimacy as an interpersonal process. In S. W. Duck (Ed.), *Handbook of personal relationships* (pp. 367–389). Chichester, England: John Wiley and Sons, Ltd.

Ross, E. A. (1908). *Social psychology*. New York: McMillan.

Ross, L., and Nisbett, R.E. (1991). *The person and the situation: Perspectives of social psychology*. McGraw-Hill.

Rozin, P. (2001). Social psychology and science: Some lessons from Solomon Asch. *Personality and Social Psychology Review, 5,* 2–14.

Rusbult, C. E. (1983). A longitudinal test of the investment model: The development (and deterioration) of satisfaction and commitment in heterosexual involvements. *Journal of Personality and Social Psychology, 45,* 101–117.

Rutter, M., Colvert, E., Kreppner, J., Beckett, C., Castle, J., Groothues, C., Hawkins, A., O'Connor, T. G., Stevens, S. E., & Sonuga-Barke, E. J. S. (2007). Early adolescent outcomes for institutionally-deprived and non-deprived adoptees. I: Disinhibited attachment. *Journal of Child Psychology and Psychiatry, 48,* 17–30.

Scinta, A., & Gable, S. L. (2005). Performance comparisons and attachment: An investigation of competitive responses in close relationships. *Personal Relationships, 12,* 357–372.

Sedikides, C., Campbell, W. K., Reeder, G., & Elliot, A. J. (1998). The self-serving bias in relational context. *Journal of Personality and Social Psychology, 74,* 378–386.

Smith, E. R., and Mackie, D. M. (2000). *Social psychology* (2nd ed.). Philadelphia, PA: Taylor and Francis.

Smith, E. R., & Semin, G. R. (2004). Socially situated cognition: Cognition in its social context. *Advances in Experimental Social Psychology, 36,* 53–117.

Smith, E. R., & Semin, G. R. (2007). Situated social cognition. *Current Directions in Psychological Science, 16,* 132–135.

Steiner, I. D. (1972). *Group process and productivity*. New York: Academic Press.

Stern, D. N. (1985). *The interpersonal world of the infant*. New York: Basic Books.

Symons, C. S., & Johnson, B. T. (1997). The self-reference effect in memory: A meta-analysis. *Psychological Bulletin, 121,* 371–394.

Taylor, S. E., Peplau, L. A., & Sears, D. O. (2000). *Social psychology* (10th ed.). Upper Saddle River, NJ: Prentice Hall.

Thibaut, J. W., & Kelley, H. H. (1959). *The social psychology of groups*. New York: Wiley.

Thompson, L., & Fine, G. A. (1999). Socially shared cognition, affect, and behavior: A review and integration. *Personality and Social Psychology Review, 3,* 278–302.

Tidwell, M. C. O., Reis, H. T., & Shaver, P. R. (1996). Attachment, attractiveness, and social interaction: A diary study. *Journal of Personality and Social Psychology, 71,* 729–745.

Wegner, D. M., Erber, R., & Raymond, P. (1991). Transactive memory in close relationships. *Journal of Personality and Social Psychology, 61,* 923–929.

Wortman, C. B., Adesman, P., Herman, E., & Greenberg, R. (1976). Self-disclosure: An attributional perspective. *Journal of Personality and Social Psychology, 33,* 184–191.

17 The Atlas of Interpersonal Situations: A Theory-Driven Approach to Behavioral Signatures

John G. Holmes
Justin V. Cavallo

Social psychologists are lost in their heads. It is our contention that the main reason that behavior has been neglected in social psychological research is that most theoretical frameworks have adopted a social construal focus that orphans behavioral prediction. We will argue that our field needs a return to more classical S–R models that link external situational features to actual behavior. The Mischel and Shoda (1995) behavioral signature model is one such approach and we will describe its virtues for advancing our understanding of behavioral responses. The weak link in the model is that one needs a "theory of situations" to predict a priori which goals will be activated and what behavior will subsequently be enacted.

We describe in some detail one attempt to create such a theory, the *Atlas of Interpersonal Situations* (2003) by H. H. Kelley and colleagues. We suggest that the application of ideas from this framework would increase the precision of behavioral prediction substantially. We discuss the advantages of this logic by focusing on an important dimension of situations, the extent of correspondence between two persons' potential interaction outcomes, otherwise known as the degree of conflict of interest. We suggest that this feature of situations triggers particular concerns and goals in people who are uncertain about others' prosocial motivations toward them, resulting in a predictable set of self-protective behavioral reactions. We then illustrate these dynamics by describing research in both the attachment and risk regulation traditions that shows the power of this form of analysis.

THE SOCIAL CONSTRUAL FOCUS: OR, HOW BEHAVIORAL PREDICTION WAS LOST

Whatever happened to traditional S–R theories that dominated thinking in psychology for so many years? The theory was central to early versions of learning and reinforcement theories, which linked stimulus features in the environment to actual behavior and its subsequent reinforcement. Little attention was given to cognition, and in the case of Skinner, cognition was seen as an "epiphenomenum," brain activity that shadowed behavior but had no effect on it. This "black box" perspective clashed forcefully with the cognitive revolution zeitgeist in social psychology in the 1970s, resulting in social construal processes becoming the central focus within the field. During this time, social psychologists began to assume that the "miracle" that linked situations with behavior could be explained by social construal processes and, like the characters in the cartoon that accompanies this volume, focused intently on elucidating it.

Two different paradigms marked this "all in the head" perspective. The first focused on social perception and explored how people perceived and interpreted external events. For instance, researchers in the interpersonal relations field studied the types of social experiences that were experienced as "rejection" (e.g., Downey, Freitas, Michaelis, & Khouri, 1998; Murray, Rose, Bellavia, Holmes, & Kusche, 2002). Other researchers devoted considerable energy to investigating perceptions of discrimination, stereotypes of social targets, and attributions for another's behavior. Indeed, these topics constitute a large part of the content of social psychology. The common thread is that the end point of research is typically the cognitive reaction to features of a social situation. The second paradigm involves theories that start with a social construal and then link it to a pattern of behavior. For example, researchers examine how hurt feelings and perceptions of rejection result in hostile behavioral reactions and distancing from others (e.g., Downey et al., 2000; Murray, Bellavia, Rose, & Griffin, 2003). They might also explore how stereotypes of a particular racial group influence behavioral reaction times to an ambiguous image of a possible gun (Payne, 2001). Behavior is indeed the focus in this paradigm, but no link is made to an external reality. The result is an inability to predict actions a priori.

MISCHEL AND SHODA'S BEHAVIORAL SIGNATURE MODEL

Clearly one could reconstitute a sophisticated S–M–R model out of these two paradigms, where M represents the cognitive-affective mechanisms intervening between the external stimulus and behavioral response.

Surprisingly, this approach was not common until Mischel and Shoda's (1995) development of a theoretical model for the cognitive-affective personality system (CAPS). The CAPS framework has had a strong influence on the field of personality psychology in recent years. Their conceptualization incorporates a person-by-situation interactionist perspective (Cantor & Kihlstrom, 1987; Endler & Hunt, 1969) into a more general social-cognitive interpretation of the meaning of "personality."

Mischel and Shoda (1995) present impressive evidence that an individual's behavioral signature is typically quite stable over time if behavior is examined within the context of *specific* situations. A person's signature is comprised of "if-then" patterns of situation–behavior associations (see Figure 17.1). The CAPS model contends that specific features of situations activate subsets of cognitive mediating units, which in turn generate responses to the different situations. That is, individuals are seen to have a distinctive behavioral signature or style of adapting to features of their social environment. In this regard, Mischel and Shoda suggest that situations need to be considered in abstract terms, redefining them "to capture their basic psychological features, so that behavior can be predicted across a broad range of contexts that contain the same features" (p. 248).

We strongly concur with this principle that features of situations need to be categorized *a priori* in terms of their psychologically critical, "active" ingredients (and indeed Holmes, 2002, developed this as a major theme in his paper on the structure of interpersonal cognition). If instead we focus on concrete or nominal details of situations, we easily become lost in the

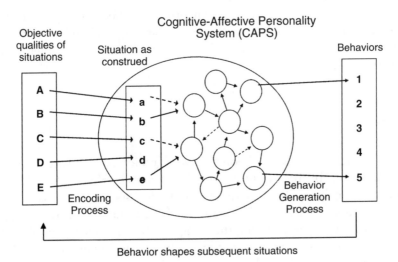

Figure 17.1. The Cognitive-Affective Personality System (CAPS; Mischel & Shoda, 1995).

minutiae of everyday life and lose predictive power. However, Mischel and Shoda's definition of the situation, the *if* in their "if-then" model, has not been particularly abstract, but instead has focused largely on another person's behavior as the context for the actor's behavior. For example, one situation in their famous summer camp study was, "Adult warned the child." This perspective is certainly not unreasonable given that focusing on what people see and hear in the social world is the most common usage of the term "situation" in social psychology (Ross & Nisbett, 1991). However, it is difficult to know what an abstract depiction of this situation would be. For instance, is the counselor giving an authoritative command (with possible consequences)? Criticizing the child's behavior? Or trying to coordinate swimming activities? In this situation, we might predict very different responses from the child depending on our theoretical depiction of it.

The problem is that we need a "theory of situations" if we are to create a model that starts with specifying abstract features of external situations and then predicts *a priori* which elements in the cognitive-affective system will be activated to adapt to or cope with the opportunities or challenges the social situation affords by its structure. The activated elements can then be related to goal processes that predict the behavior generation process. Put another way, explaining the link between situations and behavior may not require the occurrence of a "miracle" at all. Rather, understanding the features of situations that precede behavioral responses may allow for behavioral prediction without any mediating variables, wondrous or otherwise. We turn to recent developments in interdependence theory to explore how this top-down theory of situations might provide a theoretical classification of situations and an analysis of the particular cognitive and motivational processes functionally related to dealing with the specific problems each situation entails.

INTERDEPENDENCE THEORY

This description of recent theoretical work on interdependence theory is adapted from *An Atlas of Interpersonal Situations* by Kelley et al., (2003). This book analyzes 20 of the most prototypical social situations in detail and presents propositions linking each to particular cognitive and goal processes. It expands upon the long intellectual tradition of social exchange analysis first presented by Thibault and Kelley (1959). Other ideas come from a book being developed by Kelley & Holmes (2003) before Hal Kelley died in 2003. Further, some of the implications of this general theory for social cognitive processes have been developed in a paper by Holmes (2002).

Generally speaking, interdependence theory (IT) expands the formula proposed by Lewin (1946) that behavior is a function of the person and the environment. In the context of a social relationship, the behavioral interaction (I) that occurs between persons A and B is a function of both persons' respective goal tendencies in relation to each other in the *particular* situation of interdependence (S) in which the interaction occurs.

Each situation specifies the ways in which two persons are dependent on and influence each other with respect to their potential outcomes in an interaction (hence the term interdependence). The theory attempts to identify the kinds of interpersonal dispositions of persons A and B—their attitudes, motives, goals—that are *functionally* relevant to dealing with decisions in each particular type of situation. Then the type of situation S, together with the relevant dispositions of A and B, determine the interaction, I (in symbols, the SABI elements; Kelley & Holmes, 2003). As this model implies, interdependence theory adopts a person-by-situation interactionist approach with a strong social psychological focus on the nature of "situations." Each paradigmatic situation is viewed as presenting the two persons with a unique set of problems and opportunities.

The Person and the Situation

To give the reader some understanding of how a situation is defined in IT terms, an example of a 2×2 outcome matrix is presented in Figure 17.2. This well-known situation involves "Exchange with Mutual Profit" (also known as the Prisoner's Dilemma). The particular numbers used to represent the consequences for the two persons of any pair of behavioral choices are intended to provide a symbolic representation of individuals' satisfaction or dissatisfaction with an interaction event, rather than concrete outcomes of any particular kind. The *abstract pattern* of numbers represents the essential social problem that a situation poses, the "dilemma" that individuals face. Thus, the abstract features of a situation as in Figure 17.2 are intended to capture the essence of many concrete interdependence problems.

Figure 17.2 is classified as an exchange situation because each person has the ability to reward or help the other (by giving 10 units through choosing option 1). If both individuals cooperate and conclude such a reciprocal exchange, they will both profit equally and benefit from "gains in trade" by dividing up a larger "pie" (20 units) than is available by any other pair of choices. Such gains in trade are so ubiquitous in everyday social life that evolutionary psychologists have even suggested that the

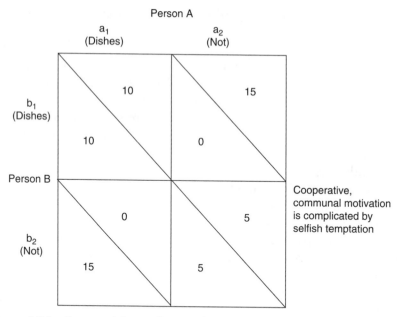

Figure 17.2. Outcome Matrix of an "Exchange with Mutual Profit" Situation.

rewards from reciprocal cooperation may have resulted in cooperative, prosocial motivations being as heritable as aggressive, selfish ones (Tooby & Cosmides, 1996).

What complicates the situation and leads to the dilemma is that each person's personal preference (of 5 units) favors the other behavioral choice, option 2. Thus, each person is tempted to defect from the cooperative exchange and to choose the second option, which could result in the most individual gain and the greatest competitive advantage (if the other person chooses option 1). For example, a husband and wife both dislike cleaning the dishes, but if both pitch in, the task is quickly accomplished and they reap the benefits of cooperation. Of course, each would be sorely tempted, if the other started the job, to just let the partner finish the unpleasant task. That way, the dishes are done and the dreaded task is once again avoided!

A central idea in the theory is that situations differ in terms of the particular interpersonal dispositions relevant to coping with the specific problems they represent. Thus, the linkages between the situation and person domains are ones of logical relevance or *affordance*. Essentially, interpersonal dispositions reflect people's preferences, or *valuations*, for the different interaction possibilities afforded by a particular situation. We conceptualize this process of evaluating behavioral options and making choices as the application of *rules*. By distinguishing the valuation rules logically applicable to various situations, we essentially summarize the various attitudes, motives, and goals that guide interpersonal behavior in each of them.

For instance, the Exchange with Mutual Profit situation in Figure 17.2 provides the opportunity through the choice of a rule for "being" a certain type of person, but not other types. This situation provides the opportunity for expressing cooperative or prosocial goals because selecting option 1 would follow valuation rules to "maximize joint profit" or "achieve equality." Alternatively, a person might have a valuation rule that specifies "maximize one's own competitive advantage" or "maximize own outcomes." However, this situation does *not* allow people to express a variety of other possible interpersonal goals, such as being dominant or submissive, showing initiative, being loyal or dependable, and so on.

Thus, the situation and person domains exist in close, complementary relation to each other. One way to describe this relation is to say that each disposition can be defined abstractly as a tendency to psychologically transform one situation into another one, or using Lewin's (1946) concept, to "restructure the field." In our current example, a cooperative person would thus be someone who turned this inherently ambiguous (i.e., mixed-motive) situation into a cooperative one by attaching particular value to the cooperative pair solution. From this perspective, one can only identify the *person* as a figure against the ground of the *situation*.

As we hope the reader will grasp intuitively from this example, however, the actor's (A) choice of rules does not occur in a vacuum. The goal person A pursues is likely to depend heavily on expectations about the other's goals and motives (B), especially the extent to which the other is expected to be responsive to one's needs (Reis, Clark, & Holmes, 2004). Indeed, Holmes (2002) has suggested that expectations about the other person's goals are the single most important and basic consideration in interpersonal relations, one that probably has evolutionary roots. Thus, not only may two partners be behaviorally interdependent, but they will frequently be *rule interdependent* as well, especially in long-term close relationships. That is, an actor's rule may be contingent on the rule the other person is expected to choose.

Put another way, the type of person one can "be" is often constrained by the type of person a partner is expected to be. In Kelley and Stahelski's (1970) pioneering research exploring the social dilemma depicted in Figure 17.2, for instance, cooperative individuals typically held contingent rules for the goal they would pursue, following a cooperative rule only if they expected the other person to reciprocate. Faced with someone they believed had a competitive goal, they could not "be themselves" and instead engaged in more competitive behaviors. Competitive individuals, in contrast, rather uniformly expected others to be self-concerned and out for themselves. Their typical response was to react in kind to the *expected* competitive behavior of the other person, whether it were true or not.

A Taxonomy of Situations

A group of scholars recently developed a systematic taxonomy of situations, described in *An Atlas of Interpersonal Situations* (Kelley et al., 2003). By applying analysis of variance logic to the 2×2 matrix depiction of situations, they demonstrated that each such situation can be characterized by four dimensions. The first dimension involves the degree of interdependence between two persons, the extent to which each has influence over the other's outcomes. A high degree of interdependence defines one sense of the term "closeness" (Berscheid, 1983). The second dimension involves the extent to which dependence is mutual or unequal, with one person having less power than the other. The third dimension involves the degree of correspondence of the two persons' outcomes, ranging from corresponding to conflicting interests. The fourth dimension involves the distinction between exchange and coordination problems. These two types of problems constitute the basis of interdependence and differ as to whether the main problem people must deal with concerns justice in terms of who gets what, or instead, mutual control and initiative in coordinating actions.

The situation depicted in Figure 17.3 is an example of the important category of situations involving coordination (rather than exchange) problems. Such situations are extremely common in close relationships. For example, the numbers in the matrix closely mirror the preference ratings from a study of dating couples deciding which movie to attend (Kelley, 1979). The large numbers in the diagonal make it clear that the two persons have a strong mutual desire to coordinate their actions so they can enjoy doing things together. However, they have different personal preferences (of five units) for which movie to attend and have to find a way to determine whose preferred movie they will attend jointly.

This situational structure is typically given the name "Hero" because it affords the opportunity for either person to show initiative and say, "let's do it your way," exerting a type of leadership by stepping forward and selecting the movie preferred by the partner. Though this initiative furthers joint goals, it is clearly considerate of the partner's feelings and benefits the partner the most. On the other hand, behavioral pre-emption could also be used in a controlling fashion by selecting one's own preferred movie, either for somewhat selfish reasons or as a result of egocentrically assuming the partner wants what you want.

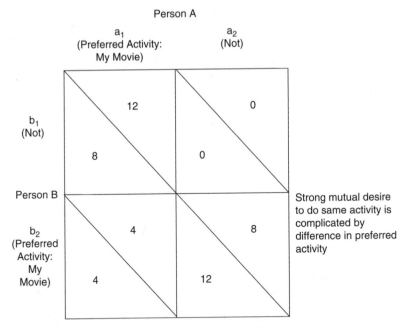

Figure 17.3. Outcome Matrix of a "Coordination" Situation.

Kelley et al. (2003) extended their analysis to include two further dimensions. The fifth dimension involves the temporal structure of the decision process (which is represented technically by a "transition list"). Some interactions have immediate consequences, whereas others are extended in time, such that the problem to be solved— the "goal" in the situation—is reached only at the end of a required sequence of intermediate steps. Two prototypical examples are delay of gratification and investment situations. Finally, a sixth dimension involves the extent to which uncertainty about outcomes is an essential feature of the situation. Whereas many situations involve quite complete information, others involve incomplete information about the other's outcomes, or uncertainty about what the future holds. The six dimensions are listed in Table 17.1.

An Interactionist Perspective on Dispositions

The analysis of situations by Kelley et al. (2003) suggests that there are approximately two dozen prototypical situations like Exchange with Mutual Profit or Hero that have distinctive and interesting properties in terms of the type of problem or opportunity that they pose for the persons. By analyzing each of these prototypical situations, Kelley and

Table 17.1. Dimensions of Situations and Interpersonal Dispositions

Dimension of Situation	Function of Rule	Interpersonal Disposition
1. Degree of interdependence 2. Mutuality of interdependence	Increase or decrease dependence on partner	Avoidance of interdependence/Comfort with dependence
3. Correspondence of outcomes	Promote prosocial or self-interested goals	Cooperative/competitive Responsive/unresponsive
	Expectations about partner's goals	Anxiety about responsiveness/Confidence or trust
4. Basis of control	Control through Exchange (promise/threat) or Coordination (initiative/follow)	[Dominant/submissive Assertive/passive
5. Temporal structure	Promote immediate or distant goal striving	[Dependable/unreliable Loyal/uncommitted
6. Degree of uncertainty	Cope with incomplete information or uncertain future	[Need for certainty/openness Optimism/pessimism

Holmes (2003) attempted to logically derive the full set of rules relevant to making choices within all the situations in our taxonomy. Clusters of rules that appear to have a common interpersonal theme or function can then be identified. (Some of these decisions would, of course, be open to interesting debate.) A quite limited number of such rule clusters or "dispositions" seems necessary for describing the set of possible adaptations to the problems encountered in prototypical social situations. Thus, through such functional analysis, we can essentially deduce an interactionist theory of interpersonal dispositions.

Such dispositions could be regarded as the dimensions of personality if they described people's consistent response tendencies across interaction partners. Or they could be regarded as relational dispositions if they were limited to a specific close relationship. (Interestingly, two partners' set of dispositions would be one way of describing the nature of their "relationship.") We believe there is much value in being able to describe personality and relational dispositions in commensurate terms so that the association between the two can be explored.

Kelley and Holmes (2003) reached some tentative conclusions about a possible set of interpersonal dispositions. The dispositions, not surprisingly, have an analogical correspondence to the dimensions of situations themselves. We have tried to make this correspondence apparent by the cross-listing in Table 17.1. The reader will note that the six dimensions of personality derived from our analysis have a rough correspondence to an integrated version of the Big Five and the two Attachment Style dimensions (with the anxiety dimension of attachment roughly corresponding to an interpersonal version of the neuroticism dimension from the Big Five). When the exact rule clusters that are the basis for the dimensions are examined in detail, they include facets of the traits that are quite different from the existing literature as well as novel interpersonal perspectives on the various dispositions.

In this paper we are not trying to persuade the reader of the virtues of this particular taxonomic system. Rather, we are using it to illustrate two crucial points. First, we need to have some means of classifying the specific *content* of people's interpersonal goals. The dispositions listed in Table 17.1 can be used not only to classify the goals of an actor (A), but also the interpersonal themes central to the actor's expectations about the interaction partner's goals (B). Second, the theory is built on the interactionist premise that situations and dispositions have a complementary relation. This suggests that features of situations should be responsible for selectively activating expectations about *relevant* dispositions. Situations are thus a key organizing principle for one's own goals as well as expectations about others' goal tendencies.

CONFLICT OF INTEREST SITUATIONS

To illustrate the situational affordance logic of IT we will describe several more detailed examples of research exploring the importance of one of the six dimensions of situations—conflict of interest or noncorrespondence of outcomes. Conflict of interest situations are those where the interests, preferences, or goals of two partners are not fully compatible. Most of these situations are mixed motive, meaning that there is some reason to cooperate and respond to a partner, but there are also temptations to look out for oneself and one's own interests. In our example in Figure 17.2, for instance, both partners dislike doing the dishes or housework and would prefer to avoid doing them; if either cares about the sensibilities of the other, however, he or she will not shirk the duties but will be communal minded and help. Such situations raise the issue of trust in the other's motivations to benefit the self. Because conflicts of interest present a partner with the temptation to avoid the costs of helping, and instead be self-interested, they represent situations marked by higher levels of interpersonal risk.

Sensitivity to situations involving risk occurs for the obvious reason of self-protection in the face of vulnerability, but also because partners' behavior in such situations is diagnostic of their orientation. That is, situations that tempt a partner to ignore the person's needs in favor of pursuing self-interested goals are the very platform for forming confident attributions (Holmes, 1991). Thus, the problem is that the goal of learning about a partner competes against the goal of protecting the self in particular situations—situations that are most diagnostic of another's motives also present the greatest risk of being hurt.

In summary, conflict of interest situations afford the opportunity for partners to demonstrate their caring and responsiveness or to act in a self-interested way that ignores one's needs. Thus, they highlight the issue of the extent of a partner's caring and are likely to activate any concerns a person might have about trust.

ATTACHMENT THEORY AND BEHAVIORAL SIGNATURES

Bowlby (1982) contended that the attachment system will only be activated to deal with circumstances involving threat, fear, and interpersonal conflict. That is, in concert with our behavioral signature perspective, he is suggesting a "stress-diathesis" analysis, whereby individuals only reveal the true colors of their personality in circumstances that are functionally relevant to the syndrome. For example, individuals high on the anxiety dimension are marked by anxiety and worry about whether significant others care for them, or instead, will reject them by not responding to their needs. Therefore, they should be schematic for identifying situations that highlight the *possibility* of rejection. They should be very sensitive to types of situations that test the strength of partners' bond, the extent of their caring and responsiveness.

Such diagnostic situations are especially likely to include those where there is a conflict of interest, where the partner might choose to follow his or her own preferences and not take the actor's interests into account. Certain prototypical situations present this dilemma quite baldly, others more subtly. For instance, the situation might be one where help from a partner would be particularly costly, creating a serious temptation not to support the person. Or the situation might be one where the partner would have to delay personal rewards and be persistent and loyal in order to reach dyadic goals, focusing on the question of whether the relationship is worth such efforts. Alternatively, the person might need the partner to provide costly help now, without knowing if or when such help will be reciprocated in the future.

Impressively, a number of attachment style studies have directly compared the behavior of anxious individuals in high-conflict situations to that in low-conflict control conditions and have been able to show that insecure attachment styles involving a lack of trust have a signature closely linked to such diagnostic situations. For example, Simpson, Rholes, & Phillips (1996) brought dating couples to the laboratory and asked them to discuss an issue in their relationship for 15 minutes. They were asked to discuss either a high-conflict issue as determined by a preliminary questionnaire, or a low-conflict, less contentious issue. Trained observers coded the quality of the couple's interaction (see Figure 17.4). The results for the low-conflict situation are quite fascinating: It is impossible to distinguish the secure individuals from the anxious ones when the situation does not provide any strong affordance for concerns about caring. This evidence suggests that poor behavior exhibited by anxious individuals in the high-conflict situation is clearly not reflective of a lack of skill, but of some other cause.

The cause seems to be the set of pessimistic expectations about being valued that were strongly activated by the high-conflict, diagnostic situation—Anxious individuals reported that their partner was treating them in a rejecting and nonresponsive way in this condition, even though observers saw no signs of that. Apparently their expectations of being rejected had been activated by the situations and then darkly colored their perceptions of the interaction. Their subsequent bad behavior was an angry *response* to the experience of rejection. On the other hand, when the high-conflict context activates beliefs in secure individuals about how much they are valued, they, paradoxically, feel more momentarily valued than controls, and react in a more positive, constructive way. When they face threatening situations that lead them to consider how they are valued by a partner, their sense of security about their partner's caring serves as a resource which promotes more closeness and interpersonal risk taking.

This research by Simpson et al. (1996) is a dramatic example of the idea that people only reveal their "true colors" when they encounter situations that are functionally relevant to the personality trait and that put stress on it to be displayed. The behavioral signature model is not only pertinent to personality, however. Research on the risk regulation model

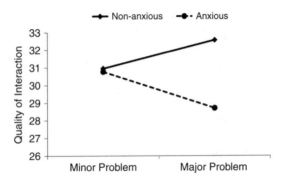

Figure 17.4. Results from Simpson, Rholes, & Phillips (1996).

(Murray, Holmes, & Collins, 2006) attests to the value of the model for predicting behavior from more social psychological variables, such as trust in a specific partner's caring and responsiveness.

THE RISK REGULATION MODEL

Given multiple layers of interdependence, people routinely find themselves in situations where they need to choose how much dependence (and thus how much potential for rejection) they safely can risk (Kelley, 1979). Throughout the course of the relationship, partners need to make iterative and often implicit choices between self-protection (decreasing dependence) and relationship promotion (increasing dependence). Consequently, to risk being in the relationship, people need a system in place that functions to keep them feeling reasonably safe in a context of continued vulnerability (Murray et al., 2006).

Optimizing Assurance: Three If-Then Contingencies Rules

The goal of the risk regulation system is to optimize the sense of assurance that is possible given one's relationship circumstances, that is, given the chronic level of confidence one feels in a partner's overall responsiveness and the level of risk inherent in particular interdependent situations. This sense of assurance is experienced as a sense of safety in one's level of dependence in the relationship—a feeling of relative invulnerability to hurt. To optimize this sense of assurance, this system functions dynamically, shifting the priority given to the goals of avoiding rejection and seeking closeness so as to accommodate the perceived risks of rejection.

The model proposes three "if-then" contingency rule systems people need to gauge the likelihood of a partner's acceptance or rejection and make the general situation of being involved in a relationship feel sufficiently safe (see Gollwitzer, Wieber, Myers, & McCrea, this volume, for more on "if-then" contingency rules). These rules involve: (1) an "appraisal" rule system that links situations of dependence and risk to the goal of gauging a partner's acceptance, (2) a "signaling" rule system that links perceptions of a partner's acceptance or rejection to the experience of gratified or hurt feelings and coincident gains or losses in self-esteem, and (3) a "dependence regulation" rule system that links perceptions of a partner's acceptance or rejection to the willingness to risk future dependence. These rule systems operate in concert to prioritize self-protection goals (and the assurance that comes from maintaining psychological distance) when the perceived risks of rejection are high or relationship promotion goals (and the assurance that comes from feeling connected) when the perceived risks of rejection are low.

The appraisal rule is essentially the first step in the CAPS model (see Figure 17.1), linking external cues to cognitions. A self-protective orientation would result in the rule, "If there are signs of risk in a particular situation, such as a conflict of interest, appraise a partner's motivations and be vigilant for rejection." A promotive orientation would link the perception of risk or threat to activating memories of a partner's typical caring and responsiveness and then looking for ways to connect more closely.

The signaling or alarm rule links cognitions about rejection to affect, within the CAPS internal units. It importantly reflects a basic assumption of the sociometer model of self-esteem. Leary and his colleagues believe that the need to protect against rejection is so important that people evolved a system for reacting to rejection threats (Leary & Baumeister, 2000). They argue that self-esteem is simply a gauge—a "sociometer"—that measures a person's perceived likelihood of being accepted or rejected by others. The sociometer is thought to function such that signs that another's approval is waning diminish self-esteem and motivate compensatory behaviors (Leary, Tambor, Terdal, & Downs, 1995). Given all that is at stake, the signal that is conveyed by this rule system needs to be sufficiently strong to mobilize action (Berscheid, 1983). The self-protective response is, "If I feel rejected, then internalize as social pain and reduced esteem." By making rejection aversive, this signaling system motivates people to avoid situations where relationship partners are likely to be unresponsive and needs for connectedness are likely to be frustrated. In contrast, perceiving acceptance should affirm people's sense of themselves as being good and valuable, mobilizing the desire for greater connection and the likelihood of having one's needs met by a partner.

The dependence regulation rule links cognition and affect to the behavior generation or response system, completing the chain of events that starts with the perception of an external situation and ends with a response to it. The self-protective adjustment is "If feel rejected, then increase psychological distance in the service of risk management." This implies feeling less close to partners, playing down their virtues, and avoiding situations of interdependence where one puts one's fate in partners' hands. In contrast, a promotive adjustment would result in finding constructive ways to connect to the partner through increasing interdependence and closeness in the face of risk.

How Perceived Regard Controls Rule Sensitivity

For a relationship risk regulation system to be functional, it needs to adapt itself to suit specific relationship circumstances. If Sally generally perceives Harry to be responsive to her needs, distancing herself from Harry at the first sign of his insensitivity is not likely to be the optimal means of sustaining the needed sense of assurance. If Sally generally perceives Harry to be unresponsive, however, such a response might be Sally's best available means of sustaining some minimal sense of safety from harm. Accordingly, to respond dynamically and adaptively to ongoing events, the regulatory system needs a heuristic means of estimating the level of risk inherent in specific situations. People's general or cross-situational sense of confidence in a partner's positive regard and love acts as such an arbiter or barometer—telling people whether it is safe to put self-protection aside and risk thinking and behaving in relationship-promotive ways (Murray et al., 2006). Specifically, feeling more or less positively regarded by a partner interacts with specific event features to control the sensitivity of the appraisal, signaling, and dependence regulation rules people adopt in specific situations.

At the first stage of this process, chronic perceptions of a partner's regard interact with specific event features to control the extent to which people categorize or code specific events as situations of risk. To the extent that Sally is unsure of Harry's regard, even the mundane choice of one movie over another could make concerns about dependence salient. However, to the extent that Sally is more confident of Harry's regard, she might only begin to entertain thoughts about her vulnerability to his actions when they try to negotiate more serious decisions in their relationship, such as deciding whose financial philosophy to follow.

The Daily Diary Study

How might this set of dynamic rules display itself in the everyday life of married couples? To illustrate, we turn to research by Murray and colleagues using a daily diary approach to studying the lives of newlyweds. This study utilized a direct measure of expectations of a specific partner's regard and tracked how couples negotiated a wide variety of dependent situations over 21 days (Murray, Griffin, Rose, & Bellavia, 2003). Participants rated how they believed their partner saw them on positive and negative interpersonal attributes (i.e., perceived regard), such as warm, critical, and responsive (Murray, Holmes, & Griffin, 2000). In each diary, participants indicated which specific situations of dependence had occurred that day (e.g., "had a minor disagreement," "partner criticized me") and completed <u>state</u> items tapping self-esteem (e.g., felt "good about myself"), how rejected or accepted they felt by their partner (e.g., "rejected or hurt by my partner," "my partner accepts me as I am"), perceptions of the partner's responsiveness (e.g., "my partner is selfish"), and closeness (e.g., "in love with my partner").

What would we expect to find in this study in terms of the appraisal rule? Imagine that Sally comes home to find Harry in an irritable mood, grumbling about the lack of food in the fridge, and the fact that Sally had promised to replenish the fridge's contents by day's end. If Sally trusts Harry's continuing positive regard, such situations might activate appraisal contingencies that link Harry's irritation to a ready excuse. She might even find some way to see such foibles as signs of Harry's acceptance and love, a motivated reconstrual of the evidence (e.g., "If Harry grumbles, he's just showing he can be himself around me"). However, if Sally generally feels less valued by Harry, she may have difficulty attributing such negative events to some specific feature of the situation, such as Harry's fatigue. Instead, Sally may attribute such grumbling to an interpersonal disposition— his broader displeasure with her (e.g., "If Harry grumbles, he's upset with me").

Following this logic, in the daily diary study, married intimates who generally felt less positively regarded by their spouse read decidedly more rejection-related meanings into negative situations than intimates who generally felt more positively regarded (Murray, Bellavia et al., 2003). For instance, people who generally felt less valued by their partner felt more rejected on days after their partner had simply reported being in a worse than average mood, a mood that had nothing to do with them or the relationship (see Figure 17.5). These feelings of rejection were especially acute after the partner reported he or she has behaved badly or a conflict had occurred. Such sensitivity to rejection was not at all characteristic of people who generally felt more positively regarded. Instead, they actually recruited more feelings of being loved and accepted by their partner on days after they reported more than their usual amount of conflict or negative partner behavior (and thus had greater actual reason to distrust their partner).

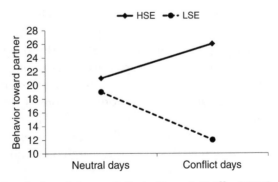

Figure 17.5. Results from Murray, Bellavia, Rose, & Griffin (2003).

What was found for the signaling system? For people who generally feel less valued by their partner, detecting drops in acceptance poses a greater proportional loss to a limited resource. For them, the signal conveyed by this rule needs to be especially strong. Relative to people who feel more positively regarded, people who feel less valued should be hurt more readily, questioning their worth in the face of perceived rejections (i.e., "If feeling acutely rejected, then internalize").

In the diary study, global perceptions of the spouse's regard determined how much daily concerns about a partner's rejection deflated state self-esteem (Murray, Griffin et al., 2003). People who generally felt less positively regarded by their partner felt worse about themselves on days after they experienced greater than usual level of anxiety about their partner's acceptance, such as after a conflict (as compared to low-anxiety days). In contrast, for people who generally felt more positively regarded, one day's anxieties about acceptance did not turn into the next day's self-doubts.

Finally, consistent with our ideas about the behavioral response system, people who felt less valued by their partner indeed responded to perceived rejection by reducing dependence (i.e., "if rejected then reduce dependence"). In the daily diary study (Murray, Bellavia et al., 2003), people who generally felt less positively regarded responded to feeling acutely rejected by their partner one day by treating their partner in more cold, critical, and negative ways the next day (according to both their *and* their partners' reports). For lows, feeling rejected activated the behavioral contingency "distance myself from my partner." These reactions emerged even though the partners of people who felt less valued were not actually upset with them when lows felt most rejected. Instead, people who felt less valued responded to an imagined rejection by treating their partner badly, according to both the person *and the partner*, leading their partners to then actually become annoyed with their bad behavior.

For people who generally feel more positively regarded, feeling acutely rejected activates "if-then" contingencies that link situations of dependence to relationship promotion goals. In the daily diary study, intimates who generally felt more positively regarded actually drew closer to their partner on days after they felt most rejected, such as the day after a conflict, a relationship-promotive response (Murray, Bellavia et al., 2003). The graph of the behavioral results for days after a conflict or control days with no conflict (Figure 17.5) has a strong resemblance to the earlier graph for Simpson et al.'s (1996) research on anxious attachment (Figure 17.4).

The Long-Term Consequences

By putting self-protection at a greater premium than relationship promotion, people who feel less positively regarded may create long-term interpersonal realities that defeat their hopes and confirm their fears. Supporting this analysis, the longitudinal part of the daily diary study suggests that the chronic activation of self-protective appraisal, signaling, and behavioral response rules has a corrosive effect on relationships over time (Murray, Bellavia et al., 2003; Murray, Griffin et al., 2003). In this sample, relationship difficulties were more likely to arise when the "if-then" contingencies underlying people's cognition, affect, and behavior mirrored the "if-then" contingencies evident among people who feel less valued by their partner.

First, satisfaction declined when people's online systems for appraising rejection threats were calibrated in a more self-protective fashion. In particular, when women linked their own personal self-doubts to their husband's lessened acceptance, their *husband* reported relatively greater declines in satisfaction over time (Murray, Griffin et al., 2003). Conversely, when women compensated for self-doubts by embellishing their partner's acceptance, their husband reported relatively greater satisfaction (Murray, Griffin et al., 2003). Second, satisfaction declined when people's signaling systems were more sensitive to rejection. When people reacted to anxieties about rejection by reporting diminished self-esteem the next day, their partner reported significantly greater declines in satisfaction. Third, when women's behavioral response to feeling rejected was to self-protect and behave negatively, their husband's satisfaction declined over the year (Murray, Griffin et al., 2003).

In summary, research exploring the chain of if-then rules linking external events to actual behavioral responses is not simply an academic exercise in studying arcane procedural rules. Through focusing on the three steps in the Mischel and Shoda (1995) CAPS model, and using an *a priori* understanding of the affordances of conflict of interest situations, this research demonstrates how appropriate models linking external situations to behavior can predict important real world outcomes.

CONCLUSION

We have argued that the lack of research in social psychology predicting behavior from identifiable stimulus features has largely resulted from a social construal approach that either begins or end in people's heads. Attempts to uncover the "miraculous" intermediary between situations and behavior have somewhat obscured the direct link between the two. In this paper we have tried to demonstrate that one possible remedy for this problem is to develop a "theory of situations" that categorizes social situations and specifies the psychologically active ingredients each situation affords. We believe that the *Atlas of Interpersonal Situations* (Kelley et al., 2003) provides one such theoretical taxonomy that will prove useful in predicting interpersonal behavior. Research on one critical dimension of situations, the degree of conflict of interest, illustrated the power of the analysis to move from features of the social environment to predicting patterns of behavior functionally relevant to coping with the challenges such situations create.

REFERENCES

Berscheid, E. (1983). Emotion. In H. H. Kelley, E. Berscheid, A. Christensen, J. H. Harvey, T. L. Huston, G. Levinger, E. McClintock, L. A. Peplau, D. R. Peterson (Eds.), *Close relationships* (pp. 110–168). NY: W. H. Freeman and Company.

Bowlby, J. (1982). *Attachment and loss*, Vol. 1 (Attachment). London: The Hogarth Press.

Cantor, N., & Kihlstrom, J. (1987). *Personality and social intelligence.* Englewood Cliffs, NJ: Prentice Hall.

Downey, G., & Feldman, S. I. (1996). Implications of rejection sensitivity for intimate relationships. *Journal of Personality and Social Psychology, 70*, 1327–1343.

Downey, G., Freitas, A., Michaelis, B., & Khouri, H. (1998). The self-fulfilling prophecy in close relationships: Rejection sensitivity and rejection by romantic partners. *Journal of Personality and Social Psychology, 75*, 545–560.

Endler, N., & Hunt, J. (1969). Generalizability of contributions from sources of variance in the S-R inventories of anxiousness. *Journal of Personality, 37*, 1–24.

Holmes, J. G. (1991). Trust and the appraisal process in close relationships. In W. H. Jones & D. Perlman (Eds.), *Advances in personal relationships*, Vol. 2 (pp. 57–104). London: Jessica Kingsley.

Holmes, J. G. (2002). Interpersonal expectations as the building blocks of social cognition: An interdependence theory perspective. *Personal Relationship, 9*, 1–26.

Kelley, H. H. (1979). *Personal relationships: Their structures and processes.* Hillsdale, NJ: Erlbaum.

Kelley, H.H., & Stahelski, A. (1970). The social interaction basis of cooperators' and competitors' beliefs about others. *Journal of Personality and Social Psychology, 16*, 66–91.

Kelley, H. H., & Holmes, J. G. (2003). *Interdependence theory: Situations, relationships, and personality.* Unpublished manuscript.

Kelley, H. H., Holmes, J. G., Kerr, N., Reis, H., Rusbult, C., & Van Lange, P. A. (2003). *An atlas of interpersonal situations.* Cambridge, UK: Cambridge Press.

Leary, M. R., Tambor, E. S., Terdal, S. K., & Downs, D. L. (1995). Self-esteem as an interpersonal monitor: The sociometer hypothesis. *Journal of Personality and Social Psychology, 68*, 518–530.

Leary, M. R., & Baumeister, R. F. (2000). The nature and function of self-esteem: Sociometer theory. In M. P. Zanna (Ed.), *Advances in experimental social psychology*, Vol. 32 (pp. 2–51). San Diego, CA: Academic Press.

Lewin, K. (1946). Behavior and development as a function of the total situation. In L. Carmichael (Rd.), *Manual of child psychology* (pp. 791–844). New York: Wiley.

Mischel, W., & Shoda, Y. (1995). A cognitive-affective system theory of personality: Reconceptualizing situations, dispositions, dynamics, and invariance in personality structure. *Psychological Review, 102*, 246–268.

Murray, S. L., Holmes, J. G., & Griffin, D. W. (2000). Self-esteem and the quest for felt security: How perceived regard regulates attachment processes. *Journal of Personality and Social Psychology, 78*, 478–498.

Murray, S. L., Rose, P., Bellavia, G., Holmes, J., & Kusche, A. (2002). When rejection stings: How self-esteem constrains relationship-enhancement processes. *Journal of Personality and Social Psychology, 83*, 556–573.

Murray, S. L., Bellavia, G., Rose, P., & Griffin, D. (2003). Once hurt, twice hurtful: How perceived regard regulates daily marital interaction. *Journal of Personality and Social Psychology, 84*, 126–147.

Murray, S. L., Griffin, D. W., Rose, P., & Bellavia, G. (2003). Calibrating the sociometer: The relational contingencies of self-esteem. *Journal of Personality and Social Psychology, 85*, 63–84.

Murray, S. L., Holmes, J. G., & Collins, N. L. (2006). Optimizing assurance: The risk regulation system in relationships. *Psychological Bulletin, 132*, 641–666.

Payne, K. (2001) Prejudice and perception: the role of automatic and controlled processes in misperceiving a weapon. *Journal of Personality and Social Psychology, 81*, 181–192.

Reis, H. T. (in press). Reinvigorating the concept of situation in social psychology. *Personality and Social Psychology Review, 12*, 311–329.

Reis, H., Clark, M., & Holmes, J. G. (2004). Perceived partner responsiveness as an organizing construct in the study of intimacy and closeness. In D. Mashek & A. Aron (Eds.), *Handbook of closeness and intimacy*. Mahwah, NJ: Lawrence Erlbaum.

Ross, L., & Nisbett, R. (1991). *The person and the situation.* New York: McGraw-Hill.

Simpson, J. A., Rholes, W. S., & Phillips, D. (1996). Conflict in close relationships: An attachment perspective. *Journal of Personality and Social Psychology, 71*, 899–914.

Thibaut, J. W., & Kelley, H. H. (1959). *The social psychology of groups.* New York: Wiley.

Tooby, J., & Cosmides, L. (1996). Friendship and the banker's paradox: Other pathways to the evolution of adaptations for altruism. *Proceedings of the British Academy, 88*, 119–143.

18 Mind–Behavior Relations in Attachment Theory and Research

Phillip R. Shaver
Mario Mikulincer

The assignment given to us by the editors was to consider the "miracle" that links the mental processes studied by contemporary relationship scientists with *behavior*. The framework that guides our research—attachment theory (Ainsworth, Blehar, Waters, & Wall, 1978; Bowlby, 1973, 1980, 1982)—makes this assignment easy. Attachment theory is one of the few conceptual frameworks in psychology that integrates evolutionary biology, primate ethology, psychodynamic conceptions of personality, lifespan cognitive and social developmental psychology, and the study of adolescents' and adults' relationships. It was constructed originally from a combination of primate ethology (see Burkhardt, 2005, for a historical overview), naturalistic and laboratory observational studies of human infants (Ainsworth, 1967; Ainsworth et al., 1978), cognitive developmental psychology (Piaget, 1953), and psychoanalysis (see Fonagy, Gergely, & Target, 2008, for an overview). This combination of intellectual influences runs the gamut from behavioral observation to clinical probing of hidden motives and idiosyncratic subjective experiences and perceptual distortions.

Attachment theory posits reciprocal relations between mental processes and behaviors, and between what Bowlby (1982) called the attachment behavioral system (guided by a need for protection in times of threat) and other behavioral systems, such as those involved in exploration (guided by curiosity), caregiving (guided by affection and empathy), and sex (guided by attraction and desire). If we use M to indicate mental states and B to indicate behavior, we can imagine breaking into the endless M → B → M → B → M stream at any point, focusing either on the way mental processes select and guide behavior or the way behaviors and behavioral outcomes influence subsequent mental states. Just as evolutionary biologists sometimes view genes as influencing animals' bodies and behavior, and at other times view bodies and behavior as mere "vehicles" used by genes to reproduce themselves (Dawkins, 2006), we social and relationship scientists can view mental states as influencing behavior or view behavior as a vehicle for creating certain mental states: "I'm feeling worn down and sad; I think I'll call my wife for some uplifting encouragement." "I gave him a big dose of affection and support, but I'm not sure he was satisfied."

In this chapter we explain Bowlby's (1982) behavioral-system construct and describe how it has been applied in the study of attachment behavior and mental processes of people at different ages. We then focus on a model of attachment-system activation and functioning in adulthood (Mikulincer & Shaver, 2003, 2007) and assess its usefulness in explaining behavior, including proximity- and support-seeking, and the ways in which attachment security and insecurity manifest themselves in close relationships and small groups. At first our discussion is fairly abstract and theoretical, because the general conceptual issue of mind–behavior relations is inherently abstract, but later we present a sampling of empirical studies to show what the abstractions refer to and explain.

BEHAVIORAL SYSTEMS DEFINED

Although Bowlby (1982) focused mainly on the formation of attachment bonds in early childhood and the self-protective and affect-regulatory functions of proximity to care providers in times of need, he also considered how evolution has shaped other kinds of human behavior, such as exploration, parenting, affiliation, and sex. For this purpose he relied on the concept of *behavioral system*, a species-universal neural program that organizes an individual's behavior in ways that increase the likelihood of survival and reproduction in the face of environmental demands. Responding to these demands—for example, dealing with threats to life and well-being by relying on what Bowlby (1982) called "stronger, wiser" caregivers, exploring environments and learning how to master them, and caring for sexual partners and dependent offspring—resulted in the evolution of distinct but interrelated behavioral systems, each with its own primary functions and characteristic behaviors.

According to Bowlby (1982), a behavioral system governs the choice, activation, and termination of behavioral sequences aimed at attaining particular "set-goals"—states of the person–environment relationship that have adaptive advantages for individual survival and genetic reproduction. The adaptive behavioral sequences are "activated" by certain kinds of stimuli or situations (e.g., sudden loud noises, pain, darkness, the presence of a stranger or predator) that make a particular set-goal salient and are "deactivated" or "terminated" by other stimuli or outcomes that signal attainment of the desired goal state (emotional support or protection, in the case of the attachment system). In Bowlby's theory, "behavior" is functionally defined in terms of its set-goal. A particular behavior, such as moving physically or psychologically closer to another person, is defined as an attachment behavior if it is intended to secure comfort, protection, or relief from stress. The same action is defined as sexual if it moves a person toward sexual intercourse and is viewed as caregiving if it occurs in the service of comforting a needy or distraught relationship partner. Similarly, the termination of one kind of behavior and the initiation of another are not defined primarily by particular motor or physical events but rather by the seeking or attainment of a particular set-goal.

According to this framework, a person's mental processes—for example, his or her hierarchy of set-goals and the chronic and contextual accessibility of a particular set-goal—govern the activation, choice among, and termination of particular behavioral sequences. Moreover, the psychological meaning of a motor or perceptual act is determined by the intrapsychic state that organizes and governs it. Although this account of Bowlby's theory probably seems to emphasize mental states rather than behavior, it can be used just as easily to analyze the influence of behavior on mental processes. For example, moving physically closer to a relationship partner and being comforted often feels good, enhances security, reduces the emphasis on security seeking, and allows other goals and mental states to arise and guide behavior. Moreover, as we show later, repeated failures of intentional actions (such as proximity seeking) to attain their set-goal (e.g., protection and security) changes the attachment system's goal structure, along with the cognitions and emotions that accompany and guide the system's functioning.

Conceptually, a behavioral system has (a) a biological function, which in the environment of evolutionary adaptation increased the likelihood of survival or reproductive success; (b) a specific set-goal, a change in the person–environment relationship that terminates the system's activity; (c) a set of activating triggers; (d) a set of interchangeable, functionally equivalent behaviors that constitute the primary strategy of the system for attaining a particular goal; (e) an internal architecture that includes if-then scripts (Gollwitzer, Wieber, Myers, & McCrea, Chapter 8, this volume), schemas, and internal working models based on past experiences; and (f) specific excitatory or inhibitory neural links with other behavioral systems. While akin to the evolutionary psychological construct of mental "module" (as used, for example, in the influential volume edited by Barkow, Cosmides, & Tooby, 1992), the behavioral system construct is more complex, applies to a broader range of behaviors, and is more evident in its behavioral effects. For example, evolutionary psychologists have postulated mental modules that reason in certain ways, detect cheaters, cause people to be attracted to sexual partners with "good genes," or arouse jealousy of particular kinds. In contrast, Bowlby (1982) focused on complex and flexible behavior patterns such as seeking proximity to a caregiver (e.g., by crying, smiling, reaching, crawling, or doing whatever is necessary to attain the goal); exploring the environment curiously and, as a result, building up a useful repertoire of physical and mental skills; and empathizing with people in distress and making an effort to comfort them.

Bowlby also assumed that behavioral systems include learned elements that reflect a person's history of behavioral system activation in particular contexts. Although behavioral systems are initially innate and presumably operate mechanistically at a subcortical level, their ability to achieve desired set-goals depends on the extent to which their operational parameters can be adjusted to fit with contextual affordances (Baron, Chapter 13, this volume) and demands. One of Bowlby's most important observations, which increased his confidence in the notion of "goal-corrected" rather than merely habitual behavior, is that particular behavioral sequences often get altered to put a person, even an infant, back on the track of goal attainment. Bowlby assumed that actual behaviors and the experiences that result from them can alter both future behaviors and mental states. Borrowing from feedback control theories developed after Bowlby wrote his attachment trilogy (e.g., Carver & Scheier, 1990), we can say that behavioral systems involve self-regulatory feedback loops that shape the systems' primary strategies and influence whether a person persists in or disengages from these strategies after discovering that they fail under certain conditions.

Over time, after operating repeatedly in the same social environment (e.g., in interactions with a primary caregiver or other emotionally significant relationship partners), a person's behavioral systems become molded so that their neural and behavioral subroutines fit better with relational constraints. These constraints can be viewed clinically as more or less optimal for long-range development—that is, as "healthy" or "unhealthy." According to Bowlby (1973), the residues of such experiences are stored in mental representations of person–environment transactions (*working models of self and others*), which organize memories of behavioral system functioning and guide future attempts to attain a behavioral system's set-goal. These representations, which operate partly unconsciously and partly consciously, become integral components of a behavioral system's programming and are responsible for both differences between individuals and within-person continuity over time.

The introduction of reciprocal relations between working models, goal-oriented behaviors, and perceptions of the results of behaviors allows us to see how a behavioral system's goals, strategies, and cognitive parameters can (a) result in still more differentiated goals and strategies, (b) create conflicts among goals, and (c) even result, at times, in confusion or dissociation between mental states and behaviors. If the primary strategy of a behavioral system repeatedly results in the attainment of its set-goal (e.g., gaining protection and comfort by seeking proximity to a relationship partner), the working models that get constructed correspond well with the normative functioning of the system (e.g., "When I encounter difficulties, I can call on my attachment figure for comfort and support, and I will then feel better and can return to other activities with a renewed sense of confidence"). This kind of working model, or script (Waters & Waters, 2006), helps to activate and organize the primary attachment strategy (optimistic proximity seeking) whenever the system's set-goal becomes salient. However, if the primary strategy repeatedly fails to attain its set-goal, the resulting working models will alter the system's strategies and some of its goals (e.g., "When I try to rely on others, they are unreliable or outright punishing"). For example, a person may become overly vigilant, intrusive, sometimes hysterical or, in contrast, wary about relying on relationship partners, emotionally closed to them, and rigidly committed to self-sufficiency.

THE ATTACHMENT BEHAVIORAL SYSTEM

During infancy, primary caregivers (usually one or both parents, but also grandparents, older siblings, daycare workers, and so on) are likely to serve as attachment figures. In adulthood, friends and romantic partners often become primary attachment figures, such that maintaining physical and psychological proximity to them in times of need becomes an important source of protection, emotional support, and reassurance (e.g., Fraley & Davis, 1997; Hazan & Zeifman, 1999). However, not every relationship partner becomes a primary attachment figure. In fact, the transformation of a relationship partner into an attachment figure is a gradual process that depends on the extent to which the person functions as

(a) a target of proximity seeking; (b) a source of protection, comfort, support, and relief in times of need (a *"safe haven,"* in the terms of attachment theory); and (c) a *"secure base"* for exploration and pursuit of important achievement goals within the context of the relationship (e.g., Ainsworth, 1991; J. A. Feeney, 2004; Hazan & Shaver, 1994; Hazan & Zeifman, 1999).

The set-goal of the attachment system is a subjective sense of protection or security (called by Sroufe & Waters, 1977, "felt security"), which normally terminates the system's activation. (This is an example of a mental state—a desire for protection or comfort—activating a behavior that results in another mental state, which in turn terminates the behavior.) The goal of attaining protective or comforting proximity is made salient by encounters with actual or imagined threats and by appraising an attachment figure as not yet sufficiently near, interested, or responsive. In such cases, the attachment system is activated, and the individual is driven to seek and reestablish actual or symbolic proximity to an external or "internalized" attachment figure. (We say more about internalized attachment figures in the next paragraph.) When the set-goal of felt security is attained, bids for proximity are terminated and the individual returns to nonattachment activities governed by other behavioral systems.

During infancy, attachment system activation includes nonverbal expressions of need and a desire for proximity, such as crying and pleading while looking at the attachment figure's face, as well as active behaviors aimed at reestablishing and maintaining proximity, such as moving toward the caregiver, reaching up, and clinging after being picked up (Ainsworth et al., 1978). In adulthood, the primary attachment strategy does not necessarily entail actual proximity-seeking behavior. Instead, felt security can be attained by calling upon soothing, comforting mental representations of relationship partners who regularly provide care and protection, or even by relying on self-representations (and self-soothing) associated with these partners (Mikulincer & Shaver, 2004). These cognitive-affective mental representations help a person deal successfully with threats and allow him or her to continue pursuing nonattachment goals without having to interrupt goal-seeking activities to engage in actual proximity bids.

Beyond considering normative features of the attachment system, Bowlby (1973) described individual differences in the system's functioning. Interactions with significant others who are available in times of need, sensitive to one's attachment behavior, and responsive to one's bids for proximity (aspects of *attachment figure availability*) support the normal functioning of the system and lead to a dispositional sense of attachment security. That is, positive expectations about others' availability and positive views of oneself as competent and valued are formed and get reinforced throughout early development, and affect-regulation strategies are organized around these positive beliefs. However, when significant others are unavailable or unresponsive to one's needs, proximity seeking fails to relieve distress, and a dispositional sense of attachment security is lost or never attained. As a result, negative representations of self and others are formed (e.g., worries about others' goodwill and doubts about one's own worth), and strategies of affect regulation other than proximity seeking (called *conditional* or *secondary attachment strategies*; Main, 1990) are developed.

Most empirical tests of these ideas by personality and social psychologists who study adolescents and adults have focused on a person's *attachment style*, the systematic pattern of relational expectations, emotions, and behavior that results from internalizing a particular history of attachment experiences and consequent reliance on a particular attachment-related strategy of affect regulation (Fraley & Shaver, 2000; Mikulincer & Shaver, 2004; Shaver & Mikulincer, 2002). Initially, research on attachment styles was based on Ainsworth et al.'s (1978) typology of attachment patterns in infancy—including secure, anxious, and avoidant attachment—and Hazan and Shaver's (1987) conceptualization of parallel adult styles in the domain of romantic relationships. However, subsequent studies (e.g., Bartholomew & Horowitz, 1991; Brennan et al., 1998; Simpson, 1990) revealed that attachment styles are best conceptualized as regions in a two-dimensional space and that the two dimensions, *attachment anxiety* and *avoidance*, could be measured with reliable and valid self-report scales. Scores on these scales are, in line with Bowlby's theory, associated with relationship functioning and affect regulation (see Mikulincer & Shaver, 2007, for a review)—and not only in dyadic relationships but in group and organizational settings as well (Davidovitz, Mikulincer, Shaver, Izsak, & Popper, 2007; Rom & Mikulincer, 2003).

In the two-dimensional (anxiety by avoidance) space, secure attachment is indicated by low scores on both anxiety and avoidance. This region is characterized by a sense of attachment security, comfort with closeness and interdependence, and reliance on support seeking and other constructive strategies for dealing with stress. The region that parallels Ainsworth et al.'s (1978) conception of anxious attachment is defined by a high score on the anxiety dimension and a low score on the avoidance dimension. This region is characterized by a lack of attachment security, a strong need for closeness, frequent worries about relationships, and fear of being rejected. People located in this region exhibit both mental states and behaviors focused on worries about rejection and abandonment and strong efforts to gain proximity and support from relationship partners. There is, in our opinion, no "mystery" or "miracle" involved in the relation between the mental states and behaviors, because the two are so closely intertwined.

The attachment pattern that Ainsworth et al. called "avoidant" corresponds to the region of the two-dimensional space in which avoidance is high and overt anxiety is low. This region, like the anxious region, is characterized by a lack of attachment security, but people with scores in this region are compulsively self-reliant and prefer to remain emotionally distant from others. The links between their mental states and behaviors are fairly circuitous and have taken clever research to uncover, but there is no "miracle" involved.

The fourth region of the space, where scores on both dimensions are high, corresponds to what Bartholomew and Horowitz (1991) called "fearful avoidance," which is, in some respects, similar to a fourth pattern of infant attachment, disorganized/disoriented, identified by Main and Solomon (1990) subsequent to the work of Ainsworth et al. (1978). People residing in this region of the two-dimensional space are especially low in trust and have often been abused, neglected, or otherwise rendered uncertain and frightened by parents or other attachment figures (Shaver & Clark, 1994).

A MODEL OF ATTACHMENT SYSTEM FUNCTIONING IN ADULTHOOD

In summarizing the hundreds of empirical studies of adult attachment processes, we (Mikulincer & Shaver, 2003, 2007) created a flowchart model of the activation and dynamics of the attachment system. This model integrates research findings with the theoretical ideas of Bowlby (1973, 1982), Ainsworth (1991), Cassidy and Berlin (1994), Cassidy and Kobak (1988), and Fraley and Shaver (2000). The model (Figure 18.1) includes three major components. The first involves the monitoring and appraisal of threatening events and is responsible for activation of the primary attachment strategy—proximity seeking. The second component involves monitoring and appraisal of the availability of external or internalized attachment figures and is responsible for individual differences in the sense of attachment security and the development of what we call *security-based strategies*. The third component involves monitoring and appraisal of the viability of proximity seeking as a means of coping with attachment insecurity and distress. This component is responsible for individual differences in the development of specific secondary attachment strategies (*anxious hyperactivating* versus *avoidant deactivating strategies*). The model includes excitatory and inhibitory pathways that result

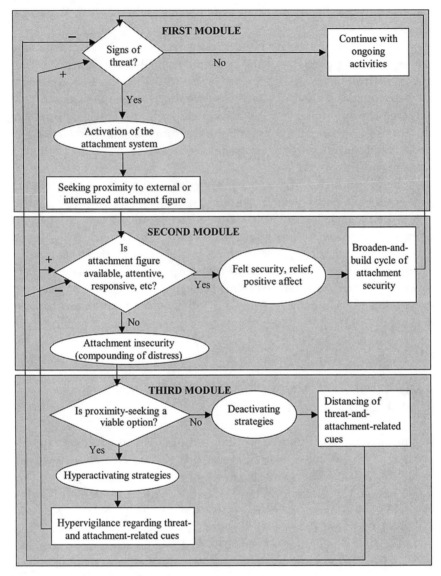

Figure 18.1. Mikulincer and Shaver's (2007) Model of the Activation and Dynamics of the Attachment System in Adulthood. (Adapted here by permission.)

from recurrent use of secondary attachment strategies. These pathways in turn affect the monitoring of threatening events and attachment figure availability.

In building this model, we (Mikulincer & Shaver, 2003, 2007) assumed that the monitoring of mental and environmental events results in activation of the attachment system whenever a potential or actual threat is encountered. That is, during encounters with physical or psychological threats, the attachment system is activated, and the primary attachment strategy is set in motion. This strategy leads adults to turn to internalized representations of attachment figures or to actual supportive others, and to maintain symbolic or actual proximity to these figures. We assume that age and development result in an increased ability to gain comfort from symbolic representations of attachment figures and internalized self-soothing routines based on interactions with attachment figures (Mikulincer & Shaver, 2004), but like Bowlby (1982, 1988) we also assume that no one of any age is completely free of actual reliance on others.

Once the attachment system is activated, an affirmative answer to the question, "Is the attachment figure literally or symbolically available?" results in a sense of attachment security and what we, following Fredrickson (2001), call a "broaden and build" cycle of attachment security. This cycle bolsters a person's resources for maintaining mental health in times of stress and broadens his or her perspectives and capacities. As a person gains experience and develops cognitively, more of the role of a security-enhancing attachment figure can be internalized and become part of personal strength and resilience. In adulthood, the question about literal attachment figure availability becomes transformed into a question about the adequacy of internal as well as external attachment-related resources for coping with stress. In many cases, internal resources, which were created originally with the help of security-providing attachment figures, are likely to be sufficient, but when they are not, the person with a secure attachment history is willing and able to depend on actual attachment figures for support.

Attachment figure unavailability results in attachment insecurity, which compounds the distress anyone might experience when encountering a threat. Shaver and Mikulincer (2002) claimed that this state of insecurity forces a "decision"—conscious or unconscious—about the viability of proximity seeking as a means of self-regulation, which in turn leads to activation of a specific secondary attachment strategy. The appraisal of proximity seeking as a viable option can result in very energetic, insistent attempts to attain proximity, support, and love. In the literature on attachment, these active, intense secondary strategies are called *anxious hyperactivating strategies* (Cassidy & Berlin, 1994); they require constant vigilance, concern, and effort until an attachment figure is perceived to be available and a sense of security is attained. Hyperactivating strategies include a strong approach orientation toward relationship partners, attempts to elicit their involvement, care, and support through clinging and controlling responses, and cognitive and behavioral efforts aimed at minimizing distance from them (Shaver & Hazan, 1993). Hyperactivating strategies are characteristic of people who score relatively high on the attachment anxiety dimension (Mikulincer & Shaver, 2007).

The appraisal of proximity seeking as nonviable can cause deactivation of proximity seeking, abandonment of the quest for support, and a decision to handle threats and distress alone. These secondary strategies of affect regulation are called *avoidant deactivating strategies* (Cassidy & Kobak, 1988) because their primary goal is to keep the attachment system deactivated to avoid frustration and further distress. Adopting this goal results in denial of attachment needs; avoidance of closeness, intimacy, and dependence in close relationships; maximization of cognitive, emotional, and physical distance from others; and strivings for self-reliance and independence. These deactivating strategies are characteristic of people who score high on the avoidant attachment dimension (Mikulincer & Shaver, 2007).

Both hyperactivating and deactivating strategies cause qualitative changes in the goal structure and functioning of the attachment system. Moreover, they sometimes produce motivational conflicts and dissociations between the set-goal of proximity seeking and actual attachment-related behavior. For example, hyperactivating strategies make the goal of controlling others' behaviors salient, which causes relationship partners to withdraw and reject the person instead of getting closer to him or her. Moreover, hyperactivating strategies include doubts about others' goodwill and supportiveness, which in turn can block proximity-seeking behaviors despite the hunger for love, comfort, and protection that anxiously attached people chronically experience (Holmes & Cavallo, Chapter 17, this volume). In contrast, deactivating strategies often require inhibiting proximity-seeking tendencies despite the fact that threats and dangers automatically tend to activate the attachment system.

Having completed this admittedly abstract account of a theory to which Bowlby (1973, 1980, 1982) devoted three long, densely referenced volumes, we can now turn to empirical studies of mental and behavioral processes related to the functioning of the attachment behavioral system in adults. In particular, we will discuss studies of the ways in which mental states, such as activation of the attachment system and global attachment orientations, are manifested in relational behavior. We will also discuss studies of the ways in which relational behaviors affect a person's mental states regarding attachment.

ACTIVATION OF THE ATTACHMENT BEHAVIORAL SYSTEM

Both attachment theory (Bowlby, 1982) and Ainsworth's (1973) behavioral observations suggest that perceived threats cause a person's attachment system to be activated. In infancy, this activation is assessed behaviorally by observing a child's reactions to sudden noises, to a stranger, or to separation from his or her mother. In adulthood, there is ample evidence that encountering a serious danger or threat elicits behaviors aimed at gaining proximity to and support from other people (e.g., Kirkpatrick & Shaver, 1988; Schachter, 1959; Shaver & Klinnert, 1982). For example, Fraley and Shaver (1998) unobtrusively observed couples waiting in the departure lounges of a public airport and found that couples who were separating were more likely than couples who were not separating to seek and maintain physical contact (e.g., by mutually gazing at each other's faces, talking intently, and touching). Theoretically speaking, the threat of separation activated these people's attachment systems and caused them to engage in proximity-seeking behavior.

The connection between experiencing stress and seeking support from attachment figures has also been documented in a diary study of couples (Collins & Feeney, 2005). Both members of each couple completed a nightly diary for 3 weeks, recording stressful life events, support-seeking behaviors, predominant mood, and thoughts and feelings about the relationship. In line with attachment theory, participants reported seeking more instrumental and emotional support from their partner on days when they experienced more stress. Another behavioral manifestation of attachment system activation was observed by Wisman and Koole (2003), who exposed participants to a severe existential threat—thoughts of their own mortality—and observed how they seated themselves for a group discussion. Death reminders caused people to sit closer to others, even if this seating preference required exposing their worldviews to potential attack (they knew that other participants would disagree with their beliefs).

However, these typical or normative behavioral manifestations of attachment system activation are moderated by attachment style. For example, Simpson, Rholes, and Nelligan (1992) invited heterosexual dating couples to a laboratory, told the woman in each couple that she was about to experience a scary, painful laboratory procedure, and then asked the woman to wait with her partner for 5 minutes while the experimenter prepared the apparatus. During this "waiting period," participants' behavior was unobtrusively videotaped, and raters later coded the extent to which each participant sought her partner's support. As expected, higher scores on the avoidance dimension were associated with less support seeking mainly when avoidant women seemed to coders to be quite distressed. These women often attempted to distract themselves by reading magazines instead of seeking comfort and support from their partner. In a subsequent study, Collins and Feeney (2000) coded support-seeking behavior while members of dating couples talked about a personal problem in the laboratory. Again, avoidance was associated with less frequent seeking of proximity or support. In addition, although attachment anxiety did not affect direct requests for support, it was associated with indirect methods of seeking support, such as conveying a need for help through nonverbal distress signals common among young children (crying, pouting, or sulking).

Interestingly, in some of our laboratory studies (Mikulincer, Birnbaum, Woddis, & Nachmias, 2000; Mikulincer, Gillath, & Shaver, 2002), we have found that these attachment-style differences in support-seeking behavior are not directly parallel to the unconscious activation of attachment-related mental representations when a person is threatened. That is, insecurely attached people show a degree of dissociation between the automatic, unconscious activation of the first step toward proximity seeking—for example, increasing the mental accessibility of an attachment figure's name—and the carrying out of subsequent steps in a behavioral sequence. Specifically, we found that subliminal priming with a threat-related word (e.g., illness, failure, separation), as compared with a neutral word (e.g., hat), increased the cognitive accessibility of attachment-related mental representations regardless of attachment style. This heightened activation was indicated by faster lexical decision times for proximity-related words (e.g., love, closeness) and names of people nominated by a participant as security-providing attachment figures (e.g., a parent, spouse, or close friend). These effects were obtained from both secure and insecure participants.

However, despite the fact that attachment style did not moderate the link between subliminal priming with a threat-related word and cognitive accessibility of attachment-related mental representations, attachment style did affect other aspects of attachment system activation. Anxious attachment was associated with hyperactivated access to attachment-related mental representations even without threats, and it was also associated with activating not only positive attachment-related representations or working models but also negative ones (e.g., words such as rejection and alone). This mental process is part of hyperactivated behavioral strategies, such as remaining hypervigilant to a partner's whereabouts and potential infidelity and expressing anger following conflicts and disagreements (Simpson, Rholes, & Phillips, 1996). Avoidant attachment was associated with deactivated access to attachment-related representations when the subliminal threat word was "separation." That is, more avoidant people took longer to access attachment-related concepts following exposure to "separation," suggesting that they have learned not to activate attachment behavior when a partner threatens separation or abandonment. In several laboratory studies (Mikulincer, Dolev, & Shaver, 2004), we found that imposing a cognitive load, such as remembering a 7-digit number, interferes with avoidant defenses and makes avoidant individuals function more like anxious ones. In more naturalistic studies (e.g., Berant, Mikulincer, & Shaver, 2008) we found that a continuing stressor that cannot be ignored, such as giving birth to a child with a congenital heart defect, also disrupts usual avoidant strategies and results, over a period of years, in worsening mental health, increased marital distress, and poorer psychological outcomes for the child.

ATTACHMENT STYLES AND RELATIONAL BEHAVIOR

The studies reviewed so far show that attachment patterns can be assessed by self-report and are related to microcognitive processes and support-seeking behaviors and behavioral tendencies. In this section, we review findings from studies showing that individual differences in attachment are evident in behavior within dating and marital relationships and in small groups.

Couple Relationships

Attachment-style differences in relational behavior have been observed in studies of conversations between dating partners. For example, Guerrero (1996) videotaped couples who were discussing personal problems and found that avoidant attachment was associated with lower levels of facial gaze, facial pleasantness, vocal pleasantness, general interest in the conversation, and attentiveness to the partner's comments. Guerrero (1996) also found that anxious attachment was associated with more vocal and physical signs of distress during taped conversations. In another study, Tucker and Anders (1998) videotaped dating couples while they discussed positive aspects of their relationship and found that more avoidant people laughed less, touched their partner less, looked less often at their partner, and smiled less during the interaction. More anxious people were rated as displaying less enjoyment during their conversations.

Attachment researchers have also assessed partners' behaviors during actual conflicts and have noticed attachment-style differences in conflict management difficulties. For example, Simpson et al. (1996), J. A. Feeney (1998), and Campbell, Simpson, Boldry, and Kashy (2005) found that insecurely attached men and women exhibited greater distress and less skillful communication tactics while discussing a major disagreement with their dating partner. J. A. Feeney (1998) also found that attachment insecurities were associated with fewer displays of warmth and affection during conflict discussions. Similar findings have been obtained in studies based on the Adult Attachment Interview (AAI), an interview focused on memories of childhood attachment relationships (e.g., Creasey, 2002; Creasey & Ladd, 2005; Crowell et al., 2002). In short, many studies converge to show that insecure attachment, measured with questionnaires or interviews, is associated with more negative behavior during conflicts in both dating and married couples.

Laboratory studies of couples have also revealed insecure people's deficiencies in providing care to a partner. In a study mentioned earlier, Simpson et al. (1992) unobtrusively videotaped dating couples while the female partner waited to undergo a frightening experience, and judges later rated (from video recordings) the female partners' expressions of distress and the male partners' caregiving behavior. Secure men recognized their partner's worries and provided greater support as their partner showed higher levels of distress, but men who scored high on avoidance actually provided less support as their partner's distress increased—a pattern also seen in Ainsworth's Strange Situation studies of avoidant mothers and their infants. In another study, Simpson, Rholes, Orina, and Grich (2002) exposed male members of couples to the threat of undergoing a frightening procedure and found that more avoidant female partners provided less support regardless of their partner's expressions of distress.

Observational studies by Collins and her colleagues have documented some of the deficiencies in anxious adults' approach to providing care to their partners. Collins and Feeney (2000), for example, videotaped dating couples while one partner disclosed a personal problem to the other partner (the "caregiver"). Caregivers scoring higher on attachment anxiety were coded (by independent judges) as less supportive during the interaction, especially when a partner's needs were not very clear (i.e., when the partner engaged in less obvious support seeking). In two subsequent laboratory experiments, B. C. Feeney and Collins (2001) and Collins, Guichard, Ford, and Feeney (2006) found that more avoidant and anxious participants were less supportive precisely when the partner most needed support.

Two observational studies of interactions between romantic relationship partners also show that attachment anxiety is associated with expressions of anger toward a romantic partner (Rholes, Simpson, & Orina, 1999; Simpson et al., 1996). In Simpson and colleagues' (1996) study, anger reactions were observed during conflictual interactions in which romantic partners were asked to identify an unresolved problem in their relationship, discuss it, and try to resolve it. Attachment anxiety was associated with the display and report of more anger, hostility, and distress during the conversation. In Rholes and colleagues' (1999) study, behavioral manifestations of anger were assessed among women who interacted with their romantic partners while waiting to engage in an anxiety-provoking activity. In this study, as mentioned earlier, self-reports of attachment anxiety were associated with more intense observable anger toward partners after the couples were told that the women would not have to perform the stressful activity. This association was particularly strong when women were more upset during the waiting period or when they sought more support from their partners.

Daily diary studies of couple interactions provide important information about attachment-style differences in everyday relational behaviors. For example, Bradford, Feeney, and Campbell (2002) found that more avoidant participants reported fewer and less intimate disclosures in their everyday conversations with dating partners and felt less satisfied with the disclosure process. Attachment-anxious individuals made more negative disclosures, and their partners rated these disclosures as relatively unsatisfying and negative in tone. In another diary study, Lavy (2006) found that more anxious participants typically reported more daily intrusive behaviors and were perceived by their partners as engaging in more intrusive behaviors, but this association was moderated by relationship satisfaction on the previous day. That is, anxious people reported relatively high levels of intrusive behavior mainly when they had been dissatisfied with their relationship the previous day. This implies that anxious intrusiveness is part of anxious people's efforts to create or restore a desired level of closeness. Like other anxious behaviors, these closeness regulation efforts are likely to backfire if they cause a partner to feel intruded upon.

This kind of closeness regulation in dating couples was also observed in a diary study assessing daily variations in seeking reassurance from a partner (Shaver, Schachner, & Mikulincer, 2005). Participants who scored higher on attachment anxiety were more likely, across the 2-week study period, to seek reassurance from their partner. In addition, anxious men sought more reassurance following days on which they experienced relationship conflicts than following days on which little or no conflict was reported.

Small Group Interactions

Attachment styles, viewed as fairly stable personality constellations, are likely to have effects that extend beyond romantic and other dyadic relationships to behavior in small groups (a topic area reviewed by Moreland, Fetterman, Flagg, and Swanenburg, Chapter 3, this volume). Exploring this possibility, Rom and Mikulincer (2003) studied small groups of new military recruits in the Israel Defense Forces (IDF), whose performance in combat units was evaluated during a 2-day screening session. Attachment anxiety was associated with poor instrumental performance during group missions, and avoidant attachment was associated with lower levels of both instrumental and socio-emotional functioning during group missions (as assessed by observers' ratings). Interestingly, group cohesion improved the socioemotional and instrumental functioning of group members and reduced the detrimental effects of attachment anxiety on instrumental behavior during group missions. From an attachment perspective, a cohesive group can be viewed as a group-level provider of approval and security, which makes anxious behavioral strategies less necessary and enables attachment-anxious soldiers to engage more fully and effectively in instrumental tasks. A sense of group cohesion, like a sense of being "close" in dyadic relationships, signals that closeness, support, consensus, and approval—all prominent goals of attachment-anxious people—have been attained, thereby freeing resources for task performance.

Attachment-related impediments to smooth group functioning have also been observed in the context of group psychotherapy. In a study by Shechtman and Rybko (2004), Israeli university students completed a self-report attachment measure before beginning a series of 12 or 13 two-hour group counseling sessions in which they were expected, with the help of a counselor, to share personal information, listen empathically to others, and help other group members deal with interpersonal problems. Both attachment-anxious and avoidant participants were rated after the first group session as sharing less intimate personal information than secure participants shared. In addition, whereas avoidant participants were rated as displaying lower levels of self-disclosure and empathy than secure ones at the end of the counseling process, anxiously attached participants were rated as working less constructively than secure ones during group sessions.

ATTACHMENT INSECURITIES AFFECTED BY OBSERVABLE PARTNER BEHAVIOR

So far, we have reviewed research findings showing that people's attachment-related mental states shape their behavior in couple relationships and small groups. We should also consider, however, whether, as Bowlby and Ainsworth maintained, mental states such as attachment security, anxiety, and avoidance are affected by relationship partners' behavior. Ainsworth and her followers have demonstrated that infants' attachment behaviors are definitely shaped by parents' behavior in their role as attachment figures (see, for example, the review by van IJzendoorn & Bakermans-Kranenburg, 2004). From early on, Ainsworth et al. (1978)

provided persuasive evidence for the impact of parental behavior on the formation of an infant's attachment style. Behavioral observations in families' homes were closely linked with infants' later behavior in the Strange Situation. For example, mothers of securely attached infants were more emotionally available in times of need; they were sensitive and responsive to their children's proximity-seeking behavior (Ainsworth et al., 1978). In contrast, mothers of avoidant infants were uncomfortable with physical closeness and were emotionally rigid, often angry, and observably rejecting of their infants' bids for close proximity. Mothers of anxious infants were inconsistently sensitive and responsive, perhaps because of their own self-preoccupation, uncertainty, and anxiety (Ainsworth et al., 1978). In subsequent decades, dozens of studies have followed up Ainsworth et al.'s (1978) findings and revealed other relevant parental behaviors, such as expressions of positive affect, helpful discussions of emotion (as the child acquires language), and encouragement of exploration, that contribute to the formation of a secure attachment and security-related patterns of behavior and affect regulation (see Atkinson et al., 2000; De Wolff & van IJzendoorn, 1997; and Thompson, 2008, for reviews).

Moreover, longitudinal studies document the formative influence of attachment figures' behavior on offsprings' later adult attachment orientations. For example, Beckwith, Cohen, and Hamilton (1999) found that maternal sensitivity and responsiveness during early childhood were associated with fewer avoidant and more secure AAI classifications in late adolescence. Relying on data from the Minnesota longitudinal study (Sroufe, Egeland, Carlson, & Collins, 2005), Roisman, Madsen, Hennighausen, Sroufe, and Collins (2001) found that more sensitive and responsive parenting when study participants were 13 years old was associated with more secure attachment at age 19. Similarly, Allen and Hauser (1996) found that secure attachment to mother at age 25 was associated with mother's encouragement of relatedness and autonomy during videotaped social interactions when the study participants were 14 years old.

In a recent longitudinal study, Dinero, Conger, Shaver, Widaman, and Larsen-Rife (2008) examined associations between the quality of observed interaction patterns in the family of origin during early adolescence (rated by trained observers from video recordings of a structured interaction task) and self-reported romantic attachment style and observed romantic relationship behaviors in adulthood (at ages 25 and 27). Both self-reported romantic attachment orientations and coded behavioral interactions with romantic partners were predictable from early adolescent interactions with parents. Moreover, as romantic relationships endured and led to marriage, one partner's social behaviors measurably influenced changes in the other's partner's attachment style. Thus, even in young adults, the attachment behavioral system is affected by observable behavioral interactions with relationship partners.

In another examination of the influence of one romantic partner's relational behavior on the other partner's attachment style, Lavi (2007) conducted a prospective 8-month study of young couples who had been dating for no more than 3 to 4 months. At the beginning of the study, Lavi randomly selected one partner in each of 100 couples to serve as the study "participant" and the other partner to serve as the "attachment figure." From the "participants" Lavi (2007) collected self-reports of relationship satisfaction, dispositional attachment anxiety and avoidance, and attachment insecurities within the specific relationship under study. She also observed interactions between the participants and their attachment figures and coded the attachment figures' sensitivity and supportiveness. Measures of sensitivity included accuracy in decoding emotional facial expressions and accuracy in decoding negative and positive emotions that participants displayed in a nonverbal communication task. Measures of supportiveness included actual supportive behaviors, coded by independent judges, during a video-recorded dyadic interaction in which participants disclosed a personal problem. Four and eight months later, participants who were still dating the same romantic partner (73% of the sample) once again completed self-report measures of within-relationship attachment orientations.

Participants' reports of within-relationship attachment anxiety and avoidance gradually decreased over the 8-month period, implying that maintenance of a dating relationship contributed to a decrease in relationship-specific attachment insecurity. However, these positive changes depended greatly on the attachment figure's previously observed sensitivity and supportiveness. Partners who were more accurate in decoding facial expressions and nonverbal expressions of negative emotions and were coded by judges as more supportive toward their partner in the dyadic interaction task brought about a steeper decline in within-relationship attachment anxiety and avoidance over the 8-month period. In fact, participants did not exhibit a significant decrease in within-relationship attachment insecurities if their partners scored relatively low on behavioral measures of sensitivity and supportiveness at the beginning of the study. These long-term changes in within-relationship attachment organization were not explained by variations in baseline relationship satisfaction and were independent of participants' general attachment orientations at the beginning of the study. That is, a partner's sensitive and supportive behaviors predicted prospective decreases in within-relationship attachment insecurities in both chronically secure and chronically insecure participants. Overall, these findings highlight the importance of a romantic partner's behavior in changing a person's attachment-related mental states.

CONCLUDING REMARKS

The findings reviewed here, as well as many more reviewed in our comprehensive book about adult attachment (Mikulincer & Shaver, 2007), flesh out the claim that social life, which means human life in general, is a very long chain of mental states and observable behaviors—a chain in which the links often involve reciprocal causal arrows. A person's mental representations of self and relationship partners—both specific partners and generalized "others"—are residues of actual experiences in relationships, sometimes amplified or shaped by imagination, rumination, worries, and wishful thinking. These mental representations color subsequent concerns, goals, and action plans, which influence actions, which shape joint self-partner situations, which are again interpreted, remembered, and ruminated upon in ways colored by pre-existing scripts or models, but which can also alter those scripts or models (usually only slightly, unless similar information is repeatedly incorporated).

Many of the details of this process have been demonstrated, at conscious and unconscious levels (and even in the brain; Gillath, Bunge, Shaver, Wendelken, & Mikulincer, 2005), using many different methods and measures. As a result, there is no "miracle" left to explain. In the same sense that a person goes to a closet and picks up an umbrella before leaving home in a rainstorm, a person who is anxious about attachment foresees rejection and abandonment and maintains vigilance for signs of partner disaffection or disloyalty, and a person who is avoidant foresees unpleasant entanglements and impositions and therefore refuses to self-disclose or become highly dependent or interdependent. For some reason, psychologists seem perversely impelled to focus on one feature of human existence at a time. Thus, behaviorism, which deliberately neglected thoughts, motives, and emotions, was supplanted by the "cognitive revolution," which proceeded to ignore motives and emotions (or, if not ignore them, try to explain them in largely cognitive terms). Eventually, emotions and motives made their way back into the story, resulting in the creation of new journals, such as *Emotion*. Now, thanks to an influential article by Baumeister, Vohs, and Funder (2007; see also Baumeister, Vohs, and Funder, Chapter 2, this volume), social-personality psychologists are worrying about the neglect of behavior. We will know we have achieved full scientific self-confidence when all of these very real aspects of human life and experience form a seamless conceptual whole, just as genes, bodies, and behavior do in biology.

It's interesting that the cartoon used by this volume's editors to highlight the supposed gap between relationship cognitions and feelings, on the one hand, and social behavior, on the other, showed what appear to be two mathematical physicists contemplating a long equation with a "miracle" inserted at a foggy area in the middle of the chain of numerical expressions. Psychologists have long felt inadequate in comparison with their idealized conception of physicists because it seemed that physicists had a much more complete picture of the phenomena they study than psychologists have of what we study. The cartoon about the mathematical physicists is funny partly because the sophistication implied by the complex equation doesn't fit with a need to postulate a miracle. We don't expect physicists to invoke miracles, even though ordinary people have, for eons, been explaining the physical world and their own experiences in terms of spirits and miracles. Behaviorally oriented psychologists have wanted to get away from spirits and miracles and focus on good old rock-solid behavior. But behavior is no more real than mental states, and behavior would not be very interesting if it took place robotically, without mental states and human meanings. It might be worthwhile, from time to time, to view behavior as just a vehicle that moves us from one meaningful mental state to another. This is no better and no worse than viewing mental states as phenomena that carry us from one behavior to another.

Oddly enough, in present-day physics it is necessary to postulate the existence of dark matter and dark energy, which no one has yet seen or measured. "Dark matter" and "dark energy" might as well be called miracles because they are cognitive placeholders for something that physicists' equations require but that observations and measurements do not yet reveal. In this sense, the study of attachment-related aspects of human relationships relies less on miracles than physics and cosmology do. There are obviously many details yet to be discovered and to be better measured, but it is already clear that mental states and behaviors are equally real and are reciprocally related, and we need postulate no miracles to explain why.

REFERENCES

Ainsworth, M. D. S. (1967*). Infancy in Uganda: Infant care and the growth of love.* Baltimore, MD: Johns Hopkins University Press.

Ainsworth, M. D. S. (1973). The development of infant-mother attachment. In B. M. Caldwell & H. N. Ricciuti (Eds.), *Review of child development research* (Vol. 3). Chicago, IL: University of Chicago Press.

Ainsworth, M. D. S. (1991). Attachment and other affectional bonds across the life cycle. In C. M. Parkes, J. Stevenson-Hinde, & P. Marris (Eds.), *Attachment across the life cycle* (pp. 33–51). New York: Routledge.

Ainsworth, M. D. S., Blehar, M. C., Waters, E., & Wall, S. (1978). *Patterns of attachment: Assessed in the Strange Situation and at home.* Hillsdale, NJ: Erlbaum.

Allen, J. P., & Hauser, S. T. (1996). Autonomy and relatedness in adolescent-family interactions as predictors of young adults' states of mind regarding attachment. *Development and Psychopathology, 8,* 793–809.

Atkinson, L., Paglia, A., Coolbear, J., Niccols, A., Parker, K. C. H., & Guger, S. (2000). Attachment security: A meta-analysis of maternal mental health correlates. *Clinical Psychology Review, 20,* 1019–1040.

Barkow, J. H., Cosmides, L., & Tooby, J. (Eds.). (1992). *The adapted mind: Evolutionary psychology and the generation of culture.* New York: Oxford University Press.

Bartholomew, K., & Horowitz, L. M. (1991). Attachment styles among young adults: A test of a four-category model. *Journal of Personality and Social Psychology, 61,* 226–244.

Baumeister, R. F., Vohs, K. D., & Funder, D. C. (2007). Psychology as the science of self-reports and finger movements: Whatever happened to actual behavior? *Perspectives on Psychological Science, 2,* 396–403.

Beckwith, L., Cohen, S. E., & Hamilton, C. E. (1999). Maternal sensitivity during infancy and subsequent life events relate to attachment representation at early adulthood. *Developmental Psychology, 35,* 693–700.

Berant, E., Mikulincer, M., & Shaver, P. R. (2008). Mothers' attachment style, their mental health, and their children's emotional vulnerabilities: A seven-year study of children with congenital heart disease. *Journal of Personality, 76,* 31–66.

Bowlby, J. (1973). *Attachment and loss: Vol. 2. Separation: Anxiety and anger.* New York: Basic Books.

Bowlby, J. (1980). *Attachment and loss: Vol. 3. Sadness and depression.* New York: Basic Books.

Bowlby, J. (1982). *Attachment and loss: Vol. 1. Attachment* (2nd ed.). New York: Basic Books. (Original ed. 1969).

Bowlby, J. (1988). *A secure base: Clinical applications of attachment theory.* London: Routledge.

Bradford, S. A., Feeney, J. A., & Campbell, L. (2002). Links between attachment orientations and dispositional and diary-based measures of disclosure in dating couples: A study of actor and partner effects. *Personal Relationships, 9,* 491–506.

Brennan, K. A., Clark, C. L., & Shaver, P. R. (1998). Self-report measurement of adult romantic attachment: An integrative overview. In J. A. Simpson & W. S. Rholes (Eds.), *Attachment theory and close relationships* (pp. 46–76). New York: Guilford Press.

Burkhardt, R. W., Jr. (2005). *Patterns of behavior: Konrad Lorenz, Niko Tinbergen, and the founding of ethology.* Chicago, IL: University of Chicago Press.

Campbell, L., Simpson, J. A., Boldry, J., & Kashy, D. A. (2005). Perceptions of conflict and support in romantic relationships: The role of attachment anxiety. *Journal of Personality and Social Psychology, 88,* 510–531.

Carver, C. S., & Scheier, M. F. (1990). Origins and functions of positive and negative affect: A control-process view. *Psychological Review, 97,* 19–35.

Cassidy, J., & Berlin, L. J. (1994). The insecure/ambivalent pattern of attachment: Theory and research. *Child Development, 65*, 971–981.

Cassidy, J., & Kobak, R. R. (1988). Avoidance and its relationship with other defensive processes. In J. Belsky & T. Nezworski (Eds.), *Clinical implications of attachment* (pp. 300–323). Hillsdale, NJ: Erlbaum.

Collins, N. L., & Feeney, B. C. (2000). A safe haven: An attachment theory perspective on support seeking and caregiving in intimate relationships. *Journal of Personality and Social Psychology, 78*, 1053–1073.

Collins, N. L., & Feeney, B. C. (2005). *Attachment processes in daily interaction: Feeling supported and feeling secure.* Unpublished manuscript, University of California, Santa Barbara.

Collins, N. L., Guichard, A. C., Ford, M. B., & Feeney, B. C. (2006). Responding to need in intimate relationships: Normative processes and individual differences. In M. Mikulincer & G. Goodman (Eds.), *Dynamics of romantic love: Attachment, caregiving, and sex* (pp. 149–189). New York: Guilford Press.

Creasey, G. (2002). Associations between working models of attachment and conflict management behavior in romantic couples. *Journal of Counseling Psychology, 49*, 365–375.

Creasey, G., & Ladd, A. (2005). Generalized and specific attachment representations: Unique and interactive roles in predicting conflict behaviors in close relationships. *Personality and Social Psychology Bulletin, 31*, 1026–1038.

Crowell, J. A., Treboux, D., Gao, Y., Fyffe, C., Pan, H., & Waters, E. (2002). Assessing secure base behavior in adulthood: Development of a measure, links to adult attachment representations, and relations to couples' communication and reports of relationships. *Developmental Psychology, 38*, 679–693.

Davidovitz, R., Mikulincer, M., Shaver, P. R., Izsak, R., & Popper, M. (2007). Leaders as attachment figures: Leaders' attachment orientations predict leadership-related mental representations and followers' performance and mental health. *Journal of Personality and Social Psychology, 93*, 632–650.

Dawkins, R. (2006). *The selfish gene* (3rd edition). New York: Oxford University Press.

de Wolff, M., & van IJzendoorn, M. H. (1997). Sensitivity and attachment: A meta-analysis on parental antecedents of infant attachment. *Child Development, 68*, 571–591.

Dinero, R. E., Conger, R. D., Shaver, P. R., Widaman, K. F., & Larsen-Rife, D. (2008). Influence of family of origin and adult romantic partners on romantic attachment security. *Journal of Family Psychology, 22*, 622–632.

Feeney, B. C., & Collins, N. L. (2001). Predictors of caregiving in adult intimate relationships: An attachment theoretical perspective. *Journal of Personality and Social Psychology, 80*, 972–994.

Feeney, J. A. (1998). Adult attachment and relationship-centered anxiety: Responses to physical and emotional distancing. In J. A. Simpson & W. S. Rholes (Eds.), *Attachment theory and close relationships* (pp. 189–219). New York: Guilford Press.

Feeney, J. A. (2004). Transfer of attachment from parents to romantic partners: Effects of individual and relationship variables. *Journal of Family Studies, 10,* 220–238.

Fonagy, P., Gergely, G., & Target, M. (2008). Psychoanalytic constructs and attachment theory and research. In J. Cassidy & P. R. Shaver (Eds.), *Handbook of attachment: Theory, research, and clinical applications* (2nd ed.). New York: Guilford Press.

Fraley, R. C., & Davis, K. E. (1997). Attachment formation and transfer in young adults' close friendships and romantic relationships. *Personal Relationships, 4,* 131–144.

Fraley, R. C., & Shaver, P. R. (1998). Airport separations: A naturalistic study of adult attachment dynamics in separating couples. *Journal of Personality and Social Psychology, 75,* 1198–1212.

Fraley, R. C., & Shaver, P. R. (2000). Adult romantic attachment: Theoretical developments, emerging controversies, and unanswered questions. *Review of General Psychology, 4,* 132–154.

Fredrickson, B. L. (2001). The role of positive emotions in positive psychology: The broaden-and-build theory of positive emotions. *American Psychologist, 56,* 218–226.

Gillath, O., Bunge, S. A., Shaver, P. R., Wendelken, C., & Mikulincer, M. (2005). Attachment-style differences and ability to suppress negative thoughts: Exploring the neural correlates. *NeuroImage, 28,* 835–847.

Guerrero, L. K. (1996). Attachment-style differences in intimacy and involvement: A test of the four-category model. *Communication Monographs, 63,* 269–292.

Hazan, C., & Shaver, P. R. (1987). Romantic love conceptualized as an attachment process. *Journal of Personality and Social Psychology, 52,* 511–524.

Hazan, C., & Shaver, P. R. (1994). Attachment theory as an organizational framework for research on close relationships. *Psychological Inquiry, 5,* 1–22.

Hazan, C., & Zeifman, D. (1999). Pair-bonds as attachments: Evaluating the evidence. In J. Cassidy & P. R. Shaver (Eds.), *Handbook of attachment: Theory, research, and clinical applications* (pp. 336–354). New York: Guilford Press.

Kirkpatrick, L. A., & Shaver, P. R. (1988). Fear and affiliation reconsidered from a stress and coping perspective. *Journal of Social and Clinical Psychology, 7,* 214–233.

Lavi, N. (2007). *Bolstering attachment security in romantic relationships: The long-term contribution of partner's sensitivity, expressiveness, and supportiveness.* Unpublished doctoral dissertation, Bar-Ilan University, Ramat Gan, Israel.

Lavy, S. (2006). *Expressions and consequences of intrusiveness in adult romantic relationships: An attachment theory perspective.* Unpublished doctoral dissertation, Bar-Ilan University, Ramat Gan, Israel.

Main, M. (1990). Cross-cultural studies of attachment organization: Recent studies, changing methodologies, and the concept of conditional strategies. *Human Development, 33,* 48–61.

Main, M., & Solomon, J. (1990). Procedures for identifying infants as disorganized/ disoriented during the Ainsworth strange situation. In M. T. Greenberg,

D. Cicchetti, & M. Cummings (Eds.), *Attachment in the preschool years: Theory, research, and intervention* (pp. 121–160). Chicago: University of Chicago Press.

Mikulincer, M., Birnbaum, G., Woddis, D., & Nachmias, O. (2000). Stress and accessibility of proximity-related thoughts: Exploring the normative and intraindividual components of attachment theory. *Journal of Personality and Social Psychology, 78,* 509–523.

Mikulincer, M., Dolev, T., & Shaver, P. R. (2004). Attachment-related strategies during thought-suppression: Ironic rebounds and vulnerable self-representations. *Journal of Personality and Social Psychology, 87,* 940–956.

Mikulincer, M., Gillath, O., & Shaver, P. R. (2002). Activation of the attachment system in adulthood: Threat-related primes increase the accessibility of mental representations of attachment figures. *Journal of Personality and Social Psychology, 83,* 881–895.

Mikulincer, M., & Shaver, P. R. (2003). The attachment behavioral system in adulthood: Activation, psychodynamics, and interpersonal processes. In M. P. Zanna (Ed.), *Advances in experimental social psychology* (Vol. 35, pp. 53–152). New York: Academic Press.

Mikulincer, M., & Shaver, P. R. (2004). Security-based self-representations in adulthood: Contents and processes. In W. S. Rholes & J. A. Simpson (Eds.), *Adult attachment: Theory, research, and clinical implications* (pp. 159–195). New York: Guilford Press.

Mikulincer, M., & Shaver, P. R. (2007). *Attachment patterns in adulthood: Structure, dynamics, and change.* New York: Guilford Press.

Piaget, J. (1953). *Origins of intelligence in the child.* London: Routledge.

Rholes, W. S., Simpson, J. A., & Orina, M. (1999). Attachment and anger in an anxiety-provoking situation. *Journal of Personality and Social Psychology, 76,* 940–957.

Roisman, G. I., Madsen, S. D., Hennighausen, K. H., Sroufe, L. A., & Collins, W. A. (2001). The coherence of dyadic behavior across parent-child and romantic relationships as mediated by the internalized representation of experience. *Attachment and Human Development, 3,* 156–172.

Rom, E., & Mikulincer, M. (2003). Attachment theory and group processes: The association between attachment style and group-related representations, goals, memories, and functioning. *Journal of Personality and Social Psychology, 84,* 1220–1235.

Schachter, S. (1959). *The psychology of affiliation.* Stanford, CA: Stanford University Press.

Shaver, P. R., & Clark, C. L. (1994). The psychodynamics of adult romantic attachment. In J. M. Masling & R. F. Bornstein (Eds.), *Empirical perspectives on object relations theories* (pp. 105–156). Washington, DC: American Psychological Association.

Shaver, P. R., & Hazan, C. (1993). Adult romantic attachment: Theory and evidence. In D. Perlman & W. Jones (Eds.), *Advances in personal relationships* (Vol. 4, pp. 29–70). London: Jessica Kingsley.

Shaver, P. R., & Klinnert, M. (1982). Schachter's theories of affiliation and emotions: Implications of developmental research. In L. Wheeler (Ed.), *Review of Personality and Social Psychology* (Vol. 3, pp. 37–71). Beverly Hills, CA: Sage.

Shaver, P. R., & Mikulincer, M. (2002). Attachment-related psychodynamics. *Attachment and Human Development, 4*, 133–161.

Shaver, P. R., Schachner, D. A., & Mikulincer, M. (2005). Attachment style, excessive reassurance seeking, relationship processes, and depression. *Personality and Social Psychology Bulletin, 31*, 343–359.

Shechtman, Z., & Rybko, J. (2004). Attachment style and observed initial self-disclosure as explanatory variables of group functioning. *Group Dynamics, 8*, 207–220.

Simpson, J. A. (1990). Influence of attachment styles on romantic relationships. *Journal of Personality and Social Psychology, 59*, 971–980.

Simpson, J. A., Rholes, W. S., & Nelligan, J. S. (1992). Support seeking and support giving within couples in an anxiety-provoking situation: The role of attachment styles. *Journal of Personality and Social Psychology, 62*, 434–446.

Simpson, J. A., Rholes, W. S., Orina, M., & Grich, J. (2002). Working models of attachment, support giving, and support seeking in a stressful situation. *Personality and Social Psychology Bulletin, 28*, 598–608.

Simpson, J. A., Rholes, W. S., & Phillips, D. (1996). Conflict in close relationships: An attachment perspective. *Journal of Personality and Social Psychology, 71*, 899–914.

Smith, E. R., Murphy, J., & Coats, S. (1999). Attachment to groups: Theory and management. *Journal of Personality and Social Psychology, 77*, 94–110.

Sroufe, L. A., Egeland, B., Carlson, E., & Collins, W. A. (2005). *The development of the person: The Minnesota study of risk and adaptation from birth to adulthood.* New York: Guilford Press.

Sroufe, L. A., & Waters, E. (1977). Attachment as an organizational construct. *Child Development, 48*, 1184–1199.

Thompson, R. A. (2008). Early attachment and later development. In J. Cassidy & P. R. Shaver (Eds.), *Handbook of attachment: Theory, research, and clinical applications* (2nd edition). New York: Guilford Press.

Tucker, J. S., & Anders, S. L. (1998). Adult attachment style and nonverbal closeness in dating couples. *Journal of Nonverbal Behavior, 22*, 109–124.

van IJzendoorn, M. H., & Bakermans-Kranenburg, M. J. (2004). Maternal sensitivity and infant temperament in the formation of attachment. In G. Bremner & A. Slater (Eds.), *Theories of infant development* (pp. 233–257). Malden, MA: Blackwell Publishing.

Waters, H. S., & Waters, E. (2006). The attachment working models concept: Among other things, we build *script*-like representations of secure base experiences. *Attachment and Human Development, 8*, 185–197.

Wisman, A., & Koole, S. L. (2003). Hiding in the crowd: Can mortality salience promote affiliation with others who oppose one's worldview? *Journal of Personality and Social Psychology, 84*, 511–527.

19 Grounding Social Psychology in Behavior in Daily Life: The Case of Conflict and Distress in Couples

Niall Bolger
Gertraud Stadler
Christine Paprocki
Anita DeLongis

The challenge put to participants at the Purdue Symposium was to discuss and perhaps remedy social psychology's neglect of behavior as a focus of research and theory. We the presenters were asked to use the "And Then a Miracle Occurs" New Yorker cartoon as a point of departure for our contributions. Not surprisingly, different presenters took different sources of mirth from the cartoon. For our group, the humor derived from the absurdity of social psychology's ignoring of behavior, of its taking for granted that internal states such as thoughts and feelings have clear implications for behavior. We believe that this is especially true when one considers behavior in the real world as opposed to the laboratory. A social psychology worthy of its name should not only encompass behavior, it should encompass behavior in the real world. Our contribution to the symposium and the edited volume is to demonstrate what social psychology has to gain by adding to its research methods the use of intensive longitudinal designs to study behavior in daily life (e.g., Bolger, Davis, & Rafaeli, 2003).

One of the most consequential behaviors for well-being in daily life is interpersonal conflict. For example, in a large community sample of married couples, interpersonal conflict accounted for over 80% of the explained variance in negative mood (Bolger, DeLongis, Kessler, & Schilling, 1989). Negativity and distress in intimate relationships are also key predictors of relationship satisfaction and divorce. In a 10-year longitudinal study, Huston, Caughlin, Houts, Smith, and George (2001) found that couples who later divorced had higher levels of negativity and distress early in their marriage than did couples who stayed happily married. Marital conflict has been associated with the onset of depressive symptoms, eating disorders, and alcohol abuse (Fincham, 2003). And although married persons generally enjoy better health than do their unmarried counterparts, marital conflict is associated with poorer physical health. It has been shown that marital conflict alters hormone levels (Kiecolt-Glaser et al., 1997; Malarkey, Kiecolt-Glaser, Pearl, & Glaser, 1994), decreases immune responses (Glaser & Kiecolt-Glaser, 1994), and raises blood pressure (Ewart, Taylor, Kraemer, & Agras, 1991). Over time, these negative marital interactions can lead to chronic health problems (for reviews, see Burman & Margolin, 1992; Kiecolt-Glaser & Newton, 2001). Indeed, marital conflicts have repeatedly been found to even predict poorer health in the children of these couples (Repetti, Taylor, & Seeman, 2002; Troxel & Matthews, 2004).

As costly as conflicts are to couples, they seem to serve an important function. Two studies of newlywed couples over their first 4 years of marriage indicate that marital conflict can allow couples to address problems in the relationship and provide an opportunity to solve them (McNulty, O'Mara, & Karney, 2008). When partners in troubled marriages used benevolent strategies that minimized the impact of negative experiences, instead of addressing them directly, they showed steep declines in relationship satisfaction by allowing problems to worsen over time. Because of these serious and varied implications of conflict, it is important to obtain a detailed picture of conflict behavior as it occurs in daily life.

Conventional measures of marital conflict are often far removed from the actual conflict behaviors. When measures of conflict are obtained, they are typically retrospective summary reports of conflict frequency that are used as components of global marital satisfaction. However, it has been found that even such summary reports of conflict frequency can be more highly predictive of well-being outcomes than the overall satisfaction scales themselves (Johnson, White, Edwards, & Booth, 1986; McGonagle, Kessler, & Schilling, 1992). For example, frequency of marital arguments has been shown to be associated with the onset and remission of clinical depression (Hooley & Teasdale, 1989; Paykel, Myers, & Dienelt, 1969) and daily distressed mood (McGonagle et al., 1992). Despite these far-reaching implications, there has been no rigorous documentation of the temporal patterning of conflicts.

Using Diary Methods

One problem that arises when studying any recurring behavior, including marital conflict, is the tendency for individuals to forget when or to what extent they enacted the behavior. It is known, for example, that retrospective frequency reports can suffer from considerable bias (Schwarz, 1999). Concurrent measurement of behavior using structured daily diaries has been proposed as an alternative that can minimize limitations of memory, problems of estimation, and bias in recall (Bolger, Davis, & Rafaeli, 2003; DeLongis, Hemphill, & Lehman, 1992). Diary measures can capture characteristics of behavior such as timing, frequency, and emotional reactivity that are hard to assess with conventional self-report measures. As Tennen, Affleck, Coyne, Larsen, and DeLongis (2006) point out, emotions are rapidly changing phenomena, and as such, can be assessed reliably only if they are measured close to their real-time occurrence. They argue that although end-of-day recollections of emotional experiences are vulnerable to the retrieval biases that affect episodic memory (Stone, Shiffman, & DeVries, 1999) and are likely to overestimate real-time affective reactions (Barrett, 1997), same-day recollections show high accuracy when compared with more frequent online reports (Thomas & Diener, 1990; Tugade, Conner, & Barrett, in press).

Bolger and Kelleher (1993) recommended that researchers use daily diaries in characterizing the quality of interpersonal relationships. Although a great deal of research has indicated the importance of marital conflict for well-being, how conflict plays out in the day-to-day lives of couples is unclear. A critical aim of daily diary data is to represent a universe of occasions, just as cross-sectional data aim to represent a population of individuals (Tennen et al., 2006). If the behavior is relatively rare, such as conflict episodes in couples, sampling at random moments during the day is inefficient and likely to miss the behavior of interest. Relatively infrequent behaviors like marital conflict can be recorded reliably, however, at day's end.

In addition to their descriptive capacity, diaries can address a variety of research questions that are relevant for understanding and predicting behavior such as (a) how often the typical person engages in a certain behavior on average, (b) the extent to which the typical person's behavior varies over time, and (c) whether people differ from one another in mean levels and variability over time. In looking at behavioral variability both within and between subjects, researchers are equipped to test theories explaining a particular behavior's antecedents and effects. In the case of marital conflict, for example, some couples seem to never get into a conflict while others fight frequently. It is likely that the typical couple does not represent this diversity well. Variability in and of itself is rarely explored, and yet it can be quite consequential for all stages of the research process. Since a goal of social psychology is to describe and explain social behavior in general, across a diversity of individuals, it makes sense to examine variability as closely as we examine mean levels. Until recently, this sort of analysis proved difficult to do, but later on in this chapter we will demonstrate how current statistical techniques allow us to more thoroughly examine variability in our sample of couples.

A Dyadic Perspective

When studying marital processes, it is important to take not only the individual into account but rather both spouses' perspectives because these perspectives can differ radically (Jacobson & Moore, 1981; Keefe & Porter, 2007; Lam, Lehman, Puterman, & DeLongis, in press). For example, within a period of stress and tension, partners might differ on the days they report that a marital conflict has occurred. Gable, Reis, and Downey (2003) explored the question of congruence and divergence in partners' perceptions of their daily interactions and found that when one partner reports a negative interaction, even if the other partner does not report such an interaction, there are significant effects on daily mood and relationship satisfaction for *both* partners. Yet very little research on the effects of marital conflict on well-being has obtained reports from both partners, instead relying on one partner's perceptions of marital tension and conflict. Given this, the pathways through which marital conflict exerts its influence on well-being is unclear. When relying exclusively on one partner's perceptions, our assumption that the conflict is critically important to the couple as a whole could be false. Indeed, such conflict and tension may exist only in the eye of the beholder. Examining concordance between spouses in reports of marital conflict and tension affords a better understanding of the influence of marital conflict on the mood of both partners.

Gender is another key variable in studying conflict processes. For example, it has been shown that there are gender-typical patterns in conflict style across husbands and wives. One such pattern that has been studied extensively is the "wife-demand/husband-withdraw" pattern, in which the wife desires a change in the relationship involving some action on the part of the husband, who responds by withdrawing from the conflict and becoming noncommunicative (Sullaway & Christensen, 1983). These findings have been replicated in both clinically distressed couples and community samples (Christensen & Heavey, 1990). However, recent findings suggest that this cycle may be less gender dependent than previously thought, and more dependent on who in the relationship wants the change (Fincham, 2003). It is the spouse who desires change, regardless of gender, who tends to approach, while the other spouse withdraws. Women more often want change, so more often approach. Women also tend to report more distress in general relative to men, and this increased reporting seems to be due to genuinely higher levels of distress, rather than a reporting bias or artifact (Mirowsky & Ross, 1995). From these findings, we might expect that in looking at frequency of reported conflicts and daily distress in couples, wives will report more conflicts than husbands, or at least report more distress related to them.

Daily Diary Study of Marital Conflict

It has now been 20 years since Bolger et al. (1989) published their report on daily stressors in a large sample of married couples. In the intervening years there have been major developments in statistical modeling that can usefully be applied to this data set. The goal of this chapter, therefore, is to revisit the Bolger et al. (1989) diary data set to provide a more fine-grained analysis of marital conflict than was possible using the statistical methods available two decades ago. The 1989 paper focused on mean levels of conflict and mood but left unaddressed the question of variability and covariability across spouses. With modern analytic methods, rigorous assessment of variability in conflict frequency and emotional reactivity can now be considered.

The specific questions that can be addressed now that could not be addressed then are (a) to what extent do couples differ from one another in their levels of marital conflict and their emotional reactivity to those conflicts, and (b) to what extent are husbands who show high levels of marital conflict exposure and reactivity paired with wives who show corresponding levels.

In our study, each partner independently filled out a background questionnaire and then a diary over a maximum period of 42 consecutive diary days. Husbands and wives were mailed their diaries separately and returned them in separate envelopes. Each partner was asked to apply adhesive strips to seal the day's diary after completion to ensure confidentiality. The diary study itself was part of the Detroit Area Study, which comprised a random community sample of 778 married couples in metropolitan Detroit. Of these, 400 couples were invited to be in a supplementary diary study. The final sample for this study is the 150 couples in which both partners filled out at least seven daily diaries regarding marital conflicts and daily distress. Further details on the sample can be found in Bolger et al. (1989). We assessed marital conflict with the item: "We would like to know about any tension or argument you had with any of these people during the past 24 hours. Please check each box that applies." If a subject had checked the box for "Your wife/husband," then we coded the day as a marital conflict day. The diary also included an inventory of 18 mood items from the Affects Balance Scale (Derogatis, 1975) designed to measure clinical levels of anxiety (e.g., nervous, tense, afraid), hostility (e.g., irritable, angry, resentful), and depression (e.g., helpless, worthless, depressed). On the basis of their emotional state over the previous 24-hour period, respondents were asked to rate each of the 18 items on a 4-point scale ranging from "not at all" to "a lot" with the instruction: "Circle the number that best describes your feelings during the past 24 hours." Responses to all items were combined and rescaled to create a summary measure of distressed mood, which ranged from 0 (all items endorsed "not at all") to 1 (all items endorsed "a lot"). The scale had high internal consistency (Cronbach's alpha $= .91$). The mean was .09, and the standard deviation was .14.

New Findings on Exposure to Daily Conflict

Although previously published papers using this data set have reported on exposure to daily conflict (Bolger et al., 1989), and heterogeneity in exposure as a function of personality (Bolger & Schilling, 1991), our approach here is in some respects more and less ambitious than the previous work. It is less ambitious in the sense that we do not attempt to explain *why* couples differ in exposure. It is more ambitious, however, in attempting to estimate the full extent of the heterogeneity. To do so we use each husband's and wife's independent report of marital conflict each day as data and estimate a multilevel logistic regression model that specifies a population distribution of probabilities of reporting conflict across all days, separately for husbands and wives. The model provides estimates of the mean and variance of these distributions and their correlation. The reader may wonder why, given that husbands and wives are reporting on the same event, we do not first of all attempt some reconciling of the reports prior to data analysis. We could have, for example, taken the average, the union, or the intersection of the two reports. We chose instead to allow the results of the multilevel analysis to tell us the extent to which husbands and wives agree or disagree about the typical level of conflict between them.

Details on the multilevel logistic model estimation are presented in the Appendix. We focus here on the key results. First, on average do husbands and wives agree on the level of conflict between them? For husbands, the log-odds of a marital conflict for any given day is −3.3, which corresponds to a probability of .036 (95% CI: .028, .046). For wives, the log-odds is −3.1, which corresponds to a probability of .043 (CI: .034, .054). Although the estimated probability of conflict for wives is somewhat higher than that for husbands, the estimates do not differ significantly ($t(148) = 1.38$, $p = .17$), and therefore we cannot rule out the hypothesis that husbands and wives are in agreement about their engagement in marital conflict. If we use the average of the two partners' estimates as the best guess as to the overall level of marital conflict, we obtain an estimate of .041, which corresponds to a little over one conflict per month. This is consistent with what others have reported, with Fincham (2003) pointing out in his review that about 80% of couples report having less than one overt disagreement per month.

A second way to assess agreement between husbands and wives is through calculating the correlation between their average reports across couples. Specifically, do husbands who have relatively high log-odds of conflict tend to be paired with wives who are also relatively high? Using the multilevel analysis we observed that the degree of correlation between husbands and wives across couples was very high, $r(148) = .86$ (CI: 0.81, 0.90), sufficiently high to meet typical standards in psychometrics for parallel measures (Nunnally & Bernstein, 1994). Note, however, that the confidence interval allows us to exclude population values greater than .90. Thus, while the correlation is impressive, we can nonetheless be very confident that the correlation between spouses is not perfect in the population. This discrepancy is interesting in its own right and deserves further investigation.

Although the key results of multilevel analyses involve estimates of population means, variances, and correlations of random effects, further insight into the data can be gained by obtaining what can be called posterior estimates of the random effects for the sample (also known as empirical best linear unbiased predictors, or EBLUPs; Littell, Milliken, Stroup, Wolfinger, & Schabenberger, 2006). In this way it is possible to see what the model's best guess is for—in the present example's case—the probability of conflict for each of the husbands and wives in each of the 150 couples in our sample. Figure 19.1, therefore, displays a scatterplot of model-estimated probabilities of marital conflict for husbands (on the y-axis) and wives (on the x-axis).

Figure 19.1 shows that although the average probability of conflict is approximately .04, there is large variability in that probability across couples. The predicted conflict engagement probabilities in the sample

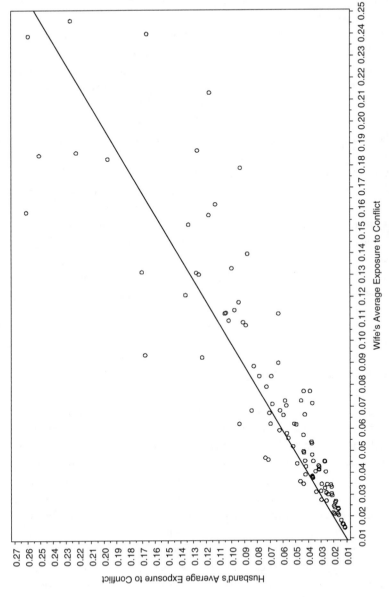

Figure 19.1. Husband's and Wife's Average Exposure to Conflicts Over 42 Diary Days: Model-Based Estimates. (Note: Each point represents one couple).

range from .01 to .24 for women and from .01 to .26 for men. Recall that these are model predictions for the sample. Consistent with these values, the estimated 95% range of *population values* based on the model is .004 to .25 for wives and from .006 to .25 for husbands. There is no evidence of population gender differences in the between-person variability ($t(148) = .63$, p $< .53$).

Figure 19.1 also shows a line of perfect agreement between spouses. Although it appears that more points fall below the line than above, a test of whether the regression lines of husband scores on wife score differs from 1.0 was nonsignificant. Similarly, a test of whether the regression of wives' scores on husbands' scores differed from 1.0 was also not statistically significant. Thus, we cannot reject the hypothesis that the means for husbands and wives are identical and also that scores are distributed evenly around a line of perfect agreement.

In summary, we have found that although rates of marital conflict reported in the diaries are low, there is substantial between-couples heterogeneity in those rates, and there is a high level of agreement between spouses regarding those rates. This high level of agreement supports the idea that the diary reports are revealing actual behavioral episodes visible to both partners. If people were not able to accurately recall the events of the day, or if they were reporting on internal states rather than behaviors they enacted, one would not expect such agreement across partners.

Daily Distress in a Dyadic Context

The second goal of this paper is to document between-couple heterogeneity in reactivity to marital conflict, and we move now to a statistical model that incorporates daily conflicts as a predictor of daily distress. Such a model allows us to distinguish days on which individuals reported that no marital conflict occurred and days on which they reported that a conflict occurred. Using that information we will focus on two outcomes: First, how distressed are husbands and wives on no-conflict days? Given that conflicts occurred approximately once a month on average, these correspond to the vast majority of days. Second, how much more distressed are husbands and wives when they experience a conflict, defined as how much more distressed they were on days when they reported having a marital conflict than on days when they did not. As in the case of the occurrence of conflicts, we will also determine the correlation between the two outcomes across couples. The appendix contains the details on the statistical model used.

Average distress on no-conflict days. The multilevel analysis produced estimates of means and standard deviations of distress on no-conflict days for husbands and wives. Overall, distress levels were very low, and we found no evidence of gender differences in distress. The average husband was estimated to have a mean distress (on a 0 to 1 scale) of 0.085 (CI: 0.073, 0.097); the average wife also had a mean distress of 0.085 (CI: 0.074, 0.096; $t_{diff}(146) = .02$, $p < .99$).

Although husbands and wives in our sample had identical distress levels on average, there was evidence of a gender difference in variability: The between-couple standard deviation was larger for husbands ($SD = .075$, CI: .066, .084) than for wives ($SD = .063$, CI: .055, .070; $t_{diff}(146) = 2.06$, $p < .041$). The confidence interval for the difference ranged from essentially no gender difference to husbands having a standard deviation of .024 greater than wives.

Figure 19.2 shows a scatterplot of the posterior estimates of the random effects for husbands' and wives' average distress on no-conflict days. They show only a slight tendency for distressed husbands to be paired with distressed wives. The between-couple correlation between these random effects is small ($r = .27$, $t(146) = 2.84$, $p < .0045$). There are plenty of examples of relatively distressed husbands who have wives who show low distress and vice versa. These findings are somewhat surprising given multiple theoretical models that posit an interrelationship in mood between members of a couple. Primary among these are models of mood contagion (Joiner & Katz, 1999), which argue that one spouse's negative affect would "infect" the other. Second, negative affect in both partners has been posited to coexist due to assortative mating. For example, evidence suggests that depressed individuals may select a similarly depressed mate (Maes et al., 1998; Mathews & Reus, 2001). Yet our findings suggest that in examining couples' mood at a day-to-day level, evidence for both mood contagion and assortative mating appears to be small.

Perhaps not surprisingly, there is a relative absence of couples who are both relatively high on distress. High distress levels in both partners could indicate that the couple is going through a mutual life stressor, or that their relationship is troubled. Such couples are likely to choose not to participate in a study of this nature because the time and commitment needed might be overwhelming. Furthermore, it could be that marriages characterized by the presence of high distress in both members of the couple are unstable and less viable in the long-term, making these couples more rare in a sample.

Reactivity to Daily Conflict. Consistent with the original Bolger et al. (1989) report, both husbands and wives show strong reactivity to marital

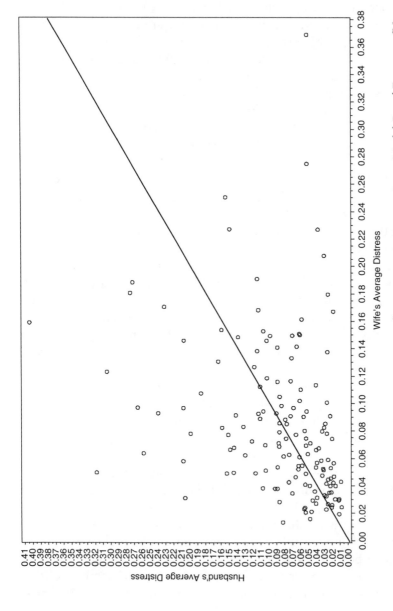

Figure 19.2. Husband's and Wife's Average Distress on No-Conflict Days Over 42 Diary Days: Model-Based Estimates (Note: Each point represents one couple).

conflict on the same day. The average coefficient for husbands is 0.110 units (CI: 0.088, 0.131); the equivalent for wives is 0.139 (CI: 0.111, 0.167). Bolger et al. concluded that wives were more reactive to marital arguments than were their husbands. Using the current statistical framework we do not have sufficient power to be confident of that claim. The confidence interval for the difference ranges from -0.002 indicating no difference in reactivity to 0.062 indicating that females could be twice as reactive as males ($t(146) = 1.81, p < .071$).

A question that was not posed by Bolger et al. (1989)—and could not have been posed given their statistical model—was whether husbands as a group were more or less variable in their reactivity than wives as a group. The standard deviation in reactivity for husbands was 0.091 (CI: 0.071, 0.111) and for wives was 0.127 (CI: 0.105, 0.149). Based on these estimates we conclude that wives are more heterogeneous than husbands in their reactivity to marital conflicts ($t_{diff}(146) = -2.48, p < .014$). Finally, as in the case of distress on no-conflict days, there is only a weak positive relationship between husbands' and wives' reactivity, $r(146) = .26, t(146) = 1.56, p < .120$.

Figure 19.3 shows a scatterplot of the posterior estimates of husbands' and wives' conflict reactivity in our sample. The univariate distributions are both positively skewed, and we have separated the plot into quadrants based on the median values in the sample. To give the reader a better understanding of the diary records for these combinations of reactivity, we present in Figure 19.4 plots of the occurrence of conflict and levels of daily distress in a selection of specific couples highlighted by circles in Figure 19.3.

By looking at the level of individual couples (see Figure 19.4), we are able to detect patterns that at the between-couples level would not be evident. For example, we can see that although on average agreement about conflict days is high, couples do not always agree on the specific days on which they argued with each other. Often, we see a pattern in which there is an overall agreement on a period of conflict, though the partners may report their conflicts a day or two off from each other. We hope to examine this further, to determine whether broad conflict periods are more highly predictive of distress than particular conflict days. This might be expected because we are able to see that at times a wife may report a conflict that her husband does not (or vice versa), but both of them experience an increase in distress on that day.

In Figure 19.4, for each of four combinations of husband-wife reactivity (high-high, low-low, average-average, high-low/low-high), two representative couples are displayed. For each couple, there is a husband panel above a corresponding wife panel. Within each panel, the higher line

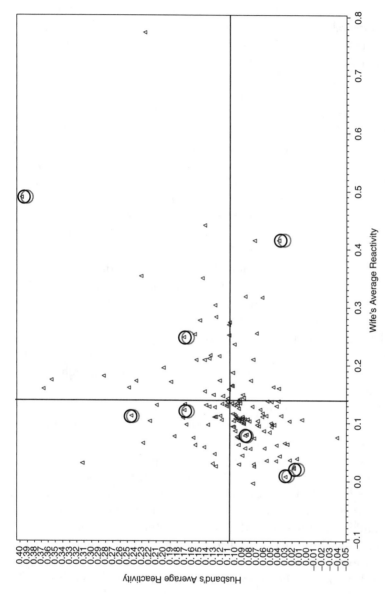

Figure 19.3. Husband's and Wife's Average Reactivity to Conflicts Over 42 Diary Days: Model-Based Estimates (Note: Each point represents one couple).

plots daily distress (on a scale from 0, no distress reported, to 1, maximum distress), and the lower line plots reports of marital conflict (on days when a conflict is reported, the lower plot spikes up from its baseline value of no conflict). This structure allows us to compare husbands' and wives' timing of conflict reports, and to compare husbands and wives on their emotional reactivity to reported conflicts.

In Figure 19.4a, the pattern represented is of a highly distressed response in both partners to a marital conflict. It can be seen that in both couples, partners agree on some of the conflict days, but not on all of them. For Couple 1 there seems to be agreement on a general period of conflict, which the husband reports on and off, and the wife reports as a multiple-day spell. In Couple 2, we see that the wife reports two days of conflict at the end of the diary period that the husband does not report, though he does have a corresponding rise in distress. Figure 19.4b displays examples of the opposite pattern of reactivity—both partners are low in

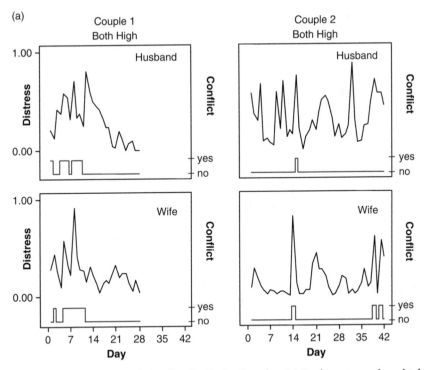

Figure 19.4. Distress and Conflict for Eight Couples. (a) Both partners show high reactivity on conflict versus nonconflict days. (b) Both partners show low reactivity on conflict versus nonconflict days. (c) Both partners show average reactivity on conflict versus nonconflict days. (d) Couples with mixed reactivity on conflict versus nonconflict days.

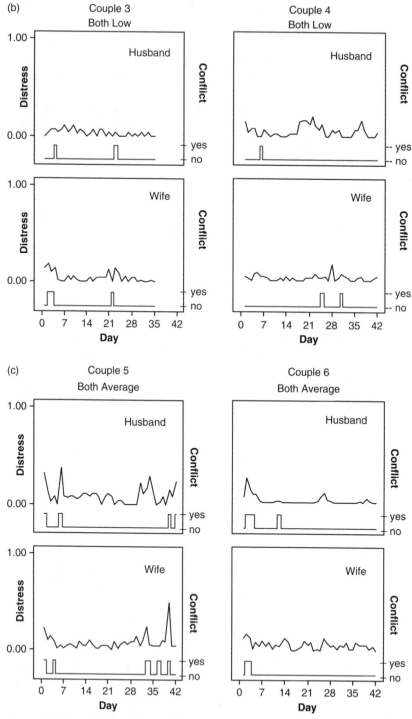

Figure 19.4. Continued.

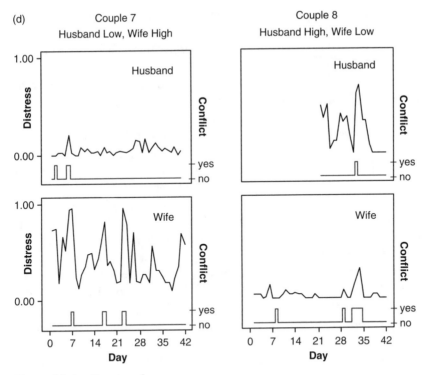

Figure 19.4.   Continued.

reactivity to conflict. We can see that both of these couples are low in distress overall, and that they do not show a distressed response on days of reported conflict. Figure 19.4c displays examples of couples in which both partners have average reactivity to conflict. Finally, Figure 19.4d shows examples of two couples in which the partners are discordant on reactivity—one partner is highly reactive to conflict, while the other partner is not.

SUMMARY AND DISCUSSION OF KEY FINDINGS

This reanalysis of the Bolger et al. (1989) data yielded two new sets of findings. The first concerned exposure to marital conflicts. We found striking heterogeneity across couples in exposure to conflict, and at the same time strong overall consensus between husbands and wives about their typical exposure. This high agreement between partners supports the claim that conflict reports correspond to actual daily interpersonal behaviors. Further, couples in the current study also showed evidence of multiday periods of tension, in which one or both partners reported conflicts over several days. This finding deserves further attention as it may indicate that couples need several attempts to resolve a marital conflict before they find a satisfactory solution (McNulty et al., 2008).

The second set of new findings concerned emotional reactivity to conflicts. Here again there were large between-couple differences, but there were also large within-couple differences. We documented these reactivity results by providing daily profiles of conflict and distress for couples with similar and different combinations of reactivity. Interestingly, we did not find an equal distribution of couples within these groups. There were very few high-high reactivity couples, perhaps due to the fact that two people who both react to conflict with a great degree of distress may not be able to function as a couple over the long-term. Ineffective coping with conflict has been shown to be predictive of divorce (Gottman & Levenson, 1999).

Note that there was also both between- and within-couple heterogeneity in distress on days of no conflict (the vast majority of days for most couples). The within-couple heterogeneity may surprise some readers in that there were approximately equal numbers of couples in which husbands were more distressed than their wives as there were couples in which wives were more distressed than their husbands on no-conflict days.

Contrary to the findings of Bolger et al. (1989), we did not find a significant gender difference in reactivity to conflict, although the confidence interval for the effect just barely included zero. Earlier research led us to expect a more highly distressed reaction to conflict in wives than in husbands, but the current results present a picture of great heterogeneity across both husbands and wives, so much so that they tend to dwarf average differences between husbands and wives. The fixed-effects analysis approach used in the 1989 study had ignored this within-group heterogeneity.

When researching behavior, how the typical person behaves and reacts is one important piece of information. Equally important, however, is the question of how much people differ in behavior and reaction (Bolger et al., 2003). The individuals in the current study varied vastly in conflict occurrence and also in distress on conflict and no-conflict days. In this case, taking into account how much individuals and couples differ is essential to describing what is actually going on in the sample. With adequate statistical models in place to describe typical levels and variability in behavior, the next step in research will be to get at the sources of variability (e.g., relationship satisfaction, communication patterns, personality).

Further research with similar designs including diary reports from both partners will help to shed light on the mechanisms explaining how marital conflict influences health (Burman & Margolin, 1992; Kiecolt-

Glaser & Newton, 2001). For example, DeLongis, Capreol, Holtzman, O'Brien, and Campbell (2004) found that only couples with low marital satisfaction tended to evidence mood disturbance when there was an absence of positive interactions with the spouse. Those high in marital satisfaction appeared to weather the natural ups and downs of married life without distress.

One limitation of the current study is that the question of the causal relation between conflict and distress cannot be answered based on the available data. Although it is highly likely that conflicts cause distress, high distress might also make conflicts more likely. Because conflict and distress were measured at the same time, we cannot be sure about the causal direction between them. To address this limitation, a study design where partners report on their distress before one or both come home from work and then again at night before going to bed would allow researchers to parse apart the contribution of distress to conflict and conflict to distress. In a study examining the effects of marital interactions on mood (DeLongis et al., 2004), negative interactions with the spouse were associated with same-day declines in mood. However, they had a significant effect on next-day mood only when there was also a dearth of positive interactions with the spouse.

A second limitation is that the behavior in question—conflict—was not directly observed. Although we have not directly observed husbands and wives in their daily arguments, we can be fairly confident that our daily diary reports are capturing actual behavior due to the level of agreement in couples on the average frequency of their conflicts. Supplementing diary data like the ones we have used for this analysis with lab sessions (e.g., conflict discussions) will allow us to further understand and describe behavior by supplementing individual reports with objective measures like observation and psychophysiological methods. However, adequately capturing behavior is an ongoing challenge for researchers. Although it has been argued that studying what couples say about themselves is not a substitute for studying how they behave (Raush, Barry, Hertel, & Swain, 1974), studies that rely exclusively on laboratory enactments of marital conflict may be anything but natural. Combining daily diary reports of behavior with observational research may be one way to find such a balance.

The most noteworthy implication of the analyses conducted here is the support they lend to the call to move beyond a focus on the typical person and to allow for a closer examination of the heterogeneity across persons. In following people across time using daily diary methods, we can study the person in a variety of naturally occurring contexts, examining how their behavior changes from day to day and from situation to situation. With new methods of data collection and analysis that allow this broader view, social psychologists are better able to ground their theories in the realities of daily behavior.

APPENDIX

This data set, based on the sample of 150 couples and 28 days, was structured such that variables from each daily report for each partner were placed on a separate data line, giving a maximum of $2 \times 42 = 84$ observations for each couple. The data set also contained two dummy variables, husband (coded 1 when a data line came from the husband and 0 when it came from the wife), and wife (coded 1 when a data line came from the wife and 0 when it came from the husband). Laurenceau and Bolger (2005) provide more details on data organization of this type.

To model average exposure to marital conflict, we used a multilevel logistic regression model where each husband and wife had his or her own log-odds of reporting a marital conflict. The level 1 equation was:

$$\log \frac{p_{it}}{1 - p_{it}} = \beta_{hi} H_{it} + \beta_{wi} W_{it}.$$

The log odds for husband in couple i, β_{hi}, and wife in couple i, β_{wi}, were assumed to vary across individuals, and this variation was assumed to be normally distributed with mean

$$\begin{bmatrix} \gamma_h \\ \gamma_w \end{bmatrix}$$

and covariance matrix

$$\begin{bmatrix} \tau_h^2 & \tau_{hw} \\ \tau_{wh} & \tau_w^2 \end{bmatrix},$$

where τ_h^2 is the variance of γ_h, τ_w^2 is the variance of γ_w, and $\tau_{hw} = \tau_{wh}$ is the covariance between husband and wife log-odds.

Using the data structure described above, this model can be estimated using the NLMIXED procedure in SAS (SAS Institute, 2002). The key SAS commands required are shown below.

```
PROC NLMIXED DATA = diarydataset;
b0h = g0h + u0h;
b0w = g0w + u0w;
eta = b0h*husband + b0w*wife;
p = 1/(1+ EXP(-eta));
MODEL conflict~BINARY(p);
```

RANDOM u0h u0w ~ NORMAL([0,0],[s2uh,chw,s2uw])
    subject = coupleid;
    PARMS g0h = −3 g0w = −3 s2uh = 1 chw = .9 s2uw = 1;

To model reactivity to conflict in the same data set, we used the following multilevel model

$$Y_{it} = \beta_{hi}H_{it} + \beta_{wi}W_{it} + \beta_{chi}CH_{it} + \beta_{cwi}CW_{it} + \epsilon_{it}.$$

We assume that the four βs are normally distributed with mean vector

$$\begin{bmatrix} \gamma_h \\ \gamma_w \\ \gamma_{ch} \\ \gamma_{cw} \end{bmatrix}$$

and covariance matrix

$$\begin{bmatrix} \tau_h^2 & \tau_{hw} & \tau_{hch} & \tau_{hcw} \\ \tau_{wh} & \tau_w^2 & \tau_{wch} & \tau_{wcw} \\ \tau_{chh} & \tau_{chw} & \tau_{ch}^2 & \tau_{chcw} \\ \tau_{cwh} & \tau_{cww} & \tau_{cwch} & \tau_{cw}^2 \end{bmatrix},$$

Given that there are a maximum of 84 observations per couple, there are also a maximum of 84 observed values for ϵ_{it}. We assume that these are normally distributed with a mean of 0 and an 84 × 84 covariance matrix that is a Kroneker product of (i) a 2 × 2 covariance matrix representing variances and covariances of husband and wife scores on an given day and a 42 × 42 covariance matrix for across time dependencies. We assume the latter to have an AR(1) structure. The error specification, therefore, is

$$\begin{bmatrix} \sigma_h^2 & \sigma_{hw} \\ \sigma_{wh} & \sigma_w^2 \end{bmatrix}_{2\times 2} \otimes \begin{bmatrix} 1 & \rho & \rho^2 & \cdots & \rho^{41} & \rho^{42} \\ \rho & 1 & \rho & \ddots & & \rho^{41} \\ \rho^2 & \rho & 1 & \ddots & \ddots & \vdots \\ \vdots & \ddots & \ddots & \ddots & \rho & \rho^2 \\ \rho^{41} & & \ddots & \rho & 1 & \rho \\ \rho^{42} & \rho^{41} & \cdots & \rho^2 & \rho & 1 \end{bmatrix}_{42\times 42}.$$

See Bolger and Shrout (2007) for more details on this approach to modeling dyadic data.

The model can be estimated using the MIXED procedure in SAS (SAS Institute, 2002). The key commands required are:

PROC MIXED data = diarydataset covtest;
CLASS coupleid sex diary_day;

MODEL distress = husband wife conflict*husband conflict
  *wife /noint solution;
RANDOM husband wife conflict*husband conflict
  *wife /subject = coupleid type = un s g gcorr;
REPEATED sex diary_day /subject = coupleid type = un@ar(1);

REFERENCES

Barrett, L. F. (1997). The relationship among momentary emotional experiences, personality descriptions, and retrospective ratings of emotion. *Personality and Social Psychology Bulletin, 23,* 1100-1110.

Bolger, N., Davis, A., & Rafaeli, E. (2003). Diary methods. *Annual Review of Psychology, 54,* 579–616.

Bolger, N., DeLongis, A., Kessler, R. C., & Schilling, E. A. (1989). Effects of daily stress on negative mood. *Journal of Personality and Social Psychology, 57,* 808–818.

Bolger, N., & Kelleher, S. (1993). Daily life in relationships. In S. W. Duck (Ed.), *Social context and relationships.* Newbury Park, CA: Sage.

Bolger, N., & Schilling, E. A. (1991). Personality and the problems of everyday life: The role of neuroticism in exposure and reactivity to daily stressors. *Journal of Personality, 59,* 355–386.

Bolger, N., & Shrout, P. E. (2007). Accounting for statistical dependency in longitudinal data on dyads. In T. D. Little, J. A. Bovaird, & N. A. Card (Eds.), *Modeling contextual effects in longitudinal studies* (pp. 285–298). Mahwah, NJ: Erlbaum.

Burman, B., & Margolin, G. (1992). Analysis of the association between marital relationships and health problems: An interactional perspective. *Psychological Bulletin, 112,* 39–63.

Christensen, A., & Heavey, C. L. (1990). Gender and social structure in the demand/withdraw pattern of marital conflict. *Journal of Personality and Social Psychology, 59,* 73–81.

DeLongis, A., Capreol, M. J., Holtzman, S., O'Brien, T. B., & Campbell, J. (2004). Social support and social strain among husbands and wives: A multilevel analysis, *Journal of Family Psychology, 18,* 470–479.

DeLongis, A., Hemphill, K. J., & Lehman, D. R. (1992). A structured diary methodology for the study of daily events. In F. B. Bryant, J. Edwards, L. Heath, E. J. Posanac, & R. S. Tinsdale (Eds.), *Methodological issues in applied social psychology* (pp. 83–109). New York: Plenum Press.

Derogatis, L. R. (1975). *Affects balance scale.* Baltimore, MD: Clinical Psychometrics Research Unit.

Ewart, C. K., Taylor, C. B., Kraemer, H. C., & Agras, W. S. (1991). High blood pressure and marital discord: Not being nasty matters more than being nice. *Health Psychology, 10,* 155–163.

Fincham, F. (2003). Marital conflict: Correlates, structure, and context. *Current Directions in Psychological Science, 12,* 23–27.

Gable, S. L., Reis, H. T., & Downey, G. (2003). He said, she said: A quasi-signal detection analysis of spouses' perceptions of everyday interactions. *Psychological Science, 14,* 100–105.

Glaser, R., & Kiecolt-Glaser, J. K. (1994). Stress-associated immune modulation and its implications for reactivation of latent herpesviruses. In R. Glaser, & Jones, J. (Ed.), *Human Herpesvirus Infections* (pp. 245–270). New York: Dekkar.

Gottman, J. M., & Levenson, R. W. (1999). Rebound from marital conflict and divorce prediction. *Family Process, 38,* 287–292.

Hooley, J. M., & Teasdale, J. D. (1989). Predictors of relapse in unipolar depressives: Expressed emotion, marital distress, and perceived criticism. *Journal of Abnormal Psychology, 98,* 229–235.

Huston, T. L., Caughlin, J. P., Houts, R. M., Smith, S. E., & George, L. J. (2001). The connubial crucible: Newlywed years as predictors of marital delight, distress, and divorce. *Journal of Personality and Social Psychology, 80,* 281–293.

Jacobson, N. S., & Moore, D. (1981). Spouses as observers of events in their relationships. *Journal of Consulting and Clinical Psychology, 49,* 269–277.

Johnson, D. R., White, L. K., Edwards, J. N., & Booth, A. (1986). Dimensions of marital quality: Toward methodological and conceptual refinement. *Journal of Family Issues, 7,* 31–49.

Joiner, T. E., Jr., & Katz, J. (1999). Contagion of depressive symptoms and mood: Meta-analytic review and explanations from cognitive, behavioral, and interpersonal viewpoints. *Clinical Psychology: Science and Practice, 6,* 149–164.

Keefe F. J., & Porter, L. (2007). Pain catastrophizing in the context of satisfaction with spousal responses: New perspectives and new opportunities. *Pain, 131,* 1–2.

Kiecolt-Glaser, J. K., Glaser, R., Cacioppo, J. T., MacCallum, R. C., Snydersmith, M., Kim, C., et al. (1997). Marital conflict in older adults: Endocrinological and immunological correlates. *Psychosomatic Medicine, 59,* 339–349.

Kiecolt-Glaser, J. K., & Newton, T. L. (2001). Marriage and health: His and hers. *Psychological Bulletin, 127,* 472–503.

Lam, M., Lehman, A. J., Puterman, E., & DeLongis, A. (in press). Spouse depression and disease course among persons living with rheumatoid arthritis. *Arthritis Care & Research.*

Laurenceau, J. P., & Bolger, N. (2005). Using diary methods to study marital and family processes. *Journal of Family Psychology, 19,* 86–97.

Littell, R. C., Milliken, G. A., Stroup, W. W., Wolfinger, R. D., & Schabenberger, O. (2006). *SAS for mixed models* (2nd ed.). Cary, NC: SAS Institute.

Malarkey, W. B., Kiecolt-Glaser, J. K., Pearl, D., & Glaser, R. (1994). Hostile behavior during marital conflict affects pituitary and adrenal hormones. *Psychosomatic Medicine, 56,* 41–51.

Mathews, C. A., & Reus, V. I. (2001). Assortative mating in the affective disorders: A systematic review and meta-analysis. *Comparative Psychiatry, 42,* 257–262.

Maes, H. H. M., Neale, M. C., Kendler, K. S., Hewitt, J. K., Silberg, J. L., Foley, D. L., et al. (1998). Assortative mating for major psychiatric diagnoses in two population-based samples. *Psychological Medicine, 28,* 1389–1401.

McGonagle, K. A., Kessler, R. C., & Schilling, E. A. (1992). The frequency and determinants of marital disagreements in a community sample. *Journal of Social and Personal Relationships, 9,* 507–524.

McNulty, J. K., O'Mara, E. M., & Karney, B. R. (2008). Benevolent cognitions as a strategy of relationship maintenance: "Don't sweat the small stuff". . . . But it is not all small stuff. *Journal of Personality and Social Psychology, 94,* 631–646.

Mirowsky, J., & Ross, C. E. (1995). Sex differences in distress: Real or artifact? *American Sociological Review, 60,* 449–468.

Nunnally, J. C., & Bernstein, I. H. (1994). *Psychometric theory* (3rd ed.). New York: McGraw-Hill.

Paykel, E. S., Myers, J. K., & Dienelt, M. (1969). Life-events and depression. *Archives of General Psychiatry, 31,* 753–760.

Raush, H. L., Barry, W. A., Hertel, R. K., & Swain, M. A. (1974). *Communication, conflict, and marriage.* San Francisco: Jossey-Bass.

Repetti, R. L., Taylor, S. E., & Seeman, T. E. (2002). Risky families: Family social environment and the mental and physical health of offspring. *Psychological Bulletin, 128,* 330–366.

SAS Institute. (2002). *SAS 9.1.3 help and documentation.* Cary, NC: Author.

Schwarz, N. (1999). Self-reports: How the questions shape the answers. *American Psychologist, 54,* 93–105.

Stone, A. A., Shiffman, S. S., & DeVries, M. W. (1999). Ecological momentary assessment. In D. Kahneman, E. Diener, & N. Schwarz (Eds.), *Well being: The foundations of hedonic psychology* (pp. 26 –39). New York: Russell Sage Foundation.

Sullaway, M., & Christensen, A. (1983). Assessment of dysfunctional interaction patterns in couples. *Journal of Marriage and the Family, 45,* 653–660.

Tennen, H., Affleck, G., Coyne, J.C., Larsen, R.J., & DeLongis, A. (2006). Paper and plastic in daily diary research: Comment on Green, Rafaeli, Bolger, Shrout, and Reis (2006). *Psychological Methods, 11,* 112-118.

Thomas, D. L., & Diener, E. (1990). Memory accuracy in the recall of emotions. *Journal of Personality and Social Psychology, 59,* 291-297.

Troxel, W. M., & Matthews, K. A. (2004). What are the costs of marital conflict and dissolution to children's physical health? *Clinical Child and Family Psychology Review, 7,* 29–57.

Tugade, M. M., Conner, T. & Barrett, L. F. (2007). Assessment of mood. Chapter to appear in S. Ayers, A. Baum, C. McManus, S. Newman, K. Wallston, J. Weinman, and R. West (Eds.), *The Cambridge Handbook of Psychology, Health, and Medicine (2nd Edition).* Cambridge UK: Cambridge UP.

20 Communication, Coordinated Action, and Focal Points in Groups: From Dating Couples to Emergency Responders

Andrea B. Hollingshead

What do dating couples, families, emergency responders (police, firefighters, and emergency medical technicians), project teams, and guilds in the popular multiplayer online game World of Warcraft have in common? For one, members of these groups have both individual and collective tasks to perform. To perform them successfully, members must coordinate their knowledge, their resources, and their actions. Effective coordination may require all individuals to take the same action, for example, finding a meeting place when family members get separated from one another at a museum. Other times, effective coordination may require members to take different actions such as police securing the perimeter of a burning building while firefighters search for victims inside. In each of these situations, group members need to be on the same page (i.e., be in cognitive synchrony) to accomplish their collective goal. In some cases, members must coordinate without visual access or otherwise being able to communicate with other members.

COORDINATED ACTION, COGNITIVE SYNCHRONY, AND COMMUNICATION

This chapter investigates the relations between coordinated action, cognitive synchrony, and communication. *Coordinated action* is "the regulation of diverse elements into an integrated and harmonious operation"

(*The Free Dictionary*, 2008; http://www.thefreedictionary.com/.) The "diverse elements" are interdependent individuals working toward a collective goal that involves taking some sort of action. Thus, each individual's actions affect their own outcomes and the outcomes of the other group members (Kelley & Thibaut, 1978.)

Synchrony is the concurrency of events in time (*Webster's Revised Unabridged Dictionary*, 1996.) *Cognitive synchrony* refers to "being in synch" or "on the same page" about what others are thinking. Individuals do not have to be thinking about the same things in the same way at the same time (although they might be) to have cognitive synchrony, but they do need to have a shared and accurate representation of what they are thinking relative to others in the group. To my knowledge, the term *cognitive synchrony* has not been used previously in the literature. I am using it here as an umbrella term for related concepts that address its different facets, precursors, processes, and consequences. Researchers have examined other types of synchrony among individuals: behavioral, emotional, and physiological, and it is helpful to have an analogous term to describe cognitive processes.[1] Although it is beyond the scope of this chapter, future research should address the interrelations between these different systems (cf. Levenson & Ruef, 1997).

Much research investigates different aspects of cognitive synchrony: expectations, knowledge content, knowledge structures, and processes (see also: socially shared cognition, Resnick, Levine, & Teasley, 1996.) With regard to expectations, *convergent expectations* occur when members have similar predictions about how others will behave (Schelling, 1960). Relevant research on the knowledge content includes: *habitual routines* (Gersick & Hackman, 1990), *shared mental models* (Klimoski & Mohammed, 1994)), *perspective taking* (Krauss & Fussell, 1991) and *group norms* (Feldman, 1984.) With regard to knowledge structures, *transactive memory*, a group level memory system that often develops in close relationships and groups has two components: (1) an organized store of knowledge contained entirely in the individual systems of group members, and (2) a set of knowledge-relevant transactive encoding, storage, and retrieval processes that occur among group members (Wegner Guiliano, & Hertel, 1985). And finally about processes: *tacit coordination* is coordination among individuals that occurs based on unspoken expectations or intentions, whereas *explicit coordination* occurs based on verbal agreements or formally adopted plans that designate who is to do what and how they should do it (Wittenbaum, Vaughan, & Stasser, 1998). *Grounding* is the process by which people establish mutual knowledge, mutual beliefs, and mutual expectations through communication, which they use for coordinating actions (Clark & Brennan, 1991).

Communication is the process by which information is exchanged between individuals through a common system of symbols, signs, or behavior (*Merriam-Webster Online Dictionary*, 2008; http://www. merriam-webster.com/.) Communication can be intentional or unintentional, occur through a variety of channels, including verbal, nonverbal, paralanguage, text, or tactile, and through direct and indirect means, for example, by a third party. It can involve the imposition of a set of procedures on a group in a top-down fashion such as the structure that a manager might provide to project team, or it can involve free-flowing discussion.

This volume is about the role of behavior in social psychology. I define behavior as observable reactions of individuals to their external, social, and internal environments. In this case both communication and coordinated action would qualify as behaviors.

Communication is perhaps the most important social behavior in which humans engage. It is the medium by which people express how they see the world, how they want it to be, and how they convince others to share their worldview. It is the means by which people create, maintain, and end relationships; display their thoughts, feelings, and intentions; and learn of their social standing relative to others. Although communication is implicated in almost every aspect of social behavior, it generally is not the first thing that comes to mind when one thinks about behavior in social psychology.

There may be many reasons for the relative lack of focus on communication by social psychologists. Communication is very difficult and time consuming to study. It is multifaceted and has verbal, paraverbal, and nonverbal components. Communication is hard to operationalize and measure as it serves many different functions in social settings from emotional expression to persuasion to collective information processing to conflict resolution. Many individual differences exist regarding how people communicate their thoughts, feelings, and their goals (and research shows that people are not very accurate at interpreting the communicated thoughts, feelings, and goals of others). Often researchers who initially set out to study communication do not observe a consistent relation between communication processes and behavior. This may in part be due to equifinality as there can be many different communication paths leading to the same behavior or outcome. For example, some groups may experience severe conflict and produce outstanding work because the most capable member stepped in and saved the day whereas other groups can be highly committed to their task, participate equally, and get along wonderfully but produce a mediocre product because no members had the requisite skills and abilities to perform the task.

This discussion leads me to the cartoon "Then a Miracle Occurs" by Sidney Harris, which all contributors to this volume were asked to interpret by the editors. As can be seen in the cartoon, two scientists are discussing some sort of mathematical proof or equation—they have the first initial step and the third final step but have not figured out the second intermediary step. So in place of the second step, the scientists have inserted the words "Then a miracle occurs." My interpretation is that most social psychologists would agree that communication is a social behavior and influences many other social behaviors, yet we do not know much about how that happens. Although social psychologists generally measure psychological states and some sort of behavior (broadly defined), very few studies explicitly measure the social processes that connect psychological states to overt behaviors, which often unfold through communication. Thus, I view communication as the intermediary "then a miracle occurred" step linking psychological states to social behaviors in many social psychological theories and studies.

Although communication can perform many different functions in social settings, the research program that I describe in this chapter examines the coordination function of communication. The central research questions are: What is the role of communication in coordinated action? When is communication essential, when is it beneficial, and when is it detrimental to coordinated action? And how might cognitive synchrony mediate the relation between the need for communication and coordinated action? I begin by posing these questions to a set of simple coordination problems, and then I present data from a research program that examines these questions empirically in increasing complexity beginning in the lab with dating couples and ending in the field with emergency responders.

Four Coordination Problems

The fundamental processes underlying collective action can be abstracted, simplified, and modeled as coordination problems. I begin by describing four coordination problems, each of which requires individuals to coordinate their actions to accomplish a collective goal. The first two are what Abele and Stasser (2008) call "matching" coordination problems: they require all individuals to engage in the same action simultaneously. The second two are "mismatching" coordination problems: they require individuals to engage in different actions simultaneously (Abele & Stasser, 2008).

Coordination Problem 1. Suppose that 100 strangers are in a room and are shown the five numbers as depicted in Figure 20.1a. They are told by a facilitator that if all 100 individuals choose the same number, they will

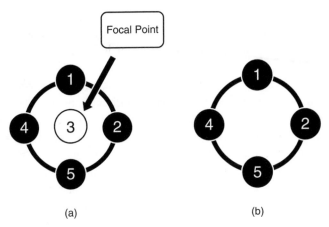

Figure 20.1. Focal Point Example.

each receive a prize. If any individual chooses a different number then no one will receive a prize. The catch is that they cannot communicate before making their choice.

I've run a similar exercise many times in my classes, and not surprisingly, all students choose the number "3". Not only is "3" is located at the center of the figure, but it is different color, and it is obvious that others would reach the same conclusion. Thus, "3" serves as what Schelling (1960) called a focal point. Mutual recognition of the focal point enables individuals to tacitly coordinate their expectations of what others will do (Schelling, 1960, p. 54). Thus, communication is not necessary for the group to figure out the solution.

Now consider a similar coordination problem with a few modifications.

Coordination Problem 2. Many aspects are kept the same (everyone must choose the same number, no communication, same prize); however, in this problem, the number of individuals in the room is reduced from 100 to only five individuals, and the number of decision alternatives is reduced from five to four, as depicted in Figure 20.1b. Rather than becoming an easier task with the reduction in the number of individuals and alternatives, the coordination task becomes much more difficult. There is no longer a focal point, so individuals are unable to coordinate their actions and reach a common solution. In this situation, communication is essential to ensure they are on the same page before making their choice.

Coordination Problem 3. A group of five individuals is given the five numbers as depicted in 1a. However, instead of instructing all individuals to choose the same number, the facilitator asks them each to choose a different number, again without communication. Like Coordination Problem 2, this problem does not have a focal point, and communication is essential in this situation for effective coordination.

Coordination Problem 4. This problem is the same as Problem 3 (five members must each choose a different number in Figure 20.1a without communication) with one additional element. Before the five individuals enter the room, each individual is given a T-shirt to wear with a different number from 1–5 displayed in the same font, colors, and exact style as in 1a. In this situation, the correspondence between the number on each T-shirt and in Figure 20.1a serves as a focal point, and the individuals are able to coordinate their actions by choosing the number depicted on each of their shirts.

In summary, when there is a focal point, group members are able to coordinate their actions successfully without communication. When there is no focal point, group members need to communicate to coordinate their actions. Figure 20.2 outlines the relations between focal points, cognitive synchrony, communication, and collective action based on these four problems. In the next section, I discuss the qualities and types of focal points involved in coordinated action.

Focal Points

Focal points tend to have two characteristics: prominence and uniqueness (Schelling, 1960). Focal points can be based on attributes of the people, situation, or norm and conventions. Of course, what is prominent or conspicuous depends upon the people, the time, and the place.

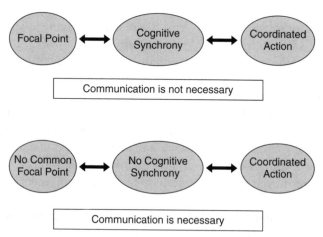

Figure 20.2. Communication, Focal Points and Coordinated Action.

In matching problems, focal points highlight what is most similar among individuals whereas focal points in mismatching problems highlight what is most different. Cultural norms and conventions can serve as focal points and enable people to coordinate their actions, for example, crossing a crowded street, driving in traffic, standing in an elevator, having a discussion, and so on (cf. Schelling, 1960). People who know one another well often develop their own conventions that become focal points when members have to coordinate their actions (cf. Hollingshead, 1998b). These conventions, when successful, can spread to other groups. For example, many large families in the United States have adopted the convention of the first person to say "shot gun" to determine who will sit in the front seat with the driver. This works well when family members are within hearing distance of one another and less well when they are not. Unexpected events can also serve as focal points and rallying points for groups. For example, a fire alarm provides a signal to team members that they should immediately end their meeting and leave the building.

In mismatching problems, characteristics of how people differ from one another may serve as focal points. Group member roles and stereotypes can serve as focal points. For example, in a patient advocacy team, members may look to the physician on the team when questions about a patient's medical condition arise. It is important to keep in mind that prominence and salience are features of the social context. For example, dimensions of demographic diversity (such as one's gender, race, or age) may be less likely to serve as focal points in highly diverse than in moderately diverse groups (Lau & Murnighan, 1998).

Most of the studies that I will describe in this chapter involve mismatching coordination problems (Abele & Stasser, 2008) such as Coordination Problems 3 and 4 above. That is, the collective task involves a division of labor, and members must perform different rather than similar actions to successfully achieve their group goal. For example, life partners often divide responsibility for household tasks, and work groups often assign members to different subtasks on team projects. In the first set of studies, I and some of my colleagues explore when and how social stereotypes can serve as focal points for coordination among newly formed groups and their cognitive and affective consequences.

Social Stereotypes as Focal Points

We examined diversity as a social context in a series of laboratory studies among newly formed dyads that had to coordinate their actions while working on a knowledge-pooling task. Members of new groups are likely to form initial impressions on the basis of group members' outstanding physical characteristics (Fiske & Newberg, 1990). We hypothesized that social stereotypes about relative knowledge would serve as a focal point in diverse dyads. (In all of the studies, the dimension underlying the dyad's similarity or diversity was made salient to participants.) This should give diverse dyads a performance advantage over similar dyads when they are not able to communicate as they work together.

For example, a group member of White European descent may judge a member of Asian descent to be more knowledgeable in math based on a cultural stereotype about Asians and expect the Asian member to perform the math-related tasks in the group. The Asian member may also think she is better able to perform math-related tasks than the white member based on the same cultural stereotype and, as a result, may expect to be assigned the math-related tasks in the group. Thus, group members are in cognitive synchrony that the Asian member will perform math-related tasks. This can happen regardless of whether the Asian member actually knows more about math than other group members, and without communication. We also tested a similar hypothesis about the role of experience in the creation of a focal point. We expected that dating couples would be able to coordinate their actions better than strangers without communication and would use their perceptions of each person's relative expertise as a focal point. (This hypothesis was also consistent with transactive memory theory, cf. Wegner et al, 1991.)

In contrast, communication should enable similar dyads to develop their own conventions and to coordinate their actions more effectively than when they cannot communicate. Thus, communication should enhance the performance of similar dyads more than diverse dyads. See Figure 20.3. And similarly, communication should enhance the

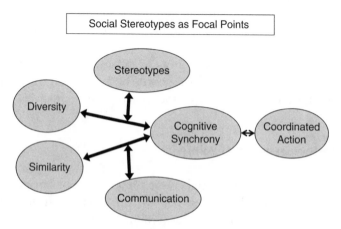

Figure 20.3. Social Stereotypes as Focal Points.

performance of strangers relatively more than dating couples. Strangers can use communication to create a common focal point regarding who will do what, which should lead to a significant performance improvement for strangers relative to their noncommunicating counterparts. In contrast, because dating couples already have a focal point—their previous knowledge of each person's relative expertise, communication should serve to reinforce their knowledge of each person's expertise and should impact performance significantly less than strangers.

We tested these hypotheses in a series of studies that examined different dimensions of diversity, which included gender (Hollingshead & Fraidin, 2003), culture (Yoon & Hollingshead, 2008), organizational role (Hollingshead, 2000), and interest diversity (Hollingshead, 2001).

All used a similar research methodology. Participants were told they would be working with another person in the study on a knowledge-pooling task and whether they would be able to interact with their partner (depending on the study and the experimental condition to which they had been assigned.) First, participants rated their own knowledge on different knowledge categories in which they would later learn information. Some knowledge categories were consistent with stereotypes; some were not. Afterward, they were "assigned" a partner, ostensibly another participant in the study. In some studies, unbeknownst to participants, participants were not assigned a real partner but instead were given the assumed partner's name (which indicated the partner's gender, culture, or organizational role depending on the study.) They were told they would be presented with information in different knowledge categories to learn and would later recall and pool it with their partner. The dyads that remembered the most information collectively received cash prizes. The main measures were the total recall of the dyad and the amount of stereotypical information recalled by individuals.

All studies showed the same effects: namely, diverse dyads coordinated their tasks and performed better on the task than similar dyads when members could not communicate. Members of diverse dyads learned and remembered significantly more stereotype-consistent information than similar dyads, signaling that they used stereotypes as a focal point to coordinate each member's actions. In the gender study, participants paired with an opposite partner were more likely to learn information consistent with their own gender stereotype than participants paired with a same-sex partner. In the culture study, participants paired with a partner from a different culture were more likely to learn information consistent with their own cultural stereotype than paired with a same-culture partner. In the organizational role study, participants were more likely to learn information related to their own functional role at the university when paired with someone with a different than with a similar functional role. And finally in the interest diversity study, participants remembered more information consistent with their own hobbies and interests when paired with someone with different than with similar hobbies and interests. All of these findings involved participants who could not communicate with their partners. Next I will describe the findings of two studies that also manipulated communication to highlight some of its benefits and costs in coordinated action.

Dating Couple and Stanger Study. Heterosexual couples that had been dating for at least 6 months participated in the study (Hollingshead, 1998). Each participant was assigned a partner, either their significant other or an opposite-sex stranger from another couple, and worked together on a knowledge-pooling task similar to the one described above.

As expected, dating couples remembered more information collectively than strangers. However, this effect was reversed when dyads could communicate: dating couples recalled less collectively than strangers. This is a counterintuitive and important finding because it suggests that, under some conditions, communication can actually impede coordination.

A closer examination of coordination strategies used by dyads revealed why dating couples performed worse in the communication than in the no-communication condition. The task used in this study was an additive task, where contributions of each member are combined into a collective group response (Steiner, 1972.) Thus, the most effective strategy for maximizing performance on the task was to divide responsibility for knowledge categories so that each member was assigned a subset of categories that they knew better than their partner. Dating couples in the no-communication category generally reported doing this in a post-task survey, but most dating couples in the communication condition did not do this. Instead, they reported using a more collaborative strategy, together creating a story, sentences, or acronyms with the information that they would not be able to recall later. This strategy was not particularly effective. They also disagreed more about who was responsible for which knowledge categories than dating couples in the no-communication condition. It appears that communication led couples to disregard or to forget about their relative expertise as an effective coordination strategy. It is important to mention that dating couples in the communication condition expressed the highest levels of enjoyment, although participants across the conditions enjoyed the experiment very much. Their coordination strategy while not as effective was more fun.

In contrast, communication facilitated the coordination of learning new information among strangers. When strangers communicated, they were able to delegate responsibility for different knowledge categories explicitly. An inspection of the self-reported learning strategies indicated that strangers were much more likely to delegate responsibility for different knowledge categories in the communication condition than in the no-communication condition. In fact, no dyads in the strangers, no-communication condition mentioned that they considered their partners at all: each individual attempted to learn all the information across all categories in every case. Although participants met their opposite-sex partner very briefly at the beginning of the experiment, they did not use stereotypes based on their partner's gender or another observable characteristic as a focal point. This finding supports the caveat described earlier in the chapter: that a stereotype must be salient and that groups members must be aware that it is salient to others before it will be used as a focal point.

Culture and Communication Study. The participants in this study were undergraduate students of white European and of Asian descent (Yoon & Hollingshead, 2008). Participants were randomly paired with a partner of the same gender. This was done to isolate the effects of cultural stereotypes. The knowledge pooling task was similar to the one described above. The design was a 2 × 2 factorial, manipulating dyad composition (same culture or mixed-culture dyads) and whether dyads could communicate during the knowledge area assignment phase (yes or no). All participants interacted and performed the task via computer using Instant Messenger.

The results confirmed the general hypotheses. As described earlier, culturally diverse dyads performed better than similar dyads when they could not communicate. However, the performance advantage of culturally diverse dyads was mitigated when dyads could communicate on the task. The data showed that communication served to reinforce cultural stereotypes in culturally diverse dyads rather than to lead members to uncover one another's true expertise—culturally diverse dyads learned a large amount of information consistent with cultural stereotypes regardless of the communication condition. In the communication conditions, dyads were explicitly instructed to share expertise and assign categories to the most knowledgeable member rather than simply to communicate with their partners. Although reliance on cultural stereotypes led to a performance advantage for culturally diverse dyads in the no-communication condition, it also had negative affective consequences. Participants were more satisfied and trusted their partners more when they were assigned knowledge areas consistent with their expertise rather than consistent with cultural stereotypes. The results also suggest that the mere opportunity to communicate and exchange knowledge in diverse work groups may not be an effective intervention to alleviate the effects of cultural stereotypes on coordinated action.

Summary. Taken together, these studies suggest that stereotyping may lead to a self-reinforcing cycle in diverse dyads. Stereotypes begin the cycle by serving as a focal point about who is likely to know most about different knowledge areas. This focal point leads to stereotypical task assignments, and those assignments can lead to members gaining knowledge consistent with stereotypes. That improvement in stereotypical knowledge may justify future stereotypical task assignments, since members in fact become experts in areas consistent with stereotypes even though they may not have had that expertise previously (cf. Fraidin & Hollingshead, 2005.) The findings of the culture study demonstrated how relying on focal points can also have negative affective consequences.

It is important to note several aspects of the research design that may limit the generalizability of these findings. The laboratory setting controlled many features of the context, which certainly could have contributed to the salience of stereotypes as a focal point. Demographic differences other than the one of interest in the study were held constant among participants to isolate the influence of stereotypes on individual perceptions and performance. Although this type of procedure is common in the social stereotyping literature, real-life work groups are likely to have diversity across multiple categories, and multiple stereotypes may operate simultaneously or differentially across group members. The unit of analysis was the dyad, and it is important to examine how these findings might scale in larger groups. Finally, the coordinated action of interest in this set of studies involved cognitive, but not physical, action. Some of these limitations were addressed in a preliminary study of communication and coordination among emergency responders, which will be described next.

MOVING INTO THE FIELD: COMMUNICATION AND COORDINATED ACTION AMONG EMERGENCY RESPONDERS

Coordinated action becomes much more difficult in the field, especially in the case of emergency responders. The 9–11 Commission Report (available at: http://www.911commission.gov) detailed communication, information sharing, and other coordination problems experienced within and between emergency response agencies (fire department, police department, Port Authority police, and the Office of Emergency Management and Interagency Preparedness). While many problems seemed to be the fault of obsolete and faulty technology (e.g., issues with the on-site repeater system, problems with radio equipment and/or channels), others were the result of coordination difficulties across the various agencies involved in the emergency response.

Emergency responders face many challenges to coordinated action. In most U.S. states, there are no formal coordination mechanisms such as common databases or communication systems between the different agencies (although that seems to be changing.) Emergency responders operate in a stressful and often very dangerous environment during emergencies, which can impair information processing and decision-making abilities (Keinan, 1987). Emergency responders have different roles, goals, and information needs in emergency situations. Police secure the area. Fire fighters put out fires and rescue trapped victims. Emergency medical technicians stabilize hurt victims. The cultures of emergency responder groups are also different. For example, firefighters have a communal culture that is built on camaraderie and trust. They spend many hours eating, talking, training, and otherwise passing the time between calls while on duty at the firehouse. During emergencies, they rely on one another for their lives. Police, on the other hand, have a culture that emphasizes security and protection—sharing information and trusting people who are outside their immediate group is not part of their culture. Common focal points do not seem to exist across the various emergency responder agencies given their different goals, cultures, and practices. As a result, effective communication is essential for effective coordination.

As part of a large interdisciplinary project supported by the National Science Foundation (NSF: ITR-0427089), we are working to gain a better understanding of coordination barriers from the perspective of emergency responders themselves. We believe this knowledge will better inform the design of training programs, policies, procedures, and technologies to facilitate information sharing and coordination during emergencies.

Our approach is informed by theory and research on transactive memory (e.g. Brandon & Hollingshead, 2004). A transactive memory system is a group level memory system that often develops in close relationships, work teams, and other groups with interdependent members. It involves the division of responsibility among group members with respect to the encoding, storage, retrieval, and communication of information from different knowledge areas, and a shared awareness among group members about each member's knowledge responsibilities (or "who knows what") (Hollingshead, in press). In transactive memory systems, this shared awareness of "who knows what" serves as a focal point enabling individuals to coordinate "who will do what" often without communication. Of course, these systems are not perfect and errors can and do occur (Hollingshead, 2005).

Research on transactive memory shows that when group members have accurate and shared views of one another's knowledge and responsibilities, they coordinate information better, perform tasks more effectively, and trust one another more. Thus, our research strategy was to compare participants' perceptions of their own expertise and responsibilities during disasters, and their perceptions of the expertise and responsibilities of other responder groups (firefighters from their department, firefighters from other departments, local police, state police, emergency medical technicians, civil engineers). We also asked about the coordination barriers that responders experienced during emergencies and examined the relations between communication, coordination, and trust among the different groups.

We conducted online surveys with 95 firefighters across the state of Illinois who participated in the annual Fire College of the Illinois Fire Service Institute in Champaign, Illinois in June 2005 (Jacobsohn, Beck, & Hollingshead, 2007.) Most firefighters in our sample were male (94%), young (mean age 32), and worked in small communities (80% lived in towns with a population under 25,000). About 40% had leadership experience as head of incident command (the highest ranking firefighter arriving first on the scene takes charge of coordinating and managing the response). It is also important to note that relatively few emergencies to which the firefighters in our sample responded were fires—only 8% on average. (Most were in fact false alarms and medical emergencies.)

The results showed that firefighters experienced environmental and technological coordination barriers more often than intergroup and interpersonal barriers during emergencies. More specifically, difficulty seeing due to smoke, hearing due to environmental noise and equipment, and quality of radio communications were mentioned most frequently. Interpersonal barriers, such as problems with the chain of command, ineffective procedures, working with incompetent people, and not knowing the location and activities of other members were also viewed as barriers but were less frequently mentioned.

We also discovered that the amount that firefighters communicated with other responder groups during emergencies was positively related to trust. Figure 20.4 shows the positive correlation between communication and trust among different responder groups (7-point scale: 1 = low; 7 = high.) Firefighters reported more communication with fellow firefighters and EMTs than with police. They also reported having greater trust in the information received from fellow firefighters and EMTs than with police and civil engineers. Thus, the degree of previous contact may

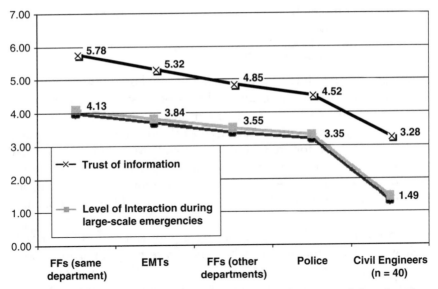

Figure 20.4. Relations between Communication and Trust in Firefighter Sample.

have had a bigger impact on trust than role similarity, as evidenced by a quote from a firefighter:

> Firefighter A: "We work with our local EMTs enough to know what they ask for, what they really need. They have always given us enough information for us to do our job, and to help them get their job done."

Unfortunately, the sentiments reported in the quote above were not the norm in our sample. A more common finding was that firefighters did not feel that responders from other agencies had a good understanding of their responsibilities, task requirements, and information needs during emergencies. They, in turn, did not feel they had a good understanding of the knowledge, task requirements, and responsibilities of the other responder groups. Participants indicated that this lack of experience with and knowledge of the other groups had an impact on the degree to which they trusted the information given by members of these agencies during emergencies. In fact some of the firefighters in our sample reported distrust in their relationships with police officers:

> Firefighter B: "We don't know what information they need, 'cause we do not understand their job. We do not train in their manner and what they do is foreign to us." Firefighter C: "The police in our town don't listen very well sometimes. Their information can get mixed up and

turn out completely wrong."Firefighter D: "In past experience, some information has been withheld (by police officers) that would have been helpful to know."

Although it seems intuitive that individuals who communicate more frequently would also have higher levels of trust, it is important to consider that many emergency situations involve individuals from agencies who may not communicate frequently. Training and continuing education programs for firefighters, police, and EMTs should be designed to teach each group about the roles and responsibilities of the other groups so that they can develop shared expectations about the goals and behaviors of each group during emergencies (cf., Liang, Moreland, & Argote, 1995.) As shown in the laboratory studies on social stereotypes described earlier in the chapter, diverse groups can perform their tasks well without communication when they have a common focal point based on shared expectations about expertise. It is also important to include simulated emergencies (and social events afterward) in training and continuing education programs to give members of different groups an opportunity to build trust and relationships and to create other focal points that may depart from role-based stereotypes. As the cultural stereotype study showed, relying solely on stereotypes to assign responsibility for tasks can lead to resentment, less trust, and lower group satisfaction.

Conclusions and Future Research Directions

Now I will return to the research questions asked at the beginning of the chapter and provide a few tentative answers. It is important to keep in mind that all studies presented in this chapter concerned mismatching problems (Abele & Stasser, 2008), the collective task involved a division of labor, and members had to perform different rather than similar actions to successfully achieve their group goal. Taken together, the studies showed that stereotypes and member roles can serve as focal points in diverse groups when members are not able to communicate as they perform their collective task.

The first question was: *What is the role of communication in coordinated action?*

On a cognitive level, communication can create, change, or reinforce cognitive synchrony. One consistent finding across experiments was that similar groups need communication to create cognitive synchrony and to coordinate their actions effectively. With respect to change, in the dating couple study, dating couples in the no-communication condition tended to use perceptions of each person's relative expertise as a focal point. In the communication condition, dating couples appeared to abandon this natural focal point and instead created a shared mnemonic for remembering task-relevant information. In contrast, communication tended to reinforce cognitive synchrony in the cultural stereotypes study. Culturally diverse dyads tended to use cultural stereotypes to assign responsibility to each member in both the no-communication and communication conditions.

On an emotional level, direct interpersonal communication can increase trust. As the firefighter study showed, interpersonal communication with other responder groups was positively associated with trust of those groups. But it can also lead to negative reactions as shown in the cultural stereotypes study when communication reinforces cultural stereotypes rather than promotes increased understanding of members' unique attributes and skills.

The second question was: *When is communication beneficial?*

The studies showed that communication is most beneficial to groups when there is no focal point, in the case of similar groups, or when subgroups have different goals, as in the case of the emergency responders. Communication enables groups to learn about one another and to establish conventions so they are better able to coordinate their actions. Although not the focus of these studies, communication is also likely to help groups correct misunderstandings and reduce the future likelihood of errors of omission and commission as members can confirm whether they are actually on the same page about each member's responsibilities.

The third and final question was: *When is communication detrimental?*

Communication can be detrimental when it interferes with preexisting modes of coordination that are effective as was shown in the dating couples study. It can also be harmful to relationships when it reinforces rather than reduces the negative influences of social stereotypes, as shown in the cultural stereotypes study.

Future Directions

There are many related topics ripe for future research. Some of the most exciting are in the area of technology and coordination. For example, there are many online contexts that relate to work, political action, social networking, and entertainment where members must coordinate to achieve individual and collective goals. One example is the popular multiplayer online game World of Warcraft. Players self-organize into guilds, in which players complete missions as a team. Players are able to choose the gender and race of their avatar. Different races have different attributes and abilities. This is a fascinating context in which to study the interplay of stereotypes and conventions in the creation of focal points by groups.

Another is technology as an intervention. As described earlier, emergency responders experience technological, cultural, and interpersonal barriers that impede their ability to coordinate their actions within and between agencies during emergencies. The preliminary results of the firefighter study suggested that a lack of direct interpersonal communication between different responder groups was positively associated with coordination problems experienced during emergencies. It may be possible to develop technologies that could bypass the need for interpersonal communication to facilitate coordination among responder groups. For example, networked sensors on uniforms could transmit and receive GPS positionings of members, communicate physical conditions such as temperature and building vibrations to others, or signal members to immediately vacate their current position and gather at a prespecified meeting point.

However, communication and other information technologies can and do fail during catastrophic events when those technologies are needed most, such as in 9/11 (9–11 Commission Report) and Hurricane Katrina (Majchzrak, Javenpaa, & Hollingshead, 2007.) When technologies fail, emergency responder groups may need to go to Plan B or to improvise on the fly. It is likely that those responders who have interacted during previous emergencies will coordinate more effectively when technological support fails. Direct interpersonal communication does more for emergency responders than promote cognitive synchrony—it also serves as a conduit for developing trust and relationships that also enhance coordinated action.

AUTHOR NOTE

[1] Concepts that relate to behavioral synchrony include: *Behavioral entrainment*, the processes whereby one person's behavior is adjusted or modified to coordinate or synchronize with another's behavior (Kelly, 1988.) *Interpersonal synchrony* or coordination involves individuals coordinating movements with the rhythmic behavior or others, for example, ballroom dancing or walking while talking with friends (Richardson, Marsh, Isenhower, Goodman, & Schmidt, 2007). *Interactional synchrony* is the coordination of movements between speaker and listener in both timing and form during conversation (Bernieri & Rosenthal, 1991).

Concepts that relate to emotional synchrony include: *Spontaneous emotional mimicry*, the tendency to spontaneously mimic the emotional expression seen in another face (Achiabou Pourtois, Schwartz, & Vuilleumier,

2008.) *Emotional rapport* refers to the emotions of one person being in synch with another (Levenson & Ruef, 1997.) *Emotional contagion* is the tendency to express and feel emotions that are similar to and influenced by those of others (cf. Hatfield, Cacioppo, & Rapson, 1994.)

Research on physiological synchrony has examined the synchrony across individuals of neuroendocrine, autonomic, and somatic systems (for a review, Levenson & Ruef, 1997).

REFERENCES

Abele, S., & Stasser, G. (2008). Coordination success and interpersonal perceptions: Matching vs. mismatching. *Journal of Personality and Social Psychology, 95,* 576–592.

Achiabou, A., Pourtois, G., Schwartz, S., & Vuilleumier, P. (2009). Simultaneous recording of EEG and facial muscle reactions during spontaneous emotional mimicry. *Neuropsychologia, 46,* 1104–1113.

Bernieri, F, & Rosenthal. R. (1991). Behavior matching and interactional synchrony. In R. S. Feldman & B. Rime (Eds.) *Fundamentals of nonverbal communication* (pp. 401–422). New York: Cambridge Press.

Clark, H. H., & Brennan, S. E. (1991). Grounding in communication. In L. B. Resnick, J. M. Levine, & S. D. Teasley (Eds.), *Perspectives on socially shared cognition* (pp. 308–327). Washington, DC: American Psychological Association.

Feldman, D. C. (1984). The development and enforcement of group norms. *Academy of Management Review, 9,* 47–53.

Fiske, S. T., & Newburg, S. L. (1990). A continuum of impression formation, from category-based to individuating process: Influences of information and motivation on attention and interpretation. *Advances in Experimental Social Psychology, 23,* 1–74.

Fraidin, S. N., & Hollingshead, A. B. (2005). "I know what I'm doing": The impact of gender stereotypes about expertise on task assignments in groups. In M. Neale, E. Mannix and M. Thomas-Hunt (Eds.), *Managing Groups and Teams* (Vol. 7—Status). Greenwich, CT: JAI Press.

Gersick, C. J. and Hackman, R. J. (1990). Habitual routines in task-performing groups. *Organizational Behavior and Human Decision Processes, 47,* 65–97.

Hatfield, E., Cacioppo, J. T., & Rapson, R. L. (1994.) *Emotional contagion.* New York: Cambridge University Press.

Hollingshead, A. B. (1998a). Communication, learning and retrieval in transactive memory systems. *Journal of Experimental Social Psychology, 34,* 423–442.

Hollingshead, A. B. (1998b). Retrieval processes in transactive memory systems. *Journal of Personality and Social Psychology, 74,* 659–671.

Hollingshead, A. B. (2000). Perceptions of expertise and transactive memory in work relationships. *Group Processes and Intergroup Relations, 3,* 257–267.

Hollingshead, A. B. (2001). Cognitive interdependence and convergent expectations in transactive memory. *Journal of Personality and Social Psychology, 81,* 1080–1089.

Hollingshead, A. B. (2005, August). *Errors of transactive memory*. Presentation at the Academy of Management Meeting (Honolulu, HI). Hollingshead, A. B. (in press). Transactive memory. In J. Levine and M. Hogg (Co-Editors) (Eds.) *Encyclopedia of group processes and intergroup relations*. Thousand Oaks, CA: Sage.

Hollingshead, A. B. & Fraidin, S. N. (2003). Gender stereotypes and assumptions about expertise in transactive memory. *Journal of Experimental Social Psychology*, *39*, 355–363.

Jacobsohn, G. C., Beck, S., & Hollingshead, A. B. (2007, June). *But can I trust you? Expertise, trustworthiness, and information sharing in first responder groups during emergencies*. Presentation at In-Group (East Lansing, Michigan).

Keinan, G. (1987). Decision making under stress: Scanning of alternatives under control. *Journal of Personality and Social Psychology, 52*, 639–644.

Kelley, H. H., & Thibaut, J. W. (1978). *Interpersonal relations: A theory of interdependence*. New York: Wiley.

Kelly, J. R. (1988). Entrainment in group interaction and task performance. In J. E. McGrath (Ed.), *The social psychology of time: New perspectives* (pp. 89–110). Thousand Oaks, CA: Sage Publications.

Klimoski, R., & Mohammed, S. (1994). Team mental model: Construct or metaphor? *Journal of Management, 20*, 403–437.

Krauss, R. M., & Fussell, S. R. (1991). Perspective-taking in communication: Representations of others' knowledge in reference. *Social Cognition, 9*, 2–24.

Lau, D. C., & Murnighan, J. K. (1998). Demographic diversity and faultlines: The compositional dynamics of organizational groups. *Academy of Management Review* 23, 325–340.

Levenson, K. W., & Ruef, A. M. (1997). Physiological aspects of emotional knowledge and rapport (pp. 44–72). In W. Ickes (Ed), *Empathic accuracy*, New York: Guilford Press.

Liang, D. W., Moreland, R. L., & Argote, L. (1995). Group versus individual training and group performance: The mediating role of transactive memory. *Personality and Social Psychology Bulletin, 21*, 384–393.

Majchrzak, A., Jarvenpaa, S. L., & Hollingshead, A. B. (2007). Coordinating expertise among emergent groups responding to disasters. *Organization Science. 18*, 147–161.

National Commission on Terrorist Attacks upon the United States. (2004) *The 9–11 Commission Report*. (http://www.911commission.gov/)

Resnick, L. B., Levine, J. M., & Teasley, S. D. (Eds.) (1996). *Perspectives on socially shared cognition*. Washington, DC: American Psychological Association.

Richardson, M. J., Marsh, K. L., Isenhower, R. W., Goodman, J. R. L., & Schmidt, R. C. (2007). Rocking together: Dynamics of intentional and unintentional interpersonal coordination. *Human Movement Science, 27*, 867–891.

Schelling, T. C. (1960). *The strategy of conflict*. Cambridge: Harvard University Press.

Steiner, I. D. (1972). *Group process and productivity*. New York: Academic Press.

Wegner, D. M., Erber, R., & Raymond, P. (1991). Transactive memory in close relationships. *Journal of Personality and Social Psychology. 61*, 923–929.

Wegner, D. M., Guiliano, T., & Hertel, P. T. (1985). Cognitive interdependence in close relationships. In W. J. Ickes (Ed.), *Compatible and incompatible relationships* (pp. 253–276). New York: Springer-Verlag.

Wittenbaum, G. M., Vaughan, S. I., & Stasser, G. (1998). Coordination in task-performing groups. In R. S. Tindale et al. (Eds), *Theory and research on small groups* (pp. 177–204), New York: Plenum Press.

Yoon, K., & Hollingshead, A. B. (2008). *Cultural stereotypes and transactive memory systems.* Manuscript submitted for review.

21 Nonverbal Behavior in Social Psychology Research: The Good, the Bad, and the Ugly

Judith A. Hall

As a nonverbal behavior researcher for the past 30 years, I can take some comfort from the fact that my field is undeniably built on the study of behavior. This behavior is measured not just in laboratories but very often in naturalistic settings. Even in the laboratory, the behavior that is studied is often high on naturalism because observation is likely to be unobtrusive. Furthermore, nonverbal behavior—by which I mean both emitted behaviors and measured skills in nonverbal communication—has obvious social psychological relevance. On these points, no defenses need be made, and no soul-searching examinations of what we mean by "behavior" are required. Still, there is much to be said about the place of nonverbal behavior research in the field of social psychology, as well as about unresolved problems and difficulties.

The goal of this chapter is to give a short overview of nonverbal research within social psychology. Of course, there is far too much accumulated knowledge about nonverbal communication to attempt much of a summary. The chapter starts with definitions and moves to a description of the two main research traditions—describing behavior and measuring communication accuracy. Then it moves to the themes of "the good, the bad, and the ugly" to convey the mixture of blessings and curses that confront researchers who take on nonverbal communication as their topic.

The "And Then a Miracle Occurs" cartoon helps us to see why nonverbal communication has broad relevance within social psychology. Understanding the process by which a phenomenon unfolds—that is, identifying mediating variables—often requires consideration of nonverbal behavior. An excellent example is interpersonal expectancy effects. How does it happen that one person's expectation can produce a change in another person? Following the path of cause and effect often leads to nonverbal cues that are inadvertently conveyed by the expecter and nonconsciously received and acted on by the target (Harris & Rosenthal, 1985). Nonverbal behavior plays a ubiquitous role in mediating many social psychological phenomena, including conformity, persuasion, bystander effects, and many more. As social psychology has matured as a field, it has progressed from simply documenting phenomena to trying to understand exactly what happens in the causal stream—that is, filling in the "Step 2" in the cartoon. Nonverbal behavior has an important place there, as well as elsewhere within social psychology.

DEFINING NONVERBAL BEHAVIOR

Nonverbal cues can be defined as all potentially informative behaviors that are not purely linguistic in content. Visible nonverbal cues include facial expressions, head movements, posture, body and hand movements, self-and other-touching, leg positions and movements, interpersonal gaze, directness of interpersonal orientation, interpersonal distance, and synchrony or mimicry between people. Auditory nonverbal cues include discrete nonlinguistic vocal sounds (e.g., sighs) as well as qualities of the voice such as pitch and pitch variation, loudness, speed and speed variation, and tonal qualities (e.g., nasality, breathiness). Several additional behaviors are often included among nonverbal cues even though they are closely related to speech: interruptions, pauses and hesitations, listener responses (such as "uh-huh" uttered while another is speaking), and dysfluencies in speech. Clothing, hairstyle, and adornments, as well as physiognomy (such as height or facial features) are also typically considered to represent nonverbal information channels.

The distinction between nonverbal *behavior* and nonverbal *communication* is important (Wiener, Devoe, Rubinow, & Geller, 1972), but not easy to apply in practice. Nonverbal behavior is simply emitted and is subject to interpretation by others even if the expressor (encoder) is not trying to communicate. In contrast, nonverbal communication refers to a more conscious active process whereby encoder and decoder emit and interpret behaviors according to a shared meaning code. Making this distinction often founders on the researcher's and even the expressor's inability to know what was intended and what was not. Enactments of nonverbal behaviors are often not in the conscious awareness of either the expressor or the decoder. The unintentional conveyance of veridical information through nonverbal cues is called "leakage" (Ekman & Friesen, 1969). Because it is so difficult to identify degrees of intentionality, I use the terms nonverbal behavior and nonverbal communication interchangeably in this chapter, even though conceptually this is an important distinction.

TRADITION #1: THE STUDY OF NONVERBAL BEHAVIOR

The first of the two main research traditions involves describing nonverbal behavior. Once it is described, it can be studied with respect to its meaning (intended or perceived) and in relation to countless different person and situation variables. Nonverbal behavior is measured using naïve raters, trained coders, and instruments. There are few standardized, "off the shelf" measurement systems. Most often, researchers decide on what to measure and how to measure it based on the nature of the research question being investigated. This section can give only a very broad picture of methodology; for a more comprehensive account see Harrigan, Rosenthal, and Scherer (2005) and Rosenthal (1987).

Methodology

Naïve Raters. Sometimes naïve raters are used to measure specific cues, and when this is done it may take more raters, whose ratings are aggregated, to achieve adequate interrater reliability (see Hall, Horgan, & Carter, 2002, for an example in the case of measuring smiling). Just as with the internal consistency reliability of a set of items on a test, the reliability of a set of raters is a joint function of the average interrater correlation and how many of them there are (Rosenthal, 1987). Though untrained raters may have more random error and therefore lower interrater correlations than would be the case for trained coders, this can be compensated for by adding more untrained raters.

Though naïve raters can be used to measure specific behaviors, the most common use for naïve raters is to gather their impressions. This is done when the researcher wants to take advantage of a viewer's or listener's inferential abilities so that the measurements tap into dimensions of meaning. The use of naïve raters implies that the researcher is interested in how "ordinary" people would respond to the nonverbal stimuli, that is, to approximate nonverbal impression formation as it might take place in "real life." Such ratings occupy positions on a continuum in terms of how much inference is asked for. To give illustrations, at a low level of inference would be ratings of speed of speech or pitch (subjective renditions of objective parameters); at a somewhat more inferential level would be ratings of fidgetiness or hurriedness of behavioral style (subjective amalgamation across different cues); at a higher level of inference would be ratings of affect such as anger or happiness (translation of perceived cues into the perception of an immediate psychological state); and at an even higher level inference would be ratings of personality (translation of perceived immediate states into inferences about latent psychological characteristics). At each advancing level of inference, information from a lower level is integrated, entailing more guesswork and/or more influence of perceivers' individual characteristics. Different raters could integrate differently or apply different judgment policies. The choice of level of inference must follow from the research question. Naïve perceivers' ratings can have high validity in terms of capturing the conveyed meaning of cues, assuming of course that interrater reliability is satisfactory.

Trained Coders. When the researcher wants to describe specific cues, without an interest in how they are interpreted, the likely choice is to use coders who are trained according to standard criteria, with the goal being that they apply the criteria in a homogeneous fashion. Examples would be timing the duration of gaze at an interaction partner, counting the frequency of smiles, or calculating the angle at which two people interact. Ideally, the choice of behaviors to measure is guided by theoretical concerns; however, researchers sometimes measure an extensive catalogue of behaviors in order to be comprehensive, sometimes without clear-cut ideas about what to expect for each of them.

Many nonverbal behaviors are rather easy to measure and do not require extensive training. An exception is FACS, the Facial Action Coding System (Ekman & Rosenberg, 1997), an anatomically based system which requires the coder to identify the action and intensity of movements of the facial muscles. Extensive training is required and coders receive certification of competence. Other systems based on muscle movements also exist (Cohn & Ekman, 2005).

Instrumentation. Finally, instrumentation can be used to measure some kinds of nonverbal cues. Computers can quantify an assortment of acoustic variables, such as fundamental frequency, amplitude, and duration of silence, and these can be averaged over time or analyzed in terms of temporal contours or variability (Juslin & Scherer, 2005). Another kind of automation involves measuring facial EMG as a way to detect facial muscle activation that is not visible to the naked eye (Dimberg, Thunberg, & Grunedal, 2002). Finally, work is progressing on artificial intelligence approaches to recognition of emotion from nonverbal cues (Cohn & Ekman, 2005).

Choices About Measurement. Regardless of which of the approaches just listed is used, the researcher still faces choices and, unfortunately, often comes to realize that there is little established wisdom to guide these choices. Consider the researcher who wants to measure smiling. Should she measure overall smile frequency, smile frequency separately while listening versus speaking, rate of smiling, total smile duration, smile duration per smile, different kinds of smiles (e.g., those with eye and mouth muscles engaged versus only mouth muscles engaged; Ekman, Davidson, & Friesen, 1990), smile intensity, or overall "how much" smiling the person displayed (which could subsume frequency, duration, and intensity)? Should she measure smiling cumulatively for the recorded interaction, or should she measure smiling within successive bins (e.g., first 30 seconds, second 30 seconds, and so forth) so that temporal trends can be examined? If so, how long should the bins be? Or, should she code only samples and not the whole interaction? If so, how long should the samples be and how should they be chosen?

All too often, researchers feel that they are stabbing in the dark when making these decisions. Perhaps the field will someday be advanced enough so that answers can be found in a textbook, but probably this will not happen. And this is not entirely bad, because measurement should be guided by theory rather than by formulas or by past tradition. The design choices made by others may not be appropriate for one's own research.

Meanings and Functions of Nonverbal Behavior

Some nonverbal behaviors are discrete (i.e., have distinct on-off properties), examples being nodding, blinking, pausing, and gestural emblems (see below). Others are continuous, such as the fluid movements of the hands while speaking (called speech-dependent gestures), vocal qualities, and movement style. Nonverbal cues often accompany spoken words, and when they do the nonverbal cues can augment or contradict the meanings of the words as well as combine with the words to produce unique messages, as in sarcasm, which involves the pairing of contradictory messages through verbal and nonverbal channels. Research has explored the impact of mixed verbal and nonverbal messages (Argyle, Alkema, & Gilmour, 1971).

Some nonverbal behaviors have distinct meanings, most notably the hand gestures called emblems that have direct verbal translations (such as the "A-okay" sign or the "thumbs up" sign in North American usage)

(Morris, Collett, Marsh, & O'Shaughnessy, 1979). However, most non-verbal cues have multiple and often ambiguous meanings that are dependent on other information for correct interpretation (associated words, situational context, antecedent events, other nonverbal cues, etc.). There is, alas, no "nonverbal cue dictionary" in existence and likely there will never be one.

The face and voice have been extensively studied in terms of emotional expression, with seven or so emotions having characteristic configurations of facial muscle movements and a variety of acoustic correlates (Ekman, 1982; Laukka, Juslin, & Bresin, 2005; Scherer, Banse, & Wallbott, 2001). Nonverbal cues can also contribute to a person's emotional experience and self-regulation via physiological feedback processes; engaging in certain behaviors can produce the associated emotions (Strack, Martin, & Stepper, 1988). Although it is commonly assumed that the main function of nonverbal behavior is to convey emotions, this is only one of several important purposes served by nonverbal behavior in daily life. Nonverbal cues are used to convey interpersonal attitudes, such as dominance, affiliation, or insult (Andersen, 1985; Hall, Coats, & Smith LeBeau, 2005). Nonverbal cues of the face, eyes, voice, and hands are used in the regulation of turn taking in conversation, and also for purposes of providing feedback regarding comprehension and interest to a speaker. Face and hand movements serve dialogic functions, for example to illustrate, comment, refer, and dramatize (Bavelas & Chovil, 1997). Speech-dependent gestures also contribute to fluent speech by facilitating word retrieval; speakers lose fluency and complexity if they are constrained from gesturing while speaking (Krauss, 1998). Nonverbal cues can also reflect ongoing cognitive activity (Barroso & Freedman, 1992).

The coordination of nonverbal behavior between people helps to produce and maintain desired levels of arousal and intimacy (Argyle & Dean, 1965; Patterson, Jordan, Hogan, & Frerker, 1981). People often mimic or reciprocate others' behavior, or adapt their movements and speech style to match an interaction partner. Such behavior matching can contribute to rapport (Chartrand & Bargh, 1999). However, behavioral compensation is also a common occurrence; one person adjusts his or her behavior to compensate for another's behaviors, for example by gazing less at another, or backing up, if the other is standing too close.

Another important function of nonverbal behavior is self-presentation, that is, to represent oneself in a desired way (e.g., as smart, honest, nice, brave, or competent; DePaulo, 1992). Related to self-presentation are societal display rules, conventions regarding what kinds of expressions are appropriate at what times and by whom (Ekman, 1982). Examples are norms for how to behave nonverbally in different social situations (when disappointed, at a funeral, etc.) and norms that produce different degrees of outward emotional expressiveness in men and women. At one extreme of self-presentation is deliberate deception (DePaulo et al., 2003).

Nonverbal cues convey information, both intentionally and unintentionally, about emotions, attitudes, personality traits, intelligence, intentions, mental and physical health, physical characteristics, sociodemographic characteristics, social group membership, relationships, deception, dominance and status, and social roles, to give a few examples. Nonverbal cues play a role in social influence, as in persuasion and interpersonal expectancy effects.

TRADITION #2: NONVERBAL COMMUNICATION ACCURACY

The second major tradition in nonverbal studies, one that originated early in the 20th century, concerns the accurate expression and judgment of nonverbal cues. Individuals and groups differ in the accuracy with which they convey information via nonverbal cues (called encoding, expression, or sending accuracy) and interpret others' nonverbal cues (called decoding or receiving accuracy, or nonverbal sensitivity).

Encoding Accuracy

Researchers measure encoding accuracy using several different paradigms, which include asking expressors to imagine or pose the intended message, observing them in specific situations that arouse an intended state, or observing them displaying their characteristic behavior styles (Friedman, Riggio, & Segall, 1980; Wagner, Buck, & Winterbotham, 1993). The cues that form the basis of generating encoding accuracy scores may be purely nonverbal or may be mixed with verbal cues. The cues may be deliberately or spontaneously conveyed. In any case, criteria must be developed so that it is clear what a "right answer" should be, such as the emotion that was intended (on an emotion recognition task), or the encoder's score on a personality scale (on a personality judgment task). Typically, observers make judgments about the encoders, which are scored for accuracy according to the criterion, and then averaged across observers for each encoder. This value becomes the operational definition of how accurate the encoder is (i.e., how well he/she can be judged). Encoding accuracy can be related to individual difference characteristics of the encoders (e.g., gender, personality) or to experimental manipulations (e.g., social power role). The measurement of encoding accuracy is laborious and methodologically nonstandard.

Decoding Accuracy

Accuracy in decoding nonverbal cues is studied far more often than encoding accuracy because it is far less individualized and time consuming in its measurement. Decoding tests can be standardized, making them easy to administer in groups and easy to score. Decoding accuracy is measured by asking perceivers to watch and/or listen to nonverbal behaviors, either live or recorded, and to make assessments of the meanings of the cues (or to recall what behaviors occurred) (Hall, Bernieri, & Carney, 2005). The content of such assessment is most often emotional or affective states, but it can also be personality, intelligence, social or ethnic group membership, deception, relationships, kinship, and hierarchical position, among others (Bernieri, 2001). If the definition of nonverbal behavior is extended beyond the physical person, then one would also include accuracy at judging manifestations of self such as are reflected in living environments and offices (Gosling, Ko, Mannarelli, & Morris, 2002).

Accuracy of interpersonal judgment is measured by researchers in a variety of ways, but, as with measuring encoding accuracy, such a test requires a criterion against which judgments can be scored as right or wrong. Thus, for example, on a test of judging the extraversion of a set of persons (targets) shown on videotape, the researcher must have a good measure of the targets' actual extraversion in order to score the test. Nonverbal decoding tests vary in how many target persons are shown, how many different kinds of content are represented, and what cue channels are included. As an example, such a test might present six targets each expressing four different emotions using facial expressions, for a total of 24 test items. On some tests, perceivers judge a full audiovisual stimulus, while on others they judge single channels such as face only or voice only. The test stimuli are typically short, ranging from less than a second to a few minutes in duration. Accuracy can be high, even when exposure to the stimulus is very brief, though this depends on what is being judged. Accuracy levels depend on many factors and are notably low for judging deceptiveness (Bond & DePaulo, 2006) and high for judging prototypical facial expressions of emotion (e.g., happy, sad, angry) (Ekman et al., 1987).

Most research on decoding accuracy is based on administering tests using recorded stimuli such as described above. A variety of validated tests of this kind are available (e.g., Costanzo & Archer, 1989; Nowicki & Duke, 1994; Rosenthal, Hall, DiMatteo, Rogers, & Archer, 1979). Some research is quite different in that it is based on judgments made during or right after a live interaction. In one such method, called the empathic accuracy paradigm, a person watches a video replay of one's own interaction with a partner and makes inferences about the partner's thoughts and feelings, which are scored against the partner's self-described thoughts and feelings (Ickes, Stinson, Bissonnette, & Garcia, 1990). In a variation of this method, the video is turned into a standardized test that new viewers can take. In the empathic accuracy paradigm, decoding accuracy has been shown to be based much more on verbal than nonverbal cues (Gesn & Ickes, 1999; Hall & Schmid Mast, 2007).

Nonverbal decoding skills advance during childhood and are typically higher in females than in males (Hall, 1984). There is also evidence for cultural expression "dialects" that allow expressions of emotions to be more accurately judged by other members of that culture, or by people with greater exposure to that culture, than by outsiders (Elfenbein & Ambady, 2002). Research shows that nonverbal decoding skills are higher in individuals with healthy mental and social functioning (Davis & Kraus, 1997; Hall, Andrzejewski, & Yopchick, in press). This includes higher empathy, affiliation, extraversion, dominance, conscientiousness, openness, tolerance for ambiguity, need to belong, better personal relationships, and internal locus of control. Decoding skill is negatively related to neuroticism, shyness, depression, and an insecure attachment style. Such individuals are also less likely to be prejudiced against minority groups (Andrzejewski, 2009).

Persons with higher decoding skill are rated by acquaintances as more interpersonally sensitive. Higher self- and acquaintance ratings of social and emotional competence are also positively related to decoding skill, as are indices of competence in workplace and clinical settings, according to supervisor or peer ratings as well as more objective indices of performance (e.g., Byron, Terranova, & Nowicki, 2007; Elfenbein, Foo, White, Tan, & Aik, 2007).

RESEARCH DESIGNS USING NONVERBAL BEHAVIOR AND NONVERBAL COMMUNICATION ACCURACY

Depending on the research question, nonverbal variables are independent or dependent variables, mediator variables, or are used in correlational designs.

Independent Variable Designs

Nonverbal behavior can be an experimentally manipulated independent variable in judgment studies (e.g., where photos or experimentally created videos are shown to participants), in confederate designs, or in studies where participants are led to position facial or body parts according to the experimenter's wishes. In most such studies, it is generally important for the participants not to realize that the manipulation has taken place or not to be consciously aware of the psychological significance of the manipulated behavior. In the confederate paradigm one has to worry whether confederates are actually able to vary certain desired nonverbal behaviors without unintentionally varying others, too (Lewis, Derlega, Shankar, Cochard, & Finkel, 1997).

Some illustrative studies from social psychology can be briefly mentioned. If persons in photographs are shown touching another person, they are perceived as more dominant and more friendly than if they do not touch (Major & Heslin, 1982). If waitpersons in restaurants touch their customers, they receive higher tips (Hubbard, Tsuji, Williams, & Seatriz, 2003). If participants in a dyadic interaction sit with postural complementarity suggestive of high and low power (sitting in an expanded vs. constricted posture, respectively), they feel more comfort in the interaction than if the postures match (Tiedens & Fragale, 2003). If children are required to use hand gestures while learning new material, they learn it better (Cook, Mitchell, & Goldin-Meadow, 2008). If people are induced to activate the Zygomaticus major muscle (i.e., the "smile" muscle) while viewing cartoons, they rate the cartoons as funnier (Strack et al., 1988). If White job applicants are treated according to how Black job applicants were observed to be treated (e.g., larger interpersonal distances, more speech dysfluencies), they perform more poorly in the interview (Word, Zanna, & Cooper, 1974). And if negotiators are instructed to mimic the movements of their partner, they achieve more favorable negotiation outcomes (Maddux, Mullen, & Galinsky, 2008).

Dependent Variable Designs

Nonverbal behavior also serves as a dependent variable in social psychological experiments. Occasionally the coding of behavior is done by live observers, but the more common approach is to record the behavior and analyze it later. When participants are assigned to have low power in a dyadic interaction, they suffer expressive deficits that make their affective state harder to judge (Hall, Rosip, Smith LeBeau, Horgan, & Carter,

2006). If participants are subtly primed with the concept of elderly persons, they walk more slowly when leaving the experiment (Bargh, Chen, & Burrows, 1996). If participants experience cognitive load while taking a nonverbal sensitivity test, it may or may not affect their accuracy, depending on which test they are taking (Phillips, Tunstall, & Channon, 2007; Tracy & Robins, 2008a). And when participants tell lies, their faces are less pleasant than when telling the truth (DePaulo et al., 2003).

Correlational Designs

Many studies using nonverbal variables are correlational, with no experimental manipulations. Though there are ambiguities about causal interpretation, these studies are often very interesting and provocative. As examples, physicians' and patients' voices are correlated in terms of anger and anxiety (Hall, Roter, & Rand, 1981). Higher nonverbal sensitivity predicts better negotiation outcomes (Elfenbein et al., 2007). Implicit anxiety as measured with a reaction time task is correlated with speech dysfluencies, nervous mouth movements, and fidgeting (Egloff & Schmukle, 2002). And persons with more dominant personalities are better at expressing various facial emotions than persons with less dominant personalities (Friedman et al., 1980).

Mediator Designs

The self-fulfilling prophecy has already been mentioned as a preeminent (and very well studied) example of how nonverbal behavior can be the medium through which social influence occurs. Teachers with high expectations for a pupil, for example, behave more warmly through nonverbal cues than teachers with lower expectations, and such behavior can, in turn, influence performance. The research of Word et al. (1974) mentioned above falls within the mediator tradition, for those authors' goal was to show that White interviewers engage in certain nonverbal behaviors towards Black interviewees which, in turn, produce deficient performance in those interviewees.

One type of design, the lens model (Brunswik, 1956), is intrisically mediational in that it measures both accuracy of communication and the cues themselves, in order to understand the process by which accuracy is achieved. Using this approach, one can find out whether accuracy exists for judging a given construct (such as a personality trait or an emotion), whether a given nonverbal cue is or is not diagnostic of that construct, and whether perceivers use a given nonverbal cue in making inferences about the construct. Putting these elements together can shed light on how perceivers are able to achieve accuracy.

The study by Murphy, Hall, and Colvin (2003) illustrates this approach for the trait of intelligence as measured by a standard IQ test. Perceivers achieved a significant degree of accuracy in judging intelligence from 1-minute excerpts of conversational behavior. Though many non-verbal cues were measured in the investigation of mediation, the following three serve to illustrate the approach. Fast speech was not a mediating cue because although perceivers rated fast speakers as being more intelligent, that cue was not in fact diagnostic of higher measured intelligence. Less fidgeting was not a mediating cue because although it was diagnostic of higher intelligence, perceivers did not rate it as such. But responsive gazing was a mediator: It was diagnostic of measured intelligence and was recognized as such by accurate perceivers.

Having provided a quick description of nonverbal methods and some illustrative findings, I now return to the tripartite theme of the chapter whereby the nonverbal field is evaluated for its qualities that are good, bad, and ugly.

THE GOOD

It Is Truly About Behavior

As already said, it is good that in this field we *do* study behavior. There is very little paper-and-pencil research in this field. Researchers and lay-people alike would agree that nonverbal behavior, both what we engage in ourselves and what we see others do, is difficult to describe in words and is often not processed at a high enough level of consciousness to justify an introspective or self-descriptive approach to its study. The relatively rare instances of paper-and-pencil research typically address questions that either intrinsically require such an approach or that cannot ethically or practically be handled otherwise. As examples, one can ask people about their patterns of intimate interpersonal touching (Jourard, 1966), about their personal liking or disliking of being touched (Andersen & Leibowitz, 1978), about how they would behave in situations too numerous or far-flung to be captured experimentally or observationally (Hall & Schmid Mast, 2009; Nagashima & Schellenberg, 1997), about their knowledge of nonverbal communication (scored for accuracy against findings in the literature; Rosip & Hall, 2004; Vrij & Semin, 1996), or about their stereotypes regarding nonverbal behavior (e.g., men versus women, Briton & Hall, 1995; persons high versus low in social power, Carney, Hall, & Smith LeBeau, 2005). Sometimes the self-reports are of interest only in relation to behavioral measurements, as when assessing how accurately people can report on their own nonverbal behavior (Hall, Murphy, & Schmid Mast, 2007) or how accurately they can appraise their own nonverbal skills (Ames & Kammrath, 2004; Patterson, Foster, & Bellmer, 2001).

It Is Interesting

But, going beyond the good fact that the nonverbal field is based on behavior, there are many other good things to be said about it. For starters, practically any finding involving nonverbal communication is interesting. Articles about nonverbal communication are hardly ever dull. Perhaps we are reminded of how close we are to our animal cousins, or perhaps we feel we are reaching towards the experience of "real life." Perhaps we are simply fascinated by the possibility of getting an empirical grip on phenomena that seem so elusive. Or, perhaps the often nonconscious or semiconscious nature of nonverbal behavior makes us believe (or hope) that it is a window into people's true inner states or character. For whatever reason, people are attracted to the topic.

It Is Widely Relevant

Researchers' interest in nonverbal communication stems from many theoretical and substantive directions. Nonverbal communication is seen as important to many different disciplines, not just psychology but also sociology, anthropology, communication studies, medicine, and ethology (to name some). Examples are the role of nonverbal cues in self-presentation (sociology: Goffman, 1959, 1979), cultural differences in nonverbal behavior (anthropology: E. T. Hall, 1966), the process of interpersonal deception (communication: Burgoon, Buller, Floyd, & Grandpre, 1996; Knapp, 2006), nonverbal communication in the social life of primates (ethology: de Waal, 2005), and the design of lifelike avatars for human–computer interaction (computer science: Bickmore & Picard, 2005).

Within psychology, though nonverbal behavior is more closely identified with social psychology than with other areas, the topic is actually studied in all areas of the discipline. This includes personality, developmental, industrial/organizational, comparative, cognitive, clinical/counseling, educational psychology, and neuropsychology. Across psychology, the list of topics related to nonverbal behavior is extremely long, but the following provides a sampling: emotions, social influence, ongoing cognition, speech production, learning, psychotherapy, psycho-pathology, gender differences and gender roles, cultural differences, social attitudes, relationships, interpersonal expectancies, conversational regulation, brain function, parent–child bonding, social adjustment, and individual differences of all kinds.

Its Star Is Rising

There is no question that nonverbal communication is gaining promi-nence as a research topic. Table 21.1 shows results from a PsycINFO search of a few relevant terms, by decades. Clearly, there is a surge in the current decade. This research appears in a huge assortment of different journals, many of which are not in social psychology per se, and it is conducted by many kinds of scholars, not just social psychologists. This wide diversity of publication outlets, reflecting the wide relevance of nonverbal communication within the behavioral sciences, is perhaps one reason why Baumeister, Vohs, and Funder (2007) did not mention nonverbal behavior in their review of behavioral variables reported on in one mainstream social psychology journal, the *Journal of Personality and Social Psychology*. (In fact, nonverbal behavior appears regularly in that journal as well as in all social psychology journals.)

Other evidence for the progress of nonverbal communication as a scientific discipline is the appearance of integrative chapters and books. There is a chapter on this topic in the *Handbook of Social Psychology* (DePaulo & Friedman, 1998). Integrative books include *The New Handbook of Methods in Nonverbal Behavior Research* (edited by Harrigan et al., 2005), *The Sourcebook of Nonverbal Measures* (edited by Manusov, 2005), the *Handbook of Nonverbal Communication* (edited by Manusov & Patterson, 2006), and *Interpersonal Sensitivity: Theory and Measurement* (edited by Hall & Bernieri, 2001). Many other monographs and edited

Table 21.1. Results of PsycINFO Search

Decade	"Nonverbal Communication"	"Facial Expression"	"Emotion Recognition"
1950–59	41	48	20
1960–69	176	75	27
1970–79	1,505	206	74
1980–89	1,875	530	241
1990–99	1,814	856	381
2000–09*	2,456*	1,988*	1,361*

* Projected

books also exist, as well as textbooks (Hickson, Stacks, & Moore, 2004; Knapp & Hall, 2005).

Another potent indicator of a field's progress is the publication of meta-analyses. These exist in abundance, on many nonverbal communication topics including predictive validity of thin slices of behavior (Ambady & Rosenthal, 1992), culture of perceivers and targets (Elfenbein & Ambady, 2002), gender (lie detection, Aamodt & Custer, 2006; interpersonal sensitivity and various nonverbal behaviors, Hall, 1978, 1984; smiling, LaFrance, Hecht, & Levy Paluck, 2003; face processing, McClure, 2000), power, status, and dominance (interpersonal sensitivity, Hall, Halberstadt, & O'Brien, 1997; various nonverbal behaviors, Hall et al., 2005), deception (accuracy of lie detection, Bond & DePaulo, 2006; cues to deception, DePaulo et al., 2003), psychosocial correlates of interpersonal sensitivity (Davis & Kraus, 1997; Hall et al., in press), personality correlates of expressiveness (Riggio & Riggio, 2002), and anti-Semitism and accuracy in distinguishing Jews from non-Jews (Andrzejewski, Hall, & Salib, 2009).

Finally, though the *Journal of Nonverbal Behavior* is not new (it has been in existence for 30 years), its impact factor is the highest it has ever been as of this writing.

Why Is Its Star Rising?

One reason for the growing recognition of nonverbal studies is the general maturation of the field. A second reason, especially relevant for social psychology, is that nonverbal behavior is relevant to many of the currently important themes within the discipline. Thus, what was once a topic of slightly oddball interest is now more than respectable, and young investigators with skills in nonverbal research are now in demand. Some of the new interest in nonverbal behavior can be traced to the "warming up" of mainstream social psychology (that is, interest in motivation and emotion, not just "cold" social cognitive processes). Examples of such mainstream work include emotional expression (Tracy & Robins, 2008b), emotional intelligence (Mayer, Salovey, Caruso, & Sitarenios, 2003), attitude formation (Wells & Petty, 1980), manifestations of racial attitudes (McConnell & Leibold, 2001), contagion/mimicry (Chartrand & Bargh, 1999), and power/dominance (Tiedens & Fragale, 2003). Some mainstream research that includes nonverbal behavior reflects efforts to unite cognition with more emotional and motivational themes; examples include implicit versus controlled processes (Dovidio, Kawakami, & Gaertner, 2002), embodied cognition (Niedenthal, Barsalou, Winkielman, Krauth-Gruber, & Ric, 2005), and ideomotor processes

(Wegner, 2002). Evolutionary social psychologists are also interested in nonverbal behavior (Floyd, 2006).

THE BAD

Clearly, nonverbal communication has a large role to play in the future of social psychology. However, there are some elements that can be called "bad," at least from some perspectives.

How Do We Fit In?

Despite a growing place for nonverbal research in social psychology, there are ambiguities about how it fits in, which has implications for professional identity. At this stage in the development of social psychology as a field, there is great emphasis placed on theory development and theory-driven research. Theory-driven research is considered prestigious, and the suggestion that a piece of research is "not theoretical enough" dooms it in mainstream journals. Nonverbal communication research, within this evaluative framework, can sometimes come up short because, speaking broadly, it is more bottom-up than top-down—that is, it is more likely to start with the exploration of interesting phenomena (nonverbal behavior or nonverbal communication skills) rather than with testing a theory. Bottom-up research, though essential in the production of knowledge and in hypothesis generation and theory generation, is not held in the highest esteem in social psychology. Thus, we are confronted with the ironic situation that, all too often, our reward for studying actual behavior is to be told by reviewers and editors that our research is deficient on theoretical grounds, or, at least, that it can't stand on its own but should rather serve the validation of higher-level theories.

Another issue for the field's identity and reputation stems from the fact that nonverbal researchers might be seen mainly as the providers of behavioral measures to be used as dependent variables in social psychological research. While not diminishing the value of this service to social psychology, I would not want the nonverbal field to be defined mainly in terms of its methodological toolbox. Nonverbal communication as a field has much more substance to offer than this.

The fact that nonverbal behavior is relevant in so many disciplines and to so many questions within social psychology creates a challenge to professional identity and to the definition of the field. The field does not have core questions or core theories; these tend to be particular to the nonverbal phenomenon being studied. Therefore, nonverbal behavior researchers may have more trouble finding common ground than those who identify as, say, social cognition researchers or as attitude researchers. This, in fact, may be a negative by-product of being a field that is defined in terms of the behavior it studies. If I study gazing, it could be in relation to many different substantive issues (e.g., physiological arousal, dominance, attraction, conversational regulation, emotion, affiliation, culture, gender, race, personality, or psychopathology). Nonverbal behavior thus cuts across substantive areas and theoretical traditions, creating ambiguity over where it belongs. Indeed, this tension is manifest in nonverbal communication textbooks because the authors have to decide whether to divide the chapters up by cue channels (face, body, voice, etc.) or by thematic topics (e.g., attraction, deception, relationships, social influence, gender and culture, etc.).

Labor Intensiveness

It is an understatement to say that nonverbal research can take a lot of time and effort. It can take years to complete a study that involves nonverbal coding. Sometimes extensive formal training and certification are required (as with the FACS), but even training research assistants in one's lab to do relatively simple coding is very time consuming. Furthermore, they find the work to be boring so it is hard to retain assistants. And because coding takes a long time, turnover among assistants (between semesters, for example) can set a project back because they leave before the coding is done, and new ones need to be recruited and trained. Even those supervising the assistants find the process exhausting and aversive. And if graduate students are involved, they may be reluctant to commit to studies that take a long time to complete, and if they do, they may end up sorry that they did.

Fortunately, there are indications that to some extent this process can be streamlined. Though much more research is needed, it is now clear that valid results can be obtained from coding less than the total amount of behavior at one's disposal. Ambady and Rosenthal (1992), in a meta-analysis, reviewed many studies showing that meaningful outcomes can be predicted from very short "slices" of behavior (5 minutes or less, sometimes much less). Ambady and Rosenthal (1993) showed that ratings and nonverbal coding made on excerpts of teacher behavior as short as six seconds predicted end-of-semester student evaluations and school principals' evaluations. Murphy (2005) showed that 3 minutes of coded nonverbal behavior (smiles, nods, gazing, self-touching, and gesturing) correlated highly with the same behaviors coded for 15 minutes, and that for some behaviors 1-minute excerpts were adequate. And Carney, Colvin, and Hall (2007) showed that accuracy for judging various personality traits was often as good for 1-minute as for 5-minute clips, and in some cases as good for five seconds as for 5 minutes.

Other evidence that long durations of behavior are not necessarily required stems from tests of judging the meanings of nonverbal cues, such as described in an earlier section. Some of the most widely used tests present stimuli for only two seconds. Matsumoto et al. (2000) based a reliable and predictive test on stimulus exposures of far less than one second. Of course, how much information is required to measure behavior adequately cannot be standardized. It will depend on what one is seeking to measure.

Finally, it has to be added that the measurement of nonverbal behavior or nonverbal skill is not a perfected science. Often, we measure behavior crudely or shallowly; for example, we might simply count the frequency of occurrence without measuring qualitative nuances or more complex temporal relations. Reliability is not always good; this is often true of tests of nonverbal decoding accuracy (Hall, 2001). Even if we measure a collection of discrete behaviors well, we are not good at reassembling them to form a coherent picture of a behaving person. The behaving person is emitting many behaviors all at once, and they occur in relation to each other, unfolding in patterns over time. The behaving person is not, therefore, simply the sum of how often she smiles, gestures, fidgets, and so forth.

THE UGLY

By "ugly" I mean complex and confusing. That is how I would describe the challenge of assigning meaning to nonverbal cues. Nonverbal cues gain meaning in context, as discussed earlier. The same behavior can mean different things or serve different functions, depending on what the expressor's inner state or intention is, or on what else is happening in the situation. Even if contextual factors are known, establishing meaning is hard because often there is no gold standard. The expressor's own opinion on the subject is hardly a gold standard, considering that often people are not aware of their own nonverbal behavior.

Furthermore, does the criterion of a cue's meaning lie in the expressor's intention or in how it is interpreted by others? To illustrate, a White person might attempt to show respect to an African American by keeping a large interpersonal distance, but this same behavior may be interpreted by the African American as a sign of rejection. The behavior "means" different things, depending on whose perspective is taken. Even when it is possible to develop a general or normative understanding of the meaning of cues, there can still be great uncertainty in specific cases.

The fact that nonverbal behavior often takes its meaning from context means that one may need to know far more than morphology and a few rules of thumb, and this is a much broader and more demanding research endeavor. Understanding the meaning of nonverbal behavior often takes us into the territory of motives and goals—*why* is the person putting on this expression? For example, observing that women smile more than men do tells us something, but not much (LaFrance et al., 2003). Are women happier than men? Are they behaving submissively? Are they simply responding to others' pleasant behaviors directed at them? Are they displaying their higher level of social communication skill? Are they trying harder to appear physically attractive? The fact that nonverbal behavior can be deliberately used for many purposes including self-presentation and deception makes the determination of "meaning" an even more complex issue.

Thus, it is all too common for a researcher to go to a great deal of trouble to measure nonverbal behaviors, only to find that their meaning is obscure. Perhaps it is partly because researchers often have to be agnostic about meaning that their work sometimes appears to be "not theoretical enough." In pointing out these difficulties, I do not intend to discourage researchers from measuring cues. But I am suggesting that they should not fall victim to behavioral reductionism, by which I mean making the assumption that measuring behavior is the only way to be scientific and rigorous.

What, then, is the alternative to behavioral reductionism? Can one study nonverbal behavior without measuring behavior? I suggest that often—depending, of course, on the research question—a researcher is more interested in imputed or observed meaning than in the behavior per se. A researcher interested in marital quality, for example, might gain much more from gathering naïve raters' impressions of anger in a videotaped interaction than from training coders to measure facial muscle movements or having a computer spit out a long list of acoustic measurements. If the researcher desires more channel specificity, she can gather these ratings based on silent video, voice only, or electronically filtered speech if no linguistic input is desired. As long as interrater reliability is achieved, raters' impressions can sensitively index a wide range of perceived psychological states. Authors have discussed the tradeoffs involved in the choice between a molecular approach on one hand, where you know what you've measured but are uncertain what it means, and a molar approach on the other, where you know what it means—at least from a perceiver's point of view—but you don't know exactly how the different behaviors contribute to the impression (Cohn & Ekman, 2005; Juslin & Scherer, 2005).

CONCLUSION

In this chapter I have tried to convey some of the excitement, as well as problems, associated with studying nonverbal communication. It is a field that is far from burned out; there are still many questions to be investigated; and there is still much room for methodological development. In one way or another, nonverbal communication is connected to virtually all of social psychology.

Although Baumeister et al. (2007), as well as Patterson (2008), who performed a similar analysis for the *Personality and Social Psychology Bulletin*, were certainly correct in noting a dearth of behavioral measures in contemporary social psychology, at least one category of behavior— nonverbal behavior—is on the rise. Furthermore, by looking only at two highly selective, mainstream journals, they may have underestimated how often nonverbal behavior appears in social psychology journals, or in studies done by social psychologists that are published in other types of journals. And, of course, all of this is just a fraction of the volume of nonverbal research that is done by scholars outside of social psychology. The nonverbal field may be fragmented, but it is large.

REFERENCES

Aamodt, M. G., & Custer, H. (2006). Who can best catch a liar? A meta-analysis of individual differences in detecting deception. *Forensic Examiner, 15*, 6–11.

Ambady, N., & Rosenthal, R. (1992). Thin slices of expressive behavior as predictors of interpersonal consequences: A meta-analysis. *Psychological Bulletin, 111*, 256–274.

Ambady, N., & Rosenthal, R. (1993). Half a minute: Predicting teacher evaluations from thin slices of nonverbal behavior and physical attractiveness. *Journal of Personality and Social Psychology, 64*, 431–441.

Ames, D. R., & Kammrath, L. K. (2004). Mind-reading and metacognition: Narcissism, not actual competence, predicts self-estimated ability. *Journal of Nonverbal Behavior, 28*, 187–209.

Andersen, P. A. (1985). Nonverbal immediacy in interpersonal communication. In A. W. Siegman & S. Feldstein (Eds.), *Multichannel integrations of nonverbal behavior* (pp. 1–36). Hillsdale, NJ: Lawrence Erlbaum Associates.

Andersen, P. A., & Leibowitz, K. (1978). The development and nature of the construct touch avoidance. *Environmental Psychology and Nonverbal Behavior, 3*, 89–106.

Andrzejewski, S. A. (2009). *Interpersonal sensitivity and prejudice.* Manuscript submitted for publication.

Andrzejewski, S. A., Hall, J. A., & Salib, E. R. (2009). Anti-Semitism and identification of Jewish group membership from photographs. *Journal of Nonverbal Behavior, 33*, 47–58.

Argyle, M., Alkema, F., & Gilmour, R. (1971). The communication of friendly and hostile attitudes by verbal and non-verbal signals. *European Journal of Social Psychology, 1*, 385–402.

Argyle, M., & Dean, J. (1965). Eye-contact, distance and affiliation. *Sociometry, 28*, 289–304.

Bargh, J. A., Chen, M., & Burrows, L. (1996). Automaticity of social behavior: Direct effects of trait construct and stereotype activation on action. *Journal of Personality and Social Psychology, 71*, 230–244.

Barroso, F., & Freedman, N. (1992). The nonverbal manifestations of cognitive processes in clinical listening. *Journal of Psycholinguistic Research, 21*, 87–110.

Baumeister, R. F., Vohs, K. D., & Funder, D. C. (2007). Psychology as the science of self-reports and finger movements: Whatever happened to actual behavior? *Perspectives on Psychological Science, 2*, 396–403.

Bavelas, J. B., & Chovil, N. (1997). Faces in dialogue. In J. A. Russell & J. M. Fernández-Dols (Eds.), *The psychology of facial expression* (pp. 334–346). New York: Cambridge University Press.

Bernieri, F. J. (2001). Toward a taxonomy of interpersonal sensitivity. In J. A. Hall & F. J. Bernieri (Eds.), *Interpersonal sensitivity: Theory and measurement* (pp. 3–20). Mahwah, NJ: Lawrence Erlbaum Associates.

Bickmore, T. W., & Picard, R. W. (2005). Establishing and maintaining long-term human-computer relationships. *ACM Transactions on Computer-Human Interaction (TOCHI), 12*, 293–327.

Bond, C. F., Jr., & DePaulo, B. M. (2006). Accuracy of deception judgments. *Personality and Social Psychology Review, 10*, 214–234.

Briton, N. J., & Hall, J. A. (1995). Beliefs about female and male nonverbal communication. *Sex Roles, 32*, 79–90.

Brunswik, E. (1956). *Perception and the representative design of experiments.* Berkeley, CA: University of California Press.

Burgoon, J. K., Buller, D. B., Floyd, K., & Grandpre, J. (1996). Deceptive realities: Sender, receiver, and observer perspectives in deceptive conversations. *Communication Research, 23*, 724–748.

Byron, K., Terranova, S., & Nowicki, S., Jr. (2007). Nonverbal emotion recognition and salespersons: Linking ability to perceived and actual success. *Journal of Applied Social Psychology, 37*, 2600–2619.

Carney, D. R., Colvin, C. R., & Hall, J. A. (2007). A thin-slice approach to accuracy of first impressions. *Journal of Research in Personality, 41*, 1054–1072.

Carney, D. R., Hall, J. A., & Smith LeBeau, L. (2005). Beliefs about the nonverbal expression of social power. *Journal of Nonverbal Behavior, 29*, 105–123.

Chartrand, T. L., & Bargh, J. A. (1999). The chameleon effect: The perception-behavior link and social interaction. *Journal of Personality and Social Psychology, 76*, 893–910.

Cohn, J. F., & Ekman, P. (2005). Measuring facial action. In J. A. Harrigan, R. Rosenthal, & K. R. Scherer (Eds.), *The new handbook of methods in nonverbal behavior research* (pp. 9–64). Oxford, UK: Oxford University Press.

Cook, S. W., Mitchell, Z., & Goldin-Meadow, S. (2008). Gesturing makes learning last. *Cognition, 106*, 1047–1058.

Costanzo, M., & Archer, D. (1989). Interpreting the expressive behavior of others: The Interpersonal Perception Task. *Journal of Nonverbal Behavior, 13*, 225–245.

Davis, M. H., & Kraus, L. A. (1997). Personality and empathic accuracy. In W. Ickes (Ed.), *Empathic accuracy* (pp. 144–168). New York: Guilford.

DePaulo, B. M. (1992). Nonverbal behavior and self-presentation. *Psychological Bulletin, 111*, 203–243.

DePaulo, B. M., & Friedman, H. S. (1998). Nonverbal communication. In D. T. Gilbert, S. T. Fiske, & G. Lindzey (Eds.), *The handbook of social psychology*, 4th ed., Vol. 2 (pp. 3–40). New York: McGraw-Hill.

DePaulo, B. M., Lindsay, J. J., Malone, B. E., Muhlenbruck, L., Charlton, K., & Cooper, H. (2003). Cues to deception. *Psychological Bulletin, 129*, 74–118.

De Waal, F. B. M. (2005). A century of getting to know the chimpanzee. *Nature, 437*, 56–59.

Dimberg, U., Thunberg, M., & Grunedal, S. (2002). Facial reactions to emotional stimuli: Automatically controlled emotional responses. *Cognition & Emotion, 16*, 449–472.

Dovidio, J. F., Kawakami, K., & Gaertner, S. L. (2002). Implicit and explicit prejudice and interracial interaction. *Journal of Personality and Social Psychology, 82*, 62–68.

Egloff, B., & Schmukle, S. C. (2002). Predictive validity of an implicit association test for assessing anxiety. *Journal of Personality and Social Psychology, 83*, 1441–1455.

Ekman, P. (Ed.) (1982). *Emotion in the human face*, 2nd ed. Cambridge, UK: Cambridge University Press.

Ekman, P., Davidson, R. J., & Friesen, W. V. (1990). The Duchenne smile: Emotional expression and brain physiology: II. *Journal of Personality and Social Psychology, 58*, 342–353.

Ekman, P., & Friesen, W. V. (1969). Nonverbal leakage and cues to deception. *Psychiatry: Journal for the Study of Interpersonal Processes, 32*, 88–106.

Ekman, P., Friesen, W. V., O'Sullivan, M., Chan, A., Diacoyanni-Tarlatzis, I., Heider, K., Krause, R., LeCompte, W. A., Pitcairn, T., Ricci-Bitti, P. E., Scherer, K., Tomita, M., & Tzavaras, A. (1987). Universals and cultural differences in the judgments of facial expressions of emotion. *Journal of Personality and Social Psychology, 53*, 712–717.

Ekman, P., & Rosenberg, E. (Eds.). (1997). *What the face reveals: Basic and applied studies of spontaneous expression using the Facial Action Coding System (FACS)*. New York: Oxford University Press.

Elfenbein, H. A., & Ambady, N. (2002). On the universality and cultural specificity of emotion recognition: A meta-analysis. *Psychological Bulletin, 128*, 203–235.

Elfenbein, H. A., Foo, M. D., White, J., Tan, H. H., & Aik, V. C. (2007). Reading your counterpart: The benefit of emotion recognition accuracy for effectiveness in negotiation. *Journal of Nonverbal Behavior, 31*, 205–223.

Floyd, K. (2006). An evolutionary approach to understanding nonverbal communication. In V. Manusov & M. L. Patterson (Eds.), *The Sage handbook of nonverbal communication* (pp. 139–157). Thousand Oaks, CA: Sage.

Friedman, H. S., Riggio, R. E., & Segall, D. O. (1980). Personality and the enactment of emotion. *Journal of Nonverbal Behavior, 5*, 35–48.

Gesn, P. R., & Ickes, W. (1999). The development of meaning contexts for empathic accuracy: Channel and sequence effects. *Journal of Personality and Social Psychology, 77*, 746–761.

Goffman, E. (1959). *The presentation of self in everyday life*. Oxford, UK: Doubleday.

Goffman, E. (1979). *Gender advertisements*. New York: Harper & Row.

Gosling, S. D., Ko, S. J., Mannarelli, T., & Morris, M. E. (2002). A room with a cue: Judgments of personality based on offices and bedrooms. *Journal of Personality and Social Psychology, 82*, 379–398.

Hall, E. T. (1966). *The hidden dimension*. Garden City, NY: Doubleday.

Hall, J. A. (1984). *Nonverbal sex differences: Communication accuracy and expressive style*. Baltimore: The Johns Hopkins University Press.

Hall, J. A. (2001). The PONS test and the psychometric approach to measuring interpersonal sensitivity. In J. A. Hall and F. J. Bernieri (Eds.), *Interpersonal sensitivity: Theory and measurement* (pp. 143–160). Mahwah, NJ: Erlbaum.

Hall, J. A., Andrzejewski, S. A., & Yopchick, J. E. (in press). Psychosocial correlates of interpersonal sensitivity: A meta-analysis. *Journal of Nonverbal Behavior*.

Hall, J. A., & Bernieri, F. J. (Eds.) (2001). *Interpersonal sensitivity: Theory and measurement*. Mahwah, NJ: Lawrence Erlbaum Associates.

Hall, J. A., Bernieri, F. J., & Carney, D. R. (2005). Nonverbal behavior and interpersonal sensitivity. In J. A. Harrigan, R. Rosenthal, & K. R. Scherer (Eds.), *The new handbook of methods in nonverbal behavior research* (pp. 237–281). Oxford, UK: Oxford University Press.

Hall, J. A., Coats, E. J., & Smith LeBeau, L. (2005). Nonverbal behavior and the vertical dimension of social relations: A meta-analysis. *Psychological Bulletin, 131*, 898–924.

Hall, J. A., Halberstadt, A. G., & O'Brien, C. E. (1997). "Subordination" and nonverbal sensitivity: A study and synthesis of findings based on trait measures. *Sex Roles, 37*, 295–317.

Hall, J. A., Horgan, T. G., & Carter, J. D. (2002). Assigned and felt status in relation to observer-coded and participant-reported smiling. *Journal of Nonverbal Behavior, 26*, 63–81.

Hall, J. A., Murphy, N. A., & Schmid Mast, M. (2007). Nonverbal self-accuracy in interpersonal interaction. *Personality and Social Psychology Bulletin, 33*, 1675–1685.

Hall, J. A., Rosip, J. C., Smith LeBeau, L., Horgan, T. G., & Carter, J. D. (2006). Attributing the sources of accuracy in unequal-power dyadic communication: Who is better and why? *Journal of Experimental Social Psychology, 42*, 18–27.

Hall, J. A., Roter, D. L., and Rand, C. S. (1981). Communication of affect between patient and physician. *Journal of Health and Social Behavior, 22*, 18–30.

Hall, J. A., & Schmid Mast, M. (2007). Sources of accuracy in the empathic accuracy paradigm. *Emotion, 7*, 438–446.

Hall, J. A., & Schmid Mast, M. (2009). *Moderators, confounders, and social power: The instructive case of beliefs about smiling*. Manuscript submitted for publication.

Harrigan, J. A., Rosenthal, R., & Scherer, K. R. (Eds.) (2005). *The new handbook of methods in nonverbal behavior research*. Oxford, UK: Oxford University Press.

Harris, M. J., & Rosenthal, R. (1985). Mediation of interpersonal expectancy effects: 31 meta-analyses. *Psychological Bulletin, 97*, 363–386.

Hickson, M., III, Stacks, D. W., & Moore, N. (2004). *Nonverbal communication: Studies and applications*, 4th ed. Los Angeles: Roxbury Publishing Company.

Hubbard, A. S. E., Tsuji, A. A., Williams, C., & Seatriz, V., Jr. (2003). Effects of touch on gratuities received in same-gender and cross-gender dyads. *Journal of Applied Social Psychology, 33*, 2427–2438.

Ickes, W., Stinson, L., Bissonnette, V., & Garcia, S. (1990). Naturalistic social cognition: Empathic accuracy in mixed-sex dyads. *Journal of Personality and Social Psychology, 59*, 730–742.

Jourard, S. M. (1966). An exploratory study of body-accessibility. *British Journal of Social and Clinical Psychology, 5*, 221–231.

Juslin, P. N., & Scherer, K. R. (2005). Vocal expression of affect. In J. A. Harrigan, R. Rosenthal, & K. R. Scherer (Eds.), *The new handbook of methods in nonverbal behavior research* (pp. 65–135). Oxford, UK: Oxford University Press.

Knapp, M. L. (2006). Lying and deception in close relationships. In A. L. Vangelisti & D. Perlman (Eds.), *The Cambridge handbook of personal relationships* (pp. 517–532). New York: Cambridge University Press.

Knapp, M. L., & Hall, J. A. (2005). *Nonverbal communication in human interaction*, 6th ed. Belmont, CA: Wadsworth.

Krauss, R. M. (1998). Why do we gesture when we speak? *Current Directions in Psychological Science, 7*, 54–60.

LaFrance, M., Hecht, M. A., & Levy Paluck, E. (2003). The contingent smile: A meta-analysis of sex differences in smiling. *Psychological Bulletin, 129*, 305–334.

Laukka, P., Juslin, P. N., & Bresin, R. (2005). A dimensional approach to vocal expression of emotion. *Cognition and Emotion, 19*, 633–653.

Lewis, R. J., Derlega, V. J., Shankar, A., Cochard, E., & Finkel, L. (1997). Nonverbal correlates confederates' touch: Confounds in touch research. *Journal of Social Behavior and Personality, 12*, 821–830.

Maddux, W. W., Mullen, E., & Galinsky, A. D. (2008). Chameleons bake bigger pies and take bigger pieces: Strategic behavioral mimicry facilitates negotiation outcomes. *Journal of Experimental Social Psychology, 44*, 461–468.

Major, B., & Heslin, R. (1982). Perceptions of cross-sex and same-sex nonreciprocal touch: It is better to give than to receive. *Journal of Nonverbal Behavior, 6*, 148–162.

Manusov, V. (Ed.) (2005). *The sourcebook of nonverbal measures*. Mahwah, NJ: Lawrence Erlbaum Associates.

Manusov, V., & Patterson, M. L. (Eds.) (2006). *The Sage handbook of nonverbal communication*. Thousand Oaks, CA: Sage.

Matsumoto, D., LeRoux, J., Wilson-Cohn, C., Raroque, J., Kooken, K., Ekman, P, Yrizarry, N., Loewinger, S., Uchida, H., Yee, A., Amo, L., & Goh, A. (2000) A new test to measure emotion recognition ability: Matsumoto and Ekman's Japanese and Caucasian Brief Affect Recognition Test (JACBART). *Journal of Nonverbal Behavior, 24*, 179–209.

Mayer, J. D., Salovey, P., Caruso, D. R., & Sitarenios, G. (2003). Measuring emotional intelligence with the MSCEIT V2.0. *Emotion, 3*, 97–105.

McClure, E. B. (2000). A meta-analytic review of sex differences in facial expression processing and their development in infants, children, and adolescents. *Psychological Bulletin, 126*, 424–453.

McConnell, A. R., & Leibold, J. M. (2001). Relations among the Implicit Association Test, discriminatory behavior, and explicit measures of racial attitudes. *Journal of Experimental Social Psychology, 37,* 435–442.

Morris, D., Collett, P., Marsh, P., & O'Shaughnessy, M. (1979). *Gestures.* New York: Stein and Day.

Murphy, N. A. (2005). Using thin slices for behavioral coding. *Journal of Nonverbal Behavior, 29,* 235–246.

Murphy, N. A., Hall, J. A., & Colvin, C. R. (2003). Accurate intelligence assessments in social interaction: Mediators and gender effects. *Journal of Personality, 71,* 465–493.

Nagashima, K., & Schellenberg, J. A. (1997). Situational differences in intentional smiling: A cross-cultural exploration. *Journal of Social Psychology, 13,* 297–301.

Niedenthal, P. M., Barsalou, L. W., Winkielman, P., Krauth-Gruber, S., & Ric, F. (2005). Embodiment in attitudes, social perception, and emotion. *Personality and Social Psychology Review, 9,* 184–211.

Nowicki, S., & Duke, M. P. (1994). Individual differences in the nonverbal communication of affect: The Diagnostic Analysis of Nonverbal Accuracy Scale. *Journal of Nonverbal Behavior, 18,* 9–34.

Patterson, M. L. (2008). Back to social behavior: Mining the mundane. *Basic and Applied Social Psychology, 30,* 93–101.

Patterson, M. L., Foster, J. L., & Bellmer, C. D. (2001). Another look at accuracy and confidence in social judgments. *Journal of Nonverbal Behavior, 25,* 207–219.

Patterson, M. L., Jordan, A., Hogan, M. B., & Frerker, D. (1981). Effects of nonverbal intimacy on arousal and behavioral adjustment. *Journal of Nonverbal Behavior, 5,* 184–198.

Phillips, L. H., Tunstall, M., & Channon, S. (2007). Exploring the role of working memory in dynamic social cue decoding using dual task methodology. *Journal of Nonverbal Behavior, 31,* 137–152.

Riggio, H. R., & Riggio, R. E. (2002). Emotional expressiveness, extraversion, and neuroticism: A meta-analysis. *Journal of Nonverbal Behavior, 26,* 195–218.

Rosenthal, R. (1987). *Judgment studies: Design, analysis, and meta-analysis.* New York: Cambridge University Press.

Rosenthal, R., Hall, J. A., DiMatteo, M. R., Rogers, P. L., & Archer, D. (1979). *Sensitivity to nonverbal communication: The PONS test.* Baltimore: The Johns Hopkins University Press.

Rosip, J. C., & Hall, J. A. (2004). Knowledge of nonverbal cues, gender, and nonverbal decoding accuracy. *Journal of Nonverbal Behavior, 28,* 267–286.

Scherer, K. R., Banse, R., & Wallbott, H. G. (2001). Emotion inferences from vocal expression correlate across languages and cultures. *Journal of Cross-Cultural Psychology, 32,* 76–92.

Strack, F., Martin, L. L., & Stepper, S. (1988). Inhibiting and facilitating conditions of the human smile: A nonobtrusive test of the facial feedback hypothesis. *Journal of Personality and Social Psychology, 54,* 768–777.

Tiedens, L. Z., & Fragale, A. R. (2003). Power moves: Complementarity in dominant and submissive nonverbal behavior. *Journal of Personality and Social Psychology, 84,* 558–568.

Tracy, J. L., & Robins, R. W. (2008a). The automaticity of emotion recognition. *Emotion, 8*, 81–95.

Tracy, J. L., & Robins, R. W. (2008b). The nonverbal expression of pride: Evidence for cross-cultural recognition. *Journal of Personality and Social Psychology, 94*, 516–530.

Vrij, A., & Semin, G. R. (1996). Lie experts' beliefs about nonverbal indicators of deception. *Journal of Nonverbal Behavior, 20*, 65–80.

Wagner, H. L., Buck, R., & Winterbotham, M. (1993). Communication of specific emotions: Gender differences in sending accuracy and communication measures. *Journal of Nonverbal Behavior, 17*, 29–53.

Wegner, D. M. (2002). *The illusion of conscious will.* Cambridge, MA: MIT Press.

Wells, G. L., & Petty, R. E. (1980). The effects of overt head movements on persuasion: Compatibility and incompatibility of responses. *Basic and Applied Social Psychology, 1*, 219–230.

Wiener, M., Devoe, S., Rubinow, S., & Geller, J. (1972). Nonverbal behavior and nonverbal communication. *Psychological Review, 79*, 185–214.

Word, C. O., Zanna, M. P., & Cooper, J. (1974). The nonverbal mediation of self-fulfilling prophecies in interracial interaction. *Journal of Experimental Social Psychology, 10*, 109–120.

INDEX